Time Out London

Penguin Books

PENGUIN BOOKS

Published by the Penguin Group
Penguin Books Ltd, 27 Wrights Lane, London W8 5TZ, England
Penguin Books USA Inc., 375 Hudson Street, New York, New York 10014, USA
Penguin Books Australia Ltd, Ringwood, Victoria, Australia
Penguin Books Canada Ltd, 10 Alcorn Avenue, Toronto, Ontario, Canada M4V 3B2
Penguin Books (NZ) Ltd, 182-190 Wairau Road, Auckland 10, New Zealand

Penguin Books Ltd, Registered Offices: Harmondsworth, Middlesex, England

First published 1989
First Penguin edition 1990
Second edition 1992
Third edition 1994
Fourth edition 1995
Fifth edition 1997
Sixth edition 1998
Seventh edition 1999
Eighth edition 2000
10 9 8 7 6 5 4 3 2 1

Colour reprographics by Westside Digital Media, 9 Bridle Lane, London W1
and Precise Litho, 34-35 Great Sutton Street, London EC1
Printed and bound by Cayfosa-Quebecor, Ctra. de Caldes, Km 3 08 130 Sta, Perpètua de Mogoda, Barcelona, Spain

WORLD
CUP'98

Edited and designed by
Time Out Guides Limited
Universal House
251 Tottenham Court Road
London W1P 0AB
Tel + 44 (0)20 7813 3000
Fax+ 44 (0)20 7813 6001
Email guides@timeout.com
http://www.timeout.com

Editorial
Editor Lesley McCave
Deputy Editor Jonathan Cox
Listings Editor Zoë Sanders
Proofreader Tamsin Shelton

Editorial Director Peter Fiennes
Series Editor Caroline Taverne

Design
Art Director John Oakey
Art Editor Mandy Martin
Senior Designer Scott Moore
Designers Benjamin de Lotz, Lucy Grant
Scanning/Imaging Chris Quinn
Picture Editor Kerri Miles
Deputy Picture Editor Olivia Duncan-Jones
Picture Admin Kit Burnet

Advertising
Group Advertisement Director Lesley Gill
Sales Director Mark Phillips
Sales Manager Alison Gray
Sales Dominic Mensah, Rhidian Thomas
Advertising Assistant Daniel Heaf

Administration
Publisher Tony Elliott
Managing Director Mike Hardwick
Financial Director Kevin Ellis
Marketing Director Gillian Auld
General Manager Nichola Coulthard
Production Manager Mark Lamond
Production Controller Samantha Furniss
Accountant Catherine Bowen

Features in this guide were written and researched by:
Introduction Lesley McCave. **London by Season** Zoë Sanders. **History** Jonathan Cox, Sarah McAlister. **London Today** John Vidal (*I could'a been a contender* Andrew White). **Sightseeing** *Central London* Jonathan Cox, Lesley McCave; *North London* Louise Gray, Zoë Sanders; *East London* Ian Cunningham, Angela Jameson; *South London* Ian Cunningham, Michael Ellis; *West London* Patrick Marmion; *Trails of the unexpected* Derek Hammond. **Accommodation** Zoë Sanders, Lesley McCave. **Restaurants** Jonathan Cox. **Pubs & Bars** Jonathan Cox. **Shopping & Services** adapted from *Time Out Shopping & Services Guide*. **Children** Sarah Halliwell, Nana Ocran. **Comedy** Andrew White. **Clubs** Frank Broughton, Dave Swindells. **Contemporary Art** (and art galleries throughout Sightseeing chapters) Michael Ellis. **Dance** Daniele Guerra. **Film** Tom Coates. **Gay & Lesbian** Stevan Alcock. **Music: Classical & Opera** Will Fulford-Jones. **Music: Rock, Roots & Jazz** Will Fulford-Jones. **Sport & Fitness** Andrew Shields. **Theatre** Patrick Marmion. **Trips Out of Town** Jonathan Cox. **Directory** Jonathan Cox, Lily Dunn, Edward Fortune, Zoë Sanders.

The Editor would like to thank:
Sophie Blacksell, Alex Brannan at the London Tourist Board, Claire Brighty and David Taylor at the New Millennium Experience Company, Jonathan Cox, Guy Dimond, Olivia Duncan-Jones; Frances Dunkels, Kirsten Jarvis and Liz Lewington at the British Museum, Lily Dunn, Peter Fiennes, Ottilie Godfrey, Sarah Guy, Ruth Jarvis, Mary McCave, James Mitchell, James Pretlove, Zoë Sanders, John Scott, Tamsin Shelton, Andrew Stern at Greenwich Council Press Office, Caroline Taverne, Jill Tulip, Simon Wallis at London River Services.
Maps by JS Graphics, 17 Beadles Lane, Old Oxted, Surrey RH8 9JG. Street maps based on material supplied by Alan Collinson and Julie Snook through Copyright Exchange.

Photography by Sarah Blee except: page 5 Glyn Kirk/Actionplus; page 10 Jon Spaull; pages 11 & 23 Hulton Getty; pages 12 & 21 Mary Evans Picture Library; pages 13 & 14 AKG; page 19 Guildhall Library, Corporation of London; page 20 Imperial War Museum; pages 27 & 32 Hayes Davidson; page 28 Dennis Gilbert/View; page 30 James Finlay; pages 36, 313, 316, Jonathan Cox; page 48 Jon Perugia; page 51 Corporation of London; page 72 Sara Hannant; page 81 Peter Mackertitch; page 124 NMEC/Hayes Davidson; page 126 NMEC; page 136 Dan McCallister; pages 57, 58, 151, 196, 205, 240 Georgie Scott; pages 166, 190 Dominic Dibbs; page 169 Luca Zampedri; pages 173, 302, 304, 310 Paul Avis; page 181, 203 James Winspear; page 195 Frank Bauer; page 231 Michael Franke; page 249 Steve Perry; page 251 Stephen White; page 257 Chris Nash; pages 100 & 277 Tony Gibson; page 295 Catherine Ashmore; page 298 Clive Barda; page 305 Trevor Ray Hart; page 320 National Trust Photographic/Andrew Butler.
The following photographs were supplied by featured establishments: pages 30, 206, 247, 269, 270, 303.

Contents

About the Guide

The eighth edition of the *Time Out London Guide* is our most comprehensive yet. For more than 30 years, *Time Out* magazine has been reporting on life in the capital, providing a definitive range of listings of films screened, books published, CDs released, plays staged, and cafés, bars, restaurants and clubs opened (and closed). The *London Guide* draws on this pool of knowledge and experience. At the same time it is part of an expanding series of city guides that now includes Amsterdam, Barcelona, Berlin, Brussels, Budapest, Dublin, Edinburgh & Glasgow, Florence, Las Vegas, Lisbon, Los Angeles, Madrid, Moscow & St Petersburg, New Orleans, New York, Paris, Prague, Rome, San Francisco and Sydney.

A good guide should not dictate an itinerary but, rather, open up a location to the curious visitor (and resident); it should inform, entertain and inspire by supplying contexts, insider knowledge and the wherewithal to encourage independent exploration. That has been our aim in preparing this Guide.

WE'VE DONE OUR BEST

All the listings information was fully checked and correct at the time of going to press, but owners and managers can change their arrangements at any time. Therefore it is always best to phone before you set out, to check opening times, dates of exhibitions, admission fees and other details.

The prices listed throughout this Guide should be used as guidelines. Exchange rates and inflation – even a change of government – can cause sudden changes. But if a particular set of prices or services varies greatly from those we have listed, ask why. (You can always go elsewhere; there's plenty of choice.) But please do tell us. We always aim to give the best, up-to-date advice, so we want to know if you think you've been ripped off.

TELEPHONES

As of 22 April 2000, the London phone codes are changing. The old 0171 and 0181 codes will be replaced by a new code, **020**, with a 7 or 8 added to the original seven-digit number to create a new eight-digit number. For example, 0171 813 3000 becomes 020 7813 3000. Although the old and new systems run in parallel until 14 October 2000, only the new numbers are listed in this Guide. After 22 April 2000, you do not need to dial the 020 to call a London number from within London. Mobile phone numbers are unaffected by this change: to dial a mobile number you need the full code.

CREDIT CARDS

The following abbreviations have been used – **AmEx**: American Express; **DC**: Diners Club; **JCB**: Japanese Credit Bank; **MC**: MasterCard; **TC**: travellers cheques in any currency ($TC, £TC denotes currency); **V**: Visa. **If credit cards aren't listed against a venue, they are not accepted.**

LET US KNOW

In all cases the information we give is impartial. No organisation or enterprise has been included because its owner or manager has advertised in our publications. We hope you enjoy the *Time Out London Guide*, but if you take exception to any of our reviews, please feel free to let us know. Readers' comments are always welcome and are taken into account when preparing later editions of the guide. There's a reader's reply card at the back of the book.

There is an online version of this Guide, as well as weekly events listings for many other international cities, at http://www.timeout.com

Introduction

London? All mouth and all trousers. A hard city to get to know. A self-absorbed, unsentimental, bad-mannered place that, beyond the superficial gloss of the tourist industry, makes little attempt to show visitors its true character. The postcard-pomp of St Paul's, Buckingham Palace, the Houses of Parliament and the Tower of London is the merest surface scratching of what is basically a strange, secretive, multi-levelled and, for all its noise and bustle, fundamentally shy city. London is, and always has been, so concerned with getting on with life and earning a crust that niceties are often forgotten. Dig deep and you'll be rewarded. Sure, go and see the big sights – many of them are worth it. But if you really want to get to know London, you'll need to step beyond the Circle Line.

Yet, for every complaint about the cost, noise and clutter of the city, there's an equal and opposite hurrah for its daring, vibrancy and sense of excitement. Two thousand years of history have created fascinating juxtapositions – architectural, cultural, sociological. Peel off one layer and there will always be another underneath. Millennium night and all its hype may be over, but in its wake come a whole range of projects and plans worthy of one of the most thrilling cities in the world.

London by numbers

If you like your information in a more digestible form, the following figures should give you some ideas about the size and diversity of the city.

Number of...	
residents	**7 million**
annual visitors	**28 million**
international air passengers passing annually through London's five airports	**90 million**
national rail termini	**12**
local rail stations	**570**
underground stations	**271**
bus routes	**700**
licensed taxis	**18,300**
seats available at cultural events on any one night	**60,000**
theatres	**200**
cinema screens	**600**
museums	**200**
restaurants/cafés	**12,000**
national/regional cuisines available	**70**
pubs/bars	**5,300**
shops	**30,000**
golf courses within M25	**100**
professional football clubs	**13**
foreign banks in London	**539**
languages spoken	**300**
resident communities with 5,000 or more people born outside the UK	**45**
Albert Halls that would fit inside the Dome	**13**
rounds in a basic royal salute	**21**
generations of corgis bred from Susan, given to Queen (then Princess) Elizabeth on her 18th birthday	**10**

The majority of the above facts and figures were provided by London First Centre (www.lfc.co.uk).

In Context

London by Season

From community celebrations to royal birthdays, sporting bashes to arts festivals – the capital's calendar isn't short on variety.

London's year has never lacked entertaining regular events and special happenings, ranging from the most starchily traditional ceremonies (Changing of the Guard) to the most relaxed, contemporary, youth-oriented gatherings (Summer Rites). So, in millennium year (if you disregard the killjoys who insist that this will *actually* be 2001 not 2000), it's no surprise to find the usual suspects augmented by a numberless host of one-off celebrations. Most of these make up the **London String of Pearls Millennium Festival** (*see page 8* **London's your oyster**). We've detailed many of these festivities under the relevant institution elsewhere in the Guide.

This chapter concentrates on the best of London's regular annual events, although there are scores more advertised in the national press and *Time Out* magazine. For some events you need to buy a ticket beforehand (sometimes several months in advance), some charge admission on the day/night, while others are free; it's always best to phone to check. All the dates given below were correct at the time of going to press, but always double check nearer the time.

For details of festivals of **dance**, *see page 258*; of **film**, *see page 261*; of **music**, *see pages 271* and *282*. For a list of public holidays in the UK, *see page 329*.

Frequent events

Many of the big museums and galleries, such as the **National Gallery** (*see page 89*) and **British Museum** (*see page 64*), hold regular talks, films, discussions and other events. Phone the individual institutions for details.

Ceremony of the Keys

Tower of London, EC3 (020 7709 0765). Tower Hill tube. **Date** 9.53-10pm daily. **Maximum** in party *Apr-Oct* 8; *Nov-Mar* 15. **Map 12 R7**

This 700-year-old ceremony starts at precisely 9.53pm, when the Chief Warder leaves the Byward Tower. It's all over just after 10pm, when the last post is sounded. Apply in writing with a stamped self-addressed envelope six to eight weeks in advance.

Changing of the Guard

Buckingham Palace, Horse Guards & St James's Palace, SW1 (recorded info 0839 123411). Victoria tube/rail/Green Park or St James's Park tube. **Ceremonies** *Buckingham Palace* 11.30am daily or on alternate days (phone for dates). **Map 7 H9**. *St James's Palace* 11.15am (dates as for Buckingham Palace). **Map 7 J8**. *Horse Guards* 11am Mon-Sat; 10am Sun. **Map 8 K8**

The most spectacular ceremony is at **Buckingham Palace**. On guard changing days the new guard and its regimental band line up in the forecourt of Wellington Barracks, Birdcage Walk, from 10.45am. It's usually one of the five regiments of Foot Guards in their scarlet coats and bearskin hats. At 11.27am they march, accompanied by a band, to the palace for the changing of the sentries, who stand guard in the palace forecourt. Note that the ceremony may be cancelled in very wet weather. At **St James's Palace**, a detachment of the old guard marches off at 11.15am and back at 12.05pm. At **Horse Guards** in Whitehall it's the Household Cavalry who mount the guard (10am-4pm daily); they ride to Whitehall via The Mall from Hyde Park for an 11am changeover.

Funfairs

Alexandra Park *Muswell Hill, N22 (020 8365 2121). Wood Green tube/Alexandra Palace rail/W3 bus.* **Dates** 20-30 Apr, 25 May-4 June, 24-29 Aug, Nov 2000 (phone to confirm exact dates).

Hampstead Heath *NW3 (020 7485 4491 for a leaflet detailing events in the park throughout the year). Belsize Park or Hampstead tube/Gospel Oak or Hampstead Heath rail/24, C11 bus.* **Dates** 21-24 Apr; 27-29 May; 26-28 Aug 2000. **Map** *see p103*

Gun Salutes

Hyde Park, W2 & the Tower of London, EC3. **Date** 7 Feb (Accession Day); 21 Apr (Queen's birthday); 2 June (Coronation Day); 10 June (Trooping the Colour, *see p7*); 4 Aug (Queen Mother's birthday); State Opening of Parliament (*see p9*). If the date falls on a Sunday, salutes are fired on the following Monday. **Map 12 R7**

The cannons are primed on important royal occasions for gun salutes. The King's Troop of the Royal Horse Artillery makes a mounted charge through **Hyde Park**, sets up the guns and fires a 41-gun

Horsing around at **Royal Ascot**. *See page 7.*

salute (at noon, except for the State Opening of Parliament) opposite the Dorchester Hotel. Then, not to be outdone, at the **Tower of London**, the Honourable Artillery Company fires a 62-gun salute at 1pm.

Spring 2000

Ideal Home Exhibition — 16 Mar-9 Apr

Earl's Court Exhibition Centre, Warwick Road, SW5 (box office 020 7373 8141/info 020 7244 0371). Earl's Court tube. **Map 3 A11**
The biggest consumer show in the UK draws in huge crowds from all around the country to drool over every conceivable household gadget and innovation. It's all a bit tacky, though.

St Patrick's Day — 17 Mar

London has the third largest Irish population of any city in the world, after New York and Dublin. There are no big parades, but head up to Kilburn (NW6) for a taste of boisterous Irish jubilation.

Head of the River Race — 18 Mar

on the Thames, from Mortlake, SW14, to Putney, SW15 (01932 220401). Mortlake rail (start), Hammersmith tube (mid-point) or Putney Bridge tube (finish).
Less well known than the Oxford and Cambridge Race but just as impressive, this one, just to be different, goes in the opposite direction, with around 420 boat crews competing for the best time. Turn up at about 2.30pm for the 3.30pm start from Mortlake. The best views of the race are to be had from Hammersmith Bridge; alternatively, watch from the finish line at Putney.

Oxford & Cambridge Boat Race — 25 Mar

on the Thames, from Putney, SW15, to Mortlake, SW14 (020 7379 3234). Putney Bridge tube (start), Hammersmith tube (mid-point) or Mortlake rail (finish).
Oxford and Cambridge Universities' fitter members race the four miles and 374 yards (6.8km) from Putney to Mortlake. The riverside pubs in Mortlake and Hammersmith are popular vantage points – but be prepared for huge crowds. The race starts at 4.10pm.

London Marathon — 16 Apr

Greenwich Park to Westminster Bridge via the Isle of Dogs, Victoria Embankment & St James's Park (020 7620 4117).
The world's biggest road race, with around 35,000 starters, including celebs and record-breakers, running the 26.3 miles (16km). To run it yourself, apply by the October before the race: your name will be entered into a ballot and you'll have a straight 50/50 chance of being allowed to run.

London Harness Horse Parade — 24 Apr

Battersea Park, Albert Bridge Road, SW11 (01733 234451). Battersea Park or Queenstown Road rail/97, 137 bus.
Working horses, traditional brewers' drays, and a variety of carts and carriages tour Battersea Park, competing for rosettes.

Rugby League Challenge Cup Final — 29 Apr

Wembley Stadium, Wembley, Middlesex (020 8902 0902). Wembley Park tube/Wembley Central tube/rail.
Highlight of the rugby league calendar.

Museums & Galleries Month 2000 — 1 May-4 June

various venues (020 7233 9796).
Museums and galleries around the country will be staging special events and activities, with exhibitions and welcome days.
Website: www.may2000.org.uk

May Fayre & Puppet Festival — 14 May

St Paul's Church Garden, Covent Garden, WC2 (020 7375 0441). Covent Garden tube. **Map 8 L7**
A free festival of Punch and Judy and other puppetry, from 10.30am to 5.30pm.

FA Cup Final — 20 May

Wembley Stadium, Wembley, Middlesex (020 8902 0902). Wembley Park tube/Wembley Central tube/rail.
The most important day of the year for footie fans. Tickets are notoriously difficult to obtain (and frighteningly expensive).

Chelsea Flower Show **23-26 May**
grounds of Royal Hospital, Royal Hospital Road, SW3 (020 7834 4333). Sloane Square tube. **Map 4 F12**
World-renowned gardening extravaganza by the river. The first two days are for members only.

Festival of Mind, Body, Spirit **28 May-4 June**
Royal Horticultural Halls, Greycoat Street, SW1 (020 7938 3788). Victoria tube/rail. **Map 7 J7**
A New Age festival featuring a mind-blowing array of approaches to health, spiritualism and the environment.

Victoria Embankment Gardens Summer Events **28 May-30 July**
Victoria Embankment Gardens, Villiers Street, WC2 (020 7375 0441). Embankment tube. **Map 8 L7**
A series of free open-air events encompassing the **Open Air Opera** season (June, July), the **Open Air Dance Festival**, **Move It Mime Festival**, **Midsummer Poetry Festival** (June) and the **Summer Season of Street Theatre** (July). Phone for the dates and times of individual events.

Summer

Beating Retreat **7-8 June**
Horse Guards Parade, Whitehall, SW1 (020 7930 4466). Westminster tube/Charing Cross tube/rail. **Map 8 K8**
For those who like loud noises with their pomp, the 'Retreat' is beaten on drums by the Mounted Bands of the Household Cavalry and the Massed Bands of the Guards Division in this colourful musical ceremony.

Derby Day **10 June**
Epsom Downs Racecourse, Epsom Downs, Surrey (enquiries/box office 01372 470047). Epsom Town Centre or Tattenham Corner rail, then shuttle bus.
The major flat race of the season is a frightfully British affair. The lower orders are herded into one enclosure, while those with fat wallets and braying voices strut about in another.

Trooping the Colour **17 June**
Horse Guards Parade, Whitehall, SW1 (020 7414 2479). Westminster tube/Charing Cross tube/rail. **Map 8 K8**
Even though the Queen's birthday is in April, she has an official birthday party on this day. She leaves Buckingham Palace at 10.40am and travels down The Mall to Horse Guards Parade, arriving at 11am. The route is always packed, but you may find space on the Green Park side of The Mall. Back home in the palace by 12.30pm, the Queen takes to the balcony to watch a Royal Air Force jet zoom past at about 1pm, and there is a gun salute at the Tower of London.

Covent Garden Flower Festival **18-25 June**
in and around Covent Garden Market (020 7735 1518). Covent Garden tube. **Map 8 L7**
The fourth annual flower festival promises blooms aplenty plus specially created gardens, display areas and street entertainment.

Royal Ascot **20-23 June**
Ascot Racecourse, Ascot, Berkshire (01344 622211). Ascot rail.
Ascot is the top toffs' horse-racing meeting of the year. On Ladies' Day (22 June), when the Queen attends, the outrageous hats worn by many of the women are as much the focus of attention as the racing results.

City of London Festival **20 June-13 July**
venues in and around the City, EC2 (box office 020 7638 8891/info 020 7377 0540).
An international line-up of soloists, string quartets, orchestras and choirs. There's also poetry and theatre in City churches (*see also p274*).
Website: www.city-of-london-festival.org.uk

Wimbledon Lawn Tennis Championships **26 June-9 July**
PO Box 98, Church Road, SW19 (020 8944 1066/ recorded info 020 8946 2244). Southfields tube/ Wimbledon tube/rail.
The one the players all want to win, and the fans all want to watch. *See p133.*

Henley Royal Regatta **28 June-2 July**
Henley Reach, Henley-on-Thames, Oxfordshire (01491 572153). Henley-on-Thames rail.
International rowing regatta and upper-class social event; the final race is on the Sunday.

Royal Academy Summer Exhibition **29 June-7 Aug**
Royal Academy, Burlington House, Piccadilly, W1 (020 7300 8000). Green Park or Piccadilly Circus tube. **Map 7 J7**
Every year around 10,000 works are submitted by artists of all styles and standards – from members of the Royal Academy to enthusiastic amateurs – and judged by a panel of eminent Academicians. The thousand or so entries on show are usually something of an artistic hotchpotch but interesting nonetheless.

Greenwich & Docklands International Festival **30 June-9 July**
various venues near the Thames at Greenwich & Docklands (020 8305 1818).
The festival features dance, theatre and music at locations along the river. *See also* 31 December.
Website: www.festival.org

BBC Henry Wood Promenade Concerts **14 July-9 Sept**
Royal Albert Hall, Kensington Gore, SW7 (020 7765 5575/box office 020 7589 8212). Gloucester Road, Knightsbridge or South Kensington tube/9, 10, 52 bus. **Map 4 D9**
Arguably the world's greatest classical music festival, presenting over 70 orchestral concerts spanning an impressive variety of composers and repertoire. *See also p270.*

London's your oyster

Throughout 2000 an unprecedented array of special events will be taking place throughout London to mark the millennium. Many of these come under the aegis of the **London String of Pearls Millennium Festival** (020 7665 1540/020 7665 1558/www.stringofpearls.org.uk), which seeks to celebrate the greatest political, cultural, social and technological achievements of the last 1,000 years. The organisers have divided these successes into 13 categories – democracy, justice, faith, freedom of speech, education, culture, commerce, community, technology, medicine, recreation, environment and defence – and liken the buildings and organisations that embody each concept to a string of pearls, stretched out along the Thames.

Rather self-congratulatory it all may be, but there's no knocking the extraordinary variety of events and unique opportunities that the festival provides to see behind the scenes at places normally closed to the public. It's always best to check that the event you're interested in is still on before you set off. Some of the longer-term events are detailed elsewhere in this Guide, under the relevant institution. Among the other highlights are…

* Twelve open days at George Gilbert Scott's spectacular **Foreign & Commonwealth Office** on King Charles Street, SW1 (*9 May-25 July* Tuesdays only; 020 7270 1500/www.fco.gov.uk). **Map 8 K9**

* Two open days (*2 & 23 July* 10am-3pm) at **Inner Temple** (020 7797 8182/www.innertemple.org.uk) and **Middle Temple** (020 7427 4830/www.middletemple.org.uk). The days consist of a service in Temple Church followed by a walk in the gardens and an afternoon concert. *See also p58.* **Map 11 N6/7**

* Gilbert and Sullivan's *Trial by Jury* performed in the **Royal Courts of Justice** on the Strand, WC2 (15-20 May; 020 7413 1410/www.cgf.co.uk) as part of the BOC Covent Garden Festival of opera and music. *See also p273.* **Map 6 M6**

* Drama production of Kate Price's *A Passionate Englishman*, looking at the possible relationship between Samuel Pepys and William Penn, performed in **All Hallows by the Tower**, Byward Street, EC3 (3-10 July; 020 7488 4772). *See also p46.* **Map 12 R7**

* Tours of the dome at 1pm, plus organ recitals at 11.30pm, at **Westminster (Methodist) Central Hall**, Storey's Gate, SW1 (*2 Apr, 7 May, 4 June, 2 July, 6 Aug, 3 Sept*/020 7222 8010/www.wch.co.uk). *See also p88.* **Map 8 K9**

Swan Upping on the Thames 17-21 July

from various points along the Thames (020 7236 1863/020 7236 7197).

This bizarre but delightfully archaic event involves a group of paddling or rowing herdsmen, who identify and mark swans as belonging to the Queen, the Vintners' or the Dyers' livery companies. The Dyers' swans get one mark (on the beak), the Vintners' two and the Queen's remain unblemished. You can watch the action from towpaths along the way. The route and departure time change daily; phone for details.

Great British Beer Festival 1-5 Aug

Olympia, Hammersmith Road, W14 (01727 867201). Kensington (Olympia) tube.

This beer fest is for real ale-lovers – literally: it's organised by CAMRA (Campaign for Real Ale). Introduce your tastebuds to 300 British ales and ciders and, despite the name of the festival, to a range of international beers.

Summer Rites 5 Aug

Brockwell Park, SW2 (020 7278 0995). Brixton tube/Herne Hill rail.

A burgeoning, gay-oriented festival, taking in a funfair, bars, market stalls, loads of live performances and disco tents run by top London clubs. At the time of going to press, the organisers were still considering staging a 'straight' event on Sunday 6 August.

Notting Hill Carnival 27-28 Aug

(020 8964 0544). Ladbroke Grove, Notting Hill or Westbourne Park tube.

This vast and ever-popular street party features steel bands, sound systems, colourful floats and excellent Caribbean food. *See also p138.*

Autumn

Chelsea Antiques Fair 15-24 Sept

Chelsea Old Town Hall, King's Road, SW3 (01444 482514). Sloane Square tube.

Open 11am-8pm Mon-Fri; 11am-7pm Sat; 11am-5pm Sun. **Admission** £6; free under-18s. **Map 4 E12**

A twice-yearly festival (also held 17-26 Mar), where anyone with a budget from £20 to £50,000 should find something of interest.

2000 Thames Festival 17 Sept

between Waterloo Bridge & Blackfriars Bridge (020 7401 3610/020 7928 8998).

An exciting festival that aims to re-ignite enthusiasm for London's great waterway with a series of events celebrating the river. A funfair and food village are open all day. The finale at 7.30pm consists of 1,500 performers following a colourful procession, to vibrant street sounds.

* A new 'Southwark cycle' of Mystery Plays by John Constable, performed at **Southwark Cathedral**, Montague Close, SE1 (*14 Apr-14 May* Fri, Sat, Sun; 020 7403 1496/ www.mysteries@southwark.org.uk). *See also p41.* **Map 11 P8**

* **Treasures of the Twentieth Century**, a major exhibition, of the silver, jewellery and art medals of the Goldsmiths' Company within the magnificent **Goldsmiths' Hall**, Foster Lane, EC2 (*25 May-21 July* 10.30am-5pm Mon-Sat; 020 7606 7010). *See also p52.* **Map 11 P6**

* The opening of **Horse Guards**, Whitehall, SW1 for guided tours (*July* 10am-4pm Sat, Sun; 020 7414 2360). **Map 8 K8**

* The spectacular tri-service millennium celebration of the **Royal Military Tattoo 2000**, Horse Guards, Whitehall, SW1 (*10-15 July*; 0870 241 0301/www.rmt2000.mod.uk). **Map 8 K8**

* A *son et lumière* spectacular entitled 'Men in Scarlet', narrated by Dame Judi Dench, in the Figure Court of Wren's **Royal Hospital Chelsea**, Royal Hospital Road, SW3 (*12-16 Sept* 8.15-9.15pm; 020 7881 5308/www. chelseapensioner.org.uk). The production records the history of the Chelsea Pensioners and their grand Chelsea home. *See also p100.* **Map 4 F12**

Great River Race — 23 Sept

on the Thames, from Richmond, Surrey, to Island Gardens, E14 (020 8398 9057).
More than 250 'traditional' boats compete in this 22-mile (35-km) 'marathon', aiming to scoop the UK Traditional Boat Championship. The race sets off from Ham House, Richmond, at 10.30am and ends at Island Gardens, opposite Greenwich, around 1.45pm.

London Open House — 23-24 Sept

various venues in London (recorded info 09001 600061).
On this weekend, the public have access to buildings of architectural interest that are normally closed, free of charge. The 500 or so participating buildings range from hulks like the Bank of England and the amazing India & Foreign Exchange to individual rooms in private homes. A snooper's paradise.
Website: www.londonopenhouse.demon.co.uk

Horseman's Sunday — 24 Sept

Church of St John & St Michael, Hyde Park Crescent, W2 (020 7262 1732). Edgware Road tube/ Paddington tube/rail. **Map 2 E6**
Dating from 1969, when local riding stables feared closure and held an open-air service to protest, a vicar on horseback blesses more than 100 horses, before the animals trot through Hyde Park.

Pearly Kings and Queens Harvest Festival — 1 Oct

St Martin-in-the-Fields, Trafalgar Square, WC2 (020 7930 0089). Charing Cross tube/rail. **Map 8 L7**
Dressed in their traditional flamboyant costumes, pearly kings, queens and princesses from all over London gather for a church service at 3pm for a harvest thanksgiving every year.

Punch and Judy Festival — early Oct

Covent Garden Piazza, WC2 (020 7836 9136). Covent Garden tube. **Map 8 L7**
Gather round in the Piazza to watch Punch and Judy duff each other up; phone for exact date.

Trafalgar Day Parade — 22 Oct

Trafalgar Square, WC2 (020 7928 8978). Charing Cross tube/rail. **Map 8 K7**
Nelson's victory at the Battle of Trafalgar (21 October 1805) is commemorated with marching bands and music performances by sea cadets. It ends with the laying of a wreath at the foot of Nelson's Column.

State Opening of Parliament — late Oct/early Nov

House of Lords, Palace of Westminster, SW1 (020 7219 4272). Westminster tube. **Map 8 L9**
Members of Parliament are welcomed back from their summer hols by the Queen. It's a private (though televised) affair, but the public at least get a chance to see the Queen as she arrives and departs in her Irish or Australian State Coach, attended by the Household Cavalry. As she enters the House of Lords, a gun salute is fired. Phone nearer the time for the exact dates.

London Film Festival — 2-16 Nov

National Film Theatre, South Bank, SE1 (020 7928 3535/box office 020 7928 3232). Embankment tube/Waterloo tube/rail. **Map 8 M8**
For three weeks a multitude of new international films are shown, at reduced prices, at the NFT and selected West End cinemas. *See also p261.*
Website: www.lff.org.uk

Bonfire Night — 5 Nov

all over the UK (020 7971 0026).
Every year Britain commemorates the failure of the Gunpowder Plot of 1605, when Guy Fawkes attempted to blow up James I and his Parliament. In celebration, we burn the 'guy' (an effigy of Fawkes) and put our lives in danger from flying fireworks. Note that most displays are held on the weekend nearest to 5 November.

London to Brighton Veteran Car Run — 5 Nov

(starting point) Serpentine Road, Hyde Park, W2 (01753 681736). Hyde Park Corner tube.
Map 2 E8
The motors, limited to an average of 20mph (32kmph), aim to reach Brighton before 4pm. The start (7.30am) at Hyde Park has a great sense of occasion, but if you can't get there, join the crowds lining the rest of the route (via Westminster Bridge).

Two facets of the **Greenwich & Docklands International Festival**. *See page 7.*

Lord Mayor's Show **11 Nov**

various streets in the City (020 7606 3030).

The City gets a facelift for one day a year with a procession of 140 floats, as the new Lord Mayor travels from Mansion House in a gilded coach. Leaving at 11am, the procession snakes through the City to the Royal Courts of Justice on the Strand at 11.50am. There, the new Lord Mayor swears solemn vows before returning to Mansion House by 2.20pm. Later, the merriment continues with fireworks launched from a barge moored between Waterloo and Blackfriars bridges.

Remembrance Sunday Ceremony **12 Nov**

Cenotaph, Whitehall, SW1. Westminster tube/ Charing Cross tube/rail. **Map 8 L8**

The Queen, the Prime Minister and other dignitaries lay wreaths and observe a minute's silence (at 11am) at the Cenotaph to commemorate those who gave their lives for their country in both world wars. Afterwards, the Bishop of London takes a short service of remembrance.

Christmas Lights & Tree **Nov-Dec**

Covent Garden, WC2 (020 7836 9136); Oxford Street, W1 (020 7629 2738); Regent Street, W1 (020 7491 4429); Bond Street, W1 (020 7821 5230); Trafalgar Square, SW1 (020 7211 2109).

Each year, in early December, London receives a fir tree from the Norwegian people in thanks for Britain's role in liberating Norway from the Nazis. The tree stands decked in lights in Trafalgar Square, and numerous main shopping streets boast impressive displays. The lights on Regent Street are switched on by a celebrity (early Nov), but other, often more charming, lights are those hanging across St Christopher's Place, W1; Bond Street, W1; and Kensington High Street, W8.

Winter

International Showjumping Championships **14-18 Dec**

Olympia, Hammersmith Road, W14 (box office 020 7373 3113). Olympia tube.

Plenty of horsing around, ranging from international riders' competitions to the Shetland Pony Grand National. There's also dog agility, and more than 100 equestrian-oriented trade stands.

New Year's Eve Celebrations **31 Dec**

Trafalgar Square, W1. Charing Cross tube/rail. **Map 8 K7**

Inebriated revellers pour into Trafalgar Square in a moronic stampede and try to jump in the fountain (emptied and switched off anyway). No self-respecting Londoner would be seen within a mile of the place. For more festivities, head to the Royal Naval College, SE10, for the **Greenwich & Docklands First Night** (020 8305 1818), an evening of entertainment and spectacle including street theatre and performances and firework displays. Because of the success of celebrations on New Year's Eve 1999, the highlight of which were fireworks by the Thames, the capital may host further similar events in future.

London International Boat Show **5-15 Jan 2001**

Earl's Court Exhibition Centre, Warwick Road, SW5 (info 01784 472222). Earl's Court tube. **Map 3 A11**

The latest in boats, equipment and holidays make up one of London's most popular events.

Website: www.bigblue.org.uk

London International Mime Festival **13-28 Jan**

venues throughout London (phone 020 7637 5661 for brochure, from Dec 2000).

No, not Marcel Marceau, but mime with a difference, with artists from all over the world.

Website: www.mimefest.co.uk

Chinese New Year Festival **24 Jan**

Chinatown, around Gerrard Street, W1 (020 7439 3822). Leicester Square or Piccadilly Circus tube. **Map 8 K7**

The high point of the Chinese calendar is marked with stalls selling crafts and delicacies, and dragons snaking their way through the streets, gathering gifts of money and food.

Masters Snooker Tournament **4-11 Feb**

Wembley Conference Centre, Wembley, Middlesex (box office 020 8902 0902). Wembley Park tube/ Wembley Central tube/rail.

The world's top potters cue up for a shot at this much-desired trophy.

Great Spitalfields Pancake Day Race **27 Feb**

Spitalfields Market, entrance on Commercial Street or Brushfield Street, E1 (020 7375 0441). Liverpool Street tube/rail. **Map 10 R5**

On the day before Lent and its 40 days of fasting comes Shrove Tuesday or Pancake Day. Would-be tossers should phone a few days in advance.

History

Two thousand years of London.

Roman to Norman London

London was founded by the Trojan prince Brutus and run by a race of heroic giants descended from the Celtic King Lud. So thought the twelfth-century chronicler Geoffrey of Monmouth, and how poetic if would have been were it true. In fact, although Celtic tribes lived in scattered communities along the banks of the Thames prior to the arrival of the Romans in Britain, there's no evidence of a settlement on the site of the future metropolis before the invasion of the Emperor Claudius' legions in AD43. During the Romans' conquest of the country, they forded the Thames at its shallowest point and, later, built a timber bridge here (near the site of today's London Bridge). On the north side of this strategically vital crossing a settlement developed over the following decade.

During the first two centuries AD, the Romans built roads, towns and forts; and trade flourished. The first mention of London (Londinium), by the Roman historian Tacitus, records it in AD60 as being 'filled with traders and a celebrated centre of commerce'. Progress was brought to a halt in AD61 when Boudicca, the widow of an East Anglian chieftain, rebelled against the Imperial forces who had seized her land, flogged her and raped her daughters. She led the Iceni in a savage revolt, destroying the Roman colony at Colchester, and then marching on London. The inhabitants were massacred and the settlement burnt to the ground. Order was restored, the town rebuilt and, *c*AD200, a two-mile (3-km) long, six-metre (18-foot) high defensive wall was constructed around London. Chunks of the wall survive today and the names of the original gates (Ludgate, Newgate, Bishopsgate and Aldgate) are preserved on the map of the city. The street London Wall traces part of its original course.

By the fourth century AD, racked by barbarian invasions and internal strife, the Empire was in decline. In 410, the last troops were withdrawn and London became a ghost town. The Roman way of life vanished; the only enduring legacies were roads and early Christianity.

A late sixteenth-century map of the city, before it had spread much beyond the Roman walls.

SAXON & VIKING LONDON

During the fifth and sixth centuries, history gives way to legend. The Saxons crossed the North Sea and settled in eastern and southern England, apparently avoiding the ruins of London; they built farmsteads and trading posts outside the walls.

In 596, Pope Gregory sent Augustine to convert the English to Christianity. Ethelbert, Saxon King of Kent, proved a willing convert and Augustine was appointed the first Archbishop of Canterbury. Since then Canterbury has remained the centre of the English Christian Church. London's first Bishop was Mellitus, one of Augustine's missionaries, who converted the East Saxon King Sebert and, in 604, founded a wooden cathedral dedicated to St Paul inside the old city walls. On Sebert's death, his followers reverted to paganism, but later generations of Christians rebuilt St Paul's.

London continued to expand. In 731, the Venerable Bede mentions 'Lundenwic' as 'the mart of many nations resorting to it by land and sea'. This probably refers to a settlement west of the Roman city in the area of today's Aldwych (Old English for 'old settlement').

In the ninth century, the city faced a new danger from across the North Sea: the Vikings. The city was sacked in 841 and, in 851, the Danish raiders returned with 350 ships, leaving London in ruins. It was not until 886 that King Alfred of Wessex (Alfred the Great) regained the city. He re-established London as a major trading centre, with a merchant navy and new wharfs at Billingsgate and Queenhithe.

Throughout the tenth century, the Saxon city prospered. Churches were built, parishes established and markets set up. Leading citizens were the Port Reeve and Shire Reeve (or Sheriff; the oldest office still existing in the City), the Bishop of London and the ealdormen (aldermen).

The eleventh century brought more Viking harassment, and the English were forced to accept a Danish king, Cnut (Canute, 1016-40). During his reign, London replaced Winchester as the capital of England. In 1042, the throne reverted to an English king, Edward the Confessor, who devoted himself to building the grandest church in England two miles (3km) west of the City at Thorn-ey ('the isle of brambles'). He replaced the timber church of St Peter's with a huge abbey, 'the West Minster' (Westminster Abbey), and moved his court to the new Palace of Westminster. The Abbey was consecrated in December 1065. A week later Edward died and was buried in his new church. Now, London grew around two hubs: Westminster as the centre for the royal court, government and law; the City of London as the commercial centre.

There be Vikings!

THE NORMAN CONQUEST

On Edward's death, there was a succession dispute. William, Duke of Normandy, claimed that the Confessor (his cousin) had promised him the English crown; the English chose Edward's brother-in-law Harold. William gathered an army and invaded. On 14 October 1066, he defeated Harold at the Battle of Hastings and marched on London. City elders had little option but to offer William the throne. He was crowned in Westminster Abbey on Christmas Day 1066.

Recognising the need to win over the prosperous city merchants by negotiation rather than force, William granted the Bishop and burgesses of London a charter (still kept at Guildhall) that acknowledged their rights and independence in return for taxes. But, 'against the fickleness of the vast and fierce population', he also ordered strongholds to be built alongside the city wall, including the White Tower (the tallest building in the Tower of London) and the now-lost Baynard's Castle at Blackfriars.

The earliest surviving written account of contemporary London was written 40 years later by a monk, William Fitz Stephen, who vividly conjured up the walled city and, outside, pastures and woods for hunting, youths wrestling and fencing in Moorfields, and skating on frozen ponds.

The Middle Ages

In the growing city of London, much of the politics of the Middle Ages (late twelfth to late fifteenth centuries) revolved around a three-way struggle for power between the king and the aristocracy, the Church, and the Lord Mayor and city guilds.

THE BIRTH OF PARLIAMENT

In the early Middle Ages, the king and his court frequently travelled to other parts of the kingdom and abroad, but in the fourteenth and fifteenth centuries the Palace of Westminster became the seat of law and government. The noblemen and bishops who attended court built themselves

A contemporary woodcut of Londoners fleeing the **Great Plague**.

palatial houses along the Strand, from the City to Westminster, with gardens stretching to the river.

The Model Parliament (agreeing the principles of government) was held in Westminster Hall in 1295, presided over by Edward I and attended by barons, clergy and representatives of knights and burgesses. The first step towards establishing personal rights and political liberty, and curbing the power of the king, had already been taken in 1215 with the signing of the Magna Carta by King John. In the fourteenth century, subsequent assemblies gave rise to the House of Lords (which met at the Palace of Westminster) and the House of Commons (meeting in the Chapter House at Westminster Abbey).

Relations between the monarch and the City were never easy – and often outright hostile. Londoners guarded their privileges with self-righteous intransigence and resisted all attempts by successive kings to squeeze money out of them to finance wars and building projects. Successive kings were forced to turn to Jewish and Lombard moneylenders, but the City merchants were as intolerant of foreigners as of royal authority. Regular rioting, persecution and the occasional lynching and pogrom were less-than-laudable features of medieval London.

CITY STATUS & COMMERCIAL CLOUT

The privileges granted to the City merchants under the Norman kings, allowing independence and self-regulation, were extended by the monarchs who followed, in return for financial favours. In 1191, during the reign of Richard I, the City of London was formally recognised as a commune (a self-governing community) and, in 1197, won control of the Thames, including lucrative fishing rights (which it retained until 1857). In 1215, King John confirmed the city's right 'to elect every year a mayor', a position of great authority with power over the Sheriff and the Bishop of London. A month later the Mayor joined the rebel barons in signing the Magna Carta.

Over the next two centuries, the power and influence of the trade and craft guilds (later the City Livery Companies) increased as trade with Europe grew. The wharfs by London Bridge were crowded with imports: fine cloth, furs, wine, spices and precious metals. Port dues and taxes were paid to customs officials, such as part-time poet Geoffrey Chaucer, whose *Canterbury Tales* became the first published work of English literature.

The city's markets, already established, drew produce from miles around: livestock at Smithfield, fish at Billingsgate and poultry at Leadenhall. The street markets or 'cheaps' around Westcheap (Cheapside) and Eastcheap were crammed with a variety of goods. As commerce increased, foreign traders and craftsmen settled around the port. The population within the city wall grew from about 18,000 in 1100 to over 50,000 in the 1340s.

THE BLACK DEATH & THE PEASANTS' REVOLT

Lack of hygiene became a serious problem in the city. Water was provided in cisterns at Cheapside and elsewhere, but the supply (more or less direct from the Thames) was limited and polluted. Houndsditch was so called because Londoners threw their dead animals into the ditch that formed the city's eastern boundary. There was no proper sewerage system, and in the streets around Smithfield (the Shambles) butchers dumped the entrails of slaughtered animals.

These conditions provided the breeding ground for the greatest catastrophe of the Middle Ages: the Black Death of 1348-9. The plague came to London from Europe, carried by rats on ships. During this period, about 30 per cent of England's population died of the disease. Though the epidemic abated, it was to recur in London on several occasions during the next three centuries.

These outbreaks left the labour market short-handed, causing unrest among the overworked peasants. The imposition of a poll tax (a shilling a head) led to the Peasants' Revolt. In 1381, thousands marched on London, led by Jack Straw from Essex and Wat Tyler from Kent. In the rioting and looting that followed, the Savoy Palace on the Strand was destroyed, the Archbishop of Canterbury was murdered and hundreds of prisoners were set free. When the 14-year-old Richard II rode out to Smithfield to face the rioters, Wat Tyler was fatally stabbed by Lord Mayor William Walworth. The other ringleaders were subsequently rounded up and hanged. But no more poll taxes were imposed.

CHURCHES & MONASTERIES

Like every other medieval city, London had a large number of parish and monastic churches, as well as the great Gothic cathedral of St Paul's. Although the majority of Londoners were allowed access to the major churches, the lives of most of them revolved around their own local parish places of worship, where they were baptised, married and buried. Many churches were linked with particular craft and trade guilds.

Monasteries and convents were established, all of which owned valuable acres inside and outside the city walls: the crusading Knights Templars and Knights Hospitallers were two of the earliest religious orders to settle, although the increasingly unruly Templars were disbanded in 1312 by the Pope, and their land eventually became occupied by the lawyers of Inner and Middle Temple.

The surviving church of St Bartholomew-the-Great (founded 1123) and the names of St Helen's Bishopsgate, Spitalfields and St Martin's-le-Grand are all reminders of these early monasteries and convents. The friars, who were active social workers among the poor living outside the city walls, were known by the colour of their habits: the Blackfriars (Dominicans), the Whitefriars (Carmelites) and the Greyfriars (Franciscans). Their names are still in evidence around Fleet Street and the west of the City.

Tudors & Stuarts

Under the Tudor monarchs (1485-1603), spurred by the discovery of America and the ocean routes to Africa and the Orient, London became one of Europe's largest cities. Henry VII brought to an end the Wars of the Roses by defeating Richard III at the Battle of Bosworth and marrying Elizabeth of York. The resulting Tudor rose can be seen in many of the surviving Tudor palaces. Henry VII's other great achievements were the building of a merchant navy and the Henry VII Chapel in Westminster Abbey (the resting place for himself and his queen).

HENRY VIII & THE ENGLISH REFORMATION

Henry VII was succeeded in 1509 by arch wife-collector (and despatcher) Henry VIII. Henry's first marriage to Catherine of Aragon failed to produce an heir so the king, in 1527, determined that the union should be annulled. As the Pope refused to co-operate, Henry defied the Catholic Church, demanding that he himself be recognised as Supreme Head of the Church in England and ordering the execution of anyone who refused to go along with the plan (including his chancellor Sir Thomas More). Thus, England began the transition to Protestantism. The subsequent dissolution of the monasteries transformed the face of the medieval city with the confiscation and redevelopment of all property owned by the Catholic Church.

On a more positive note, Henry developed a professional navy, founding the Royal Dockyards at Woolwich in 1512 and at Deptford the following year. He also established palaces at Hampton Court and Whitehall, and built a residence at St James's Palace. Much of the land he annexed for hunting became the Royal Parks, including Hyde, Regent's, Greenwich and Richmond parks.

There was a brief Catholic revival under Queen Mary (1553-8), and her marriage to Philip II of Spain met with much opposition in London. She had 300 Protestants burned at the stake at Smithfield, earning her the nickname 'Bloody Mary'.

ELIZABETHAN LONDON

Elizabeth I's reign (1558-1603) saw a flowering of English commerce and arts. The founding of the Royal Exchange by Sir Thomas Gresham in 1566 gave London its first trading centre, allowing it to emerge as Europe's leading commercial centre. The merchant venturers and the first joint-stock companies (Russia Company and Levant Company) established new trading enterprises, and Drake, Ralegh and Hawkins sailed to the New World and beyond. In 1580, Elizabeth knighted Sir Francis Drake on his return from a three-year circumnavigation. Eight years later, Drake and Howard defeated the Spanish Armada.

As trade grew, so did London. By 1600, it was home to 200,000 people, many living in dirty, overcrowded conditions, with plague and fire constant hazards. The most complete picture of Tudor London is given in John Stow's *Survey of London* (1598), a fascinating first-hand account by a diligent Londoner, whose monument stands in the City church of St Andrew Undershaft.

The glory of the Elizabethan era was the development of English drama, popular with all social classes but treated with disdain by the Corporation of London, which went so far as to ban theatres from the City in 1575. Two famous rival theatres,

The 'Armada Portrait' of **Elizabeth I.**

the Rose (1587) and the Globe (1599), were erected on the south bank of the Thames at Bankside. It was here that the plays of Marlowe and Shakespeare were performed. Deemed 'a naughty place' by royal proclamation, Bankside was the Soho of its time – home not just to the theatre, but also bear-baiting, cock-fighting, taverns and the 'Stewes' (brothels).

The Tudor dynasty ended with Elizabeth's death in 1603. Her successor, the Stuart King James I, narrowly escaped assassination on 5 November 1605, when Guy Fawkes and his gunpowder were discovered underneath the Palace of Westminster. The Gunpowder Plot was a protest at the failure to improve conditions for the persecuted Catholics, but only resulted in several messy executions and an intensification of anti-papist feelings in ever-intolerant London. The date is commemorated as Bonfire Night. It was James I who employed Inigo Jones to design court masques and the first examples of classical Renaissance style in London, the Queen's House in Greenwich (1616) and the Banqueting House in Westminster (1619).

CIVIL WAR

Charles I succeeded his father in 1625, and gradually fell out with the City of London (from whose citizens he tried to extort taxes) and an increasingly independent-minded and antagonistic Parliament. The last straw came in 1642 when he intruded on the Houses of Parliament in an attempt to arrest five MPs. The country slid into a civil war (1642-9) between the supporters of Parliament (led by Puritan Oliver Cromwell) and those of the King.

Both sides knew that control of the country's major city and port was vital for victory. London's sympathies were firmly with the Parliamentarians and in 1642 24,000 citizens assembled at Turnham Green, west of the city, to face Charles's army. Fatally, the King lost his nerve and withdrew. He was never to seriously threaten the capital again and, eventually, the Royalists were defeated. Charles was tried for treason and, although he denied the legitimacy of the court, he was declared guilty and, on 30 January 1649, was beheaded outside the Banqueting House in Whitehall.

For the next 11 years the country was ruled as a Commonwealth by Cromwell. The closing of the theatres, banning of the supposedly Catholic superstition of Christmas and other Puritan strictures on the wickedness of any sort of fun meant that the restoration of the exiled Charles II in 1660 was greeted with considerable relief and rejoicing by the populace.

PLAGUE, FIRE & THE 'GLORIOUS REVOLUTION'

Two major catastrophes, however, marred the first decade of Charles's reign in the capital. In 1665, the most serious outbreak of bubonic plague since the Black Death devastated the capital's population. By the time that the winter cold put paid to the epidemic nearly 100,000 Londoners had died.

Just as the city was breathing a sigh of relief, a second disaster struck. The fire that spread from a carelessly tended oven in a bakery in Pudding Lane in September 1666 was to rage for three days and consume four-fifths of the city, including 87 churches, 44 livery company halls and more than 13,000 houses.

Here was the chance to rebuild London as a spacious, rationally planned modern city. Many blueprints were drawn up and considered, but, in the end, Londoners were so impatient to get on with business as soon as possible that the city was reconstructed largely on its medieval street plan, albeit this time in brick and stone rather than wood. The towering figure of the period is the extraordinarily prolific Christopher Wren, who personally oversaw the work on 51 of the 54 churches that were rebuilt, including his masterwork, the new St Paul's, which was finished in 1711 and was effectively the world's first Protestant cathedral.

After the Fire, many well-to-do former City residents moved to new residential developments that were springing up in the West End. In the City, the Royal Exchange was rebuilt, but merchants increasingly used the new coffee houses to exchange news. With the expansion of the joint-stock companies and the chance to invest capital, the City was emerging as a financial (rather than manufacturing) centre.

Anti-Catholic feeling still ran high, so the accession of Catholic James II in 1685 aroused fears of a return to Catholicism, and resulted in the Dutch Protestant, William of Orange, being invited to take the throne with his wife Mary Stuart (James's daughter). James fled to France in 1688 in what became known (by its beneficiaries) as the 'Glorious Revolution'. One of the most significant developments in William III's reign was the founding of the Bank of England, in 1694, to finance the King's wars with France.

Georgian London

In accordance with the Act of Settlement (1701), after the death of Queen Anne the throne passed to George, great-grandson of James I, who had been born and brought up in Hanover, Germany. Thus, a German-speaking king (who never learned English) became the first of four long-reigning Georges in the Hanoverian line. During his reign (1714-27), and for several years after, the Whig party – led by Sir Robert Walpole – had the monopoly of power in Parliament. Their opponents, the Tories, supported the Stuarts and had opposed the exclusion of the Catholic James II.

Walpole chaired, on the King's behalf, a group of ministers (the forerunner of today's Cabinet), becoming, in effect, Britain's first prime minister. He was also presented with 10 Downing Street as a residence; it remains the official home of all serving prime ministers.

During the eighteenth century, London grew with astonishing speed, both in terms of population and built-up area. New squares and streets of Georgian terraced houses spread over Bloomsbury, Soho, Mayfair and Marylebone as wealthy landowners and speculative developers took advantage of the demand for leasehold properties. Horse and carriage stabling, built behind the terraces, has become today's fashionable mews housing. South London became more accessible with the opening of the first new bridges, Westminster Bridge (1750) and Blackfriars Bridge (1763). Until then, London Bridge had been the only bridge over the Thames. The old city gates, most of the Roman Wall and the remaining houses on Old London Bridge were demolished, allowing easier access to the City for traffic and people.

POVERTY & CRIME

In the older districts, however, people lived in terrible squalor and poverty, far worse than that of Victorian times. Some of the most notorious slums were around Fleet Street and St Giles (north of Covent Garden), only a short distance from streets of fashionable residences maintained by large numbers of servants. To make matters worse, gin ('mother's ruin') was readily available at very low prices, and many poor Londoners drank excessive amounts in an attempt to escape from the horrors of daily life.

Worse still, the well-off seemed totally complacent. They regularly amused themselves at the popular Ranelagh and Vauxhall Pleasure Gardens, and with organised trips to Bedlam (Bethlehem or Bethlem Hospital) to mock the mental patients, while public executions at Tyburn (near today's Marble Arch) were among the most popular events in the social calendar.

The outrageous imbalance in the distribution of wealth encouraged crime: robberies in the West End often took place in broad daylight. Reformers were few, though there were some notable exceptions. Henry Fielding, the satirical writer and author of the picaresque novel *Tom Jones*, was also an enlightened magistrate at Bow Street Court. In 1751, he established, with his blind brother John, a volunteer force of 'thief-takers' to back up the often ineffective efforts of the parish constables

Oldest swinger in town

In the days before Arsenal v Spurs and Pavarotti in the Park, there was no public spectacle Londoners loved more than a good old public execution. Tyburn was the Wembley Stadium of capital punishment. From 1388 to 1783 (when hangings moved to outside Newgate Prison), it was primarily to this spot near today's Marble Arch that the majority of London's condemned travelled to meet their maker (*see also page 67*). The first permanent gallows was set up here in 1571 and attracted much ooh-ing and aah-ing in the hangmen's world for its groundbreaking triangular design, which allowed eight people to be dispatched on each of its three arms. How economical.

It was hoped that letting the people see what became of lawbreakers would act as a deterrent. Often the opposite was the case. London's legion of unruly apprentices were given a day off for 'the hanging match' and frequently lionised the more notorious and glamorous criminals such as Jack Sheppard, whose death in 1714 was witnessed by an estimated 200,000 people. The prisoner's progress from Newgate Prison to Tyburn (along present-day Oxford Street) would often take around two hours and resemble a triumphal procession, with the condemned waving to onlookers and stopping off at taverns along the way for a final pint or two (often arriving at Tyburn drunk).

Enormous crowds would gather, and the erection of a grandstand during the eighteenth century, known as 'Mother Proctor's Pews', made its owner a fortune. Pepys, present at the execution of Colonel Turner in 1664, paid one shilling to stand on a cartwheel to get a better view. It was fairly common for riots to ensue if a last-minute reprieve arrived and the mob was denied its fun.

It was the hangman's jealously guarded privilege to sell his used rope to gruesome souvenir hunters and to keep the executees' clothes. Once, in 1447, five men were hanged, taken down when still alive, stripped and marked for quartering when their pardon arrived. The hangman refused to give them their clothes back and they had to walk home naked.

The unruliness of the crowds and unseemliness of the spectacle finally forced the government to move executions to within Newgate Prison in 1868. When this was demolished in 1902, they took place in other London jails. The last execution in the UK was in 1964.

and watchmen who were the only law-keepers in the city. This group of early cops, known as the Bow Street Runners, were the forerunners of today's Metropolitan Police (established in 1829).

Disaffection was also evident in the activities of the London mob during this period. Riots were a regular reaction to middlemen charging extortionate prices, or merchants adulterating their food. In June 1780, London was hit by the anti-Catholic Gordon Riots, named after ringleader George Gordon, which were the worst in the city's violent history, leaving 300 people dead.

Some attempt to alleviate the grosser ills of poverty was made by the establishment of five major new hospitals by private philanthropists. St Thomas's and St Bartholomew's were already long established as monastic institutions for the care of the sick, but Westminster (1720), Guy's (1725), St George's (1734), London (1740) and the Middlesex (1745) went on to become world-famous teaching hospitals. Thomas Coram's Foundling Hospital for abandoned children was also one of the remarkable achievements of the time.

It was not only the indigenous population of London that was on the rise in the eighteenth century. Country people (who had lost their own land because of enclosures and were faced with starvation wages or unemployment) drifted into the towns in large numbers. The East End was increasingly the focus for poor immigrant labourers, especially towards the end of the eighteenth century with the buildings of the docks. By 1801, London's population had grown to almost a million, the largest in Europe. And by 1837 (the year Queen Victoria came to the throne), five more bridges and the capital's first railway line (from London Bridge to Greenwich) were further signs of the expansion to follow.

The Victorian era

As well as being the administrative and financial capital of the British Empire, spanning a fifth of the globe, London was also its chief port and the world's largest manufacturing centre, with breweries, distilleries, tanneries, shipyards, engineering works and many other grimy industries lining the south bank of the Thames. On the one hand, London boasted splendid buildings, fine shops, theatres and museums; on the other, it was a city of squalor, poverty, disease and prostitution. The residential areas were becoming polarised into districts with fine terraces, maintained by squads of servants, and overcrowded, insanitary, disease-ridden slums.

The growth of the metropolis in the century before Victoria came to the throne had been spectacular enough, but during her reign (1837-1901) thousands more acres were covered with housing, roads and railway lines. Today, if you pick any street at random within five miles (8km) of central London, the chances are its houses will be mostly from the Victorian era. By the end of the nineteenth century the city's population had swelled to over six million.

Despite the social problems (most memorably depicted in the writings of Charles Dickens), major steps had been taken to improve conditions for the great majority of Londoners by the turn of the century. The Metropolitan Board of Works installed an efficient sewerage system, street lighting and better roads, while the worst slums were replaced by low-cost building schemes funded by philanthropists (such as the American George Peabody) and by the London County Council (created in 1888).

THE RAILWAYS

The Victorian expansion of London would not have been possible without an efficient public transport network to speed workers into and out of the city from the new suburbs. The horse-drawn bus appeared on London's streets for the first time in 1829, but it was the opening of the first passenger railway, from Greenwich to London Bridge, in 1836, that hailed the London of the future. In 1863, the first underground line – which ran between Paddington and Farringdon Road – proved an instant success, attracting more than 30,000 travellers on the first day. The world's first electric track in a deep tunnel (the 'tube') opened in 1890 between the City and Stockwell (it later became part of the present-day Northern Line).

THE GREAT EXHIBITION

The Great Exhibition in 1851 captured the spirit of the age: confidence and pride, discovery and invention. Prince Albert, the Queen's Consort, was involved in the organisation of this triumphant event, for which the Crystal Palace, a giant building in iron and glass (designed not by a professional architect but by the Duke of Devonshire's talented gardener, Joseph Paxton), was erected in Hyde Park. During the five months it was open, the Exhibition drew some six million visitors from Great Britain and abroad, and the profits inspired the Prince Consort to establish a permanent centre for the study of the applied arts and sciences: the result is the South Kensington museums and Imperial College. After the Exhibition, the Palace was moved to Sydenham and used as an exhibition centre until it was destroyed by fire in 1936.

When the Victorians were not colonising the world by force, they had the foresight to combine their conquests with scientific developments. The Royal Geographical Society sent navigators to chart unknown waters, botanists to bring back new species, and geologists to study the earth. Many of the specimens that were brought back ended up in the Royal Botanic Gardens at Kew.

A bridge too far

Until the eighteenth century the city's only river crossing was building-cluttered Old London Bridge – tremendously picturesque but hopelessly impractical. The capital's bridge builders since then, as if in reaction, have gone to the other extreme and, with the exception of Tower Bridge, there's been little place for dash or whimsy in the multitude of crossings that now join the north and south banks of the Thames. It could have been so different…

WATERLOO BRIDGE

In the 1770s, **Thomas Sandby** proposed an extraordinarily ornate bridge on the site of today's Waterloo Bridge. Lined with columns, arches and colonnades, featuring domed wings and Italianate buildings, it was adorned, and all but overwhelmed, by almost every known form of classical ornamentation. This design was later elaborated on by Sandby's pupil Sir John Soane (*see page 61*).

(John Rennie's graceful granite Waterloo Bridge was built in 1811-17. Described by Canova as 'the noblest bridge in the world', it was demolished, amid great protests, to be replaced by the current cantilevered concrete bridge by Sir Giles Gilbert Scott in 1937-42.)

CHARING CROSS BRIDGE

The ugly iron Charing Cross (or Hungerford) rail bridge, completed in 1864, replaced Brunel's Hungerford Suspension Footbridge. The rail bridge, located at one of the prime Thames sites, was never popular, and one of the most striking plans to replace it was dreamed up by **TE Colcutt** in 1906. Assuming that the railway line would terminate on the south side of the river, the bridge was to provide a link on an axis from Trafalgar Square to Waterloo Station. It was to be lined with colonnades containing 50 shops on each side. Later, Sir Edwin Lutyens also proposed a new bridge – an audacious combined road and rail bridge with six rail tracks below and an 18-metre (60-ft) wide road bridge above.

(The original rail bridge remains in place, although two new, graceful footbridges are to be built alongside it, the first by December 2000 and the second by April 2001.)

ST PAUL'S BRIDGE

In the mid-nineteenth century it was deemed necessary for a new bridge to link St Paul's with Southwark. Francis Bennoch came up with a bold plan but it was shelved; the next schemes didn't materialise until after an Act of Parliament

The twentieth century

During the brief reign of Edward VII (1901-10), London regained some of the gaiety and glamour lacking in the last dour years of Victoria's reign. A touch of Parisian chic came to London with the opening of the Ritz Hotel in Piccadilly; the Café Royal was at the height of its popularity as a meeting place for artists and writers; while 'luxury catering for the little man' was provided at the Lyons Tea Shops and new Lyons Corner Houses (the Coventry Street branch, opened in 1907, could accommodate 4,500 people). Meanwhile, the first American-style department store, Selfridges, opened to an eager public on Oxford Street in 1909.

Entertainment for the little man (and woman) meant a night out at the music hall. Audiences cheered and jeered at the songs and jokes of Max Miller and Marie Lloyd right into the 1930s, when the variety shows lost out to cinema, radio and, eventually, television.

Road transport was revolutionised. Motor cars put-putted around the city's streets. The first motor bus was introduced in 1904, and by 1911 the use of horse-drawn buses had been abandoned. Electric trams (double-deckers) started running in 1901 (though not through the West End or the City) and continued until 1952.

WORLD WAR I (1914-18)

London suffered its first air raids in World War I. The first bomb over the city was dropped from a Zeppelin near Guildhall in September 1915, to be followed by many nightly raids. Bombing raids from planes began in July 1917. Cleopatra's Needle, on Victoria Embankment, was a minor casualty, receiving damage to the plinth and one of its sphinxes that can still be seen. In all, around 650 people lost their lives as a result of Zeppelin raids.

BETWEEN THE WARS

Political change happened quickly after World War I. Lloyd George's government averted revolution in 1918-19 by promising (but not delivering) 'homes for heroes' for the embittered returning soldiers. But the Liberal Party's days in power were numbered and, by 1924, the Labour Party had enough MPs to form its first government, led by Ramsay MacDonald.

After the trauma of World War I, a 'live for today' attitude prevailed among the young upper classes in the 'roaring twenties', who flitted from parties in

of 1911 approved the building of a bridge. Decades of wrangles over designs and sites came to nothing and the idea had lapsed by the 1940s. *(There is still no road bridge at St Paul's, although Sir Norman Foster's Millennium Bridge, designed with the sculptor Anthony Caro, which will link the Tate Modern gallery to the north bank of the river near St Paul's Cathedral, will be completed by April 2000.)*

LONDON BRIDGE

In 1800, **George Dance the Younger** conceived an audacious scheme for the proposed new London Bridge (*see picture*). His plans were, in fact, for two parallel bridges, 100m (328ft) apart and each incorporating a drawbridge to allow ships through, with immense crescents of houses sweeping from one bridge to the other around great piazzas. Another famed but failed design was **Thomas Telford**'s impressive single-span cast-iron bridge, shelved because of problems with the approaches rather than the bridge itself. *(In 1823-31 John Rennie's five-arch stone bridge was built; it was superseded by the present unprepossessing concrete structure in 1967-72).*

TOWER BRIDGE

Around the middle of the nineteenth century it became clear that the volume of cross-river traffic necessitated a bridge close to the Tower of London. Of the range of plans for Tower Bridge, the weirdest was that of **Sidengham Duer**'s high-level metal bridge. Hydraulic lifts carried carts, horses and pedestrians up 24 metres (80ft) to the bridge and then down the other side. *(London's best-known bridge was completed in 1894. Sir Horace Jones' fashionable Victorian Gothic towers conceal a steel frame.)*

Mayfair to dances at the Ritz. But this meant little to the mass of Londoners, who were suffering in the post-war slump. In 1921, Poplar Council in east London refused to levy the rates on its impoverished population. The entire council was sent to prison but later released, having achieved an equilisation of the rates over all London boroughs that relieved the burden on the poorest ones.

Civil disturbances, caused by rising unemployment and an increased cost of living, resulted in the nationwide General Strike of 1926, when the working classes downed tools in support of the striking miners. Prime Minister Baldwin encouraged volunteers to take over the public services and the streets teemed with army-escorted food convoys, aristocrats running soup kitchens and students driving buses. After nine days of chaos, the strike was called off by the Trades Union Congress (TUC).

The economic situation only worsened in the early 1930s following the New York Stock Exchange crash of 1929. By 1931, more than three million people were unemployed in Britain. During these years, the London County Council began to have a greater impact on the city's life, undertaking programmes of slum clearance and new housing, creating more parks and taking under its wing education, transport, hospitals, libraries and the fire service. London's population increased dramatically between the wars, peaking at nearly 8.7 million in 1939. To accommodate the influx, the suburbs expanded at a tremendous rate, particularly to the north-west with the extension of the Metropolitan Line (an area that became known as Metroland). Identical gabled, double-fronted houses sprang up in their hundreds of thousands, from Golders Green to Surbiton.

And all these new Londoners were entertained by the new media of film, radio and, later, TV. London's first radio broadcast was beamed from the roof of Marconi House in the Strand in 1922. Soon families were gathering around their enormous Bakelite wireless sets to hear the latest sounds from the British Broadcasting Company (the BBC; from 1927 called the British Broadcasting Corporation). Television broadcasts started on 26 August 1936, when the first BBC telecast went out live from Alexandra Palace studios.

WORLD WAR II (1939-45)

Neville Chamberlain's policy of appeasement towards Hitler's increasingly aggressive Germany during the 1930s finally collapsed when the

Germans invaded Poland. On 3 September 1939 Britain declared war. The government implemented precautionary measures against the threat of air raids – including the digging of trench shelters in London parks, and the evacuation of 600,000 children and pregnant mothers – but the expected bombing raids did not happen during the autumn and winter of 1939-40, a period that became known as the 'Phoney War'. In July 1940 Germany began preparations for an invasion of Britain with three months of aerial attack that came to be known as the Battle of Britain.

For Londoners, the Phoney War came to an abrupt end on 7 September 1940 when hundreds of German bombers dumped their loads of high explosives on east London and the docks. Entire streets were destroyed; the dead and injured numbered over 2,000. The Blitz had begun. The raids on London continued for 57 consecutive nights, then intermittently for a further six months. Londoners reacted with tremendous bravery and stoicism and the period is still nostalgically referred to as 'Britain's finest hour'. After a final massive raid on 10 May 1941, the Germans focused their attention elsewhere, but by the end of the war about a third of the City and the East End was in ruins.

From 1942 the tide of the war began to turn, but Londoners still had a new terror to face – the V1 or doodlebug. In 1944, dozens of these explosive-packed pilotless planes descended on the city, causing widespread destruction. Later in the year, the more powerful V2 rocket was launched. Over the winter, 500 V2s dropped on London, mostly in the East End; the last one fell on 27 March 1945 in Orpington, Kent. Victory in Europe (VE Day) was declared on 8 May 1945. Thousands of people took to the streets of London to celebrate.

Bomb damage around St Paul's Cathedral.

POST-WAR LONDON

World War II left Britain almost as shattered as Germany. Soon after VE Day, a general election was held and Churchill was heavily defeated by the Labour Party under Clement Attlee. The new government established the National Health Service in 1948, and began a massive nationalisation programme that included public transport, electricity, gas, postal and telephone services. But for all the planned changes, life for most people was drab, regimented and austere.

In London, the most immediate problem was a critical shortage of housing. Prefabricated bungalows provided a temporary solution (though many were still occupied 40 years later), but the huge new high-rise housing estates that the planners began to erect were often badly built and unpopular with residents.

There were bright spots, however, during this otherwise rather dour time. London hosted the Olympic Games in 1948 and three years later came the Festival of Britain (100 years after the Great Exhibition), a celebration of British technology and design. The exhibitions that took over derelict land on the south bank of the Thames for the Festival provided the incentive to build the South Bank Centre, now the largest arts centre in Europe.

THE 1950S & 1960S

As the 1950s progressed, life and prosperity gradually returned to London, leading Prime Minister Harold Macmillan in 1957 to proclaim that 'most of our people have never had it so good'. The coronation of Queen Elizabeth II in 1953 had been the biggest television broadcast in history and there was the feeling of a new age dawning.

However, many Londoners were moving out of the city. The population dropped by half a million in the late 1950s, causing a labour shortage that prompted huge recruitment drives in Britain's former colonies. London Transport and the National Health Service were particularly active in encouraging West Indians to emigrate to Britain. Unfortunately, as the Notting Hill race riots of 1958 illustrated, the welcome these new emigrants received was rarely friendly. One of the few relatively tolerant areas of the city was Soho. During the 1950s, it became famed for its seedy, bohemian pubs, clubs and jazz joints, such as the still-jumping Ronnie Scott's.

By the mid-1960s London had started to swing. The innovative fashions of Mary Quant and others broke the stranglehold of Paris on couture; boutiques blossomed along King's Road, while Biba set the pace in Kensington. Carnaby Street became a byword for hipness, as the city basked in its newfound reputation as the music and fashion capital of the world.

The year of student unrest throughout Europe, 1968, saw the first issue of *Time Out* (a fold-up sheet for 5p) appear on the streets in August. The decade ended with the Beatles naming their final album *Abbey Road* after their recording studios in London NW8, and the Rolling Stones playing a free gig in Hyde Park (July 1969) that drew around half a million people.

THE 1970S & 1980S

The bubble had to burst: many Londoners remember the 1970s as a decade of economic strife. Inflation, the oil crisis and international debt caused chaos in the economy; and the IRA began its bombing campaign on mainland Britain. The explosion of punk in the second half of the decade, sartorially inspired by the idiosyncratic genius of Vivienne Westwood, provided some nihilistic colour.

History will regard the 1980s as the Thatcher era. When the Conservatives won the general election in 1979, Britain's first woman prime minister – the propagandist for 'market forces' and Little Englander morality – set out to expunge socialism and the influence of the 1960s and 1970s. A monetarist policy and cuts in public services savagely widened the divide between rich and poor. While the professionals and 'yuppies' (Young Urban Professionals) profited from tax cuts and easy credit, unemployment soared. In London, riots erupted in Brixton (1981) and Tottenham (1985); mass unemployment and heavy-handed policing methods were seen as contributing factors.

The Greater London Council (GLC) mounted spirited opposition to the Thatcher government, a sin for which it was abolished in 1986. Since then, London has been without an elected governing body, but a referendum in May 1998 returned a resounding vote in favour of creating a mayor with authority over the whole of the city, which will happen in 2000 (*see page 26* **I could'a been a contender**).

The spectacular rise in house prices at the end of the 1980s (peaking in August 1988) was followed by an equally alarming slump and the onset of a severe recession that only started to lift in the mid-1990s. The Docklands development (one of the Thatcher enterprise schemes, set up in 1981 in order to create a new business centre in the docklands to the east of the City) has faltered many times. Although it can now be counted as a qualified success in terms of attracting business to the Isle of Dogs, the bleakness of the surrounding area and lack of infrastructure make it unpopular with Docklands' office workers, and the locals in the area resent the intrusion of the yuppies.

Official guide to the 1951 **Festival of Britain**.

THE 1990S

The replacement of Margaret Thatcher by John Major as leader of the Conservative Party in October 1990 signalled an upsurge of hope in London. A riot in Trafalgar Square had helped to see off both Maggie and her inequitable Poll Tax.

Yet the early years of the decade were scarred by continuing recession and an all-too-visible problem of homelessness on the streets of the capital. Shortly after the Conservatives were elected for yet another term in office in 1992, the IRA detonated a massive bomb in the City, killing three people and obliterating the Baltic Exchange. This was followed by a second bomb a year later, which shattered buildings around Bishopsgate. Another Docklands bomb in February 1996 broke a fragile 18-month ceasefire. Yet now, with the Good Friday Agreement and the devolution of power to Belfast, there's a real chance of a permanent peace in the province, and the terrorist threat to the capital has been massively reduced.

In May 1997, the British people ousted the tired Tories. Tony Blair's notably unsocialist Labour Party swept to victory on a huge wave of enthusiasm. Though the Labour Government has not yet delivered all its promises, its popularity hasn't waned (thanks in part to the lack of any credible opposition) and the general mood in London today remains one of optimism.

Follow my leader

Over the last couple of hundred years Britain's relatively liberal political climate has provided haven and intellectual succour to countless foreign political activists and radical thinkers. Michael Collins, Sun Yat Sen, Marcus Garvey, Lenin and Ho Chi Minh all spent time here (the latter as a washer-up at The Savoy) before returning home to run an uprising or revolution.

The ten-mile (16-km) walk below – stretching in a crescent from Earl's Court in west London, through Regent's Park via Notting Hill, and then south to Bloomsbury, ending in Soho – takes in the one-time homes (all marked by Blue Plaques) of ten major international figures.

(Directions are given only for the areas outside those covered by the maps at the back of this Guide.)

(Take the District Line or Piccadilly Line tube to West Kensington or Baron's Court.)

1 Mahatma Gandhi (1869-1948)
20 Baron's Court Road, W14 (just off **Map 3 A11**)

On the road running parallel to (and just south of) the traffic-choked Talgarth Road is one of the houses where the young Mohandas Karamchand Gandhi lived while studying law at Inner Temple in the 1880s. At that time, Gandhi thought England 'the land of philosophers and poets, the very centre of civilisation' and dressed in a rather flash and foppish western style. The leaders of his caste disagreed and expelled him.

(Cross the main road at West Kensington station and walk north up North End Road, then right at the junction with Hammersmith Road at Olympia Exhibition Centre; Russell Road is second on the left.)

2 Mohammed Ali Jinnah (1876-1948)
35 Russell Road, W14 (just off **Map 3 A9**)

Only a mile away from Gandhi's student digs are those of the eventual founder of Pakistan while he was studying at Lincoln's Inn in 1895. At first, Jinnah found England 'a strange country', 'but I soon settled down and was quite happy'.

(From Russell Road, take Napier Road across Holland Road and straight on along Melbury Road to Holland Park. Walk north through Holland Park, emerging at the street, Holland Park. Turn right on Holland Park Avenue then left up Ladbroke Grove. Elgin Crescent is the eighth road on the left.)

3 Jawaharlal Nehru (1889-1964)
60 Elgin Crescent, W11 (just off **Map 1 A6**)

The third west London Indian law student connection is the house where the first prime minister of India lived in 1910 and 1912 while reading for the bar at Inner Temple (and living the high life). Nehru was the most anglicised of the three, having been educated at Harrow and Trinity College, Cambridge.

(At the east end of Elgin Crescent, turn right into Kensington Park Road and then second left into Chepstow Villas.)

4 Lajos (Louis) Kossuth (1802-94)
39 Chepstow Villas, W11 (**Map 1 A6**)

Regarded as the father of Hungarian democracy, Kossuth, a liberal editor and lawyer, advocated independence for Hungary in 1848. He was forced to flee the country the following year and, after a spell as a prisoner in Turkey, was warmly and sympathetically welcomed in England in 1851. He stayed at this house in Notting Hill before moving on to the USA and back again.

(Continue down Chepstow Villas, which turns into Pembridge Villas, and on to Westbourne Grove (which, along with Queensway, has great places for lunch). Head for Warwick Avenue tube station. Warrington Crescent leads away from the station.)

5 David Ben-Gurion (1886-1973)
75 Warrington Crescent, W9 (just off **Map 1 C4**)

The future first prime minister of Israel lived in this Maida Vale house in 1920 while in Britain rallying support for his proposed Jewish homeland in Palestine. (He packed out the Royal Albert Hall on one occasion.)

(Walk back to Warwick Avenue tube station, turn left along Clifton Gardens/Clifton Road, over Maida Vale/Edgware Road and down St John's Wood Road past Lord's Cricket Ground. At the end of the road turn right on to Park Road.)

6 José de San Martin (1778-1850)
23 Park Road, NW1 (north of **Map 1 F4**)

The Argentine soldier and statesman played a major part in gaining his country independence from Spain.

(Walk north across Regent's Park, emerging on Prince Albert Road, then left onto Albert Terrace and over Primrose Hill on to Regent's Park Road. Chalcot Crescent comes off Regent's Park Road on the east side of Primrose Hill.)

7 Dr José Rizal (1861-96)
37 Chalcot Crescent, NW1 (north of **Map 5 G2**)

The writer and national hero of the Philippines lived here while touring Europe between 1882 and 1887. He published his classic novel *Noli me*

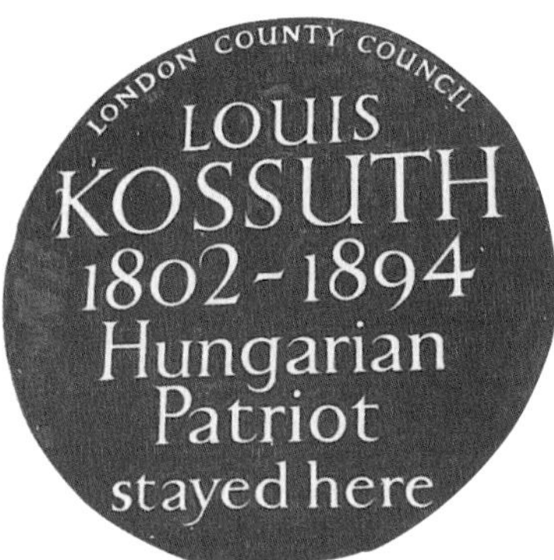

Tangere in 1886 – its condemnation of the Catholic Church in the Philippines for its support of Spanish colonialism, and his support of (non-violent) nationalism, made him a marked man at home. In 1896, Rizal was arrested and executed by firing squad.

8 Friedrich Engels (1820-95)
121 Regent's Park Road, NW1 (north of **Map 5 G2**)
The German political philosopher, who, with Marx, wrote *The Communist Manifesto*, spent most of his life in England. He lived at this house from 1870 to 1894.

(Walk down Regent's Park Road or Gloucester Avenue, then turn right on to Albany Street. Continue down to Great Portland Street tube station then turn left. Gower Street is the sixth road on the right, by Euston Square tube station.)

9 Giuseppe Mazzini (1805-72)
183 Gower Street, NW1 (**Map 6 K4**)
Mazzini, one of the liberal leaders of Italy's Risorgimento, was banished from his homeland, and then expelled from France and Switzerland, taking refuge in London in 1837. He lived here in poverty, teaching and helping the Italian organ-boys, before returning to Italy to take part in the Italian revolution.

10 Karl Marx (1818-83)
28 Dean Street, W1 (**Map 6 K6**)
The German political, social and economic theorist moved to London in 1849 after a decade of writing and editing radical newspapers and formulating the basics of communism in Germany, Paris and Brussels. From 1851 to 1856 Marx and his family lived in poverty in Soho, but during this time he began his researches in the nearby British Library (in its original site on Great Russell Street) that led to the publication of *Das Kapital*.

The funeral of Princess Diana at Westminster Abbey in September 1997 prompted extraordinary scenes and a thoroughly un-British outpouring of emotion. Far more British was the speed with which life got back to normal – the supply of flowers outside Kensington Palace dried up and the local residents started grouching about the planned 'Diana Memorial Garden' (now downgraded to a monument, to be built in one of the royal parks).

Nimby-ism (Not In My Back Yard) is also threatening far more worthwhile projects such as Sir Norman Foster's scheme to pedestrianise part of Trafalgar Square and Westminster. But plenty of big schemes are going ahead (*see pages 27-30*), and if the Dome turns out to be as big a waste of money as some fear, then there are at least a clutch of excellent projects (particularly the magnificent **Tate Modern** on the South Bank) that will spruce up the capital in time for the start of the new century.

Expensive public transport, traffic choked roads and environmental pollution remain major problems in London, but tourism in the capital has never been stronger, the city is building on the international renown for the excellence of its shops, restaurants, clubs and creative talent, and, in 2000, the long-overdue election of a Mayor with genuine powers to bring about change should at last give Londoners a positive voice in how their city is run in the next millennium.

Carnaby Street, *in the days when it swung.*

Key events

AD43 Roman invasion of Britain; building of bridge over Thames and foundation of Londinium.
61 Boudicca burns Londinium; the city is rebuilt and designated provincial capital.
200 City wall built; Londinium becomes capital of Britannia Superior.
410 Evacuation of Roman troops from Britain.
c600 Building of Saxon London, west of Roman city.
604 First St Paul's built by King Ethelbert; Mellitus appointed Bishop of London.
841, 851 Norse raids on London.
c871 Danes occupy London.
886 King Alfred of Wessex retakes London.
1013 Danes take London again.
1042 Edward the Confessor builds new palace and 'West Minster' upstream from city.
1066 Death of Harold at Hastings; William I crowned in Westminster Abbey; London granted a charter.
1067 Building of Tower of London started.
1176 Work starts on first stone London Bridge.
1185 Temple church consecrated.
1191 Henry Fitzalwin becomes London's first mayor.
1213 St Thomas's Hospital founded at Southwark.
1215 Mayor of London is one of signatories of Magna Carta; this strengthens power of City.
1240 First Parliament sits at Westminster.
1290 Jews expelled from London.
1327 First Common Council of City of London.
1348-9 Black Death devastates London.
1381 Wat Tyler's Peasants' Revolt.
1397 Richard Whittington becomes Lord Mayor.
1411 First Guildhall built.
1476 First printing press set up by William Caxton at Westminster.
1513 Royal Dockyard at Woolwich and Deptford founded by Henry VIII.
1534 Henry VIII breaks with the Catholic Church.
1566 Thomas Gresham opens the Royal Exchange.
1577 First theatre in London built at Shoreditch.
1598 John Stow's *Survey of London* published.
1599 Globe Theatre built at Southwark.
1605 Guy Fawkes' failed Gunpowder Plot to blow up James I and Parliament.
1642 Start of the Civil War; Royalists defeated at Turnham Green.
1649 Charles I executed; Commonwealth established under Oliver Cromwell.
1664-5 The Great Plague.
1666 The Great Fire.
1675-1711 Building of new St Paul's after the Fire.
1692 First insurance market opens at Lloyd's.
1694 Bank of England established.
1717 Hanover Square and Cavendish Square laid out; start of development of the West End.
1732 10 Downing Street offered to Sir Robert Walpole as official residence.
1750 Building of Westminster Bridge.
1759 Foundation of Royal Botanic Gardens, Kew.
1766 City wall demolished.
1780 The anti-Catholic, anti-Irish Gordon Riots.
1802 Stock Exchange founded.
1803 First public railway – horsedrawn from Croydon to Wandsworth.
1812 Prime Minister Spencer Perceval assassinated at House of Commons.
1824 National Gallery founded.
1827-8 Regent's Park Zoo opened.
1829 London's first horse-drawn bus, from Paddington to the City; Metropolitan Police Act.
1833 London Fire Brigade established.
1835 Madame Tussaud's waxworks opens.
1836 First passenger railway opened, from Greenwich to London Bridge; University of London founded.
1837-52 Rebuilding of the Houses of Parliament after fire.
1841 Last Thames frost fair.
1843 Trafalgar Square laid out.
1848-9 Major cholera epidemic.
1851 Great Exhibition held in Hyde Park.
1853 Harrods opened.
1858 'The Great Stink', pollution of the Thames.
1863 Opening of the world's first underground railway, the Metropolitan Line.
1864 First Peabody buildings, providing cheap housing for the poor, built in Spitalfields.
1865 Metropolitan Fire Brigade founded.
1866 Last major cholera outbreak; Sanitation Act.
1868 Last public execution at Newgate Prison.
1877 First Wimbledon tennis tournament.
1884 Greenwich Mean Time established.
1888 Jack the Ripper murders terrorise East End.
1889 London County Council created.
1890 Housing Act enables LCC to clear slums; opening of first electric underground railway, from Bank to Stockwell.
1915-18 Zeppelins bomb London.
1940-4 The Blitz devastates much of London.
1948 Olympic Games held in London.
1951 Festival of Britain.
1953 Coronation of Queen Elizabeth II.
1966 England win the World Cup at Wembley.
1982 Closure of last of London's docks.
1984 Thames Flood Barrier completed.
1986 Abolition of the Greater London Council.
1990 Poll tax riot in Trafalgar Square.
1991 Riot in Brixton.
1992 Opening of Canary Wharf development; IRA bomb the Baltic Exchange in the City.
1997 Funeral of Princess Diana at Westminster Abbey.
2000 London elects its Mayor; opening of the Tate Modern and Tate Britain galleries, the Dome, the Millennium Bridge, the London Eye observation wheel and a host of other millennium projects.

London Today

Live and unplugged.

It was a miserable, raining and almost freezing Sunday when I first glimpsed the London Eye, that great new wheel on the south bank of the Thames. I'd missed the slow drama of it being lifted up over the river and had been away when the Spanish eco-protesters climbed up it within hours of it being raised. But now I was at Waterloo. I turned left and saw this thing poking over County Hall. I shrieked. It was like a new moon had fallen into the river. I rounded another corner and there it was again, this time a grey sliver hard against an office block. Then it was a cheeky quadrant peeping between buildings, in turns an arc, a wink, a smile and finally a full, but empty face. From the south bank I could see right through it to the cruel, Gothic, aspiring upward lines of the Houses of Parliament and the cold stone of colonial Westminster. From over the river, it just hung there, reflecting itself in the water, touching the low grey sky. If the gigantic Dome, ten long miles to the east, is a noisy, crass corporate lecture about 'change' and 'progress' and a reflection of what politicians and designers think we the British are supposed to be, the wheel is altogether simpler and more naïve. It just goes round, letting us muse about London for ourselves. It says 'see for yourself', 'try a new perspective', 'be amazed'.

Don't ya just love our feathered friends?

REFLECTING ON THE PAST

Surrounded by the secrecy of Whitehall, the impenetrability of government, the choked streets and the urgency of life in the megalopolis, the wheel is the first genuine new observation point in a century of progressive privatisation of space and the closing down of London vistas. It fits a city – and a country – trying to get a new perspective on itself, eager to come to terms with its past and searching for a new way forward. How can a city this size, this rich, this important to so many people, turn the democratic selection of a mayor into a West End farce? How can £758 million be spent on a structure (the Dome) that only a few politicians ever wanted and which will be dismantled in a year or two? How could the room I paid £20 a week to rent only 15 years ago now be 'worth' £150,000? Pass.

London is the most human and alien of cities. It is not an English city. It's certainly not a European city. It is rather a world city, a crossroads and meeting place for cultures, with all the pleasures and horrors such an identity implies. If it could talk it would be in an unintelligible babble of 300 languages. If it saw a doctor it would be sent for treatment on the spot. There's a sense that both body and mind are deteriorating. The circulation is awful, its extremities neglected and its heart distinctly unhealthy.

WARTS AND ALL

Yet, in spite of (or perhaps because of) all its faults, Londoners love their city. I hate the way the unique is being ironed out, to be replaced by the same global chains of shops, bars, restaurants, shows and hotels that you'll find now in Rome or Paris. I might loathe the way space is being corporatised, the centre made richer at the expense of the margins, but you might approve of the way Brick Lane and other beloved corners are being sanitised and turned to new bars, new clubs, new flats. We might both hate the lousy schools and the fact that it costs a small fortune to see a football match, yet love the soaring new glass walls, the prospect of new bridges, fireworks, carnivals, the return of beaches to the river, the vibrancy of the villages and the clubs.

It's the excluded parts of the city that act as a dampener to unbridled optimism, however. Out in the run-down areas of Manor House, Southall, and other grey suburbs, the very idea of Fulham, Chelsea or Belgravia seems somehow irrelevant. In these overripe, cocooned oases, the smugness and arrogance is tangible.

WE'LL DO IT OUR WAY

So each Londoner makes their own London, their own islands and networks of profession, degrees of wealth, neighbourhood, speed of life, street and self-interest. We learn who to trust and where and what to avoid. We watch the human ecology, the way one area or group feeds off another and is in turn consumed by others. We hear the politicians trumpeting that London is the capital of commerce, design, good living, environmental excellence and tranquillity, the richest area of Europe. And, whether or not we believe them, we learn to live with the city's downsides.

From the top of the wheel, the city spread below us, our perspectives slowly changing, we can see the city's limits and physicality. We see how the city evolved, first hugging its banks, sprawling west and east and now erupting everywhere. The concrete forest, the empty river curling through it, the infinite shades of green, blue and grey. On a bad day it all seems rather alien, remote and untouchable. On a good day we feel a real part of it and sense the thrill of the new, the history and get the feeling that the world is changing under our feet. For a moment at least we understand we are at some centre, a turning point to be celebrated. The humanity of it all then physically hurts.

John Vidal is environment editor of the Guardian.

I could'a been a contender

May 2000 sees a watershed in the political life of the capital. For the first time in London's history, the good folk of the metropolis will have the chance to vote for their own city leader. While the City, that square mile of London that is the capital of capitals, has long had its own liveried Lord Mayor – from Dick Whittington, philanthropist and cat-lover, to the current incumbent, Alderman Clive Martin – this new London Mayor will preside over the whole city, and be elected by over five million voters, making him or her the most personally endorsed political figure in the country.

But attempts to select the candidates proved chaotic and farcical, with the party leaderships embarrassed by their efforts to influence the outcome of a selection process supposedly left to the grass-roots membership. New Labour were troubled by the prospect that 'Red' Ken Livingstone, the newt lover who led the previous London Authority, the Greater London Council, could indeed prove to be the people's choice, and has led to allegations that the party hierarchy has interfered with the internal election process. Tony Blair's preferred choice, the ex-Health Secretary, Frank Dobson, is a Yorkshireman with the charisma, and appearance, of Father Christmas. Glenda Jackson, cinema's one-time Queen Elizabeth, was Labour's third candidate.

The Conservative Party allowed the blue-rinse brigade to choose the darling of the party faithful, Lord Archer, a man long suspected of being economical with the truth. As many predicted, details of past transgressions emerged that forced Archer to withdraw from both the race and public life. The runner-up in the Tory vote, Steven Norris, has had a high public profile, not least because of his colourful love life. He was always open about his philandering, but such a background may have left the Tories nervous of supporting him.

Which leads to Susan Kramer, the Liberal Democrat's candidate. She took to the streets, quietly pounding the pavement, trying to increase her public profile and to focus the people's attention on the issues. Unfortunately for her, she was hampered by her apparent integrity and skeleton-free cupboard, her party's efficient and steadfast decision-making, and by the fact that there was no one with whom to argue the issues.

So what are the issues? The new Mayor will provide a strategic influence over areas such as transport, policing, public health and the environment. But crucially, s/he will not have broad tax-raising powers, and will still have to leave most of the implementation of policies to the boroughs. It is perhaps the prospect of a toothless tiger at the helm that has led to the policy differences playing second fiddle to the personalities. And, as if to prove the point, at the end of 1999 Malcolm McLaren, former manager of the Sex Pistols and godfather of punk, threw his hat in the ring, to be followed, days later, by Cockney songsters Chas and Dave.

Yet by the time you read this, the chances are that the back-biting and the in-fighting will be but distant memories. A mayor will have been chosen and the real business of discovering what difference they can make to the life of the city begins.

Building for the Future

A round-up of the capital's constructions.

Take the Central Line to St Paul's, walk to the south side of the cathedral, cross the road and continue walking until you come to the river – here you will see, in microcosm, all the tensions, ambiguities and contradictions that is London's architecture. Immediately in front of you will be the spanking new Millennium Bridge; ahead is the aged Bankside Power Station, a brick monolith cleverly converted into one of the largest galleries of modern art in the world; and to its left is the Globe Theatre, a brand-new complex built in the style of the sixteenth century – timber framing, thatched roof, the lot.

So what's going on? London is engaged in the largest building spree since the nineteenth century, a phenomenon triggered by a combination of factors including a general sense of prosperity, the advent of the National Lottery and millennium fever. But London is not, and never has been, a city for the master-planner; it is, instead, a curious mixture of just about every architectural style since Roman times. And since the abolition of the Greater London Council in the mid-'80s, the city's planning officers have been employed by a loose collection of councils, authorities and corporations that take little notice of each other – resulting in a complete absence of vision for London's architecture, transport and services.

It is also worth noting that London is ringed by an area called the 'green belt', a slice of protected countryside that prevents the city from spreading out into the whole of south-east England. This, and the vocal army of conservationists who slap preservation orders on anything more than a generation old has forced architects to respect their heritage and reuse old buildings rather than pull them down. The new is often grafted on to the old in a way that is invisible from street level and visitors will often be surprised by the way contemporary interiors have been inserted into elderly buildings. Fortunately, this does not mean that modern, landmark buildings are not going up – you just have to know where to look.

HI-TECH

It is a cause of wonder, then, that London is now showcasing some of the most extraordinary new buildings in Europe. Impossible to ignore, whether you want to or not, is the **Dome** in Greenwich (*see pages 124*). Whatever you think of this £758-million tent, there's no denying the impressive list of architects brought in to work on the project.

Computer-generated image of the **Millennium Bridge** *next to the* **Tate Modern**. *See page 29.*

The end of the line

Jubilee-ve this is **Canary Wharf** *station?*

It is curious that one of the more significant additions to London's architecture is buried undergound. The long-awaited **Jubilee Line Extension**, joining Green Park in the West End with Stratford in the east, is a showcase of different architectural talent. Each station and bus depot along the ten-mile (16-km) route is the product of a different design practice, and it is well worth an architectural buff's time to explore every one.

Alsop, Lyall & Störmer's station at **North Greenwich** didn't need to win the civic and community division of the Sterling Architecture Prize (which it shared with Stratford station) to boost its public image: it's the nearest station to the Millennium Dome. A composition of steel, cobalt mosaics and electric blue lighting, the station is a dramatic architectural departure for the tube system. The £110-million building even suspends its concourse over the tracks, so that its 12,000 hourly passengers can look down on to the platforms below. The redevelopment at **Stratford**, a relative bargain at £25 million, is an overland station and features an extraordinary cantilevered roof that seems to pay homage to the great railway buildings of the nineteenth century.

For sheer scale, however, get off at **Canary Wharf** – where the station is further evidence of the ubiquity of Norman Foster. As long as the neighbouring tower block is tall, you can't help but be awed by the concrete gull-wing structure that towers overhead. If you want to see the sort of space that architectural writers have in mind when they use the term 'cathedral-like', buy a ticket to Canary Wharf.

These include Zaha Hadid, Shigeru Ban and Nigel Coates (designer of the beautiful, if not so well-known, extension to London's interior design showcase, the **Geffrye Museum**; *see page 111*).

Aside from this obvious act of extravagance, visitors may be surprised to discover that large sums of money are being spent on the city's museums, sports stadiums, bridges and even its neglected transport system. A fair chunk of this work is emerging from the founding fathers of the UK's hi-tech movement, **Richard Rogers** (sorry, Lord Rogers of Riverside) and **Norman Foster** (or rather, Lord Foster of Thames Bank).

Rogers, responsible for the Dome, tends to confine his work to corporate jobs, which generally means restricted access for the public. Broadly, if the clean lines of office and apartment blocks are suddenly interrupted by the conspicuous presence of heating ducts, water and electricity pipes, and the like, the chances are that this is the work of Richard Rogers. Used to great effect in his 1986 **Lloyd's Building** (Lime Street, EC3; *see page 49*) and the **Channel 4 Building** on Horseferry Road, SW1 (1994; *see page 87*), Rogers has shown that industrial aesthetics and stainless steel can sit comfortably with brick and granite. Now 14 years on, the revolutionary design of the Lloyd's Building far outclasses many more recent buildings. Look out for the 'Open House' weekend in September, which provides the only opportunity you will get to see inside this unique structure (*see page 9*).

Rogers' friend and rival Norman Foster has had more success in erecting public buildings, an arena that has allowed him to explore the possibilities of the glass roof – a device used to great success in his remodelling of Berlin's Reichstag. The translation of this technology to London will be seen in Foster's audacious extension to the **British Museum** (*see page 64*), which is due to open in November 2000 after a £98-million refit. The nineteenth-century BM contains a huge central court originally intended as a garden for the museum's visitors; soon deemed an extravagant waste of space, however, this court quickly became the site for the British Library. But when the Library moved into a (controversial) building of its own two years ago, this overcrowded museum was suddenly given a new lease of life. Having stripped away everything but the central circular Reading Room, Foster has roofed over the football pitch-sized courtyard with 1,000 tons of glass and steel. Having bowed to pressure from local conservationists, appalled at the prospect of the BM actually being visibly improved, the roof dips, bends and curves its way around the court in order that it cannot be seen from street level. The newly restored area beneath will boast exhibition spaces, educational facilities and the obligatory restaurant – but best of all, the round Reading Room will open as a public library for the first time.

Foster has also pulled off a bit of a coup by winning the competition to build the parliament building for the new **Greater London Authority**, the city-wide council being reinstated after mayoral elections in May 2000. After Thatcher abolished the GLC in a fit of right-wing pique, she then sold the property to a consortium, which wrecked a once-proud building by filling it with hotel rooms, an aquarium, a computer games emporium and a McDonald's outlet. The Labour government's plans to replace what the Conservatives destroyed prompted the need for a new building. After muddling through what was a pretty botched competition, Foster carried the day with a low-energy building that has been variously described as a giant crash helmet, headlamp and testicle. Whatever it looks like, this glass and steel edifice will certainly enliven the defunct space next to Tower Bridge once it is completed in 2003. It will be open to the public, with a viewing gallery for 200 people minded to observe the machinations of the city's government, and will also boast a top-floor observation platform to get a bird's-eye view of the city.

THAMES VIEWS

Foster will undoubtedly join Hawksmoor, Nash and Wren in London's architectural pantheon. His **Millennium Bridge**, designed in conjunction with sculptor Anthony Caro and due to open in 2000, is London's first new river crossing for over a century. Purely a pedestrian route, this thin blade of a suspension bridge will carry people between St Paul's Cathedral and the new arts venues on the south bank of the river.

It is a pity, though, that this new crossing has been given a higher priority than the route between Charing Cross and the South Bank Centre near Waterloo. **Hungerford Bridge**, shared by pedestrians and railway traffic, has long been an embarrassment to the city: views of the Houses of Parliament to the west are obscured by the fencing that keeps people and trains apart, while the crowded walkway is too narrow and rarely free of puddles and beggars. Plans are now afoot to rectify this mess with the construction of two footbridges either side of the railway crossing. Slung from cables beneath seven huge steel pylons, it is hoped that the new decks will carry seven million people a year – twice the present number. This increased traffic is partly due to the fact that the west-side walkway will offer views not seen for 100 years, an opportunity that might entice commuters off the overcrowded tube lines between Embankment and Waterloo. This bridge is due to be opened in December 2000, with its downstream twin opening in April 2001.

If you're into bridges, then it's worth a trip on the DLR to the **Royal Victoria Dock** in London's East End. Here, the architects of the £26-million regeneration of Hungerford Bridge, Lifschutz Davidson, have completed an unusual bridge, which had to be high enough for yachts to pass beneath and low enough to present no danger to planes landing at the nearby City Airport. The architects opted for a structure that involves taking a lift to the top, a windswept walk high above the dock, followed by taking the lift down at the other side. Kitted out in steel and wood that weathers to a complementary silver, the bridge is a well-crafted and elegant structure that stands out against the rather bleak, post-industrial landscape.

But if it's a river view you want, forget the bridges and make a beeline for the **British Airways London Eye** (*see page 36* **Wheel life**), that gigantic new fairground attraction over the river opposite the Houses of Parliament. This 135-m (443-ft) high structure, the world's largest observation wheel, was assembled on its side over the water and then hauled upright in an operation that had to be called off on the first attempt after a cable snapped – giving the press an opportunity to do what it does best, which is to scoff at innovation and predict failure. Happily, the wheel is now in its correct position and fully equipped with its 32 glass capsules and fully functioning. There are plans to move it in 2005, but many, quick to point out that the Eiffel Tower was only supposed to be temporary, are hopeful that it will become a permanent feature on London's skyline.

MUSEUMS & GALLERIES

One of the major architectural events of 2000 will be the opening of **Tate Modern** (*see page 39* **Tate of the art no.1**), a major new gallery space created out of the cathedral-like spaces of the redundant Bankside Power Station. Swiss architects Herzog and de Meuron have endeavoured to respect the integrity of the original building (designed, incidentally, by Sir Giles Gilbert Scott, also responsible for the much-loved red phone box) while adding two floors by building a glass box along the length of the roof. This will create seven floors of gallery space, part of which has been carved out of the old turbine hall, enabling truly monumental sculptures to be accommodated. Dedicated to twentieth-century international art, this £143-million development is due to open in May 2000.

Two months prior to this opening, the Tate's traditional home further upstream near Pimlico will open as **Tate Britain** after a major refit. Work will continue, however, until 2001, when a 35 per cent increase in gallery space and a new entrance in Atterbury Street will be revealed.

The art establishment is also due to receive a further boost in May 2000 with the opening of an extension to the **National Portrait Gallery** (*see page 90*), the National Gallery's poor relation tucked quietly around the corner of Trafalgar Square. Happily, the National Portrait Gallery shunned postmodern pastiche (as practised by its big brother in its own decade-old extension) and opted instead for a little drama. The entrance hall is to be pierced by a new escalator, which delivers you to a new set of galleries, effectively increasing the building's exhibition space by 50 per cent.

For drama, however, no one can hold a candle to plans being developed by the venerable **Victoria & Albert Museum** (*see page 96*). Long overdue for an extension, the museum has commissioned Daniel Libeskind to build an £80-million pile of shiny, white, wonky box-like structures known as the 'Spiral'. Still blushing from the admiration heaped on his Holocaust Museum in Berlin, Libeskind has designed a building that will catapult London into the architectural Big League much as Gehry's new Guggenheim put Bilbao on the map. Formed from a series of interlocking, inclined planes, the structure, when completed in a few years' time, will provide a set of exhibition spaces so unusual that it is a minor miracle that it received planning permission. The new Materials Gallery in the **Science Museum** (*see page 96*) and the planned glass and terracotta Darwin Centre extension to the **Natural History Museum** (*see page 96*) are further evidence that the Kensington arts complex is finally looking to the future, rather than resting on past glories.

On the matter of arts complexes, plans are still afoot to improve the barren concrete landscape that is collectively the **South Bank Centre** (*see pages 256 & 271*). Since Richard Rogers' proposal to top the whole lot with an undulating glass roof was shelved, plans for the area's regeneration have been put in the capable hands of American architect Rick Mather – currently remodelling the **Dulwich Picture Gallery** (*see page 129*) in south London and the **Wallace Collection** in Marylebone (*see page 70*). Mather has been coy about revealing his ideas, most of which centre upon whether or not to retain the **Hayward Gallery** (the example par excellence of the 1970s Brutalist movement; *see page 39*) or demolish it and erect a new building in the nearby Jubilee Gardens. Whatever the outcome, nothing will happen until at least the end of 2000.

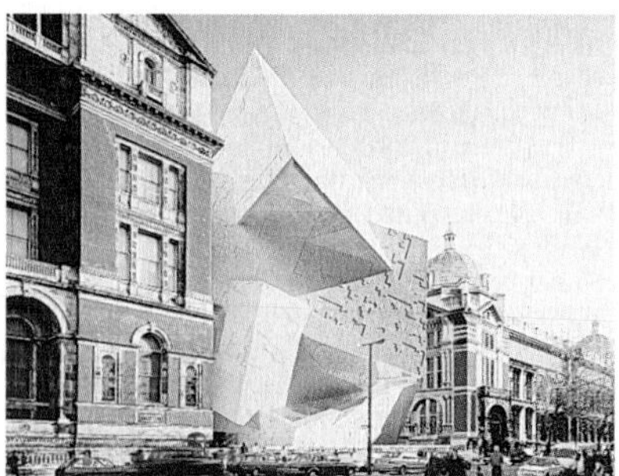

How the **V & A***'s 'Spiral' extension will look.*

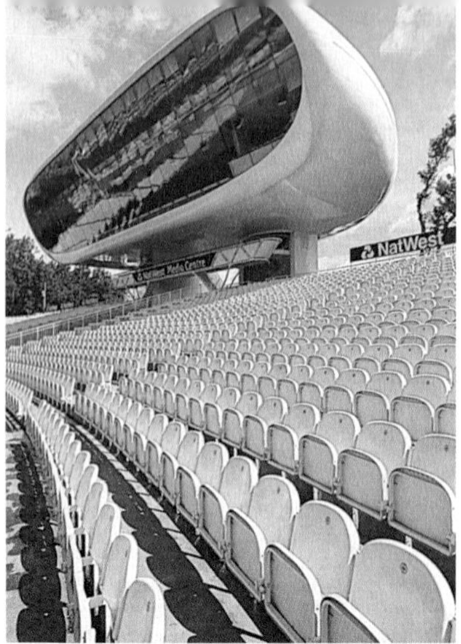

Good Lord's! New **Natwest Media Centre***.*

SPORTING VENUES

As part of Britain's bids to host future world sporting events, plans are now under way to completely replace the much-loved (but inadequate) **Wembley Stadium** (*see page 292*). Major public schemes are never simple, it seems, and at the end of 1999 the project was rapidly turning into a fiasco, with the architects being sent back to the drawing board almost as soon as their revised plans were published. On the other hand, the architectural success of the year was also a sport-related building. The **NatWest Media Centre**, hovering like a giant bar of soap over the stands of **Lord's Cricket Ground** (*see pages 102 & 290*), is a truly innovative building. Designed by Future Systems, a small practice that makes its living by throwing the rule book out the window, this aluminium structure was built in a boatyard using yacht technology. Seating up to 140 reporters in a pale blue interior inspired by a 1950s Chevvy, the iconic building well deserved its £20,000 Sterling Prize, administered by RIBA in late 1999.

Incidentally, the Marylebone Cricket Club also won the award for Client of the Year, a factor that was instrumental in getting its media stand built with the minimum of fuss. Such enlightenment in a client is unusual in Britain, which is why many of the projects outlined in this chapter have been subjected to planning delays, funding crises and media criticism. It's worth remembering, then, that Christopher Wren was put on half pay before being sacked as architect of St Paul's, that Charles Barry was threatened with a public hanging after completing the Houses of Parliament and that criticism and overwork brought Edmund Street, architect of the Royal Courts of Justice, to an early grave. Who'd be an architect in this town?

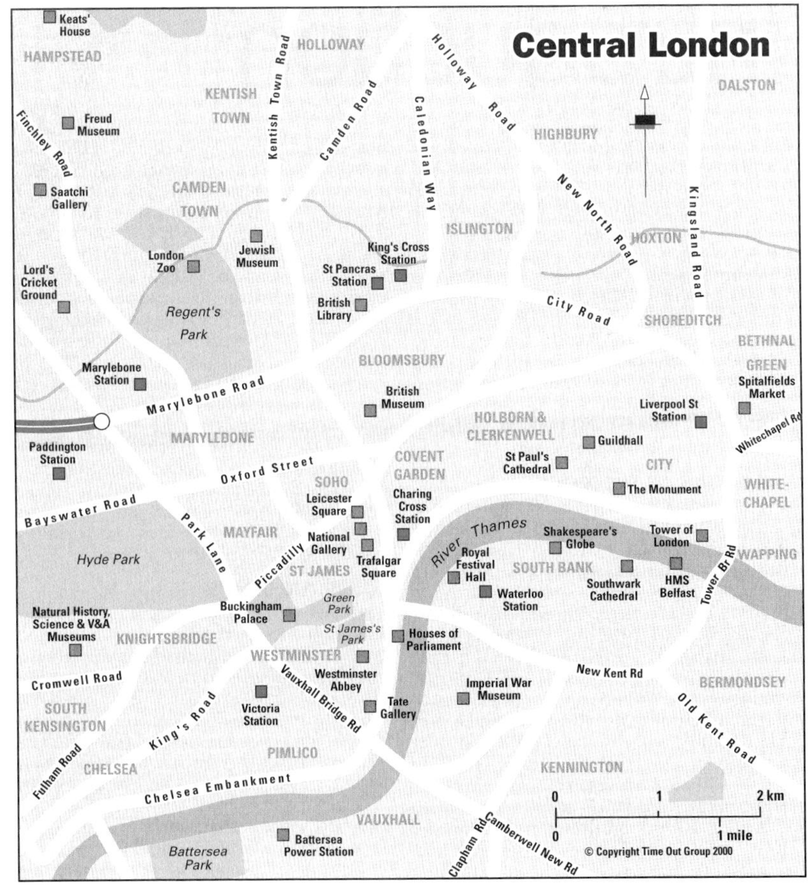

Sightseeing

Introduction

Millennium fever has caused unprecedented stirrings amid London's sights, museums and galleries. It seems that every institution has its millennium project, many of which show considerable ambition. Among the more significant developments over the next year or so are the **British Museum**'s Great Court project, the Wellcome Wing of the **Science Museum**, the new Holocaust Galleries at the **Imperial War Museum**, the creation of the African Worlds Gallery at the **Horniman Museum** and the expansion of the exhibition space at the **Wallace Collection**. Because of all this frantic activity, some parts of museums may be temporarily closed, so phone first to check what is and what isn't open.

THE SHOCK OF THE NEW

Several museums beat the rush and completed their millennium brush-ups during 1998-9. The **Geffrye Museum** unveiled a stylish new extension, the **National Maritime Museum** proudly revealed its Neptune Court project and the **Courtauld Institute of Art** emerged in improved surroundings. At the end of 1999 the revamped **Royal Opera House** in Covent Garden opened to great acclaim. A rather different, but equally welcome, opening was the Wildlife and Wetlands Trust's **Wetland Centre** in Barnes, south-west London.

In 2000, two new collections will go on show alongside the Courtauld in Somerset House. In May the **Gilbert Collection** of gold snuff boxes, European silver and Italian mosaics will open; in autumn the **Hermitage Rooms at Somerset House** will follow suit, showing treasures from Russia's premier museum. Also in May, Britain's oldest public gallery, the **Dulwich Picture Gallery**, will reopen after a major remodelling. Perhaps the highest-profile project, though, is the magnificent new **Tate Modern** in the former Bankside Power Station on the South Bank (also opening in May). The old Tate Gallery, revamped and renamed **Tate Britain**, reopened in March.

Many of the sights and museums listed are putting on special events as part of the **London String of Pearls Millennium Festival** (*see page 8* **London's your oyster**). Always phone to check the details of these events before setting out.

FREE FOR ALL?

The issue of whether or not to charge for entrance into the major national collections has been vexing the Labour Government ever since it was elected in May 1997. Initially it seemed to be continuing its Tory predecessor's policy of pressurising the biggest museums and galleries into paying their own way via entrance charges, but in 1998 it announced a volte face – all entry fees were to be scrapped at the major institutions. But, in early 2000, the plan seemed close to collapse as some of the big boys (including the Natural History and Science museums) refused to drop admission charges as, they claim, the Government is not prepared to compensate them enough for lost revenue. The first part of the plan – to allow free entry for children – has been in place since April 1999; the idea was for pensioners to have free admission in 2000 and everyone else in 2001. At the time of going to press it was unclear whether this last phase of the scheme would be implemented.

Note that entry to a number of the major museums (British Museum, National Gallery, National Portrait Gallery, the Tate) has always been free and that a number of the others allow visitors in free after a certain time (often 4.30pm).

GOSEE THE SIGHTS

If you plan to pack a lot of sights, museums and galleries in to a short period of time, it may be worth buying a **GoSee Card** (although be aware that some museums may eventually scrap their admission charges; *see above*). This three-day or seven-day pass allows unlimited entry to more than 16 sights, museums and galleries within the specified time period. Participating institutions are marked '*' in the index opposite. **Prices are**: individual adult card £16 for three days, £26 for seven days; family card £32 for three days, £50 for seven days. The cards can be purchased from any of the participating museums and galleries and most tourist information centres. For further details, check out the website at *www.london-gosee.com*.

Interior of the impressive new **Tate Modern**.

Museums & sights index

The following list is not comprehensive, but includes the city's major sights. Places marked '*' below are members of the GoSee Card scheme (*see p32*).

The big seven museums

Key art galleries

Other art galleries & exhibition spaces

Royal palaces & other major sites

Animals, wildlife & nature

Applied art & design

Childhood & toys

Film, TV & theatre

Historic houses & buildings

Literary & historical figures

Medicine & science

Military & war

Prisons & dungeons

Religion

Sport

Transport & maritime

Others

The South Bank

Take me to the river.

MAPS 8, 11 & 12

The south bank of the Thames, between Lambeth and Tower bridges, may seem an unorthodox place to start a tour of central London, but, in terms of history, culture and the wealth of millennium developments, there's no more absorbing and rewarding part of the city. Indeed, if you're returning to London after a few years away, chances are you'll hardly recognise the area, such is its new image and atmosphere. The south bank's greatest asset is that, while most of the north side of the river is dominated by fume-filled expressways, the entire length of the south side can be walked without coming into contact with a single car. The opening of the south bank 'spine route' in 1997 heralded a new beginning for the area. The route, running parallel to the river along the previously dingy and unappealing Upper Ground, Belvedere Road and Concert Hall Approach, was given a new feel by the introduction of boulevards with trees, wide pavements and warm lighting. New fingerpost signs, street name plates and illuminated map boards run throughout the area, and 66 banners have been hung from specially designed street lights to create London's longest open-air gallery. The **Millennium Mile** walk has also helped (*see page 42* **A shore thing**).

LAMBETH BRIDGE TO HUNGERFORD BRIDGE

Just north of Lambeth Bridge huddle the red-brick buildings of **Lambeth Palace**, official residence of the Archbishops of Canterbury since the twelfth century. The palace is not usually open to the public, but during most of 2000, as part of the **London String of Pearls Millennium Festival** (*see page 8* **London's your oyster**), visitors will be able to take a tour of its historic rooms, including the crypt, chapel and library (phone 020 7898 1198 for details). Next door is the absorbing **Museum of Garden History** (*see page 40*) in the deconsecrated church of St Mary-at-Lambeth. St Thomas's Hospital, containing the **Florence Nightingale Museum** (*see page 39*), stands on one side of Westminster Bridge, but the dominant presence here is the looming bulk of the revamped **County Hall**. Home of the Greater London Council until its abolition in 1986, it now contains two hotels (*see page 158*), Chinese and Italian restaurants, a McDonald's, the **London Aquarium** (*see page 40*), the two-floor arcade-game nirvana of **Namco Station**, and the **FA Premier League Hall of Fame** (*see page 38*).

Next door, **Jubilee Gardens** became a major focus of attention in autumn 1999, when crowds gathered to watch the hoisting of the stunning **British Airways London Eye** (*see page 36* **Wheel life**). Standing 135m (450ft) tall, it is London's fourth tallest structure; rides were due to start in early 2000. The gardens themselves have been returfed and revamped. **Hungerford Bridge** (alongside Charing Cross rail bridge) is currently the subject of an ambitious new project; the present footbridge will be demolished and a new one built either side of the railway bridge. The upstream bridge is expected to be completed by December 2000; the downstream one by April 2001 (*see also page 29*).

HUNGERFORD BRIDGE TO BLACKFRIARS BRIDGE

The arts complex on the south bank, known, imaginatively, as the **South Bank Centre**, represents London at its most self-consciously modern. Denys Lasdun's **Royal Festival Hall** (*see pages 256* and *271*) was built to mark the let's-all-cheer-up-after-the-war 1951 Festival of Britain. Accordingly, the new buildings were a showcase for contemporary architectural and building skills. It would be fair to say that it is not universally admired, although appreciation is not made easier by the raised concrete walkways that stranglingly swirl about it and the proximity of the true smack-in-the-face brutalism of the **Hayward Gallery** (*see page 39*). Plans to humanise the area have been mooted since at least the 1980s, but only in late 1999 was architect Rick Mather finally appointed master-planner and given the go-ahead to evaluate each building individually. The Royal Festival Hall will remain (and indeed was recently granted £12 million of Lottery money for restoration, which will hopefully go some way to improving the acoustics inside), but the unloved buildings housing the Hayward, the **Queen Elizabeth Hall** and the **Purcell Room** will be demolished, along with the concrete walkways (this has already happened to the one on the Belvedere Road side of the Royal Festival Hall), to be reborn on the other side of Hungerford Bridge in a new low-rise building. In their place, a new film complex will be constructed to house the **National Film Theatre** (*see page 260*) and the **Museum of the Moving Image** (**MOMI**; closed until 2003) – both currently crouched under Waterloo Bridge – as well as the **BFI London IMAX Cinema** (*see pages 36* and *261*) and a new headquarters for the British Film Institute.

Next door, and also due for some improvements, is the immense, boxy **Royal National Theatre**, which is also being redeveloped as part of the south bank project (*see page 294*). The glorious view over to the City from **Waterloo Bridge**, especially fine at dusk, inspired the 1967 Kinks' hit *Waterloo Sunset*. On the riverside walk under the bridge is a regular book market.

Between Waterloo and Blackfriars bridges, the most distinctive building is undoubtedly the beautifully restored **Oxo Tower Wharf**. The cleverly conceived art deco tower incorporates the word 'OXO' into its design, thereby circumventing council rules against large-scale advertising. The building now contains flats and small retail crafts units, and is topped by a glitzy restaurant and bar (*see page 166*), run by the people behind Harvey Nichols' **Fifth Floor** restaurant (*see page 165*). Anyone can enjoy the views from the top from the eighth-floor public viewing gallery. A new museum, the intriguingly titled **The Museum of...** (*see page 40*) opened here in late 1998. The tower and much of the surrounding housing (plus the cutesy shops of **Gabriel's Wharf**) are maintained by the admirable, non-profit-making Coin Street Community Builders, who have done much to retain the integrity of this fast-developing area and ensure that the original inhabitants are not priced out. The annual **Coin Street Festival** is a multifaceted celebration of local life and the arts (June-Sept). Another exciting project, a floating, Olympic-sized lido, is planned for the stretch of the Thames by the Oxo Tower.

AROUND WATERLOO

A pathway links the Royal Festival Hall to **Waterloo Station**, where Eurostar trains arrive and depart from under Nicholas Grimshaw's glass-roofed terminus. This short walk once involved negotiating a complicated, unpleasant route across busy roads and down stinking alleys, but, again, great strides are being taken to make the experience easier and more pleasant. The roundabout outside Waterloo Station was once home to legions of homeless people who camped out in 'cardboard city'. No longer. The huge £20-million **BFI London IMAX Cinema** (*see page 261*) has been built on the site, featuring a ten-storey high screen, the biggest in Europe.

Behind and below the station on the other side, **Lower Marsh** has a lively market on weekdays, and leads on to the curiously named **The Cut**, home of the **Young Vic** (*see page 300*) and the **Old Vic** theatres (*see page 293*). The former contains the excellent **Konditor & Cook** café (*see page 180*), while other good eating options here include the lively tapas bar **Mesón Don Felipe** (no.53), the excellent seafood of **Livebait** (nos.41-43; *see page 172*) and the airy bar-restaurant, the **Fire Station** (150 Waterloo Road; *see page 197*).

Wheel life

Whether or not the Dome turns out to be a white elephant, there's one millennium project that has no shortage of admirers. Cantilevered out over the Thames, the **British Airways London Eye** was finally hoisted into place in late 1999 after months of erection problems, so to speak (at one point, a Virgin hot air balloon with the words 'BA can't get it up' was spotted overhead). Despite the digs, it's a stunning structure, visible from many parts of central London, which isn't surprising when you realise that, at 135m (443ft), it's the tallest observation wheel in the world (don't call it a Ferris wheel; Ferris wheels are supported on both sides and have open capsules that hang down). The 32 capsules (with up to 25 people in each) will turn continuously, giving passengers a gentle 30-minute journey and views of up to 25 miles (40km) on clear days. With the public barred from London's three tallest buildings (Canary Wharf Tower, NatWest Tower and BT Tower), the London Eye, as the city's fourth tallest structure, can fairly claim to offer an unparalleled picture of the capital.

British Airways London Eye

Jubilee Gardens, next to County Hall, SE1 (0870 500 0600). Waterloo tube/rail or Westminster tube. **Open** *Apr-Oct* 9am-dusk daily; *Nov-Mar* 10am-6pm daily. **Admission** £7.45; £4.95 5s-15s; £5.95 OAPs; free under-5s. **Map 8 M8**
Website: www.ba-londoneye.com

BANKSIDE

The original Blackfriars Bridge (1760-9) was the third to span the Thames. It was under here that Italian banker Roberto Calvi was found hanging in 1982. The area between here and London Bridge, known as **Bankside**, was, for many centuries, London's pleasure zone. As it was outside the puritanical jurisdiction of the City, theatres, bear-baiting pits, bawdy houses, inns and other dens of iniquity could freely prosper. There's no little irony that Bankside (officially deemed 'a naughty place' by royal proclamation in 1547) fell within the sway of the Bishops of Winchester. Far from condemning the depravity, the Church made a tidy sum from its regulation, and if anyone got too unruly they could always be cast into the dank depths of the Clink Prison. The prison was destroyed in 1780, but its site, on one of the area's most appropriately dismal and Dickensian streets, is now home to the **Clink Exhibition** (*see page 38*). Next door are the scant remains of **Winchester Palace** – little is left beyond the rose window of the Great Hall. If you fancy a drink but aren't tempted by any of the riverside pubs around here (though the **Anchor Bankside** is worth a visit, *see page 196*), kill two birds with one stone and visit **Vinopolis, City of Wine** (*see page 42*), just around the corner from the Clink.

Modern Bankside's commanding presence is that mighty monolithic temple of industry, **Bankside Power Station** (which only operated for 17 years before being closed in 1980). Like Battersea Power Station upriver (*see page 132*), it was designed by Sir Giles Gilbert Scott and will make a magnificent home for the **Tate Modern**'s art collection when it opens in May 2000 (*see page 39*). The building will contain one of the most stunning spaces in the city, running the length, height and almost half the width of the mammoth structure – and it'll be open to all, not just those visiting the gallery. Tiny in comparison, and a reminder of the Bankside of old, is its neighbour – the reconstructed **Shakespeare's Globe** (*see page 41* and *page 294*). Standing somewhat in its shadow, figuratively and almost literally, is another theatre dating from the sixteenth century, the **Rose Theatre**.

Next to the Globe is a curious little terrace, containing the house in which Wren is said to have lived during the construction of St Paul's. One of the most worthwhile of the millennium projects will be the **Millennium Bridge**, a footbridge across the river from outside the new Tate Modern to the area south of St Paul's Cathedral. The sightlines on the north bank will be cleared so that the view that Wren enjoyed of his masterwork from the south side will be restored. Two minor attractions nearby are the **London Fire Brigade Museum** on Southwark Bridge Road (*see page 40*) and the **Bankside Gallery** at 48 Hopton Street, home to the Royal Watercolour Society and the Royal Society of Painter/Printmakers.

BOROUGH

If you like literature, you'll love Borough. One of the area's biggest draws is the magnificent pub **The George**, London's sole surviving galleried coaching inn. Before custom-built theatres were introduced, plays were performed in the courtyard while people watched from the galleries. The White Hart Inn, where Mr Pickwick first meets Sam Weller in *The Pickwick Papers*, stood in White Hart Yard (it was pulled down in 1889). Talbot Yard marks the site of the Tabard Inn, where Chaucer's pilgrims meet at the beginning of *The Canterbury Tales*. The church of **St George-the-Martyr** (corner of Borough High Street and Long Lane) is mentioned in Dickens' *Little Dorrit* – the heroine is born in Marshalsea Prison, which used to stand a few doors away. The author's father was imprisoned in Marshalsea for debt in 1824.

Borough has always been a congested place. Until 1750, London Bridge was the only crossing point into the City, and Borough High Street became a stagecoach terminus. The seventeenth-century poet Thomas Dekker described the street as 'a continued ale house with not a shop to be seen between'. The chaotic and raucous Southwark Fair was held here every September from 1462 to 1763, until it was suppressed by the spoilsport Corporation of London.

All but submerged under sweeping road and rail lines, **Southwark Cathedral** (*see page 41*) is in the throes of a Lottery-funded redevelopment project. Not such good news is that Borough's unique streets, little touched this century and long popular for period film sets, are still threatened by a rail improvement scheme. The greatest tragedy would be the destruction of covered **Borough Market** – a fruit and vegetable market has been on the site since the thirteenth century. The good news is that the area has been given a new lease of life by the weekly Saturday food markets held here, selling gourmet cheese, meat and bread (*see also page 223*). The presence of other new interests, such as the acclaimed **fish!** restaurant and shop (*see page 171*), have also helped raise the profile of the area.

Not far from the cathedral, the impressive replica of Sir Francis Drake's **Golden Hinde** (*see page 39*) is well worth a visit, particularly for kids. Several attractions are clustered around London Bridge Station: the **Old Operating Theatre, Museum & Herb Garret** (*see page 41*), opposite Guy's Hospital, **Winston Churchill's Britain At War Experience** (*see page 42*) and the gory **London Dungeon** (*see page 40*).

TOWER BRIDGE & BERMONDSEY

The stretch of the river from London to Tower bridges is dominated by the uncompromising bulk of **HMS Belfast** (*see page 40*) and the massive, soaring, glass-roofed arcade of Hay's Galleria. Its centrepiece is David Kemp's splendidly silly *The Navigators* mechanical sculpture. This is the start of **Bermondsey**, an area that was long a focus for Christianity – **Tooley Street** was once home to no fewer than three abbots, a prior and the church of St Olave's. Its near-namesake, **St Olaf House**, a fabulous art deco 1930s warehouse, is worth a look. The area immediately west of Tower Bridge is set to be transformed in a few years' time by the construction of the new Norman Foster-designed HQ for the **Greater London Authority** (GLA), due to be completed in 2003 (*see also page 26*).

The capital's most spectacular bridge, **Tower Bridge**, is a relatively recent addition to the London skyline, opening not much more than a century ago in 1894. If you want to find out more about it, undergo the **Tower Bridge Experience** (*see page 55*). East of here, **Butler's Wharf** is the home of a trio of Sir Terence Conran restaurants and, just a little further on, the excellent **Design Museum** (*see below*), which Conran, the man who did much to bring good household design to the ordinary punter, helped to establish. Around the corner is the more idiosyncratic charm of the **Bramah Tea & Coffee Museum** (*see below*).

Much of this area has a Dickensian feel to it – check out **St Saviour's Dock**, a muddy creek between towering warehouses, visible over a low parapet in Jamaica Road. In Dickens' day, the streets around here formed a notorious slum called Jacob's Island, where Bill Sikes gets his comeuppance in *Oliver Twist*. Bermondsey Square is home to a superb antiques market, frequented by serious collectors and dealers (*see page 223*).

Sights

Bramah Tea & Coffee Museum

corner of Gainsford Street & Maguire Street, SE1 (020 7378 0222). London Bridge tube/rail/P11, 15, 42, 47, 78 bus. **Open** 10am-6pm daily. **Admission** £4; £3 5s-15s, OAPs, disabled, ES40s; £10 family. **Credit** AmEx, JCB, MC, £TC, V. **Map 12 S9**

Though he's been in the business for half a century, it was only in the early 1990s that Edward Bramah, a former tea taster, set up this unusual museum to chart the history of tea and coffee drinking. The new premises allow the two infusions to be studied separately, and their important role in British society to be documented. There's also an impressive collection of coffee makers and teapots (including the world's largest) and a café where you can try out the real thing.

Website: www.bramahmuseum.co.uk

Clink Exhibition

1 Clink Street, SE1 (020 7378 1558). London Bridge tube/rail. **Open** 10am-6pm daily. **Admission** £4; £3 5s-15s, OAPs, disabled, students, ES40s; £9 family. **Credit** AmEx, JCB, MC, £TC, V. **Map 11 P8**

A better job could have been made of bringing to life Bankside's ribald past than the couple of recreated cells, piped music and illustrations on display here. This was the site of the Bishops of Winchester's small jail that, until its destruction during the Gordon Riots of 1780, held misbehaving actors, prostitutes and drunks dragged from the raucous taverns, theatres and whorehouses of Bankside. The expression 'in the clink', meaning in prison, originated from this dismal place.

Website: www.clink.co.uk

Design Museum

Butler's Wharf, off Shad Thames, SE1 (020 7403 6933). London Bridge tube/rail/15, 78, 100 bus. **Open** 11.30am-6pm daily (last entry 5.30pm). **Admission** £5.50;£4 5s-18s, students, disabled, ES40s; free under-5s. *GoSee Card member (see p32).* **Credit** AmEx, MC, £TC, V. **Map 12 S9**

This beautifully designed 1930s-style, sparkling white building is stark and spacious within – the perfect setting for a collection of innovative design. Incredibly user-friendly, the museum consists of just two levels with a minimum of exhibits. The first floor holds the **Review Collection** (state-of-the-art innovations from around the world) and the **Temporary Exhibition Gallery**. Temporary exhibitions for 2000 include **Bauhaus Dessau** (10 Feb-4 June), an in-depth look at the significance of the period when the Bauhaus was based in Dessau (1925-32), the **Life and Work of Buckminster Fuller** (15 June-15 Oct) and **Five Designs of Mr Brunel** (26 Oct-25 Feb 2001).

The **Collection Gallery**, devoted to the study of design for mass production, is housed on the second floor. Arranged thematically, it concentrates on different types of product. The car is one such focus – look for the wooden model made up from drawings by the architect and designer Le Corbusier dating from 1928. There are also early televisions, washing machines, telephones, chairs (including one designed by Rennie Mackintosh) and a collection of tableware. Temporary shows in the Collection Gallery during 2000 include **Dr Martens Airwair** (Mar-May) and **Hong Kong Architecture: Aesthetic of Connection** (1 June-31 July). The **Blue Print Café**, which shares the building, with its balcony overlooking the Thames, is an appropriately stylish establishment (but be warned, it's a restaurant rather than a café, with prices to match).

Website: www.designmuseum.org

FA Premier League Hall of Fame

County Hall, Riverside Building, Westminster Bridge Road, SE1 (020 7928 1800). Westminster tube or Waterloo tube/rail. **Open** 10am-6pm daily (last entry 5pm). **Admission** £9.95; £6.50 4s-15s; £7.50 OAPs, disabled, students, ES40s. **Credit** AmEx, MC, £TC, V. **Map 8 M9**

Not a bad stab at giving a history of football from its origins to the present day (although you might want to give the first exhibit, the lamentable Football Physics Laboratory, a miss). The exhibition mostly comprises information panels and interesting interactive screens, with the odd dummy here

Tate of the art no.1

On 12 May 2000 one of the most eagerly awaited of London's millennium projects is due to open: the new home of the Tate's collection of international modern art from 1900 to the present. Appropriately, it is housed in Sir Giles Gilbert Scott's modern icon, the former Bankside Power Station. This monolithic post-war brick building has been remodelled (at a cost of £134m), and a new glass structure has been added at roof level to give two more floors, bring in more light and provide wonderful views over the city.

The **Tate Modern** will be exhibiting its superb collection thematically, using the size of the new gallery to display a far greater range of works than was ever possible at Millbank. An agreement with the **V&A** (*see page 96*) means that the two museums will regularly exchange works of art – 1920s and 1930s photographs from the V&A will be on display at the opening of the Tate Modern. As part of the **Unilever Series**, the Tate will be showcasing the work of French-born American artist **Louise Bourgeois** (12 May-Oct), which will include a newly commissioned large-scale piece for the 152-m (500-ft) long, 30-m (100-ft) high Turbine Hall (further large works will be commissioned for the hall, one a year for five years). Also, the architects of the Bankside conversion, Swiss firm **Herzog & de Meuron**, get to blow their own trumpets with an exhibition devoted to their work (12 May-Dec).

By the time the gallery opens, the appealing **Millennium Bridge** – designed by Norman Foster, Anthony Caro and Ove Arup – will lead the way from the Tate Modern to St Paul's Cathedral, just across the river from the site. There are also plans to link the Tate Modern by boat, shuttle bus and bicycle and pedestrian routes to the former Tate Gallery, now the **Tate Britain**, *see page 91* **Tate of the art no.2**.

Tate Modern

25 Sumner Street, SE1 (020 7887 8000). Southwark tube. **Open** *from 12 May 2000* 10am-6pm Mon-Thur, Sun; 10am-10pm Fri, Sat. **Admission** free. **Map 11 O7**

and there, but disappointingly few bits of memorabilia. Not surprisingly, much is made of England's World Cup victory in 1966. The final two exhibits are a bit of a letdown: the eponymous Hall of Fame, with lifelike but few models of famous footballers such as David Seaman, Alan Shearer and co (but, surprisingly, no Michael Owen), and the section where you get to play on footie video games.
Website: www.hall-of-fame.co.uk

Florence Nightingale Museum

St Thomas's Hospital, 2 Lambeth Palace Road, SE1 (020 7620 0374). Westminster tube/Waterloo tube/rail. **Open** 10am-5pm Mon-Fri (last entry 4pm); 11.30am-4.30pm Sat, Sun (last entry 3.30pm). **Admission** £4.80; £3.60 5s-15s, OAPs, students, ES40s; £10 family. **Credit** AmEx, MC, £TC, V. **Map 8 M9**

The world's most famous nurse is celebrated in the well thought-out displays of this small museum, close to Westminster Bridge. Nightingale's chief achievement in a long career of social campaigning was to establish nursing as a disciplined profession (indeed, 'her lady and the lamp' care in the Crimea was but a small part of her life's contribution to medicine); and she set up the first nursing school at St Thomas's in 1859.
Website: www.florence-nightingale.co.uk

Golden Hinde

St Mary Overie Dock, Cathedral Street, SE1 (020 7403 0123). Monument tube or London Bridge tube/rail. **Open** 10am-6pm daily (phone to check). **Admission** £2.50; £1.75 4s-13s; £2.10 OAPs, students, disabled, ES40s; £6.50 family. **Credit** MC, V. **Map 11 P8**

This full-size reconstruction of Sir Francis Drake's sixteenth-century flagship looks impressively pristine considering the two decades it has spent circumnavigating the world as a seaborne museum. It's hard to believe that the dinky ship travelled over 100,000 miles, many more than the original. Years of research went into producing this authentic reproduction, now in a dry dock, and it shows: the interior has been recreated in minute detail and the diminutive proportions of the gun deck and hold feel painfully real. The atmosphere on board is fleshed out by 'crew' in Elizabethan costume. A big hit with kids. Tickets are sold from the card shop next to the ship.
Website: www.goldenhinde.co.uk

Hayward Gallery

Belvedere Road, SE1 (box office 020 7960 4242/ recorded info 020 7261 0127). Embankment tube/ Waterloo tube/rail. **Open** *during exhibitions* 10am-6pm Mon, Thur-Sun; 10am-8pm Tue, Wed. **Admission** varies (phone for details). *GoSee Card member (see p32).* **Credit** AmEx, DC, MC, V. **Map 8 M8**

The Hayward, part of the south bank's thriving arts scene, is one of London's finest venues for temporary exhibitions of contemporary and historical art. The relatively high admission charges are usually justified by the quality of the work. A feature of

recent exhibitions has been the policy to involve celebrated architects such as Zaha Hadid and Rem Koolhaas in adapting the space for specific exhibitions. The Hayward flits between big names in art, such as Bruce Nauman, Anish Kapoor, Lucio Fontana and Chuck Close, and themed shows, such as twentieth-century fashion and 1999's **Cities on the Move**. In 2000 the startling technological sculptures of Belgian artist **Panamarenko** will be followed by **Sonic Boom** (27 Apr-18 June), **Force Fields** (13 July-17 Sept) and **Know Thyself** – an exhibition exploring the art and science of the human body from Leonardo da Vinci to the present day (19 Oct-14 Jan 2001).
Website: www.sbc.org.uk

HMS Belfast

Morgan's Lane, Tooley Street, SE1 (020 7940 6328). London Bridge tube/rail. **Open** *Mar-Oct* 10am-6pm daily (last entry 5.15pm); *Nov-Feb* 10am-5pm daily (last entry 4.15pm). **Admission** £5; £3.90 students, OAPs; free under-16s. **Credit** MC, £TC, V. **Map 12 R8**

One of the most spectacular sights on the Thames, the 11,500-ton battlecruiser, built in 1938, was instrumental in the sinking of the German battleship *Scharnhorst* during World War II and remained in active service until just after the Korean War. Exploring its seven decks, boiler and engine rooms and massive gun turrets is great fun – especially for children. Interestingly, the front two turrets are trained on the Scratchwood motorway services on the M1, 12½ miles (20km) away to the north-west of London – more, one assumes, to demonstrate the guns' great range than to comment on the quality of motorway food.
Website: www.hmsbelfast.org.uk

London Aquarium

County Hall, Riverside Building, Westminster Bridge Road, SE1 (020 7967 8000). Westminster tube or Waterloo tube/rail. **Open** 10am-6pm daily (last entry 5pm). **Admission** £8.50; £5 3s-14s, £6.50 students, OAPs; £24 family; free under-3s, wheelchair-users. **Credit** MC, £TC, V. **Map 8 M9**

A three-level display of hundreds of varieties of sea life and fish – from huge to dinky – from around the world. It's a hit with children – who especially love the touchable rays – although adults will be far from bored. The interactive displays and nod to environmental awareness (information about endangered species such as the nautilus, the tiny poison dart frog and coral reefs – the latter is part of the new **Coral Reef Conservation Experience**) are laudable, if, frankly, rather overshadowed by the most popular residents, the sharks. One word of criticism, though – it's a bit cheeky to charge extra (albeit 30p) for a leaflet about the exhibition.
Website: www.londonaquarium.co.uk

London Dungeon

28-34 Tooley Street, SE1 (020 7403 7221). London Bridge tube/rail. **Open** *Oct-Mar* 10am-5pm (last entry) daily; *Apr-Sept* 10am-5.30pm daily. **Admission** £9.95; £6.50 4s-14s; £8.50 students; £6.50 OAPs, disabled; free under-5s, wheelchair users. **Credit** AmEx, MC, £TC, V. **Map 12 Q8**

It's hard not to feel uneasy about the glorification of pain, horror and death at the London Dungeon; it's equally hard to deny that the punters – and gore-adoring older kids in particular – love it: they pile in by the coachload. Peer through railings amid a dank, dark, musty maze of gloomy arches and eerie nooks, and thrill at the scenes of medieval torture and the screams as the rack is tightened another notch. Groups of visitors are herded into a mock courtroom, before being sentenced by a 'judge'. The punishment, it seems, is a scary boat ride that, frankly, isn't. The last part of the museum centres on one of the grizzliest episodes from British history – the ever-popular tale of jolly old woman-mutilator Jack the Ripper: actors in costume take you on the hunt for the madman through rooms made to look like the East End (in pre-curry house days). New from Easter 2000 is **Firestorm! 1666**, an exhibition about the Great Fire of London. Chilling and fun or exploitative and sick? Only you can decide.
Website: www.dungeons.com

London Fire Brigade Museum

94A Southwark Bridge Road, SE1 (020 7587 2894). Borough or Southwark tube. **Guided tours** 10.30am, 12.30pm, 2.30pm, Mon-Fri by appointment only. **Admission** £3; £2 7s-14s, students, OAPs, ES40s; free under-7s. **Credit** MC, £TC, V. **Map 11 O9**

Book in advance for a two-hour guided tour of the museum, which explains the history of firefighting in London since 1666, the year of the Great Fire. Old firefighting appliances are among the exhibits, and visitors might glimpse firefighting recruits training at the adjacent centre.

The Museum of...

The Bargehouse, Oxo Tower Wharf, Bargehouse Street, SE1 (020 7928 1255). Waterloo tube/rail or Southwark tube. **Open** 11am-6pm Tue-Sun (last entry 5.30pm). **Admission** free. **Map 11 N7**

A unique venture that aims to 'challenge the way we think about museums and… ask questions about our relationship with material culture'. What this means in practice is five separate museums running for 16 weeks each. Details of upcoming museums weren't available at the time of going to press, but in 1999, the enigmatic exhibitions included the Museum of Collectors, the Museum of Me and the Museum of the Unknown.

Museum of Garden History

St Mary-at-Lambeth, Lambeth Palace Road, SE1 (020 7261 1891). Waterloo tube/rail/C10, 507 bus. **Open** *Feb* 11am-2pm Mon-Fri; *5 Mar-Dec* 10.30am-4pm Mon-Fri; 10.30am-5pm Sun. **Admission** free; donations appreciated. **Map 8 L10**

Inside St Mary-at-Lambeth church, antique horticultural tools and photographic panels on famous garden designers and plant hunters illustrate the development of the English passion for gardening. The tireless John Tradescant, gardener to James I and Charles I, is given particular prominence. A replica of a seventeenth-century knot garden has been created in the tiny church courtyard. One of the sarcophagi here contains the remains of Captain Bligh, who was abandoned by his mutinous crew in the middle of the Pacific.

Old Operating Theatre, Museum & Herb Garret

9A St Thomas's Street, SE1 (020 7955 4791). London Bridge tube/rail. **Open** 10am-4pm Tue-Sun, most Mons (phone to check). **Admission** £2.90; £1.50-£2 concs; £7.25 family. **Map 12 Q8**

The only surviving example of an early nineteenth-century operating theatre is reached via a narrow flight of stairs to the belfry of an old church. Here, in an adjoining room, ancient banks of viewing stands rise in semicircles around a crude wooden bed. Close your eyes and you can almost hear the screams from an unanaesthetised, blindfolded patient as a blood-stained surgeon carefully saws through his leg. Exhibits in the garret illustrate the history of surgery, herbal medicine and nursing at Guy's and St Thomas's hospitals.

Rose Theatre

56 Park Street, SE1 (020 7593 0026). London Bridge or Cannon Street tube/rail. **Open** 10am-5pm daily (last entry 4.30pm). **Admission** £3; £2 5s-15s; £2.50 students, OAPs, disabled. **Credit** MC, V. **Map 11 P8**

The remains of the sixteenth-century Rose, the first of four playhouses to be built at Bankside, were rediscovered in 1989 during excavations on a site where new office buildings were due to be erected. The extensive remnants, some two-thirds of the original site, would have been built over were it not for the campaigning of a group of actors, scholars and ordinary theatre-loving punters. Currently there's a sound and light exhibition, with a video narrated by Sir Ian McKellan, aimed at raising awareness of the Rose. In the longer term, the Rose Theatre Trust wants to see the site fully excavated (during which time the public can watch the archaeologists at work) and open to all – this is pending further funding being raised.

Website: www.rdg.ac.uk/rose

Taking in the view from **Waterloo Bridge**.

Shakespeare's Globe

New Globe Walk, Bankside, SE1 (020 7902 1500). Mansion House or Southwark tube/London Bridge tube/rail. **Open** *May-Sept* 9am-12.30pm daily; *Oct-Apr* 10am-5pm daily. **Admission** £7.50; £5 5s-15s; £6 students, OAPs; £23 family. *GoSee Card member (see p32).* **Credit** MC, £TC, V. **Map 11 O7**

The original Globe theatre, where many of Shakespeare's plays were first performed, burned down in 1613 during a performance of *Henry VIII*, when a cannon spark set fire to the roof; the only minor casualty was a man whose breeches caught fire. Nearly 400 years later, the Globe has been rebuilt not far from its original site, using construction methods and materials as close to the originals as possible. Productions (staged from May to September only) are authentically Elizabethan, relying chiefly on natural light, a simple, unchanging set and with audience participation encouraged. The admission price includes a fascinating guided tour (by lively and well-informed guides who inject a real passion into their work) and entrance to the exhibition, in the vast space beneath the Inigo Jones theatre (where performances will ultimately be held in winter). The new multimedia exhibition explores all aspects of the Bard's work and the role of the actor, audience and architecture of the theatre. There's an excellent café and restaurant on the site already, and plans for another shop, lecture theatre and workshop space to be built nearby by the end of 2000. Note that there are no guided tours in the afternoon from May to September, when performances are held (though visitors still have access to the exhibition).

Throughout 2000, as part of the **London String of Pearls Millennium Festival** (*see p8* **London's your oyster**), the Globe will be hosting a series of temporary exhibitions and open days; phone for details.

Website: www.shakespeares-globe.org

Southwark Cathedral

Montague Close, SE1 (020 7367 6700). London Bridge tube/rail. **Open** 8am-6pm daily (closing times vary on religious holidays). **Services** 8am, 8.15am, 12.30pm, 12.45pm, 5.30pm, Mon-Fri; 9am, 9.15am, 4pm, Sat; 9am, 9.15am, 11am, 3pm, Sun. **Admission** free; donations appreciated. **Map 11 P8**

Originally the monastic church of St Mary Overie, this splendid but little-visited building became an

A shore thing

Walks & events

With the opening of three major Thames-side millennium projects in 2000 (the **Tate Modern**, the **Millennium Bridge** and the **British Airways London Eye**, plus, further down the river, **the Dome**, for which *see pages 124-6*), the south bank is gearing up to attract many more visitors. A free leaflet, 'Explore the Millennium Mile', details two walking routes of, not surprisingly, one mile each, which take in these new attractions and many others included in this chapter. The most appealing of the two routes hugs the river, starting in the west at **County Hall**, passing the **South Bank Centre**, **Gabriel's Wharf**, the **Oxo Tower Wharf**, **Shakespeare's Globe** and the **Rose Theatre, Vinopolis, City of Wine** and the **Golden Hinde**, where it meets the second walk, which continues past **HMS Belfast** and **Tower Bridge**, ending at the **Design Museum** and the **Bramah Tea & Coffee Museum**. The leaflet is available from any of the participating sights along the way or by calling 020 7928 6193.

The Thames is also the focus for the year-long **London String of Pearls Millennium Festival** (*see page 8* **London's your oyster**): sights from the Royal Botanic Gardens in Kew to the Old Royal Naval College at Greenwich are staging events throughout the year.

Getting around

In addition to the tube and rail connnections in the area (which have been boosted by the opening of the Jubilee Line Extension), the south bank is finally taking advantage of the river by increasing riverboat services, and building new piers for their use. The piers are marked on the maps at the back of this Guide. For a full list of passenger services, *see page 338-9.*

Anglican cathedral in 1905. The first church on the site may date from as early as the seventh century; the oldest parts of the present building are twelfth-century. After the Reformation, the church fell into disrepair and was partially used as a bakery and a pigsty. Heavy-handed Victorian restoration added to the fascinating mix of architectural styles, including a fine Gothic choir. John Harvard, benefactor of Harvard University, was born in Southwark in 1607 and baptised in the church; more recently, the John Harvard Chapel was the setting for the film *The Slipper and the Rose*. The cathedral is currently in the stages of an ambitious Lottery-funded millennium project, which will involve, among other things, adding a two-storey wing containing a refectory and teaching library, a new entrance to the north of the cathedral, and, as part of the **London String of Pearls Millennium Festival** (*see p8* **London's your oyster**), the building of a new Visitors' Centre and exhibition about the history of the cathedral and surrounding area. Work is due to be completed at the end of 2000 but the cathedral is open as usual in the meantime.
Website: www.dswark.org

Tate Modern

See p39 **Tate of the art no.1**.

Vinopolis, City of Wine

1 Bank End, SE1 (0870 4444777). London Bridge tube/rail. **Open** 10am-5pm daily (last entry 4.30pm). **Admission** £11.50; £4.50 5s-18s; £10.50 OAPs; £1 discount if booked in advance. **Credit** AmEx, JCB, MC, £TC, V. **Map 11 P8.**

The motto of this oenophile's attraction, which opened in July 1999, is 'Explore, taste, enjoy'. They got the first two right. You pick up a headset and, later, a wine glass and embark on a tour of the history of wine across the world. Huge blow-up photos of vineyards and luxury chateaux set the scene, but the commentary, from the likes of famous wine experts Jancis Robinson, Hugh Johnson *et al*, is made up of soundbites so short that you don't feel like you're learning much. Still, on the plus side, included in the (not inconsiderable) entry fee are vouchers to taste five wines, provided by informative servers (try, if you dare, a Romanian or a Georgian). The much-publicised trip through a vineyard on a Vespa, is, frankly, a bit of a waste of time. Still, it's all a good excuse to drink during the day. There are further attempts to push booze in your face in the form of a Majestic wine warehouse at the end of the tour, in addition to a rather good shop selling all manner of vinous accoutrements (corkscrews, wine racks, books, etc), and gourmet food.
Website: www.vinopolis.co.uk

Winston Churchill's Britain at War Experience

64-66 Tooley Street, SE1 (020 7403 3171). London Bridge tube/rail. **Open** *Apr-Sept* 10am-5.30pm (last entry 5pm); *Oct-Mar* 10am-4.30pm (last entry 4pm). **Admission** £5.95; £2.95 5s-16s; £3.95 students, OAPs; £14 family. **Credit** AmEx, MC, £TC, V. **Map 12 Q8**

This 'real life' experience is, inevitably, nothing of the sort. What you get is a rather shabby attempt to evoke Blitz-time London, with rickety speakers blaring out '40s radio broadcasts and showtunes, and awkward-looking dummies dressed up in period costumes. There is a lot of fascinating memorabilia, though, if you care to look for it among the muddled wall displays, and children might enjoy the atmospheric reproductions of an air raid shelter, dance hall and a huge darkened bombsite.
Website: www.britain-at-war.co.uk

The City

Because of its rich history (in more ways than one), London's moneypot also boasts some of its most ancient sights.

MAPS 9-12

Despite a working population of 250,000, only 6,000 live within the governance of the City's ruling body, the Corporation of London. Come on a Saturday or Sunday or after 9pm on a weekday and you'll be wandering a ghost town of deserted office buildings, shut-up shops and pubs, and empty streets. Yet visit on a weekday and you will feel something of Charlotte Brontë's excitement.

Founded as a port, commerce has always been the City's *raison d'être*: according to Tacitus, in AD60 Roman Londinium was already 'filled with traders and a celebrated centre of commerce'. And if the trading is now in virtual rather than actual commodities, it's still possible to trace a direct lineage from the chaotic, cacophonous stalls of medieval Cheapside to the chaotic, cacophonous dealing rooms of today's City. This is one of the key financial centres on the planet – there are more foreign banks in London than in any other city (around 540) and the foreign exchange market is the largest in the world. This position was bolstered by the 1999 decision of Nasdaq, the US-based technology stock market, to base its forthcoming (electronic) European market in London. The very air seems to vibrate with millions being made and lost. Yet the City is more than blokes in suits shouting into phones.

For most of the capital's history, the City of London *was* the city of London – hence, that all-important, self-important capital letter. Apart from a brief Saxon excursion westward, it was only in the seventeenth century that there was significant, systematic building outside the boundaries of the old Roman wall.

Today's City – its 320 hectares (1¼ square miles) almost accurately known also as the Square Mile – subsumes the original site of Roman Londinium. Its boundaries are defined by Temple Bar to the west, Smithfield and Moorfields to the north, Tower Hill in the east and the Thames in the south. Flattened by the Great Fire of 1666, and again by the 1940-1 Blitz, the City has always been in such a hurry to rebuild, to get back to business, that no grand Haussmann-like scheme to rationalise the place has ever been able to get off the ground. But the City, though proud of its lack of sentimentality, hasn't entirely forgotten its past. Uninspiring office blocks may line many of the streets today, but these streets

Say cheese... snapping the **Tower of London**. *See page 55.*

still largely follow their medieval courses, their names speaking their history – Old Jewry, Ironmonger Row, Poultry, Bread Street. Several excellent museums and a magnificent crop of seventeenth-century churches (*see pages 46-7*) provide further links to the City's proud and colourful past.

ALONG FLEET STREET

Fleet Street, once synonymous with Britain's national daily and Sunday newspapers, leads eastwards from the Strand towards Ludgate Hill and St Paul's. It still bustles, but the bitterly fought departure of the papers to Wapping and Docklands in the late 1980s has torn the heart out of Fleet Street; its individual character has gone. No more do the hot metal presses clatter into the night; no more do the booze-fuelled hacks teeter from their offices to the pub and back again. The grandiose, fieldstone grey *Daily Telegraph* building (no.135) is now occupied by finance houses; the ground-breaking black glass-and-chrome *Daily Express* building at nos.121-128 (the first glass-curtain structure in Britain when it was built in 1932) stands empty. Only the Reuters/Press Association building (no.85) remains as a reminder of the 500-year association of Fleet Street with the printed word. It all started when William Caxton's successor, Wynkyn de Worde, brought his presses here from Westminster in 1500 and set up shop at **St Bride's** (*see page 46*). It's still affectionately thought of as the printers and journalists' church, although these are not professions renowned for their piety.

Literary figures too were familiar with the hostelries and chophouses of Fleet Street. A plaque on Child's bank (no.1) marks the site of the Devil's Tavern, where Ben Jonson, Samuel Pepys and Samuel Johnson all supped. Johnson was also a regular at the most famous of the Fleet Street pubs, the still-standing, charmingly creaky **Ye Olde Cheshire Cheese** (on the corner with Wine Office Court). The corpulent doctor's only surviving London home in Gough Square, restored and opened to the public as, logically enough, **Dr Johnson's House** (*see page 51*), is a handy one-minute's stagger away. Nearby is Johnson's Court, where Charles Dickens delivered what was to become his first published story, 'stealthily one evening in twilight, into a dark letterbox in a dark office up a dark corner of Fleet Street'.

As you head down into the Fleet valley (the river is now underground) towards Ludgate Circus, the view of St Paul's – particularly at night, floodlit and apparently floating over the City – is magical.

AROUND ST PAUL'S

Wren's masterwork may now be forced to jostle for position with graceless office blocks, but **St Paul's Cathedral** (*see page 54*) still stands proud as a symbol of British resilience, largely thanks to wartime photos of the flame-licked, but apparently untouched, cathedral weathering the Blitz. It actually suffered direct hits on several occasions, and in one night alone a total of 28 incendiary bombs fell in the immediate vicinity – but the Kipling-esque imagery of brave St Paul's keeping its head while all about it were losing theirs was just the tonic the nation needed.

Adjoining **Paternoster Square** fared less well: all but flattened by the Luftwaffe, it was rebuilt in the 1960s as a precinct of shops and offices that almost immediately became a byword for architectural ugliness. After a ten-year wrangle, plans were finally agreed a few years back to rebuild the square in a mixture of classical and modern styles; the project is currently under way.

The old marketplace of medieval London, **Cheapside** ('ceap' or 'chepe' is the Old English word for market), runs down from the cathedral to Bank. Shakespeare and John Donne used to drink in the raucous taverns here that once quenched the thirsts of the hoarse street sellers, while the surrounding area echoed to the work of craftsmen (no prizes for guessing what was sold and made in Milk Street and Bread Street).

Bow Lane, by the side of **St Mary-le-Bow** (*see page 47*), is now an appealing, narrow pedestrianised street, lined with shops, sandwich bars and pubs. At its southern end, **St Mary Aldermary** is one of Wren's rare experiments with the Perpendicular style, based on the pre-Fire church. Over Queen Victoria Street is Garlick Hill, its medieval name proving false the supposed antipathy between the English and the pungent bulb. At the bottom of the street is Wren's church of **St James Garlickhythe**, which has the highest roof in the City (after St Paul's). Its light-filled interior remains much as it was in the seventeenth century, and has earned the church the nickname of 'Wren's Lantern'. Between here and Cannon Street is wine and Whittington territory. The four-times Mayor of London lived on half-cobbled College Hill (a plaque on nos.19-20 marks the site of his house). He was buried in **St Michael Paternoster Royal** at the foot of the hill. Inside, 1960s stained glass by John Hayward depicts an anachronistically flat-capped Dick, together with his apocryphal cat. The name of this Wren church derives from two ancient thoroughfares nearby – Paternoster Lane (where rosaries were once made) and La Réole, a wine-making region near Bordeaux, popular with London's medieval wine importers. The **Vintners' Hall** (*see page 52* **A league of their own**) is close by, across Upper Thames Street.

South of St Paul's lies a little explored but delightful tangle of alleyways, concealing shops, pubs and the dinky Wren church of **St Andrew by the Wardrobe**. Built in 1685-95, the church's curious name dates from 1361, when the King's Wardrobe (the ceremonial clothes of the royal family) were moved to the adjoining building. Nearby, two other Wren creations, **St Benet** and **St Nicholas Cole**

Abbey, are, unfortunately, usually closed. Facing the former across scruffy Queen Victoria Street is the unexpectedly neat red-brick, seventeenth-century mansion of the **College of Arms** (*see page 51*), which still industriously examines and records the pedigrees of those to whom such things matter. Just west of here, at traffic-swept **Blackfriars**, the Dominicans – the 'black friars' – once had a monastery (it was dissolved in 1538; all that remains is a chunk of wall in Ireland Yard), and the Normans built one of their defensive forts, **Baynard's Castle**, to keep the unruly Londoners in check.

Just east of here is Foster's spectacular **Millennium Bridge**, which will be unveiled in May 2000 to coincide with the opening of the new Tate Modern gallery on the South Bank (*see page 39* **Tate of the art no.1**). The reasoning behind the bridge is to create a straight line of sight from the Tate right up to St Paul's.

North of Blackfriars station is **Apothecaries' Hall**, one of the most charming of the livery halls (*see page 52* **A league of their own**), and, close by on Ludgate Hill, stands the church of **St Martin within Ludgate**, its lead spire still visible over the surrounding buildings as Wren intended (which, alas, is more than can be said for those of most of his other churches). After reflecting on the works of God, ponder upon the sins of man around the corner in the most famous court in the land, the **Old Bailey** (*see page 54*), built on the site of the infamous Newgate Prison.

NORTH TO SMITHFIELD

The two major presences north of St Paul's are Smithfield Market and St Bartholomew's Hospital. Both have ancient roots. Smithfield was originally 'smooth field' – it had no blacksmithery connections, although there was an equine link. William Fitz Stephen, in 1173, wrote of 'a smoth field where every Friday there is a celebrated rendezvous of fine horses to be sold'.

As a large open space near to the City, Smithfield was much in demand for all manner of public events – jousts, sports matches, tournaments, executions and the most famous of all London's once-numerous annual fairs. Founded in 1123, **Bartholomew Fair** was renowned as a cloth fair before transmogrifying into the raucous entertainment fest that Ben Jonson captured so vividly in his seventeenth-century play of the same name. The spoilsport City authorities finally suppressed the fair in 1855, blaming it for encouraging public disorder, and built **Smithfield Market** on the site (it opened in 1868). Livestock had been traded here for centuries, but now the slaughtering took place elsewhere and Smithfield became – and remains – a meat market (or, rather, four linked markets). Now officially known as London Central Markets, a £70-million refit and refurbishment has left Horace Jones's immense Victorian East and West Markets looking splendid, repainted in their original colours of deep blues, reds and green with gold stars. If you want to see the working market, an early rise will be necessary – kicking off at around 3am, all the action is over by 8am – but you can reward your dedication with a fried breakfast and a pint with the meat porters in one of the nearby pubs (which have special early licences). Traders are normally happy to sell meat to the public, but you'll have to buy in bulk.

The instigation of Bartholomew Fair was only one of the actions of Rahere, court jester to Henry I, who almost died from malarial fever on a pilgrimage to Rome, and vowed to build a hospital on his return. He kept his promise, establishing **St Bartholomew's Hospital**, as well as a priory and the wonderfully atmospheric church of **St Bartholomew-the-Great** (*see page 46*). Although under a seemingly permanent threat of closure (the accident and emergency department has already been axed), Bart's retains its position as London's oldest and best-loved hospital. It was to here that Wat Tyler was brought after being stabbed at Smithfield by the Lord Mayor in 1381, although he was immediately dragged out and beheaded by the King's men (*see page 13*). A small museum of the hospital's history can be visited (*see page 54*). North of here, off St John Street, is the **Museum of the Order of St John** (*see page 54*), next to an original early sixteenth-century gateway.

AROUND BANK

The City has no indisputable centre, but if any place can lay claim to being the heart of the Square Mile, it's the great convergence of streets at **Bank**, overlooked by the unshakeable, self-confident triumvirate of the **Bank of England**, the **Royal Exchange** and the Lord Mayor's official residence, **Mansion House** (*see page 53*).

Britain's national bank was founded in 1694 to provide William III with the necessary finance to fight the French. It had its ups and downs, but eventually secured its position as the government's banker, with the authority to print and issue banknotes, and the responsibility of storing the country's gold reserves, managing the national debt and safeguarding the value of the British currency. The present building dates from 1925 to 1939, although the outer 'curtain' walls of Sir John Soane's 1788 structure have been retained. The admirably accessible exhibition of the bank's past and present in the **Bank of England Museum** (*see page 50*) is worth a look. Behind the bank is the modern **Stock Exchange** (closed to the public).

Overshadowing the bank is the massive neoclassical portico of the Royal Exchange, built by William Tite and opened by Queen Victoria in 1844. Sir Thomas Gresham created the Exchange in 1566 as a meeting and trading centre for merchants – he is honoured by a statue over the entrance in Exchange Buildings and his

City churches

Before the Great Fire of 1666, nearly 100 churches stood within the City walls. Of these, 87 were destroyed during the conflagration. Sir Christopher Wren was responsible for 51 of the 54 churches that were rebuilt. Thus, not only do the great majority of City churches date from a very narrow historical period (the late seventeenth century), but, uniquely, they are also almost all the work of one man. The fact that this has not resulted in a monotony of style is a testament to Wren's incomparable genius, particularly as he was forced to work only on the original cramped sites. The churches exhibit an extraordinary diversity of design and decoration although many do share certain features in common – light interiors, painted in white and gold, clear glass windows, fine wood carving, painted altarpieces and imaginative use of ironwork. The Victorian 'improvers', preferring the dim light and stained glass of the Gothic style, mangled many of Wren's churches, and bomb damage in World War II destroyed 11 more. Today, only 38 remain; St Ethelburga's in Bishopsgate – one of the few medieval churches to survive both the Great Fire and the Blitz – was almost completely destroyed by an IRA bomb in 1993 (*see page 49*). Many City churches put on free lunchtime concerts (*see page 274*).

All Hallows by the Tower

Byward Street, EC3 (020 7481 2928). Tower Hill tube. **Open** 9am-5.45pm Mon, Wed, Fri; 8am-5.45pm Tue; 9am-6.45pm Thur; 10am-5pm Sat, Sun. **Map 12 R7**

Samuel Pepys surveyed the progress of the Great Fire from the tower of All Hallows – the church survived the disaster, only to be all but destroyed by Luftwaffe bombs in 1940. Only the walls and seventeenth-century brick tower were left standing, but the post-war rebuilding has created a pleasingly light interior. A Saxon arch testifies to the church's ancient roots (seventh century); other interesting relics include Saxon crosses; a Roman tessellated pavement; Tudor monuments, sword-rests and brasses; a superb carved limewood font cover (1682) by Grinling Gibbons; and a collection of model ships. William Penn was baptised and John Quincy Adams married at All Hallows.

St Bartholomew-the-Great

West Smithfield, EC1 (020 7606 5171). Farringdon tube/rail. **Open** *mid-Nov-mid-Feb* 8.30am-4pm Mon-Fri; 10.30am-1.30pm Sat; 2-6pm Sun; *mid-Feb-mid-Nov* 8.30am-5pm Mon-Fri; 10.30am-1.30pm Sat; 2-6pm Sun. **Map 9 O5**

This church is the only surviving part of the Norman priory founded by Rahere in 1123, and London's oldest and most atmospheric parish church. The nave once extended the entire length of the churchyard to the thirteenth-century gateway, now the entrance from Smithfield. Although the nave was torn down during Henry VIII's monastic purge, leaving only one-third of the structure standing, it's still a wonderfully evocative place – most of the Norman arches are original. Look out for Rahere's early sixteenth-century tomb. Hogarth was baptised here, and in the Lady Chapel – once leased out for commerce – Benjamin Franklin served a year as a journeyman printer.

St Botolph Aldgate

Aldgate, EC3 (020 7283 1670). Aldgate tube. **Open** 10am-4pm Mon-Fri; 9.30am-1pm Sun. **Map 12 R6**

The original St Botolph, built by the City's east gate, may date back to the tenth century. The galleried interior of the current plain brick, stone-dressed structure (built by George Dance in 1744) is notable for John Francis Bentley's weird if highly original ceiling, lined with angels. Daniel Defoe was married here in 1683. St Botolph has a distinguished history of campaigning on social issues and it maintains the tradition today; its crypt is currently used as a day centre for the homeless.

St Bride's

Fleet Street, EC4 (020 7353 1301). Blackfriars tube/rail. **Open** 8am-4.45pm Mon-Fri; 9am-4.30pm Sat; 9.30am-12.30pm, 5.30-7.30pm, Sun. **Map 11 N6**

Completed by Wren in 1703, St Bride's is one of the finest examples of the Italian style in England. The spire, at 69m (226ft), is the architect's tallest; the four octagonal arcades of diminishing size are said to have been the inspiration for the first tiered wedding cake. The church was gutted in the Blitz, revealing Roman and Saxon remains, which are now effectively displayed and labelled in the crypt, along with information on the long-standing connections between St Bride's and the printing and newspaper publishing businesses. The press may have deserted Fleet Street, but St Bride's, where Wynkyn de Worde set up the first printing press in the City, is still known as the journalists' or printers' church.

St Helen Bishopsgate

Great St Helen's, EC3 (020 7283 2231). Bank tube/Liverpool Street tube/rail. **Open** 9am-5pm Mon-Fri. **Map 12 R6**

Having survived the Great Fire and weathered the Blitz, St Helen's was badly damaged by the 1992 and 1993 IRA bombs in the City. Founded in the thirteenth century, the spacious building incorporates fifteenth-century Gothic arches and a fourteenth-century nuns' chapel. The unusual double nave shows that this was once two churches side by side, one belonging to a Benedictine nunnery. St Helen's is known as the 'Westminster Abbey of the City' because of its splendid collection of medieval and Tudor monuments to City dignitaries. **St Andrew Undershaft**, nearby, and **St Olave's**, on Hart Street, are also pre-Fire churches.

St Magnus the Martyr

Lower Thames Street, EC3 (020 7626 4481). Monument tube. **Open** 10am-4pm Tue-Fri; 10.30am-1pm Sun. **Map 12 Q7**

The road leading to Old London Bridge (which stood downstream of the current bridge) passed by the door of the medieval church, which was rebuilt by Wren. In *The Waste Land*, TS Eliot described its interior as an 'inexplicable splendour of Ionian white and gold'. St Magnus was probably a twelfth-century Norwegian Lord of the Orkneys.

St Mary Abchurch

Abchurch Yard, Abchurch Lane, EC4 (020 7626 0306). Bank tube/Cannon Street tube/rail. **Open** 10.30am-2pm Mon-Fri. **Map 12 Q7**

The simple, Dutch-influenced red-brick exterior of this Wren church (1681-6) conceals a splendidly rich yet light interior, largely unaltered by subsequent 'improvers'. Below the shallow dome (painted by William Snow) is superb seventeenth-century woodwork. The highlight, however, has to be the limewood reredos (altar screen) – the only one in the City that can be attributed with certainty to Grinling Gibbons. The original church on the site dates from the twelfth century and may have been named 'up church' because it was upriver from its then-owner, the Priory of St Mary Overie (now Southwark Cathedral).

St Mary-le-Bow

Cheapside, EC2 (020 7248 5139). Bank or St Paul's tube. **Open** 6.30am-6pm Mon-Thur; 6.30am-4pm Fri. **Map 11 P6**

Wren's graceful white tower and spire (1670-3), topped by a huge dragon weathercock, is one of the architect's finest works. German bombers put paid to the original interior – what you see now is a post-war reconstruction. The tradition that only those born within earshot of 'Bow Bells' can claim to be a true Cockney probably dates from the fourteenth century, when the bells first rang the City's nightly curfew. The crypt of the original Norman church survives (its arches, or 'bows', give the church its name) and is now home to **The Place Below** vegetarian restaurant (*see p188*).

St Mary Woolnoth

Lombard Street, EC3 (020 7626 9701). Bank tube. **Open** 8am-5pm Mon-Fri. **Map 12 Q6**

Wulnoth, a Saxon noble, is believed to have founded this church on the site of a Roman temple to

Another Wren gem: **St Bride's**. *See p46.*

Concord. It was rebuilt many times, most recently by Nicholas Hawksmoor in 1716-17, and its tiny but beautifully proportioned interior, based on the Egyptian Hall of Vitruvius, is one of the architect's finest. Edward Lloyd, in whose coffee shop Lloyd's of London was founded, was buried here in 1713. When Bank tube station was built in 1897-1900 the church was undermined, the dead removed from the vaults and lift shafts sunk directly beneath the building.

St Stephen Walbrook

39 Walbrook, EC4 (020 7283 4444). Bank, Mansion House or Monument tube/Cannon Street tube/rail. **Open** 10am-4pm Mon-Thur; 10am-3pm Fri. **Map 11 P6**

Arguably Wren's finest parish church, St Stephen Walbrook was a practice run for many of the ideas that he brought to fruition in St Paul's. Its cross-in-square plan surmounted by a central dome creates a marvellous feeling of space and light and is an ingenious use of the relatively cramped site. Although badly damaged in the Blitz, the church has been superbly restored – largely thanks to the support of Lord Palumbo, who commissioned the amorphous, Roman travertine central altar by Henry Moore. The rector, Prebendary Dr Chad Varah, founded the Samaritans here in 1953. The original seventh-century Saxon church stood on the bank of the long-vanished River Walbrook.

grasshopper emblem on the bell tower. The Royal Exchange is now HQ of the futures market, but trading no longer takes place on the premises.

Further west is the centre of the City's civic life, **Guildhall** (*see page 51*), base of the Corporation of London, as well as an excellent library, the **Clockmakers' Company Museum** (*see page 51*), the church of **St Lawrence Jewry**, and the **Guildhall Art Gallery** (*see page 52*), housing the Corporation of London's art collection, which opened in 1999.

Next to Mansion House stands one of the City's finest churches, **St Stephen Walbrook** (*see page 47*), Wren's trial run for St Paul's. Nearby is the heap of stones that was once the Roman **Temple of Mithras** (*see page 55*). Other notable churches in the vicinity include Nicholas Hawskmoor's idiosyncratic **St Mary Woolnoth** at the junction of King William Street and Lombard Street and Wren's exquisite **St Mary Abchurch** off Abchurch Lane (for both, *see page 47*). Around the corner from St Mary Abchurch, set into the wall of the Overseas-Chinese Banking Corporation at 111 Cannon Street, is one of the City's most esoteric and, frankly, unimpressive sights: **London Stone** (*see page 53*).

As is the case all over the City, wandering where the fancy takes you is the best way to get to know this enigmatic part of London. Further north, a brief foray off Cornhill down St Michael's Alley takes you to the **Jamaica Wine House**, a popular pub on the site of the Jamaica Coffee House. Opened in the 1670s, sea captains and traders would meet at the Jamaica to discuss business with the West Indies and buy the best rum to be found in London.

AROUND THE TOWER OF LONDON

For more than 900 years, the **Tower of London** (*see page 55*) has acted as the eastern anchor of the City – there is no more potent symbol of the capital. Yet, for Londoners, the symbolism has always been complex. Built to protect the Norman conquerors and subdue their new subjects, the Tower came later to be seen also as a stern sentinel, guarding London's freedoms from those who sought to diminish them. Sometime palace, sometime prison, sometime place of execution, the Tower's associations, stories and legends are legion. Add to this the fact that it is Britain's most perfect medieval fortress, and it comes as no surprise that the Tower is one of London's top five visitor attractions.

The entire Tower Hill area, unappealingly bisected by a busy road, is a major focus for visitors. Just outside Tower Hill tube station in Wakefield Gardens is one of the most impressive surviving chunks of London's **Roman wall**. Although medieval additions have increased the height of the wall from around 6m (20ft) to 10m (35ft), its scale still impresses. A 1.7-mile (2.8-km) walk, punctuated by 21 explanatory plaques, follows the course of the old wall from the Tower to the **Museum of London** (*see page 53*). The tourist-targeted **Tower Bridge Experience** (*see page 55*) and St Katharine's Dock are nearby, but a far greater insight into London's past – and present – can be had by stepping a little off the tourist trail.

Samuel Pepys lived and worked on Seething Lane – there's a bust of the promiscuous diarist in the tiny green oasis of Seething Lane Gardens. Also here is the church of **St Olave Hart Street** (dubbed by Dickens 'St Ghastly Grim' after the grinning skulls around the entrance to the churchyard) where Pepys and his wife worshipped and are buried. Opposite the bottom of Seething Lane stands **All Hallows by the Tower** (*see page 46*), from the tower of which Pepys surveyed the progress of the Great Fire.

Between here and London Bridge stand two reminders of London's great days as a port: the early nineteenth-century **Custom House**, with a façade by Robert Smirke, and, next door, the former **Billingsgate Market**. For many centuries, Billingsgate wharf was famed for two things: the landing of fish and the foul language of its porters. The market was moved to a larger site on the Isle of Dogs in 1982, but Horace Jones's 1870s market building has been impressively restored (look for the fish on top of the weather vanes).

The lanes behind the waterfront are a rewarding hunting ground for church-spotters. **St Magnus the Martyr** (*see page 47*), **St Mary at**

Lovely **Leadenhall Market**. *See page 49.*

Hill, **St Margaret Pattens** and **St Dunstan in the East** are all within a couple of minutes' walk of each other. The gardens of the latter are a wonderfully lush haven in which to relax after struggling to the top of **The Monument** (*see page 53*). In nearby Pudding Lane, in the early hours of 2 September 1666, a fire started in a bakery that was to blaze for three days, destroying four-fifths of medieval London. Although, remarkably, only nine people are thought to have died, more than 13,000 houses, 87 churches and 44 livery halls were reduced to ashes. The Lord Mayor, woken soon after the fire started, lived to regret his immediate dismissal of the danger with the words, 'Pish! A woman might piss it out.' Thankfully, though, the fire put paid to the City's brown rats, carriers of the Great Plague, which had wiped out around 100,000 of the capital's population the previous year.

A little further north, around Bishopsgate, is the area with the greatest concentration of City tower blocks. Manhattan it ain't, and the lack of architectural imagination, daring and flair is depressing. The **NatWest Tower** (on Bishopsgate) is typically unexciting, although, with 52 storeys and at 373m (660ft) high, it at least had the distinction of being the tallest office block in Europe when it was built in 1980.

The one outstanding exception is Richard Rogers' extraordinary **Lloyd's Building** (1986), on Lime Street. Its guts-on-the-outside design draws much from Paris's Pompidou Centre, also by Rogers, and is the sort of daring, uncompromising architectural vision that is so rarely seen in the conservative City. Part of the façade of the old 1928 building (on Leadenhall Street) has been left standing. Lloyd's of London, the largest insurance market in the world, is a remarkable and unique organisation; a society of underwriters ('Names') that accepts all insurance risks for personal loss or gain. It traces its roots back to Edward Lloyd's coffee shop in Tower Street in the 1680s. Traditionally, being a Name seemed to involve nothing but waiting for regular fat cheques to pop through your letterbox. That this was all too good to be true was made brutally clear in the early 1990s, when a series of disasters caused Lloyd's to suffer record losses of over a billion pounds. Many Names were personally ruined and the company came to the brink of collapse.

Next door is one of the City's most delightful surprises: **Leadenhall Market**. 'Foreigners' – meaning anyone from outside London – were allowed to sell poultry here (and, later, cheese and butter) from the fourteenth century. The current arcaded buildings, painted in green, maroon and cream with wonderful decorative detail, are the work of Horace Jones (architect also of Smithfield Market and Tower Bridge). One of the market's greatest characters was a gander from Ostend called Old Tom. Somehow he avoided the fate of 34,000 other geese who were slaughtered in the space of two days, and became a much-loved feature of Leadenhall, waddling around the local pubs to be fed tit-bits. He died in 1835 at the venerable age of 38 and was buried in the market. Today, Leadenhall remains a great place to wander, particularly around lunchtime. Reassuringly, the fresh produce stalls haven't been displaced – there are still fabulous cheesemongers, butchers and fishmongers.

Between Leadenhall and Liverpool Street rail station there are more churches to discover: **St Helen Bishopsgate**, off Bishopsgate (*see page 46*), **St Andrew Undershaft** on St Mary Axe, **St Botolph Aldgate** (*see page 46*) and **St Katharine Cree** on Leadenhall Street. The latter, one of the few churches to be built in England during the years preceding the Civil War, is an extraordinary hybrid of classical and Gothic styles.

Near here is Britain's oldest synagogue, the superbly preserved **Bevis Marks Synagogue**, in a courtyard off Bevis Marks; it was built in 1701 by Sephardic Jews who'd escaped from the Inquisition in Portugal and Spain. This area suffered considerable damage from the IRA bombs of April 1992 and April 1993, although most have now been fully restored. The tiny pre-Fire church of **St Ethelburga** (built 1390) on Bishopsgate was devastated, but, appropriately, is to be rebuilt at a cost of £4.5 million as a 'Centre for Reconciliation and Peace' and a world research centre investigating the role of religion in ending conflict.

AROUND LIVERPOOL STREET STATION

The broad expanse of **Finsbury Circus** offers vital breathing room for local office workers – a rare commodity in the City, where open spaces are seen less as enhancements to the quality of life than wasted development opportunities. Tall sweeps of offices (none of the early nineteenth-century originals survives) overlook an agreeable, almost provincial, scene of manicured gardens, a bowling green, bandstand and small restaurant.

Metropolitan values unmistakably reassert themselves in the huge **Broadgate** office development along the west side of Liverpool Street Station. Design-wise, like so many City buildings, it's all very macho and conservative, yet the area around the arena, with its atria and cascading foliage, is a pleasant spot to shop, eat or drink, and the venue for concerts in the summer and an open-air ice rink in the winter (*see page 286*). Spacious, if somewhat isolated, **Exchange Square**, with its view into Liverpool Street Station, is also worth a look (if only for a quick peek at the modern piece of sculpture there – the Beryl Cook-esque, and rather fancifully named, *Broadgate Venus*).

Liverpool Street Station is one of London's busiest, daily pumping in the City's lifeblood – tens of thousands of commuters – and then returning them back to their East Anglian homes at the end of the day. An impressive redevelopment of the station in the late 1980s/early 1990s has made it fit for the twenty-first century. On its east side, Charles Barry's venerable late-Victorian Great Eastern Hotel has been totally refurbished and reopened in early 2000 (*see page 145*). That the hotel is aiming high is suggested by the fact that the catering in all four restaurants, and the interior design, are being provided by the ubiquitous Sir Terence Conran (in partnership). Within striking distance of here, to the east, are the shops and food stalls of **Spitalfields Market** (*see pages 109 & 223*) and, further east, the curry houses of **Brick Lane** (*see page 110*).

NORTH OF LONDON WALL

Extending from the Barbican to close to Liverpool Street Station, **London Wall** follows the northerly course of the old Roman fortifications. Part of the wall, and the remains of one of the gates into the Cripplegate Roman fort, can be seen in **St Alfage Gardens**. The area just to the north of here was levelled during the Blitz. Rather than encourage lucrative office developments, the City of London and London County Council laudably purchased a 14-hectare (35-acre) site in 1958 to build 'a genuine residential neighbourhood, incorporating schools, shops, open spaces and amenities'. Unfortunately, what we ended up with was the **Barbican**.

In the brave new post-war world, it must have looked great on paper. This was how we would all live in the future: 6,500 state-of-the-art flats, some in blocks of 40 storeys and more, rising higher than 135m (400ft) – the tallest in Europe at the time – a huge arts centre with concert halls (home to the London Symphony Orchestra), a theatre (London base of the Royal Shakespeare Company), a repertory cinema, art gallery, exhibition space, cafés and restaurants. The complex also incorporates one of the city's best museums, the **Museum of London** (*see page 53*), the **Barbican Art Gallery**, with its wide-ranging exhibitions (*see page 50*), the Guildhall School of Music and Drama and the City of London School for Girls.

Tragically – considering the immense cost of the Barbican (the arts centre alone accounted for over £150 million) – the ideas behind the development were already out of date by the time it was completed in the early 1980s. Granted, occupancy rates are high (there is little choice of residence if you want to live in the City; five-sixths of the inhabitants of the Square Mile live here) and the events programmes at the arts centre are usually first rate – it's just that, try as hard as you can to like the place, it has no soul, no warmth, no sense of community. It's a clumsy, charmless colossus, notorious for its confusing layout.

Marooned amid the towering blocks is the only pre-war building in the vicinity – the heavily restored sixteenth-century church of **St Giles**, where Oliver Cromwell was married and John Milton buried. The Nonconformist connection continues further north-east. **Bunhill Fields** was set aside as a cemetery during the Great Plague, although seemingly not used at that time. Instead, because the ground was apparently never consecrated, it became popular for Nonconformist burials, gaining the name of 'the cemetery of Puritan England'. Much of the graveyard is now cordoned off, but it's still possible to walk through and see the monuments to John Bunyan, Daniel Defoe and that most unconformist of Nonconformists, William Blake. On adjoining Bunhill Row, John Milton lived from 1662 until his death in 1674, writing some of his greatest works here, including *Paradise Lost*. Opposite Bunhill Fields on City Road is the **Museum of Methodism** and **John Wesley's House** (*see page 53*). The founder of Methodism lived his last years in the Georgian house and is buried by the unexpectedly ornate chapel. There's a museum in the crypt, while upstairs, in 1951, Denis Thatcher married Margaret Hilda Roberts. So it seems there was methodism in her madness after all.

Sights

City Information Centre

St Paul's Churchyard (south side of the cathedral), EC4 (020 7332 1456). St Paul's tube. **Open** *Apr-Sept* 9.30am-5pm daily; *Oct-Mar* 9.30am-5pm Mon-Fri; 9.30am-12.30pm Sat. **Map 11 O6**

A source of information on sights, events, walks and talks within the Square Mile.

Bank of England Museum

Bartholomew Lane, EC2 (020 7601 5545). Bank tube. **Open** 10am-5pm Mon-Fri. **Admission** free. **Map 12 Q6**

This unexpectedly interesting museum centres on a restoration of the bank's Stock Office, designed by Sir John Soane in 1793, complete with figures in period costume and a stuffed tabby cat. Well thought-out displays tell the bank's 300-year story, explaining its vital role in providing the stability and wherewithal for Britain to build up a global empire, and give an enlightening, informal course in national finance for beginners. Visitors come tantalisingly close to a stack of gold bars, learn via interactive screens about the complexities of banknote production and security, and budding City high-flyers can play at foreign exchange trading.

Barbican Art Gallery

Level 3, Barbican Centre, Silk Street, EC2 (box office 020 7638 8891/enquiries 020 7638 4141). Barbican tube/Moorgate tube/rail. **Open** 10am-6pm Mon, Tue, Thur-Sat; 10am-8pm Wed; noon-6pm Sun. **Admission** £6; £4 under-16s, concs; £15 family. *Gosee Card member (see p32).* **Credit** AmEx, MC, £TC, V. **Map 9 P5**

The main gallery of this notoriously disorienting City arts centre regularly mounts interesting exhibitions of modern and historical works, frequently showcasing major photographic exhibitions, such as 1999's retrospective of David Bailey. The Barbican also takes on art in a wider context, with shows focusing on fashion and design. The 2000 programme looks to be particularly eclectic. **The Art of Star Wars** (13 Apr-3 Sept) is the first UK exhibition devoted to George Lucas's cult films. Two contrasting exhibitions are held simultaneously from 5 October to 10 December: **The Wilde Years: Oscar Wilde and his Times** places Wilde's achievements in the context of the art and culture of his time, while **Rock Style** looks at the influence of rock and pop on twentieth-century fashion with outfits worn by Elvis, Madonna and Bono.

Meanwhile, the Concourse Gallery will house the **Carnegie Art Award**, a celebration of contemporary Nordic painting shown for the first time outside Scandinavia (20 Apr-21 May); **Paris sur Scène**, a selection of photographs from the Maison Européene de la Photographie in Paris (5 June-6 Aug); and **Time**, an exhibition of specially commissioned work by **Andy Goldsworthy** (31 Aug-29 Oct), accompanied by a season of documentary films about the sculptor. Fans should note that Goldsworthy's vast snowballs will be on display in selected outdoor locations around the City from 21 to 25 June – or until they melt.
Website: www.barbican.org.uk

Clockmakers' Company Museum

The Clockroom, Guildhall Library, Aldermanbury, EC2 (020 7332 1868/1870). Bank, Mansion House or St Paul's tube/Moorgate tube/rail. **Open** 9.30am-4.45pm Mon-Fri. **Admission** free. **Map 11 P6**
This cramped but easily digestible collection of timepieces is the world's oldest. It includes the watch that Sir Edmund Hillary wore on the first successful ascent of Everest in 1953 and John Harrison's eighteenth-century prizewinning chronometer. Anyone familiar with Dava Sobel's surprise bestseller *Longitude* will want to take a look at the latter – a remarkable invention that made it possible for ships at sea to chart their exact position, giving the edge to Britain's empire builders.

College of Arms

Queen Victoria Street, EC4 (020 7248 2762). Blackfriars tube/rail. **Open** 10am-4pm Mon-Fri. Closed public hols. **Admission** free. **Map 11 O7**
The College of Arms has been granting coats of arms and checking family pedigrees since 1484. Its seventeenth-century mini-mansion has been beautifully restored. Only the Earl Marshal's Court (the wood-panelled entrance room hung with paintings of various worthies) can be viewed without notice. Book a tour if you want to see the Record Room and the artists at work on the elaborate certificates. If you wish to trace your roots, ask to see the Officer in Waiting, though you may be charged a small fee for him to look up the information. It's also helpful if you bring any details you already have on your family background.
Website: www.kwtelecom.com/heraldry/collarms

Dr Johnson's House

17 Gough Square, off Fleet Street, EC4 (020 7353 3745). Chancery Lane or Temple tube (both closed Sun) or Blackfriars tube/rail. **Open** *May-Sept* 11am-5.30pm Mon-Sat; *Oct-Apr* 11am-5pm Mon-Sat. **Admission** £3; £1 10s-18s; £2 students, OAPs, ES40s, disabled; free under-10s. **Map 11 N6**
When a man is tired of London, he is probably tired of all the interminable Samuel Johnson references. This is the only surviving London residence – he had 17 – of the inimitable and inescapable doctor. Johnson lived in this late seventeenth-century house from 1748 to 1759, while working on the first comprehensive English dictionary. Visitors can wander through his home, guided by descriptions, anecdotes and quotes on laminated sheets; there's not much in the way of furniture – it's mainly engravings and paintings. The top room is the long garret, which was 'fitted out like a counting-house' when Johnson and his six clerks did their lexicographing here. A video provides insights into aspects of Johnson's life and work. Curios include a brick allegedly from the Great Wall of China donated to the house (Johnson never managed to fulfil his wish to go there). Look out for the statue of the doctor's cat, Hodge, in Gough Square.
Website: www.drjh.dircon.co.uk

Guildhall

off Gresham Street, EC2 (020 7606 3030/guided tours ext 1460). Bank tube. **Open** 9am-5pm daily. **Admission** free. **Map 11 P6**
For more than 800 years Guildhall has been the centre of the City's local government (as well as the site of major trials such as those of Lady Jane Grey and Archbishop Cranmer in 1553). The stunning fifteenth-century Great Hall was gutted during the Great Fire and again in the Blitz, but has been sensitively restored. It is decorated with the banners and shields of the 100 Livery Companies; the windows record the names of every Lord Mayor since 1189; and there are monuments to Mayor William Beckford, Wellington, Nelson, Churchill and the two Pitts. Look out for the almost oriental-looking statues of legendary giants Gog and Magog guarding the West Gallery. They are post-war replacements for originals destroyed in the Blitz; the phoenix on Magog's shield symbolises renewal after fire. Meetings of the Court of Common Council (governing body for the Corporation of London, presided over by the Lord Mayor) are held here once a month on a Thursday at 1pm, except during August (visitors welcome; phone for dates). The hall is also used for banquets and ceremonial events. Below the Guildhall is the largest medieval crypt in London.

Guildhall *'s gorgeous Great Hall.*

The buildings alongside house Corporation offices, the **Guildhall Library** (partly financed by Mayor Dick Whittington's estate and the first local authority-funded public library), a shop selling books on London and the **Clockmakers' Company Museum** (*see p51*). *See also below* **Guildhall Art Gallery**.
Website: www.corpoflondon.gov.uk

Guildhall Art Gallery

Guildhall Yard, off Gresham Street, EC2 (020 7332 1632/1856/recorded info 020 7332 3700/guildhall.artgallery@corpoflondon.gov.uk). Bank tube. **Open** 10am-5pm Mon-Sat; noon-4pm Sun. **Admission** £2.50; £1 under-18s, concs; £5 family. **Map 11 P6**

In late 1999, the Guildhall Art Gallery opened its doors to the public for the first time since the original, established in 1885, was destroyed by fire during World War II. Of the Corporation of London's 4,000 paintings only about 250 can be displayed at any one time, thus part of the space will be given over to rolling exhibitions in order to air the more obscure elements of the collection. Generally, the paintings are more of historic than artistic interest: a group of London cityscapes stretching from the seventeenth century to the present; portraits of former mayors and other dignitaries; and a selection of battle paintings that includes John Singleton Copley's massive opus *The Defeat of Floating Batteries, September 1782*. Of more aesthetic, but equally sentimental appeal are the Pre-Raphaelite works, which include Millais' *The Woodman's Daughter* and Frederic Lord Leighton's *The Music Lesson*; there is also one rather grand oil sketch by Constable – *Salisbury Cathedral from the Meadows*. A digital gallery – accessible at terminals dotted throughout the building – allows you to search on screen for the many paintings held in store.
Website: www.guildhall-art-gallery.org.uk

A league of their own

The City of London's **guilds** or **livery companies** are the old union headquarters of once-powerful trades that largely no longer exist. The Barber-Surgeons, Cordwainers and Periwig-Knitters may have lost their magnificent halls to the Great Fire or the Blitz, but they still vie in a medieval league table of self-importance. The livery companies do a lot of work for charity, dress up in ruffles and big-buckled shoes for the Lord Mayors' Show, pull strings Masons-style, and still own 15 per cent of the City. With persistence and luck, access may be gained to view the architecture and treasures of the most interesting of the remaining halls. Top of the curiosities is at the eighteenth-century **Fishmongers' Hall** (London Bridge, EC4; 020 7626 3531) where, amid a jumble of precious loot, is preserved the 12-inch dagger used by fishmonger-Mayor William Walworth to stab Wat Tyler in the back and put down the Peasants' Revolt of 1381. There's even a lifesize wooden statue of the murderous Walworth, dagger in hand. In comparison, the pride of the **Skinners' Hall** (Dowgate Hill, EC4; 020 7236 5629) – exquisite panelling and an overblown eighteenth-century Russian glass chandelier – seem almost tame. The **Vintners' Hall** (Upper Thames Street, EC4; 020 7236 1863) is the oldest surviving HQ, dating back as far as 1671; the **Apothecaries' Hall** (Blackfriars Lane, EC4; 020 7236 1180) boasts a Reynolds sketch and portraits of James I and Charles I; while the Renaissance-style **Goldsmiths' Hall** (Foster Lane, EC2; 020 7606 7010) is one of the easiest to visit, staging occasional exhibitions (chief among those planned for 2000 is 'Treasures of the Twentieth Century', as part of the **London Millennium String of Pearls Festival** (*see page 8* **London's your oyster**), featuring silver, jewellery and art medals, from 25 May to 21 July).

Swanky but shy **Apothecaries' Hall**.

London Stone

set in wall of Overseas-Chinese Banking Corporation, 111 Cannon Street, EC4. Cannon Street tube.
Map 11 P7

One of London's oldest, least known and least spectacular sights is the rough-hewn chunk of Clipsham limestone, barely visible behind an iron grille and glass in the wall opposite Cannon Street Station. The origins of this unremarkable-looking stone, unmarked but for two grooves on the top, are murky. It probably dates from Roman times and may have been a milestone, but was already a landmark in 1198 when it was referred to as 'Lonenstane'. It was originally set in the ground on the opposite side of the road, before being swapped to the north side of the street in 1742 and embedded in the wall of St Swithin's (now demolished) church on this site in 1798. No one has ever been very sure about the purpose of the stone, but it was considered, in some vague unspecified way, to be the symbolic cornerstone of the City. In 1450, Jack Cade, leader of the Kentish rebels, calling himself John Mortimer, is believed to have struck the stone with his sword and proclaimed, 'Now is Mortimer Lord of the City.'

Mansion House

Walbrook, EC4 (020 7626 2500). Bank tube. **Open** for group visits by written application to Ms Sarah Jane Mayhew, at least two months in advance (min 15, max 40 people). **Admission** free. **Map 11 P6**

Squaring up to the Bank of England and the Royal Exchange is another neo-classical portico – that of the Lord Mayor's official residence, Mansion House. Designed by George Dance, it was completed in 1753 and contains sumptuous state rooms, such as the Egyptian Hall, scene of many an official banquet. Mansion House is the only private residence in England with its own Court of Justice, complete with 11 cells – including one for women, 'the birdcage', where Emmeline Pankhurst was once imprisoned.
Website: www.cityoflondon.gov.uk

The Monument

Monument Street, EC3 (020 7626 2717). Monument tube. **Open** 10am-5.40pm daily.
Admission £1.50; 5s-15s. **Map 12 Q7**

Erected in 1671-7 by Christopher Wren and Robert Hooke, this simple Doric column, topped with a flaming urn of gilt bronze, commemorates the Great Fire of 1666 (*see p15*). At 61m (202ft) – the distance from here to the site of the bakery on Pudding Lane where the Fire began – the Monument was the tallest isolated stone column in the world in its time. Anyone who labours up the 311 steps won't find that hard to believe (although you will at least get a certificate for your trouble on the way out). Unless you're terminally unfit, it's worth the effort for the wonderful views from the top. Although the gallery is entirely enclosed in an iron cage (it had been a notorious spot for suicides), those who suffer from vertigo may agree with James Boswell that it is 'horrid to be so monstrous a way up in the air'. Look for the gap at the bottom of the Latin inscription on the side of the Monument. After telling of how the Fire was finally extinguished, the words '(but Popish frenzy, which wrought such horrors, is not yet quenched)' were added in 1681. Not until 1830 were these bigoted (and foundationless) words erased.

Museum of London

150 London Wall, EC2 (020 7600 3699/24hr info line 020 7600 0807/info@museumoflondon.org.uk). Barbican or St Paul's tube/Moorgate tube/rail. **Open** 10am-5.50pm Mon-Sat, public hols; noon-5.50pm Sun; 10am-7.50pm 1st Wed of month. **Admission** (tickets valid for one year) £5; £3 students, OAPs; free under-16s, registered disabled; **free** after 4.30pm. *GoSee Card member (see p32).* **Credit** MC, V. **Map 9 P5**

The concrete 'drawbridge' across a 'moat' of traffic makes an appropriate, if daunting, approach to this exploration of London's history. The museum, named Best Large Attraction of the Year 1999 as part of the London Tourism Awards, opened in 1976, purpose-built in the middle of a busy City roundabout, on the site of the Roman fort. Inside, you'll find one of the most imaginatively designed museums in the capital. Visitors can trace the growth of London from prehistoric times up to the present day with an absorbing combination of models, artefacts and reconstructions. Plans for redevelopment in 2000 will increase gallery space to allow more comprehensive coverage of post-1945 history.

In the meantime, it's well worth lingering over the impressive Roman interior, with its original mosaic pavement; the Cheapside hoard (a staggering cache of fine jewels, dating from 1560 to 1640, found in a box under a shop); and the **Great Fire Experience**, an illuminated model with sound effects and commentary depicting the fire that destroyed four-fifths of London in 1666. Reconstructions of Newgate prison cells, and the Lord Mayor's ceremonial coach and shop/restaurant interiors from Victorian and Edwardian London (including Selfridges' splendid art deco elevator) all help to create an atmospheric and informative experience.

The temporary exhibitions are usually excellent and, in 2000, include **High Street, Londinium**, a re-creation of Roman London (21 July-Easter 2001). The new **Voices Gallery**, billed as an 'oral history presentation', will open at the end of May.
Website: www.museumoflondon.org.uk

Museum of Methodism & John Wesley's House

Wesley Chapel, 49 City Road, EC1 (020 7253 2262). Old Street tube/rail. **Open** 10am-4pm Mon-Sat; noon-2pm Sun. **Admission** *museum & house* £4; £2 5s-15s, OAPs, ES40s; additional visits free within same month. **Map 10 Q4**

Appropriately enough, Bunhill Fields (*see p50*), just across the City Road, is the burial ground of many of London's religious dissenters. John Wesley's unorthodox assemblies resulted in the establishment of a church that now has a following of over 50 million around the world. In 1778, Wesley opened this chapel for worship, and in 1981 a museum of the man's work opened in the crypt. Highlights include the pulpit and a large oil portrait of the scene at his death bed. His house next door has been restored to its original Georgian interior design, right down to the paint it's thought that Wesley would have chosen. In the kitchen and study you can see his nightcap, preaching gown and, bizarrely, his personal experimental electric-shock machine.

Museum of the Order of St John

St John's Gate, St John's Lane, EC1 (020 7253 6644). Farringdon tube/rail. **Open** 9am-5pm Mon-Fri; 10am-4pm Sat. *Guided tours* 11am, 2.30pm Tue, Fri, Sat. **Admission** free; donations requested. **Map 9 O4**

The surviving 1504 gateway was once the entrance to the Priory of St John of Jerusalem, founded in the twelfth century, and is now the HQ of the British Order of St John. Beside the gate is a small museum tracing the history of the Order from the swashbuckling days of the crusading Knights Hospitallers, to the more mundane but more useful work of today's St John Ambulance Brigade. The Chapter Hall, Council Chamber, Old Chancery, new church and Norman crypt (the only remaining part of the original building) can only be seen on the guided tours. All that remains of the priory's original circular church is its outline, traced in cobbles, in St John's Square, just north of the gate.

Old Bailey

corner of Newgate Street & Old Bailey, EC4 (020 7248 3277). St Paul's tube. **Open** 10.30am-1pm, 2-4pm, Mon-Fri. **Admission** free (no under-14s admitted, 14s-16s accompanied by adults only). **Map 11 O6**

The Old Bailey – or Central Criminal Court – has dealt with some of the most publicised criminal cases in London's history (including Oscar Wilde in 1895, Dr Crippen in 1910, William 'Lord Haw-Haw' Joyce in 1945, and Peter Sutcliffe in 1981). The court was built on the site of the notorious Newgate Prison (demolished in 1902) and the bronze figure of Justice on the copper-covered dome overlooks the area where convicts were once executed. Stones from the prison made up the façade with Pomeroy's sculpted group over the main entrance – representing the Recording Angel supported by Fortitude and Truth. The tradition of judges carrying a posy of flowers into court has its origin in the need to mask the foul stench and ward off germs emanating from the prison. The public are admitted to watch trials.

St Bartholomew's Hospital Museum

West Smithfield, EC1 (020 7601 8152/guided tours 020 7837 0546). St Paul's tube. **Open** 10am-4pm Tue-Fri. *Guided tours* 2pm Fri. **Admission** free. *Guided tours* £4; £3 OAPs, ES40s, disabled. **Map 11 O5**

London's oldest and best-loved hospital, threatened with closure for many years, has thankfully been saved (for the time being at least). Inside the grounds are a small but informative museum of its history and the only survivor of its original four chapels, **St Bartholomew-the-Less**. The **Great Hall** and the staircase, its walls decorated with epic biblical murals by William Hogarth, can also be viewed from the museum, but the seasonal weekly tours offer a better view, while also taking in Smithfield and the surrounding area.

St Paul's Cathedral

EC4 (020 7236 4128). St Paul's tube. **Open** 8.30am-4pm Mon-Sat; *galleries, crypt & ambulatory* 10am-4pm Mon-Sat. Last entry 4pm. **Admission** *cathedral, crypt & gallery* £5; £2.50 6s-16s; £4 OAPs, students, ES40s, disabled; *audio guide* £3; £7 family; £2.50 OAPs, students, ES40s, disabled; *guided tour* £2.50; £1 6s-16s; £2 OAPs, students, ES40s, disabled. *Guided tours* 11am, 11.30am, 1.30pm, 2pm Mon-Sat. **Credit** *shop* MC, £TC, V. **Map 11 O6**

Impressive enough today, the effect that Sir Christopher Wren's masterpiece must have had in the seventeenth century can only be wondered at. A Roman temple dedicated to Diana probably stood on the site where King Ethelbert built the first wooden church in AD604. Two more Saxon cathedrals followed (all three burned down), before the Normans constructed 'Old St Paul's' at the end of the eleventh century. This colossal Gothic building, destroyed in the 1666 Great Fire, was, amazingly, even larger and taller than Wren's successor. Today's St Paul's is one of the few cathedrals ever to be designed by one architect, supervised by one master builder (Thomas Strong) and built within their lifetimes (construction lasted 35 years). Wren's epitaph, inscribed on the wall by his simple tomb in the crypt, could not be more appropriate: 'If you seek his monument, look around.'

Rather like St Peter's in Rome, the scale of the thing means that any feeling of sanctity is sacrificed on the altar of grandeur, but there's a wonderful sense of proportion, space and harmony that even the endless stream of coach parties can't spoil. One of the biggest surprises is the dazzlingly rich, almost Byzantine-like mosaics of the Creation in the **Choir**; these, like Holman Hunt's incongruous *Light of the World* hanging in the south aisle, are late nineteenth-century additions. In the clock tower on the West Front hangs **'Great Paul'**, the heaviest swinging bell in England, some 3m (5ft) in diameter. It is tolled daily at 1pm.

High up in the dome, frescoed with stories from the life of St Paul by James Thornhill, people in the **Whispering Gallery** strain to hear reverberating voices above the muffled din. Higher still are the viewing galleries: the **Stone Gallery** (at the base of the dome) and the **Golden Gallery** (at the top). It's a long, hard climb, involving 530 steps, but worth it for the unrivalled views over London. The bright, whitewashed **Crypt** (one of the largest in Europe) centres around grandiose monuments to the Duke of Wellington and Admiral Nelson; it raises a wry smile to see a modest monument to Florence Nightingale amid all the military bigwigs who did so much to keep her supplied with customers. **Painters' Corner** contains memorials to Reynolds, Lord Leighton, Alma-Tadema, Turner, Millais and Holman Hunt. The most interesting item in the **Treasury** is an extraordinary cope (a ceremonial cape), embroidered with the spires of 73 churches. Also down here are a decent café and restaurant.

It's worth doing one of the lively, anecdote-packed guided 'Supertours', which allow access to areas you're not normally allowed into, such as the magnificent choir area, with carving by Grinling Gibbons.
Website: www.stpaulslondon.anglican.org

Temple of Mithras

On the raised courtyard in front of Sumitomo Bank/Legal & General Building, Temple Court, 11 Queen Victoria Street, EC4. Mansion House tube. **Open** 24 hours daily. **Admission** free. **Map 11 P6**

During the third century AD, the rival cults of Mithraism and Christianity were battling for supremacy. The worship of the macho Persian god Mithras appealed particularly to Roman soldiers, and the troops on the British frontier built the small temple to their champion near this spot (cAD240-50). The reconstructed foundations (looking as they did when they were unearthed in 1954) aren't much to look at, but show the Roman influence on the later design of churches: rounded apse, central nave and side aisles. The difference is that Christian churches were built in the shape of a cross with the altar facing east. The story of the temple, and the marble sculptures found buried underneath, can be found in the **Museum of London** (*see p53*).

Tower Bridge Experience

SE1 (020 7403 3761). Tower Hill tube or London Bridge tube/rail. **Open** *Apr-Oct* 10am-6.30pm, *Nov-Mar* 9.30am-6pm, daily (last entry 1hr 15mins before closing). **Admission** £6.25; £4.25 5s-15s, OAPs, students; £18.25 family. *GoSee Card member (see p32).* **Credit** AmEx, MC, £TC, V. **Map 12 R8**

Despite its mock-Gothic appearance, Tower Bridge was actually a pioneering steel-framed structure. The 'Tower Bridge Experience' might sound a bit naff, but visitors do get a fact-packed insight into the history of London's famous bridge, which opened in 1894 and was once described as 'a colossal symbol of the British genius'. The tour is helped along by lively animatronics, interactive displays and the 'ghost' of Horace Jones, the original architect of the bridge, who died shortly after foundation work began. A collection of photos of the bridge, taken during its first 100 years, are displayed along the elevated walkways. The views from here are far-reaching, if somewhat obscured by the glass and metal of the corridors. The tour ends in the engine rooms, which house the steam pump engines used to raise the bridge until 1976 (it's all done by electrics now). To find out when the bridge will next be lifted (usually at least once a day), and the name and type of vessel passing beneath, phone 020 7378 7700. *Website: www.towerbridge.org.uk*

Tower of London

Tower Hill, EC3 (020 7709 0765). Tower Hill tube/ Fenchurch Street rail. **Open** *Mar-Oct* 9am-5pm Mon-Sat; 10am-5pm Sun; *Nov-Feb* 10am-4pm Mon, Sun; 9am-4pm Tue-Sat. **Admission** phone for prices. **Credit** AmEx, MC, £TC, V. **Map 12 R7**

The Tower has been a castle, a palace and a prison during its long history and it remains one of the capital's most important sights. Be warned that 2.5 million people annually traipse around the Tower; arrive early if you want to avoid the worst of the crowds. A good introduction is provided by the entertaining, free, hour-long guided tours that depart every half hour, hosted by the snappable Beefeaters (more soberly known as Yeoman Warders).

The oldest part of the complex is William the Conqueror's **White Tower**, begun in 1076 (its name refers to the period during Henry III's reign when it was whitewashed). It now houses a portion of the extensive **Royal Armouries** and, on the second floor, the exquisite, austere **Chapel of St John**, which, dating from 1080, is the oldest church in London.

Although popularly notorious as a site of aristo beheadings, only seven people were ever executed on **Tower Green** (a plaque in the centre of the green records their names). The proprietorial ravens that squawk about the green have been protected by royal decree for more than 300 years and are a reminder of the extensive menagerie that was kept at the Tower from 1235 until it was transferred to London Zoo in 1831. The nineteenth-century Waterloo Barracks, north of the White Tower, contain the celebrated **Crown Jewels**, the centrepiece of which is the Imperial State Crown, set with a 317-carat diamond. Their popularity is such that viewing time is strictly rationed.

South of the White Tower is the gloriously named **Bloody Tower**. It was here in 1483 that the 12-year-old Edward V and his ten-year-old brother were incarcerated by their uncle, the future Richard III. Subsequent Tudor propaganda asserted that Richard had the boys murdered – and the skeletons of two children were discovered in the tower in 1674 – but the true fate of the young princes remains one of history's great mysteries. A hundred years later, Sir Walter Ralegh was imprisoned in the tower on three separate occasions, the last being for six weeks in 1618 before his execution at Westminster. On the waterfront, south of the Bloody Tower, is **Traitors' Gate**, by which prisoners used to enter the Tower, having been ferried down the Thames from the law courts at Westminster. The gate is part of **St Thomas's Tower**, which, with neighbouring **Wakefield Tower**, has been converted to resemble Edward I's medieval palace.

During 2000, the Tower will be holding several free exhibitions as part of the **London String of Pearls Millennium Festival** (*see page 8* **London's your oyster**), including the **Royal Armouries Millennium Exhibition** (15 Apr-31 Dec), detailing the 2,000-year history of the Tower through a series of specially commissioned works of art; and various performances and parades. **Sir Thomas More's Cell** will be open for the first time, until 10 December.

In 1999, the Tower Environs Scheme was given the go-ahead, with the aim of humanising the area by creating a new visitor centre, pathway and entrance area to the Tower. The project is due to take place over the next couple of years.

Despite its outward glitter, the Tower is a strangely antiseptic, soulless place, and pricey with it. It could take some lessons from **Hampton Court Palace** (*see p135*), which puts on a far more convincing, evocative and entertaining historical show.

For the most up-to-date information, visitors are advised to pick up one of the regularly updated leaflets at the Tower, which detail the current events. Note that tickets can be purchased at all London Underground ticket offices.

Holborn & Clerkenwell

A mix of trendy and traditional.

MAPS 6 & 9

The character of Holborn (pronounced 'Hó-bun'), sandwiched between commercial Covent Garden, learned Bloomsbury and the money-mad City, owes something to all three districts, but is primarily formed by the straggling, anachronistic **Inns of Court** (*see page 58* **Inns & outs**).

AROUND ALDWYCH

The long-vanished Holebourne river was once a tributary of the not-so-long-ago-vanished Fleet, which ran along the course of today's Farringdon Road. The western flank of modern Holborn is formed by the uncompromising car-filled conduit of Kingsway, which was carved out of slum-lined streets in the early 1900s in an attempt to relieve traffic congestion, and culminating in the crescent of Aldwych. The handsome **Meridien Waldorf** hotel, built here soon afterwards, and **One Aldwych** (*see page 147*), one of London's newest and most stylish luxury hotels, face a trio of unashamedly Imperial buildings: India House, Australia House and Bush House, once intended to be a huge trade centre and now home to the BBC's much-loved and much-threatened World Service. BBC mementoes and spin-offs can be bought from the shop by the entrance (*see page 220*).

Between here and the Thames lie **King's College** (its hideous 1960s buildings sitting uncomfortably with Robert Smirke's graceful 1829-31 originals) and William Chambers' grandiose late eighteenth-century **Somerset House**, which has been restored and is due to reopen to the public in May 2000. The central courtyard will be the site of a series of cultural events, and the River Terrace, with stunning views of the Thames, has a café and is connected to Waterloo Bridge by a glass and steel bridge. Somerset House's main attractions, though, are its museums: the **Courtauld Gallery**; the mosaics, gold and silver of the **Gilbert Collection** (for both, *see page 59*); and, from autumn 2000, the **Hermitage Rooms at Somerset House**, which will hold regularly changing exhibitions from the great St Petersburg museum.

Two nearby curiosities are worth a glance. On Temple Place is one of a handful of still-functioning **cabmen's shelters**. These rather dainty, green-painted sheds are a legacy of the Cabmen's Shelter Fund, set up in 1874 to provide cabbies with an alternative to pubs (Victorian cab drivers were overfond of a pint) in which to hide from the elements and get a hot meal and (non-alcoholic) drink. Around the corner on Strand Lane is the **'Roman' bath**, reached via an alley off Surrey Street. David Copperfield took many a cold plunge here. It can be viewed through a window if you don't manage to pass by during its official opening times (10am-12.30pm Mon-Fri).

No, not the Tardis, but a **cabmen's shelter**.

Back on the Strand are the churches of **St Mary-le-Strand** (James Gibbs' first public building; built 1714-17) and **St Clement Danes** (*see page 61*), both isolated on traffic islands. Samuel Johnson was a regular and 'solemnly devout' member of the

Chowing down in hip Clerkenwell.

congregation at the latter. Just north of here loom the suitably imposing neo-Gothic **Royal Courts of Justice** (*see page 61*), opened in 1882 by Queen Victoria. The stress of the commission was such that the architect GE Street's crowning achievement brought him to an early grave. The fiercesome bronze griffin in the middle of the road near here marks the site of **Temple Bar** and the official boundary of the City. Just beyond is the church of **St Dunstan in the West** (*see page 61*) and the little-known, seventeenth-century **Prince Henry's Room** (*see page 61*). South of here are the labyrinthine alleyways of the **Middle** and **Inner Temples** (officially lying within the boundaries of the City; *see page 58* **Inns & outs**).

AROUND LINCOLN'S INN FIELDS

The winding streets to the west of the courts bear the names of several of the now-defunct **Inns of Chancery**, such as New Inn and Clement's Inn, and are home to one-time cradle of left-wing agitation, the **LSE** (London School of Economics). Nearby, at 13 Portsmouth Street, is the **Old Curiosity Shop**, the supposed (though this is much disputed) inspiration behind the eponymous Dickens novel. It dates from about 1567.

The broad expanse of **Lincoln's Inn Fields** is London's largest square and Holborn's focal point. On the north side is the fine **Sir John Soane's Museum** (*see page 61*); to the east are the buildings of the Inn itself. Chancery Lane, running up from the Strand to High Holborn – site of Mid-City Place, an ambitious new steel and glass office block – is home of the Public Records Office and the Law Society. At its northern end are the weird, subterranean shops of the **London Silver Vaults** (*see page 201*), selling everything from silver spoons to antique clocks. On the south side of the square, and not for the squeamish, are the various components of the **Museums of the Royal College of Surgeons** (*see page 59*).

Around the corner, heading towards Holborn Circus, teeter the overhanging, half-timbered Tudor buildings of **Staple Inn**, which is one of the former Inns of Chancery. Across the road, by the ancient Cittie of Yorke pub, is an alley leading into the most northerly of the Inns of Court, **Gray's Inn**.

CLERKENWELL

North and east of here lies the fashionable district of **Clerkenwell**. In the twelfth century, a hamlet grew up here around the religious foundations of the Priory of St John of Jerusalem and the now-vanished St Mary's Nunnery and, from the fourteenth century, the Carthusian monastery of **Charterhouse** (now an upmarket OAP home).

The original **Clerk's Well**, first mentioned in 1174, and long thought lost, was rediscovered by chance in 1924. It can now be viewed through the window of 14-16 Farringdon Lane. Over the centuries, a strong crafts tradition grew up in Clerkenwell as French Huguenots and other immigrants settled to practise their trades away from the restrictions of the City guilds. The area was thought 'an esteemed situation for gentry' until the early nineteenth century when population pressure and increasing dilapidation led to an influx of Irish, and then Italian, immigrants, looking for cheap accommodation. (Evidence of the once 10,000-strong Italian community can still be seen in **St Peter's Italian Church**, nearby on Clerkenwell Road, and **L Terroni & Sons**, the excellent deli next door.) Radicals were also attracted to Clerkenwell at this time. Clerkenwell Green was a political meeting point – Lenin edited 17 editions of the Bolshevik paper *Iskra* from a back room (which has been preserved) in the **Marx Memorial Library** (at no.37A).

DICKENSIAN CLERKENWELL

By the late nineteenth century, the district had become a 'decidedly unsavoury and unattractive locality': prime Dickens territory. Long after the demise of the saffron crocus fields, the notorious rookeries of **Saffron Hill** were depicted in all their desperate horror in *Oliver Twist*. **Bleeding Heart Yard**, off Greville Street, was where Arthur Clennam became a partner in the engineering firm of Doyce and Clennam in *Little Dorritt*, and where the ineffectual Mr Pancks tried to collect rent from his impecunious tenants. It supposedly owes its name to the brutal murder here of Elizabeth Hatton in 1646 – her heart was ripped out and said to be still pumping blood on to the cobbles when found the next morning. You can ponder the likely veracity of the legend while indulging at the **Bleeding Heart Restaurant & Wine Bar** (*see page 193*).

In nearby **Ely Place**, David Copperfield met Agnes Wakefield and renewed his friendship with Tommy Traddles. This fascinating enclave was once the site of the Bishop of Ely's London palace; all that remains is the delightful church of **St Etheldreda** (which contains a good lunchtime café; *see page 61*). The private, gated road, now lined by Georgian houses, is crown property and

Pick up an old bag in **Exmouth Market**.

remains outside the jurisdiction of the City of London. Pub-lovers should not miss the **Olde Mitre Tavern**, on this site since 1546, secreted up a narrow alley off Ely Place. West of here, the long-established, no-nonsense **Leather Lane Market** sells clothes, food and dodgy videos, and supports a number of cheap caffs. Running parallel is **Hatton Garden** – now the centre of London's diamond trade.

TRENDY CLERKENWELL

The slums were eventually cleared, but little was built in their place. Consequently, the population plummeted and Clerkenwell stagnated. Since the late 1980s, however, property developers have wised up to the attractions of an area so close to the City and the West End. The tourism potential of the district is also being increasingly exploited. There's now a heritage walk, as well as the spooky **House of Detention** (*see page 59*) and the sixteenth-century **St John's Gate** and **Museum of the Order of St John** (*see page 54*).

If a gauge of a district's desirability is the number of quality restaurants it maintains, then Clerkenwell has most assuredly arrived. St John Street is home to the offal-biased excellence of **St John** (no.26; *see page 168*), the relentlessly classy **Stephen Bull Smithfield** (no.71; *see page 167*) and the hip bar and oriental snacks of **Cicada** (no.126; *see page 193*). Running almost parallel to St John Street, Farringdon Road is nesting place for **The Eagle** (no.159; *see page 186*), the gastro-pub

Inns & outs

London's quiet, sprawling **Inns of Court** offer a pleasant afternoon's archaic amusement. Here, members of the legal profession wander safely out of touch with reality, bewigged but quite serious, selling (or learning to sell) our wonderful British justice. Wander around Lincoln's Inn and Gray's Inn, and sample the joys of passing 'by unexpected ways, into its unexpected avenues, into its magnificent ample squares, its classic green recesses', as essayist Charles Lamb laid it on thick at the end of the eighteenth century. Today, the quiet alleys and open spaces of the Inns that he described remain a blessed haven from the endless traffic and choking fumes of central London. The Inns have restricted opening times, so phone to check before you set off. During 2000, however, as part of the **London String of Pearls Millennium Festival** (*see page 8* **London's your oyster**), some of the buildings will be more accessible to casual visitors. Specially printed tour guides will be available for the public to use to visit **Lincoln's Inn**, **Inner Temple** and **Middle Temple** from 10am to 5pm Mon-Fri; available from the Tudor Street Gate. In addition, the Middle Temple will house an exhibition, One Thousand Years of the Middle Temple (10am-noon, 3-4pm, Mon-Fri).

Gray's Inn (Gray's Inn Road, WC1; 020 7458 7800) was the last Inn to be founded, in 1569. Its Hall contains a superb screen, said to be made from the wood of a galley from the Spanish Armada. On a guided tour of **Lincoln's Inn**'s Old Hall and Great Hall (Lincoln's Inn Fields, WC2; open on application during 2000, except August – phone 020 7405 6360 to arrange a visit; otherwise open by written application only; phone 020 7405 1393 for details), it's still possible to relive scenes from *Bleak House*, Dickens' ferocious attack on the legal system: virtually nothing has changed. South of the Strand, **Middle Temple** (Middle Temple Lane, EC4; 020 7427 4800) and **Inner Temple** (Inner Temple Treasury Office, EC4; 020 7797 8250) are built around a maze of courtyards and passageways, especially atmospheric after dark, when they're gaslit. Of the old halls and buildings open to the public, only **Temple Church** (Inner Temple, King's Bench Walk; 020 7353 1736), which was built in 1185, is stuffed with recumbent Knights Templars and grimacing gargoyles, though somehow it doesn't feel very old. The four remaining Inns of Court are situated to symbolise the law's role as mediator in the historical battle for power between the City and royal Westminster: nowhere is this tension felt so much as at Temple Bar on the Strand, past which rampant griffin the Queen cannot stray without the Lord Mayor's permission. Plans are afoot to end the Hertfordshire exile of Wren's original arch – the last of the eight City gates – placing it in the revamped Paternoster Square by St Paul's.

that pioneered the idea of top-notch nosh in a boozer; meanwhile the ultra-hip, modern Spanish **Moro** (*see page 186*) is leading the development of increasingly trendy **Exmouth Market** (nos.34-36).

The only hitch in Clerkenwell's inexorable rise is that the predominantly 'loft' accommodation drawing in most of the new blood is of a type and price to exclude all but the young, high-earning professional. Ad executives and solicitors may soon swamp the few remaining locals and artists who had previously found a haven in one of central London's quietest yet most interesting districts.

Sights

Courtauld Gallery

Somerset House, Strand, WC2 (020 7848 2526). Covent Garden or Temple tube (closed Sun). **Open** 10am-6pm Mon-Sat; noon-6pm Sun. **Admission** £4; free under-18s; £3 students, OAPs; *joint ticket with Gilbert Collection* £7; £5 OAPs. **Map 8 M7**

Housed in the superb eighteenth-century **Somerset House**, the rest of which opens to the public in May 2000, the Courtauld Gallery represents the sum of several donated private collections. At its heart are the paintings of textile magnate Samuel Courtauld, which account for the bulk of the impressionist and post-impressionist works. These include excellent examples of the respective styles, such as Manet's *A Bar at the Folies-Bergère* and a version of his *Le Déjeuner sur l'Herbe*, Cézanne's *The Card Players* and Gauguin's *Nevermore*. This collection is augmented largely by the munificence of Count Antoine Seilern, who gave the institute a wealth of fourteenth- to twentieth-century paintings, resulting in a roomful of Rubens and a group of wonderful early Flemish and Italian paintings. Highlights include Fra Angelico's *Man of Sorrows*, Cranach's *Adam and Eve* and Quentin Metsys' almost-translucent *Virgin and Child with Angels*.

Temporary exhibitions in 2000 will include a special millennium visual art and poetry exhibition, **About Time**, combining works by the likes of Rembrandt, Manet, Shakespeare and Larkin (24 Feb-11 June); an impressive selection of **Modern Still Lives** from the reserve collection (29 June-15 Oct); and **The Nativity**, tracing the changing artistic portrayal of the Christian story (2 Nov 2000-21 Jan 2001).

Website: www.courtauld.ac.uk

Gilbert Collection

Somerset House, Strand, WC2 (020 7240 4080). Covent Garden or Temple tube (closed Sun). **Open** 10am-6pm Mon-Sat; noon-6pm Sun (last entry 5.15pm). **Admission** £4; free under-18s, UK full-time students, ES40s; £3 part-time & foreign students; £2 disabled & helpers. *Joint ticket with Courtauld Gallery* £7; £5 OAPs. **Credit** AmEx, MC, V. **Map 8 M7**

From May 2000, the South Building of Somerset House will be home to London's newest museum of decorative arts. The three-pronged collection of London-born Arthur Gilbert is made up of over 800 items, and focuses on a fabulous array of gold snuff boxes, European silver and Italian *pietre dure* mosaics. An audio guide is included in the admission price. There's also a café and a shop.

Website: www.gilbert-collection.org.uk

Somerset House, *restored to its former glory.*

House of Detention

Clerkenwell Close, EC1 (020 7253 9494). Farringdon tube/rail. **Open** 10am-6pm daily (last entry 5.15pm). **Admission** £4; £2.50 5s-16s; £3 students, OAPs; £10 family. **Map 9 N4**

In the nineteenth century you could find yourself clapped in irons here for begging, attempting suicide or even 'stealing two grapes'. There has been a prison on this site since 1616, but it was at its busiest in 1846-78, receiving some 10,000 inmates a year. Brave the underground passageways (all that remain of the prison), and you'll get an all-too-real feeling of the dank, dark conditions that prisoners had to endure. The individual cells, at the end of the marked route, display a collection of torture weapons that go by the delightful names of 'tongue-tearer' and 'throat-catcher'. Bags of atmosphere (the BBC filmed part of *Great Expectations* here in late 1998), but not somewhere to be caught during a power cut.

Museums of the Royal College of Surgeons

35-43 Lincoln's Inn Fields, WC2 (020 7973 2190/ recorded info 020 7312 6694/museums@rcseng.ac.uk). Holborn tube. **Open** 10am-5pm Mon-Fri. **Admission** free; donations encouraged. **Map 6 M6**

The Royal College of Surgeons runs four museums under one roof: the **Hunterian**, the **Odontological**, and the **Wellcome Museums of Pathology** and

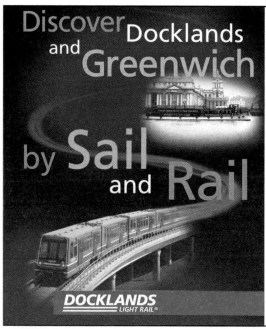

Anatomy (open by appointment only). The Hunterian Museum (perhaps the most impressive), in Lincoln's Inn Fields, consists of a collection of anatomical and pathological specimens, purchased by the British government in 1799 from John Hunter (1728-93); it's not for visitors with weak stomachs. Tall glass-fronted display cabinets hold jars of numerous (human and animal) internal organs along with foetuses at different stages of their development. The skeleton of the 'Irish Giant' and a dwarf woman are also on display. Jaws, casts and skulls can be seen in the Odontological Museum, as well as the famous Waterloo teeth, extracted from the corpses on the field of battle to replace those lost by the living. The dental and surgical instruments serve to reinforce the value of anaesthetics.
Website: www.rcseng.ac.uk

Prince Henry's Room

17 Fleet Street, EC4 (020 7936 4004). Temple tube (closed Sun). **Open** 11am-2pm Mon-Sat. **Admission** free. **Map 11 N6**

Built in 1611 and named in honour of James I's eldest son, this is one of the few City buildings to have survived the Great Fire, with oak panelling and plaster ceiling intact. It now houses a collection of Samuel Pepys memorabilia.

Royal Courts of Justice

Strand, WC2 (020 7936 6000). Temple tube (closed Sun). **Open** 9.30am-4.30pm Mon-Fri (no court cases during Aug & Sept recess). **Admission** free. **Map 6 M6**

Anyone is free to take a pew at the back of any of the 88 courts. It's a fascinating and somehow reassuring experience to thus exercise one's democratic right to witness the creaky British justice system in action. The interior of the building is as impressive as the façade, and also houses a coffee shop and a small exhibition of legal garb.

Throughout 2000, in conjunction with the **London String of Pearls Millennium Festival** (*see p8* **London's your oyster**), an exhibition and video about the legal system, past, present and future, will be shown in the Main Hall (9am-4.30pm Mon-Fri; admission free). Guided tours are also planned.
Website: www.open.gov.uk

St Clement Danes

Strand, WC2 (020 7242 8282). Temple tube (closed Sun). **Open** 8.30am-4.30pm Mon-Fri; 9am-3.30pm Sat; 9am-12.30pm Sun. **Map 6 M6**

The curious name of this Wren church (with a tower extension by James Gibbs) may date back to its use by Danes married to English wives who were allowed to stay behind when Alfred the Great expelled most of their countrymen from the kingdom. Its name is immortalised in the children's nursery rhyme 'Oranges and lemons, Say the bells of St Clement's'; the bells still ring out the tune, and children at St Clement Danes Primary School are given an orange and a lemon after the annual service. (Pity that the church in the rhyme almost certainly wasn't this one, but St Clement Eastcheap, which is near to the wharves where citrus fruit used to be unloaded.) Most of the interior was gutted during the Blitz, and has been renovated as a suitably sedate and stately central church for the RAF. Outside the front of the church is the controversial 1992 memorial to Marshal of the RAF, Sir Arthur 'Bomber' Harris, the man behind the devastating saturation bombings of German cities towards the end of World War II.

St Dunstan in the West

Fleet Street, EC4 (020 7242 6027). Chancery Lane tube. **Open** 10am-2pm Tue; 2-6pm Sat; 9am-2pm Sun (occasional concerts on Fri). **Map 11 N6**

The first mention of this church was in 1185, but the present early Gothic-revival building dates only from 1831-3, when a widening of Fleet Street required it to shift slightly northwards. John Donne was rector here (1624-31); Izaak Walton (whose *Compleat Angler* was published in the churchyard in 1653) held the bizarrely named posts of 'scavenger, questman and sidesman' (1629-44); and Samuel Pepys popped in one day in 1667 to hear a sermon and unsuccessfully try to fondle one of the local maidens ('…at last I could perceive her to take pins out of her pocket to prick me if I should touch her again').

St Etheldreda

Ely Place, EC1 (020 7405 1061). Chancery Lane tube. **Open** 7.30am-7pm daily. **Map 9 N5**

Britain's oldest Catholic church (built in the 1250s) is the only surviving building of the Bishop of Ely's once-extensive London residence. The simple chapel, lined with the statues of local martyrs, is London's only remaining example (excepting parts of Westminster Abbey) of Gothic architecture from the reign of Edward I. The strawberries that were once grown in the gardens were said to be the finest in the city (and received plaudits in Shakespeare's *Richard III*); every June the church holds a 'Strawberrie Fayre' in Ely Place.

Sir John Soane's Museum

13 Lincoln's Inn Fields, WC2 (020 7405 2107). Holborn tube. **Open** 10am-5pm Tue-Sat; 6-9pm 1st Tue of every month. **Admission** free; donations appreciated. **Guided tours** 2.30pm Sat (£3; free concs). **Map 6 M5**

One of London's most delightful and idiosyncratic museums. Sir John Soane (1753-1837) was not only one of the leading architects of his day, but an inveterate and inspired collector. The word 'eclectic' does not do justice to the extraordinary accumulation of treasures stuffed (much as they were in Soane's time) into the house he reconstructed himself. Highlights include Hogarth's *Rake's Progress* and *The Election* series, the sarcophagus of Pharaoh Seti I, Indian drawings, Christopher Wren's watch, numerous chunks and casts of ancient sculpture, a monument to Soane's wife's dog ('Alas, poor Fanny') and Soane's own architectural plans and models. The house's atmosphere is at its most magical when lit by candles in winter on the evening openings on the first Tuesday of the month. Note that tickets for the guided tours go on sale at 2pm in the library dining room, on a first-come first-served basis.
Website: www.soane.org

Bloomsbury

Literary and academic London meet in this distinctive district, home to some of the country's greatest historic institutions.

MAPS 5 & 6

Between Gower Street and Great Portland Street, Euston Road and Oxford Street lies the area that during the 1930s and 1940s became known as **Fitzrovia**. Aspiring and expiring artists and writers (including Dylan Thomas) were drawn to this seductively louche northern extension of Soho to drink away their talent in basement dens and pubs such as the **Fitzroy Tavern** on Charlotte Street. In his *Memoirs of the Forties*, Julian Maclaren-Ross recalls being warned by Tambimuttu, Sinhalese editor of *Poetry London*, to '...beware of Fitzrovia... you will stay there always day and night and get not work done ever'. The fact that few people have heard of him today suggests he failed to heed the warning.

Today, Fitzrovia's backstreets can often seem curiously devoid of life – few tourists venture north of Oxford Street, and few local workers stray from the gaggle of no-longer-very-appetising pubs in the area around **Charlotte Street** (although the restaurants here are good). The area is, however, slowly reviving as Soho overspills northwards and trendy bars such as **Jerusalem** (on Rathbone Place; *see page 195*) open up.

Beyond **Pollock's Toy Museum** (*see page 66*), **All Saints** Margaret Street (*see page 63*), and the omnipresent (620-ft) **British Telecom Tower** (not open to the public), sights are few, but there's still a certain neglected charm to Fitzrovia, providing you keep clear of the scruffy, car-fume-filled canyon of Tottenham Court Road. Not much more than a century ago this was still a quiet rural road lined by cow sheds; now it's the place to head for electronic goods and computers, and classy furniture and household wares (at **Heal's**, **Habitat** and **Purves & Purves**, *see page 219*). The southern end of the road, though, has been revived somewhat by the construction of an impressive glass mini-shopping complex, with big-name stores such as Sainsbury's and Boots breathing some life back into the area.

BOOKISH BLOOMSBURY

West of Fitzrovia, and approximately bounded by Euston Road, Gray's Inn Road and Theobald's Road/Bloomsbury Way/New Oxford Street, is an area with more heavyweight literary and academic associations: **Bloomsbury**. Its main selling point is undoubtedly the magnificent **British Museum** (*see page 64*), which tops the list of London's most-visited tourist attractions. The other main influence in the area is the **University of London**, whose most striking building is the 130-m (210-ft) tower of Senate House (built in the 1930s in Portland stone), looming massively over the Malet Street campus like an Orwellian Ministry of Truth. Many of the buildings in Bloomsbury's fine Georgian squares contain offshoots of the university, including the **Percival David Foundation for Chinese Art** (*see page 66*) and the **Petrie Museum of Egyptian Archaeology** (*see page 66*). The university bookshop, **Waterstone's**, on the corner of Torrington Place and Gower Street, is one of London's biggest and best.

The name Bloomsbury is derived from 'Blemondisberi', meaning 'the manor of (William) Blemond', who acquired the area in the early thirteenth century. It remained largely rural until the 4th Earl of Southampton built **Southampton** (now **Bloomsbury**) **Square** around his house in the 1660s. Close by on Bloomsbury Way is the eighteenth-century church of **St George Bloomsbury** (*see page 66*), identified by its unique, stepped steeple. The construction of Southampton Square marked the start of a trend and many more followed, including Bloomsbury's only surviving complete Georgian square, **Bedford Square** (1775-80), once the haunt of book publishers, and enormous **Russell Square** (laid out in 1800), dominated by the red-brick-and-terracotta fantasy of the Russell Hotel, and with a handy café in the square gardens.

Few original houses remain of 1820s **Gordon Square**, but this is nevertheless still the area most closely associated with the **Bloomsbury Group**. In various houses around here (look out for the blue plaques), Virginia and Leonard Woolf, Lytton Strachey, Roger Fry, Vanessa and Clive Bell, Duncan Grant and John Maynard Keynes flounced about practising GE Moore's belief that 'by far the most valuable things... are... the pleasures of human intercourse and the enjoyment of beautiful objects'.

HIDDEN CORNERS

Further east are some of Bloomsbury's most charming corners, including pedestrianised **Woburn Walk** (off Upper Woburn Place), with its bow-windowed shops and cafés. Equally

Bloomsbury's finest: **Bedford Square**.

appealing are the small-scale restaurants and shops lining **Marchmont Street**, the pleasant kids' park of **Coram's Fields** (*see page 234*), the excellent pubs on Lamb's Conduit Street (**The Lamb** is particularly recommended; *see page 191*) and **Dickens' House** on Doughty Street (*see page 65*), the author's only surviving London residence.

Traffic-packed Southampton Row, leading down to Holborn, forms Bloomsbury's lower backbone. Try the noisy, old-fashioned **Princess Louise** (on the corner of High Holborn and Newton Street) for a pint, or lunch in the blissfully quiet **October Gallery Café** (*see page 180* **Cafés, coffees & light lunches**) on Old Gloucester Street, before browsing the second-hand books at **Skoob Books** (*see page 204*) in the curious, pedestrianised, colonnaded Sicilian Avenue.

IT'S GRIM UP NORTH

The north of Bloomsbury is decisively bounded by the endless traffic hurtling along Euston Road. Here stands the utilitarian **Euston Station**, simultaneously the oldest and newest of London's mainline termini. Opened in 1837, and described at the time as 'a railway station without equal', its magnificent classical portico, screen and Great Hall were, criminally, demolished in 1963 to make way for the current structure.

Equally controversial has been the endlessly criticised, hopelessly over-budget and woefully behind-schedule **British Library** (*see page 63*), next to **St Pancras Station** (which will be the terminus of the high-speed Channel Tunnel link in 2003). Looking more like an out-of-town shopping mall than a temple of knowledge, the library finally opened to the public in spring 1999.

St Pancras Station itself is a Victorian wonder. The glass-and-iron train shed, spanning 73m (240 ft) and over 30m (100ft) high at its apex, is a remarkable feat of engineering and is fronted by Sir George Gilbert Scott's exuberant High Gothic fairytale of a building, formerly the **Midland Grand Hotel**, a structure the architect accurately if immodestly described as 'possibly too good for its purpose'. It's now known as **St Pancras Chambers** – there's a small exhibition about the hotel and the building's future in the lobby (at the west end of the building; open 11.30am-3.30pm Mon-Fri). If you want to see more, fill in a form available in the lobby for one of the occasional guided tours of the building. Marriott Hotels is planning to convert part of it back into a hotel.

Next door is the more functional but unlovely **King's Cross Station**. Much of the surrounding area is seedy – unpleasantly so at night – and in desperate need of regeneration.

Sights

All Saints

Margaret Street, W1 (020 7636 1788).
Open 7am-7pm daily. **Services** phone for details.
Map 5 J5

This 1850s church is the major work of William Butterfield, whose dread hand scarred countless London churches with his Victorian Gothic 'improvements'. The site of All Saints, however, was too small for Gothic proportions so, instead, he used an extraordinary – but surprisingly triumphant – mishmash of fourteenth-century-style details, red brick and humbug-like black stone bands à la Siena Cathedral. Look for the Pre-Raphaelite Minton tile paintings on the walls.
Website: www.ucl.ac.uk/~ucgbmxd/allss.htm

British Library

96 Euston Road, NW1 (info 020 7412 7332/box office 020 7412 7222). King's Cross St Pancras or Euston Square tube/Euston rail. **Open** 9.30am-6pm Mon, Wed, Thur, Fri; 9.30am-8pm Tue; 9.30am-5pm Sat; 11am-5pm Sun. **Admission** free; donations appreciated. **Map 6 K3**

You either love or hate the new postmodern, red-brick British Library building next to St Pancras Station. Yet even those who fall into the latter category can't deny that the library puts on some excellent exhibitions and services for the public.

British Museum

The British Museum is easily London's number one tourist attraction – and it's not difficult to see why. This is one of only two institutions in the world – the other being the Smithsonian in Washington DC – that fulfil the Enlightenment concept of gathering all branches of human knowledge under one roof: a real-life encyclopaedia. The museum's beginnings can be traced to royal physician Dr Hans Sloane's 'cabinet of curiosities' (bequeathed to the nation in 1753), a substantial miscellany of books, paintings, classical antiquities and stuffed animals. Over the next century the plunder of empire, including the Elgin Marbles and various massive Egyptian monuments, overwhelmed the storage space available. In 1847, Robert Smirke designed the present impressive neo-classical edifice, with its grand colonnaded façade and ample interior.

It had to happen, though. With more than five million visitors a year and an ever-expanding list of exhibits, the British Museum could hardly justify the close to one-hectare (two-acre) expanse at its centre, around the edge of the Reading Room, that lay occupied only by bookstacks belonging to the British Library. The museum's 250th anniversary (actually in 2003) seemed like a fitting time to resolve the situation once and for all.

The first part of the plan was the move of the **British Library** to Euston Road in 1997 (*see page 63*), which in total freed up 40 per cent of the building's space. The following year work began on Norman Foster's £97-million plan for the **Great Court** (*see picture*). This will create new space for galleries, greatly improved access to the existing galleries and a central plaza with shops and cafés, which will stay open after the galleries have closed. The idea is to make the museum a place to hang out as well as to visit. Also here will be the **Wellcome Gallery of Ethnography**, which introduces themes in adjacent galleries dedicated to the arts of Africa, the Americas, Australia and the Pacific. The **Reading Room** has been restored to its original splendour and will contain a public reference library and COMPASS, a multimedia system allowing the public electronic access to the museum's collections. But the showpiece is undoubtedly Foster's **glass roof**, a great undulating wave of glass and metal with no visible supports.

In addition, the original Robert Smirke façades of the courtyard will be restored and the southern portico reinstated. The museum's **Ethnography Collections** make a welcome return from the Museum of Mankind in Mayfair; they will be displayed at several locations within the museum, including the **Sainsbury African Galleries**. With the aim of improving the museum's already-excellent educational facilities, the **Clore Centre for Education** is being created in the Great Court, with two auditoria for lectures, film and video, plus academic conferences, concerts and other performances.

Running until 24 April 2000 is **Apocalypse**, a temporary exhibition examining the depiction of apocalyptic episodes throughout history.

Note that the Great Court and galleries mentioned above are, unless stated otherwise, due to open in November 2000; until then visitors' services, such as disabled access and access to toilets, may be interrupted and galleries closed at short notice.

GETTING TO GRIPS WITH THE BM

The cardinal rule is: don't try to see everything on one visit. Even if it were physically possible to do so, you'd end up with nothing but glazed eyes, throbbing feet and only the haziest of memories of anything you had seen. You should focus your attention on specific areas of interest. If you're not sure what you want to see, buy one of the excellent souvenir guides (£5) and take your pick of the highlights, or try one of the four suggested tours on the £1 leaflets. Alternatively, book one of the 90-minute tours of the museum's top treasures at the information desk (£7) or join one of the free 'Eye Openers' tours, which concentrate on one aspect of the museum's collections (such as 'Europe: Medieval to Modern' or 'Treasures of the Islamic World').

HIGHLIGHTS

Selected highlights of the museum's permanent collection are listed below. Note that as this Guide went to press there were plans to renumber the galleries.

Ancient Egypt – the monumental **statues of the pharaohs** and the **Rosetta Stone**, inscribed with a decree in two languages and three scripts, which enabled Egyptian hieroglyphics to be deciphered for the first time; *room 25.*

Ancient Assyria – the vivid **reliefs** of battles and hunting scenes from Nineveh; *rooms 17, 19 & 21.*

Ancient Greece – the reconstructed tomb of one of the rulers of Xanthos, known as the **Neried Monument**; *room 7.* The sculptures from the Parthenon, better known as the **Elgin Marbles**; *room 8.*

The Celts – the **Lindow Man**, preserved in peat, having been ritually killed c300 BC; *room 50.*

Roman Britain – the **Mildenhall Treasure** – fourth-century silver tableware; *room 49.*

Middle Ages – the seventh-century **Sutton Hoo ship burial**, containing a fabulous cache of Anglo-Saxon treasure; *room 41.*

Islamic World – the unsurpassed collection of **Iznik pottery** from Ottoman Turkey; *John Addis Islamic Gallery.*

China – the Tang dynasty (AD618-906) **tomb figurines** buried with General Kiu Tingxun in 728; *Joseph E Hotung Gallery of China, South & South-east Asia.*

Chase Manhattan Gallery of North America – a series of changing exhibitions about Native North America's art and culture; *room 33d.*

South-east Asia – the close-to lifesize **figure of the goddess Tara** from the eighth century; *Sir Joseph Hotung Exhibition Gallery.*

British Museum

Great Russell Street, WC1 (020 7636 1555/ recorded info 020 7323 8783/disabled info 020 7636 7384/minicom 020 7323 8920). Holborn, Russell Square or Tottenham Court Road tube.
Open galleries 10am-5pm Mon-Sat; noon-6pm Sun; *Great Court* phone for details. **Admission** free; donations appreciated. Prices of temporary exhibitions vary; phone for details. **Map 6 K5**
Website: www.british-museum.ac.uk

Dominating the piazza in front of the library is Sir Eduardo Paolozzi's huge statue of William Blake's famous image of Isaac Newton, plotting the immensity of the universe with his compasses. Of the permanent exhibitions inside the building, the **John Ritblat Gallery**, housing the **Treasures of the British Library**, is undoubtedly the best, showcasing the library's collection of rare and historic items such as the Lindisfarne Gospels (c700), the Magna Carta (1215) and the Gutenberg Bible (1455). Also of interest are the **Workshop of Words, Sounds and Images**, a hands-on gallery tracing the history of book production, and the **Philatelic Exhibition**, described as 'probably the best permanent display of diverse, classical stamps in the world'.

At the heart of the building is the stunning **King's Library**, the library of George III (a gift from George IV to the nation in 1823), housed in a six-storey glass-walled tower (it's next to the café-restaurant, but even if you're not stopping for refreshments you can catch a glimpse). **The Pearson Gallery of Living Words** is based around five themes: the Story of Writing, Children's Books, the Scientific Record, Images of Britain and the Art of the Book. It is also used for temporary exhibitions, including, in 2000, **Chapter & Verse – 1,000 Years of English Literature** (10 Mar-15 Oct), exploring themes to which writers have returned through the ages, such as love, identity and faith; and **Oscar Wilde: Spendthrift of a Genius** (10 Nov-4 Feb 2001), curated by the writer's grandson, which will explore the main episodes in Wilde's life. Phone for times and prices of the guided tours, some of which feature a visit to one of the Reading Rooms (for information about Readers' Tickets call 020 7412 7677), and for details of events, discussions and lectures held at the library.
Website: www.bl.uk

Dickens' House

48 Doughty Street, WC1 (020 7405 2127). Chancery Lane or Russell Square tube.
Open 10am-5pm Mon-Sat. **Admission** £4; £2 5s-15s; £3 students, OAPs, disabled, ES40s; £9 family. **Credit** *shop* AmEx, MC, V. **Map 6 M4**
This Georgian terrace house is the sole survivor of Charles Dickens's many London residences. He was able to move into this elegant (then-private) street on the strength of the phenomenal success of *The Pickwick Papers* and, although he lived here for just two and a half years (Apr 1837-Dec 1839), he managed to pen *Oliver Twist* and *Nicholas Nickleby* during that time. Only the first-floor drawing room has been restored to its original appearance, but the house is packed with Dickens memorabilia, including portraits of himself and his family, his desk, bars from the Marshalsea Prison where his father was incarcerated for debt and the room in which his sister-in-law, 16-year-old Mary Hogarth (with whom he had fallen in love), died. Every Wednesday evening from mid-

March to the end of September, a one-man show, 'The Sparkler of Albion', brings the author and his characters entertainingly to life.
Website: www.dickensmuseum.com

Percival David Foundation of Chinese Art

53 Gordon Square, WC1 (020 7387 3909). Euston Square, Goodge Street or Russell Square tube/Euston tube/rail. **Open** 10.30am-5pm Mon-Fri. **Admission** free; donations appreciated (under-14s must be accompanied by an adult). **Map 6 K46**
The late Percival David's collection of Chinese ceramics is the finest outside China. Temporary exhibitions are held on the ground floor. The 1,700-odd items of the permanent collection are found on the first and second floors. Most date from the tenth to eighteenth centuries although there are some earlier pieces, such as a rather portly hare from the Tang dynasty (eighth to tenth centuries). Aficionados will be drawn to the very rare Ru and Guan wares and the unique pair of blue-and-white Yuan dynasty temple vases (1351). Curiosity seekers, look out for the late seventeenth-century Dehua ware figure of Guanyin with a swastika hanging on his chest.
Website: www.soas.ac.uk

Petrie Museum of Egyptian Archaeology

University College London, Malet Place, WC1 (020 7504 2884). Goodge Street tube. **Open** 1-5pm Tue-Fri; 10am-1pm Sat. **Closed** Christmas & Easter. **Admission** free; donations appreciated. **Map 6 K4**
Father of Egyptian archaeology Sir Flinders Petrie bequeathed the result of his desert digs, a collection of the minutiae of ancient Egyptian life, to **University College London** in 1933. It's hard to find (it's best to ask a security guard once in the grounds), but even Indiana Jones would consider the effort worthwhile. On display among ranks of traditional glass cabinets full of pots, carvings and ornaments, you'll discover the oldest piece of clothing in the world (from 3000 BC) and the Qua bead-net raunchy undergarment (2400 BC). More disturbing exhibits include the exhumed pot-burial in a corner with its skeletal occupant squatting inside, and the coiffured head of a mummy with eyebrows and lashes still intact.

Pollock's Toy Museum

1 Scala Street, W1 (020 7636 3452). Goodge Street tube. **Open** 10am-5pm Mon-Sat. **Admission** £3; £1.50 3s-18s; free under-3s. **Credit** *shop* MC, V. **Map 5 J5**
An unlikely location – tucked away behind Goodge Street – but this museum is well worth tracking down. Most of the exhibits date from the last two centuries (but look out for the rare Egyptian clay mouse from 2000 BC), and include optical toys with such mind-boggling names as the Phenakistoscope and Heliocinegraphe. The puppet cabinets feature more familiar faces along the lines of Sooty and Sweep, Punch and Judy, and Muffin the Mule. The large collection of dolls' houses, fine examples of changing décor over the decades, display incredible attention to detail. It's also interesting to witness the evolution of teddy bears: from veteran Eric ('born' 1905) to a decidedly larger and cuddlier specimen only a few years later. Toy theatre performances can be booked for parties of children (minimum 10).
Website: www.pollocks.cwc.net

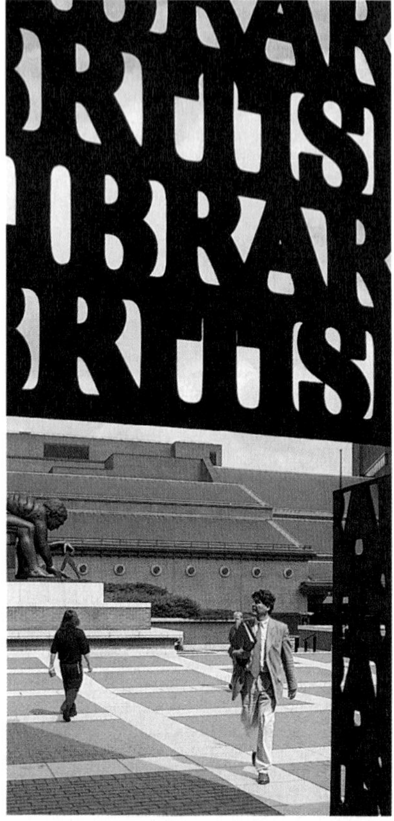

The controversial **British Library**. *See p63.*

St George Bloomsbury

Bloomsbury Way, WC1 (020 7405 3044). Holborn tube or Tottenham Court Road tube. **Open** 9.30am-5.30pm Mon-Fri; 9am-5pm Sun. **Map 6 L5**
A classical portico leads from the smoke-blackened exterior of this episcopal Hawksmoor church (1716-31) into its genteelly flaking interior (a restoration is planned). Despite its sky-blue ceiling and gilding, there's a mournful air to the place. George I, looking inappropriately heroic in a Roman toga, surmounts the remarkable tiered steeple, inspired by Pliny's description of the Mausoleum at Halicarnassus. There are free concerts in summer (1.10pm Tue) and services on a Sunday, often with opera singers (phone for details).

Marylebone

Marylebone is at last seeing the fruits of its investment, with shops, restaurants and sights to rival the rest of the West End.

Stately **Cumberland Terrace**, *one of Nash's masterpieces. See page 68.*

MAPS 2 & 5

Roughly defined by Oxford Street, Edgware Road, Regent's Park and Great Portland Street, the ancient manors of Lileston (Lisson) and Tyburn were thoroughly disreputable, violent places by the fourteenth century. The infamous gallows were set up at Tyburn in 1388 where they remained in use until 1783 (their site is marked by a plaque on the traffic island at the junction of Bayswater and Edgware roads; *see also page 16* **Oldest swinger in town**). Local residents petitioned the Bishop of London for their frequently ransacked church to be moved half a mile away, to a safer site by the Tyburn stream (or bourne). The church, St Mary by the bourne, eventually gave its name to the entire district, Marylebone.

The small-scale shops, restaurants and pubs along today's snaking Marylebone Lane and Marylebone High Street create an agreeably laid-back, if rather upmarket, small-town ambience in contrast to the frenzy of nearby Oxford Street. Yet this coexists amid a grander, land-that-time-forgot world of sedate Georgian squares and streets.

GEORGIAN MARYLEBONE

In the sixteenth century, the northern half of Marylebone (now Regent's Park) became a royal hunting ground, while the southern section was bought up by the Portman family. Two centuries later, the Portmans developed many of the elegant streets and squares that lend much of this relatively unvisited part of the city its dignified air.

One of these squares, Manchester Square, is home to the paintings, armour and other goodies of the **Wallace Collection** (*see page 70*). Nearby is Harley Street, renowned since the mid-nineteenth century for its high-charging medical specialists, while, running parallel, Wimpole Street was immortalised (not very complimentarily) by Tennyson in *In Memoriam* as a 'dark unlovely street'. It was from no.50 that Elizabeth Barrett scandalously eloped with Robert Browning in 1846; they were secretly married at **St Marylebone Parish Church** on Marylebone Road.

Stately **Portland Place**, leading up to Regent's Park, was the glory of eighteenth-century London and, although many of its houses have been

Home comforts at the **Conran Shop**.

rebuilt, its spacious proportions have been maintained. At its kink, where it links at Langham Place with Nash's Regent Street, is the BBC's HQ, **Broadcasting House**, and home to the **BBC Experience** (*see below*). Next door is Nash's delicate little Thunderbird of a church, **All Souls** (1822-4), much ridiculed in its time for the slenderness of its spire. Over the road is the expensively restored Langham Hilton, the first of London's grand hotels, opened in 1865.

REGENT'S PARK & BAKER STREET

Portland Place emerges to the north at Nash's sublimely proportioned **Park Crescent** (1812-18), originally intended to be a full circus. A decade or so later, the architect's most elegant terrace, **Cumberland Terrace**, was built on the east side of **Regent's Park** (*see page 70*) as part of his hugely influential scheme to transform this former royal hunting ground into an urban idyll. On the west side of the park is the London Central Mosque, built in 1978 to service the spiritual needs of the city's many Muslims, whose shops, cafés and restaurants are a feature of nearby **Edgware Road** and **Bayswater** (*see page 136*). The northern edge of the park is home to one of the city's major visitor attractions, **London Zoo** (*see page 69*), while the area's other main tourist draw is the permanently besieged **Madame Tussaud's** (*see page 70*) – and the **London Planetarium** next door (*see page 69*), on Marylebone Road. Nearby Baker Street is synonymous with the fictional junkie-detective Sherlock Holmes; devotees flock to the **Sherlock Holmes Museum** (*see page 70*).

ALL STREET AND NO OXFORD

Discreet Marylebone hits snooty Mayfair at **Oxford Street**. **Marble Arch**, yet another Nash creation, marks its western extent. This almost apologetically unremarkable monument was intended to be the entrance to Buckingham Palace but, found to be too small, was moved to its current site in 1851 where it now stands, marooned on a traffic island.

London's most famous shopping street, accurately judged by Peter Ackroyd's fictional Oscar Wilde (in *The Last Testament of Oscar Wilde*) to be 'all street and no Oxford', is a scruffy, people-packed canyon of uncontrolled commerce. It's a curious mix of trash and class. Next to the tourist tat stalls and dodgy geezers flogging counterfeit perfumes on the street are huge flagship department stores (**Selfridges**, **John Lewis**, **Marks & Spencer** *et al*; *see pages 216-7*). Filling the middle ground are countless cheap clothes and shoe stores, music megastores and other high-street favourites like Gap and Next. More individual shops can be found on Marylebone High Street, which is constantly being tipped as 'the next big thing' in terms of shopping and eating. The chances of this happening have been boosted by relatively recent arrivals such as swish eco-friendly toiletries store **Aveda** (no.28-29; *see page 221*), cool French designer **Agnès b** (no.41), and Sir Tel's **Conran Shop** (no.55; *see page 219*), showcasing the best of modern furniture and household design, and topped with the excellent **Orrery** restaurant.

Desirable food and drink destinations – formerly not abundant in the area – are multiplying rapidly. Try restaurant-cum-deli **Villandry** at 170 Great Portland Street, sausage and beer emporium **RK Stanley** (6 Little Portland Street) or noodle joint **Wagamama** (101A Wigmore Street; *see page 163*). Marylebone High Street is short on options; Orrery (*see page 166*) and the superlative Italian cooking of **Ibla** (no.89; *see page 175*) are exceptions.

Sights

BBC Experience

Broadcasting House, Portland Place, W1 (0870 603 0304). Oxford Circus or Regent's Park tube.
Open 11am-6pm Mon; 10am-6pm Tue-Sun. *Last tour* 4.30pm daily. **Admission** *by tour only* £6.95; £4.95 5s-16s, students; £5.95 OAPs; £19.95 family. *GoSee Card member (see p32)*. **Credit** MC, V. **Map 5 H5**
Within months of being occupied by the BBC in 1932, Broadcasting House was found to be too small for the burgeoning company, yet this gleaming Portland-stone construction (designed by G Val Myers, with an external sculpture of Shakespeare's Ariel by Eric Gill) has become so synonymous with 'Auntie' that it remains the heart of the nation's public service broadcasting. Daily BBC radio programmes first emanated from Savoy Hill (next to the Savoy Hotel) on 14 November 1922. In 1997, as part

of celebrations marking the 75th anniversary of the Beeb, the BBC Experience was opened.

The semi-guided tour (book in advance to ensure admission) includes an exhibition on Marconi, a look at BBC TV from the 1950s to the 1990s, a short but excellent behind-the-scenes film of the BBC today and the chance to participate in a mock radio show (the highlight of the tour). The tour finishes with various interactive exhibits including the chance to 'direct' a short, pre-filmed scene from *EastEnders* and present the weather. All in all it's a pleasant but rather superficial glimpse of one of the country's greatest institutions.

It is now also possible to find out what really goes on behind the camera with a tour of **Television Centre** at Wood Lane, White City, W12. Tours must be pre-booked (0870 603 0304) and are only available to visitors aged 16 or over.
Website: www.bbc.co.uk/experience

London Planetarium

Marylebone Road, NW1 (020 7935 6861). Baker Street tube. **Open** *June-Aug* 10.20am-5pm daily; *Sept-May* 12.20-5pm Mon-Fri; 10.20am-5pm Sat, Sun. **Admission** £6.30; £4.20 5s-15s; £4.85 OAPs. *Combined ticket with Madame Tussaud's* £12.95; £8.50 5s-15s; £9.80 OAPs. **Credit** AmEx, MC, $£TC, V. **Map 5 G4**

Be sure to plan your visit to the Planetarium – the main 'attraction' is a 30-minute show, but a 40-minute gap between performances means that if you arrive just after a show begins, you're in for a long wait. Even this is a disappointment – visitors sink back into the comfy chairs to watch an extremely simplified and dated looking history of space and the universe (as far as we know it), projected on to the dome.
Website: www.madame-tussauds.com

London Zoo

Regent's Park, NW1 (020 7722 3333). Baker Street or Camden Town tube then 274, C2 bus. **Open** *Nov-Mar* 10am-4pm daily; *Apr-Oct* 10am-5.30pm daily. **Admission** £9; £7 3s-14s; £8 students, OAPs. **Credit** AmEx, JCB, MC, £TC, V. **Map 5 G2**

London Zoo celebrated its 170th birthday in 1998. Whatever your view on the morality of keeping wild beasties in cages, the importance of zoos in conservation work is unquestionable. The zoo, understandably, promotes this side of its remit to the full – as well as the popular 'adopt an animal scheme' (£25 for a piranha; £6,000 for an elephant). One of its proudest achievements is the hand-rearing of a black rhinoceros (called Rosie), a feat rarely achieved. It's a marvellous place for kids – feeding times and special events are posted on notice boards, and close encounters of a furry kind are available at the Children's Zoo. The

Trails of the unexpected...

Marylebone madness.

Marylebone is central to some of the biggest scandals of the nineteenth and twentieth centuries. So, if you want to know how to get your name in the papers, read on…

It was at no.21 Shouldham Street, between Gloucester Place and Edgware Road, that superswindler the '**Tichbourne Claimant**' (aka Arthur Orton, aka Sir Roger Charles Doughty Tichbourne, recently the subject of a film) died on, appropriately, April Fool's Day, 1898, having successfully fooled Rog's mum that he was back from the dead (never mind the fact that he had somehow turned into a fat, destitute Cockney).

A couple of streets south, at no.5 Bryanston Court, a block of luxury flats (on the corner of George Street and Seymour Place), **Mrs Wallis Simpson** began entertaining the **Prince of Wales** (the future King Edward VIII) in 1933. As a direct consequence, he lasted only ten months as monarch, choosing love over duty.

East of here, the other side of Baker Street, lies Manchester Street. Back in 1814, the eyes of the nation were on the resident of no.38: 64-year-old **Joanna Southcott** was pregnant! Alas, this was not due to the imminent Second Coming, as was widely inferred, but instead a tragic and terminal bout of flatulence.

Off Marylebone Lane lies Bentinck Street. It's hard to believe now that this quiet, secluded place was the site of some of the twentieth-century's most debauched goings-on. During World War II, a flat at no.5 was rented by **Guy Burgess** and **Anthony Blunt**, where the pair brought home Top Secret files from MI5 and MI6 respectively, before passing them on to the Russians. Burgess was found out relatively early, in the '50s, but it wasn't until 1979 that his flatmate was unmasked, disgraced and stripped of his knighthood pretty sharpish.

North-east of here, Wimpole Mews hit the headlines in 1963 along with the Profumo Affair. It emerged that the resident of no.17, osteopath **Stephen Ward**, had here 'introduced' his pretty 'friends' **Mandy Rice-Davies** and **Christine Keeler** to men including Cold War minister John Profumo... and sundry Russian diplomats. The story ended in tragedy when Ward took an overdose, dying before the judge could deliver the jury's verdict of guilty.

gardens are beautifully landscaped and it's easy to spend the best part of a day wandering between the enclosures. The buildings include some gems of modern architecture: look out for the Penguin Pool (1936) by Lubetkin and Tecton, Hugh Casson's Elephant House (1965) and Lord Snowdon's Aviary (1963-4).

New to the Zoo is the **Web of Life** exhibition, aimed at promoting conservation in the natural world. Housed in an environmentally friendly glass pavilion, it features live animals, interactive displays and on-show breeding facilities. *See also p236.*
Website: www.londonzoo.co.uk/londonzoo

Madame Tussaud's

Marylebone Road, NW1 (020 7935 6861). Baker Street tube. **Open** *May-Sept* 10am-5.30pm daily; *Oct-June* 10am-5.30pm Mon-Fri; 9.30am-5.30pm Sat, Sun. **Admission** £10.50; £7 5s-15s; £8 OAPs. *Combined ticket with Planetarium* £12.95; £8.50 5s-15s; £9.80 OAPs. **Credit** AmEx, MC, $£TC, V. **Map 5 G4**

If you're a child or gaspingly credulous, you'll enjoy Madame Tussaud's, but it's hard to see what anyone over the age of 16 could get from the place beyond the chance to have your photo taken sticking your tongue out at Saddam Hussein. Some (but not all) of the models are spookily accurate – including a Tony Blair looking more false than in real life and a rather smug Paddy Ashdown – but there's very little information about any of the figures, no interactivity and little animatronic action. Entertainment and sporting heroes (including a lycra-clad Linford Christie) mill around at the 'garden party', while close by the smouldering Pierce Brosnan/James Bond figure attracts perhaps unwanted attention (repeated female gropings caused it to be taken out of commission not long ago for retouching work, as it were).

In the main hall dummies are grouped by profession – monarchs, US presidents, dictators, etc – though the inclusion of some figures remains critically questionable (Wilde, Dickens, Shakespeare and, er, Agatha Christie?). The once-legendary Chamber of Horrors seems somewhat tame these days, particularly now that the **London Dungeon** (*see p40*) does this sort of thing more graphically, although this section does at least contain a few genuine exhibits (such as the guillotine blade that dispatched Marie Antoinette). Finally, punters can take a break in the café, before embarking in a 'time taxi', the 'Spirit of London', on a breakneck trip through 400 years of London history – a ride of such extraordinary brevity and nonsensicality that the blinking, saluting Benny Hill at journey's end seems entirely appropriate. Book in advance to avoid the queues.
Website: www.madame-tussauds.com

Regent's Park

NW1 (020 7486 7905/tennis courts 020 7486 4216). Baker Street, Camden Town, Great Portland Street or Regent's Park tube. **Open** *park & Queen Mary's Gardens* 5am-30mins before dusk daily; *tennis courts Apr-Oct* 9am-dusk daily; *May-Sept* 8am-dusk; *playgrounds* 10am-30mins before dusk daily. **Map 5 G3**

Laid out in 1817-28 by John Nash, Regent's Park (named after Nash's faithful patron) remains central London's most well-mannered park. Originally part of the Middlesex Forest, and later a royal hunting ground, the park is particularly lively in summer, with a boating lake (herons live on the islands), three playgrounds, bandstand music, tennis courts, a café and a celebrated open-air theatre that's been running since 1932 (*see p298*). The Outer Circle, the main road running around the park, is over two miles (3.2km) long. It's bordered to the south by Marylebone Road and Park Crescent, on the west and east by Palladian mansions, and to the north by Regent's Canal. Strolling in Queen Mary's Gardens (inside the Inner Circle) on a summer evening is one of the best reasons for being in London.

Sherlock Holmes Museum

221B Baker Street, NW1 (020 7935 8866). Baker Street tube. **Open** 9.30am-6pm daily. **Admission** £6; £3.50 under-16s. **Credit** AmEx, JCB, MC, £TC, V. **Map 5 G4**

This re-creation of the great sleuth's fictional lodgings is well done, but you won't find any genuine historical treasures or information about Conan Doyle or the Edinburgh surgeon upon whom he based his famous detective. Six quid is rather steep for a bit of atmosphere. Fans might also like a peek at the new statue of the great detective outside Baker Street station.
Website: www.sherlock-holmes.co.uk

Wallace Collection

Hertford House, Manchester Square, W1 (020 7935 0687/admin@the-wallace-collection.org.uk). Bond Street tube. **Open** 10am-5pm Mon-Sat; 2-5pm Sun. **Admission** free. **Map 5 G5**

The hallway and the state drawing room of Sir Richard Wallace's late eighteenth-century house have been meticulously restored to the splendour of his original design, down to the crimson silk hangings and damask curtains. The illegitimate heir of the Marquis of Hertford, Wallace nevertheless inherited the ardent Francophile's extraordinary collection of furniture (including a writing desk belonging to Marie Antoinette), paintings and porcelain purchased for safe keeping in London after the Revolution. An impressive clutch of Old Masters, including Franz Hals' *The Laughing Cavalier* and Rubens' *Rainbow Landscape*, vie for space with magnificent European and Asian arms and armour and a display of Catherine the Great's crockery.

The house seems like a delightfully peaceful nineteenth-century anachronism, although this may be threatened by a current building project, which will create four new galleries and extensive educational facilities. The new space will house temporary exhibitions, the **Watercolour Gallery**, an interactive **Materials and Techniques Gallery** and the entire **Reserve Collection**. In addition, the courtyard, covered by a glass roof, will form a sheltered space for the Sculpture Garden Restaurant. Work is due for completion by June 2000, when the gallery celebrates its centenary as a national museum. Until then, public access to the exhibitions is limited. While you're there, don't miss the splendidly tiled toilets.
Website: www.the-wallace-collection.org.uk

Mayfair

Posh homes, posh shops.

MAP 7

The late seventeenth century was a time of great dynamism in the development of London. New districts – such as Covent Garden and Soho – were laid out, and enjoyed brief vogues as fashionable addresses before the well-to-do looked further west for grander residences. The elegant Georgian streets and squares of **Mayfair** and **St James's** were part of the next wave, largely occupying their current sites by the mid-eighteenth century, but their social cachet, unlike that of their eastern neighbours, has never wavered to this day.

PICCADILLY CIRCUS

Piccadilly Circus is one of central London's pivotal points, as its constant streaming traffic indicates only too clearly. The name derives from the speciality of a tailor, Robert Baker, who made his fortune selling stiff collars known as 'picadils' and lived near here in the early seventeenth century. The commercial connection is apposite, for the posh shops of Mayfair, Piccadilly and Regent Street have long been a fixture of the district.

The Circus's great bank of neon – so untypically flashy for London – can trace its origins back to at least 1910. The other defining feature is the statue of **Eros** – a misnomer on two counts: it's actually a memorial fountain to the philanthropic Lord Shaftesbury, not a statue; and represents the Angel of Christian Charity, not the god of love. Although Eros is an enduringly popular symbol of London, the stumpy memorial, no longer marooned on a traffic island, is unimpressive. It might have been far more pleasing had the designer, Alfred Gilbert, not met with constant interference from the organising committee and council. He refused to attend the unveiling in 1893 and remained traumatised by the experience for the rest of his life.

Two big tourist attractions lie just to the east of the Circus – the bafflingly popular **Rock Circus** (*see page 77*) and the more obviously exciting fun palace of the **Pepsi Trocadero** (*see page 76*).

Leading south from here, **Haymarket**'s associations are with older forms of fun. The market, after which the street is named, traded until 1830; by then Haymarket was already famed for its theatres (the Theatre Royal opened in 1720, Her Majesty's Theatre in 1705) and notorious for its prostitutes. Today it's short on charm of any variety.

Green Park – *it's green, it's a park. And that's about it. See page 76.*

The mock-Tudor **Liberty** *department store.*

REGENT STREET

Curving away north-westwards from Piccadilly Circus and southwards towards Pall Mall, **Regent Street** was conceived by John Nash in the early 1800s as a dramatic boulevard to clear away unsightly slums, improve transport links and connect the Prince Regent's residence, Carlton House, with Regent's Park. His plans were continually frustrated by a variety of vested interests, but the sweep of the section just north of Piccadilly Circus – known as the Quadrant – still impresses. Nash also intended Regent Street to act as a *cordon sanitaire* between the scruffs of Soho and the toffs of Mayfair. The distinction still holds good.

Shops 'appropriated to articles of fashion and taste' were a fixture of Regent Street from the beginning. Some of the capital's most famous retailing names – the mock-Tudor department store **Liberty** (*see page 216*), the kiddie-heaven of **Hamleys** toy store (*see page 230*) – still survive amid the encroaching mainstream chains. Here too is the **Café Royal**, at no.68, ultra-fashionable bohemian hangout for artists and writers a century ago.

PICCADILLY

Extending from Piccadilly Circus past **Green Park** (*see page 76*) to Hyde Park Corner, **Piccadilly** is (along with Oxford Street) one of the ancient roads heading west out of London. Despite the attractions of the street's almost equally ancient emporia such as the bookshop **Hatchards** at no.187 (founded in 1797) and **Fortnum & Mason** (*see page 216*), the constant traffic means that more pleasant window shopping can be had in the arcades leading off Piccadilly. **Burlington Arcade**, running down the side of Burlington House, now home of the **Royal Academy of Arts** (*see page 77*), is the most celebrated. The arcade was built in 1819 by the house's then-owner, Lord George Cavendish, to stop passers-by throwing rubbish over the wall into his garden. Even today, uniformed beadles ensure that shoppers don't hum, carry large packages or do anything else to upset Regency decorum.

Piccadilly is also home to several of London's luxury hotels; chief among them is **The Ritz**. Soon after the hotel opened in 1906, it became a byword for a level of glamour, glitz and extravagance unparalleled in London. Even today, the word 'ritzy' conjures up high-class luxury. Taking afternoon tea is the cheapest way to gain access to the opulent Louis XVI interior (*see page 178*).

Those seeking escapism of a more low-key kind should duck in to Wren's delightful **St James's Church Piccadilly** (*see page 77*). The churchyard hosts a regular craft market, and the Aroma café next door has good food and outdoor seating in the summer.

Those in search of a good read, meanwhile, should head straight for **Waterstone's** (nos.203-206; *see page 203*), Europe's largest bookstore, on eight floors. Regardless of whether you agree with the critics who say it lacks atmosphere, you can't knock the sheer number of books it holds.

RETRO ST JAMES'S

The tiny enclave bounded by Piccadilly, Green Park, the Mall and Haymarket is a corner of London that will be forever England – that is, if your idea of England is Victorian-throwback, pinstriped old duffers puffing on cigars, reddening their faces with countless bottles of claret and lamenting the decline of empire. This is clubland – and we're not talking Ministry of Sound.

The majority of these exclusive (in every sense) establishments are lined up along **St James's Street** and **Pall Mall** (named after a croquet-like game once played here). They evolved from the seventeenth-century coffee houses as meeting places for gentlemen, although most date only from the nineteenth century. Ultra-aristocratic **White's** (Prince Charles had his stag party here), at 37 St James's Street, is the oldest (founded in 1693); the **RAC Club** (89 Pall Mall), which celebrated its centenary in 1997, is the most recent and, reputedly, the least class-conscious. The 1832 Reform Act spawned both the 'radical' **Reform Club** (104 Pall Mall) and the reactionary **Carlton Club** (69 St James's Street); the latter remains an unshakeable bastion of all-male Toryism –

Margaret Thatcher had to be made an honorary man to secure entrance. **Brooks**, on the corner of St James's Street and Park Place (so exclusive it doesn't have a street number), was famed for the prodigious gambling of its members, particularly during the 1770s when Charles James Fox would drink and gamble all night before wandering down to the House of Commons to dazzle the members with the wit and erudition of his speeches.

The material needs of the venerable gentlemen of St James's are met by the fabulously anachronistic shops and restaurants of **Jermyn** (pronounced 'jér-mun') **Street** and St James's Street. If you ignore the fact that well-to-do tourists make up most of the clientele these days, it's still a thrill to see the lovingly crafted quality of the goods and the time-warp shopfronts. For details of the best of the old St James's stores, *see page 226* **Victorian values**.

EXPLORING ST JAMES'S

Few visitors (and equally few Londoners) venture further into St James's than Jermyn Street, yet its streets, mews and alleyways make for rewarding wandering. In particular, don't miss lively **Crown Passage** off King Street.

St James's Square was the most fashionable address in London for the 50 years after it was laid out in the 1670s, boasting no fewer than seven dukes and seven earls as residents by the 1720s. The Prince Regent was attending a ball at no.16 in 1815 when a bloodied and dirty major arrived to announce the victory at Waterloo, much to the dismay of the hostess who was 'much annoyed with the Battle of Waterloo as it spoilt her party'. Alas, no private houses survive on the square today. In the north-west corner is the prestigious **London Library**, a private library founded by Thomas Carlyle in 1841 in disgust at the inefficiency of the British Library (a common complaint until recent times).

A huddle of great aristocratic houses stand in the south-west corner of St James's, the most notable being **St James's Palace**. Built by Henry VIII on the site of St James's Hospital, the palace was one of the principal royal residences for more than 300 years and is still used by Prince Charles and various minor royals. Most of what you see today is the result of a Nash remodelling in the early nineteenth century. (Nash was also responsible for **Clarence House** next door, home of the Queen Mum.) Tradition still dictates that foreign ambassadors to the UK are officially known as 'Ambassador to the Court of St James'. Although the palace is closed to the public, it is possible to explore Friary Court on Marlborough Road and attend the Sunday services at the **Chapel Royal** (October to Good Friday; 8.30am, 11.30am). It was here that Charles I took holy communion on the morning of his execution, and Victoria and Albert (and many other royals) were married in the chapel.

Across Marlborough Road from St James's Palace, the **Queen's Chapel** was the first classical church built in England. Designed by Inigo Jones in the 1620s for Charles I's intended bride of the time, the Infanta of Castile, the chapel now stands in the grounds of **Marlborough House** and is only open to the public during Sunday services (Easter to July; 8.30am, 11.30am). The house itself was built by Christopher Wren (both father and son) for Queen Anne's bosom chum, Sarah, Duchess of Marlborough, and, as requested, is 'strong, plain and convenient'.

Further east, overlooking the Mall, is gleaming **Carlton House Terrace**, built by Nash in 1827-32 on the site of Carlton House. When the Prince Regent came to the throne as George IV he decided that his then-home was not ostentatious enough for his newly elevated station and levelled what Horace Walpole had described as 'the most perfect palace' in Europe. The terrace splits at the **Duke of York's Column**, erected in 1833. Not only did the 'Grand Old Duke' march his 10,000 men to the top of the hill and down again, but he also docked them a day's wages to pay for his own monument.

Two other notable St James's mansions overlook Green Park. At the Mall end is neo-classical **Lancaster House**, rebuilt in the 1820s by Benjamin Dean Wyatt for Frederick, Duke of York. Now used mainly for government receptions and conferences, the house much impressed Queen Victoria with its splendour (on one visit she remarked to her hostess: 'I have come from my house to your palace'). It is closed to the public. A couple of doors further north is beautiful, eighteenth-century **Spencer House** (*see page 77*), ancestral townhouse of Princess Diana's family and now open as a museum and art gallery.

MAYFAIR

To the casual observer, the huge expanse of **Mayfair**, filling the space between Oxford Street, Regent Street, Piccadilly and Park Lane, can seem little more than a homogeneous mass of mansions. But there is much of interest in this vast area, named after the raucous annual fair, which moved to the site of today's Curzon Street and Shepherd Market from Haymarket in 1686 and was suppressed by the local nobs less than a century later for lowering the tone of the neighbourhood. Today, the narrow, winding streets around **Shepherd Market**, lined with restaurants, pubs and shops, make up Mayfair's quirkiest corner. The area has long held a reputation as a haunt of a better class of prostitute. Whether the oldest profession still flourishes here is a matter of debate, but the curious can always settle themselves in the congenial **Ye Grapes** pub, wave a wad of tenners around conspicuously and see what happens.

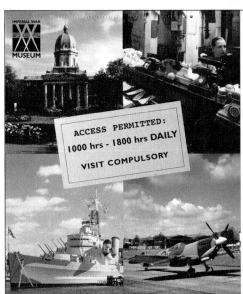

Just south of here, on **Down Street**, distinctive maroon glazed tiles betray the former entrance to the eponymous, and now disused, tube station. The Duke of Wellington's London home, **Apsley House** (*see page 76*), stands not far away at Hyde Park Corner.

Three great squares dictate the feel of the northern portion of Mayfair: Hanover Square, Berkeley Square (where no nightingales have sung in living memory) and immense **Grosvenor Square**, second in size only to Lincoln's Inn Fields. Laid out between 1725 and 1731, it has always been a prestigious address, although disappointingly few of its original houses survive. Today, the square is dominated by the looming presence of the immense US Embassy on the west side. Built in 1958-61 by Eero Saarinen, it was described by Nikolaus Pevsner as 'an impressive but decidedly embarrassing building'. A statue of Franklin D Roosevelt in the centre of the square furthers the American connection, and the **Grosvenor Chapel** on South Audley Street (where radical MP John Wilkes is buried) is still a favourite with American expats. Nearby are the peaceful **Mount Street Gardens**, next to the **Church of the Immaculate Conception** on Farm Street. One of London's few Catholic churches at which a sung Latin mass is celebrated, this splendid Gothic revival building is the British HQ of the Jesuits.

One unlikely Mayfair resident in 1968 was Jimi Hendrix, who lived at no.23 Brook Street, next door to the house where George Frederick Handel spent the last 35 years of his life. ('I haven't heard much of the guy's stuff, but I dig a bit of Bach now and again,' Jimi said of his neighbour.) Plans to set up the Handel House Museum at nos.23-25 have finally come to fruition, though the work will not be completed until at least spring 2001 (phone 020 7495 1685 for details).

Not far from here, on Brook Street and Carlos Place, are two of Mayfair's poshest and most history-laden hotels, respectively, **Claridge's** and **The Connaught**. Towards Piccadilly, on Albemarle Street, is another classic London hotel, **Brown's**, from where Alexander Graham Bell made the first successful telephone call in 1876. Another scientific pioneer, Michael Faraday, is commemorated in the **Faraday Museum** (*see page 76*) in the basement of the Royal Institution, further up the street, at no.21.

The eastern side of Mayfair is largely devoted to commerce, albeit of a very upmarket kind. Savile Row has long been home to gentlemen's outfitters of a fiercely traditional stamp. At the junction of **Savile Row** and Vigo Street old meets new, with the venerable firm of **Gieves & Hawkes** (*see page 226* **Victorian values**) squaring up opposite the dazzling, iconoclastic tailoring of **Ozwald Boateng** (*see page 215*).

St James's Church Piccadilly. *See page 77.*

Bond Street is equally famed for its frighteningly opulent yet clinical temples of art, couture, jewellery and antiques. In fact, there is no Bond Street as such, but, rather, **New Bond Street** and **Old Bond Street**. Here also are two of London's best-known auction houses: **Sotheby's**, at 34-35 New Bond Street (020 7293 5000), and **Phillips** (020 7629 6602), at 101 New Bond Street. Don't be reluctant to pop in and view items that are coming up for sale. Art fans might also like to cruise the many commercial galleries of Cork Street and Dering Street (*see page 250*), while antique buffs shouldn't miss the **Bond Street Antiques Centre** (124 New Bond Street; 020 7493 1854) and **Grays Antique Market** (*see page 201*). Nearby, pedestrianised **South Molton Street** offers more chic and bank-breakingly pricey shops.

A moment's peace from the commercial bustle can be had in the church of **St George** (1721-4) on St George Street near Hanover Square, where Handel regularly played the organ. This was the first London church to have a portico and has long been a favourite venue for society weddings.

Food options in Mayfair tend towards the unimaginative and extortionate, though there are exceptions. Marco Pierre White's exemplary **Mirabelle** (*see page 173*) and the renowned south Indian vegetarian cooking at **Rasa W1** (*see page 174*) are two prime examples.

Trails of the unexpected...

Sheer clarse.

Ian Fleming usually lunched at **Boodle's** (28 St James's Street) because he 'liked dull clubs', and was put off the aristocratic **White's** (just up the road, at nos.37-38) because 'the members gassed too much'. Here Ronnie Kray was a regular guest of his alleged lover, Lord Boothby. To save the blushes of Boodle's and White's, Fleming made M a member of 'Blade's', an amalgamation of the two, and had James Bond drop by to savour the freshly minted change and the ironed newspapers; also to dissuade the suspiciously 'un-English' Sir Hugo Drax – a psychotic, disfigured ex-Nazi intent on A-bombing London – from cheating at cards.

Just round the corner, in the smoking room of the **Reform Club** (104-105 Pall Mall), Phileas Fogg took the bet – on a fine point of principle and gentlemanly high-jinks, what-ho! – that he could travel 'Around the World in Eighty Days'.

Perhaps the ultimate high-roller's gambling club to survive from Regency times, though, is **Crockford's** (now at 30 Curzon Street, over the other side of Piccadilly). If you can afford the funds to lose sufficiently, you're welcome. Founder William Crockford is said to have died from a broken heart after his highly fancied horse was beaten by a ringer in the Derby.

The nearby **Clermont Casino** (44 Berkeley Square) is another top people's venue designed to help you shed your unwanted millions; then straight downstairs to shed your inhibitions with Arab princes and Joan/Jackie Collins-alikes at **Annabel's**, 'the best nightclub in the world...'. 'According,' scoffs London gadabout Richard Jobson, 'to those few pampered men and women who have never been in a real nightclub'.

Sights

Apsley House – The Wellington Museum

149 Piccadilly, W1 (020 7499 5676). Hyde Park Corner tube. **Open** 11am-5pm Tue-Sun. **Admission** £4.50; £3 students, OAPs, ES40s, disabled; free under-18s. *GoSee Card member (see p32).* **Credit** AmEx, DC, MC, V. **Map 7 G8**

This grand house (once known as 'No.1 London' – it was the first building you came to en route from the village of Kensington to London), built by Robert Adam in the 1770s, was the London residence of the Duke of Wellington from 1817 until his death in 1852. His descendants still live here, but ten rooms, restored to their original state, are open to the public. They contain the paintings, sculpture, ceramics, silverware and memorabilia belonging to the Iron Duke (so nicknamed not for his indomitable will but for the iron shutters he installed after rioters broke his windows in protest over his Reform Bill). Exhibits include an equestrian portrait of the great man by Goya. One of the more eccentric touches is a huge 3.4-m (11ft 4-in) statue by Canova of the diminutive Napoleon. The basement contains an exhibition on the Duke's death, including his death mask. An audio guide is included in the entrance fee.

Faraday Museum

Royal Institution, 21 Albemarle Street, W1 (020 7409 2992). Green Park tube. **Open** 9am-5pm Mon-Fri. **Admission** £1. **Map 7 J7**

The achievements of Michael Faraday, one-time professor at the Royal Institution and 'father of electricity', are celebrated in this small, interesting museum. Exhibits include a re-creation of the lab where Faraday discovered the laws of electromagnetics.

Green Park

SW1. Green Park tube. **Open** dawn-dusk daily. **Map 7 H7**

This literally named park was enclosed by Henry VIII and made into a Royal Park by Charles II. The park was the site of a number of early balloon ascents and firework displays. Handel composed his *Music for the Royal Fireworks* for the most famous of these pyrotechnical extravaganzas, celebrating the Peace of Aix-la-Chapelle in 1748. Today, Green Park is one of the duller of central London's open spaces, though it's an agreeable enough spot to snooze away an hour in a deckchair.

Pepsi Trocadero

1 Piccadilly Circus, W1 (09068 881100). Piccadilly Circus tube. **Open** 10am-midnight Mon-Fri daily. **Admission** varies (*see below*). **Credit** varies. **Map 8 K7**

The shy and retiring would be wise to steer clear of this entertainment mega-complex; kids, on the other hand, flock here in droves. Spend time – and no doubt piles of money – on the various video games and virtual reality rides of **Funland** (020 7287 8913), spread over the six floors of the Trocadero; check out the **007 Licence to Thrill, The James Bond Ride** (£5.95; £3.95 children), where you can get close to undercover gadgetry and test out your suitability for MI6; or, if you think your stomach can take it, have a go on the **Pepsi Max drop ride** (£3), where you get strapped into a seat that plummets the six storeys in two seconds. The **Pepsi London IMAX Theatre** (*see p261*) is a less frenetic choice. Further attractions include **Internet Exchange**, and **Old-Time Photography**, where you get kitted out in historical costumes and have your photo taken.

Rock Circus

London Pavilion, 1 Piccadilly Circus, W1 (020 7734 7203). Piccadilly Circus tube. **Open** *Mar-Aug* 10am-8pm Mon, Wed, Thur, Sun; 11am-8pm Tue; 10am-9pm Fri, Sat; *Sept-Feb* 10am-5.30pm Mon, Wed-Sun; 11am-5.30pm Tue. **Admission** £8.25; £7.25 concs; £6.25 under-16s. **Credit** AmEx, EC, MC, £$TC, V. **Map 8 K7**

Despite a major facelift, this Madame-Tussaud's-for-pop-fans remains highly priced and only mildy diverting. While a few of the dummies are surprisingly lifelike (including Lenny Kravitz), most are either laughable (a camp Elvis), out of date (George Michael stuck in a late-'80s time warp) or completely unrealistic (such as a black Michael Jackson – whatever next?). Every 20 minutes visitors are 'treated' to 'the Greatest Rock'n'Roll Show on Earth' – an overblown title for rockumentary clips, interspersed with animated dummies playing 'live' songs. Though the footage is watchable (if unrevealing), the lifeless, jolting models make the Thunderbirds look like the Royal Shakespeare Company. Less embarrassing are the re-creations of London hotspots in the '60s and '70s including Carnaby Street, Denmark Street and Sex – Westwood and McLaren's shop on the King's Road from where the Sex Pistols were launched. However, the most bizarre, not to say macabre, section is the rock cemetery, where waxworks of dead heroes – Marc Bolan, Jimi Hendrix, Marvin Gaye and Kurt Cobain – stand around in the semi-darkness surrounded by ivy-covered tombstones. An adjoining 'vault' has unsettling footage of Michael Hutchence being measured up for his wax double, just weeks before he died.

Royal Academy of Arts

Burlington House, Piccadilly, W1 (box office 020 7300 5959/020 7300 8000/boxoffice@royalacademy.org.uk). Green Park or Piccadilly Circus tube. **Open** 10am-6pm Mon-Thur, Sat, Sun; 10am-8.30pm Fri. **Admission** varies. *GoSee Card member (see p32).* **Credit** AmEx, MC, £TC, V. **Map 7 J7**

Britain's first art school (opened in 1768), the Royal Academy of Arts also held the country's first annual open exhibitions of living artists. This persists as the **Summer Exhibition** (29 May-7 Aug 2000), which attracts huge numbers of people for its thousands of paintings, sculptures and architectural designs. The temporary shows here throughout the rest of the year are the most visited of any London exhibition, and booking is sometimes a necessity – 1999's **Monet in the Twentieth Century** was reckoned the most popular art exhibition ever held in Britain. Shows to look out for in 2000 include the work of **Jean-Baptiste-Simeon Chardin** (11 Mar-29 May); the **Scottish Colourists** (29 June-24 Sept); a showcase of **Terry Frost**, one of Britain's leading abstract painters (12 Oct-12 Nov); and **The Great Watercolours of JMW Turner**, a major commemorative exhibition marking the 150th anniversary of the great man's death (2 Dec-11 Feb 2001). Usually, two exhibitions run concurrently, one in the main exhibition space and one in the Norman Foster-designed Sackler Galleries.

Website: www.royalacademy.org.uk

The courtyard of the **Royal Academy of Arts**.

St James's Church Piccadilly

197 Piccadilly, W1 (020 7734 4511). Piccadilly Circus tube. **Open** 8am-7pm daily (phone for details of evening events). **Map 7 J7**

Offering a tranquil haven from the traffic pounding along Piccadilly, this charming Wren church (1676-84) is, surprisingly, the only church the prolific architect built on an entirely new site. It was also one of the architect's favourites of his works: 'I think it may be found beautiful and convenient'. The limewood reredos, carved by Grinling Gibbons, was much admired by John Evelyn. Gibbons was also responsible for the font and organ case. James Christie, the auctioneer, and James Gillray, the caricaturist, are among the many distinguished people buried here. A crafts market is held in the churchyard every Thursday to Saturday.

Spencer House

27 St James's Place, SW1 (020 7499 8620). Green Park tube. **Open** *Feb-July, Sept-Dec* 11.45am-4.45pm Sun. **Admission** £6; £5 10s-16s (no children under 10). **Map 7 J8**

The (compulsory) guided tours of one of the capital's most splendid Palladian mansions (and Princess Diana's family's ancestral London house) take in a number of restored state rooms. The most notable features are the extravagant murals of the Painted Room and the beautiful painted ceiling in the Great Room. James Vardy, James Stuart and Robert Adam all worked on the house, which was completed in 1766 for Earl Spencer.

Soho

Drinking, shopping, dining, bopping.

MAPS 5-8

From hunting ground to boozing and cruising ground – Soho's come a long way in not much over 300 years. Sliced off from the rest of London by Oxford Street, Regent Street, Shaftesbury Avenue and Charing Cross Road, Soho is an island in the centre of the city – distinctive, proud, particular.

The integrity of this unique district has undoubtedly benefited from its lack of 'attractions', in the conventional sense. The streets are narrow, the buildings mean; there are no museums or galleries, and precious little greenery – people, not things, are the sights of Soho. While older brother Covent Garden has sobered up and scrubbed itself down, the mantle of London's pleasure zone has passed westward. Scruffier, dirtier and noisier, Soho is where media London works and where the rest of London plays.

Most of the district was laid out in the 1670s and 1680s as part of a general expansion westward from the overcrowded City. Soho (the name derives from an old hunting call) was completed just in time to absorb an influx of Greek Christians (hence, Greek Street) fleeing Ottoman persecution, and a larger wave of French Protestants (Huguenots), forced out of France by Louis XIV's bigotry. Many were talented craftsmen and set up leather, silver and furniture workshops. Thus, from the outset, Soho has acted as a sponge and haven for outcasts and misfits; a spirit of toleration was born out of necessity, and remains one of the area's defining characteristics.

Those who didn't like what they saw got out – most of the early well-to-do residents left their Soho Square mansions for the grander, more exclusive developments of Mayfair in the early eighteenth century – and in moved the artists, writers, radicals and yet more foreign immigrants (particularly Italians). By the nineteenth century, John Galsworthy, in *The Forsyte Saga*, summed up Soho as: 'untidy, full of Greeks, Ishmaelites, cats, Italians, tomatoes, restaurants, organs, coloured stuffs, queer names…'

As the resident population dropped in the twentieth century, the area became increasingly known for its entertainments (legal and otherwise) and cheap restaurants. Jazz came to Soho in the 1950s (**Ronnie Scott's** at 47 Frith Street celebrated its 40th birthday in 1999) and the sex industry expanded rapidly in the 1960s. By the mid-1970s, with operators and police in cahoots, Soho was in danger of being overrun by the sex trade. A major clampdown – which included the prosecution of several high-ranking police officers for bribery and corruption – saw the number of premises used by the sex trade drop by five-sixths in the 1980s. At the same time, Soho was regaining its dynamism, thanks largely to its increasingly visible and energetic gay scene. Pubs like the Golden Lion on Dean Street had long been the haunt of gay servicemen, but now gay cafés, late-night bars and clubs, and fetish shops appeared along Old Compton Street, injecting a much-needed vitality and *joie de vivre* into a district in danger of becoming the sole province of dirty old men in raincoats.

That Soho is now more popular than ever is a cause for both celebration and concern. A 24-hour culture is developing, people are taking to the streets – eating, drinking, promenading; coming over all continental. Yet the chains are moving in too, bringing with them those fainthearts who previously found Soho too grimy and seedy for their tastes. No lover of cranky, louche old Soho can fail to worry at the sight of long queues at the doors of huge, characterless booze barns like the Pitcher & Piano and All Bar One on Dean Street.

THE HEART OF SOHO

The core of Soho today is **Old Compton Street** – a shopping centre since its earliest days – and its surrounding streets. Here is Soho at its most heterodox and lively – gay bars, off-licences, delis, heaving boozers, pâtisseries and cheap to chic restaurants. Perhaps the most evocative way to enter Soho, however, is via the arch of the Pillars of Hercules pub leading from Manette Street to Greek Street. The sense of passing through a portal into a different world has entranced more than one Soho neophyte in the past. Just north of here is shady **Soho Square**, initially known as King Square (a weather-beaten statue of the king in question, Charles II, stands close to the mock-Tudor hut in the centre). In summer, office workers munch their lunchtime sandwiches on the grass; while, around the square's edge, London's one remaining French Protestant church and St Patrick's Catholic church provide spiritual nourishment.

The short streets leading down from here to Old Compton Street are brimful of eateries and historical associations. On **Greek Street**, Casanova and Thomas de Quincey once lodged and Josiah Wedgwood had his London showroom; famous old restaurants like **L'Escargot** (no.48; *see page 172*)

Don't fancy yours much...

and the Hungarian **Gay Hussar** (no.2) still survive; notorious Soho soak Jeffrey Bernard's favourite hangout, the undistinguished **Coach & Horses**, is at no.29.

Neighbouring **Frith Street** has been home to John Constable, Mozart and William Hazlitt (at no.6 – now one of London's most charming and discreet hotels; *see page 150*). Over the ever-vibrant **Bar Italia** (no.22; *see page 181*), with its constantly blaring TV, are, appropriately, the rooms where John Logie Baird first demonstrated the wonder of television. The Vietnamese culinary delights of **Saigon** (no.45; *see page 188*) add to the multicultural feel of the place.

Next along is **Dean Street**, site of such famed drinking haunts as the **French House** (no.49; unofficial HQ of De Gaulle and the Free French during World War II; *see page 196*) and the Colony Club (no.41), second homes to Francis Bacon and assorted literary and artistic layabouts from the 1950s, and of the **Groucho Club** (no.44), a focus for today's arts and media crowd. In two cramped rooms over **Quo Vadis** restaurant (no.28), Karl Marx and family lived in 1851-6.

West of here, work begins to get an equal billing with play. **Wardour Street** has long associations with the film industry and remains home to a number of film production companies, as well as Sir Terence Conran's mega **Mezzo** restaurant (no.100), which stands on the site of the legendary Marquee Club. At the street's southern end is the churchyard of **St Anne** – only the early nineteenth-century tower of the church survived the Blitz, but it's worth a look to read the memorial slabs of William Hazlitt and the unfortunate Theodore, King of Corsica, who died penniless.

At the eastern end of **Brewer Street** sex shops, shows and clip joints dominate (it may only be £3 to get in, but you'll be fleeced for 100 times that before you get out); the western portion contains a number of Japanese restaurants and quirky shops. Leading south to Shaftesbury Avenue is **Rupert Street** market, majoring in clothes, jewellery and CDs, while to the north is another one of Soho's portals. The tiny arch of Walkers Court leads past Paul Raymond's Revue Bar into **Berwick Street**, home to several excellent record and CD shops and central London's only surviving fruit and veg market (*see page 223*).

Branching off west is **Broadwick Street**, birthplace of William Blake (every inch the Soho misfit) and centre of a severe cholera outbreak in 1854. Local doctor John Snow became convinced that the disease was being transmitted by polluted water and had the street's water pump chained up. That Snow was proved correct led to a breakthrough in epidemiology. The doctor is commemorated by a handleless replica water pump and in the name of the street's pub (appropriately enough; the only locals who survived the outbreak were those who drank beer rather than water).

'WEST SOHO'

Broadwick Street leads on to pedestrianised **Carnaby Street**, supposed heart of the invented district of 'West Soho'. So long has this been home to pedlars of tat and tourist trash that it's hard to believe the street could even have entered the Oxford English Dictionary in the 1960s as a byword for 'fashionable clothing for young people'. Yet, perhaps, the area is slowly coming full circle, with newcomers such as **Lush** (no.40; *see page 221*), selling toiletries made from fresh, natural products. On tiny, cobbled, parallel Newburgh Street are some of the city's most genuinely cutting-edge clothing stores, while nearby Foubert's Place counts hypertrendy cosmetics shop **MAC** (no.28) and **Ted Baker** (nos.5-7), selling branded casualwear, among its residents.

CHINATOWN

Curving **Shaftesbury Avenue**, extending from New Oxford Street to Piccadilly Circus, was driven through an area of slums in the 1880s, although care was taken to preserve the shape of Soho to the north. Over the next 20 years seven theatres were built along the street; six still stand, and Shaftesbury Avenue revels in being known as the heart of Theatreland. Here are also a handful of Chinese opticians, herbalists, restaurants and travel agents, providing an introduction to London's compact Chinatown.

Trails of the unexpected...

Soho music venues of yesteryear.

It's likely that as you wander round Soho today, you'll inadvertently walk past the sites of venues that made the headlines in their day. Most went the way of the dinosaur, one or two have survived.

In the mid- to late-'60s, the basement **Bag O' Nails** (9 Kingly Street, parallel with Regent Street) was the place to be seen. With any luck you'd have stopped by on the night that Stevie Wonder, Mick Jagger and Eric Clapton jammed together on stage – while Jimi Hendrix got stoned at the bar. It was also here that a certain Paul McCartney met a certain Linda Eastman, in May 1967.

Just east of here, at 7 Broadwick Street, the **Bricklayers Arms** (now a violin repair shop) was the site of the Rolling Stones' first audition in 1962. Brian Jones had placed an ad in a music paper for people to join the group. Apparently, when Mick and Keith turned up Jones was impressed less by their musical ability than their dishevelled appearance, which fitted the bill perfectly, so he hired them on the spot.

Top of the list of club survivors, though, must be the Whiskey-a-Gogo or **Wag Club** (33-37 Wardour Street, just round the corner), where the equally important **Flamingo Club** flourished in the basement from 1960 to 1976. Over the years this address has seen it all, from smoky, speedy R&B via disco and futurism to the percussion drill/ambient choice of today's club scene.

The year before, rival group the Beatles had played their first gig in London, at the now-vanished **Blue Gardenia Club**, St Anne's Court, off Wardour Street. A few years later they went on to record tear-jerker *Hey Jude* and other songs just a few doors down at the Trident Studios (which they'd turned to in favour of Abbey Road Studios because it was more technologically advanced).

Every Friday during the Summer of Love, the basement of the scruffy **Blarney Club** at 31 Tottenham Court Road (just up from the Oxford Street/New Oxford Street junction) was transformed via dope and joss sticks into the all-night **UFO Club**. It was here that resident house band Pink Floyd cut their teeth. Now, all that stands in their place are hi-fi shops. A fitting tribute, they might think.

In the 1950s, many Chinese (mainly from Hong Kong and London's original Chinatown, near the docks in Limehouse) were drawn to **Gerrard Street** and **Lisle Street** by cheap rents. Today, the ersatz oriental gates, stone lions and silly pagoda-topped phone booths suggest a Chinese theme park rather than a genuine community. Yet, despite the fact that the majority of London's Chinese live elsewhere, Chinatown remains a closely knit residential and working enclave with (beyond the many restaurants; *see pages 169*) few concessions made to tourism. The focus of the year here is the Chinese New Year celebrations (late Jan/early Feb; *see page 10*), which fill the streets with dancing dragons, firecrackers and revelry. Oriental foodies shouldn't miss the amazing **New Loon Fung** supermarket on Gerrard Street, below the rooms where John Dryden once lived.

LEICESTER SQUARE

Leading down from Lisle Street to Leicester Square is Leicester Place, home to one of London's cheapest yet most comfortable cinemas, the **Prince Charles** (*see page 260*) and the French Catholic church of **Notre Dame de France**. This circular symphony in concrete contains some fetching 1960 murals by Jean Cocteau.

Leicester Square itself is one of the city's great tourist meeting points. Although it started out as a chic aristo hangout in the seventeenth and eighteenth centuries (when Leicester House fronted the north side), the attractions of the theatre and the flesh had taken over by the mid-nineteenth century. Latterly, the square had become notorious as a haven for winos, junkies and general tawdriness until Westminster Council got its act together and tarted the place up in the mid-1990s.

Today, the convex-cambered square is a pleasing space, although done few favours by the undistinguished, monumental buildings that surround it. Here are London's biggest cinemas, the **Empire** and the monolithic, black-clad **Odeon** (for both, *see page 260*), venues for many a glitzy film première. Here, too, is the Society of West End Theatres' **Half-Price Ticket Booth** (*see page 294*) and, in the north-west corner, the hideous **Swiss Centre** – where the bizarre, hourly chiming cowherd clock exerts an inexplicable fascination on the milling masses. A newcomer to the Square is the much vaunted **Home** nightclub (*see page 96* **Three of a kind**).

Covent Garden

Having recovered from its down-and-out days, Covent Garden has become a tourist magnet, with shops, sights and bags of atmosphere.

The **Royal Opera House** *– it's got some front.*

MAPS 6 & 8

The designation '**Covent Garden**' nowadays refers to anywhere within the bounds of Charing Cross Road, Strand, Kingsway, High Holborn and Shaftesbury Avenue. The focus, however, remains the pedestrianised piazza where gift shops, market stalls and street entertainers vie for visitors' attention. Covent Garden's name is a corruption of the 'convent garden' of the Abbey of St Paul at Westminster, which originally stood on the site. In the 1630s, the would-be property speculator 4th Earl of Bedford brought in Inigo Jones to develop the centre of Covent Garden into an area 'fitte for the habitacions of *Gentlemen* and men of ability'. Under the influence of the Italian neo-classicism of Palladio, Jones designed the bluff, no-nonsense church of **St Paul's** (*see page 85*) looking on to tall terraces over an arcaded, three-sided square (none of the original houses survives).

London's first planned square was an immediate hit with the well-to-do, but as the fruit and vegetable market grew to uncomfortable proportions, and newer, more exclusive developments sprung up further west, Covent Garden's reputation slumped. Coffee houses, taverns, Turkish baths and brothels thrived – John Cleland's archetypal tart-with-a-heart, Fanny Hill, picked up trade and lodged here for a while. Later, the area's grandiose Victorian gin palaces acted as 'the lighthouses which guided the thirsty soul on the road to ruin'. To the north, the squalor of the rookeries around Seven Dials and St Giles was notorious, evoking in Dickens 'wild visions of prodigies of wickedness, want and beggary'.

THEATRICAL COVENT GARDEN

Yet throughout these years, Covent Garden remained a fashionable venue for theatre and opera (as celebrated at the **Theatre Museum**; *see page 85*). From the time the first **Royal Opera House** (*see pages 256 & 270*) opened in Bow Lane in 1732, London's beau monde has gingerly picked its way through the filth and rotting vegetables to enjoy the glittering pleasures of the stage. The **Theatre Royal** in Drury Lane was the other main attraction; it was here that Nell Gwyn performed and David Garrick revolutionised English theatre. The Royal Opera House finally opened in December 1999 after a long and controversial (not to mention hugely expensive, at £214 million) redevelopment and expansion programme. The stunning new structure, which features the impressive cast-iron and glass façade of the Floral Hall, links Bow Street with Covent Garden piazza (and houses several shops), and is now the permanent home of the Royal Ballet as well as the Royal Opera. In an attempt to gag critics who claim the Royal Opera House is elitist, the building is now open to the public throughout the day, for drinks, snacks, full meals and guided tours (phone 020 7304 4000).

TOURIST MECCA

It's easy to be cynical about today's tourist-oriented Covent Garden and the influx of chain restaurants and shops – yet Covent Garden works. It's one of London's all-too-few extensive pedestrianised public spaces and, while it's true that some of the shops and market stalls dispense cheap tat, many do not. Even in the central market, there are decent goods (such as some of the

jewellery on the **Apple Market** stalls in the market building) and quality entertainment (live musicians and the quirky **Cabaret Mechanical Theatre**, *see page 84*). The **Jubilee Market**, on the south side of the piazza, now contains mainly clothes and tatty souvenir stalls, while the old Flower Market has been converted into the **London Transport Museum** (*see page 85*).

QUALITY SHOPPING

Covent Garden's concentration of hip clothes shops, many selling clubby gear, is a major draw. Floral Street, in particular, offers rich pickings for dedicated followers of fashion, while many of the more mainstream chains are represented on parallel Long Acre. Pedestrianised **Neal Street** has an agreeably offbeat ambience, with small, quirky retailers predominating, and everything from kites to oriental tea sets on offer. **Neal's Yard** (off Shorts Gardens), a hippie haven of health food and natural remedies, is a reminder of the 'alternative' scene that did so much, through its mass squats and demonstrations, to prevent the brutal redevelopment of Covent Garden after the market moved out to Battersea in 1974.

Notable shops include the fabulous cheese-feast of **Neal's Yard Dairy** at 17 Shorts Gardens (*see page 217*) and the lush, exotic splendour of the **Wild Bunch** flower stall in nearby Earlham Street by Seven Dials (*see page 215*). The musical instrument shops of Denmark Street (close to the parish church of **St Giles-in-the-Fields**; *see page 85*) are as legendary in the rock world as the bookshops of Charing Cross Road are to the literate classes. In addition to the big book chains, including **Borders** (formerly Books Etc, at no.120), the idiosyncratic doyen of the London book trade, **Foyles** (*see page 201*), has been trading from nos.119-125 since 1904. Look out also for the many second-hand and specialist book stores (*see page 203*).

ELSEWHERE IN COVENT GARDEN

East of the piazza, in **Bow Street**, stands the Magistrates' Courts. During the 1750s and 1760s the courts were presided over by novelist and barrister Henry Fielding, and his blind half-brother John, 'the blind beak' – who was said to be able to recognise 3,000 thieves by their voices alone. It was Henry Fielding who, horrified by the lawlessness and danger of Georgian London, established the Bow Street Runners, precursors of the modern police force. Nearby on Great Queen Street stands the monolithic HQ of the United Grand Lodge of England – otherwise known as **Freemasons' Hall** (*see page 85*). Surprisingly, perhaps, the normally ultra-secretive Masons run guided tours of the building.

Connoisseurs of the London pub should not miss the **Lamb & Flag** (*see page 192*), at 33 Rose Street, off Garrick Street. Built in 1623, it is one of central London's few surviving wooden-framed buildings. Another delightful echo of the past is the tiny alley of **Goodwin's Court**, running between St Martin's Lane and Bedfordbury, which contains a row of bow-fronted seventeenth-century houses, still lit by clockwork-operated gas street lighting. St Martin's Lane is also home to Ian Schrager's lavish hotel of the same name (*see page 147*), which opened in 1999.

Chilling out in Covent Garden **piazza**.

DO THE STRAND

Skirting the south of Covent Garden, the **Strand** (or articleless 'Strand' as it's officially known) has a much more ancient pedigree. Originally a muddy bridle path, it ran directly alongside the river until Victoria Embankment was constructed in the 1860s. Built to link the City with Westminster and lined with the palatial homes of the aristocracy from the thirteenth century, it turns southward at **Charing Cross**. In front of the railway station is an 1863 monument commemorating the original cross, erected near here by the sorrowful Edward I to mark the passing of the funeral procession of his queen, Eleanor, in 1290. An appealing tradition says that Charing is a corruption of 'Chère Reine', but there was a village of Charing here long before Eleanor's body passed through.

The Strand became as notorious for pickpockets and prostitution as Covent Garden (Boswell recalls: '… last night… I met a monstrous big whore in the Strand, whom I had a great curiosity to lubricate'), but within 100 years Disraeli thought it the finest street in Europe. The building of the grand **Savoy** hotel (*see page 149*) in 1884-9 enhanced this reputation, thanks to the managerial skills of César Ritz and culinary genius of Auguste Escoffier. Around the corner in Savoy Street, the sixteenth-century **Savoy Chapel** was a fashionable venue for society weddings 100 years ago. The original chapel was part of John of Gaunt's Savoy Palace, burnt down during the Peasants' Revolt of 1381. Today's Strand, brimming with traffic and lined with offices, shops, theatres, and the odd pub and restaurant, still has grand scale, but without its former grace and distinction, it's a harsh, rather forlorn place; an impression reinforced by the many homeless people who sleep in its doorways.

THE EMBANKMENT

From the Strand, pedestrianised Villiers Street leads down past Terry Farrell's monster-toy-brick **Embankment Place** development, and the claustrophobic but character-packed **Gordon's** wine bar (*see page 192*), to **Embankment Gardens** and Embankment tube station. The grand York House stood here from the thirteenth to the end of the seventeenth century. All that remains of it is the **York Watergate** (on Watergate Walk), which once let on to the Thames. Across from the gardens, sandwiched between the river and the Embankment's constant traffic, is **Cleopatra's Needle** (*see below*).

Just down from here is **Hungerford Bridge**, subject of a spectacular millennium makeover. The existing footbridge will be demolished and two new ones built either side of the railway bridge. In addition, one of Brunel's original piers, the Surrey Pier, will be connected to the South Bank by two lower walkways, and will have an exhibition centre. The upstream bridge is scheduled to be completed by December 2000; the downstream one by the following April. *See also page 29.*

Walk over Hungerford Bridge towards the South Bank Centre to enjoy one of the best views of London's riverscape, particularly at night. The huge white **New Adelphi** building, with the giant clock, stands on the site of the Adam brothers' celebrated Adelphi, built in 1768-72. This terrace of 11 houses over arches and vaults was more of an architectural than commercial success, but it was mindless vandalism that the whole thing was pulled down in 1936.

Neal's Yard – *hard to beat.*

Sights

Cabaret Mechanical Theatre

33-34 The Market, Covent Garden, WC2 (020 7379 7961). Covent Garden tube. **Open** 10am-6.30pm Mon-Fri; 10am-7pm Sat; 11am-6.30pm Sun. **Admission** £1.95; £1.20 5s-16s, OAPs, students, ES40s; £4.95 family. **Credit** AmEx, MC, JCB, £TC, V. **Map 8 L7**

Sue Jackson's unique venture is not a cabaret, or a theatre, but it is mechanics in their most delightful form. More than 60 hand-built automata whirl and jump and spin at the touch of a button. Many are a form of animated cartoon, and heart-warmingly witty. Well worth the admission for the novelty value alone. It's possible to try out the coin-operated machines by the small shop without entering the exhibition – have a chat with Elvis on the 'Hotline to the King', or dare to entrust your fingers to the Great Chopandoff.

Website: www.cabaret.co.uk

Cleopatra's Needle

Victoria Embankment, WC2. Embankment tube. **Map 8 L7**

Nothing to do with Cleopatra, this 37-m (60-ft) high, 186-ton granite obelisk dates from around 1475BC. Presented to Britain in 1819, it was long thought to be too awkward to transport to Britain. It did, however, finally make the long journey in 1877-8. Buried beneath the needle are various objects including, bizarrely, photographs of 12 of the best-looking English women of the day. The sphinxes at the base were accidentally replaced facing the wrong way after being cleaned in the early years of this century.

Freemasons' Hall

Great Queen Street, WC2 (020 7831 9811). Covent Garden or Holborn tube. **Open** 10am-5pm Mon-Fri; 10.30-11.30am Sat. **Admission** free. **Map 6 L6**

You need to book a tour to enter the precincts of this monumental, strangely disturbing art deco edifice: the Grand Lodge of the Freemasons. Though the building includes around 20 temples, the centrepiece is undoubtedly the Grand Temple – possibly the quietest spot in central London – with its beautiful carved doors, superb mosaic ceiling and stained-glass windows. Freemasons' Hall is the central meeting place for the UK's 8,660 Masonic lodges, but, in a bid to update the Masons' notorious reputation for secretiveness, is also open for concerts and other public events in addition to the informative guided tours (days and times vary; phone for details).

London Transport Museum

Covent Garden Piazza, WC2 (020 7379 6344). Covent Garden tube. **Open** 10am-6pm Mon-Thur, Sat, Sun; 11am-6pm Fri (last entry 5pm). **Admission** £5.50; £2.95 5s-16s, students, OAPs, disabled, ES40s; free under-5s; £13.95 family. *GoSee Card member (see p32).* **Credit** MC, £TC, V. **Map 8 L6**

This award-winning museum traces the history of public transport in London from the days of the first buses and cabriolets in the 1820s to the present. It's popular with kids, not least because they get to clamber aboard an early tram and have a go at being a bus conductor, but also gets the thumbs-up from parents, who certainly won't get bored. True, some of the interactive stuff could do with a revamp (such as the clonky screens showing old footage of former methods of transport), but this is a minor criticism. The museum generally manages to strike the right balance between fun and education (children get given a **Kidzones** card that they then stamp at various sites along the way) – and there are interesting facts such as the frightening prediction that road traffic in London is predicted to increase by 98 per cent by 2025. As well as tracing the roots of public transport, the museum also looks forward to the future, with its **>>Fast Forward/Rewind<<** section on the first floor, showcasing ideas of future methods of transport (some of them, such as the Sky Car, a personalised hover car, seem ridiculous at the moment, though perhaps in a few years' time we won't be laughing at them so much). This exhibition runs until July 2000, when it will be replaced by an exhibition specifically about traffic congestion.

The museum shop is worth a mention – quirky 'Mind the Gap' T-shirts sit alongside books detailing the history of the London Underground. And, if it all gets too much for you, sit back and relax in the Aroma café attached.

Website: www.ltmuseum.co.uk

St Giles-in-the-Fields

St Giles High Street, WC2 (020 7240 2532). Tottenham Court Road tube. **Open** 9am-3.30pm Mon-Fri. **Map 6 K6**

It's hard to believe, but this church (founded in 1101) was once surrounded by fields. The Great Plague started in the parish of St Giles in 1665; the number of corpses buried here was so high that subsidence caused severe structural damage to the church. The competition to design a replacement was won by Henry Flitcroft; his church, influenced by Gibbs's newly completed **St Martin-in-the-Fields** (*see p90*), is little changed since the eighteenth century. The poet Andrew Marvell was buried here in 1678, the painter Sir Godfrey Kneller in 1723.

Website: store.yahoo.net/giles-in-the-fields

St Paul's

Bedford Street, WC2 (020 7836 5221). Covent Garden tube. **Open** 9.30am-4.30pm Tue-Fri. **Map 8 L7**

When the parsimonious 4th Earl of Bedford asked Inigo Jones to build a church on newly developed Covent Garden piazza, he said, 'I would not have it much better than a barn,' to which Jones replied, 'Well then, you shall have the handsomest barn in England.' The result (completed in 1633) was a suitably plain Tuscan pastiche that is, indeed, little more than a huge box inside (refreshingly uncluttered, some might say). With Covent Garden being so intertwined with theatre, it's no surprise that it has long been known as the actors' church. Lining the interior walls of the church are memorials to stars such as Charlie Chaplin, Boris Karloff and Vivien Leigh, interspersed with those of lesser-known, but undoubtedly just as great in their way, entertainers such as Pantopuck the Puppetman.

Theatre Museum

Tavistock Street (entrance off Russell Street), WC2 (020 7836 7891/2330). Covent Garden tube. **Open** 10am-6pm Tue-Sun. **Admission** £4.50; £2.50 students, OAPs, ES40s, disabled; free under-16s. *GoSee Card member (see p32).* **Credit** AmEx, MC, £TC, V. **Map 8 L6**

Appropriately sited near the West End's oldest theatre, Theatre Royal Drury Lane, the basement galleries of the excellent Theatre Museum feel like an aquarium of theatre history. Instead of water and fish, the rows of tanks contain illustrations and artefacts from Elizabethan theatre to present-day productions. The theatrical effect is enhanced by low lighting in the long corridors and flickering neon advertisements. In another gallery, **From Page to Stage** invites visitors to explore the creative development of the National Theatre's acclaimed production of *The Wind in the Willows*: try on Toad's webbed gloves, play at being stage manager, or watch videos of rehearsals in progress. The museum also holds the National Video Archive of Stage Performance (access by appointment). **Picturing the Players** is the Somerset Maugham collection of portraits of legendary thespians and theatres: look out for Elizabeth I's startling resemblance to Bette Davis in the first painting.

Fans might like to note that the acclaimed **Forkbeard – Architects of Fantasy**, an interactive exhibition with props such as a giant eyeball and a 2-m (7-ft) rabbit with a 'sinister twitching nose', has been extended to the end of April 2000.

Westminster

Pomp, politics and a palace or two.

MAPS 7 & 8

Ever since Edward the Confessor built his 'West Minster' and palace on the unpromisingly marshy Thorney Island, three miles west of the City, in the eleventh century, Westminster has been the centre of London's religious and royal life. The first Parliament met in the abbey in the fourteenth century and politics remains the lifeblood of the district to this day. Shops and restaurants may be few, but here are London's most spectacular group of buildings and some of the easiest and most rewarding sightseeing in the capital.

TRAFALGAR SQUARE

Expansive and somewhat bleak in appearance, **Trafalgar Square** only came into existence 170 years ago, when it was laid out on the site of the demolished King's Mews. Its appearance would undoubtedly be improved if it were not, in effect, a huge traffic island (although plans are currently being considered to rectify this situation), and if the verminous rats with wings that infest the place were eradicated. Visitors, however, seem uncommonly attached to the pigeons. In summer 1999 the birds seemed a little put out by the arrival of a modern-day statue of Christ, which was hoisted on to the plinth that had previously stood empty for 150 years. The work is one of three that will be displayed one after another until May 2001, when a permanent replacement will be chosen.

The disappointingly low-key, low-rise buildings on the north side of the square, built in 1832-8, don't seem a grand enough home for the magnificent collection of the **National Gallery** (*see page 89*; the **National Portrait Gallery**, *see page 90*, can be accessed around the corner on Charing Cross Road). A more impressive structure, standing on the north-east corner of the square, is James Gibbs's perky **St Martin-in-the-Fields** (*see page 90*), the crypt of which contains a café.

Trafalgar Square's centrepiece, **Nelson's Column**, surrounded by Sir Edwin Landseer's splendid lions, commemorates Britain's most famous sailor. The friezes around the base of the 51-m (171-ft) column, erected in 1843, were cast from metal from French and Spanish cannon captured at the Battle of Trafalgar in 1805.

AROUND ST JAMES'S PARK

From Trafalgar Square, the grand processional route of **The Mall** (home of the **ICA Gallery**; *see page 89*) passes under Admiralty Arch and past St James's Park to the Victoria Memorial in front of **Buckingham Palace** (*see page 88*). Up close, the palace seems rather small, squat and unimposing. More satisfying is a wander around the carriages of the **Royal Mews** behind the Palace, or a stroll in **St James's Park** (*see page 90*) – one of London's most beautiful. On the south side of the park, the Wellington Barracks, home of the Foot Guards, contains the **Guards' Museum** (*see page 88*). Nearby are the wonderfully intact Georgian terraces of Queen Anne's Gate and Old Queen Street.

WHITEHALL TO PARLIAMENT SQUARE

Back in Trafalgar Square, Nelson gazes, with his one good eye, down the long, gentle curve of **Whitehall** into the heart of British governmental bureaucracy. Lined up along the street, many of the big ministries maintain at least the façade of heart-of-the-empire solidity. Halfway down the street, the Horse Guards building (try to pass by when the mounted scarlet-clad guards are changing; *see page 5*) faces the **Banqueting House** (*see page 87*), central London's first classical-style building and site of Charles I's execution. Near here is Edwin Lutyens's ascetically plain memorial to the dead of both world wars, the **Cenotaph**, and, on **Downing Street**, the disappointingly anonymous official homes of the prime minister and the chancellor of the exchequer (closed off by iron security gates since 1990).

At the end of King Charles Street, the **Cabinet War Rooms** (*see page 88*) is the effectively restored operations centre used by Churchill and his cabinet during World War II air raids.

Parliament Square was laid out in 1868 on the site of what was then a notorious slum. Architecture here is on a grand scale. **Westminster Central Hall**, with its great black dome, built on the site of the old Royal Aquarium in 1905-11, is used for conferences (the first assembly of the United Nations was held here in 1946) as well as Methodist church services. Following a lengthy facelift, **Westminster Abbey** (*see page 90*) is now resplendent in its original pristine white (for years, many Londoners assumed it was black). Similarly shaped but much smaller, **St Margaret's Westminster** (*see page 90*) stands in the shadow of the abbey, rather like a promising child next to an indulgent parent. Both Samuel Pepys and Winston Churchill were married here.

Few buildings in London dazzle – the **Houses of Parliament** (*see page 89*) are an exception. Built between 1834 and 1858 by Charles Barry, and fancifully decorated by Augustus Pugin, their Disneyland Gothic chutzpah simultaneously raises a smile and a gasp. Although formally still known as the Palace of Westminster, the only surviving part of the medieval royal palace is **Westminster Hall** (and the **Jewel Tower**, just south of Westminster Abbey; *see page 89*).

London icon though it is, Parliament's clock tower, **Big Ben**, seems rather stumpy when viewed close up. The tower originally contained a small prison cell – Emmeline Pankhurst, in 1902, was its last occupant. A statue of the suffragette stands in **Victoria Tower Gardens**, by the river on the south side of Parliament. Here too is a cast of Rodin's glum-looking *Burghers of Calais* and a splendid Gothic revival drinking fountain. In the shadow of Big Ben, at the end of Westminster Bridge, stands a statue of Boudicca and her daughters gesticulating ambiguously towards Parliament – the Queen of the Iceni was no friend to Londoners, having reduced Roman Londinium to ruins and massacred its inhabitants in AD61.

MILLBANK

Millbank runs along the river from Parliament to Vauxhall Bridge. Just off here is **St John's Smith Square**, built as a church in 1713-28 by Thomas Archer, and now primarily a venue for classical music concerts (*see page 271*). This exuberant baroque fantasy has not been without its detractors – Dickens thought it 'a very hideous church with four towers at the corners, generally resembling some petrified monster, frightful and gigantic, on its back with its legs in the air'.

By the river, just north of Vauxhall Bridge, stood the Millbank Penitentiary – an attempt to build a model prison, based on the ideas of Jeremy Bentham. But it was a grim place, lasting only 70 years until 1890, before being demolished and replaced by the rather more enlightened Tate Gallery, now the **Tate Britain** (*see page 91* **Tate of the Art no.2**). Overshadowing the Tate is the 240-m (387-ft) high **Millbank Tower** – a 1960s office block that is not without its fans – while, over the river, the giant toy-town-building-block bulk of **Vauxhall Cross** is the surprisingly conspicuous HQ of the internal security service, MI6.

VICTORIA

Victoria Street, stretching from Parliament Square to Victoria Station, links political London with backpackers' London. Victoria Coach Station is a short distance away in Buckingham Palace Road; Belgrave Road provides an almost unbroken line of cheap (and fairly grim) hotels.

The area has seldom stayed the same for long. In the eighteenth and early nineteenth centuries, it was dominated by the Grosvenor Canal, but in the 1850s much of this was buried under the new Victoria Station. A century later, many of the shops and offices along Victoria Street were pulled down and replaced by the anonymous blocks that now line it on both sides.

Partly screened by office blocks and set well back from Victoria Street behind its own piazza, **Westminster Cathedral** (*see page 91*) always comes as a pleasant surprise, coming into view only when you draw level with it. Built between 1896 and 1903, the cathedral's interior has never been finished.

Further down Victoria Street, the grey concrete monstrosity that is the **Department of Trade and Industry** HQ represents 1960s architecture at its near-worst. The **Albert** pub, on the corner of Victoria Street and Buckingham Gate, standing in the shadow of two enormous office blocks, provides an oddly effective juxtaposition of old and new.

Continuing along Victoria Street, you come to **Christchurch Gardens**, burial site of Thomas ('Colonel') Blood, the seventeenth-century rogue who very nearly got away with stealing the Crown Jewels. A memorial is dedicated to the suffragettes, who held their first meetings at **Caxton Hall**, visible on the far side of the gardens and badly in need of repair. **New Scotland Yard** – with its famous revolving sign – is in Broadway, down at the end of Caxton Street.

Strutton Ground, on the other side of Victoria Street, is home to a modest all-purpose market, flanked by sandwich shops. At the other end, the zippy **Channel Four Building**, with its outside lifts and spindly exterior design, is worth a look (corner of Chadwick Street and Horseferry Road).

Pimlico fills the triangle of land formed by Chelsea Bridge, Ebury Street, Vauxhall Bridge Road and the river. Thomas Cubitt began building elegant streets and squares here in the 1830s, as he had in Belgravia, albeit on a less grand scale. The cluster of small shops and restaurants around Warwick Way forms the heart of Pimlico, but Belgrave Road, with its rows of solid, dazzling-white terraces, is its backbone. Close by are many dignified, beautifully maintained townhouses.

Sights

Banqueting House

Whitehall, SW1 (020 7930 4179). Westminster tube or Charing Cross tube/rail. **Open** 10am-5pm Mon-Sat (sometimes closed at short notice; phone to check). **Admission** £3.60; £2.30 5s-15s; £2.80 students, OAPs, ES40s, disabled. **Credit** MC, V. **Map 8 L8**

Looking perfectly in step with Whitehall buildings 200 years its junior, Inigo Jones's groundbreaking, classically inspired Banqueting House (1619-22) is the only part of the former Whitehall Palace that survived the devastating fire of 1698. There's a video and small exhibition in the undercroft, but the chief glory is the first-floor hall, designed for court ceremonials, and magnificently adorned with ceiling paintings by Rubens (1635). Charles I commissioned the Flemish artist and diplomat to glorify his less-than-prepossessing father James I and celebrate the divine right of the Stuart kings. There is no little irony that, on 30 January 1649, Charles walked beneath these very paintings on his way to stepping out of a first-floor window on to the scaffold at the front of the building to make his appointment with the executioner's axe. An excellent audio guide explaining the paintings and the hall's functions is included in the admission price.

As part of the **London String of Pearls Millennium Festival** (*see page 8* **London's your oyster**), Banqueting House will stage a series of concerts throughout 2000.

Buckingham Palace & Royal Mews

SW1 (020 7930 4832/recorded info 020 7799 2331/credit card bookings 020 7321 2233/disabled info 020 7839 1377/info@royalcollection.org.uk). St James's Park/Green Park tube or Victoria tube/rail. **Open** *6 Aug-1 Oct* 9.30am-4.15pm daily. *Royal Mews Oct-July* noon-4pm (last entry 3.30pm), *Aug-Sept* 10.30-4.30pm (last entry 4pm), Mon-Thur. **Admission** £10.50; £5 5s-16s; £8 OAPs. *Royal Mews* £4.30; £2.10 5s-16s; £3.30 OAPs; £10.70 family. **Credit** AmEx, JCB, MC, £TC, V.
Map 7 H9

Built in 1703 for the Duke of Buckingham, the original Buckingham House was bought by George III and converted into a palace by his son George IV. In 1837, the young Queen Victoria decided to make Buckingham Palace her home, and it has been the London residence of the royal family ever since. The Royal Standard flies above the palace when the Queen is in London. During August and September (the exact dates vary each year), while the royals are on their hols, the State Apartments, used for banquets and investitures, are open to the public. The 18 rooms on view include the Throne Room, State Dining Room and Music Room, and, while some of the works of art are gems, there really is little of interest unless you're after tips on how to do up your house with upmarket knick-knackery. Tickets go on sale from 9am on the day at the ticket office on Constitution Hill. To avoid the queues, book in advance by credit card over the phone, or by requesting an application form from the Visitor Office (although note that only £10.50 tickets are available in advance). The **Queen's Gallery**, featuring highlights of Lizzie's vast art collection, is closed for remodelling until 2002.

Just around the corner, on Buckingham Palace Road, the **Royal Mews** is home to the royal carriages. The gilt palm-wood Coronation Coach, the elegant Glass Coach, the immaculately groomed horses and the finely crafted, sleek, black landaus make the Mews one of the capital's better-value collections. Top dog in the pecking order is Her Majesty's State Coach, a breathtaking double-gilded affair and the earliest royal carriage still in existence (built 1761). Closed during Royal Ascot week (June) and on state occasions.
Website: www.royal.gov.uk

Get a peek of **Westminster Abbey**. See p90.

Cabinet War Rooms

Clive Steps, King Charles Street, SW1 (020 7930 6961). St James's Park or Westminster tube. **Open** *Oct-Mar* 10am-6pm, *Apr-Sept* 9.30am-6pm, daily (last entry 5.15pm). **Admission** £4.80; £3.50 students, OAPs; £2.20 ES40s; £1.80-£2.40 disabled. **Credit** AmEx, MC, V. **Map 8 K9**

The austere underground HQ of Churchill's War Cabinet during World War II has been faithfully preserved. A guided audio tour takes you through the rooms rather quickly (though you can play further clips of information on subjects that interest you). What you don't get is a feel for the stress, smells, noises and (controlled) chaos that must have filled the rooms at the height of the war. Highlights include the key Map Room (manned day and night throughout the war to monitor the movements of Allied and Axis troops), Churchill's bedroom (complete with nightshirt and chamberpot), and the telephone hotline to the White House.
Website: www.iwm.org.uk

Guards' Museum

Wellington Barracks, Birdcage Walk, SW1 (020 7414 3271). St James's Park tube. **Open** 10am-4pm daily (last entry 3.30pm). **Admission** £2; £1 5s-16s, students, OAPs; £4 family. **Map 7 J9**

This small museum records the history of the British Army's five Guards regiments, which were founded in the seventeenth century under Charles II. The oldest medal (awarded by Oliver Cromwell to officers of his New Model Army at the Battle of Dunbar in 1651) and a bottle of Iraqi whisky captured in the Gulf War notwithstanding, this is predominantly an exhibition of uniforms and oil paintings accompanied by stirring martial music. That said, the museum is trying to emphasise its collection of curios from the everyday life of your ordinary guardsman down the ages. See the Guards in ceremonial action (every day Apr-Aug, every other day Sept-Mar, at 10.50am) when they form up to march to St James's Palace and Buckingham Palace to relieve their comrades on guard duty. The toy soldier shop at the museum claims to be the largest of its kind in London.

Houses of Parliament

Parliament Square, SW1 (Commons info 020 7219 4272/Lords info 020 7219 3107). Westminster tube. **Open** (always phone to check) *House of Commons Visitors' Gallery* from 2.30pm Mon, Tue; 9.30am-2pm Wed; 11.30am-7.30pm Thur; 9.30am-3pm Fri. *House of Lords Visitors' Gallery* from 2.30pm Mon-Wed; from 3pm Thur; from 11am Fri. **Admission** free. **Map 8 L9**

Originally set on an island, the first Parliament was held here in 1275. Westminster became Parliament's permanent home in 1532, when Henry VIII upped sticks to Whitehall. Parliament was originally housed in the choir stalls of St Stephen's Chapel, where members sat facing each other from opposite sides; the tradition continues today. The only remaining parts of the original palace are **Westminster Hall**, with its hammer-beam roof, and the **Jewel Tower** (*see below*); the rest burned down in a great fire (1834) and was rebuilt in neo-Gothic style by Charles Barry and Augustus Pugin. There are 1,000 rooms, 100 staircases, 11 courtyards, eight bars and six restaurants (though, alas, none of them is open to the public).

Anyone can watch the Commons or Lords in session from the visitors' galleries; queuing outside gives you access to the central lobby, and eventually the visitors' galleries. If you arrive after 6pm (the chamber sits until at least 10pm Mon-Thur) you shouldn't have to queue. The best spectacle, however, is Prime Minister's Question Time at 3pm on Wednesdays (though note you will need tickets in advance for this – arrange with your MP or embassy). There's no minimum age but children must at least be able to sign their name in the visitors' book.

Parliament takes a break at Christmas, Easter and during the summer, but the galleries remain open to the public for pre-booked guided tours (which are not free). The procedure for booking is somewhat lengthy, so it's best to phone for details.

During summer 2000, the Houses of Parliament will be more accessible to casual visitors: as part of the **London String of Pearls Millennium Festival** (*see p8* **London's your oyster**), the public will be able to see **Voters of the Future** (1 Aug-15 Sept; 9.30am-5pm; admission free), an exhibition detailing the workings of Parliament, past, present and future.

Website: www.parliament.uk

ICA Gallery

The Mall, SW1 (box office 020 7930 3647/ membership enquiries 020 7873 0062). Piccadilly Circus tube/Charing Cross tube/rail. **Open** noon-7.30pm daily. **Membership** *daily* £1.50, £1 concs Mon-Fri; £2.50, £2 concs Sat, Sun; *annual* £25, £15 concs. **Credit** AmEx, DC, JCB, MC, £TC, V. **Map 8 K8**

At the Institute of Contemporary Arts' opening in 1948, the art historian and anarchist Herbert Read declared that this would be different from all other galleries. Much to its credit, it has largely maintained its reputation for being a challenging place to witness all forms of artistic expression. The Upper Gallery hosts exhibitions of every type of avant-garde work; the Concourse Gallery attracts more attention because of its position by the café. Many leading artists had their first London exposure at the ICA, including Moore, Picasso, Ernst and, more recently, Helen Chadwick, Damien Hirst, Gary Hume and the Chapman brothers. Its somewhat ramshackle feel ensures that exhibitions here are never particularly slick, but they frequently provoke reaction and debate, even when flawed by an inability to pull off the grander intentions.

Among the events scheduled for 2000 are the **Beck's Futures Awards**, a new prize and exhibition of British artists (18 Mar-14 May); and the architectural work of **Daniel Libeskind** and **Julie Becker** (June-July), as well as the first major UK show of video work by Iranian-American Shirin Neshat (July-Sept).

Website: www.ica.org.uk

Jewel Tower

Abingdon Street, SW1 (020 7222 2219). Westminster tube. **Open** *Apr-Sept* 10am-6pm daily; *Oct-Mar* 10am-4pm daily. **Admission** £1.50; 80p 5s-16s; £1.10 students, OAPs, ES40s. **Credit** MC, £TC, V. **Map 8 L9**

Along with Westminster Hall, the moated Jewel Tower is a survivor from the medieval Palace of Westminster. It was built in 1365-6 to house Edward III's gold and jewels (and *not* the Crown Jewels, as a notice outside reiterates). From 1621 to 1864, the tower stored records of the House of Lords. Restored, it now contains an informative, if rather plainly presented, exhibition, and a livelier video on Parliament past and present.

National Gallery

Trafalgar Square, WC2 (020 7747 2885). Leicester Square tube/Charing Cross tube/rail. **Open** 10am-6pm Mon, Tue, Thur-Sun; 10am-9pm Wed; Micro Gallery 10am-5.30pm Mon, Tue, Thur-Sun; 10am-8.30pm Wed. **Admission** free. **Map 8 K7**

Founded in 1824 with just 38 pictures, the National Collection of Paintings now contains more than 2,000 western European paintings from the mid-thirteenth century to 1900 – it's indisputably one of the finest collections in the world. The quality and range of pictures on display are stunning, with leather chesterfield sofas, lashings of marble and creaking wooden floors adding to the hallowed atmosphere. There's a good introductory guided tour, which concentrates on the major paintings on the ground floor, or you can pick up the excellent free audio guide from either of the two main entrances.

The exterior of Robert Venturi and Denise Scott Brown's **Sainsbury Wing** has its detractors, but the exhibition space provides a superb setting for the fine collection of early Renaissance (Italian and northern) works as well as playing host to numerous temporary exhibitions throughout the year. And don't miss the **Micro Gallery**, where, at the touch of a screen, you can see any painting in the collection, print out a reproduction or construct a customised tour around your own favourites, which might include Van Gogh's *Sunflowers*, Van Eyck's *The Arnolfini Portrait*, Bellini's *Portrait of the Doge Leonardo Loredan*, Constable's *The Hay Wain*, Turner's *The Fighting Temeraire* or Leonardo's cartoon of *The Virgin and Child with Saint John the Baptist and Saint Anne*.

Exhibitions planned for 2000 include **Seeing Salvation: The Image of Christ** (until 7 May 2000), which is part of the the **London String of Pearls Millennium Festival** (*see p8* **London's your oyster**), and which will explore how Christ has been represented visually over the past two millennia; and **Close Encounters: New Art from Old** (14 June-17 Sept), during which more than 20 established artists such as Lucian Freud and Claes Oldenburg will choose a work from the gallery and respond to it with a new work of their own. Also scheduled is **Telling Time** (18 Oct-14 Jan 2001), examining the relationship between time and painting.
Website: www.nationalgallery.org.uk

National Portrait Gallery

2 St Martin's Place, WC2 (020 7306 0055). Leicester Square tube/Charing Cross tube/rail. **Open** 10am-6pm Mon-Sat; noon-6pm Sun. **Admission** free; £4 for selected exhibitions. **Map 8 K7**

You can trace the history of the nation in the faces of its key players down the ages at the National Portrait Gallery. Founded in 1856 to collect pictures of royal and political figures, it now boasts as one of its most prized exhibits the only known portrait of the non-royal, non-political William Shakespeare. A new wing for this packed gallery will open in May 2000, creating extra space for the oldest and newest elements of the collection in the form of the **Tudor Gallery** and the **Balcony Gallery**, while also adding a rooftop restaurant.

For a chronological tour of the gallery, start on the top floor and work your way downwards (although be prepared for some disruption as the gallery extends its exhibition space). The present generation of the royal family is on Level 2, including Brian Organ's portrait of the Princess of Wales. Exhibitions planned for 2000 include **Photographs by Snowdon – A Retrospective** (25 Feb-14 June) and **Painting the Century** (20 Oct-Feb 2001). The winner and best-of-the-rest of the **BP Amoco Portrait Awards** are on show from 23 June to 17 September. Stop for sustenance in the Portrait Café.
Website: www.npg.org.uk

St James's Park

The Mall, SW1 (020 7930 1793). St James's Park tube. **Open** dawn-dusk daily. **Map 8 K8**

In the seventeenth century, Charles II had the deer park of St James's Palace converted into a garden by French landscape gardener Le Nôtre, and it was landscaped further by John Nash in the early nineteenth century. The view of Buckingham Palace from the bridge over the lake is wonderful, particularly at night when the palace is floodlit. The lake is now a sanctuary for wildfowl – pelicans (fed at 3pm daily), ducks, geese and Australian black swans. There's a playground at the Buck Palace end, and refreshments at the new, if rather uninspiring, café that replaced the unloved concrete Cake House. Many Londoners rate St James's as the loveliest and most intimate of the capital's central parks.

St Margaret's Westminster

Parliament Square, SW1 (020 7222 5152). Westminster tube. **Open** 9.30am-4.30pm Mon-Fri (last entry 3.45pm); 9.30am-2.45pm Sat (last entry 1.45pm); 2-5pm Sun (last entry 4pm). **Services** 11am Sun (phone to check). **Map 8 K9**

Founded in the twelfth century but rebuilt in 1486-1523 and restored many times since, it is easy to overlook this historic church, dwarfed by the adjacent abbey. The impressive east window (1509), in richly coloured Flemish glass, commemorates the marriage of Henry VIII and Catherine of Aragon. Later windows celebrate Britain's first printer, William Caxton, buried here in 1491; the explorer Sir Walter Ralegh, executed over the road in Old Palace Yard; and the writer John Milton (1608-74) who worshipped, and married his second wife, here. John Piper's Braque-like windows on the south side date from 1966.
Website: www.westminster-abbey.org

St Martin-in-the-Fields

Trafalgar Square, WC2 (020 7930 1862). Charing Cross tube/rail. **Open** 8am-6.30pm daily. **Map 8 L7**

A church has stood here since the thirteenth century, when it was 'in the fields' between the City and Westminster. The present church, designed by James Gibbs (1726), is embellished inside with dark woodwork and ornate Italian plasterwork; note the Royal Box to the left of the gallery – this is officially the parish church for Buckingham Palace. Free lunchtime concerts take place here on Mondays, Tuesdays and Fridays at 1.05pm (*see p271*). The crypt contains a café, a gift shop and the London Brass Rubbing Centre.
Website: www.stmartin-in-the-fields.org

Tate Britain (formerly the Tate Gallery)

See p91 **Tate of the art no.2**.

Westminster Abbey

Dean's Yard, SW1 (020 7222 5152/guided tours 020 7222 7110). St James's Park or Westminster tube. **Open** *Nave & Royal Chapels* 9.30am-4.45pm Mon-Fri (last entry 3.45pm); 9am-2.45pm Sat (last entry 1.45pm). *Chapter House Nov-Mar* 10am-4pm daily (last entry 3.30pm); *Apr-Oct* 10am-5.30pm daily (last entry 5pm). *Pyx Chamber & Abbey Museum* 10.30am-

Tate of the art no.2

From spring 2000, the Tate Gallery's current collection (comprising international modern art and historical and modern British art) will be split between the Millbank site and the new **Tate Modern** at Bankside (*see page 39* **Tate of the art no.1**). The creation of a new building means that, between them, the galleries will be able to show about 60 per cent of their total holdings, a vast improvement on the current figure of 15 per cent. The Millbank building, scheduled to open on 24 March 2000 as the **Tate Britain**, will cover work from the sixteenth century to the present day (shown thematically rather than chronologically during 2000). More space will be freed up for contemporary British art, and rooms will be dedicated to major artists such as Blake, Constable, Spencer and Bacon. The Clore Gallery extensions, specially designed by James Stirling, will continue to house the marvellous collection of works by Turner.

Visitors may find some overlap between the two galleries, however, when it comes to contemporary British work, with the Tate Modern showing British artists in an international context and the Tate Britain continuing to house the **Turner Prize** exhibition. Events in 2000 include **New Acquisitions in British Art 1990-2000** (23 Mar-28 May), **Ruskin, Turner & the Pre-Raphaelites** (9 Mar-28 May), the triennial **New British Art 2000** (6 July-24 Sept) and **William Blake** (9 Nov-11 Feb 2001), a multifaceted look at the multifaceted oddball genius. Other exhibitions include **Romantic Landscape: the Norwich School of Painters 1803-1833** (24 Mar-16 Sept) and, in the Duveen Sculpture Gallery, the challenging works of **Mona Hatoum** (24 Mar-3 July). New galleries and visitor facilities are planned for 2001. By May 2000, when the Tate Modern reopens, visitors will be able to move easily from one gallery to the other using a shuttle bus and boat services, and bicycle and pedestrian routes.

Tate Britain

Millbank, SW1 (020 7887 8000). Pimlico tube/ C10, 77A, 88 bus. **Open** 10am-5.50pm daily. **Admission** free; special exhibitions prices vary. **Map 8 K11**

4pm daily. *College Garden Apr-Sept* 10am-6pm Tue-Thur; *Oct-Mar* 10am-4pm Tue-Thur. **Admission** *Nave & Royal Chapels* £5; £2 11s-15s; £3 students, OAPs; £10 family. *Chapter House, Pyx Chamber & Abbey Museum* £2.50; £1 with main entrance ticket; free with audio guide; *audio guide* £2. **Map 8 K9**

Since Edward the Confessor built his church to St Peter (consecrated in 1065) on the site of the Saxon original, the abbey has been bound up with British royalty. With two exceptions, every king and queen of England since William the Conqueror (1066) has been crowned here; many are buried here too – the royal chapels and tombs include Edward the Confessor's shrine and the Coronation Chair (1296).

Of the original abbey, only the **Pyx Chamber** (the one-time royal treasury) and the Norman **Undercroft** remain; the Gothic nave and choir were rebuilt by Henry III in the thirteenth century; the **Henry VII Chapel**, with its spectacular fan vaulting, was added in 1503-12; the west towers (by Hawksmoor) completed the building in 1745. The interior is cluttered with monuments to statesmen, scientists, musicians and poets. The centrepiece of the wonderfully light, octagonal **Chapter House** (1253) is its thirteenth-century tiled floor, while the **Little Cloister**, surrounding a pretty garden, offers a welcome respite from the crowds, especially during the free lunchtime concerts on Thursdays in July and August. Worth a look too are the **statues** of ten twentieth-century Christian martyrs in fifteenth-century niches over the west door.

If you can avoid the dispiriting tour-group throng, you'll get much more out of a visit to the abbey. Come as early or late as possible or on midweek afternoons, when the coach parties have moved on to St Paul's. The rather patronising audio guide ('We'll keep talking while you walk') is hardly brain-taxing, but it's a good way of getting to grips with the somewhat bewildering scale of the abbey.

Special exhibitions, sermons, concerts and lectures are planned in the abbey during 2000 as part of the **London String of Pearls Millennium Festival** (*see p8* **London's your oyster**).

Website: www.westminster-abbey.org

Westminster Cathedral

Victoria Street, SW1 (020 7798 9055). Victoria tube/rail. **Open** 7am-7pm Mon-Fri, Sun; 8am-7pm Sat. **Admission** free; donations appreciated; *audio guide* £2.50; £1.50 5s-16s, students, OAPs, ES40s. **Map 7 J10**

Britain's premier Catholic cathedral is a delightfully bizarre neo-Byzantine confection, with its candy-striped stone and brick bands. The structure was completed in 1903 by John Francis Bentley, but the decoration still isn't finished, and the domes are bare. Nevertheless, the columns and mosaics (made from over 100 kinds of marble) are magnificent; the nave is the widest in Britain, Eric Gill's sculptures of the Stations of the Cross (1914-18) are especially fine and the view from the campanile is superb.

Website: www.westminstercathedral.org.uk

Knightsbridge

Whether you want to flex those credit cards, further your education or relax in the park, Knightsbridge has everything to satisfy you.

Going for gold: **Albert** *sitting pretty. See p93.*

MAPS 2, 4 & 7

The village of **Knightsbridge** was once renowned for its taverns and notorious for its highwaymen. The only danger of daylight robbery today comes from the inflated prices of the exclusive shops along Sloane Street and Brompton Road. Whether or not there's any truth in the suspiciously literal legend that a fight between two knights on a bridge over the now-subterranean Westbourne river (near Albert Gate in Hyde Park) gave the area its name, there's no doubt that Knightsbridge today is as posh as London gets.

The majority of visitors get no further than a devotional visit to that fabled temple of retailing, **Harrods** (*see page 216*). But, if it's Knightsbridge cachet you're after, follow the ladies-who-lunch up the road to the hipper **Harvey Nichols** (food and fashion are its strengths; *see page 216*), where the **Fifth Floor** restaurant (*see page 165*) continues to be *the* shop-and-scoff destination for those who consider 'work' to be deciding whether to wear the Christian Lacroix or Dolce & Gabbana number today; the Fifth Floor Café, and the Foundation restaurant, in the basement, are Harvey Nick's other commendable options. If your lunch budget is closer to £5 than £50, you'll be relieved to discover one of London's bargain **Stockpot** restaurants on nearby Basil Street (*see page 184* **Dead-cheap dinners**), where it has been serving up ludicrously cheap, if basic, grub since 1956.

The fashion triangle of Sloane Street, Brompton Road and Beauchamp (pronounced, heaven knows why, 'bée-chum') Place contains just about every big couture name on the planet. If the staggering price tags don't freeze you to the spot, the icy stares of the cooler-than-thou assistants surely will.

BELGRAVIA

East of Sloane Street lies **Belgravia**. Until it was developed by Lord Grosvenor and Thomas Cubitt in the 1820s, the area comprised open fields and was popular as a site for duels. As soon as the first grand stucco houses were raised, Belgravia established a reputation as a highly exclusive, largely residential district. It retains it today, although the judgement of Benjamin Disraeli that Belgravia was 'monotonous… and so contrived as to be at the same time insipid and tawdry' might be echoed by anyone who has found themselves lost in this curiously characterless embassyland. Characterful relief is provided in the **Grenadier** pub, in Old Barrack Yard, off Wilton Row (*see page 195*), once frequented by the Duke of Wellington and said to be haunted by the ghost of one of his officers, beaten to death for cheating at cards.

HYDE PARK

Knightsbridge (the street), leading westward via Kensington Road into Kensington High Street, borders the largest of London's royal parks, **Hyde Park** (*see page 95*), site of the outstanding **Serpentine Gallery** (*see page 95*). Every morning, at 10.28am (9.28am on Sundays), soldiers of the Household Cavalry emerge from their barracks to ride through the park to Horse Guards Road for the **Changing of the Guard** (*see page 5*). Merging into Hyde Park is **Kensington Gardens** (*see page 95*), containing Queen Victoria's birthplace and the former home of Diana, Princess of Wales, **Kensington Palace** (*see page 95*). Perhaps surprisingly, vehement local opposition caused a plan to build a £10-million Diana memorial garden here to be abandoned, though a memorial to her in one of London's Royal Parks may yet still be erected.

SOUTH KENSINGTON MUSEUMLAND

Prince Albert's greatest legacy to the nation lies south of here in **South Kensington**. With the £186,000 profit of the 1851 Great Exhibition, and a matching government grant, he oversaw the purchase of 35 hectares (87 acres) of land for the building of institutions to 'extend the influence of Science and Art upon Productive Industry'. Although the Prince didn't live to see the completion of 'Albertopolis', the scheme was an unqualified success. Concentrated in this small area are Imperial College, the Royal Geographical Society, the Royal College of Art, the Royal College of Music (with a small museum), plus the heavyweight museum triumvirate of the **Science Museum**, the **Natural History Museum** and, arguably the best of the lot, the magnificent fine and applied art collection of the **Victoria & Albert Museum** (for all, *see page 96* **Three's company**).

Albert is commemorated by the extravagant **Albert Memorial** (*see page below*) on the edge of Hyde Park and, opposite, the Roman-influenced **Royal Albert Hall**, venue for the annual 'Proms' concerts (*see pages 7 & 270*). Another nearby attraction renowned for its musical tradition is the florid, Italianate **Brompton Oratory** (*see below*). During the Cold War this church was used by the KGB as a dead letter box. Other eastern European connections in the area include the **Russian Orthodox Church** off Ennismore Gardens and the timeless Polish restaurant, **Daquise**, by South Kensington tube at 20 Thurloe Street.

Well-to-do residential area South Kensington stretches down to meet Chelsea somewhere around Fulham Road. Near its northern end, at no.81, stands the unique, exuberant, art nouveau **Michelin Building**, designed by Espinasse for the tyre manufacturers in 1905. It now houses book publishers, the beautiful, if pricey, **Bibendum** restaurant (*see page 165*) and Sir Terence Conran's design shrine, the **Conran Shop** (*see page 219*). Fulham Road, lined with swish antique shops, bars and restaurants (**Wok Wok** at no.140 is good for a bowl of noodles; *see page 183*), continues down to Chelsea's football ground, **Stamford Bridge**, and on through Fulham towards Putney Bridge.

Sights

Albert Memorial

Kensington Gardens, SW7. Knightsbridge or High Street Kensington tube then 9, 33, 49, 52, 73 bus.
Map 2 D8

This grandiose memorial to the beloved husband of Queen Victoria was finally unveiled by the Queen in October 1998 after a decade-long restoration programme. Designed by Sir George Gilbert Scott and finished in 1872, it centres around a gilden Albert, holding a copy of the catalogue of the 1951 Great Exhibition. It is hard to believe that the modest German Prince, who explicitly said, 'I would rather not be made the prominent feature of such a monument', would have approved of the pompous finished product, or the fact that its restoration cost £11 million (although this was £3 million under budget, and completed a year earlier than expected). It's quite a sight though. Guided tours of the memorial can be booked on 020 7495 0916/www.tourguides.co.uk; they allow you to get closer to the memorial and examine, in particular, the superbly crafted and wonderfully detailed marble frieze of 168 leading literary and artistic figures from history.

Flowers at **Kensington Palace**. *See p95.*

Brompton Oratory

Thurloe Place, Brompton Road, SW7 (020 7808 0900). South Kensington tube. **Open** 6.30am-8pm daily. **Admission** free; donations appreciated.
Map 4 E10

Easily overlooked but worth stepping inside if only to escape the roaring traffic outside, Brompton Oratory is a monument to the late nineteenth-century English Catholic revival. Built in 1880-4 to the designs of little-known (and unfortunately named) architect Herbert Gribble, after an open competition, it is a shameless attempt to imitate a florid Italian baroque church. Many of the ornate internal decorations predate the building, including Mazzuoli's late seventeenth-century statues of the apostles, which previously stood in Siena Cathedral.

ONE OF THE MOST NATURAL SELECTIONS IN THE WORLD.
THE NATURAL HISTORY MUSEUM
Monday-Saturday 10am-5.50pm
Sunday 11am-5.50pm Cromwell Road, London SW7.
Nearest Underground: South Kensington.
Free admission for children.

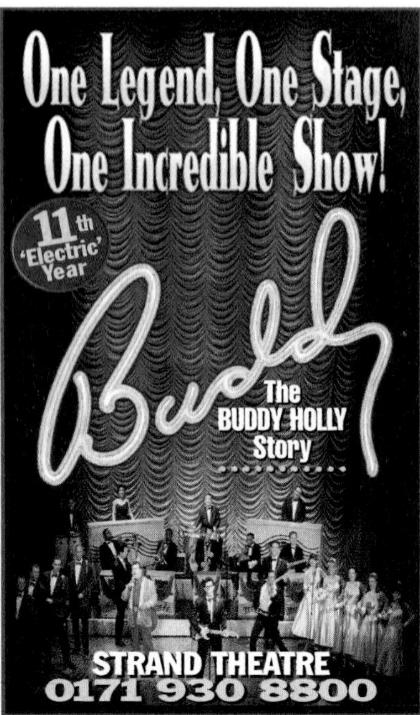
One Legend, One Stage, One Incredible Show!
11th 'Electric' Year
Buddy
The BUDDY HOLLY Story
STRAND THEATRE
0171 930 8800

SCIENCE MUSEUM
If they want to play with electricity, let them
WARNING
OFF
ON
WHERE KIDS RUN FREE
THE SHOCK MACHINE IN 'THE SECRET LIFE OF THE HOME'
16s AND UNDER GO FREE
The Science Museum Exhibition Road London SW7 2DD Telephone: 020 7942 4000 Nearest tube station: South Kensington www.sciencemuseum.org.uk

Art in the park: the **Serpentine Gallery**.

Hyde Park

W2 (020 7298 2100). Hyde Park Corner, Knightsbridge, Lancaster Gate, Marble Arch or Queensway tube. **Open** 5am-midnight daily. **Map 2**

Hyde Park is central London's largest park – one-and-a-half miles long and just under a mile wide – and the first to be opened to the public (in the early seventeenth century). The park later developed a reputation as a fashionable place to see and be seen, despite being plagued by highwaymen and duelling nobles. Queen Caroline, a keen landscape gardener, was behind the damming of the Westbourne river to form the park's central feature, the **Serpentine**, in the 1730s. Joseph Paxton's magnificent Crystal Palace stood between the lake and the Prince of Wales Gate. This was the venue for the '**Great Exhibition** of the Works and Industry of All Nations' in 1851. Although phenomenally successful and visited by over six million people in less than six months, the palace was dismantled and rebuilt in south-east London in 1854; it burned down in 1936.

Today, Hyde Park's distractions are equally numerous – lounging in a deckchair, playing softball, boating on the lake, trotting a horse down **Rotten Row** (a corruption of 'route du roi', which William III laid out from the West End to Kensington Palace), listening to the Sunday soapbox orators revive the flagging British tradition of free speech at **Speaker's Corner** near Marble Arch – although its relative lack of vegetation can give it a barren appearance during the bleaker months. On royal anniversaries and other special occasions, a 41-gun salute is fired in the park, opposite the Dorchester Hotel in Park Lane.

Kensington Gardens

W8 (020 7298 2117). Bayswater, High Street Kensington, Lancaster Gate or Queensway tube. **Open** dawn-dusk daily. **Map 1**

The attraction of **Kensington Palace**'s (*see below*) extensive gardens (John Evelyn thought them 'very delicious') was part of the reason that William and Mary bought the house. Although the gardens now merge into Hyde Park, they were, in the early eighteenth century, laid out in a distinct formal Dutch style; they now have a considerably more natural appearance. Wander through the sunken garden, take tea at the **Orangery**, or gaze at the paintings in the **Serpentine Gallery** (*see below*). The huge **Round Pond** in the middle is a focus for little boys (most of them over 40) sailing their model boats. Close to the Long Water is the **Peter Pan statue**. Also for children, look out for Elfin Oak, puppet shows in summer and two playgrounds (one off Broad Walk and one near Black Lion Gate).

Kensington Palace

W8 (020 7937 9561). Bayswater, High Street Kensington or Queensway tube. **Open** 10am-4pm daily. **Admission** £9.50; £7.10 5s-15s; £7.70 OAPs, students, ES40s; £29.10 family. **Credit** AmEx, JCB, MC, £TC, V. **Map 1 B8**

Living near the river at Whitehall aggravated William III's chronic asthma, so, in 1689, he and Mary, looking for a more healthful home, bought the modest Jacobean mansion then known as Nottingham House. Wren and Hawksmoor (and, later, William Kent) were drafted in to redesign the building. Kensington Palace remained the favoured royal residence until the reign of George III, who preferred Buckingham House. The future Queen Victoria was born in the palace in 1819, and it has latterly been known as the last home of Princess Di (although she was only one of a number of royal residents). Plans were put forward a couple of years ago to convert the palace into a permanent memorial to the Princess and a home for the magnificent (but currently scattered) Royal Collection of art. The **Princess's dresses** are on show until the end of March 2000, after which the project may go ahead. Whether or not this happens, the palace is open for tours of the State Apartments, including the room where Queen Victoria was baptised, the King's Gallery with its fine seventeenth-century paintings, and the royal dress collection.
Website: www.hrp.org.uk

Serpentine Gallery

Kensington Gardens (nr Albert Memorial), W2 (020 7402 6075). Lancaster Gate or South Kensington tube. **Open** 10am-6pm daily. **Admission** free. **Map 2 D8**

The Serpentine has pursued an independent and lively curatorial policy that has won it many regular visitors. It is housed in a tranquil former tea pavilion with french windows looking out on to Hyde Park, imbuing the exhibitions with varying qualities of natural light (depending on the weather). In 2000 the Serpentine, in collaboration with the Natural History Museum (*see p96*), will present **The Greenhouse Effect**, a major exhibition of work by 20 young international artists exploring how art can reinvent or recreate the 'natural' world (3 Apr-28 May). Other planned events include a solo exhibition of Cuban conceptual artist **Felix Gonzalez-Torres** to coincide with the gallery's 30th birthday gala (2 June-16 July) and a show of new work by the American painter **Brice Marden** (Nov-Jan 2001).
Website: www.serpentinegallery.org

Three's company

A trip to London wouldn't be complete without a visit to at least one of the big three museums in South Kensington. They are located near to each other but it's unlikely you'll get around all three in one day (and it would be insane to try to do so). You're better off dedicating a day to each of them, though even this isn't usually enough time to appreciate their collections in full.

Note that all three museums sell an adult ticket that covers entry to the three museums for a year; it costs £24 (£42 for two adults; £13 concessions).

Natural History Museum

Cromwell Road, SW7 (020 7942 5000). South Kensington tube. **Open** 10am-5.50pm Mon-Sat; 11am-5.50pm Sun. *Guided tours* hourly 11am-4pm daily. **Admission** £6.50; £3.50 students, OAPs, ES40s; free under-16s; **free** for all after 4.30pm Mon-Fri; after 5pm Sat, Sun, public hols. *GoSee Card member (see p32).* **Credit** AmEx, MC, £TC, V. **Map 4 D10**

The Natural History Museum – built on the site of a second not-so-Great Exhibition, in 1862 – opened in 1881 to display the British Museum's burgeoning collection of natural history specimens. Split between the **Life Galleries** and the **Earth Galleries**, this is one of London's most innovative, absorbing and enjoyable museums. Alfred Waterhouse's stunning pink and gold, brick and terracotta building is as extraordinary as its contents, particularly the exquisitely painted ceiling and carved fauna details in the Central Hall where the famed cast of a Diplodocus skeleton stands.

The Life Galleries include the ever-popular **Dinosaurs**, the interactivity-rich **Human Biology** section, the **Creepy Crawlies** and the excellent **Mammals** and **Ecology** galleries. The opening of the Earth Galleries has transformed the old Geological Museum and achieved the seemingly impossible – making rocks interesting. An escalator ride up through a rotating globe takes you below the earth's crust to **The Power Within**: feel the force of an earthquake in a mock-up Kobe supermarket, and witness the eruption and devastation caused by a volcano. **From the Beginning** looks at the earth's history and development, and poses some searching questions about its future, particularly pertinent in the first year of the new millennium. A textbook example of how to make education fun.

The **British Natural History** exhibition is due to reopen in early 2000, as is the newly developed **Investigate** – a hands-on gallery for children.

Towards the end of 1999 plans were revealed for the creation of the ambitious **Darwin Centre**, aimed at increasing public understanding of science by allowing greater access to its collections. The first phase of the project is due to be completed by 2002.

Website: www.nhm.ac.uk

Science Museum

Exhibition Road, South Kensington, SW7 (020 7942 4454/4455/sciencemuseum@nmsi.ac.uk). South Kensington tube. **Open** 10am-6pm daily. **Admission** £6.50; £3.50 students, OAPs; season tickets available; free under-16s, ES40s, registered disabled & carer; **free** for all after 4.30pm daily. *GoSee Card member (see p32).* **Credit** AmEx, MC, £TC, V. **Map 4 D9**

The Science Museum makes the most of Britain's pioneering industrial heritage. Many of the original machines that powered civilisation towards the millennium are lovingly preserved here. Handily located and easy-to-use interactive screens help visitors negotiate five floors of technological wizardry, and the daily tours and shows, on a wide range of topics, are lively and fascinating. The place is crammed full of information; the **Synopsis** (in a side gallery), which gives an overview of the exhibits, is practically a museum in itself. Big hardware includes Stephenson's Rocket, a V2 missile and the Apollo 10 command module. Also exhibited are inventions that were spurned in their time, such as Charles Babbage's counting machine, a precursor of the computer.

If this all sounds a bit dry, don't be fooled: this place is a huge hit with kids, particularly the **Launch Pad** – a hands-on technological adventure playground, the **Flight Lab** where you can test the principles of flight, and **On Air**, where secondary-school children can produce their own radio shows. The basement is entirely given over to younger visitors, with hugely fun hands-on games and experiments for three- to 12-year-olds.

A recent addition to the museum's treasure trove is the **Challenge of Materials**, a permanent exhibition, which explores the design, creation, use and disposal of natural and manmade products, with loads of interactive exhibits and activities. The centrepiece is a stunning glass and steel bridge linking the two sides of the first-floor gallery, which responds to the pressure of people walking across it with video, sound and light effects. The second-floor exhibition focusing on the achievements of **Leonardo and Renaissance Engineers**, complete with working models and animated drawings, runs until 24 April 2000. There is an extra charge of £3 (adults) and £2 (children) for this exhibition.

The big news for 2000, however, is the opening of the £48-million **Wellcome Wing** in June. This vast extension, featuring four floors of exhibition space, will present the cutting edge of

contemporary science, medicine and technology using state-of-the-art exhibits and multimedia, and will also house an IMAX cinema. A new permanent exhibition, **Making the Modern World**, with displays drawn from existing collections, will link the old and new parts of the museum. In the meantime, visitors should note that some sections of the museum are likely to be closed.
Website: www.sciencemuseum.org.uk

Victoria & Albert Museum

Cromwell Road, SW7 (020 7938 8500). South Kensington tube. **Open** 10am-5.45pm daily (seasonal late view on Wed 6.30-9.30pm; phone for details). **Admission** £5; £3 OAPs; free under-18s, students, disabled & carer, ES40s; **free** for all after 4.30pm Mon-Fri, after 5pm Sat, Sun, bank hols; £15 season ticket. *GoSee Card member (see p32).* **Credit** AmEx, MC, V. **Map 4 E10**

The Victoria & Albert Museum (commonly known as the V&A) houses the world's greatest collection of decorative arts, as well as the national sculpture collection. Founded in 1852, and housed in Aston Webb's immense, sprawling, exceptionally grand building (1890), the V&A offers a staggering cross-cultural view of human achievement.

The **Art & Design** galleries are arranged thematically by place and date; the **Materials & Techniques** galleries by type of material. It is best to concentrate on certain areas of interest – it would be insane (and probably physically impossible) to try to cover all 145 galleries on one visit. Perhaps sample the world's largest collection of art from **India** outside the subcontinent, or the exceptional **Japanese Gallery** (look out for Hokusai's famous *Great Wave*), or the **Samsung Gallery of Korean Art**, with ceramics dating back to around AD300. Or come more up to date in the **Frank Lloyd Wright Gallery**, with some of the architect's applied art designs. The V&A's most famous exhibits are the **Raphael Cartoons** – seven vast designs for tapestries, based on episodes from the Acts of the Apostles, but almost equally popular are the superb **Dress** and **Jewellery** collections (*see picture*). The **British Galleries** are currently undergoing a massive £31-million refit (due to open in 2001).

Major exhibitions planned for 2000 include **Art Nouveau 1890-1914** (6 Apr-30 July), featuring paintings, sculpture, ceramics, glass, textiles and furniture, and **Brand New** (19 Oct-14 Jan 2001), which takes a look at the rise of global consumerism via a series of installations by young and influential designers.

The V&A held the first-ever exhibition of photography in 1858, so it's an appropriate home for the National Collection of the Art of Photography. The **Canon Photography Gallery** shows regularly changing displays – in 2000 these will include **Breathless: Photography and Time** (10 Feb-17 Sept), 'exploring movement, speed, growth and reflection through the photographer's lens'.

The museum shop is also excellent, as is the (pricey) café, and the jazz brunch/lunch every Sunday has become an institution (£9.50 including entrance to the museum).

In 1999, plans for Daniel Libeskind's eight-storey ceramic '**Spiral**' extension to the museum – due to be completed in 2004 – were given the go-ahead, although its construction could still be thwarted by conservative killjoys.
Website: www.vam.ac.uk

Chelsea

In a world of its own.

MAP 4

The name still has cachet. Chelsea may no longer be a 'village of palaces', as it was in the sixteenth century; it may now be too pricey to support an impoverished but formidably talented artistic community, as it did in the nineteenth century; the cutting-edge King's Road fashions of the 1960s and punk may have passed into folk memory; but Chelsea still thrives. This wedge-shaped piece of land, sandwiched between Kensington and the Thames, is now the province of identikit gorgeous blonde babes (mobile phones glued to their ears, noses held high), of long-resident, venerable *grandes dames*, and of the odd well-to-do writer (the century-old Chelsea Arts Club, at 143 Old Church Street, remains as popular as ever). It is the maintenance of this arts connection, together with abundant shopping opportunities, that give Chelsea a life and spark that districts like nearby Knightsbridge – where wealth is the sole god – can only envy.

Chelsea's central axis is the ever-vibrant **King's Road**. Once the private royal route to Hampton Court, it stretches south-west from snooty Sloane Square, gradually becoming more downmarket, particularly as it rounds the bend at World's End, where the pub of the same name stands, and then proceeds (as New King's Road) all the way to Putney Bridge.

The arts and commerce stare each other in the face in **Sloane Square**, where upmarket department store **Peter Jones** (housed in one of Britain's first glass-curtain buildings, built 1935-8) faces the ground-breaking **Royal Court Theatre** (*see page 293*). Among the works premièred here were many of George Bernard Shaw's plays, John Osborne's *Look Back in Anger* and Arnold Wesker's *Roots*, and the theatre continues to pioneer challenging new works.

Shopping has long been King's Road's *raison d'être*, and fashion remains dominant. Amid the high-street chains numerous boutiques survive, providing relatively affordable garb for a mainly youthful market. Just beyond the King's Road kink is Vivienne Westwood's **World's End** clothes store (no.430; *see also page 207*), with its sloping floor and backward-spinning clock. Known as Sex in the mid-1970s, it was here that the look of punk was born. Antiques are also much in evidence – try the excellent **Antiquarius** (nos.131-141; *see page 200*). Contemporary household desirables are available from **Habitat** (no.206; *see page 219*) and **Heal's** (no.224; *see page 219*). The most welcome development of recent years on King's Road is Sir Terence Conran's **Bluebird** gastrodome (no.350; *see pages 165 & 218*), combining a restaurant, a café, a cook shop and a fabulous food hall. Surprisingly, apart from the Bluebird, this is not a fruitful area for gourmets – high prices and a lack of imagination are the norm. Budget diners can eat for remarkably little at **Chelsea Kitchen** (no.98) or the **Stockpot** (no.273), while those with a little more to spend are probably best heading for the selection of eating spots in the peaceful Chelsea Farmers' Market on Sydney Street, near Kensington and Chelsea Town Hall.

DOWN BY THE RIVER

Chelsea's non-commercial attractions, and historical and artistic associations, are found between King's Road and the river. Just south of the huge Lots Road Power Station (providing much of the

A prospective customer of **World's End***?*

juice for the London underground network) is the somewhat spooky **Chelsea Harbour** development. Apartments for the super-rich, a hotel, offices, unapproachably swish designer shops and a handful of restaurants cluster around the mega-yachts in the marina. But where are all the people?

More rewarding sightseeing is provided further north on **Cheyne** (pronounced 'chain-ee') **Walk**. Handsome, blue plaque-bespattered houses testify to the extraordinary concentration of artistic and literary talent that was drawn to the area in the nineteenth century. George Eliot lived the last few weeks of her life at no.4; Dante Gabriel Rossetti, Algernon Charles Swinburne and George Meredith moved into no.16 (Queen's House) in 1862, where Rossetti kept a small but noisy menagerie, much to the irritation of his neighbours; Henry James lived and died in Carlyle Mansions. Other distinguished residents of the street include Mrs Gaskell (no.93), James McNeill Whistler (no.96), Hilaire Belloc (no.104) and JMW Turner (no.119).

Nearby, Oscar Wilde lovingly decorated his house at 16 Tite Street (now no.34) in whites, yellows, reds and blues. The more sober-minded historian, Thomas Carlyle, entertained the Victorian great and good at his home at 24 Cheyne Row. **Carlyle's House** (*see below*) has been preserved much as it was in those days.

The first big-name resident in Chelsea was that man for all seasons, Thomas More, who fell foul of axe-happy Henry VIII in 1535 for refusing to acknowledge the King's divorce from Catherine of Aragon. More's manor house has long since disappeared, but a gilt-faced statue of the 'scholar, saint, statesman' sits outside **Chelsea Old Church** (*see below*), where he built his own chapel, stoically gazing at the traffic pounding along Chelsea Embankment.

Past the delightful walled **Chelsea Physic Garden** (*see below*) on Royal Hospital Road is the impressive **National Army Museum** (*see page 99*). Appropriately housed in a bunker-like building, it offers an unexpectedly accessible insight into military life over the centuries. After a lifetime of service, a lucky few veterans might find themselves passing their twilight years next door in Wren's majestic **Royal Hospital Chelsea** (*see page 99*). Part of the hospital's grounds were once the location of **Ranelagh Gardens**, celebrated during the eighteenth century as a haunt of pleasure-seeking toffs. 'You can't set your foot without treading on a Prince, or Duke of Cumberland,' as Horace Walpole wrote. The eight-year-old Mozart gave a concert here in 1764. Canaletto's painting of the gardens can be seen in the National Gallery.

It's worth bearing in mind that most of this area is poorly served by the underground, so unless you're prepared for a fair bit of walking from Sloane Square tube, the best way to reach the sights is by bus.

Sights

Carlyle's House

24 Cheyne Row, SW3 (020 7352 7087).
Sloane Square tube/11, 19, 39, 45, 49, 219 bus.
Open *Apr-Oct* 11am-5pm Wed-Sun.
Admission £3.50; £1.75 5s-16s. **Map 3 E12**

Such was the contemporary renown of the 'Sage of Chelsea', the historian Thomas Carlyle, that within a few years of his death in 1881, the red-brick Queen Anne house where he'd lived since 1834 had been converted into a museum by public subscription. In the care of the National Trust since 1930, it is now watched over by a delightful live-in custodian who will regale visitors with stories of the many eminent visitors Carlyle and his feisty wife Jane entertained here, including Dickens, Thackeray, George Eliot and Ruskin. The roomy yet modest house remains much as it was in the Carlyles' time; it's easy to imagine the tempestuous couple in residence. Carlyle and Tennyson would smoke by the chimney in the basement kitchen, so that Jane didn't have to endure the smell.

Chelsea Old Church

Cheyne Walk, SW3 (020 7352 5627).
Sloane Square tube/11, 19, 39, 45, 49, 219 bus.
Open noon-4pm Mon-Fri; 8am-1pm, 2-7pm, Sun.
Admission free, donations welcome. **Map 4 E12**

It doesn't look very old – from the outside at least – but All Saints (as it's also known) traces its origins back to 1157. World War II bombing all but flattened the church, though the (rather cluttered) interior has a few points of interest, including the south chapel, built in 1528 by Sir Thomas More for his own private worship; a font from 1673; monuments to eminent local families such as the Lawrences and the Cheynes, and a memorial to Henry James. Look out also for the only chained books in a London church, the gift of Sir Hans Sloane, whose monument stands outside in the churchyard. Henry VIII is said to have married Jane Seymour in the church before their state wedding.
Website: www.domini.org/chelsea-old-church

Chelsea Physic Garden

66 Royal Hospital Road (entrance in Swan Walk), SW3 (020 7352 5646). Sloane Square tube/11, 19, 22, 239 bus. **Open** *2 Apr-29 Oct* noon-5pm Wed; 2-6pm Sun. **Admission** £4; £2 5s-16s, concs (not incl OAPs). **Credit** *shop only* MC, £TC, V. **Map 4 F12**

The walled confines of London's first botanical garden – it predates Kew Gardens by a century – provide blessed relief from the streaming traffic on Chelsea Embankment (note, though, the restricted opening hours). Established by the Apothecaries' Company in 1676, the garden was developed by Sir Hans Sloane in the early eighteenth century for 'the manifestation of the glory, power and wisdom of God, in the works of creation'. Today, it is primarily a research and educational facility, but even the uninitiated will make enlightening discoveries. Among the dye plants you'll find woad, which pre-Roman Britons fermented in stale urine to produce a violent blue face paint. In the greenhouses are the

Wing your way to foodie heaven at Conran's **Bluebird**. *See page 97.*

types of yams from which modern contraceptives and steroids were synthesised, as well as meadowsweet, source of the active ingredient of aspirin, discovered in 1899. The garden's other points of interest include a Grade I-listed rockery. Cotton seed sent from Chelsea to Georgia in 1732 helped to establish the American cotton industry. The gardens enjoy a microclimate, as evidenced by some of the trees found growing here – olive and cork among them. Guided tours are held if there is enough demand; otherwise there are two self-guided tours. From 9 July to 3 September 2000 a photographic show, **Timely Cures: Pharmaceutical Plants at the Millennium**, will run.
Website: www.cpgarden.demon.co.uk

National Army Museum

(by the Chelsea Royal Hospital) Royal Hospital Road, SW3 (020 7730 0717). Sloane Square tube/11, 19, 239 bus. **Open** 10am-5.30pm daily. **Admission** free. **Map 4 F12**

An admirable attempt to make the history of the British soldier – from Agincourt to Bosnia – accessible for the non-martially inclined. The imaginatively displayed permanent exhibits include **The Victorian Soldier**, which traces the history of the British Army in peace and war from 1816 to 1914 across the world; **The Road to Waterloo** (featuring a huge model of the battle, complete with 75,000 mini-soldiers and three specially commissioned films); and **The Modern Army**, with exhibitions on the Gulf War and Bosnia, where you can brush up on army slang and test your map-reading skills. All this is done with lifesize figures of soldiers from different eras, plus film footage and memorabilia such as letters from POWs in Japan, and more quirky exhibits such as the skeleton of Napoleon's beloved Arab stallion, Marengo. The **Art Gallery** contains portraits by Reynolds and Gainsborough. Phone for details of temporary exhibitions. The museum also contains a small café and a shop.

Throughout 2000, as part of the **London String of Pearls Millennium Festival** (*see page 8* **London's your oyster**), the museum will be holding a series of talks about life in the army.
Website: www.national-army-museum.ac.uk

Royal Hospital Chelsea

Royal Hospital Road, SW3 (020 7730 5282). Sloane Square tube/11, 19, 22, 137 bus. **Open** *museum, chapel & hall* 10am-noon, 2-4pm, Mon-Sat; 2-4pm Sun (closed Sun in winter). **Admission** free. **Map 4 F12**

The grandest old age pensioners' home in the country, the Royal Hospital was inspired by Louis XIV's Hôtel des Invalides in Paris. Charles II wanted an equally splendid home for his veteran soldiers and, in 1682, commissioned Christopher Wren to construct the present structure around three courtyards. 'Quiet and dignified and the work of a gentleman,' in the words of Thomas Carlyle, the hospital is still home to around 400 ex-servicemen, whose uniforms of navy blue (for everyday wear) and scarlet (for ceremonial occasions) are nationally recognised. Visitors can peek at the harmonious, barrel-vaulted chapel, with its florid depiction of the *Resurrection* by Sebastiano Ricci over the altar, and the equally fine hall opposite, still in use as the pensioners' refectory. In the central, south-facing courtyard stands a bronze statue of Charles II in Roman garb by Grinling Gibbons (1676), gazing across the grounds (site of the Chelsea Flower Show every May, *see p7*) and the river to Battersea Power Station. On Oak Apple Day (29 May), pensioners parade in the courtyard and dress the statue in oak foliage to commemorate the King's birthday and his escape from the Battle of Worcester when he hid in the Boscobel Oak. The museum has a collection of medals, and records of the hospital dating back to its foundation.

North London

Sights or scenery... the choice is yours.

Camden Town

You have to throw yourself in at the deep end with **Camden**; there is no shallow end. As you walk out of the tube station on to the grubby high street, waves of goths, punks, ravers and hippies try to stuff flyers advertising small clubs or tiny shops into your hands; the well-scrubbed denizens of the area's more respectable streets expertly sidestep incoherently cackling winos; the pungent aromas of fried onions and takeaway kebabs fill the air; cranked-up sound systems pulse out. It's all part of the Camden experience. Most people come for the cram-packed markets, some for the quieter pleasures of Sunday afternoon bookshop browsing or a cruise down the canal. More realistically, after a few hours spent here at the weekend – Camden's busiest time, when all the markets are open – your favourite place is likely to be a seat on the tube, taking you to comparative calm elsewhere.

Camden Town, an area that – in the vernacular, at least – stretches from Victorian politician Richard Cobden's statue at Mornington Crescent, up Camden High Street to the borders of **Chalk Farm**, has undergone a sea change in the past 30 years. From 1816, when the Regent's Canal and, later, the railway were laid out, the area became built up with cheap lodging houses, which had a reputation for rough characters. After 1905, artist Walter Sickert, who lodged at Mornington Crescent and Fitzroy Street, led the so-called Camden Town Group, who rebelled against high-brow and symbolist composition.

Irish and, after 1945, Greek Cypriots, migrated to Camden; traces of the latter are still visible in the scattered Greek tavernas and cafés, and the Greek Orthodox church near the Royal Veterinary College (founded in 1791) on Royal College Street. Until the late 1960s, this was still a slum area; a surge in property prices, coupled with Camden's popularity with hippies as a (relatively) cheap bohemian hangout (it's no coincidence that the struggling actors in the film *Withnail & I* live here) brought the place into new repute. Then the professional classes (and media celebs such as Alan Bennett and Michael Palin) moved in, renovating houses in some of Camden's lovely crescents. The influx of money shows itself in buildings, such as Nicholas Grimshaw's hi-tech Sainsbury's supermarket on Camden Road, and the new **Glass Building** on Jamestown Road – ultra-popular noodle chain **Wagamama** and **The Body Shop** have recently moved in here; the upper floors are luxury loft apartments.

Camden and its environs have plenty to offer visitors. First, and definitely foremost, are the **markets** (*see page 222* **Market forces**). Since the early 1970s, these have expanded massively, becoming one of London's most popular tourist attractions. On market days the tube station now strains at the seams, and fears for passenger safety have caused London Transport to make Camden Town tube an entry-only station. At the weekends visitors are forced to leave the area from either Mornington Crescent or Chalk Farm stations, the latter being a more pleasant (and shorter) walk from the market. The crush may be relieved further if plans to pedestrianise the High Street north of Camden Town tube station come to fruition.

The impressive **Jewish Museum** (*see page 102*) on Albert Street, just off Parkway, also deserves a visit – a reflection, along with a variety of restaurants and bars, of the area's cultural diversity. Try the hip Caribbean **Mango Room** (*see page 169*), the irreverent moules-frites minimalism of **Belgo Noord** (*see page 168*) or the top-rank foodie pub, the **Engineer** (*see page 186*).

If it's a scorcher outside, cool down with one of the great sorbets or ice-creams at **Marine Ices**, opposite Chalk Farm tube. Close by is the famous **Roundhouse** on Chalk Farm Road, originally a turning point for trams, and now a multipurpose venue for everything from exhibitions and plays to circuses, gigs, the odd illegal rave and (during 1999 and extending into 2000) the unclassifiable Argentinian hi-energy dance/music/circus extravaganza De La Guarda. There are plans to convert the maze of tunnels underneath the Roundhouse into a creative arts centre, housing multimedia production suites and community workshops.

AROUND CAMDEN

Moving north, green relief is provided by charming **Primrose Hill** and, at the edge of Hampstead Heath, **Gospel Oak,** from which the kite-flyers of **Parliament Hill** are a short walk away. As Camden has grown it seems to have swallowed its neighbours. Fat cat retail outlets have moved in, causing small local shops in neighbouring areas to suffer. **Kentish Town** has now become a series of bargain stores and cheap eateries, linking Camden to **Highgate** and **Tufnell Park**. There have been, nevertheless, benefits from the social

Get as high as a kite on **Hampstead Heath**. *See page 104.*

elevation of its southern neighbour, such as the ceaseless conversions of traditional London boozers into modern 'gastropubs' (although not everyone sees this as 'progress'). Travel along Highgate Road, past one of London's busiest music venues, the **Forum** (*see page 276*), and stop for nosh and a pint at **The Vine** or the **Bull & Last** (at nos.86 and 168 respectively; *see page 186*).

Squeezed between Camden and King's Cross is **Somers Town**, dominated by huge '60s and '70s council housing developments, and blighted further by ongoing tensions between its young white and Asian communities. Eversholt Street boasts the extraordinary **Transformation** (motto: '*From He to She*'), the world's largest transvestite emporium. The window display is worth a picture in itself. A little further east, the **Camley Street Natural Park** offers a much-needed injection of bucolic charm amid the railway sheds and gas works. The **Regent's Canal** runs along one side of the park and enthusiasts for man-made waterways might like to check out the nearby **Canal Museum** (*see below*).

Canal Museum

12-13 New Wharf Road, N1 (020 7713 0836). King's Cross tube/rail. **Open** 10am-4.30pm Tue-Sun. **Admission** £2.50; £1.25 8s-16s, students, OAPs. **Map 6 L2**

The warehouse housing this small museum on the Regent Canal's Battlebridge Basin was built in the 1850s by an Italian immigrant, Carlo Gatti, who made his fortune importing ice from Norway. The blocks were carried from the docks on canal boats and stored here in huge ice wells. The museum tells the story of Gatti's life and the families who made their living on the canals.

Website: www.charitynet.org/~LCanalMus

Jewish Museum, Camden

129-131 Albert Street, NW1 (020 7284 1997). Camden Town tube. **Open** 10am-4pm Mon-Thur, Sun. **Admission** £3; £1.50 5s-16s; £2 students, OAPs, disabled; free under-5s.

London's two-sited Jewish Museum (*see also p108* **Jewish Museum, Finchley**) has been recognised as one of Britain's pre-eminent museums. It's easy to see why. Although both sites are relatively small, they contain a wealth of information. Camden's branch is more formal: three galleries detailing Jewish British history, an exhibition area and, upstairs, a floor of effectively displayed ceremonial objects such as a series of rimmonim (the decorative silver tops of Torah scrolls), Hanukkah lamps and a magnificent Venetian synagogue ark, dating from the sixteenth century. This quiet building, smelling of fresh wood, lends itself to a thoughtful experience: there are helpful volunteers on hand always ready to furnish further information. A major exhibition, **Judaica 2000 – Contemporary British Jewish Ceremonial Art** (late Mar/early Apr-3 Sept 2000), features outstanding examples of contemporary Judaica made in Britain, including examples of textiles, metalwork and stained glass.

Website: www.jewmusm.ort.org

St John's Wood

To the west of Regent's Park is a wealthy enclave containing, perhaps, the world's most famous cricket ground, **Lord's**, home to the **MCC Museum** (*see below*). Grove End Road leads from here into **Abbey Road**, where the Beatles recorded their legendary LP at EMI Studios (no.3). The zebra crossing outside is always busy with Japanese and American tourists capturing that ineffable Beatles moment on film and scrawling their names on the wall. Further up Abbey Road, at 98A Boundary Road, is the former paint factory that's now home to the **Saatchi Gallery** (*see page 103*). One of London's major spaces for contemporary art, the gallery has helped turn fringe Britpack artists into the current mainstream.

MCC Museum

Marylebone Cricket Club, Lord's Ground, St John's Wood Road, NW8 (020 7432 1033). St John's Wood tube/13, 46, 82, 113, 274 bus. **Open** *guided tours* (phone for availability) *Oct-Mar* noon, 2pm, daily; *Apr-Sept* 10am, noon, 2pm, daily. **Admission** *guided tours* £6; £4.40 5s-15s, students, OAPs, ES40s.

Cricket fans will be delighted by this entertainingly anecdotal exhibition of the some of the game's most famous memorabilia. Among the paintings, photographs and significantly battered bats, there's a reconstruction of the notorious shot that killed a passing sparrow in 1936, complete with stuffed bird and the ball. The Ashes reside here: not much bigger than an egg cup, the sport's most hard-won trophy contains the charred remains of one of the bails from the 1882-3 Test series between England and Australia. The informative guided tour allows visitors to view the empty ground from the Mound stand, and continues with a lingering wander through the pavilion, the visitors' dressing room and the historic Long Room. When not in use (most of the time in winter), the impressive, startlingly-designed NatWest Media Centre (*see also p30*) forms part of the tour.
Website: www.lords.org

Saatchi Gallery

98A Boundary Road, NW8 (020 7624 8299/ 7328 8299). St John's Wood or Swiss Cottage tube/ 139, 189 bus. **Open** noon-6pm Thur-Sun. **Admission** £4; £2 concs; free under-12s. **Credit** MC, V.
Charles Saatchi's advertising fortune enabled him to become a mover and shaker in the art world. A decade ago he visited the Freeze exhibition in Docklands and fell in love with contemporary British art. Whoever he buys now, everyone else will be watching. Similarly, whoever he sells is also noted. Not surprisingly, the large, purpose-built space has also seen some extraordinary temporary exhibitions. The traits of the ad man have not left Saatchi, and the knack for a good phrase is still there. Having created the half-truth of the Young British Artists, he's since been attempting to come up with a term for a brand new movement. Neurotic

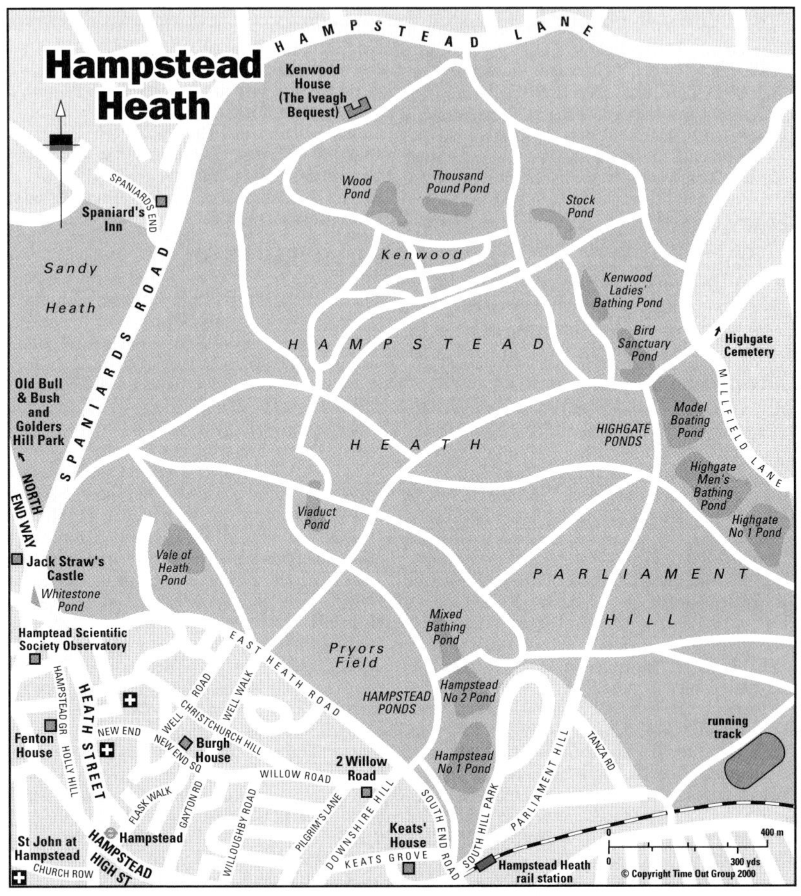

Realism is the result, a phrase that sounds good but hardly sums up the work chosen for the two exhibitions that were handed this title. **Neurotic Realism Part Two**, which ran until December 1999, included work by Dexter Dalwood, Peter Davies, David Falconer, Mark Hosking and Tom Hunter. Time will tell if the phrase gains currency. For early 2000 (until April) Saatchi presents **Eurovision**, featuring painting and photography by five artists from Germany, Holland, Finland, Switzerland and Spain. Richard Wilson's *20:50*, an installation in sump pump oil and galvanised steel, is the sole fixture at this gallery (in an adjacent room); this alone makes a visit worthwhile.

Hampstead

Perched at the top of a hill alongside the 325-hectare (800-acre) Heath, insular, villagey **Hampstead** has long been popular with the literati and chattering classes (although not with Ezra Pound, who thought it 'a more hideous form of Boston'). Pope and Gay took the waters here during its brief time as a spa; Wilkie Collins, Thackeray and Dickens drank at **Jack Straw's Castle** (on North End Way); and Keats strolled on the Heath with Coleridge and Wordsworth. Much of Keats's best work was composed in his house in Wentworth Place; it was in its garden that he heard his nightingale. Happily, Hampstead's hilly geography has prevented the sort of urbanisation that Camden has suffered, and it remains, together with **Highgate**, a haven for much of London's (monied) intelligentsia and literary bigwigs. It's entirely appropriate that Hampstead's MP is ex-actress Glenda Jackson.

A TOUR OF HAMPSTEAD

Hampstead tube station stands at the top of the steep High Street, lined with opulent but unthrilling shops and bars. Running north, and further uphill, from here is Heath Street. Don't miss the dark and inviting **Louis Pâtisserie** (no.32) for tea and fabulously sticky mittel-European cakes. It's a reminder of how much German, Viennese and Hungarian émigrés have contributed to NW3 since the 1930s. Just off the southern end of Heath Street is **Church Row**, one of Hampstead's most beautiful streets, with twin lines of higgeldy-piggeldy terraces leading down to **St John at Hampstead**, where painter John Constable and his wife lie at rest in the sylvan graveyard. Close by, on Holly Hill,is possibly Hampstead's nicest pub, the **Hollybush** (*see page 197*); while another minute's climb brings you to **Fenton House** (*see page 105*) on Hampstead Grove, with its fine porcelain and paintings. The celestially inclined might like to gaze skyward at the nearby **Hampstead Scientific Society Observatory** (Lower Terrace; 020 8346 1056; open Sept-Mar 8-10pm Fri, Sat; 11am-1pm Sun and for times of interest such as when comets are passing; admission free). On Hampstead's southern fringes, in Maresfield Gardens, is the house where Sigmund Freud lived the last year of his life, having fled Nazi persecution in Vienna in 1938 (now the **Freud Museum**; *see page 105*). Nearby is **Camden Arts Centre** (*see page 105*), with its eclectic programme of exhibitions.

East of Heath Street is a maze of attractive streets that shelters **Burgh House** on New End Square (a Queen Anne house that now houses a small museum) and **2 Willow Road** (*see page 106*), a modernist house built by Hungarian-born Ernö Goldfinger for himself in the 1930s. Ian Fleming hated the work of Goldfinger (who also designed Trellick Tower; *see page 137*) so much he named one of his Bond villains after him. Nearby, off Keats Grove, is **Keats' House** (*see page 105*). Around the corner, on South Hill Park, Ruth Ellis shot her former boyfriend outside the Magdala pub in 1955 (look for the bullet holes in the wall). She had the dubious claim to fame of being the last woman to be hanged in Britain.

Nearby, on Rosslyn Hill (the southern continuation of Hampstead High Street), is one of the area's few stylish all-day eating and drinking venues: **Giraffe** (no.46; *see page 184*), as well as the foodie delights of the excellent **Rosslyn Delicatessen** (no.56).

HAMPSTEAD HEATH

The **Heath** (*see map page 103*) is Hampstead's chief and enduring glory. A Sunday afternoon tramp across its varied landscapes is essential therapy for any jaded Londoner, while a dip in the swimming ponds and a picnic at one of the summer lakeside concerts at **Kenwood House** (*see page 106*) are equal institutions.

Not far from Kenwood, on the northern perimeter, is the old **Spaniard's Inn** pub (haunted, it is said, by the ghost of a highwayman). To the west lies the weather-boarded pub **Jack Straw's Castle** (named after one of the leaders of the 1381 Peasants' Revolt) and **Whitestone Pond**, where grown men play with model boats. Ignoring, if you wish, the gay men cruising about the **West Heath**'s leafy undergrowth, head off for **Golders Hill Park**, with its small menageries of deer, goats and birds. While you're here, drop into the **Old Bull & Bush** pub on North End Road to sing a few choruses of the music hall song, 'Come, come, come and make eyes at me/Down at the old Bull and Bush.'

Or, if you want utter tranquillity, follow the long stone walkway on the left behind the new housing development on North End Way (coming up from Jack Straw's Castle) until you stumble upon the all-but-secret **Hill Garden** with its goldfish pond and wonderful collections of plants and rare trees set in landscaped grounds. On a clear day, the views from here are superb.

Gorgeous, eclectic **Fenton House**.

Camden Arts Centre

Arkwright Road, corner of Finchley Road, NW3 (020 7435 2643). Finchley Road tube.
Open 11am-7pm Tue-Thur; 11am-5.30pm Fri-Sun.
Admission free.

The borough of Camden's community arts centre includes three gallery spaces, which host contemporary exhibitions and one historical show a year. There is a programme of talks by artists, usually responding to the current exhibitions (phone for details). During 2000 the centre will be exhibiting work by **John Riddy** and **Juan Cruz** (31 Mar-21 May), **Yinka Shonibare** (June-July), **Martin Creed** and **Simon Starling** (Nov-Jan 2001); plus the international group show **Dream Machine** – contemporary and historical works selected by Susan Hiller (June-July).

Fenton House

Hampstead Grove, NW3 (020 7435 3471). Hampstead tube. **Open** *Apr-Oct* 2-5pm Wed-Fri; 11am-5pm Sat, Sun, public hols (last entry 4.30pm).
Admission £4.20; £2.10 5s-15s.
Map *see p103.*

This gem of a house, built in 1693 in William and Mary style, is one of the earliest and largest houses in Hampstead. It houses the excellent Benton Fletcher Collection of Early Keyboard Instruments, which can be heard in action during the summer at fortnightly baroque concerts (phone for details). Other exhibits include a quirky range of pottery poodles in the Rockingham Room and Chinese snuff-boxes and ninth-century porcelain in the Oriental Room. The four attic rooms have retained the atmosphere of a seventeenth-century property with impressive views over London. Entry to the garden (one side is beautifully landscaped; the other contains an orchard and vegetable patch) is free.

Freud Museum

20 Maresfield Gardens, NW3 (020 7435 2002/5167). Finchley Road tube/Finchley Road & Frognal rail. **Open** noon-5pm Wed-Sun. **Admission** £4; £2 students, OAPs, disabled, ES40s; free under-12s.
Credit AmEx, MC, V.

This Arts and Crafts-style house is where Sigmund Freud spent his last year (1938-9) after leaving Vienna and Nazi persecution. It was here that he finished his final master work, *Moses and Monotheism*, and received visitors such as HG Wells and Salvador Dalí. On the ground floor is a faithful reproduction of Freud's Viennese study, complete with rug-bedecked couch and a few of the antique figurines he loved to collect. Upstairs are artefacts belonging to his daughter Anna, a leading child analyst who lived here until her death in 1982. Various displays and a short video illuminate the Freud clan (including a young Lucian) in action. Freud heritage merchandise and a small range of books is sold.
Website: www.freud.org.uk

Hampstead Heath

NW3 (Parliament Hill 020 7485 4491/Golders Hill 020 8455 5183). Belsize Park or Hampstead tube/Gospel Oak or Hampstead Heath rail/24, C2, C11 bus. **Open** 24 hours daily. **Map** *see p103.*

One of London's most popular and varied green spaces, the rolling, semi-landscaped Heath has something for everyone. You can jog, stroll, sunbathe, picnic, swim in the ponds or Parliament Hill Lido (*see p288*), walk the dog, play football, fish, or fly a kite from the top of Parliament Hill. Alternatively, just sit and admire the views, which, on a clear day, take in the whole of central London. There are band concerts on summer Sunday afternoons on Golders and Parliament hills, as well as bowls (020 7284 3779) and guided walks (020 7482 7073). Visit **Kenwood House** to see the wonderful **Iveagh Bequest** (*see p106*) collection of paintings, and look for one of Kenwood's hidden treasures: the beautifully restored **Romany Buckland Caravan**, in a small building near the Coach House restaurant. On Saturday evenings in summer, thousands make their way to Kenwood for the lakeside **concerts** (*see p274*). Funfairs are held, at the upper and lower ends of the Heath, on the Easter, May and August bank holidays (*see p5*). A diary of events taking place on the Heath is available at information points.
Bathing ponds: men only, women only & mixed (summer 7am-sunset daily; admission free).
Tennis courts (020 7284 3779).

Keats' House

Wentworth Place, Keats Grove, NW3 (020 7435 2062). Hampstead Heath rail/Hampstead tube/24, 46, 168 bus. **Open** phone to check. **Admission** free.
Map *see p103.*

Keats wrote some of his best-loved poems and fell in love with Fanny Brawne while living in this cutesy Regency cottage (1818-20). A plum tree in the garden marks the site of the original tree beneath which he is thought to have penned his *Ode to a Nightingale*. Cabinets within the house contain original manuscripts, and visitors can nose around the poet's bedroom, living room and kitchen. The house reopened in 1998 after major restoration work on the roof. More work is planned, so phone to check that the house is open before setting off.

Kenwood House/Iveagh Bequest

Kenwood House, Hampstead Lane, NW3 (020 8348 1286). Golders Green tube then 210 bus.
Open *Apr-Sept* 10am-6pm daily; *Oct-Mar* 10am-4pm daily. **Admission** free, donations appreciated.
Map *see p103.*
This elegant mansion overlooking Hampstead Heath from its northern fringe was rebuilt in classical style for the Earl of Mansfield by Robert Adam in 1767-9 and bequeathed to the nation in 1927. Inside, the house contains a number of fine pieces of furniture, but the chief attraction is the **Iveagh Bequest** collection of paintings. Look out for one of Rembrandt's self-portraits (a guaranteed original, unlike so many others); a rare Vermeer in the dining room; and Romney's portrait of Nelson's mistress, Lady Hamilton, dressed up as a nun. Botticelli, Guardi and a couple of classic flirtatious Bouchers round out this wonderful collection. The sumptuous library is also worth a gawp. Exhibitions planned for 2000 include **The British at Table: 1600-2000**, an exhibition focusing on food and eating habits (27 June-24 Sept).

2 Willow Road

2 Willow Road, NW3 (020 7435 6166). Hampstead Heath rail/Hampstead tube.
Open *Apr-Oct* noon-5pm Thur-Sat (last entry 4pm). **Admission** £4.20; £2.10 5s-15s. **Map** *see p103.*
Ernö Goldfinger's pioneering piece of domestic modernist architecture looks as striking today as it did when it was built in 1939. Its purchase by the National Trust was a brave move, but one that has paid off. Before being taken on an informative guided tour of the house, visitors watch a short video explaining Goldfinger's philosophy of design described as 'structural rationalism'. Space is used economically throughout the building, with beds and bathrooms in closets, and a unique spiral staircase through the centre of the house. This was the Goldfinger family home and still contains much of its original contents including furniture he designed himself. There is also a collection of twentieth-century art, including works by Henry Moore and Max Ernst. Hour-long tours run from 12.15pm to 4pm every 45 minutes.
Website: www.nationaltrust.org.uk

Highgate

East of Hampstead Heath, and perched on a hill of its own, is graceful **Highgate**. Once a remote settlement, impassable in winter snows, the area gets its name from an old tollgate that once stood on the site of the **Gate House** pub on the High Street; dinky shops now predominate. There are fine views from the top of **Highgate Hill**. At the foot of the hill, it's said that **Dick Whittington**, on the point of leaving town, heard Bow bells peel out 'Turn again Whittington, thrice Lord Mayor of London Town'. (The bells underestimated his potential – he became mayor on four occasions in the late fourteenth/early fifteenth century.) This momentous and entirely fictitious event is commemorated on the Whittington Stone, near the eponymous hospital. He didn't have a cat either.

Top Marx for **Highgate Cemetery**.

North of Highgate tube station, **Highgate Wood** and **Queen's Wood** offer shady walks plus refreshments in the former at **Oshobasho Café** (closed on Mondays). Highgate's best-known sight is **Highgate Cemetery** on Swain's Lane (*see below*), one of London's great burial grounds. Adjoining the cemetery is beautiful **Waterlow Park** (*see below*). Further down Swain's Lane, you can peep through the Gothic entrance to **Holly Village**, a private village built in 1865, complete with its own village green. Hornsey Lane, on the other side of Highgate Hill, leads you to the **Archway** (or 'Suicide Bridge'), a Victorian viaduct built high over what is now the A1 and offering vertiginous views of the City and East End.

Highgate Cemetery

Swain's Lane, N6 (020 8340 1834). Archway tube/ C11, 271 bus. **Open** *East Cemetery Apr-Oct* 10am-5pm Mon-Fri; 11am-5pm Sat, Sun; *Nov-Mar* 10am-4pm Mon-Fri; 11am-4pm Sat, Sun. *West Cemetery tours Apr-Oct* noon, 2pm, 4pm, Mon-Fri; 11am, noon, 1pm, 2pm, 3pm, 4pm, Sat, Sun; *Nov-Mar* 11am, noon, 1pm, 2pm, 3pm, Sat, Sun. **Admission** *East Cemetery* £2; *West Cemetery tour* £3.
Opened in 1839, Highgate is London's most famous and exotic graveyard. The East Cemetery, apart from being the last resting place of Karl Marx, is rather drab, and something of a let-down, although it's worth seeking out the tomb of Mary Anne Evans (alias George Eliot). The West Cemetery, however, is a romantic wilderness of tombs and catacombs, but can only be visited on one of the excellent guided tours. Highlights include the mystical, family vault-lined Egyptian Avenue, the eerie catacombs and the elaborate mausoleum of seventeenth-century media tycoon Julius Beer. Eminent Victorians residing here include such contrasting figures as chemist Michael Faraday and celebrated barefist-fighter Tom Sayers (whose funeral attracted a crowd of 100,000). Note that children of eight and under are not allowed on the tours. Photography in the cemetery is only allowed with a camera permit (£2).

Waterlow Park

Highgate Hill, N6 (020 7272 2825). Archway tube/C11, 271 bus. **Open** 7.30am-dusk daily.

A small, beautiful park next to Highgate Cemetery, with steep slopes, ponds, magnificent trees and a mini-aviary. It was bequeathed to the people by former owner Sydney Waterlow as 'a garden for the gardenless'. As well as tennis courts, a putting green and a dog-free play area for the under-fives, there's a garden café in sixteenth-century **Lauderdale House** (020 8348 8716). The park takes part in London's annual **Jazz in the Park** festival in June (phone for details). For 2000 there are plans to exhibit sculptures in the park, and hold organised performance trails whereby audiences follow actors around the park as they act out different scenes.

Islington

MAP 9

Islington's fortunes have ebbed and flowed over time. Henry VIII owned several houses here and liked to hunt nearby. 'Merry Islington', then a village on a hill, was renowned for its dairy farms and local spring water. In the nineteenth century, it was known for its smart shopping streets, theatres and music halls, but its fortunes plummeted in the early twentieth century and the area became depopulated and run-down.

These days Islington is decidedly of two parts. Like so much of London, its Georgian squares and Victorian terraces have been gentrified in the past 25 years and rising property prices have succeeded in pushing out some of its poorer population. This means that the middle classes (and until a few years ago, that epitome of focaccia socialism, Richmond Crescent's Tony Blair and family) have colonised Islington. They are appropriately served by **Camden Passage**'s antique shops, **Waterstone's** bookshop (once the Collins Music Hall), bijou restaurants (including **Granita** – *see page 166* – where Blair and cohorts hatched their idea of New Labour), an independent cinema (the **Screen on the Green**; *see page 260*), music at the gorgeous Victorian **Union Chapel** (*see page 282*), and theatre at the **King's Head** (*see page 298*) and wonderful **Almeida** (*see page 297*) – a home to contemporary classical music and high-quality fringe theatre. It's easy to forget that Islington and its chic Canonbury and Highbury neighbours are close to ramshackle housing projects like Essex Road's Marquess Estate.

Islington is best taken at a stroll, starting at **Angel** tube station, and walking along **Upper Street**, past the glass façade of the **Business Design Centre** (which hides the former Royal Agricultural Hall) and triangular Green and up to Highbury, where the swimming pool is bordered by an award-winning children's playground. This way, you'll take in the shops – such as the art deco lamps at **Out of Time** on 21 Canonbury Lane, and the vinyl delights of **Reckless Records** (79 Upper Street). For sustenance, try the fish and chips at the **Upper Street Fish Shop** (no.324; *see page 172*) or a slap-up fry-up at **Alfredo's**, opposite Islington Green on Essex Road. Indian restaurants around Penton Street and the vegetable stalls at **Chapel Market** round out the picture. The area's famous residents include Charles Lamb (64 Duncan Terrace) and Joe Orton, killed by his lover, Kenneth Halliwell, at their top-floor bedsit at 25 Noel Street in 1967.

Before striking out for **Highbury** and beyond, sample the architectural delights of Regency **Canonbury Square** and **Compton Terrace**, both well-maintained pieces of architectural history. The square, once home to George Orwell (no.27) and Evelyn Waugh (no.17A), houses the **Canonbury Tower**, which affords great views (phone the Canonbury Academy on 020 7359 6888 to arrange admission). This is Islington's oldest monument, with possibly Roman foundations. In its present state, however, it is all that remains of Tudor mansion **Canonbury House**, whose former residents include Sir Francis Bacon and Oliver Goldsmith. Restored in 1907, two of the tower's rooms contain Elizabethan oak panels. Also on the square is the dedicated **Estorick Collection of Modern Italian Art** (*see below*).

The **Little Angel Theatre** (*see page 237*) is past **St Mary's Church** (where Wesley preached) on Dagmar Passage, and, just beyond, the fine eighteenth-century houses of Cross Street line the slope towards Essex Road. **Highbury Fields**, at the north end of Upper Street, was where 200,000 Londoners fled to escape the Great Fire of 1666 (*see page 16*). Beyond this open space, on the way to Finsbury Park, lies compact **Highbury Stadium**, home to **Arsenal** Football Club: nicknamed 'the Gunners', the team's origins lie in south London's Woolwich munitions works.

Estorick Collection of Modern Italian Art

39A Canonbury Square, N1 (main entrance Canonbury Road; 020 7704 9522). Highbury & Islington tube/rail/271 bus. **Open** 11am-6pm Wed-Sat; noon-5pm Sun. **Admission** £3.50; free under-16s; £2.50 concs.

Housed in a Georgian listed building, the Estorick is Britain's first museum dedicated to modern Italian art. The collection of American academic and art dealer Eric Estorick and his wife Salome contains a truly wonderful selection of futurist work, including pieces by leading lights Luigi Russolo, Umberto Boccioni and Gino Severini. Many other major Italian artists are represented, including Modigliani and de Chirico. Long-term loans from other private collections and a café complete the picture. In 2000, the temporary exhibition programme features **Primo Conti: A Futurist Prodigy** (15 Mar-21 May); **Futurist Photography 1911-1939** (2 June-17 Sept); and **Fortunato Depero** (4 Oct-22 Dec).

Website: www.estorickcollection.com

Dalston & Stoke Newington

Bishopsgate in the City passes through Shoreditch and becomes Kingsland High Street, otherwise known as the A10, the busy main road that runs out through Dalston, Stoke Newington, past the Hassidic enclave of Stamford Hill, via Tottenham and out of London altogether.

Though scruffy and, at times, intimidating, **Dalston** is also a vibrant place: there are several kosher shops, including the round-the-clock **Bagel Bakery** at 13-15 Ridley Road, and, along the same road, bustling market stalls selling Afro-Caribbean vegetables. Lots of the small cafés and late-night restaurants reflect the Turkish influx into the area.

Middle-class house buyers started moving in to **Stoke Newington** in a big way after 1980. Green spaces can be found at **Clissold Park** (which includes a small zoo and tearooms) and the rambling old boneyard of **Abney Park Cemetery**, which took over from Bunhill Fields as a burial ground for dissenters and Nonconformists; General Booth, founder of the Salvation Army, is buried here. Attractive, villagey Stoke Newington Church Street contains a number of good restaurants: **Rasa** (no.55; *see page 174*) is famed for its superlative vegetarian south Indian cooking, and the hippie café **Blue Legume** (no.101) has a great laid-back vibe. **Vortex** (no.139; *see page 283*) combines jazz venue, café and wine bar in one atmospheric building. At weekends, the street is enlivened by a small arts and crafts market.

Further north

Moving towards the northern perimeter of London, dull suburban streets are enlivened by the immigrant communities that have made them their home. **Golders Green**, **Hendon** (where the impressive **Royal Air Force Museum** is located; *see below*) and **Finchley** have large Jewish communities; you'll still find plenty of Jewish restaurants and shops selling kosher delicacies. Finchley is home to London's second **Jewish Museum** (*see below*). Golders Green is also the focus of a growing population of Chinese and Japanese City workers. There has been a Jewish cemetery on Hoop Lane since 1895 – the cellist Jacqueline du Pré is buried here. Across the road, the fires of **Golders Green Crematorium** have consumed hundreds of notable bodies, including those of TS Eliot, Marc Bolan and Anna Pavlova.

Tottenham and **Haringey** retain a strong Greek Cypriot and Turkish Cypriot identity. Both areas are fun for the sweet-toothed wanting to try a few honey-soaked pastries, or the fabulous kebab shops of Green Lanes. **Cricklewood**'s Indian population has also contributed a marvellous array of shops, stocking all kinds of sugary goodies. **Muswell Hill**'s prime attraction is the giant glasshouse of **Alexandra Palace**, within **Alexandra Park** (*see below*), with its wonderful views.

Alexandra Park

Muswell Hill, N22 (park 020 8444 7696/info 020 8365 2121). Wood Green tube/Alexandra Palace rail/ W3, W7, 84A, 144, 144A bus. **Open** 24 hours daily.

The views over London from Alexandra Palace, at the top of this steeply sloping park, are impressive on a clear day. The Palace (informally known as Ally Pally) once housed the BBC's first television studio. Now, it's an entertainment and exhibition centre with an indoor ice rink. The park's public gardens have plenty of kids' attractions and sports facilities, including a pitch-and-putt course. There are bank holiday funfairs (*see p5*) and a free fireworks display on Bonfire Night (5 Nov, but usually held on the nearest Saturday).

Boating (020 8889 9089). Jazz concerts in the Grove (summer; 020 8883 7173).

Website: www.alexandrapalace.com

Jewish Museum, Finchley

80 East End Road, N3 (020 8349 1143). Finchley Central tube/13, 82, 112, 143, 260 bus.

Open 10.30am-5pm Mon-Thur; 10.30am-4.30pm Sun. **Closed** Sun in Aug, Jewish festivals, public hols & public hol weekends, 24 Dec-4 Jan. **Admission** £2; £1 students, OAPs, disabled, ES40s; free under-12s.

Located in the Sternberg Centre for Reform Judaism, the museum's Finchley branch may lack the gilt-edged splendour of its NW1 sibling (*see p102*), but it compensates admirably with its fascinating displays on many aspects of Jewish social history. On two levels, there is a functional sewing workshop, detailing sweatshop life at the turn of the century, plus artefacts relating to East End life and practical information for refugees from Germany. Upstairs, a Holocaust exhibition follows the life of Leon Greenman, a British Jew who, alone of his family, survived Auschwitz. Overseen by friendly staff, this branch also has a 12,000-strong photographic archive, augmented by 2,000 oral history tapes.

Website: www.jewmusm.ort.org

Royal Air Force Museum

Grahame Park Way, NW9 (020 8205 2266/ recorded info 020 8205 9191). Colindale tube/ Mill Hill Broadway rail/32, 226, 292, 303 bus.

Open 10am-6pm daily. **Admission** £6.50; £3.25 5s-16s, students; £4.90 OAPs; free registered disabled; £16.60 family. **Credit** MC, £TC, V.

Hendon Aerodrome bills itself as the birthplace of aviation in Britain and here you can see how baby has grown. The hi-tech Phantom jet dwarfs the Spitfire and Hurricane fighters that won the Battle of Britain. You can have a close look at these on a guided tour (book in advance by phone). The main hangar houses planes plucked from aviation history. Opposite you'll find the harbingers of the terrible rain from Bomber Command. There's also a Red Arrows flight simulator, a 'touch and try' Jet Provost cockpit and a walk-through Sunderland flying boat. Children will enjoy the 'fun 'n' flight' interactive gallery.

Website: www.rafmuseum.org.uk

East London

In addition to a surprising number of museums and sights, East London is packed with atmosphere and enthusiasm.

Whitechapel & Spitalfields

MAPS 10 & 12

Whitechapel has always been the City's poor, rather embarrassing next-door neighbour. Situated on the main route from London to Essex, it first developed as a home for bell-founders and other metalworkers who were expelled from the City for being too noisy; the **Whitechapel Bell Foundry** (established 1570) and **Gunmakers' Company Proof House** still survive in Fieldgate Street and Commercial Road respectively. By Victorian times, the area was wretchedly poor, a contemporary social historian describing it as 'a shocking place… an evil plexus of slums that hide human creeping things'. Only crime – and especially prostitution – thrived.

Poverty meant low rents – an attraction for the successive waves of immigrants who have enriched Whitechapel over the last few centuries. First, it was the French Protestant refugees, the Huguenots, in the early eighteenth century; then the Irish and Germans in the early nineteenth century; Jewish refugees from eastern Europe from 1880 to 1914; and, as the Jews prospered and moved north, Indians and Bangladeshis, who between the 1950s and 1970s took over textile businesses on Commercial Street and Commercial Road.

Is it me? **Whitechapel Road Market.**

EXPLORING THE EAST END

The best way to enter the East End is to take the 15 bus through the City and get off at Aldgate East at the stop between Goulston Street and Old Castle Street (look out for Tubby Isaacs' jellied eel stall – established 1919 – by the Aldgate Exchange pub). Commercial Street, which sweeps off to the left through Spitalfields towards Shoreditch, is largely a wide swathe of Victorian warehouses.

Halfway up Commercial Street is the covered **Spitalfields Market** (*see page 223*). The famous fruit and vegetable market, established in 1682, moved north-east to Leyton some years ago. An organic market continues where the old one left off, surrounded by a plethora of different market traders who enjoy a thriving weekend trade in books, music, clothing, both second-hand and new, household accessories and various arts and crafts. Cheap eateries, among them the inimitable **Arkansas Café** (*see page 167*), edge the hall.

Opposite the market is Hawksmoor's magnificent **Christ Church Spitalfields** (*see page 111*). After dark, this stretch of Commercial Street has a distinctly Hell's Kitchen look to it, with prostitutes standing at intervals along the kerb and anonymous figures clustering around the all-night mobile caff parked outside the church railings.

Fournier Street, which runs alongside Christ Church to link Commercial Street with Brick Lane, is altogether more respectable – a reminder of the Huguenots, whose skill at silk weaving brought them prosperity in the East End. Their tall houses, with distinctive shutters and ornate, jutting porches, line the street. Similar houses are to be found in nearby Elder Street and Folgate Street, where the unique, recreated Georgian residence, **Dennis Severs' House** (*see page 111*), can be distinguished by its flickering gas flames over the front door.

BARGAINS & BALTIS

Once, the two main reasons for visiting **Brick Lane** and the immediate area were **Brick Lane Market** and the plethora of cheap curry restaurants. Many of the latter are, alas, uninspiring these days – notable exceptions are (at the basic end of the scale) **Sweet & Spicy** (no.40) and (rather posher) **Le Taj** (no.134). Brick Lane's Jewish heritage survives in the **Beigel Bake** at no.159 (open 24 hours daily). Playwright Arnold Wesker was brought up in nearby Fashion Street, and *Oliver!* composer Lionel Bart lived above the shop on the corner of Brick Lane and Princelet Street, opposite the Eastern Eye restaurant. The **Pride of Spitalfields** in Heneage Street is one of the few good old-fashioned pubs remaining in this area, and it attracts a friendly local crowd. Several younger, trendier brasseries and bars have struck roots in the area, the best known being the **Vibe Bar** (no.91). These additions reflect the changing face of Brick Lane's social mix as it heads into the twenty-first century. Hip folk come to the area to catch the latest in designer furniture, clothing and art since the Truman Brewery and immediate environs opened up to entrepreneurs cut from an altogether savvier, artier pattern than their '80s forebears.

Many more visitors to Whitechapel pour in for the Sunday markets at Brick Lane and nearby **Petticoat Lane** (*see page 222*), but the whole area is worth exploring. The art nouveau **Whitechapel Art Gallery** (*see page 111*) on Whitechapel High Street specialises in contemporary art. The lobby of **Whitechapel Public Library** is adorned with a painted-tile depiction of the hay market that was held in the High Street for 300 years until its abolition in 1928. A modest clothing market continues to thrive further along Whitechapel Road. Fieldgate Street (running behind the huge **East London Mosque**) is worth a detour for a look at the grim, derelict, Victorian bulk of **Tower House**, built as a hostel for the homeless. Stalin and Lenin stayed here while attending the Fifth Congress of the Russian Social Democratic Labour Party in nearby Fulbourne Street. The 'Elephant Man', Joseph Merrick, was exhibited at what is now the Bombay Saree House, before Sir Frederick Treves, a surgeon at the **Royal London Hospital** opposite, spotted him and provided a home for him in the hospital buildings. The hospital is now topped by a helipad and contains a museum with a section on Merrick plus a general rundown on the history of medicine and the hospital itself (*see page 111*).

MURDER IN WHITECHAPEL

The **Blind Beggar** pub (corner of Whitechapel and Cambridge Heath roads) is best known for its criminal connections. It was here, on 8 March 1966, that gangster George Cornell was shot dead by Ronnie Kray (allegedly for calling him a 'fat poof'). For ten years Ronnie and his twin brother Reggie had dominated organised crime from Woolwich to the City; Cornell was a member of the rival Richardson gang. Today, the Blind Beggar is a comfortable, rather ordinary pub, popular with traders and visitors to Whitechapel Road Market. **Sidney Street**, which leads off Whitechapel Road opposite Cambridge Heath Road, was the site of a famous siege on 3 January 1911. Several anarchists barricaded themselves into a house and took potshots at the police and soldiers outside before the house caught fire. Two charred bodies were recovered but the gang's leader, the enigmatically named Russian, Peter the Painter, was never found.

For decades, the alley at **Wood's Buildings** (down the side of the Bombay Saree House, across Whitechapel Road from the Royal London Hospital) led to what was arguably the most desolate spot in the whole of the East End: an almost-forgotten tract of land, dominated by a huge, ruined Victorian school. It was here that **Jack the Ripper** claimed his first victim. The school may now have been converted into luxury flats, but the view back along the alley towards Whitechapel Road is still tinglingly Dickensian. The old East End is disappearing fast – catch it while you can.

Hawksmoor's **Christ Church**. *See p111.*

Christ Church Spitalfields

Commercial Street, E1 (020 7247 7202). Aldgate East tube/Liverpool Street tube/rail/67 bus. **Open** for services 10.30am, 7pm Sun; phone for details of other times. **Map 10 S5**

One of Nicholas Hawksmoor's masterpieces, Christ Church is best seen at night, when its floodlit bulk looms massively above the darkened warehouses of Commercial Street. Built in 1714 to provide a place of worship for the Huguenot silk-weavers, it later fell into disrepair and is currently undergoing restoration (mainly on the inside), though it remains open to the public.

Dennis Severs' House

18 Folgate Street, E1 (020 7247 4013). Liverpool Street tube/rail. **Open** 2-5pm 1st Sun of month; evening 1st Mon of month; or by appointment (phone to book). **Performances** 7.30pm. **Admission** £7 Sun; £10 Mon. **Map 10 R5**

The current owner of this beautifully restored Georgian red-brick terraced house (built in 1724), the eccentric American-born Mr Severs, invites visitors to travel through time (for two and a half hours) and become the guests of an imaginary family who lived in the house from 1685 to 1919. As a kind of still-life radio drama, it's a highly atmospheric portrayal of lives during 250 years of east London history. You should book about three weeks in advance for the shows, though it's always worth phoning to see if there's been a cancellation. Sunday and candlelit Monday evening tours omit the theatrical element but are still worthwhile. A word of warning: Dennis discourages children and the 'average' businessman and tourist from coming, and expects everyone to get totally immersed in the experience. It's expensive, sure, but quite unforgettable.

Royal London Hospital Archives & Museum

St Philip's Church, Newark Street, E1 (020 7377 7608). Whitechapel tube. **Open** 10am-4.30pm Mon-Fri. **Admission** free.

Joseph Merrick, 'the Elephant Man', was a patient, and then an exhibit, at the Royal London Hospital in the late 1880s. Part of the hospital's museum is devoted to this tragic figure. The rest charts the history of the hospital, and nursing and medicine in general. It includes a section on the heroic nurse Edith Cavell, who was executed by the Germans in 1915 for helping Allied soldiers to escape from occupied Belgium.

Website: www.mushm.link.com

Whitechapel Art Gallery

80-82 Whitechapel High Street, E1 (020 7522 7888/recorded info 020 7522 7878). Aldgate East tube/15, 253 bus. **Open** 11am-5pm Tue, Thur-Sun; 11am-8pm Wed. **Admission** free. **Map 12 S6**

A fine gallery space on two floors, the Whitechapel remains one of the most interesting independent galleries in London, putting on a continually challenging series of temporary shows. In 1999 the gallery hosted a major retrospective of Rosemary Trockel's work and the attention-grabbing Speed exhibition. Shows for 2000 include the provocative Mexican artist **Francisco Toledo** (14 Apr-7 June). The format and timing of the 2000 biennial **Whitechapel Open**, the only major show devoted to east London's heaving colony of artists, was unconfirmed at the time of going to press. The gallery also organises a lecture and workshop programme.

Shoreditch & Hoxton

Shoreditch – or Score's Ditch as it was known in Anglo-Saxon times – was formed at the intersection of two Roman roads: Old Street, running east-west, and Kingsland Road, running north-south. Not quite the City or the East End, the place seems uncertain of its identity, and its main focal point, around Old Street tube station, is dour and run-down. But it has seen more cheerful times. James Burbage founded London's first theatre on the corner of Great Eastern Street and New Inn Yard. Called simply The Theatre, it lasted barely 20 years before decamping to Southwark and becoming the **Globe** (*see page 294*). The same year, 1598, Ben Jonson, then Britain's foremost playwright after Shakespeare, fought a duel with an actor named Gabriel Spencer at Hoxton Fields (now Hoxton Square) and killed him. Since he was also a clergyman, Jonson escaped the gallows, but had his left thumb branded; his victim was buried in **St Leonard's Church**, in Shoreditch High Street.

Hoxton is the section of Shoreditch north of Old Street and west of Kingsland Road. From Victorian times until the outbreak of World War II it was known chiefly for its overcrowded slums and its music halls. Both features have since disappeared under unappealing blocks of flats, but an influx of artists, musicians and other bohemian types in recent years has given pockets of Hoxton an unexpected chic. Centred around **Hoxton Square**, home of the fine **Lux Cinema** (*see page 260*), cool bars (such as **Home** and the **Shoreditch Electricity Showrooms**; for both *see page 198*) are now legion in Hoxton, yet shops, restaurants and other basic facilities remain conspicuous by their absence. Near here is one of the city's best museums, the **Geffrye Museum** (*see below*).

Geffrye Museum

Kingsland Road, E2 (020 7739 9893/recorded info 020 7739 8543/info@geffrye-museum.org.uk). Old Street tube/rail then 243 bus/Liverpool Street tube/rail then 149, 242 bus. **Open** 10am-5pm Tue-Sat; noon-5pm Sun, bank holiday Mon. **Admission** free (under-8s must be accompanied by an adult). **Map 10 R3**

These beautiful almshouses, built in 1715, were converted into a museum of furniture and interior design in 1914 and are now one of London's most fascinating and delightful museums. A series of rooms, reconstructed in period style, amounts to an informative and atmospheric voyage through the ages of British domestic interiors from the Elizabethan era to the present day. The twentieth-century rooms and exhibits are displayed in the new £5.3-million extension. Edwardian, 1930s and 1960s living rooms and a spookily authentic 1990s loft conversion are arranged in a loop around a sinuous, skeletal staircase leading down to a design centre, educational art rooms, and a temporary exhibition gallery.

The **Geffrye Design Centre** is a showcase gallery for contemporary designer-makers based locally in the East End. Exhibitions during 2000 include **Contemporary Furniture 1 & 2** (until 2 July) and **Glass** from 5 July. The temporary exhibition space will show work by **Matthew Hilton**, one of the country's leading furniture designers (until 9 July), followed by **The House Beautiful: Oscar Wilde and the Aesthetic Style** (18 July-21 Jan 2001). Every December, the Geffrye's popular **Christmas Past** season transforms the museum's atmosphere as all the rooms are decorated with original artefacts and historically accurate replicas to reflect four centuries of Christmas traditions. In summer, free jazz and world music concerts are given on the front lawns. A bright, airy restaurant separating the old and new sections of the museum looks out over the walled herb garden, which provides a pleasant 'outdoor room' in fine weather.
Website: www.geffrye-museum.org.uk

Bethnal Green & Hackney

In Victorian times **Bethnal Green** was the poorest district in London. In 1889, nearly half the population lived below subsistence level, with the **Jago**, around Old Nichol Street, containing the worst ravages of poverty and squalor. The area has been completely transformed in the twentieth century, with wholesale slum clearance and the building of huge council estates, but, despite pockets of gentility, Bethnal Green remains impoverished. The **Bethnal Green Museum of Childhood** on Cambridge Heath Road (*see below*), originally the east London branch of the Victoria & Albert Museum, opened in 1872. Almost as ancient is the art deco inlaid Anglo-Italian caff **E Pellicci** (332 Bethnal Green Road), which has been run by the friendly Pellicci family for a century.

Hackney, to the north, was originally an extended village, popular in the fifteenth and sixteenth centuries with merchants who wanted to live near, but not too near, the City. Hackney's oldest house, **Sutton House** (*see below*), dates from this period. In his diary entry for 11 June 1664, Pepys records that he went 'with my wyfe only to take ayre, it being very warm and pleasant, to Bowe and Old Ford; and thence to Hackney. There... played at shuffle board, ate cream and good cherries; and so with good refreshment home.' The rural idyll continued until the nineteenth century, when Hackney's market gardens were gradually buried under terraced houses and workshops, themselves to be replaced by housing estates after World War II.

A large, mainly poor area, Hackney is best approached selectively. **Columbia Road** (*see page 223*) and **Ridley Road** have excellent markets; the former also has a number of pottery shops specialising in terracotta. You won't go hungry, either: the **Ridley Bagel Bakery** (13-15 Ridley Road) is open 24 hours, and fish and chip shops don't come much better than **Faulkners** (424-426 Kingsland Road). Thanks to the local Kurdish community, there are also plenty of Turkish restaurants nearby.

Mare Street features the splendid **Hackney Empire** (*see page 277*), in its heyday one of London's great music halls and still a popular theatre. Look out for the striking paintwork, forming a human face, on the brick building diagonally opposite. Hackney Central Hall was built as a Methodist meeting hall in 1907, and until recently contained the eclectic Hackney Museum. The building is currently undergoing a major redevelopment and when it reopens in September 2000 will house the **Ocean Music Venue**, which will include three performance spaces for a wide variety of music, as well as rehearsal rooms, bars and so on. A Technology and Learning Centre will also be built on the south side of the Town Hall Square, which will incorporate the new Central Library and Hackney Museum.

Bethnal Green Museum of Childhood

Cambridge Heath Road, E2 (020 8983 5200/ recorded info 020 8980 2415). Bethnal Green tube/ rail. **Open** 10am-5.50pm Mon-Thur, Sat, Sun. **Admission** free (under-8s must be accompanied by an adult).

This mammoth collection of dolls, trains, cars, children's clothes, books and puppets is housed in a nineteenth-century building. The dolls' houses in cabinets, originating in seventeenth-century Holland, and the Japanese ceremonial dolls, should not be missed. On the upper gallery, a selection of educational toys can be handled, but the museum is of more interest to nostalgic adults than kids. The museum has art workshops on Saturdays and a soft play session on Sundays; phone for times.
Website: www.vam.ac.uk

Sutton House

2 & 4 Homerton High Street, E9 (020 8986 2264). Bethnal Green tube then 253, 106, D6 bus/ Hackney Central rail. **Open** *historic rooms Feb-Nov* 11.30am-5.30pm Wed, Sun, public hols (last entry 5pm). **Admission** £2.10; 60p 5s-16s; £4.70 family. **Credit** MC, V.

This National Trust-owned red-brick Tudor mansion is the oldest house in east London. It was built in 1535 for Henry VIII's first secretary of state. The house opened as a community centre in the late 1980s after a fierce debate over its future that thank-

A place for sittin' in **Sutton House**. *See p112.*

fully led to the superb restoration now on view. There are Tudor, Jacobean and Georgian interiors, as well as the Edwardian chapel and medieval foundations in the cellar. It also boasts what is possibly London's oldest loo: a sixteenth-century 'garderobe'. There's even a protected wall of graffiti, believed to have been done by squatters in the early '80s. The café and shop here are open all year round.

Docklands

The history of London's **Docklands** (stretching east from Tower Bridge to the Isle of Dogs and beyond) is the history of Britain in microcosm. As the British Empire expanded in the eighteenth and nineteenth centuries, so too did the traffic along the River Thames, as ships arrived laden with booty from all corners of the globe. Different docks were built to specialise in various types of cargo: rum and hardwood at West India Docks on the Isle of Dogs; wool, sugar and rubber at St Katharine's Dock by Tower Bridge; ivory, coffee and cocoa at London Docks in Wapping. During World War II the docks suffered heavy bombing (including 57 consecutive nights of firebombing), but by the 1950s they had again reached full capacity. When it came, the end was sudden. The collapse of the Empire, a series of crippling strikes and, above all, the introduction of deep-water container ships led to the closure, one by one, of all of London's docks from Tower Bridge to Barking Creek between 1967 and 1984.

REGENERATION

In 1981, the Conservative government set up the London Docklands Development Corporation (LDDC). Its brief was to regenerate the eight-and-a-half square miles (2,200 hectares) of derelict land by building new offices and homes and attracting new businesses. Accused from the outset of favouring wealthy outsiders over the needs of local people, the LDDC came badly unstuck in the recession of the early 1990s, when developers found themselves with brand-new empty buildings on their hands and no one to move into them. Since then, the situation has improved: the population of Docklands increased from 39,400 in 1981 to 77,000 by the time the organisation ceased operation in March 1998. Its responsibilities have been taken over by a range of other bodies.

Docklands remains one of the most intriguing areas of London to visit, and it's becoming more accessible. New, imaginatively designed pedestrian bridges across the water-filled docks have made the place more people-friendly. The Docklands Light Railway (DLR) was joined in 1999 by the stations of the long-awaited Jubilee Line extension.

ST KATHARINE'S

Just east of Tower Bridge on the north bank of the Thames, **St Katharine's** once housed over 1,000 cottages, a brewery and the twelfth-century church of St Katharine – all of which were demolished (without compensation) to make way for a grandiose new docklands development scheme in 1828. St Katharine's Dock, which was built over the old settlement, remained open until 1968, re-emerging in 1973 as the first of the Docklands redevelopments. **St Katharine's Haven** is now a yacht marina; one corner of the dock houses a squadron of russet-sailed, turn-of-the-century barges. The restaurants, cafés and pubs around the dock pull in tourists by the coachload.

WAPPING: CRIME, PUNISHMENT & PUBS

In 1598, London historian John Stowe described Wapping High Street as a 'filthy strait passage, with alleys of small tenements or cottages… built and inhabited by sailors' victuallers'. Today, it is a quiet, rather sunless thoroughfare – though not without charm – hemmed in on either side by warehouses (those in Wapping Wall are the most spectacular) and new flats.

The river at **Wapping**, to the east of St Katharine's, brims with history. Until well into the nineteenth century, convicted pirates were taken at low tide to **Execution Dock** (near the River Police station at Wapping New Stairs), hanged, and left there in chains until three tides had washed over them. The **Captain Kidd** pub (108 Wapping High Street) commemorates one of the most famous recipients of this brand of rough justice – Kidd had been dispatched by the government to capture pirates in the Indian Ocean but decided to become one himself. Another historic pub, the **Town of Ramsgate** (62 Wapping High Street), is where the bloodthirsty Judge Jeffreys, who sent scores of pirates to Execution Dock, was himself captured as he tried to escape to Hamburg disguised as a sailor (he died in the Tower of London). 'Colonel' Blood was also caught here after attempting to steal the Crown Jewels in 1671.

While you're here, have a look at **Scandrett Street** (leading off Wapping High Street, opposite Wapping Old Stairs). This was once a miniature community containing a pub, a church and a school, built in 1760 and bearing plaster figures of an eighteenth-century schoolboy and schoolgirl over the main entrance.

Dating from 1520, the **Prospect of Whitby** (57 Wapping Wall; *see page 198*) is the oldest and most famous of the Wapping riverside pubs. Pepys, Dickens, Whistler and Turner were all regulars. The **White Swan & Cuckoo** (corner of Wapping Lane and Prusom Street) lacks a riverside view but is friendly and serves good food.

The streets north of The Highway are solidly working-class tenements. Though not outwardly prepossessing, this area too has a colourful past. A large mural at St George's Town Hall, a few minutes' walk away in **Cable Street**, commemorates the battle between local people and marching blackshirts, led by fascist leader Sir Oswald Mosley, on 4 October 1936. The march, intended to intimidate the local Jewish population, was abandoned and the blackshirts were never seen in such numbers again in the East End. The church of **St George-in-the-East**, just off The Highway on Cannon Street Road, was built in 1714-29 to the designs of Nicholas Hawksmoor. Although the interior was rebuilt after the Blitz, the exterior and monumental tower are typical of the architect.

LIMEHOUSE

Sandwiched between Wapping and the Isle of Dogs, **Limehouse** was named after the medieval lime kilns that once stood here. But, like Wapping, Limehouse's prosperity came from the sea. In 1610, a census revealed that half the working population were mariners, and Limehouse later became a centre for shipbuilding. The straw-coloured **Sail Makers' & Ship Chandlers' Building** still stands at 11 West India Dock Road.

The importance of Limehouse is reflected in the immense size of **St Anne's Limehouse** (corner of Commercial Road and Three Colt Street). Built between 1712 and 1724 in what were then open fields, this is probably Nicholas Hawksmoor's most dramatic creation. The clock tower is the second highest in Britain after Big Ben and was built by the same makers.

Britain's first wave of Chinese immigrants (mainly seamen) settled in Limehouse in the nineteenth century. Their influence survives in some of the street names (Ming Street, Canton Street) and in the few Chinese restaurants that remain around West India Dock Road. In Victorian times, Limehouse was notorious for its gambling and drug dens (Oscar Wilde's Dorian Gray comes here to buy opium) and it features in stories by Sax Rohmer (creator of oriental villain Fu Manchu) and Sir Arthur Conan Doyle. Dickens knew Limehouse well: he regularly visited his godfather in Newell Street and used the tiny, dark, and still superb, **Grapes** inn (76 Narrow Street; *see page 198*) as the model for the Six Jolly Fellowship Porters in *Our Mutual Friend* (1865). The canal path on the other side of Narrow Street takes you to Limehouse Basin, which, despite renovation and the various pleasure-crafts moored there, still looks somewhat desolate.

Visitors coming by car should note that, during 2000, stringent parking restrictions apply to a two-mile radius around the Dome. This starts roughly east of Limehouse and includes the Isle of Dogs.

ISLE OF DOGS

For many people, the **Isle of Dogs** *is* Docklands. Redevelopment has been at its most intense here, focusing on **Canary Wharf**. Cesar Pelli's rocket-shaped 500-m (800-ft) tower is the tallest building in the UK and has dominated the London skyline since it was erected in 1991. The only pity is that owing to fear of IRA attack (a massive bomb at South Quay in February 1996 caused a huge amount of damage and killed two people) the public aren't allowed access to enjoy the view from the top. Still, the sight of the tower through the glass-domed roof of CanaryWharf DLR station is spectacular in itself (*see page 28* **The end of the line**).

There's little about the Isle that isn't subject to dispute. Some insist that it isn't an island at all, but a peninsula (though the main section of West India Docks effectively splits it in two) and no one can agree on whether 'Dogs' refers to the royal kennels that were once kept here or whether it's a corruption of the dykes that were built by Flemish engineers in the nineteenth century. Above all, argument continues to rage over whether the Isle of Dogs is a crucible of economic progress or a monstrous adventure playground for big business.

The best way to see Docklands is from the overhead Docklands Light Railway. At the undeveloped southern end of the Isle is **Mudchute City Farm** (a big hit with kids; *see page 236*). **Island Gardens**, at the very tip, offers an unparalleled

Trails of the unexpected...

Historic East End boozers.

Early in 1888, any male visitor to the **Ten Bells** (Commercial Street) would have run the risk of being propositioned by one of Jack the Ripper's desperate future victims, all of whom frequented this rub-a-dub-dub of ill repute. These days, he's just as likely to be greeted by an oily teenager wiggling naked on the floor in front of the yellowing Ripperabilia. Cockney rhyming slang for a stripper, by the way, is 'Jack the Ripper'. Confusing, that.

According to various London guidebooks, Reggie Kray's bullet holes are 'lovingly preserved' at the **Blind Beggar** (337 Whitechapel High Street, a little further east). Unfortunately, they don't say exactly where, and it seems somehow rude to ask at the very bar that was sprayed with George Cornell's brains back in 1966. Cornell's crime had been to call Reggie a 'fat poof'. Brother Ronnie had already dispatched Jack 'The Hat' McVitie, and Reggie was keen to even the score. So he shot Cornell in broad daylight, in a crowded bar, believing no one would ever dare say a word against him. Bang went the Krays' East End reign of extortion and terror. In 1969, they were each jailed for a minimum of 30 years, the judge commenting that 'society has earned a long rest from your activities'.

Heading south, in the basement of the medieval **Town of Ramsgate** (62 Wapping High Street) there are wall-irons that held convicts before transportation to Australia. Before their little disagreement over the *Bounty*, Captain Bligh (Trevor Howard) and Fletcher Christian (Marlon Brando) supped together here. The Thameside patio is in the exact location of the old river pirates' hanging dock, just yards from Wapping Old Stairs, where Colonel Blood (Errol Flynn) was caught with the Crown Jewels secreted under his cloak.

Just along Wapping Wall from the Town of Ramsgate, at no.57, is the **Prospect of Whitby** – London's oldest riverside pub, rebuilt in 1549! Until 1777 it was known as the Devil's Tavern, a deeply dodgy fencing gaff for smugglers and river pirate gangs (Mudlarks, Heavy Horsemen, Scuffle Hunters et al), though it's now a bit touristy and not as authentically atmospheric as the Town of Ramsgate. Finally, straight over the river from the Town of Ramsgate is the **Angel** (101 Bermondsey Wall). This is the boozer where gangster Bob Hoskins was bombed in *The Long Good Friday*. There's nowhere better to get totally blasted with great views of Tower Bridge from the balcony.

view across the Thames towards **Greenwich** (the DLR has now been extended across the river as far as Lewisham, so visitors no longer have to get out at Island Gardens and walk under the foot tunnel). Alternatively, since the completion of the Jubilee Line extension, you could arrive in one of the most expansive (and expensive) tube stations in the world; the Foster-designed Canary Wharf tube station, resplendent in glass and steel, is said to be as long as Canary Wharf Tower itself is high. Nearby, at West India Quay, is the site of the new **Museum in Docklands**. Housed in a Grade-I listed building, the museum will explore the history of London as a trading city. The museum was due to open in early 2000 but exact details were not known as this Guide went to press; call 020 7515 1162 for further information.

Eating and drinking options on the Isle of Dogs are not abundant. The greatest concentration of places is in the Canary Wharf complex, but most are pricey and sterile. A better bet is **Landy's at the Space** (269 Westferry Road) at Island Gardens, which offers good breakfasts and lunches upstairs from the Space arts venue.

Mile End, Bow & Stratford

Mostly common land until the sixteenth century, **Mile End** experienced a minor population explosion in the nineteenth century as industrialisation took hold. The area never really experienced the ravages of poverty suffered by neighbouring Whitechapel and Bethnal Green. Nevertheless, it was here that the **Trinity Almshouses** were built in 1695 (near the junction with Cambridge Heath Road) for 'twenty-eight decayed masters and commanders of ships'. Look out for the model galleons, on either side of the entrance. In the 1860s, William Booth founded the Salvation Army in Mile End.

Much of Mile End Road is filled by **Queen Mary and Westfield College**, which was opened by Queen Victoria in 1887 as a working men's institute. Further east, beyond Mile End tube station, lies little-known and quietly impressive **Tredegar Square** and its offshoots, Tredegar Road and Lichfield Road, each lined with beautifully restored and maintained 1830s terraced houses.

To the south-west, **Mile End Park** borders Copperfield Road, home to the **Ragged School Museum** (*see below*) and **Matt's Gallery** (*see page 252*). The park was, until recently, divided rather bluntly by the less-than-picturesque Mile End Road; a £25-million redevelopment scheme is creating new themed areas within the park, such as the Garden of the Senses (due to be completed in summer 2000), emphasising the colour, scent and touch of plants; while Piers Gough's 25-m (82-ft) wide **Green Bridge** aims to provide a much-needed link between the two sides of the park. To the north is **Victoria Park** (*see below*), a welcome slice of green stretching towards Hackney.

Bow, to the east, has played a major role in the growth of London. In the twelfth century, the narrow Roman bridge over the River Lea at Old Ford was supplemented by a new bridge downriver. Its bow shape gave the whole area its name. Grain was transported by boat from Hertfordshire and unloaded at mills along the river. In the mid-nineteenth century, new factories sprang up, notably the Bryant and May match factory, scene of a bitter but ultimately successful match-girls' strike in 1888. A quarter of a century later, Bow struck another blow for women's rights when Sylvia Pankhurst (sister of Emmeline) launched the East London Federation of Suffragettes.

Stratford ('street by the ford') formed north of the twelfth-century bridgehead. A wealthy Cistercian monastery, Stratford Langthorne Abbey, helped put Stratford on the map. The abbey was dissolved by Henry VIII in 1538, but by then Stratford's prosperity was ensured, thanks to the development of early industries such as gunpowder manufacture. In the mid-nineteenth century much of the area was covered by railway lines and marshalling yards. Stratford remains a busy transport nexus, boasting a railway, tube and DLR station, as well as a glittering new bus station resembling an upside-down umbrella.

Modern Stratford has a busy, well-defined centre, focused on Broadway, where an obelisk commemorates the nineteenth-century philanthropist Samuel Gurney. Look out too for the distinctive green dome and globe of the Transport and General Workers Union building in nearby West Ham Lane. Make your way through the big indoor shopping centre and you come to **Gerry Raffles Square**. Here the sparkling new glass-and-neon **Stratford Picture House** faces the venerable **Theatre Royal Stratford East**, which is currently closed for extension on to the adjacent site by Newham Council; a new arts centre, **Stratford Circus**, which will include a rehearsal space and a bar, is due to open in autumn 2000. Joan Littlewood's Theatre Workshop was based here during the 1950s and 1960s, providing an early boost for the musical talents of Lionel Bart.

Ragged School Museum

48-50 Copperfield Road, E3 (020 8980 6405). Mile End tube. **Open** 10am-5pm Wed, Thur; 2-5pm 1st Sun of every month. **Admission** free.

'Ragged schools' were established to educate and feed poor children. Founded by Dr Barnardo, this canalside warehouse was one of the largest ragged schools in London (there were 144 in total). Now restored to its original form, it contains a reconstructed Victorian classroom, complete with role-playing for pupils when schools visit. Free events are organised for children during school holidays and on the first Sunday of each month, and there are also good temporary exhibitions on subjects of local interest. The café is a useful refuelling stop as the museum is somewhat out of the way.

During 2000 the museum is holding a special Millennium exhibition, which will be housed in a new gallery on the ground floor. Using photos, objects and interactive displays, the exhibition will relate the history of the area now known as Tower Hamlets, focusing on the last two centuries.

Website: www.ics-london.co.uk/rsm

Victoria Park

Old Ford Road, E3 (020 8533 2057). Mile End tube/ Cambridge Heath rail/2, 8, 26, 30, 55, 253, 277, S2 bus. **Open** 6am-dusk daily.

Fringed by the Hertford Union Canal, Victoria Park is a useful detour for those weary of Hackney's plains of cement. At the main Sewardstone Road entrance, look out for the deranged-looking Dogs of Alcibiades, which have stood here since 1912. The park's large ponds and tearooms provide it with an atmosphere reminiscent of Regent's Park.

Walthamstow

The name comes from the Old English word 'Wilcumestowe': a place where guests are welcome. It's a description that still applies today – **Walthamstow** is noticeably friendly. Its borders are ancient ones: **Epping Forest** (*see page 320*) to the north, **Walthamstow Marshes** to the west. The first settlers lived here in the Bronze Age, when the whole area was still thickly forested. In medieval times much of the forest was cleared and replaced by farmland. It wasn't until the nineteenth century that Walthamstow became a wholly urban area, though most of its largely working-class population has been spared the tenements and tower blocks that litter other parts of east London.

Walthamstow has two main thoroughfares. The narrow **High Street** contains the longest and, after Brixton, most varied market in London. **Walthamstow Market** stretches for more than a mile and is lined by inexpensive shops. The second thoroughfare is undulating **Hoe Street**, consisting of a mainly uninspiring selection of kebab shops and mini-marts, although the **Dhaka Tandoori** (no.103) is rather good.

North of Forest Road, streets such as Holmes Avenue, Diana Road and Winns Avenue are inimitably Walthamstow: ruddy brick terraced houses, with deep porches and creaking iron gates. It's the sort of dreaming suburbia immortalised in William Sansom's 1949 novel *The Body*.

Lloyd Park contains the **Waltham Forest Theatre** and a variety of imported water birds. The aviary and manicured bowling green, frequented by white-clad elderly locals, make it particularly pleasant on a summer afternoon. The eighteenth-century building with its back imperiously turned to the park is the **William Morris Gallery** (*see below*). From here, a short walk up Forest Road will be amply rewarded by the dramatic view of the art nouveau **Walthamstow Town Hall**. This is one of the most startling pieces of municipal architecture in London; its beautiful proportions, green-and-gold clock tower and circular reflecting pool have graced many a film and TV production (in pre-glasnost days it frequently stood in for Moscow or Leningrad).

The area's oldest buildings can be found in a well-concealed enclave known as **Walthamstow Village**. Vestry Road is the site of the **Vestry House Museum** (*see below*) and the **Monoux Almshouses**, built in 1795 and 'endowed for ever… for the use of six decayed tradesmen's widows of this parish and no other'. The squat exterior of nearby **St Mary's Church** conceals a modest but tranquil interior. Timbered **Ancient House**, opposite the churchyard, was once a farmhouse. Restored in 1934, it sags like an unsuccessful fruit cake. The Village continues along Orford Road, with its Italian restaurants and cosy pub.

Vestry House Museum

Vestry Road, E17 (020 8509 1917). Walthamstow Central tube/rail. **Open** 10am-1pm, 2-5.30pm, Mon-Fri; 10am-1pm, 2-5pm, Sat. **Admission** free.
This diminutive but charming museum offers a fascinating photographic history of Walthamstow, as well as focusing on two of the area's favourite sons: Alfred Hitchcock, from Leytonstone, and Frederick Bremer, designer of Britain's first motor car (the 1894 vehicle is on display). Strangely, there's nothing about Britain's first powered flight, by AV Roe over Walthamstow Marshes in 1909. The costume and toy sections are well worth a look.
Website: www.lbwf.gov.uk/vestry/vestry.htm

William Morris Gallery

Lloyd Park, Forest Road, E17 (020 8527 3782). Walthamstow Central tube/rail then 34, 97, 215, 257 bus. **Open** 10am-1pm, 2-5pm, Tue-Sat; 1st Sun of every month. **Admission** free. **Credit** MC, £TC, V.
Opened in 1950, this was the childhood home of William Morris, the influential late-Victorian designer, craftsman and socialist. In four rooms on the ground floor, Morris's biography is expounded through his work and political writings. Upstairs are galleries devoted to his associates – Burne-Jones, Philip Webb and Ernest Gimson – who assisted in contributing to the considerable popularity Morris's style retains today. There are also paintings by one-time apprentice to Morris, Frank Brangwyn.
Website: www.lbwf.gov.uk/wmg

Leyton & Leytonstone

Badly bombed during World War II, **Leyton**'s post-war development has been haphazard, and it lacks the cohesion and charm of neighbouring Walthamstow. Much of the land originally consisted of marshy, fertile farmland, and during the eighteenth century the area was best known for its market gardening. The inevitable industrialisation of the mid-nineteenth century led to much of the marshland being covered by railways and gas works, and to a downturn in the area's fortunes as the population swelled with low-paid railway workers. The proliferation of discount supermarkets and second-hand furniture and electrical shops testifies to the fact that Leyton remains one of London's poorer areas. Its best-known 'attraction' is probably its endearingly underachieving football team, **Leyton Orient**.

Leytonstone, to the east of Leyton, took its name from a milestone on the Roman road from the City to Epping Forest. The petrol station on the corner of Leytonstone High Road is on the site of a greengrocer's shop where **Alfred Hitchcock** spent his early childhood. Late in life, he recalled how, following some forgotten mischievousness, his father gave him a note and told him to take it to the nearby Harrow Green police station. There, the sergeant on duty read the note and proceeded to lock the future Master of Suspense in a cell for 20 minutes, explaining, 'This is what we do to naughty boys.'

Further east

Although the London Dockland Development Corporation remit to revive the London Docks extended well to the east of the Isle of Dogs, there is little to interest visitors beyond **Blackwall**. **Canning Town**, huddled next to the River Lea, lost its main industry as early as 1912, with the closure of the Thames Ironworks and Shipbuilding Company on Bow Creek. Much of the area was flattened by German bombers in World War II, and large, unsympathetically designed post-war housing estates did nothing to revive the area's fortunes. Neighbouring **Newham** fared even worse: the collapse of a tower block, Ronan Point, in 1968 caused several deaths. **Beckton**, to the east, has been more fortunate, with better-than-average new housing. South of Beckton, **London City Airport** was opened in 1987, using the long, narrow quay between Royal Albert Dock and George V Dock as a runway for short-haul airliners (there's a good view of the airport from the DLR).

South London

From Greenwich to Richmond, there's far more to south London that north Londoners would have you believe.

Charlton House: *what a beauty. See p119.*

Charlton, Woolwich & Eltham

In centuries past, few travellers relished the prospect of a journey along the Old Dover Road. At **Shooters Hill** in particular the road was steep and the countryside wild; this was a favourite spot for footpads and highwaymen to lie in wait for easy prey. Robbers who were caught were themselves shown no mercy: they were hanged at a gallows at the bottom of Shooters Hill and their bodies displayed on a gibbet at the summit. In 1661, Samuel Pepys recorded that he 'rode under a man that hangs at Shooters Hill, and a filthy sight it was to see how the flesh is shrunk from his bones'.

Charlton was a nearby village, built around the Jacobean manor **Charlton House** (*see page 119*). Nearby **Hornfair Park** takes its name from the Charlton Horn Fair, which was held every year until 1872. According to local tradition, the fair was started after King John seduced the wife of a local miller and, in recompense, gave her wronged husband all the land visible from Charlton to Rotherhithe. The miller's neighbours named the riverside boundary of his new land Cuckold's Point and established the annual Horn Fair (horns being the symbol of cuckoldry). Hornfair Park is now tucked away at the corner of a housing estate; **Maryon Park**, used in Antonioni's film *Blow-Up* and closer to the river, is more pleasant.

One of the most spectacular sights on the river is the **Thames Barrier**, which stretches between Silvertown on the north bank and Woolwich on the south. The nearby **Visitors' Centre** details the history of the structure (*see page 135*).

Woolwich itself attracts fewer visitors than its more glamorous neighbour Greenwich, although it does have plenty to offer, including an above-average shopping centre. Long, pedestrianised Powis Street also boasts two spectacular buildings at the river end: the ruddy Edwardian Central Stores building and, opposite, the creamy-tiled, art deco Co-op.

The character of Woolwich has been shaped by strong military and naval associations. Woolwich Arsenal was established in Tudor times as the country's main source of munitions. Over the centuries it spread to colossal proportions – at its peak during World War I the site stretched 3½ miles (5½ km) along the river and employed 72,000 people. When it closed down in 1967, much of the land was used to build the new town of **Thamesmead**, and the remaining buildings – including historic gatehouses, foundries and engraving shops – fell into disrepair. Greenwich Council has announced plans to restore the buildings to their former grandeur and open them to the public for the first time. In the meantime, you can admire **Woolwich Garrison**, historic home of the Royal Artillery, which boasts the longest Georgian façade in the country. It's best seen from Woolwich Common or from Grand Depot Road, where the remains of the **Royal Garrison Church of St George** have been left as consecrated ground after being hit by a flying bomb in 1944 (the end walls and altar still stand). For military aficionados there is the **Museum of Artillery** (*see page 119*).

Henry VIII established the Royal Dockyard at Woolwich in 1512, initially so that his new flagship, the *Great Harry*, could be built there. The dockyard closed in 1869 and moved to Chatham. Just downstream from the Woolwich Ferry terminal, the stretch of river known as Gallions Reach was the scene of the Thames' worst-ever shipping accident. In 1878, a crowded pleasure steamer, the *Princess Alice*, was struck broadside by a collier, with the loss of some 700 lives.

The Woolwich Ferry has existed since the fourteenth century; the old paddle steamers were replaced by diesels as late as 1963. (There is also a foot tunnel.) Today, the seating area outside the Waterfront Leisure Centre, next to the terminal, is a fine spot to watch a great river at work. Railway enthusiasts might like to take the ferry across the river to the **North Woolwich Old Station Museum** (*see below*).

Despite being despoiled by numerous bleak housing estates, there are a surprising number of green spaces in this part of south-east London, connected by the excellent **Green Chain Walk** (call 020 8312 5884 for maps). This takes in wonderful ancient woodlands such as **Oxleas Wood** (accessible from Falconwood rail station), a couple of miles south of Woolwich. A mile and a half south-west of here was the site of one of the most splendid of medieval royal palaces, the now-restored **Eltham Palace** (*see below*).

Charlton House

Charlton Road, SE7 (020 8856 3951). Charlton rail/ 53, 54, 380, 442 bus. **Open** 8am-11pm Mon-Fri; 9am-5.30pm Sat.

The finest Jacobean house in London, and possibly in the country, red-brick Charlton House was built in 1612 as a retirement gift for Adam Newton, tutor to Prince Henry, son of James I. It's not known for definite who the architect was, though John Thorpe is the most likely contender. The orangery, on the other hand, is almost certainly the work of Inigo Jones. The building now enjoys a useful if humdrum existence as a public library and community centre.

Eltham Palace

off Court Road, Eltham, SE9 (020 8294 2577). Eltham rail. **Open** *Apr-Sept* 10am-6pm Wed-Fri, Sun; *Oct* 10am-5pm Wed-Fri, Sun; *Nov-Mar* 10am-4pm Wed-Fri, Sun. **Admission** *house & grounds* £5.90; £3 5s-16s; £4.40 students, OAPs, disabled, ES40s; **grounds only** £3.50; £1.80 5s-16s; £2.60 students, OAPs, disabled, ES40s. **Credit** MC, V.

The name Eltham Palace is a little misleading, for this is really a wonderful homage to the 1930s. It is true that the oldest part of the building, the medieval Great Hall, is a remnant of the royal palace that once stood here, but the particular joy of this house is the art deco interior. In the mid-1930s the once-grand hall was a crumbling relic, and it was patron of the arts Stephen Courtauld who bought the wreck and, with the aid of gifted architects and designers, grafted a country home on to the old hall (which itself was restored to its medieval glory). In art deco style, the interior plays with geometry, line and contrasts of light and dark, from the deep wooden veneers to the truly modern concrete and glass dome in the light-filled entrance hall. A rare building indeed, and a fine place for the Courtaulds' pet ring-tailed lemur, which would scamper around these elegant rooms in their 1930s' heyday. The gardens are splendid as well, with views across to the distant city and out to the greenery of Kent. The palace is about a 20-minute walk from Eltham rail station (which is 25 minutes by train from Charing Cross Station). The ticket price includes an audio guide.

Website: www.english-heritage.org.uk

Eltham Palace'*s superb art deco interior.*

Museum of Artillery

The Rotunda, Repository Road, SE18 (020 8316 5402). Woolwich Dockyard rail. **Open** 1-4pm Mon-Fri. **Admission** free.

Worth visiting if only for the fine eighteenth-century architecture by John Nash. But you'll also find artillery pieces here ranging from a 1346 Bombard (a kind of stubby mortar) to a four-barrelled 14.5mm anti-aircraft gun used in the Gulf, and a section of Saddam Hussein's massive supergun, which nearly brought down a British government without firing a shot. Model weapons, guidance systems and other weaponry are dotted across the grounds. Note that the museum is gradually moving to a new site – the Royal Artillery Museum, which will open in 2001. At the time this Guide went to press it was not known whether the Museum of Artillery will stay open after then.

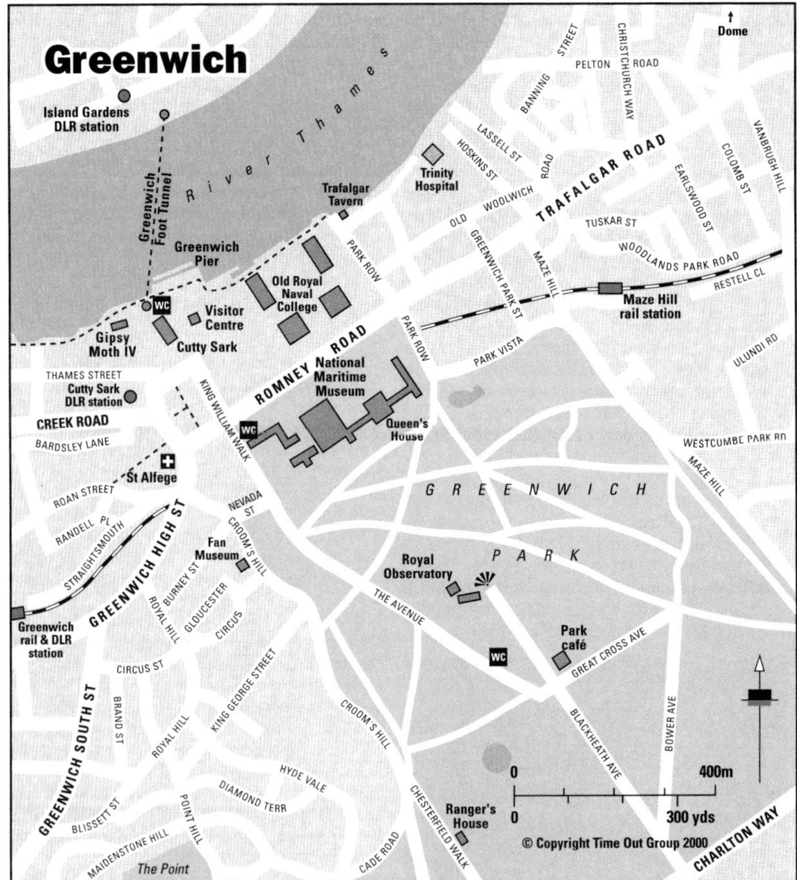

North Woolwich Old Station Museum
Pier Road, E16 (020 7474 7244). Beckton DLR/ North Woolwich rail/Woolwich Dockyard or Woolwich Arsenal rail then foot tunnel/riverboat to North Woolwich Pier. **Open** *Jan-Nov* 1-5pm Sat, Sun; *school holidays* phone for details. **Admission** free.
Dedicated to the London & North Eastern Railway, this museum is at its best on the first Sunday of summer months when the Coffee Pot and Pickett steam engines chug up and down outside. Inside, trains, tickets, station signs and a 1920s ticket office are on display. For railway enthusiasts it's worth a journey to this rather charmless part of London.

Greenwich & Blackheath

Greenwich was the playground of kings and queens. Henry VIII and his daughters Mary I and Elizabeth I were born here, and Greenwich Palace (then called Placentia) was Henry's favourite residence. He could hunt in Greenwich Park and visit his beloved home fleet ('the wood wall of England') at anchor along the river. It was at Greenwich that Sir Walter Ralegh put his cloak over a puddle so Elizabeth I wouldn't get her feet wet.

After the Tudors, the palace fell on hard times. Under Oliver Cromwell, it became first a biscuit factory, then a prison. In 1660, the newly restored Charles II embarked on an ambitious scheme to return Greenwich to its former glory. Work began on a new palace, though in the event only one riverside wing was actually built. William and Mary, who succeeded Charles, preferred the royal palaces at Kensington and Hampton Court and ordered Sir Christopher Wren to design another wing for the unfinished building, to create the Royal Naval Hospital. Better known today as the **Old Royal**

Naval College (the Navy moved out in 1998; *see page 127*), this is the great façade you see from the river today, with a central gap to allow an unobscured view of **Queen's House** behind (*see page 127*), now part of the superb **National Maritime Museum** (*see page 127*). It's for good reason that maritime Greenwich was designated a UNESCO World Heritage Site in 1997.

The best way to arrive at Greenwich is still by river to Greenwich Pier (*see page 42* **A shore thing**), from where the Greenwich shuttle boat also leaves to the Dome (*see also page 126* **Getting to the Dome**). Previously, visitors coming from north of the river had to alight at Island Gardens station and take the foot tunnel under the Thames to get to Greenwich; now they can travel all the way to Greenwich on the Docklands Light Railway (DLR) – the Cutty Sark and Greenwich stations both serve the major sights. Either way, you'll find yourself in the shadow of the **Cutty Sark** (*see page 123*), built in 1869 and in dry dock here since 1954, after an adventurous life as one of the fastest tea clippers in the world. Dwarfed in comparison is the yacht **Gipsy Moth IV** (currently closed for restoration; phone 020 8858 2698 from 2001 to find out when it will reopen), in which Sir Francis Chichester made the first solo round-the-world voyage in 1966-7 (on his return he was knighted with the same sword that Elizabeth I used to ennoble Francis Drake). The new **Greenwich Tourist Information Centre** (0870 608 2000) is based in Pepys House beside the *Cutty Sark*, and provides full details on sights and transport in the area, plus tickets for and information on travel to the Dome. On the other side of the ship is the site of **Greenwich Reach**, an award-winning leisure and retail development, which, when finished, will include a ten-screen cinema, bars, restaurants, luxury flats and the city's first central cruise liner terminal. The first stage of the project should be completed in 2000.

National Maritime Museum. *See page 127.*

Greenwich is a busy, traffic-ridden place. Visitors flood in every weekend to peruse the arts and crafts stalls of sprawling **Greenwich Market** (*see page 222*). Punters aren't exactly spoilt for choice when it comes to eating establishments in the area; many fill up at **Goddard's Ye Old Pie House** at 45 Greenwich Church Street, which has been serving home-baked pies since 1890; **Time** and the **North Pole** (for both *see page 125* **Dome truths**) are two decent alternatives. Non-residents of the area, though, should note that throughout 2000 stringent parking restrictions within two miles of the Dome mean that parking in marked bays is limited to two hours between 10am and 9pm and that drivers cannot return within three hours.

The church of **St Alfege Greenwich** (1712-18), on Greenwich High Road, takes its name from the Archbishop of Canterbury who was martyred on the site by marauding Vikings in 1012, after courageously refusing to sanction a demand for ransom that would have secured his release. The church is normally closed to visitors except at weekends but will be open daily for a small exhibition from 10am to 4pm throughout 2000 as part of the **London String of Pearls Millennium Festival** (*see page 8* **London's your oyster**).

A Thames-side walkway by the *Cutty Sark* takes you past the riverside front of the Old Royal Naval College to the **Trafalgar Tavern**, built directly on to the river and a favourite of literary chums Dickens, Thackeray and Collins, who came regularly for seafood dinners. (Dickens set the wedding feast here in *Our Mutual Friend.*) Tiny Crane Street, on the far side of the pub, takes you past Victorian cottages and disused Highbridge Wharf to the bizarre, white, castellated Trinity Hospital, which, since 1617, has been home to '21 retired gentlemen of Greenwich'. Despite its proximity to Greenwich town centre, this is one of the most peaceful spots anywhere on the urban Thames. The residents must have been horrified as the huge power station next door took shape in 1903, though its quiet bulk has its own grandeur. The path continues until it reaches the **Cutty Sark Tavern**, dating from 1695. Seats outside give a good view of still-active wharfs downstream, as well as the controversial **Dome** (*see*

Cutty Sark *ahoy!*

pages 124-6) a couple of miles downriver. It's around a 30-minute walk from the centre of Greenwich to the Dome, and a further 20 minutes to the Thames Barrier (*see page 135*).

Hilly **Greenwich Park** (*see page 127*) is topped by the **Royal Observatory** (*see page 128*), built during the reign of Charles II. Temporally speaking, this is the centre of the planet. Greenwich Mean Time, introduced in 1890, sets the world's clocks. Here too you can straddle the Greenwich Meridian Line and stand simultaneously in the eastern and western hemispheres. Every day since 1833, the red time-ball on the north-eastern turret of the observatory has dropped at precisely 1pm as a signal to shipmasters on the river to adjust their chronometers. At the southern end of the park stands the eighteenth-century **Ranger's House** (*see page 128*), exhibiting paintings from Jacobean to contemporary times. Visitors wishing to avoid the long hike up the hill can take advantage of the Shuttle Bus (020 8859 1096), a royal blue minibus that meets the boats at Greenwich Pier to transport visitors up through Greenwich Park stopping at the National Maritime Museum and the Royal Observatory. Tickets for the hop-on, hop-off service are valid all day and cost £1.50 for adults and 50p for children.

A long road, Maze Hill, runs south from Trafalgar Road, forming the eastern boundary of Greenwich Park. At the top of the hill, at the corner of Maze Hill and Westcombe Park Road, is the castle-like house built by the architect-playwright John Vanbrugh, who lived here from 1719 to 1726. From here, the view back towards the Old Royal Naval College and the City is superb. On Croom's Hill, west of the park, is the simply titled **Fan Museum**.

Maze Hill brings you to the edge of windswept **Blackheath**. Blackheath Village, on the far side of the heath, lies just beyond the **Princess of Wales** pub, where the first ever rugby union club, Blackheath FC, was founded in 1858. The field-stone **All Saints Church** stands nearby, its unusually tall, sharp spire giving the building the shape of a witch's hat. With its multiplicity of restaurants and estate agents, Blackheath Village exudes middle-class values. **The Paragon**, a crescent on the edge of the heath, lined with prestigious colonnaded houses, was built in the late eighteenth century with the express purpose of attracting the right sort of people to the area when it was still struggling to lose its reputation as a no-go area, plagued by highwaymen. Allowed to fall into disrepair in the 1920s and 1930s, and badly bombed during World War II, the crescent has since been restored to its original state.

Sticking out into the Thames, Greenwich Peninsula is, of course, famous as the site of the controversial **Dome** (*see pages 124-6*). The true legacy of the Dome, which is due to be emptied in 2001 and may be pulled down unless someone can come up with a good reason to keep it, is that it has provided the motivation to turn an enormous slab of polluted wasteland into a place to which people wish to travel and even live. In addition to the structure itself, a £250-million **Millennium Village** is being planned, which will raise ten per cent of its energy needs through wind and solar power. Sadly this development is way off course – originally intended for early 2000, the first phase of this housing complex is now at least 18 months behind schedule.

Cutty Sark

King William Walk, SE10 (020 8858 3445). Greenwich DLR/rail or Cutty Sark DLR. **Open** 10am-5pm daily (last entry 4.30pm). **Admission** £3.50; £2.50 5s-15s, students, OAPs, disabled, ES40s; £8.50 family; free under-5s. *Combined ticket with National Maritime Museum and Royal Observatory* £12; £9.60 students, OAPs, disabled, ES40s; £2.50 under-16s. **Credit** MC, V. **Map** *see p121*

The world's only surviving tea and wool clipper, this 1869 vessel smashed speed records. Visitors are free to roam the beautifully restored decks and crew's quarters, and gaze up at the rigging. Inside are collections of prints and naval relics, plus the world's largest collection of carved and painted figureheads. On summer weekends there are popular costume storytelling sessions, reliving life aboard the ship.
Website: www.cuttysark.org.uk

Fan Museum

12 Crooms Hill, SE10 (020 8305 1441). Greenwich DLR/rail or Cutty Sark DLR. **Open** 11am-5pm Tue-Sat; noon-5pm Sun. **Admission** £3.50; £2.50 7s-15s, students, OAPs; free under-7s, OAPs, disabled 2-5pm Tue. **Credit** MC, £TC, V. **Map** *see p121*

Housed in two attractive converted Georgian town-houses, this is one of only two permanent exhibitions of hand-held folding fans and other breeze-stirring contraptions in the world (the other is in Paris). True to their coy usage, only part of the enormous collection is ever on view at one time: their elasticity necessitates periodic rest. The fans are displayed by theme, such as design, provenance or social history. Among the exhibitions planned for

continued on page 127

Dome sweet Dome?

After all the hype, controversy and criticism the Dome is finally open. So, is the Millennium Experience 'the most spectacular millennial event anywhere in the world', or is it the most spectacular millennial waste of money anywhere in the world? As fast as the PR people have pumped it up, the press have deflated it. Now you can decide for yourselves.

There's no denying that the structure itself is something else. Designed by the Richard Rogers Partnership, the largest roof in the world (covering 8 hectares/20 acres) is stretched over 12 masts, providing a vast internal space (enough to squeeze in 13 Albert Halls, if that means anything to you). There's far more controversy over what the Dome represents. Entertainment? Education? National self-promotion? The Millennium Experience's avowed aim for visitors of 'exploring the possibilities of their own personal futures in the next millennium through a spectacular array of attractions and events' sounds laudable and impressive enough (if rather woolly), but does it deliver?

Teething problems encountered by many visitors – in particular the huge queues for the more popular exhibits such as the Body zone – may well be ironed out over the course of 2000 (after which time the Millennium Experience is due to be dismantled), but initial public reaction was so disappointing that extra attractions may be added during the year. Supporters of the Dome may recount how many ambitious, pioneering projects met hostility and negativism in their early stages yet were eventually judged as triumphs (the Eiffel Tower, Festival of Britain, etc). Nevertheless, the (heavily sponsored and branded) exhibits do come across as little more than second-rate mind candy, and the lack of a coherent, imaginative, innovative vision is all too evident. In this sense, the Dome could be said to capture the essence of new Britain, especially the casual acceptance of dumbed-down mediocrity. It may well provide an entertaining day out, especially for those with kids in tow, but it'll have to do a lot more than this if we're to feel that the £758 million cost (not to mention the individual cost to the visitor) was money well spent.

Key to exhibits

The numbers of the 'zones' match those on the plan opposite.

1 Home Planet A virtual tour of the Earth.

2 Living Island A re-creation of a typical British seaside resort, with a beach, bandstand, pier and lighthouse; and, er some cliffs made from scrap metal.

3 Shared Ground A look at how our private spaces (bedroom, lounge, etc) reflect our personalities, and the potential for shared experiences.

4 Play One of the most fun exhibits, where kids (and parents) can score a goal, play a concerto and frolic in the electronic playground.

5 Body Journey through an abstract human form, learning of the challenges of advances in science, genetics and medicine.

6 Main entrance

7 Learning & Work Relive your school days in an outsize school corridor. See how the world of work has changed and will change further; test your skills by playing interactive challenges.

8 Mind Senses and perception are explored in this imagination-enhancing zone.

9 Faith A celebration of 2,000 years of the many religions that make up today's multi-faith Britain.

10 Self Portrait Modern Britain as reflected by the attitudes, images and cultures of the British.

11 Journey A virtual reality trip from past modes of transport through to possible future ones (with the inevitable nod towards 'green' solutions).

12 High Way Inner path within the Dome.

13 Mast Way Outer path within the Dome.

14 Money What it is, how we use it and how the global market works.

15 Our Town Stage A venue for performances from local communities. International visitors will perform during the World Stage Season.

16 Rest Relax in a mental flotation tank, where sounds, light and shapes provide a relaxing antidote to the activity outside.

17 Talk An exploration of means of communication; take part in a live TV show.

18 The Millennium Show Arena Taking place in the 12,000-capacity central arena, this huge spectacle will include acrobats, trapeze artists, dance, theatre, trampolining and abseiling, creating an allegorical love story.

Outside the Dome

Skyscape By day see a specially commissioned episode of *Blackadder* on the big screen; by night see live concerts and events.

Learning Experience Centre

Greenwich Pavilion The story of time, Greenwich and the Dome.

Dome truths

Where to buy tickets

Tickets are available from the country's 25,000 National Lottery Retailers (including many newsagents), the Dome Ticket Line (0870 606 2000, subject to a £2.50 booking fee), the Millennium Experience website (www.dome2000.co.uk, subject to a £1 booking fee) and railway stations, bus stations and tour operators. **Note that visitors cannot turn up at the Dome without a ticket.**

Where to eat & drink

The Dome has more than 50 places to eat, from (many) fast food outlets to restaurants (among the better ones are Seabar and Acclaim!) and the Red Boot pub. Alternatively, head to **Greenwich** – options include **Time** (7A College Approach; 020 8305 9767), serving refined Modern European food; the **North Pole** (131 Greenwich High Road; 020 8853 3020), dishing up pricey-but-worth-it cuisine; and the **Trafalgar Tavern** (Park Row; 020 8858 2437), a huge pub with better-than-average food and great views of the Dome. **Blackheath**, meanwhile, boasts the upmarket **Lawn** (1 Lawn Terrace; 020 8355 1110) and the imaginative food of **Chapter Two** (43-45 Montpelier Vale; 020 8333 2666).

Admission prices

Adults £20; 5s-15s £16.50; under-5s free; OAPs £18; students £16.50; ES40s £12; family (two adults and three children or one adult and four children) £57, working out at £11.40 per person. There are discounts for groups of 15 or more.

Opening times

Gates open at 9am-6pm, and the Dome at 10am, daily during 2000. Extra evening sessions are planned during April 2000 (6-11pm).

Other facilities

These include gift and souvenir shops, cash machines, toilets, baby-changing facilities and a Tourist Information Centre.

Facilities for disabled visitors

Seats, ramps, lifts and wheelchair-height payphones, plus a free wheelchair loan service (call 0870 241 0540). Deaf and speech-impaired callers with their own text phone should call 0161 238 5117 for information. Audio guides are also available for non-English-speaking visitors and for disabled visitors.

General information

Visit the website at www.dome2000.co.uk or phone 0870 603 2000.

Please note that all information was correct at the time of going to press.

Getting to the Dome

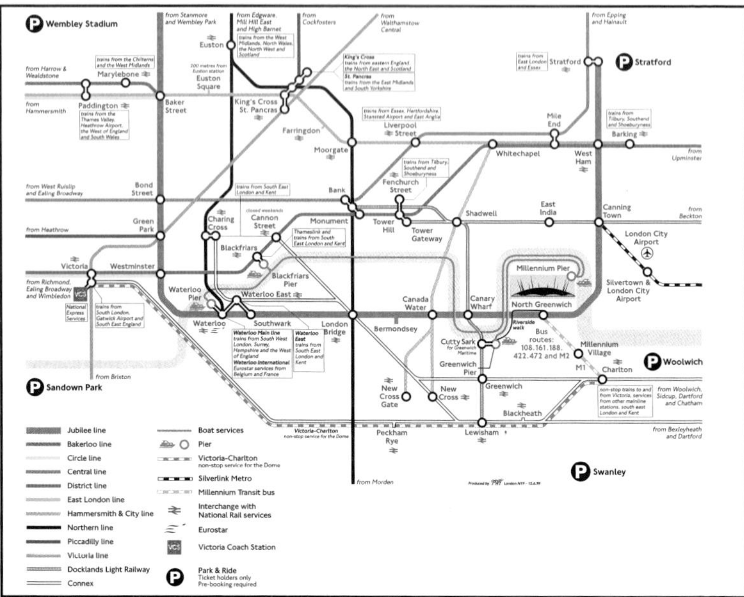

The Dome is accessible by virtually any method you choose – except car, that is (during 2000 there's no parking in the vicinity of the Dome, and a two-mile restricted parking zone around it). Here's the low-down on how to get there.

By tube: the Dome is next to North Greenwich tube station on the Jubilee Line. Visitors travelling by tube to the Dome can buy a one-day Millennium LT Card (£3.50 adults, £1 children), valid for unlimited travel on the tube, buses and DLR at any time on the day of a Dome visit (buy them from Dome Ticket Line on 0870 606 2000 not less than seven days before a visit). Alternatively, they can be bought from any tube station no more than four days before a Dome visit, and visitors must show a valid Dome admission ticket. For London Travel Information phone 020 7222 1234 or visit www.londontransport.co.uk. Transport advice for disabled passengers is available on 020 7918 3312.

By train then transit bus: direct trains run from Victoria Station to Charlton Station, where they are met by the M1 'Millennium Transit' bus for the short trip to the Dome. The M2 'Millennium Transit' bus runs from Greenwich rail station (accessible from Charing Cross Station) to the Dome.

By boat: **City Cruises** run the Millennium Express service from Waterloo and Blackfriars piers direct to the Dome every 30 minutes (for details, call 020 7740 0400 or see www.citycruises.com). **White Horse Fast Ferries** operates the Greenwich Shuttle service from Greenwich Pier to the Dome about every 15 minutes (for details, call 0870 240 3240 or see www.whitehorse.co.uk/dome).

By bus & coach: local buses M1, M2, 108, 161, 188, 422 and 472 all run to the North Greenwich Transport Interchange by the Dome. Local coach companies may run services direct to the Dome.

By foot, cycle or motorcyle: a 1½-mile (2-km) riverside cycle/walkway links Greenwich town centre to the Dome, where there is a secure bike park.

By road: there are five Dome 'park and ride' car parks around London, based at Wembley Station, Stratford, Woolwich, Swanley and Sandown Park. Visitors should phone 0870 241 0541 to book and pay for a space, for directions and details of onward travel to the Dome.

Only **taxis** and **minicabs** can drop off and pick up at the Dome. Parking is available for motorbikes, pre-booked coaches and minibuses. The only car parking is for **Orange Badge holders**, who should ring 0870 241 0540 to book a space.

2000 are **Commemorative Fans** (until 23 Apr), which looks at fans created especially for important events; the museum itself now also has its own specially designed Millennium Fan, which is displayed on site.
Website: www.fan-museum.org

Greenwich Park

Charlton Way, SE10 (020 8858 2608). Blackheath or Maze Hill rail/Cutty Sark DLR/Greenwich DLR/rail. **Open** *pedestrians* 6am-dusk daily; *traffic* 7am-dusk daily. **Map** *see p121*
The remains of 20 Saxon grave mounds and a Roman temple have been identified within its precincts, but this beautiful riverside park is more famous for its Tudor and Stuart history. Henry VIII was born at Greenwich Palace and it remained his favourite residence, surrounded by a magnificent park for hunting and hawking. In 1616, James I commissioned Inigo Jones to rebuild the Tudor palace. The result was **Queen's House** (*see p127*), England's first Palladian villa. In the 1660s, the park was redesigned by André Le Nôtre, who landscaped Versailles, but Charles II's plan for a new palace was later adapted to become the **Old Royal Naval College** (*see p127*). Crowning the hill at the top of the park are the **Royal Observatory** (*see p128*) and Flamsteed House, both designed by Wren. The **Ranger's House** (*see p128*), in the south of the park, is also well worth a visit. The view from the observatory towards the river is one of the finest in London. In summer, brass bands perform in the afternoon, and there are puppet shows in the playground during August.

National Maritime Museum

Romney Road, SE10 (020 8858 4422/info 020 8312 6565). Greenwich DLR/rail or Cutty Sark DLR. **Open** 10am-5pm daily. **Admission** £7.50; £6 students, OAPs, disabled, ES40s; free under-16s. *Combined ticket with Cutty Sark & Royal Observatory* £12; £9.60 students, OAPs, disabled, ES40s; £2.50 under-16s. *GoSee Card member (see p32).* **Credit** AmEx, MC, £TC, V. **Map** *see p121*
Don't be put off if you're not nautically inclined: this ever-improving museum is enjoyable for all but the terminally incurious. A series of entertaining galleries does a good job of putting Britain's maritime heritage in perspective, cleverly combining traditional exhibits with interactive elements. At its heart is the **Neptune Court** (opened in spring 1999), a large, airy covered space with exhibition galleries on four sides around a central display area.

A slightly bewildering colour-coded floor plan guides you through the themed exhibitions. In the **Maritime London** section, old prints and lithographs provide a reminder of the capital's marine history, while video installations explore the city's current role as the financial hub of the shipping industry. Two **Explorers** galleries feature man's attempts to push back the boundaries of the known world; displays look at navigation, marine archaeology, early journeys of discovery made by Polynesians and Vikings, as well as the imperialist drive of European exploration. Among many fascinating exhibits are a reindeer-hide sleeping bag used on Scott's fateful expedition to the Antarctic, and the scanty remains of the equally doomed attempt by Sir John Franklin to find a north-west passage from the Atlantic to the Pacific in 1845. Other innovations include **Rank & Style** – a survey of naval costume and its influence on fashion; **Art and the Sea**, which explores the role of the sea in European art; and the ecology-oriented **Future of the Sea** display.

Despite the lure of the new exhibitions, the **Nelson Gallery** remains one of the most popular sections of the museum. A comprehensive monument to the naval hero, it charts his achievements at sea and liaisons on land. Not surprisingly, the Battle of Trafalgar features heavily: look out for JMW Turner's biggest ever painting (of the battle) and, on a more morbid note, the blood-soaked uniform Nelson was wearing when fatally wounded.

All Hands and the **Bridge** are hands-on, interactive galleries, where younger visitors can get to learn how to send a distress signal using Morse code, flags or radio; and try their hands at steering a Viking longboat, a paddle steamer and a modern passenger ferry.
Website: www.nmm.ac.uk

Old Royal Naval College

King William Walk, SE10 (020 8269 4744). Greenwich DLR/rail or Cutty Sark DLR. **Open** 10am-5pm Mon-Sat; 12.30-5pm Sun (last entry 4pm). **Admission** £5; £3 students, OAPs, disabled, ES40s; free under-16s with an adult. **Map** *see p121*
Founded by William III as a naval hospital, designed by Wren and built on the site of Greenwich Palace, the Royal Naval College was split in two in order to give an unimpeded view of **Queen's House** (*see below*) from the river, and vice versa. After 125 years in residence, the Navy vacated the buildings in 1998 and the University of Greenwich took up residence. The spectacular Painted Hall (decorated by James Thornhill in 1708-27) and the chapel are open to the public, as before, and in addition a space has been opened up for temporary exhibitions, with guided tours and concerts throughout 2000 as part of the **London String of Pearls Millennium Festival** (*see p8* **London's your oyster**). An investigation of Tudor Britain is also planned for 2000.
Website: www.greenwichfoundation.org.uk

Queen's House

Romney Road, SE10 (020 8858 4422/info 020 8312 6565). Greenwich DLR/rail or Cutty Sark DLR. **Open** 10am-5pm daily. **Admission** £7.50; £6 students, OAPs, disabled, ES40s; £3.75 5s-16s; free under-5s; £20 family. *GoSee Card member (see p32).* **Credit** AmEx, DC, JCB, MC, £TC, V. **Map** *see p121*
Furnished as it would have been in the seventeenth century, this was the first Palladian-style villa in Britain. It was designed by Inigo Jones in 1616 for James I's wife, Anne of Denmark, who died before it was finished. During 1999 the building was upgraded to improve disabled access, security and its suitability as an exhibition space. Until 24 September 2000, the house will play host to

The Story of Time, a comprehensive survey of what time means around the world and throughout the ages. Art works with reference to time, featuring paintings by Titian and Canaletto, will be included, as will sundials and an array of other mechanical equipment for measuring and quantifying the hours, days, months and years.

Ranger's House

Chesterfield Walk, SE10 (020 8853 0035). Blackheath rail or Greenwich DLR/rail/53 bus. **Open** *Apr-Sept* 10am-6pm daily; *Oct* 10am-5pm daily; *Nov-Mar* 10am-4pm Wed-Sun. **Admission** £2.50; £1.30 5s-15s; £1.90 students, OAPs, disabled, ES40s. **Map** *see p121*
This lovely red-brick eighteenth-century villa houses the Suffolk collection of Jacobean and Stuart portraits. The ground-floor gallery shows contemporary work, with exhibitions changing every three months or so. The Greenwich printmakers, exhibitions of textiles and the work of artist Tom Phillips have all been shown recently. In the Coach House there's a study centre dedicated to English urban architecture from the seventeenth to the nineteenth centuries.
Website: www.english-heritage.org.uk

Royal Observatory

Romney Road, SE10 (020 8858 4422/recorded info 020 8312 6565). Greenwich DLR/rail or Cutty Sark DLR. **Open** 10am-5pm daily. **Admission** £6; £4.80 students, OAPs, disabled, ES40s; free under-16s. *Combined ticked with Cutty Sark & National Maritime Museum* £12; £9.60 students, OAPs, disabled, ES40s; £2.50 under-16s. *GoSee Card member (see p32).* **Credit** AmEx, DC, JCB, MC, £TC, V. **Map** *see p121*
The Royal Observatory was founded in 1675 by Charles II to find a solution to the problem of determining longitude at sea. It was clockmaker John Harrison, no doubt encouraged by the £20,000 prize money, who eventually found the solution in 1763. No official astronomical observation has been made here since 1954, and the cluster of buildings now houses a detailed exhibition charting the build-up to the establishment of Greenwich Mean Time and zero meridian (which divides the globe into East and West), both based here. There's a **planetarium** too, which puts on informative shows lasting around 40 minutes, usually at 2.30pm from Monday to Friday (£2; £1.50 children, concs), but phone first to check.

Rotherhithe

Upriver from Greenwich, the Thames curves past down-at-heel **Deptford** (where the Royal Naval Yards once built the warships with which Britain controlled the world's seas) to **Rotherhithe**. Pepys knew Rotherhithe as Redriffe, though both names may derive from the Anglo-Saxon words 'redhra' and 'hyth' – 'mariner's haven'. The old name still holds good: Rotherhithe is relatively undisturbed by visitors, with superb views across the Thames to Wapping and two of the best riverside pubs in London. The infamous Judge Jeffreys is said to have used **The Angel** (101 Bermondsey Wall East) as a vantage point to watch pirates being executed on the opposite bank. The grassy area opposite the pub, with the remains of a few walls, is all that exists of a moated manor house, built by Edward III around 1355. A short walk away is **The Mayflower** (117 Rotherhithe Street; *see page 198*), dating from 1550 and, like the Angel, built on piles so it stands directly over the river. It was given its present name when *The Mayflower* docked here in 1620 before beginning her voyage to America. Captain Christopher Jones, who commanded her, is buried in nearby **St Mary's Rotherhithe** (*see below*). Look out for the old school opposite the church, with its carved figures of eighteenth-century schoolchildren.

St Mary's Rotherhithe

St Marychurch Street, SE16 (020 7231 2465). Rotherhithe tube. **Open** 7am-6pm Mon-Thur; 8am-6pm Sat, Sun. **Admission** free.
A gem of a church, built in 1715 by local sailors and watermen. Today, thanks to acts of burglary and vandalism, the interior can only be viewed through glass, under the watchful eye of a video camera. The communion table in the Lady Chapel and two bishop's chairs were made from timber salvaged from the warship *Fighting Temeraire*, the subject of Turner's painting now hanging in the National Gallery.

Peckham, Dulwich & Camberwell

Much of south London is stigmatised as a dull, amorphous sprawl. But this (predominantly north Londoner) prejudice masks a patchwork of communities of often individual character and (sometimes hidden) charm.

Finding such charm in **Peckham** is, admittedly, a challenge. Like many districts of south London, this was a quiet rural area until the Industrial Revolution. It was a favourite stopping place for cattle drovers on their way to markets in the City; they would leave their herds grazing on the common, **Peckham Rye**, while they refreshed themselves at the inns along Peckham High Street. As a child, William Blake saw a vision of angels on the Rye, and in her novel *The Ballad of Peckham Rye* (1960), Muriel Spark refers, apparently without irony, to 'the dusky scope of the Rye's broad lyrical acres'. (Drinkers: she also maps out a useful pub crawl on page one.) The Victorian terraces that feature in the novel have now mostly gone, replaced by monolithic council estates and tower blocks. Peckham may yet surprise us, though: a £5-million library, designed by architects Alsop & Stormer, is the focus of a new public square and park that should be completed by January 2000. The library itself is impressive, cantilevered out over the concrete below, with little in the way of visible support.

West of here, long **Lordship Lane** is the main thoroughfare through more sedate **Dulwich**. (Its only pub of real distinction is the **East Dulwich**

Tavern, on the corner of Spurling Road, but there are plenty of decent cheap restaurants.) **Dulwich Park**, with its dramatic view of the Crystal Palace TV transmitter (in **Crystal Palace Park**; *see below*), and adjoining **Dulwich Village** lie at the southern tip of Lordship Lane. Dotted with modern sculpture, the grounds of **Dulwich Picture Gallery** (*see below*) are a pleasant place to sit (the gallery itself reopens in May 2000 following extensive refurbishment). The rarefied atmosphere of the Village, with its distinctive dark brick, is as great a contrast to rough-and-tumble Peckham as you could imagine. Heading south out of the Village, College Road is lined with fine detached houses. At **Dulwich Common** a spectacular sight greets you: palatial, red-brick **Dulwich College**, serene in its verdant grounds. Old boys include PG Wodehouse and Raymond Chandler. Close by is the marvellously eccentric **Horniman Museum** (*see below*).

Between Brixton and Peckham, **Camberwell** was a country village until the mid-nineteenth century. The composer Felix Mendelssohn lived in Southampton Street; his 'Spring Song', written in 1842, was originally entitled 'Camberwell Green', after the former village green (tarted up in recent years) next to what is now the junction of Camberwell Road and Denmark Hill. Camberwell's best feature is **Camberwell Grove**, a steep hill lined with tall Georgian houses. Its golden-lit drawing rooms, reminiscent of Henry James novels, are an enticing sight at dusk. At the eastern end of Camberwell Church Street, **St Giles Church**, built to the designs of Sir George Gilbert Scott (1844), has grown mossy over the years and, with its 72-m (210-ft) spire, now seems embarrassingly big for its surroundings.

Crystal Palace Park

SE19 (no phone/museum 020 8676 0700). Crystal Palace rail/2B, 3, 63, 108B, 122, 137, 157, 227, 249 bus. **Open** *park* dawn-dusk daily. *Museum* 11am-5pm Sun, bank holiday Mon. **Admission** free; donations requested.

Built to house the 1851 Great Exhibition, the all-glass Crystal Palace was originally erected in Hyde Park (*see p95*). After the Exhibition closed, the building was moved to Sydenham, where it was used for exhibitions, plays and concerts. The extensive grounds contained an amusement park and, dotted here and there, life-sized models of dinosaurs. In 1936, the Crystal Palace caught fire and burned to the ground; the small but informative **Crystal Palace Museum**, housed in the old engineering school where John Logie Baird invented television, chronicles the history of the palace (note its limited opening times). The model dinosaurs, which survived the blaze and are now classified as listed buildings, are a reminder of how quirky the whole place was in its heyday. Views from the park – which contains the **National Sports Centre** (*see p292*) – are stunning.

Dulwich Picture Gallery

College Road, SE21 (020 8693 5254). North Dulwich or West Dulwich rail/3, 12, 37, 176, P4 bus. **Open** *from end May 2000* 10am-5pm Tue-Fri; 11am-5pm Sat, Sun. **Admission** £3; £1.50 concs; free under-16s, and for all Fri. **Credit** MC, V.

Dulwich Picture Gallery – the oldest public gallery in Britain – is set to reopen towards the end of May 2000. The building, designed by Sir John Soane, has been revamped by Rick Mather Architects, restoring some of the building's original features while adding new facilities, such as a café, a practical art room (for the gallery's educational programme) and extra space for temporary exhibitions of more contemporary work. During the gallery's closure, much of the collection embarked upon a worldwide tour (generating much-needed revenue), but the Old Master paintings from the seventeenth and eighteenth centuries will return to their newly polished home.

Horniman Museum

100 London Road, SE23 (020 8699 1872/recorded info 020 8699 2339). Forest Hill rail/63, 122, 176, 185, 312, 352, P4, P13 bus. **Open** 10.30am-5.30pm Mon-Sat; 2-5.30pm Sun. **Admission** free.

It's a testament to this idiosyncratic museum that a journey from central London is worthwhile to discover its multifaceted charms; children enjoy the place enormously. The essence of nineteenth-century tea merchant Frederick Horniman's endearingly peculiar collection is on view in the natural history hall. Here an immense stuffed walrus presides gruffly over an eclectic display of other specimens. The surprising Apostle's Clock enacts a famous episode from the Gospels daily at 4pm. Equally popular is the Living Waters Aquarium, which demonstrates the life in a river on its way to the sea. In summer, the formal and sunken gardens with fine views are an added attraction, as is the small zoo containing farmyard animals.

The museum is in the middle of a major redevelopment programme, due for completion in late 2001, and until then there will be disruption with some galleries closed (the entire museum will shut for around three months in early 2001; call to check before setting out). When work is finished, the Horniman will have new spaces for the music and anthropology collections, and a new temporary exhibitions gallery, education section, shop and café. The most exciting development, however, will be Britain's first permanent gallery, **African Worlds**, devoted to African art and sculpture. There's also a wide range of events and activities for both adults and children.

Stockwell, Kennington & Vauxhall

Stockwell was, at one time, a medieval manor, with the manor house on the site of present-day Stockwell Gardens, off Stockwell Road. Until the feverish house- and railway-building of the 1840s, Stockwell remained a country village. South Lambeth Common, on which cattle used to graze, has now been reduced to the scrap of green bearing the clock tower and war memorial outside Stockwell tube station.

St Mark's Church, between Prima Road and Camberwell New Road, was built in 1824 on the site of a gallows; many of the Jacobites who fought in the 1745 rebellion were hanged, drawn and quartered here. Nearby **Kennington Park** was originally Kennington Common. In the eighteenth and nineteenth centuries, preachers – among them John Wesley – addressed large audiences here. Today, Kennington is best known for its sporting connections. The **Foster's Oval** cricket ground (*see page 290*) is the home of Surrey County Cricket Club. Opened in 1845, it has hosted not only Test matches but most of the football FA Cup Finals between 1870 and 1890.

The continuation of Kennington Lane beyond the junction with Kennington Road brings you to some of south London's most delightful streets – **Cardigan Street**, **Courtney Street** and **Courtney Square** are lined with clean, neat, light-brown terraced houses, all dating from 1914 and featuring matching white ironwork porches and railings. The rather unexpected glimpse of the Palace of Westminster from Cardigan Road is a reminder of how close the area is to central London.

Vauxhall lies between Kennington and the Thames. The wasteland bounded by Tyers Street, Goding Street and Glasshouse Walk is all that remains of the eighteenth-century pleasure park, **Vauxhall Gardens**. Henry Fielding's novel *Amelia* and Thackeray's *Vanity Fair* give a taste of the Gardens at their peak.

Nineties Vauxhall is not a pretty sight. Its hub, near Vauxhall station, consists of a formidable road junction, bisected by a railway viaduct. Late on Friday and Saturday nights, the area tries to put on a cheerful face, when the **Royal Vauxhall Tavern** (*see page 265*), one of south London's most popular gay venues, throbs into life. There is also a lively Portuguese community in the area (and some good restaurants, notably **Bar Estrela**, 111-115 South Lambeth Road). Lambeth Road, meanwhile, is home to one of the capital's best museums, the **Imperial War Museum** (*see below*).

Imperial War Museum

Lambeth Road, SE1 (020 7416 5320/ mail@iwm.org.uk). Lambeth North or Southwark tube/Waterloo tube/rail. **Open** 10am-6pm daily. **Admission** £5.20; £4.20 students, OAPs, ES40s; £2.60 disabled; free under-16s; free (for everyone) 4.30-6pm daily. *GoSee Card member (see p32).* **Credit** MC, £TC, V. **Map 11 N10**

The early nineteenth century's most famous lunatic asylum, known as Bedlam, now houses the country's memorial to the wars of the twentieth century. A rotating clock-hand in the basement symbolises the cost of war in terms of human lives, an estimated body count that has already passed 100 million.

In the vast atrium, you can see pristine restored and cut-away examples of a selection of hardware, including a Sopwith Camel, a V2 rocket and a Spitfire. The lower ground floor galleries hold the excellent four-part permanent exhibition of the history of warfare in the twentieth century. Two of the most popular exhibits, or rather 'experiences', are **The Blitz** and **The Trench**, which do a good job of bringing history to life while avoiding vicarious thrills. **Secret War** on the first floor attempts to shed light on the clandestine world of espionage from 1909 to the present day. Exhibits range from Brezhnev's uniform to an original German 'Enigma' encrypting machine. The second floor is devoted to the museum's art collections, including the huge *Gassed* painted in 1919 by John Singer Sargent and works by CRW Nevinson and Stanley Spencer.

Since 1999 the museum has been undergoing major redevelopment work, due for completion in 2001. Central to the programme is the creation of the third-largest **Holocaust Museum** in the world, covering two floors of new gallery space. This will replace the small but harrowing **Belsen** exhibition currently on the lower ground floor and should open to the public in July 2000. The redeveloped gallery space will also house **The Age of Total War** exhibition and extensive educational facilities.

The major exhibition (designed by Sir Terence Conran) chronicling the changing face of Britain from 1945 to 1965 – **Post War Britain: From the Bomb to the Beatles** – continues until May 2000.
Website: www.iwm.org.uk

Brixton

Brixton has existed, in various guises, for around a thousand years, of which the first 985 or so were relatively uneventful. The small settlement here in the early nineteenth century underwent intense development between the 1860s and 1890s, as railways and trams linked it with the heart of London. Around the turn of the century, the social character of Brixton began to alter, as the large houses built along the trunk roads 100 years earlier were turned into flats and boarding houses. The latter were popular with theatre people working in the West End.

Brixton's ethnic identity changed during the 1940s and 1950s, with the arrival of immigrants from the West Indies. A generation later, simmering hostility between the black community and the police, combined with economic decline, culminated in serious rioting in 1981, 1985 and 1995.

Yet today the mood in Brixton is ostensibly upbeat. Problems (particularly drug-related) certainly remain, and this contributes to a volatile edge that is prone to sparking up now and again. But the influx of youngish, middle-class residents with a bit of money to burn has fuelled some of the bar, club and restaurant enterprises that continue to spring up around the centre of Brixton, giving it a rather cool kudos.

By day, however, Brixton is fairly unassuming. The market and vendors around the tube station get going early, but not much else shakes a leg until late morning. After work things ease into their stride. Cinema-goers congregate outside the **Ritzy** (*see page 259*), and drinking and dancing joints such as the **Dogstar**, the **Bug Bar** (for both, *see page 244*), the **Isobar**, and the **Fridge Bar** (*see page 245*) start to fill, while **Fujiyama** and the **Satay Bar** get their first cocktail- and saki-sipping, noodle- and rice-eating punters. Later on, full-on clubs such as **Mass** and **The Fridge** (for both, *see page 245*) take over. Food options include the crypt-ensconced vegetarian **Bah Humbug** (*see page 187*), the modern international fare of **Helter Skelter** (*see page 173*), the exemplary Caribbean cuisine of the rum-soaked **Brixtonian Havana Club** (*see page 168*), and the freshest newcomer on the block, **Ichiban** sushi bar, on Atlantic Road. Brixton is also home to London's friendliest gay B&B, **Number Seven** (*see page 267*).

Brixton is more than just ragged around the edges, however. It's true to say there are encouraging signs: a chunk of the centre is currently being redeveloped to provide more shopping facilities, and over the past year or so a handful of fashion, furniture and objets d'art boutiques have sprung up along Coldharbour Lane and Atlantic Road. For the time being, though, much is still run-down and grimy. Emerging from the tube station to a chorus of shouts from incense-sellers, *Big Issue* vendors, drunks and the multitude of religious groups with a hankering for a hold on your soul can be quite a shock for the unwary. And there's plenty more noise, chaos and colour in evidence in **Brixton Market** (*see page 222*), which offers the widest selection of African and Caribbean food in Europe, as well as everything from wigs to ironing boards. And if you want to take a breather from the bustle of the market, sit at one of the tables outside tiny **Eco Brixton** (4 Market Row) or, if it's too busy, **Pangaea** at 15 Atlantic Road. The market sprawls – partly under cover – between Electric Avenue and Brixton Station Road. The former was so named in the 1880s when it became the first street in the area to be lit by electricity (and was later immortalised in song by Eddy Grant). More serene attractions of the area include hilly **Brockwell Park**, 15 minutes' walk from the tube station, with its 1930s-built lido (*see page 288*).

Clapham

Clapham has two centres: **Clapham Junction** (technically part of Battersea) and **Clapham Common**. Until the railways arrived, Clapham Junction was a country crossroads, with **The Falcon** providing refreshment for travellers. Nowadays, the pub provides respite for shoppers: Clapham's own department store, **Arding & Hobbs**, opposite, has been serving the area since 1885. With more than 2,500 trains passing through every day, Clapham Junction is one of the busiest stations in the world.

Battersea Rise, leading towards the Common, is a somewhat arty stretch, with a huge choice of restaurants, including **La Pampa**, an Argentinian grill joint (*see page 167*). **Northcote Road**, running at right angles to Battersea Rise, is a rapidly developing bar and restaurant alley that still (just) clings on to its street fruit and vegetable market. Beyond the junction with Bramfield Road is a stretch of antique shops. **The Hive**, at 53 Webb's Road (parallel to Northcote Road), is one of the most extraordinary shops in south London. Devoted entirely to bees and their products, it features a huge glass hive containing 20,000 live bees, linked to the outside world by a tunnel opening on to the street.

Battersea Rise eventually becomes Clapham Common North Side, the eastern reaches of which contain tall, stately houses with enviable views of the Common. A flat, grassy expanse within a triangle of roads, **Clapham Common** is somewhere between a park and a wild place; its bleak atmosphere has never been more vividly evoked than in Graham Greene's *The End of the Affair*. After dark, parts of the Common have gained a reputation as gay cruising grounds (and brought to an end the career of Welsh Secretary Ron Davies who experienced his ill-explained 'moment of madness' here in late 1998).

The streets around the north end of Clapham Common are transforming from down-at-heel to desirable at an extraordinary rate. A sure sign of this is the proliferation of good new bars and restaurants (try laid-back French **Gastro** at 67 Venn Street; the pizzas at trendy **Eco**, 162 Clapham High Street; or cheap Thai scoff at **Pepper Tree**, 19 Clapham Common Southside).

There's more than a whiff of snobbery about genteel **Clapham Old Town**, just north-east of the Common, but it's worth a visit, if only to take in the villagey atmosphere – especially at its central point, where eighteenth-century pubs face on to an approximate square (complete with a small, countryish bus terminus). The 88 bus, rather self-consciously styled 'The Clapham Omnibus', starts its pleasantly circuitous route from here.

Famous for its lush setting on the edge of the common, **Holy Trinity Church** was well known in the nineteenth century as the headquarters of the Clapham Sect, a group of wealthy Anglicans who advocated 'muscular Christianity'; one of them was William Wilberforce, the anti-slavery campaigner. The church was rebuilt after being hit by a V2 in 1945. For breakfast, or a spot of afternoon tea, the determinedly camp **Tea-time**, at 21 The Pavement, is recommended.

Battersea

In Saxon times, **Battersea** was a small settlement known as Batrices Ege (Badric's Island), bounded by the Thames to the north and marshes to the south. Known for centuries as a centre for market gardening (part of it is still called Lavender Hill), the character of Battersea changed dramatically with the Industrial Revolution. In the nineteenth century, scores of factories sprang up, and the area was covered by a dense network of railway lines.

Battersea is still best approached by rail. The journey from Victoria Station will give you the greatest view of its best-known landmark, Sir Giles Gilbert Scott's gargantuan **Battersea Power Station** (built 1929-33). Closed in 1983, it has been subject to innumerable development plans. Occasional events are held in the shell of the building, but its long-term future remains uncertain.

Battersea Park (*see below*), bordering the river, has a bloody history: in 1671 Colonel Blood hid in reeds near what is now the boating lake, waiting to shoot King Charles II as he bathed (Blood's nerve failed him); and in 1829 the Duke of Wellington fought a pistol duel here with Lord Winchilsea, who had accused him of treason for introducing the Catholic Emancipation Bill.

Battersea has long been a favourite spot for artists and writers: the old **Battersea Bridge** was the subject of Whistler's moody *Nocturnes*; Turner used to paint the river and its sunsets from **St Mary's Battersea** (and William Blake married the daughter of a local market gardener here); more recently, the Pogues celebrated Battersea Bridge's next-door neighbour in 'Misty Morning, Albert Bridge'.

Battersea Park

Albert Bridge Road, SW11 (020 8871 7530). Sloane Square tube/Battersea Park or Queenstown Road rail. **Open** 8am-dusk daily (later during events). **Map 4 F13**

Lively Battersea Park, opened in 1858 by Queen Victoria, was conceived as a means of keeping the lower orders orderly with healthful recreation. These days its patrons are more mixed, though still generally well behaved. Its most famous feature, **Festival Gardens**, was one of the attractions of the 1951 Festival of Britain. There are sports facilities and playgrounds, a boating lake, a café, a children's zoo, Bank Holiday funfairs and other events throughout the year. The Peace Pagoda by the Thames was built by Japanese monks and nuns in 1985 to commemorate Hiroshima Day. The park is currently undergoing a massive £12-million restoration, with the first works starting in spring 2000. New features will include a pier with services to the Dome and a new boathouse. Longer-term plans include the restoration of the sub-tropical gardens, the elegant promenade along the Thames and the Festival Gardens.

Rambling in **Richmond Park**. *See page 134.*

Putney, Barnes, Mortlake & Kew

Originally a fishing and farming community, **Putney** ('Putta's landing') can claim to be London's first suburb. Thomas Cromwell was the most senior among the scores of Tudor courtiers who bought homes in the village and travelled to their jobs in the royal palaces around west London.

Away from the narrow, busy High Street, Putney is a peaceful place, especially if you head west from the bridge along the Embankment, with its ubiquitous canoe trailers hitched to Land Rovers. The annual **Boat Race** (*see page 6*) is held between here and Mortlake.

Striking inland across the base of the Putney peninsula eventually brings you to **Mortlake**. On the way, the main road, Queen's Ride, crosses a railway line at **Barnes Common**. On the western side of the humpbacked bridge, there's a spindly tree invariably decorated with flowers and other offerings to Marc Bolan. On 16 September 1977, the T-Rex singer's Mini collided with the tree, killing him instantly. Barnes is also the setting, from May 2000, for **WWT The Wetland Centre** (*see page 133*), a unique mosaic of wetland habitats created from scratch from what were the Thames Water Barn Elm reservoirs and water works.

Like Putney, Mortlake is a former riverside village that was gradually overtaken by genteel suburbia. A little of its original character remains in Christ Church Road, with its brick workers' cottages and the cosy white-painted **Plough** (*see page 155*). Mortlake High Street takes you past the old brewery and **The Limes** (123 Mortlake High Street), a Georgian mansion built for the Countess of Strafford and now used as offices.

Kew is all but synonymous with **Kew Gardens** (more properly known as the **Royal Botanic Gardens**; *see page 133*), which maintains its position as the world's principal botanical research centre. In cutesy Kew Village you can find refreshment at the **Flower & Firkin** pub, whose conservatory backs on to the station platform, and the airy, arty **Hothouse** café-bar.

If you're heading for the gardens themselves, Lichfield Road takes you to Kew Road and one of the gardens' entrances. A few hundred metres to the north is the old-fashioned **Maids of Honour** teashop (288 Kew Road), with its fine home-made cakes and pastries, **Kew Green**, with its cricket ground surrounded by pubs, and, in a corner, long, low, elegant **St Anne's Church**, built for Queen Anne in 1714. Its interior, with fine stained glass, is superbly clear and bright.

Royal Botanic Gardens (Kew Gardens)

Richmond, Surrey (020 8332 5000/recorded info 020 8940 1171). Kew Gardens tube/rail/ Kew Bridge rail/riverboat to Kew Pier. **Open** 9.30am daily; closing times vary according to time of year: 4.30pm midwinter-7.30pm midsummer. **Admission** £5 adults; £2.50 5s-16s; £3.50 students, OAPs, disabled, ES40s; £13 family; free under-5s. **Credit** MC, £TC, V.

Hugging the curve of the Thames, Kew Gardens was developed in the seventeenth and eighteenth centuries in the grounds of today's **Kew Palace** (closed for restoration until at least early 2001). It was landscaped by William Chambers and 'Capability' Brown, and planted with specimens from all continents by Sir Joseph Banks. The gardens were donated by the crown to the state in 1841. Since then, Kew has become a world-renowned centre for horticultural research (it boasts the world's largest collection of orchids).

The **Palm House** (Decimus Burton and Richard Turner, 1848) is the finest surviving glass-and-iron structure in the country, and is best seen from the galleries where you look down on a warm, damp jungle of palm and fern. The **Temperate House** is also by Burton and Turner. Don't miss the steamy **Aroid House** (John Nash, 1836), where you step into a tropical rainforest. Surrounding the glasshouses are 120ha (300 acres) filled with every imaginable variety of tree, shrub and flower. Hidden among the trees are some interesting buildings and sculptures, including the **Great Pagoda** (William Chambers, 1762) and a Japanese gateway. The **Marianne North Gallery** and the small **Wood Museum** are also open to visitors. The former name of Jacobean **Kew Palace** was the Dutch House, because of its distinctive gables. Built in 1631, it was bought by George III in 1781 and used as a country retreat by the royal family until about 1820.

Website: www.kew.org

WWT The Wetland Centre

Queen Elizabeth's Walk, SW13 (020 8409 4400/ info@wetlandcentre.org.uk). Hammersmith tube then 33, 72, 209, 283 bus/Barnes rail. **Open** *from end May 2000 summer* 9.30am-6pm daily; *winter* 9.30am-5pm daily. Last entry *summer* 5pm, *winter* 4pm. **Admission** £6.50; £4 children; £5.25 OAPs. **Credit** to be confirmed.

It's remarkable to find a wildlife-rich wilderness so close to the centre of London, but the late Sir Peter Scott's Wildfowl and Wetlands Trust (WWT) has done a marvellous job in creating this multiple-habitat reserve from a disused water works. In 42½ hectares (105 acres) visitors can scour the open water lakes, reedbeds, seasonally inundated grasslands and open mudflats (much of it via CCTV cameras located throughout the site). There's also the Peter Scott Visitor Centre, an exhibition space, a restaurant, café and shops. The centre opens at the end of May 2000.

Wimbledon

Just as most people think of Kew as its gardens, most non-Londoners equate **Wimbledon** with its two-week tennis tournament (*see page 7*) or with the cuddly, litter-collecting Wombles. For the rest of the year, the place is pretty much left to its own devices. **Wimbledon Broadway** is dominated by the massive **Centre Court** shopping centre, and, a little further east, **Wimbledon Theatre** – an entertaining example of Edwardian architecture at its most feverish. There's a scattering of decent bars and restaurants here if you don't fancy the hike up the formidably steep Wimbledon Hill Road to **Wimbledon Village**. The latter is a moneyed, country-townish sort of place that looks down its nose at the suburbia at the bottom of the hill. Best of the pubs here is the seventeenth-century **Rose & Crown** (near the junction of Marryat Road and Parkside).

Beyond lies **Wimbledon Common**, a huge, partially wooded expanse, criss-crossed with paths and horse tracks; it's easy to get lost here. The windmill towards the north-east corner dates from 1817. Baden-Powell wrote part of *Scouting for Boys* while living in the windmill in 1908. The museum it now houses closes during the winter, although the large tearoom is open all year round. **Putney Vale Cemetery**, in the north-east corner of the Common (accessible from Roehampton Vale), is one of the largest graveyards in London. Lillie Langtry was buried here in 1929.

On the east side of the common, the disused **Bluegate Gravel Pit** forms an idyllic lake, whose peace and quiet is barely disturbed by the murmur of traffic on Parkside. Cross the road and go down Calonne Road to discover Wimbledon's biggest surprise. Amid prime south London suburbia (all pre-war villas and new Rovers at rest) is a fully fledged Thai Buddhist temple, the **Buddhapadipa Temple**. Visitors are free to look around (1-6pm Sat; 8.30-10.30am, 12.30-6pm, Sun). Close by is the All England Lawn Tennis Club and the **Wimbledon Lawn Tennis Museum** (*see below*). Next door, **Wimbledon Park** has public tennis courts and a large boating lake.

Wimbledon Lawn Tennis Museum

Church Road, SW19 (020 8946 6131). Southfields tube/39, 93, 200 bus. **Open** 10.30am-5pm daily; spectators only during championships. **Admission** £4; £3 5s-16s, students, OAPs. **Credit** MC, V.

More than 150 years of social and sporting history are encapsulated in this newly designed, well-lit museum. More interesting than the rows of cases filled with racquets and balls are a mock-up of an

Edwardian tennis party and the section on tennis since 1968, with touch-screen commentaries on past and present Wimbledon stars and videos of past championships. The place is packed with unusual information: yellow balls were first used in 1986; they are stored at 20°C and can reach a speed of 140mph (224kmph). Only fanatical tennis groupies will thrill at the collection's array of personal memorabilia, such as some of Pat Cash's headbands and Boris Becker's autograph.

Richmond

It's not so difficult to envisage **Richmond** as the busy, cramped English country town it once was – though the rural calm has long since been supplanted by heavy traffic and the roar of low-flying jets approaching Heathrow. Until the early sixteenth century, the whole area was called Sheen, receiving its new name when Henry VII acquired the local manor house and named it after his earldom in Yorkshire. Elizabeth I spent the last few summers of her life at Richmond and died there in 1603, but Richmond Palace fell into neglect. All that remains of the palace is a gateway on Richmond Green, bearing the arms of Henry VII, and Old Palace Yard beyond. The long building on the left is the Wardrobe, which was once used to house the palace furnishings.

Richmond station stands opposite the **Bull & Bush** pub – formerly the Station Hotel and, in its heyday in the early to mid-1960s, HQ of the British blues scene. The Rolling Stones were the house band in their early days, and Elton John, Rod Stewart, the Small Faces and Long John Baldry all cut their musical teeth here.

George Street and **The Quadrant** form Richmond's nexus, lined with shops and restaurants. Alley-like Brewer's Lane, with its rows of antique shops, takes you to **Richmond Green**, bigger and less appealing than Kew Green, though it is enlivened at one end by the twin-cupola'd **Richmond Theatre**. The church of **St Mary Magdalene**, in Paradise Road, is worth a look for its hectic combination of architectural styles, dating from 1507 to 1904.

Despite its period look, **Richmond Riverside**, near **Richmond Bridge**, was built in the 1980s, the mock Georgian-style façades concealing ordinary offices and flats. The genuinely Victorian town hall houses the public library, tourist office and **Museum of Richmond** (*see below*).

Good eating options are scarce in Richmond. Exceptions are the seafood and pancake-based **Chez Lindsay** (*see page172*) and the hip **Canyon** (*see page 167*) by Richmond Bridge. For Sunday lunch try the **White Cross** on the riverside, at the bottom of Water Lane.

Ultimately, Richmond is a place for enjoying the Great Outdoors. With the exception of Epping Forest, **Richmond Park** (*see below*) is the last vestige of the great oak forests that surrounded London until medieval times. In 1727, the poet James Thomson exclaimed of **Richmond Hill**: 'Heavens! What a goodly perspective spreads around, of hills and dales and woods and lawns and spires and glittering towns and gilded streams.' The view has changed little, except that the glittering towns have merged to form a glittering city. Close to the top of Richmond Hill, the **Terrace Gardens** descend steeply towards the river (there's a café halfway down). If the river isn't flooding, you can follow its meandering course towards **Petersham** and **Ham**. The Thames is at its most tranquil here and, in the early morning and evening, **Petersham Meadows** are almost impossibly pastoral – brown cattle grazing on water meadows beside the misty river.

Museum of Richmond

Old Town Hall, Whittaker Avenue, Richmond, Surrey (020 8332 1141). Richmond tube/rail.
Open *May-Oct* 11am-5pm Tue-Sat; 1-4pm Sun; *Nov-Apr* 11am-5pm Tue-Sat. **Admission** £2; £1 students, OAPs, ES40s; free under-16s.

The focus here is on Richmond's popularity as a royal resort, but the museum also traces the area's history from its role as a prehistoric settlement (weapons and other implements frequently turn up in the river) to life in the town during World War II. The staff are friendly and well informed.

Richmond Park

Richmond, Surrey (020 8948 3209). Richmond tube/rail then 371 bus. **Open** *Mar-Sept* 7am-dusk daily; *Oct-Feb* 7.30am-dusk daily.

Once a royal hunting ground, Richmond Park covers a massive 1,010ha (2,500 acres) and offers superb views over London and Surrey. It's ideal for rambling, cycling and riding, and is also home to much wildlife – most famously red and fallow deer. Notable buildings in the park include **Pembroke Lodge** (now a café), which was the childhood home of philosopher Bertrand Russell, and the fine Palladian villa, **White Lodge**. Don't miss the exquisite **Isabella Plantation**, a woodland haven landscaped with a stream, ponds and spectacular floral displays.

Further south

Following the Thames south from Richmond (a delightful walk or bike ride) takes you close to a clutch of fine country villas. **Marble Hill House** and neighbouring **Orleans House** square up across the river to **Ham House** (for both, *see page 135*). Past **Twickenham** (home to the **Museum of Rugby**; *see page 135*) is Horace Walpole's idiosyncratic home, **Strawberry Hill**, before the river reaches the busy shopping centre of **Kingston** and curves around to magnificent **Hampton Court Palace** (*see page 135*).

Ham House

Ham, Richmond, Surrey (020 8940 1950). Richmond tube/rail then 371 bus. **Open** *house Apr-Oct* 1-5pm Mon-Wed, Sat, Sun; *gardens* 10.30am-6pm/dusk Mon-Wed, Sat, Sun. **Admission** £5; £2.50 5s-15s; £12.50 family; *garden only* £1.50; 75p 5s-15s. **Credit** AmEx, MC, £TC, V.

The uniqueness of this handsome, red-brick, riverside mansion is due to the original seventeenth-century furniture, paintings and décor that still adorn its rooms. From the house, water meadows lead down to the Thames, while the formal gardens are currently being restored to their original state. Part of the grounds is known as the wilderness, an area that is in fact a carefully planted, almost maze-like section, divided into garden rooms.

Hampton Court Palace

East Molesey, Surrey (020 8781 9500). Hampton Court rail/riverboat from Westminster or Richmond to Hampton Court Pier (Apr-Oct). **Open** *Palace Apr-Oct* 10.15am-6pm Mon; 9.30am-6pm Tue-Sun; *Nov-Mar* 10.15am-4.30pm Mon; 9.30am-4.30pm Tue-Sun (last entry 45mins before closing). *Park* dawn-dusk daily. **Admission** *Palace, courtyard, cloister & maze* £10.50; £7 5s-15s; £8 students, OAPs, disabled, ES40s; £31.40 family. *Maze* only £2.50; £1.60 5s-15s. **Credit** AmEx, MC, £TC, V.

Yup, it sure is pricey – but, as you can easily spend the best part of a day wandering the corridors and gardens of Hampton Court, it's also good value for money. In 1514, the powerful Cardinal Wolsey started to build up Hampton Court as his country seat. After his fall from favour in 1529, Henry VIII took over the palace – his additions include the fabulous vaulted ceiling of the **Chapel Royal**, which took 100 men nine months to complete. In the 1690s, William and Mary commissioned Christopher Wren to rebuild the **State Apartments** in classical Renaissance style (the **King's Apartments**, damaged by fire in 1986, have been splendidly restored).

Sensibly, the palace has been split into six bite-size tours. Highlights include the **Renaissance Picture Gallery**, Henry VIII's hammer-beam-roofed **Great Hall**, and the **Tudor Kitchens**. The latter is perhaps the most fun part of the whole palace – period-dressed minions make sixteenth-century dishes, turn meat on a spit and chat to visitors. Elsewhere, costumed guides lead tours and there's foolery several times a day in **Clock Court**, overlooked by the magnificent Astronomical Clock, made for Henry VIII in 1540 by Nicholas Oursian.

The extensive gardens are an attraction in themselves. Look out for the **Great Vine**, which is the oldest-known vine in the world. It was probably planted by 'Capability' Brown around 1770 and still produces an annual crop of 230-320kg (500-700lbs) of black grapes, which are sold to visitors. Another must-see, or rather, must-get-lost-in, is the famous maze. Many a cynic has come unstuck here.

Website: www.hrp.org.uk

Marble Hill House

Richmond Road, Twickenham, Middlesex (020 8892 5115). Richmond tube/rail/33, 90, 290, H22, R70 bus. **Open** *Apr-Oct* 10am-6pm daily; *Nov-Mar* 10am-4pm Wed-Sun. **Admission** £3; £1.50 5s-15s; £2.30 students, OAPs, ES40s. **Credit** MC, V.

Marble Hill House, overlooking the Thames in Marble Hill Park, is a perfect Palladian villa. It was built for Henrietta Howard, the mistress of George II, and later occupied by Mrs Fitzherbert, George IV's secret wife. The interior Cube Hall has beautiful moulded decoration, and the house has been immaculately restored with original Georgian furnishings. On Sunday evenings in summer there are concerts in the park (*see p274*).

Museum of Rugby/ Twickenham Stadium

Gate K, Twickenham Rugby Stadium, Rugby Road, Twickenham, Middlesex (020 8892 2000). Hounslow East tube then 281 bus/Twickenham rail. **Open** 10am-5pm Tue-Sat; 2-5pm Sun (last entry 4.30pm). **Admission** *combined ticket* £5; £3 5s-15s, students, OAPs, disabled, ES40s; £15 family. **Credit** JCB, MC, £TC, V.

Rugby's increasing popularity might mean that more fans make the journey to this interactive celebration of the sport at its mecca in Twickenham. Its collection includes touch-screen information points on clubs and players, a scrum machine and a reconstruction of the old West Stand changing rooms. The tour round the spectacular stadium, from the dressing rooms to the hallowed turf itself, is excellent.

Website: www.rfu.com

Orleans House

Riverside, Twickenham, Middlesex (020 8892 0221). St Margaret's rail. **Open** *Apr-Sept* 1-5.30pm Tue-Sat; 2-5.30pm Sun; *Oct-Mar* 1-4.30pm Tue-Sat; 2-4.30pm Sun. **Admission** free.

Built in 1710 for James Johnston, William III's secretary of state for Scotland, this was later home to the exiled Duke of Orléans – hence the name. The building was demolished in 1926, with the exception of the Octagon, an eight-sided turret that had formed part of the west wing. A gallery was subsequently built on the site of the main house, and both it and the Octagon are used for exhibitions.

Thames Barrier Visitors' Centre

1 Unity Way, SE18 (020 8305 4188). North Greenwich tube/Charlton rail/riverboats to & from Greenwich Pier (020 8305 0300) & Westminster Pier (020 7930 3373)/177, 180 bus. **Open** 10am-5pm Mon-Fri; 10.30am-5.30pm Sat, Sun. **Admission** £3.40; £2 5s-16s, OAPs; £7.50 family. *Greenwich ticket.* **Credit** MC, V.

Since its completion in 1982, at a cost of over £500 million, the Thames Barrier has been raised more than 20 times to protect London from flooding. When in use, the four main gates are each the height of a five-storey building (normally they lie flat on the riverbed, allowing ships to pass over them). The Visitors' Centre has working models and an audio-visual presentation explaining how the structure was built. The barrier is usually raised once a month (dates and times vary; phone for details).

Website: www.environment-agency.gov.uk

West London

It's not all Notting Hill, you know... charming Chiswick and handsome Holland Park mean west is a contender for best.

Paddington & Bayswater

MAPS 1 & 2

The name **Paddington** derives from the ancient Anglo-Saxon chieftain Padda, but most contemporary Londoners associate this district north of Hyde Park with the railway station and its magnificent cathedral-like iron girder roof, designed by Isambard Kingdom Brunel in 1851. It was the building of the station, along with the Grand Junction Canal (1801), that precipitated the population boom in Paddington and neighbouring **Bayswater** in the mid-nineteenth century – the area was previously considered off residential limits thanks to the infamous Tyburn gallows near present-day Marble Arch. Despite another dip in fortune in the early twentieth century, when the district became synonymous with prostitution, poverty and neglect, these areas are now relatively prosperous, owing to their centrality and the popularity of their classic Victorian white stuccoed townhouses. There's also an agreeably cosmopolitan ambience thanks to Middle Eastern, Greek and Jewish communities. Although tourist hotels and hostels abound, the **Alexander Fleming Laboratory Museum** (*see below*) in St Mary's Hospital is as close as the area comes to conventional tourist attractions. Nearby **Paddington Station**, meanwhile, has recently been given a new lease of life by an ambitious £63 million overhaul; the centrepiece is **The Lawn**, a swanky new glass and steel space featuring shops, cafés and airline check-in desks for passengers taking the Heathrow Express from the station.

Queensway is the heart of Bayswater, but, despite some decent restaurants (particularly Chinese; *see page 169*), it's something of a gaudy tourist trap. The palatial Whiteley's shopping mall labours under the ignominy of being one of Adolf Hitler's favourite buildings, but it makes up for this with a number of cafés, an eight-screen cinema and a good assortment of shops.

A left turn at the north end of Queensway opens up the richer pickings of **Westbourne Grove**, once known as the 'curry corridor'. The Indian restaurants here are no longer very good, but there are some excellent Middle Eastern and African eateries, such as Sudanese **Mandola** (*see page 186*). As the road continues westward towards Portobello Road and Notting Hill, antique shops begin to proliferate. Look out also for London's most stylish public toilet (a big green-tiled triangular structure), complete with its own upmarket flower stall, **Wild at Heart** (*see page 215*), at the junction with Colville Road . Design shrines such as **Aero** and **Space** (*see page 227*) also feature.

Alexander Fleming Laboratory Museum

St Mary's Hospital, Praed Street, W2 (020 7725 6528). Paddington tube/rail/7, 15, 27, 36 bus.
Open 10am-1pm Mon-Thur and by appointment 2-5pm Mon-Thur, 10am-5pm Fri. **Admission** £2; £1 concs. **Map 2 D5**

On 3 September 1928, when a Petri dish of bacteria became contaminated with a mysterious mould, Alexander Fleming realised something peculiar was going on. This chance discovery of penicillin had momentous consequences and this re-creation (in the very same room) of his laboratory is backed up with displays and a video providing insights into his life and the role of penicillin in the fight against disease.

Maida Vale, Kilburn & Queen's Park

North of the divisive Westway lies Edgware Road, Maida Vale, Kilburn and Queen's Park. Dead-straight Edgware Road follows the course of ancient Watling Street – a traffic-clogged thoroughfare, redeemed only by some of London's best kebab shops (try **Patogh**; *see page 183*), courtesy of the thriving local Middle Eastern community.

Maida Vale (named after the British victory against the French at the Battle of Maida in southern Italy in 1806) is an affluent area characterised by Edwardian purpose-built flats, and prettified by the locks round **Little Venice**. You can walk from here along the canals to **London Zoo** (*see page 69*) – or even take a boat.

Kilburn High Road, meanwhile, is well known for its boisterous pubs, patronised primarily by the Irish expats. **Kilburn** is also a good place for bargain shopping, and its predominantly Afro-Caribbean and Irish populations are well served by one of London's more popular and enterprising local arts complexes, the **Tricycle** (*see page 300*).

Queen's Park is a sanctuary away from the bedlam of Kilburn High Road and offers an excellent children's playground, a little pitch-and-putt golf course beside six well-maintained hard tennis courts and a good café.

Classy bird in **Holland Park**.

Notting Hill

MAP 1

Once upon a time a ghettoised slum, **Notting Hill** is now full of models, media-ites and bohemian roués wining, dining and making films about themselves. But it was not ever thus. Until a wave of white stuccoed buildings mapped out Notting Hill in the early 1800s, there was little but piggeries in the area. The district's fortunes declined in the twentieth century and it became solidly white and working class. During the1950s, an influx of West Indian immigrants under the exploitative thumb of slum landord Peter Rachman triggered serious race riots.

Notting Hill Gate itself is little more than a busy through road, although it does boast two cinemas: the **Gate** and the **Notting Hill Coronet** (for both, *see page 260*), the latter being one of the last cinemas in town where you can smoke. Opposite is artist Damien Hirst's medical gimmick bar and restaurant Pharmacy, while round the corner on Pembridge Road over the Prince Albert pub is the tiny **Gate Theatre** (*see page 298*) – one of the best pub-theatres in town. However, when people talk about Notting Hill they really mean **Portobello Road**. This narrow, snaking thoroughfare, most famed for its **market** (*see page 223*) and antique shops, forms the spine of the neighbourhood. There are cafés, bars, restaurants, curiosity shops and delicatessens, all patronised by the indigenous trustafarians (semi-aristocratic white Rastas living off parental trust funds). The section around Westbourne Park Road and Talbot Road, together with the northern end of Kensington Park Road, was made famous and, perhaps now destroyed, by the Hugh Grant/Julia Roberts film. Further up, Portobello Road under the Westway, there is a massive free-for-all flea market of modish second-hand clothes on Fridays and Saturdays.

At the north end of Portobello Road past another series of cafés lies **Golborne Road** – a great place to buy Portuguese and Moroccan groceries and pâtisseries. The other main feature of Golborne Road is **Trellick Tower** – seen as a hideous carbuncle by some and by others as a seminal piece of modern architecture. Built in 1973 by Ernö Goldfinger (Ian Fleming hated his work so much he used his name for the notorious Bond villain), it was the tallest residential block in the country at the time and is distinguished by a separate lift shaft linked to the main building by concrete corridors. Despite Fleming's vilification, residents are said to enjoy living here and the flats fetch high prices. (*See also page 106* **2 Willow Road**.) Going east along Westbourne Park Road from Portobello Road past All Saints Road (one-time crack cocaine centre, now ultra-hip eating alley), the **Westbourne** pub (*see page 199*) is crammed with hard-core fashion and pop-star wannabes all year round.

Up at the top of Ladbroke Grove, past the gigantic Sainsbury's superstore, is **Kensal Green Cemetery** on Harrow Road. Opened in 1833, it's a huge and beautiful resting place for many a famous Londoner, including Thackeray, Trollope and Isambard Kingdom Brunel, who were joined in 1997 by London's most celebrated 'lowlife' drinker, Jeffrey Bernard.

Kensington & Holland Park

MAPS 1-4

No doubt to the delight of its heritage-conscious upper-class residents, **Kensington** gets a mention in the Domesday Book of 1086. In the seventeenth century the district grew up around Holland House (1606) and Campden House (1612) and was described by one contemporary historian in 1705 as a place 'inhabited by gentry and persons of note' with 'an abundance of shopkeepers and artificers'. *Plus ça change, plus c'est la même chose.* Both aspects of Kensington are in evidence around the High Street. A lively mix of chain stores and individual shops stretch along the ever-busy thoroughfare while the nearby streets and squares are lined by large townhouses. The most famous of the squares, **Kensington Square**, sports an generous array of blue plaques denoting residents

Carnival time!

If west London is internationally famous for anything, it's Europe's biggest street party: the **Notting Hill Carnival**. Every year, the Carnival attracts more than a million revellers over its two-day duration, on the Sunday and Monday of the August bank holiday weekend (**27-28 August 2000**). Started as a small-scale local community event in the 1960s by the area's West Indian residents, the Carnival is now so huge and all-encompassing that many Notting Hill residents flee their homes for the duration. If you can stand the heaving crowds, however, you'll enjoy this spectacular event which centres on the massive costume parades and steel bands that inch their way around the three-mile (5-km) route via Ladbroke Grove, Westbourne Grove, Chepstow Road and the Great Western Road. Various stages feature live music (Portobello Green, Powis Square and outside Sainsbury's at the top of Ladbroke Grove), food stalls dole out great spicy street grub, and sound systems blast out everything from lovers' rock to drum 'n' bass. Sunday is ostensibly (but not exclusively) oriented towards kids, while the big day is Monday, with the streets sardine-packed to the point of immobility. The action gets under way around midday and winds down by 7-8pm. There are often parties afterwards but they are mostly private affairs. Despite now attracting many more tourists and Londoners from outside Notting Hill than locals, the Carnival remains an Afro-Caribbean event at heart. Happily, it has also managed to shake off its volatile reputation after disturbances in the 1970s and 1980s. However, it's still wise to be wary – travel light, don't wear jewellery or carry bags or wallets. Also, be sure to bring your own booze to save yourself paying the outrageous mark-ups, but watch your liquid intake – toilet facilities are always woefully inadequate.

of distinction, such as William Makepeace Thackeray (no.16) and the philosopher John Stuart Mill (no.18).

Kensington Square is just behind the art deco splendour of **Barker's** department store (built 1905-13). Next door, on the sixth floor of the former Derry & Toms, is one of Europe's largest **roof gardens** (accessed from the entrance on Derry Street). It's also an upmarket club/restaurant (*see page 241 & 246*). Over the road from here, at the foot of Kensington Church Street, is the church of **St Mary Abbots**, distinguished by the tallest steeple in London (85m/250ft) and the pleasantly secluded gardens to its rear. **Kensington Market** is now a shadow of its former self. Opposite is the trendy **Urban Outfitters** (*see page 210*); you'll find **Amazon** (*see page 206*), with its bargain-priced designer togs, in several shops in nearby Kensington Church Street. Further west down the High Street there is a classic Odeon cinema from 1926, and opposite, behind a small wood of flagpoles, lurks the **Commonwealth Institute**, a monument to flimsy 1950s design.

Behind the Institute is **Holland Park** (*see below*), the most action-packed of all London's parks. At the south end of the park is **Holland House**, named after an early owner, Sir Henry, Earl of Holland. The house suffered serious bomb damage during World War II and only the ground floor and arcades survived; the restored east wing contains the most romantically sited youth hostel in town (*see page 160*).

Among the local historic houses worth a visit are **Leighton House** (*see below*), the nineteenth-century home of the painter Lord Leighton, and **Linley Sambourne House**, home of Edward Linley Sambourne (*see below*), cartoonist for the satirical magazine *Punch*.

Holland Park

Entrances on Holland Park, Abbotsbury Road, Holland Walk & Kensington High Street, W8. High Street Kensington or Holland Park tube. **Open** 7.30am-30mins before dusk daily. **Map 1 A8**

This is one of the most romantic parks in London, with beautiful woods and formal gardens surrounding the reconstructed Jacobean **Holland House**. The summer ballroom has been converted into a stylish contemporary restaurant, **The Belvedere**; there's also a café. Open-air theatre and opera under an elegant canopy are staged in the park during the summer (*see page 274*). For children, there's an adventure playground with tree-walks and rope swings, while tame rabbits, squirrels and peacocks patrol the grounds. The Kyoto Japanese Garden provides a tranquil retreat from the action.

Leighton House

12 Holland Park Road, W14 (020 7602 3316). High Street Kensington tube. **Open** 11am-5.30pm Mon-Sat. **Admission** free; donations appreciated.

Located on a quiet Kensington side street, Leighton House was designed by one-time president of the Royal Academy Frederic Lord Leighton (1864-79) in collaboration with George Aitchison. Leighton spent much of his life travelling the world, and it is from the East that the house takes most of its inspiration; its most striking feature is the exotic Arab Hall, added in 1879, and based on a Moorish palace in Palermo, Sicily. The audio tour, though slightly patronising in tone, gives an anecdote-filled insight into Leighton's life. A charge is levied for guided tours (noon Wed, Thur); phone for details.

Leighton, himself a distinguished artist, collected a variety of Victorian works of art by his contemporaries that are now on permanent display. The house also hosts temporary exhibitions, which, in 2000, will include **Shaker Hassan El Said** (17-29 Apr); **Patricia Milns** (8-20 May); **Fibre Art** – a collaborative art textile exhibition (30 May-10 June); **Khosrow Hassan Zadeh** (19 June-1 July); **Ghanoum and Faraj** (4-16 Sept); **Galliardi Gallery** (25 Sept-14 Oct); the **Silver Show** (23 Oct-4 Nov) and the **Leighton Open**, the annual exhibition for artists who live, work or study in the Royal Borough of Kensington and Chelsea (mid-July-late Aug).

Linley Sambourne House

18 Stafford Terrace, W8 (enquiries 020 8994 1019). High Street Kensington tube. **Open** *Mar-Oct* 10am-4pm Wed; *guided tours* 2.15pm, 3.15pm, 4.15pm, Sun. **Admission** £3.50; £2 5s-15s; £2.50 students, OAPs, disabled, ES40s. **Map 3 A9**

Dating from the 1870s, the former home of the noted late Victorian and Edwardian *Punch* cartoonist retains its magnificent interior, complete with pictures by Sambourne and his peers. An exceptional example of a Victorian townhouse, it's a rare chance to see how a successful artist lived and worked, and is a monument to the Arts & Crafts movement with original wallpaper by William Morris.
Website: www.victorian-society.org.uk

Earl's Court & Fulham

MAPS 3 & 4

Earl's Court changed from hamlet to built-up urban area with the arrival of the Metropolitan Railway in 1860, and from 1914 many of its imposing houses were subdivided into flats. To this day it remains a district where many people have lived but few have settled. Previously known as Kangaroo Valley, thanks to Antipodean trekkers seeking cheap accommodation in its warren of bedsits and budget hotels, it has always had something of a seedy, though not dangerous, reputation. In the late 1970s and 1980s it became the gay centre of London, with the action centering most famously on the **Coleherne** pub (corner of Brompton and Coleherne Roads). One of England's more famous dominatrixes, Lindy St Clair (aka Miss Whiplash), set up parlour on Eardley Crescent until bankrupted by the Inland Revenue. Freddie Mercury also lived around here, at Garden Lodge, 1 Logan Place, and Earl's Court retains a strong gay vibe.

The area is, perhaps, more widely known as the site of the hulking **Exhibition Centre**, opposite the tube station. The 1937 structure, in its time the largest reinforced concrete building in Europe, was used as an internment camp in World War II.

The pleasantly laid-out **Brompton Cemetery** is sometimes exploited for sexual encounters (the proximity to graves presumably sharpening the experience), although an unmolested stroll, searching perhaps for the grave of Emmeline Pankhurst, is perfectly possible. The peace is only broken on Saturday afternoons when **Chelsea FC** are playing at home; the massive bulk of their Stamford Bridge stadium overlooks the tombs.

Neighbouring **Parsons Green** and **Fulham** are not as colourful or promiscuous as Earl's Court, being home to déclassé toffs. Parsons Green is centred around a small green that once, logically enough, supported a parsonage. Residents will be relieved to know that it was considered the aristocratic part of Fulham even in 1705 when Bowack pronounced it to be inhabited by 'Gentry and persons of Quality'. The heaving **White Horse** pub (*see page 199*) on the green serves one of the best selections of cask and bottled beers in London.

Apart from the hugely posh **Hurlingham Sports Club** and the **Queen's (Tennis &**

Fulham Palace, *fit for a bishop.*

Rackets) Club, which hosts the Stella Artois pre-Wimbledon tournament, there is one place in Fulham you can enter without the requirement of a ridiculous bank balance: **Fulham Palace** (*see below*). Next door, small but perfectly formed **Bishop's Park** contains a paddling pool and offers beautiful leafy walks by the side of one of the prettiest stretches of the Thames.

Fulham Palace

Bishop's Avenue, off Fulham Palace Road, SW6 (020 7736 3233). Putney Bridge tube/220, 74 bus. **Open** *museum Mar-Oct* 2-5pm Wed-Sun; *Nov-Feb* 1-4pm Thur-Sun. **Admission** *museum* £1; 50p students, OAPs, disabled, ES40s (accompanied children free); *guided tours* £2; free under-16s.

From 704 until 1973, Fulham Palace was official residence of the Bishops of London. The present brick house is a mishmash of periods and architectural styles; the oldest part is from 1480, while William Butterfield's neo-Gothic chapel is relatively recent, dating from 1866. The site also boasted one of the largest moats in Britain until it was filled in 1921, while the quirky museum, which traces the building's history, counts a mummified rat among its exhibits. The lovely grounds are open daily, but to see the palace interior go to one of the informative tours, held twice a month in summer and once a month in winter (on a Sunday; phone for dates).

Shepherd's Bush & Hammersmith

The approach to **Shepherd's Bush** from Holland Park Avenue is marked by Shepherd's Bush roundabout, with the **Thames Water Tower** springing out of its centre. The tower, which looks like a state-of-the-art toilet cistern, is in fact a 15-m (50-ft) surge pipe for London's underground ring main. Designed by students at the Royal College of Art, it doubles as a huge barometer.

Shepherd's Bush Common used to be called Gagglegoose Green and formed the centre of what was, only 150 years ago, a 'pleasant village'. The name Shepherd is thought to be a personal one, but a more quaint story ascribes the origin of Shepherd's Bush to the habit of shepherds watching sheep on the green while hiding in thorn bushes. Now, however, the Common is a scruffy traffic island overlooked by one of London's ugliest edifices: the Shepherd's Bush Centre.

All is not gloom in W12, however, for this is home to one of London's most prestigious new-writing theatres, **The Bush** (*see page 297*), and the neighbouring **Shepherd's Bush Empire** concert venue (*see page 277*). Shepherd's Bush **market** (between Shepherd's Bush and Goldhawk Road tubes) is one of west London's busier markets and, unlike Portobello Road, is very much geared to the local (Afro-Caribbean) population.

Shepherd's Bush and neighbouring **White City** are also the main base of BBC TV – **Television Centre** on Wood Lane can be readily identified by its massive satellite dishes combing the skies. Nearby is Loftus Road, the home of perennial under-achievers **Queens Park Rangers FC**. The wide open spaces of **Wormwood Scrubs** to the north are marred by one of London's most famous and forbidding Victorian jails. Less than a mile down Goldhawk Road, **Ravenscourt Park** is a much more agreeable space with an adventure playground and a number of tennis courts.

Hammersmith, south of Shepherd's Bush, is less depressing than its neighbour, but, on a similar note, is best known for its huge traffic interchange and the stone-clad corporate monstrosity of the Broadway Centre. The district is not, however, without its more notable architectural landmarks. There's the **Olympia Exhibition Centre** on Hammersmith Road, and the brown, shipshape curiosity called the **London Ark**, the city's first ecologically friendly building, which, ironically, leans across one of the city's least ecologically friendly roadways, the A4. Then there's the **London Apollo**, formerly the Hammersmith Odeon, where many a famous rock band has gigged. Finally, the knobbly **Hammersmith Bridge**, built in 1824 with a span of 144m (422ft), was London's first suspension bridge (currently closed to traffic; it's great for promenading). **Lower**

Mall, running along the river from the bridge, is a pleasant spot for a stroll or a pint at one of several riverside pubs (**The Dove** is the pick; *see page 199*).

Nor is Hammersmith without culture. On the main shopping route of King Street stands the **Lyric** theatre (*see page 298*), while the **Riverside Studios** (*see pages 256 & 299*) on Crisp Road is a three-theatre contemporary arts centre with a gallery and arthouse repertory cinema.

Chiswick

A leafy suburb coveted by BBC senior management, actors and minor celebrities, **Chiswick** is in a world of its own. Turning your back on the tarmacked swoops of Hammersmith and walking west by the river from Hammersmith Bridge, **Chiswick Mall** gives off a very different vibe. Lining this mile-long riverside stretch is an assortment of grand seventeenth- to nineteenth-century townhouses with be-flowered, wrought-iron verandahs. The nearby **Fuller's Griffin Brewery** on Chiswick Lane South has stood on the same site since the seventeenth century and offers hour-and-a-half-long tours (020 8996 2063; tours at 11am, noon, 1pm and 2pm, Mon, Wed-Fri; £5). Chiswick Mall ends at the church of **St Nicholas**. Only the ragstone tower of the original fifteenth-century building remains; the rest of the church is nineteenth-century. Grave stones commemorate local painters Hogarth and Whistler, but they are buried elsewhere. North of here, the pleasant shops and restaurants along Chiswick High Road signify the area's growing affluence. The street culminates at villagey **Turnham Green**, where cricket is still played in the summer.

Other Chiswick attractions include the Palladian magnificence of **Chiswick House** (*see below*) and **Hogarth's House** (*see page 142*), the country retreat of the famous eighteenth-century satirical artist. Further west is the **Kew Bridge Steam Museum** (*see page 142*), housed in an impressive nineteenth-century pumping station. South of here, overlooking Kew Gardens from the opposite side of the river, is **Syon House** (*see page 142*). A cutesy riverside promenade, just east of Kew Bridge on the north side of the river, runs by the mini-village of **Strand-on-the-Green**, and takes in three of the best pubs in the area.

Chiswick House

Chertsey Road, W4 (020 8995 0508). Turnham Green tube then E3 bus to Edensor Road, or Chiswick rail or Hammersmith tube/rail and then 190 bus.
Open *Apr-Sept* 10am-6pm daily; *Oct* 10am-5pm daily; *Nov-Mar* 10am-4pm Wed-Sun (last entry 30mins before closing). **Admission** £3.30; £1.70 5s-16s; £2.50 students, OAPs, ES40s. **Credit** MC, £TC, V.

Lord Burlington's 1727 design for this mansion is based on Palladio's Villa Capra (the Rotonda) in Vicenza. The interior is decked out in baroque splendour, with the lavish Blue Velvet Room winning the prize for most over-the-top décor. The formal gardens are peopled with statues, temples and obelisks as well as living picnickers. There's a good café too. Jonathan Swift, Alexander Pope and George Frideric Handel were all guests here.
Website: www.english-heritage.org.uk

Trails of the unexpected...

Notting Hill silver screen.

Where better to start a tour of cinematic Notting Hill than in Hugh Grant's travel bookshop in **Notting Hill**? Situated just off the Portobello Road, at 13 Blenheim Crescent, it's somewhat prosaically called The Travel Bookshop. It does exactly what it says on the awning, and does it well – and never mind the increasing statistical chance of film fans bumping into one another and falling head-over-heels in instant lust…

Michelangelo Antonioni shot **Blow Up!** on Notting Hill's streets in 1966. Even though Maryon Park, where David Hemmings unwittingly photographed the film's murder, is in Charlton, his bachelor-pad studio was on Princedale Road. Quite fittingly, Nic Roeg and Donald Cammell subsequently slammed the door in the decade's face nearby with the unsettling **Performance**, filmed at 25 Powis Square.

A Disneyfied cardboard version of the Portobello Road appeared in **Bedknobs and Broomsticks**. Here, servicemen from all around the world were pressed to perform their national dance along with corresponding members of the local population – West Indian military calypso, Gurkha banghra, Irish jigs with golden-hearted good-time girls. Could this perhaps be lost footage of the first-ever Notting Hill Carnival?

As for Portobello's strangest filmic claim? No, not Paddington Bear's pad at Mr Brown's antique shop. During World War II, local mass-murderer-cum-necrophiliac John Christie (played so creepily by Richard Attenborough in **10 Rillington Place**) was the projectionist at the historic 1910-vintage Electric Cinema (191 Portobello Road).

Idyllic **Strand-on-the-Green**. *See page 141.*

Hogarth's House

Hogarth Lane, Great West Road, W4 (020 8994 6757). Turnham Green tube/Chiswick rail.
Open *Apr-Oct* 1-5pm Tue-Fri; 1-6pm Sat, Sun; *Nov, Dec, Feb, Mar* 1-4pm Tue-Fri; 1-5pm Sat, Sun.
Admission free.

Hogarth's country retreat has been fully restored to its eighteenth-century condition and provides wall space for over 200 of the social commentator's prints, though his most famous work, *The Rake's Progress*, is a copy. (The original is in the Sir John Soane's Museum; *see page 61*).

Kew Bridge Steam Museum

Green Dragon Lane, Brentford, Middlesex (020 8568 4757). Gunnersbury tube/Kew Bridge rail/ 65, 237, 267, 391 bus. **Open** 11am-5pm daily.
Admission *Mon-Fri* £3; £1 5s-15s; £2 students, OAPs, disabled; £7 family; *Sat, Sun, public hols* £4; £2 5s-15s; £3 students, OAPs, disabled; £10.50 family. **Credit** MC, £TC, V.

A Victorian riverside pumping station, close to the north end of Kew Bridge, is now home to this museum of water supply. The Water for Life exhibition details the history of London's use and abuse of the world's most precious commodity and includes a unique walk-through sewer experience. At 3pm on weekends one of the largest working steam engines in the world, the 229-cm (90-in) Cornish Beam engine (built in 1845 for use in the tin mines), stirs ponderously into motion. Like the working waterwheel and five other steam engines, it has been restored by enthusiastic volunteers to its former working order.

Syon House

Syon Park, Brentford, Middlesex (020 8560 0881). Gunnersbury tube/Kew Bridge rail/ 237, 267 bus. **Open** *house mid-Mar-Oct* 11am-5pm Wed, Thur, Sun, public hols; *gardens* 10am-dusk daily. **Admission** *house & gardens* £6; £4.50 5s-15s, OAPs, disabled, ES40s; £15 family ticket; *gardens only* £3; £2.50 5s-15s, OAPs, disabled, ES40s; £7 family ticket.
Credit MC, £TC, V.

Once a wealthy monastery, Syon was established by Henry V and used by Henry VIII as a prison for his wife Katherine Howard while she awaited execution. Home of the Percy family since the 1590s, Robert Adam remodelled the interior in 1761, creating one of the most lavish and splendid eighteenth-century interiors in London. Among the many paintings on display are works by Lely, Gainsborough, Reynolds and Van Dyck. The riverside gardens, modelled by the ubiquitous 'Capability' Brown, now contain an impressive nineteenth-century conservatory, a miniature steam train, a garden centre and the **London Butterfly House**. Children, meanwhile, love the **Aquatic Experience**, featuring fish, reptiles, amphibians, birds and small mammals in their natural habitats (*see also p234*).

Further west

A couple of miles west of Chiswick in the middle of gigantic **Osterley Park** is **Osterley House** (*see below*), yet another west London Robert Adam revamp.

Just north of here are the colour and curries of **Southall**. Like many of the previously sleepy parts of west London, Southall has been given a new lease of life by Indian immigrants. The predominantly Punjabi community retains a strong identity and provides a great opportunity to sample authentic north Indian cuisine in the countless cheap restaurants that line the **Broadway** (*see page 174*). Try to visit on a Sunday, when the locals promenade among the market stalls, sari stores and Bollywood-packed video shops. To the north, **Wembley** has been similarly enlivened by the mainly Gujarati community, although this deeply suburban district is better known as the home of the national sports stadium (*see page 292*), with its famous twin towers (added in 1963 to celebrate the 100th anniversary of the football league). The stadium is expected to undergo a massive redevelopment and its twin towers may now go the way of the dinosaurs.

Nearby **Neasden** is another piece of sprawling suburbia, once satirised mercilessly by the Monty Python team. Then a Hindu sect built the multi-billion-rupee **Shri Swaminarayan Mandir**, replicating the Akshardam outside Ahmedabad in Gujarat, western India. Constructed in 1995, the temple required 5,000 tons of marble and limestone and employed 1,500 sculptors for an enterprise unprecedented in this country since building the cathedrals in the Middle Ages. Visitors are welcome (dress discreetly) and there's also an informative 'Understanding Hinduism' exhibition and a good, cheap Indian café. Neasden will never be the same again.

Osterley House

Osterley Park, off Jersey Road, Isleworth, Middlesex (020 8568 7714/recorded info 01494 755566). Osterley tube. **Open** *park* 9am-dusk daily; *house Apr-Oct* 1-4.30pm Wed-Sun.
Admission £4.10; £2.05 5s-15s; £10.25 family.

Osterley House was built for Sir Thomas Gresham (founder of the Royal Exchange) in 1576 but transformed by Robert Adam in 1761. His revamp is dominated by the imposing colonnade of white pillars before the courtyard of the house's red-brick body. The splendour of the state rooms alone makes the house worth the visit, but the still-used Tudor stables, the vast parkland walks and the ghost said to be lurking in the basement add to Osterley's allure.
Website: www.nationaltrust.org.uk

Consumer London

Good Value Accommodation
in Central London

WESTPOINT HOTEL

170–172 SUSSEX GARDENS, HYDE PARK, LONDON W2 1TP

- Pleasant central location
- Convenient for all major sights, museums & theatres
- Close to all shopping districts, Oxford Street & Piccadilly Circus
- Clean, comfortable, well decorated rooms
- All rooms with ensuite shower, toilet, colour TV & radio
- Lift to all floors
- Free luggage room facility
- 2 minutes from Paddington Station, Heathrow Express & Airbus

RATES PER PERSON PER NIGHT

	LOW SEASON	HIGH SEASON
Singles	*from* £39	*from* £46
Doubles	*from* £24	*from* £33
Triples	*from* £22	*from* £26
Family room	*from* £19	*from* £22

include continental breakfast, service charge & all taxes

Tel: (0207) 402 0281
Fax: (0207) 224 9114
*www.*westpointhotel.com
e-mail info@westpointhotel.com

ABBEY COURT HOTEL

174 SUSSEX GARDENS, HYDE PARK, LONDON W2 1TP

- Convenient location 2 minutes from Paddington Station, Airbus & Heathrow Rail Express
- Easy access to all London's important tourist sights, shopping districts and theatres
- Ensuite shower and w.c. in all rooms
- Lift to all floors
- Each room with colour TV, radio & intercom
- Car parking by arrangement

RATES PER PERSON PER NIGHT

	LOW SEASON	HIGH SEASON
Singles	*from* £40	*from* £47
Doubles	*from* £25	*from* £34
Triples	*from* £23	*from* £27
Family room	*from* £20	*from* £23

include continental breakfast, service charge & all taxes

Tel: (0207) 402 0704
Fax: (0207) 262 2055
*www.*abbeycourt.com
e-mail info@abbeycourt.com

SASS HOTEL

11 CRAVEN TERRACE, HYDE PARK, LONDON W2 3QD

Sass Hotel offers superb value for money accommodation in a convenient, quiet location, just 3 minutes walk from Hyde Park and Lancaster Gate tube station. Paddington station with Heathrow Rail Express and Airbus is just 5 minutes away. Easy access to all London's famous sights and entertainment.

- All rooms with ensuite shower, toilet & colour TV
- Friendly personal service
- Car parking by arrangement

RATES PER PERSON PER NIGHT

	LOW SEASON	HIGH SEASON
Singles	*from* £35	*from* £48
Twin	*from* £24	*from* £28
Doubles	*from* £23	*from* £26
Triples	*from* £21	*from* £24

include continental breakfast, service charge & all taxes

Tel: (0207) 262 2325
Fax: (0207) 262 0889
*www.*sasshotel.com
e-mail info@sasshotel.com

Accommodation

Whether you want to splash out or just crash out, our round-up of the best of the city's many options will save you from hotel hell.

Another week, another hotel. 1999 was a boom year in terms of new accommodation in London. Unveiled were Ian Schrager's eagerly anticipated **St Martins Lane** (*see page 147*; to be followed in 2000 by **Sanderson** on Berners Street, W1), small but perfectly formed **No.5 Maddox Street** (*see page 150*) and the feng shui heaven of **myhotel bloomsbury** (*see page 150*). Two newcomers to primarily business-oriented areas, but no doubt attractive to leisure travellers as well, were the **Four Seasons Hotel Canary Wharf** (Westferry Circus, E14 8RS; 020 7510 1999), which opened in December 1999, and the **Great Eastern Hotel** (Liverpool Street, EC2M 7QN; 020 7618 5000), featuring a Conran-designed interior and Conran restaurants.

Despite this flurry of activity, demand still far outstrips supply, and it is not advisable or desirable to turn up in the city without a hotel booking. It may be an easy option to book into a chain hotel (and we list the central numbers for the main ones; *see page 153* **The chain gang**) but there are loads of more characterful, personal and friendly options – if you know where to look.

But beware. There is no getting away from the unpalatable fact that hotel rooms in London are a) overpriced, b) small, and c) stylistically challenged. So be prepared for the implied parentheses in some of the comments below – 'rooms are a good size' (for London), 'prices are reasonable' (for London), etc. It is all too easy to end up in unsavoury accommodation with a severe dent in your bank balance. Unfortunately, style only comes at a price as yet. London remains desperately short of classy budget options. (It's quite telling that, in our listings, the 'moderate' price range starts at £100 for a double room). The award-winning **Highfield Guesthouse** (*see page 158*) is a notable exception. Below we have attempted to sift the class from the dross, in every price bracket.

There is good news, however. It seems that hoteliers are finally becoming aware that the Empire is long gone and not every visitor to London wants to sip Darjeeling to the sound of a string quartet. Anouska Hempel's **Blakes** (*see page 146*) was a groundbreaker in this respect, bringing discreet 1980s chic to a fusty market. Her follow-up, **The Hempel** (*see page 147*), is 1990s minimalism taken to the extreme. Others are starting to muscle in on the style-hotel act. That's not to say that luxury and comfort no longer feature in London's hotels: newcomers **St Martins Lane** (*see page 147*), **No.5 Maddox Street** (*see page 150*) and **One Aldwych** (*see page 147*) are just three examples of a new breed where understated extravagance is the byword.

INFORMATION & BOOKING

If you have not booked ahead, London Tourist Board (LTB) information centres will help (*see page 330*). There is a booking fee of £5. In addition, if you book more than a few weeks in advance, a deposit for the room may also be required. *London – Where to Stay & What to Do* (£4.99), published annually by the LTB, can be found in information centres and large bookshops. Many hotels now have e-mail and/or website addresses via which reservations can be made.

London Tourist Board Hotel Booking Line *(020 7604 2890/www.londontown.com).*
Open 9am-5.30pm Mon-Fri; 9am-1pm Sat.

Visitors with disabilities

Disabled visitors are advised to phone the hotel of their choice before booking to find out about its disabled facilities. The **Holiday Care** service is also very useful. *See also page 341* **Access all areas?**

Holiday Care *2nd floor, Imperial Buildings, Victoria Road, Horley, Surrey RH6 7PZ (01293 774535/fax 01293 784647/holiday.care@virgin.net).*
Open 9am-5pm Mon-Fri. **Credit** AmEx, MC, V.
This advisory service can help disabled visitors find suitable accommodation.
Website: freespace.virgin.net/hol.care

COMPLAINTS

If you have a complaint about anywhere you stay in London, you should personally inform the management at the time of the incident, and then in writing. In some circumstances, the LTB may look into complaints (regardless of whether or not you used its booking service). Please let us know if any of the hotels listed do not come up to scratch.

Hotels

You will find most of London's best-known hotels in Mayfair, while budget accommodation is often clustered around railway stations. The latter can be rather seedy, but Ebury Street, SW1 (near Victoria), and Gower Street, WC1 (near Euston), have some good-quality, cheap hotels. There are also many

Pillow talk, **myhotel bloomsbury**. *See p150.*

hotels in the Earl's Court area and around Queensway, W2. For accommodation catering for a primarily gay and lesbian clientele, *see page 267.*

PRICES & CLASSIFICATION

Until recently the official classification of hotels was hopelessly confused, with a variety of systems used by different organisations. Thankfully, a standardised star rating system (ranging from one star for a decent B&B to five stars for the classiest luxury hotel) has at last been brought in (although only in England; the Scots and the Welsh have gone their own way).

We do not indicate star ratings below. Instead, we classify hotels according to the price of the cheapest **double** room for one night, **inclusive** of 17.5 per cent VAT. Many expensive hotels quote prices exclusive of VAT so do check (where they have quoted us prices without VAT, we have added it on). **Prices were correct at the time of going to press but are subject to annual increases of around five per cent**. Hotel prices tend to remain the same throughout the year; but it is always worth asking if there are any special deals available (especially weekend breaks).

All 'Deluxe' and 'Expensive' hotels will have an en suite bath and/or shower and toilet. Most 'Cheap' hotels have shared bathroom facilities. 'Including breakfast' means continental breakfast, which may consist of little more than tea/coffee and toast. 'English breakfast' is more substantial and generally of the fry-up variety.

Deluxe (£235 and up)

Even if you are unable to afford to stay in London's most famous hotels, their restaurants and bars are open to the public, and most serve afternoon tea (*see page 178* **Tea time**). Unless otherwise stated, every hotel in this category offers babysitting, business services, conference facilities, currency exchange, fax, laundry, 24-hour room service, a safe, multilingual staff, a limousine service and valet parking, will have non-smoking rooms available, and has at least one bar and restaurant; all rooms have air-conditioning, are equipped with hairdryers and modem points, a minibar, radio, safe, telephone and satellite TV.

Blakes

33 Roland Gardens, SW7 3PF (020 7370 6701/ fax 020 7373 0442/blakes@easynet.co.uk). Gloucester Road or South Kensington tube. **Rooms** 51. **Rates** *single* £182; *double* £259-£364; *suite* £570-£715. **Credit** AmEx, DC, JCB, MC, TC, V. **Map 4 D11**

A unique designer hotel within the dark green shell of two Victorian mansions. Characterised throughout by Anouska Hempel's daring and dramatic design details – in black, ochre, cardinal red and white – the individually decorated rooms are inspired by the themes of travel and history; one room houses the original bed of Napoleon's Empress Josephine. Blakes prides itself on protecting the privacy of its clients, a policy that hints at the type of guest it attracts. It's discreet, but fully conscious of its fashionable status. The secluded courtyard garden and restaurant are further draws. Only some rooms have air-conditioning.

Hotel services *Courtyard. Roof terrace.*
Room services *CD player. Fax (on request). Mobile phone (on request). VCR.*
Website: www.hempelhotel.com

Covent Garden Hotel

10 Monmouth Street, WC2H 9HB (020 7806 1000/ fax 020 7806 1100/covent@firmdale.com). Covent Garden or Leicester Square tube. **Rooms** 50. **Rates** *single* £205; *double* £235-£299; *suite* £347-£681. **Credit** AmEx, MC, TC, V. **Map 6 L6**

In the midst of theatreland, Tim and Kit Kemp's Covent Garden Hotel is an appropriate stage for guests with a sense of the dramatic. All rooms are individual in terms of their size and impressive décor (in luxurious, bold colours). Quirky furniture and vivid upholstery plus matching tailor's mannequins (the hotel's trademark) make this a fun place to stay. Bathrooms, meanwhile, are mahogany and granite. There is a new florist's in the hotel, which provides the striking flowers in the lobby. **Brasserie Max** serves light meals and snacks. The Kemps also own the distinguished **Pelham** (*see p150*).

Hotel services *Gym.* **Room services** *CD player (some rooms). Fax. Mobile phone. VCR.*
Website: www.firmdale.com

The Halcyon

81 Holland Park, W11 3RZ (020 7727 7288/fax 020 7229 8516/halcyon_hotel@compuserve.com). Holland Park tube. **Rooms** 42. **Rates** *single* £165; *double* £270; *suite* £305-£600. **Credit** AmEx, DC, MC, TC, V.

The Halcyon prides itself on being a discreet retreat for the rich and famous. Wonderfully arranged

flowers scent the air of the reception rooms, where antique furniture is set off against the racing green carpet and draped cream curtains. The invitingly spacious bedrooms may not be at the forefront of modern design but their light, soothing tones, frills and flounces have a reassuringly English retro vibe. In the restaurant, the softly lit, unassuming interior belies a brilliantly executed menu with modern touches playing to the tastes of its younger, glitzier clientele. If you want to splash out in more ways than one, request a room with a Jacuzzi.
Hotel services *Terrace. Parking.* **Room services** *CD player (some rooms). Fax (some rooms). Mobile phone (on request). VCR (some rooms).*
Website: www.lewisfield.co.uk/halcyon

The Hempel

31-35 Craven Hill Gardens, W2 3EA (020 7298 9000/fax 020 7402 4666/the-hempel@easynet.co.uk). Lancaster Gate or Queensway tube/Paddington tube/rail. **Rooms** 40; 6 apartments. **Rates** *double* £288-£335; *suite* £529-£1,410. **Credit** AmEx, DC, JCB, MC, TC, V. **Map 1 C6**
London's most minimalist hotel certainly packs a punch. Its precise, clinical design even affects the flora; on a large table almost the size of the lobby, 200 fresh white orchids stand to attention. The jaw-dropping white-on-white reception, with an atrium that extends up to the fifth floor, has no decoration or furniture except four antique Burmese oxen carts that serve as tables. The individually designed rooms are kitted out in natural fabrics; the bathrooms sport slate and sand-blasted glass. A Zen-style garden, Shadows Bar and the appropriately minimal **I-Thai** (Italian/Thai – ho, ho) restaurant complete the design package.
Hotel services *Disabled rooms (2). Garden.* **Room services** *CD player. Fax. Mobile phone (on request). VCR.*

The Lanesborough

Hyde Park Corner, SW1X 7TA (020 7259 5599/ fax 020 7259 5606/info@lanesborough.co.uk). Hyde Park Corner tube. **Rooms** 95. **Rates** *single* £285-£345; *double* £382-£505; *suite* £600-£4,700. **Credit** AmEx, DC, JCB, MC, TC, V. **Map 7 G8**
Behind the relatively sober façade of the former St George's Hospital, the Lanesborough's unabashed magnificence dazzles. The luxurious Regency décor extends from the bedrooms to the Withdrawing Room and the Library Bar, which boasts one of the best collections of cognacs in London. The Conservatory restaurant, modelled on Brighton Pavilion, is the antithesis of such grandeur, reflecting a light chinoiserie theme, and serving Mediterranean/Pacific Rim cuisine (with a particularly impressive vegetarian selection) among potted palms and tinkling fountains. Only captains of industry and Lottery winners with £4,000+ to burn should enquire after the Royal Suite.
Hotel services *Disabled room (1). Gym. Parking.* **Room services** *CD player. Fax. Mobile phone. VCR.*
Website: www.lanesborough.com

The Metropolitan

Old Park Lane, W1Y 4LB (020 7447 1000/fax 020 7447 1147/sales@metropolitan.co.uk). Green Park or Hyde Park Corner tube. **Rooms** 155. **Rates** *single* £258; *double* £288-£400; *suite* £482-£1,645. **Credit** AmEx, DC, JCB, MC, TC, V. **Map 7 G8**
Christina Ong, owner of the more business-oriented but equally stylish **Halkin** (5 Halkin Street, SW1; 020 7333 1000), splashed out £45 million to create her most exclusive hotel yet on the site of the former Londonderry. This isn't the place for the easily intimidated: service, by the posse of model-like, DKNY-clad staff, is assertively attentive. If you want to feel like a star, though, you're on home territory: just recline on the cream leather suites in the lobby to the sounds of piped New York hip hop, and try to foster an air of studied nonchalance. Décor in the rooms is resolutely contemporary, minimalist chic, with a well thought-out use of hardwoods, marble and natural fabrics. More wannabes try (and fail) to gain entry into the star-spangled **Met Bar** than virtually any other. The Japanese restaurant, **Nobu** (*see p177*), is a cut above.
Hotel services *Beauty salon. Gym. Parking (limited).* **Room services** *CD player. Fax. VCR (on request).*
Website: www.metropolitan.co.uk

One Aldwych

1 Aldwych, WC2B 4BZ (020 7300 1000/fax 020 7300 1001/sales@onealdwych.co.uk). Charing Cross, Covent Garden or Temple tube. **Rooms** 105. **Rates** *single* £299-£375; *double* £320-£385; *suite* £465-£1,060. **Credit** AmEx, DC, JCB, MC, TC, V. **Map 8 M7**
Winner of several major awards (among them the AA Hotel of the Year 2000), One Aldwych is one of a new breed of London hotels: modern, chic, sharply stylish. The imposing grey façade gives way to a sleek, white-tiled, tall-windowed lobby, featuring modern sculpture and small but perfectly formed cocktail bar. The co-owner, Gordon Campbell Gray, has made this a multimillion-pound homage to modern art – there are over 300 pieces from his own collection here. In the rooms, bold tones strike out from calm backdrops (think: minimalist luxury – even the two pieces of fruit on a simple white plate manage to look chic). From the mini-gymnasiums in the deluxe suites to the underwater Mozart symphonies in the lap pool, the clientele is bathed in luxury at every turn. The health club offers personal training, massage and beauty treatments. Sustenance comes in the form of **Axis**, in the basement, reached via a stunning spiral staircase, and **Indigo**, both serving modern European food.
Hotel services *Disabled rooms (6). Gym (with pool).* **Room services** *CD player. Fax. Mobile phone (on request). VCR (some rooms).*
Website: www.onealdwych.co.uk

St Martins Lane

45 St Martin's Lane, WC2N 4HX (reservations 0800 634 5500/020 7300 5500/fax 020 7300 5501). Covent Garden or Leicester Square tube. **Rooms** 204. **Rates** *single* £230-£500; *double* £253-£524; *suite* £405-£1,469. **Credit** AmEx, DC, JCB, MC, £$TC, V. **Map 8 L7**
It only opened in September 1999, but the first London hotel from Ian Schrager (who also gave us

the Paramount and Royalton in New York and the Delano in Miami) is already a winner. While Schrager's ethos is always to create a 'hotel as theatre', co-star Philippe Starck aims to avoid overdecoration. The result? Rooms that are minimalist yet inviting (crisp white sheets, walk-in showers, lighting in colours you can change to suit your mood, a single pot plant, and Starck gadgets here and there). You don't have to be a guest to take advantage of the hotel's dining options – **Asia de Cuba**, with its free-standing bookcases and globally influenced food that hasn't met with universal approval from the critics; the pristine **Sea Bar**, serving sushi; the excellent if pricey **Saint M** brasserie, plus the **Light Bar**.
Hotel services *Disabled rooms (10). Terrace. Gym. Parking.* **Room services** *CD player. Fax (on request). VCR.*

The Savoy

Strand, WC2R 0EU (020 7836 4343/fax 020 7240 6040/info@the-savoy.co.uk). Covent Garden or Embankment tube/Charing Cross tube/rail.
Rooms 207. **Rates** *single* £329; *double* £393-£417; *suite* £535-£1,610. **Credit** AmEx, DC, JCB, MC, TC, V. **Map 8 L7**
Built by Richard D'Oyly Carte in 1889, the Savoy retains a reputation for effortless grandeur and trad British style (although the art deco rooms are the most thrilling). The great Escoffier first put the Savoy on the culinary map, and it's still possible to dine handsomely in the restaurant (where Ho Chi Minh was once a washer-up – honest), take tea in the Thames Foyer and eat lunch amid assorted MPs in the refined **Grill Room**. In addition, The Savoy is blessed with lavish banqueting rooms, a fitness centre and a swimming pool.
Hotel services *Beauty salon. Gym (with pool).* **Room services** *CD player. Fax. Mobile phone (on request). VCR.*
Website: www.savoy-group.co.uk

Expensive (£150-£235)

Unless otherwise stated, all hotels in this category have 24-hour room service, at least one bar, a hotel safe, multilingual staff, can arrange babysitting or a limousine service, and offer fax, business and laundry services; all rooms are equipped with a hairdryer, telephone and a TV. The services listed below each review are in addition to the above.

Blooms

7 Montague Street, WC1B 5BP (020 7323 1717/ fax 020 7636 6498/blooms@mermaid.co.uk). Holborn or Russell Square tube. **Rooms** 27 (all en suite). **Rates** (inc English breakfast) *single* £130; *double/twin* £195-£205; *four-poster* £205.
Credit AmEx, DC, JCB, MC, £TC, V. **Map 6 L5**
This smart and elegant Bloomsbury hotel is on the doorstep of the British Museum. The eighteenth-century house is kitted out with furniture in keeping with the era, and impressive finishing touches include fresh flowers in every room. A walled garden at the back offers refuge from the busy road at the front. One of the few hotels of its size with a lift.

Best for...

- **when the boss is paying**
  The Lanesborough, *p147.*
- **gawping at media-whore stars**
  The Metropolitan, *p147;* St Martins Lane, *p147.*
- **avoiding eye contact with stars who want to be left alone**
  Blakes, *p146;* Hazlitt's, *p150.*
- **interior design junkies**
  The Hempel, *p147.*
- **great value for money**
  Five Sumner Place, *p153.*
- **totally organic, feng shui-ed chill out experience**
  myhotel bloomsbury, *p150.*
- **top central London location at a bargain price**
  London County Hall Travel Inn Capital, *p158.*
- **getting to the Millennium Dome (both near to Waterloo tube station, on the Jubilee Line)**
  London County Hall Travel Inn Capital, *p158;* The Mad Hatter, *p159.*

Hotel services *Conference facilities. Garden.* **Room services** *Minibar. Radio. Satellite TV.*
Website: www.bloomshotel.co.uk

Dorset Square Hotel

39-40 Dorset Square, NW1 (020 7723 7874/fax 020 7724 3328/dorset@firmdale.com). Baker Street tube/ Marylebone tube/rail. **Rooms** 38 (all en suite). **Rates** *single* £115-£123; *double* £153-£264. **Credit** AmEx, MC, £$TC, V. **Map 1 F4**
Located just south of Regent's Park on a grand garden square, this elegant hotel manages to retain an air of intimacy lost to some of its larger peers. The rooms have a plush, Regency feel, combining boldly patterned walls with heavy floral drapery, and in the newly fitted lounge the guests congregate on sofas around an open fire. In comparison, the feel of the Potting Shed restaurant, which serves basic English fare, is surprisingly humble.
Hotel services *Currency exchange. No-smoking rooms.* **Room services** *Air-conditioning. Minibar. Mobile phone (on request). Modem point. Radio. Safe. Satellite TV. VCR (on request).*
Website: www.firmdale.com

The Gore

189 Queen's Gate, SW7 5EX (020 7584 6601/ fax 020 7589 8127/reservations@gorehotel.co.uk). Gloucester Road tube. **Rooms** 53. **Rates** *single* £128; *double* £194; *suite* £331-£338. **Credit** AmEx, DC, JCB, MC, TC, V. **Map 4 D9**

The mini-palms at the Gore's entrance add a touch of the exotic to this highly traditional Victorian hotel. Open for over a century, the Gore has retained its period charm, with mahogany wall panelling and deep scarlet curtains, but its relaxed, unpretentious staff manage to keep it on the right side of stuffiness. Individual touches add to the appeal: the hotel's collection of 5,000 sketches graces the walls, the Tudor Room has wonderful oak beams and a minstrel's gallery, and a carved, gilded bed once belonging to Judy Garland sits in the Venus room. The buzzing **Bistro 190** (*see p179*) serves imaginative Mediterranean food, if not at bistro prices.
Hotel services *Conference facilities. Currency exchange. No-smoking rooms.* **Room services** *CD player (on request). Minibar. Modem point. Safe. VCR (on request).*

Hazlitt's

6 Frith Street, W1V 5TZ (020 7434 1771/fax 020 7439 1524/reservations@hazlitts.co.uk). Tottenham Court Road tube. **Rooms** 23. **Rates** *single* £165; *double* £200; *suite* £353. **Credit** AmEx, DC, JCB, MC, £TC, V. **Map 6 K6**

Favoured by the author Bill Bryson as 'intentionally obscure', this small, unobtrusive hotel oozes quirky charm, and enjoys a great Soho location. Essayist William Hazlitt spent his final days in one of the houses of which it is made up, and it remains a favourite haunt of literary and media types: the bookcase in the lounge contains signed copies of books by former guests, and a glance over the shelves reads like a Who's Who of '90s literati. The 23 rooms, named after previous distinguished residents and guests, are exquisitely decked out with antique four-posters, panel-backed beds and free-standing claw-footed baths. There's no bar in the hotel, but step outside and you needn't look far.
Room services *Modem point. Safe. VCR (on request).*

myhotel bloomsbury

11-13 Bayley Street, WC1B 3HD (020 7667 6000/fax 020 7667 6001/guest_services@myhotels.co.uk). Goodge Street or Tottenham Court Road tube. **Rooms** 76. **Rates** *single* £176-£200; *double* £205-£229; *suite* £346-£393. **Credit** AmEx, DC, JCB, MC, TC, V. **Map 6 K5**

A newcomer to the London hotel scene (it opened in March 1999), this curiously named hotel is the brainchild of owner Andrew Thrasyvoulou. Superlative service is the name of the game, with one 'personal assistant' looking after each customer (tipping is discouraged). Décorwise it's East meets West with interiors and furniture coming from the Conran Design Partnership and a full feng shui treatment ensuring plenty of free-flowing positive energy. This concept follows through to the bar (**mybar**) and restaurant (**mychi**), which serves well-executed food of an oriental bent. *See picture p146.*
Hotel services *Conference facilities. Currency exchange. Gym. No-smoking rooms.* **Room services** *Air-conditioning. CD player. Fax. Minibar. Mobile phone (on request). Modem point. Radio. Safe. Satellite TV. VCR (on request).*
Website: www.myhotels.co.uk

No.5 Maddox Street

5 Maddox Street, W1R 9LE (020 7647 0200/fax 020 7647 0300/no5maddoxst@living-rooms.co.uk). Oxford Circus tube. **Rooms** 12. **Rates** *one-bedroom suite* £195-£275; *two-bedroom suite* £345; *three-bedroom suite* £495. **Credit** AmEx, DC, JCB, MC, £TC, V. **Map 5 J6**

Stunning is the only word to describe this boutique hotel, which opened in February 1999. The feel of the rooms (which are all suites) is organic yet luxurious, with tactile natural materials, plush sofas and bamboo floors. Deluxe suites have the added attractions of an open fireplace and decked balcony. Guests can don their linen kimono and raid their 'Big Bar', stocked with 'good' and 'bad' groceries. There's nothing the staff won't do to keep residents happy, from ordering in an expert from the Jet Lag Clinic to hiring out bikes. There's no bar or restaurant but you're spoilt for choice for places to eat and drink within the area. Well worth splashing out on, but with only 12 rooms, it gets booked up quickly.
Room services *Air-conditioning. CD player. Fax. Minibar. Modem point. Radio. Safe. Satellite TV. VCR.*
Website: www.living-rooms.co.uk

Number Sixteen

16 Sumner Place, SW7 3EG (020 7589 5232/fax 020 7584 8615/toll-free from US 1 800 592 5387/reservations@numbersixteenhotel.co.uk). South Kensington tube. **Rooms** 36 (33 en suite). **Rates** (incl breakfast) *single* £90-£125; *double/twin* £160-£195; *suite* £205. **Credit** AmEx, DC, MC, £$TC, V. **Map 4 D11**

A smart yet homely (and pricey) B&B taking up four Victorian townhouses on a tree-lined street. Rooms are named by colour, and decorated with sober good taste. In winter guests can huddle around the open fire in the drawing room or browse in the library, while the conservatory and meandering garden, with fountain and statuettes, are delights in warmer weather. No business services.
Hotel services *Garden. No-smoking rooms.* **Room services** *Minibar. Radio. Room service (7am-11pm). Safe.*
Website: www.numbersixteenhotel.co.uk

The Pelham

15 Cromwell Place, SW7 2LA (020 7589 8288/fax 020 7584 8444/pelham@firmdale.com). South Kensington tube. **Rooms** 50 (all en suite). **Rates** *single* £171; *double* £206-£264; *suite* £335-£411. **Credit** AmEx, DC, JCB, MC, TC, V.

Kit and Tim Kemp (who also own the **Covent Garden Hotel**; *see p146*) personally designed each room at this luxury townhouse. The classically English-style bedrooms have contemporary granite bathrooms and an array of modern gadgetry. Plush communal areas, including a restaurant, lounge and honesty bar, have solid English antiques and equestrian prints. Knightsbridge and Hyde Park are a short walk away.
Hotel services *Conference facilities. Currency exchange. No-smoking rooms. Parking. Valet parking.* **Room services** *Air-conditioning. Minibar. Mobile phone. Modem point. Radio. Safe (some rooms). Satellite TV. VCR.*

Portobello Hotel

22 Stanley Gardens, W11 2NG (020 7727 2777/ fax 020 7792 9641/reception@portobello-hotel. demon.co.uk). Holland Park or Notting Hill Gate tube. **Rooms** 24. **Rates** (incl breakfast) *single* £115; *double* £155-£260. **Credit** AmEx, MC, £TC, V. **Map 1 A6**

The Portobello's white Victorian façade gives no clue to the wacky curios that characterise its delightfully idiosyncratic interior. The circular bed in one of the suites is particularly exquisite. All rooms are different and, amid the clutter, you might stumble across globes, potted palms, or a wonderful Heath-Robinson bathing machine spouting taps and pipes. The restaurant, in contrast, is light and airy.

Hotel services *Gym (with pool).* **Room services** *Air-conditioning (some rooms). Minibar. Mobile phone (on request). Modem point. Radio. Satellite TV. VCR.*

Website: www.portobello-hotel.demon.co.uk

The Rookery

12 Peter's Lane, Cowcross Street, EC1M 6DS (020 7336 0931/fax 020 7336 0932/reservations@ rookery.co.uk). Farringdon tube/rail. **Rooms** 33 (all en suite). **Rates** *single* £165; *double* £200; *suite* £270-£411. **Credit** AmEx, DC, JCB, MC, £TC, V. **Map 9 O5**

The discreet doorway to this small hotel can be found along a Dickensian lane close to Smithfield meat market. Popular with business people, the Rookery (sister hotel to **Hazlitt's**; *see p150*) is reminiscent of a gentleman's club. The traditional décor steers clear of chintz and fuss, and favours a more masculine smart and sturdy style. Each bedroom has a work space with antique desk, complete with fax and modem line. All bathrooms have Victorian claw-foot bath tubs with showers, standing on plinths. If you're staying here for a special occasion, try to book the stunning master suite – the Rook's Nest – which comes complete with a retractable hexagonal ceiling opening to a private lounge area. Guests can choose to take breakfast either in their room or the conservatory-style lounge area.

Hotel services *Conference facilities. Courtyard. No-smoking rooms.* **Room services** *Fax (on request). Minibar. Mobile phone (on request). Modem point. Safe. Satellite TV. VCR (on request).*

Moderate (£100-£150)

In addition to the services listed below, all hotels in this category have multilingual staff, and offer fax and laundry services, and all rooms have a TV and telephone.

Abbey Court

20 Pembridge Gardens, W2 4DU (020 7221 7518/ fax 020 7792 0858/info@abbeycourthotel.co.uk). Notting Hill Gate tube. **Rooms** 22 (all en suite). **Rates** (incl breakfast) *single* £99; *double/twin* £140-£160; *triple* £170; *four-poster/suite* £180. **Credit** AmEx, DC, MC, £TC, V. **Map 1 A7**

An elegant, comfortable hotel close to Notting Hill Gate. The well-sized rooms are individually decorated, many with Designers Guild fabrics, antique furniture and dressing tables, while the old-fashioned marble bathrooms have the added bonus of a relaxing Jacuzzi bath. The communal areas include a lovely, comfy reception lounge and a small but cosy conservatory. Highly recommended.

Rook's Nest suite at **The Rookery**. *Zzzzzzz*

Hotel services *Babysitting. Bar. Business services. No-smoking rooms. Terrace.* **Room services** *Hairdryer. Radio. Room service (24 hours). Safe.*

Website: www.abbeycourthotel.co.uk

Academy Hotel

17-25 Gower Street, WC1E 6HG (020 7631 4115/ fax 020 7636 3442/restaurant 020 7636 7612). Goodge Street or Tottenham Court Road tube. **Rooms** 50 (all en suite). **Rates** (incl English breakfast) *single* £115; *double* £145; *suite* £185. **Credit** AmEx, DC, JCB, MC, V. **Map 6 K4**

A £1-million development programme has left the sleek, classy Academy with gleaming pastel-painted walls and an extra 17 rooms, which are large and airy. Two patio gardens, a conservatory and a library are among the facilities. Rooms at the front of the building suffer remarkably little from traffic noise. The hotel is very well located for the British Museum. Staff are friendly.

Hotel services *Babysitting. Bar. Business services. Conference facilities. Garden. Library. No-smoking rooms. Restaurant. Terrace.* **Room services** *Air-conditioning. Minibar. Room service (7am-midnight). Tea/coffee. Safe. Satellite TV.*

Commodore Hotel

50 Lancaster Gate, W2 3NA (020 7402 5291/fax 020 7262 1088/reservations@commodore-hotel.com). Lancaster Gate tube. **Rooms** 90 (all en suite). **Rates** (incl breakfast) *single* £99; *double* £129; *triple* £160; *suite* £180-£250. **Credit** AmEx, DC, JCB, MC, £TC, V. **Map 2 D7**

Just a stroll away from Hyde Park, the Commodore provides easy access to London's sights and bustling Queensway, in quiet surroundings. The elegant, recently refurbished lobby features antique furniture and chandeliers, a theme echoed in the superb galleried suites (worth the extra cash); the standard rooms, though fairly basic, are good value.
Hotel services *Bar. Business services. Conference facilities. No-smoking rooms. Restaurant. Safe.*
Room services *Hairdryer. Modem point. Radio. Room service (8am-8pm). Tea/coffee.*
Website: www.commodore-hotel.com

Cranley Gardens Hotel

8 Cranley Gardens, SW7 3DB (020 7373 3232/ fax 020 7373 7944). Gloucester Road tube.
Rooms 85 (all en suite). **Rates** (incl breakfast) *single* £79-£89; *double* £109-£119; *triple* £135.
Credit AmEx, DC, JCB, MC, £TC, V. **Map 4 D11**
Four converted Victorian townhouses make up this family-run hotel. In contrast to the lovely plant-bedecked entrance, welcoming lounge and panelled wood bar, the rooms are nothing thrilling, but are nonetheless comfortable, with modern furniture. Guests can fuel up for a day of sightseeing in the bright, yellow-painted restaurant.
Hotel services *Babysitting. Bar.* **Room services** *Hairdryer. Radio. Room service (7am-midnight). Satellite TV.*

Five Sumner Place

5 Sumner Place, SW7 3EE (020 7584 7586/fax 020 7823 9962/reservations@sumnerplace.com). South Kensington tube. **Rooms** 13 (all en suite). Rates (incl English breakfast) *single* £99; *double/twin* £140-£150; *triple* £165. **Credit** AmEx, JCB, MC, £TC, V.
Map 4 D11
Situated in a smart tree-lined street in South Kensington, this gem of a B&B offers large rooms with superior furnishings – dark wood, high ceilings and floral prints. The airy blue/yellow conservatory is a lovely place to enjoy breakfast and afternoon tea. Deserved winner of the London Tourism Awards' Best B&B of 1999. *See picture p154.*
Hotel services *Lift. No-smoking rooms. Safe. Terrace.* **Room services** *Hairdryer. Minibar. Radio. Refrigerator. Room service (8am-10pm). Tea/coffee.*
Website: www.sumnerplace.com

London Elizabeth Hotel

4 Lancaster Terrace, W2 3PF (020 7402 6641/ fax 020 7224 8900). Lancaster Gate tube.
Rooms 49 (all en suite). **Rates** (incl breakfast) *single* £100; *double* £115-£150; *suite* £135-£250.
Credit AmEx, DC, MC, £$TC, V. **Map 2 D6**
Located close to Hyde Park's Italian gardens, this hotel was converted from three townhouses. The rooms vary in size and décor, with the suites, not surprisingly, offering more comfort than the more straightforward standard rooms (the Hyde Park Suite, featuring original Victorian fireplace and mirrors, is good value at £250). Service is impeccable, and the restaurant's menu incorporates fresh herbs plucked from the hotel garden.
Hotel services *Babysitting. Bar. Business services. Conference facilities. Currency exchange. Garden. No-smoking rooms. Parking. Restaurant. Safe.*
Room services *Air-conditioning. Disabled rooms. Hairdryer. Radio. Room service (24-hour). VCR.*
Website: www.londonelizabethhotel.co.uk

Mornington Lancaster Hotel

12 Lancaster Gate, W2 3LG (020 7262 7361/ fax 020 7706 1028/london@mornington.co.uk). Lancaster Gate tube. **Rooms** 66 (all en suite).
Rates (incl breakfast) *single* £110; *twin* £135-£150; *double* £125-£145; *mini-duplexes* £140.
Credit AmEx, DC, JCB, MC, £$TC, V. **Map D7**
Part of a small sub-group of Swedish-run Best Westerns, the Mornington is a curious mix of English formality and Scandinavian pragmatism. The traditional dark greens and heavy wood veneers of the lobby and library bar are at odds with the simple pastel and pine décor of the bedrooms, but it's a combination that works surprisingly well. The light and airy breakfast room is well stocked with cereals, freshly squeezed juices and, er, herrings (that's the Swedish connection). Service is friendly, so it's no surprise that many guests come back year after year.
Hotel services *Bar. Conference facilities. Currency exchange. Modem point. No-smoking rooms. Parking. Safe.* **Room services** *Hairdryer. Radio. Tea/coffee. VCR.*
Website: www.mornington.se

The chain gang

Sometimes you're simply not bothered about staying in the most charming hotel in town. Below we list the central phone numbers for the larger chains, plus their reservation line opening times and the number of hotels they own in Greater London.

Best Western *(0345 747474/ www.bestwestern.co.uk).* **Open** 8am-8pm Mon-Fri; 9am-6pm Sat, Sun. **Hotels** 13.

Forte Hotels Reservations Line *(0345 404040/www.forte-hotels.co.uk).* **Open** 7am-10pm daily. **Hotels** 16.

Hilton *(0800 856 8000/www.hilton.com).* **Open** 8am-11pm Mon-Fri; 9am-6pm Sat, Sun. **Hotels** 12.

Holiday Inn *(0800 897121).* **Open** 7am-10.40pm daily. **Hotels** 17.

Marriott *(0800 221222/ www.marriotthotels.com).* **Open** 24 hours daily. **Hotels** 6.

Radisson Edwardian *(0800 374411/ www.radisson.com).* **Open** 24 hours daily. **Hotels** 11.

Travel Inn *(01582 414341/ www.travelinn.co.uk).* **Open** 8am-6pm Mon-Fri; 8am-4pm Sat, Sun. **Hotels** 4.

Award-winning **Five Sumner Place**. *See p153.*

Pembridge Court Hotel

34 Pembridge Gardens, W2 4DX (020 7229 9977/ fax 020 7727 4982/reservations@pemct.co.uk). Notting Hill Gate tube. **Rooms** 20. **Rates** (incl English breakfast) *single* £115-£155; *double* £145-£185; *triple/quad* £190-£195. **Credit** AmEx, DC, MC, £TC, V. **Map 1 A7**

Handy for Portobello Road market and Notting Hill's oh-so-trendy restaurants, the Pembridge Court is a cheery place. Many of the rooms are decorated in floral fabrics, and on the walls hang a fascinating collection of Victoriana, including fans, gloves and handbags. The restaurant, **Caps**, offers an inventive European menu. Two of the hotel's best-loved guests are the cats, Spencer and Churchill, who often prowl the picturesque patio. A place that exudes warmth, making it easy to relax and feel at home.

Hotel services *Bar. Business services. Babysitting. Limousine service. Room service (24 hours).*
Room services *Air-conditioning. CD player. Hairdryer. Radio. Safe. Satellite TV. VCR.*
Website: www.pemct.co.uk

Sandringham

3 Holford Road, NW3 1AD (020 7435 1569/ fax 020 7431 5932/sandringham.hotel@virgin.net). Hampstead tube. **Rooms** 17 (15 en suite). **Rates** *single* £75-£95; *double/twin* £125-£140; *triple/quad* £115-£180; *junior suite* £150. **Credit** AmEx, DC, JCB, MC, TC, V.

This elegant hotel is stylishly decorated and has a distinctive country house feel. The ground-floor bedrooms tend to be more spacious, while upstairs they have great views of the city. Close to Hampstead Heath, the Sandringham is surrounded by good walks and plenty of fresh air, while central London is only a 15-minute tube journey away.

Hotel services *Bar. Parking (for 5 cars). Garden. Limousine service. Lounge. No-smoking rooms. Safe.* **Room services** *Hairdryer. Room service (24-hour). Tea/coffee.*

Topham's Belgravia

28 Ebury Street, SW1W 0LU (020 7730 8147/ fax 020 7823 5966/Tophams_Belgravia@ compuserve.com). Victoria tube/rail. **Rooms** 40 (38 en suite). **Rates** (incl English breakfast) *single* £115; *double/twin from* £130; *four-poster* £150; *triple* £170; *family room* £260. **Credit** AmEx, DC, JCB, MC, £TC, V. **Map 7 H10**

This pretty hotel in the heart of Belgravia has an unassuming, home-from-home feel, providing a welcome respite from Victoria Station a couple of streets away. The bright and spacious rooms, most of which have recently been redecorated, are decked out in cutesy pastel pinks and whites. Staff are welcoming, as evidenced by the fact that many visitors come back year after year. The cosy feel of the place is enhanced by the homely lounge; guests can also have a drink in the newly refurbished bar or dine in the cosy red restaurant.

Hotel services *Bar. Conference facilities. Lift. Restaurant. Safe.* **Room services** *Hairdryer. Tea/coffee.*
Website: www.tophams.co.uk

Moderate to cheap (£70-£100)

Unless stated to the contrary, all hotels in this category have a fax machine; all the rooms are equipped with telephones and TVs, and have hairdryers in the rooms or available on request. The services listed below each review are in addition to the above.

Crescent Hotel

49-50 Cartwright Gardens, WC1H 9EL (020 7387 1515/fax 020 7383 2054). Russell Square tube/ Euston tube/rail. **Rooms** 27 (21 en suite). **Rates** (incl English breakfast) *single* £42-£65; *double/twin* £80; *triple* £90; *quad* £100. **Credit** MC, £TC, V. **Map 6 L3**

Run by the same family since 1956, this pleasant Regency house is dotted with antiques. Breakfast is served from a Georgian kitchen bench, discovered during recent renovations. Guests have use of nearby tennis courts.

Hotel services *Lounge. Multilingual staff. Safe.*

Gate Hotel

6 Portobello Road, W11 3DG (020 7221 0707/fax 020 7221 9128/gatehotel@thegate.globalnet.co.uk). Notting Hill Gate tube. **Rooms** 6 (5 en suite). **Rates** (incl breakfast) *single* £50-£65; *double* £80-£85. **Credit** MC, £TC, V. **Map 1 A6**

A stone's throw from Portobello Market and Notting Hill's hip bars and restaurants, the Gate enjoys a prime location. Accommodation is fairly simple, but rooms are well equipped, there's a profusion of fresh flowers and the proprietors are friendly. Note that there is a 3% surcharge on credit card payments. **Room services** *Radio. Refrigerator. Tea/coffee.*

Harlingford Hotel

61-63 Cartwright Gardens, WC1H 9EL (020 7387 1551/fax 020 7387 4616). Russell Square tube/ Euston tube/rail. **Rooms** 43 (42 en suite). **Rates** (incl English breakfast) *single* £68; *double/twin* £85; *triple* £95; *quad* £105. **Credit** AmEx, DC, JCB, MC, £TC, V. **Map 6 L3**

At the end of a pretty Regency crescent, the Harlingford's Bloomsbury location is relatively peaceful for central London. Recently refurbished, the rooms all have new bathrooms, and there's an impressive large and bright breakfast room. Use of tennis courts.

Hotel services *Safe.* **Room services** *Tea/coffee.*

Hart House Hotel

51 Gloucester Place, W1H 3PE (020 7935 2288/ fax 020 7935 8516/reservations@harthouse.co.uk). Baker Street or Marble Arch tube. **Rooms** 16 (11 en suite). **Rates** (incl English breakfast) *single* £53-£65; *double/twin* £75-£93; *triple* £110; *quad* £130. **Credit** AmEx, JCB, £$TC, V. **Map 5 G6**

This good-looking Georgian hotel located on a smart terrace close to Oxford Street is within easy reach of both Hyde Park and Regent's Park. The rooms are simply furnished and well maintained, and staff are friendly and competent.

Hotel services *Safe.* **Room services** *Tea/coffee.*

Hotel 167

167 Old Brompton Road, SW5 0AN (020 7373 0672/fax 020 7373 3360). Gloucester Road tube. **Rooms** 19 (18 en suite). **Rates** (incl breakfast) *single* £72-£86; *double* £90-£99; *triple* £115. **Credit** AmEx, MC, £TC, V. **Map 4 D11**

Featured in Jane Soloman's novel of the same name, Hotel 167 offers comfortable accommodation with flair. The peaceful rooms are decked out in subtle, soft tones and pine furniture. The bright reception-cum-breakfast room features marble tables and large modern paintings.

Hotel services *Multilingual staff. Safe.*
Room services *Refrigerator. Room service (8am-11pm). Satellite TV. Tea/coffee.*

Kensington Gardens Hotel

9 Kensington Gardens Square, W2 4BH (020 7221 7790/fax 020 7792 8612). Bayswater or Queensway tube. **Rooms** 17 (13 en suite). **Rates** (incl breakfast) *single* £50-£55; *double* £75; *triple* £95. **Credit** AmEx, DC, MC, £TC, V. **Map 1 B6**

Set on a quiet Victorian square, this comfortable B&B offers very good room facilities for the price and boasts a great location, overlooking a private leafy square near to the restaurants and multicultural buzz of Queensway. Rates are set to rise slightly in 2000.

Hotel services *Lounge. Multilingual staff.*
Room services *Minibar. Room service (2-11pm). Satellite TV. Tea/coffee.*

Morgan Hotel

24 Bloomsbury Street, WC1B 3QJ (020 7636 3735/ fax 020 7636 3045). Tottenham Court Road tube. **Rooms** 21 (all en suite). **Rates** (incl English breakfast) *single* £50-£60; *double/twin* £75; *triple* £110; *suite* £95 for two people, £130 for three people. **Credit** MC, £TC, V. **Map 6 K5**

The friendly owners of this Georgian terrace hotel by the British Museum are Londoners and proud of it: Beefeaters on the walls and toby jugs lining the breakfast room windowsill are among the give-aways. Bedrooms are clean and comfortable. The hotel is split between two houses, the second of which contains a number of suites and larger rooms, let to loyal guests or those making extended stays. There's a surcharge of 3% for credit card bookings.

Hotel services *Iron.* **Room services** *Air-conditioning (most rooms). Safe.*

The Plough

42 Christchurch Road, SW14 7AF (020 8876 7833/ fax 020 8392 8801/ploughthe@hotmail.com). Richmond tube then 33, 337 bus/Mortlake rail. **Rooms** 8 (all en suite). **Rates** (incl English breakfast) *single* £60; *double* £80; *triple/quad* £100. **Credit** AmEx, MC, TC, V.

A little gem. This lovely sixteenth-century inn retains its beamed ceilings and thick walls, some still in wattle and daub, while providing an impressive array of modern comforts. Breakfast is served in the pub downstairs, where you can mingle with locals. Richmond Park and the river are within walking distance.

Hotel services *Parking. Garden. Laundry. Multilingual staff. Pub. Restaurant. Safe.*
Room services *Room service (noon-3pm, 7-9.30pm). Satellite TV. Tea/coffee.*

Riverside Hotel

23 Petersham Road, Richmond, Surrey TW10 6UH (tel/fax 020 8940 1339). Richmond tube. **Rooms** 22 (all en suite). **Rates** (incl English breakfast) *single* £60; *double* £80; *triple* £90-£95; *suite* £115. **Credit** AmEx, MC, TC, V.

Located in Richmond town centre, only a 20-minute tube ride from London, this agreeable B&B enjoys stunning views of the Thames. Other plus points include clean and comfortable rooms of a reasonable size, and notably friendly owners. Ask for a

Brekkie at **30 King Henry's Road**. *See p157.*

room with a river view, or room 22, which has a private garden.
Hotel services *Currency exchange. Garden. Laundry. Multilingual staff. Safe.* **Room services** *Tea/coffee. Satellite TV.*

Rushmore

11 Trebovir Road, SW5 9LS (020 7370 3839/6505/ fax 020 7370 0274). Earl's Court tube. **Rooms** 22 (all en suite). **Rates** (incl breakfast) *single* £59-£69; *double* £79-£85; *triple* £89-£95; *quad* £99-£110. **Credit** AmEx, MC, £TC, V. **Map 3 B11**
A delightful hotel, with rooms decorated in an imaginative range of styles and colours, using *trompe l'oeil* techniques and draped fabrics – each one is different. The Rushmore's Italian feel extends to the wrought-iron Tuscan furniture and glass tables in the airy conservatory, where breakfast is served.
Hotel services *Conference facilities. Laundry. Lounge. Multilingual staff. No-smoking rooms. Safe.* **Room services** *Satellite TV. Tea/coffee.*

Swiss House Hotel

171 Old Brompton Road, SW5 0AN (020 7373 2769/ fax 020 7373 4983/recep@swiss-hh.demon.co.uk). Gloucester Road tube. **Rooms** 15 (all en suite). **Rates** (incl breakfast) *single* £65; *double* £80-£90; *triple* £104; *quad* £118. **Credit** AmEx, DC, JCB, MC, £TC, V. **Map 4 D11**
This building, formerly owned by Swiss Air, has an attractive façade covered with trailing ivy and flower boxes. Inside, the rooms are large and many have their original fireplaces. Breakfast is served by friendly staff in a country-style dining room.
Hotel services *Laundry. Multilingual staff. No-smoking rooms. Safe.* **Room services** *Room service (noon-9pm). Satellite TV.*
Website: www.swiss-hh.demon.co.uk

30 King Henry's Road

30 King Henry's Road, NW3 3RP (020 7483 2871/ fax 020 7483 4587/ingram30kh@aol.com). Chalk Farm tube. **Rooms** 3 (all with private bathrooms). **Rates** (incl breakfast) *single* £65; *double* £90. **Credit** £TC.
This stylish and homely Victorian B&B in Primrose Hill offers lovely rooms and a relaxed atmosphere. Owners Carole and Andrew Ingram undertake to treat everyone as if they were a friend coming to stay. Guests are served breakfast in the impressive traditional kitchen complete with Aga. *See picture p155.*
Hotel services *Garden. Multilingual staff. No smoking throughout.* **Room services** *Radio.*

Vicarage Hotel

10 Vicarage Gate, W8 4AG (020 7229 4030/fax 020 7792 5989/reception@londonvicaragehotel.com). High Street Kensington or Notting Hill Gate tube. **Rooms** 18 (1 en suite). **Rates** (incl English breakfast) *single* £45; *double* £74; *triple* £90; *quad* £98. **Credit** £$TC. **Map 1 B8**
Overlooking a pretty Victorian square, this grand building contains a cosy B&B. The rooms are basic but clean. Close to Kensington Gardens and Palace, and to the shops of Kensington High Street.
Hotel services *Payphone. TV lounge.* **Room services** *Tea/coffee. Washbasin.*

Cheap (under £70)

All hotels in this category have a fax machine, in addition to the services listed below each individual hotel.

Abbey House

11 Vicarage Gate, W8 4AG (020 7727 2594). High Street Kensington or Notting Hill Gate tube. **Rooms** 16 (none en suite). **Rates** (incl English breakfast) *single* £43; *double* £68; *triple* £85; *quad* £95; *quin* £105. **Credit** £$TC. **Map 1 B8**
One of the best quality B&Bs in this price range, Abbey House is an elegant Victorian house, retaining many of its original fittings, with spacious, simply decorated rooms and comfy orthopaedic beds. *See picture p158.*
Hotel services *Multilingual staff. Payphone. Tea/coffee.* **Room services** *Washbasin.*

Arosfa

83 Gower Street, WC1E 6HJ (tel/fax 020 7636 2115). Goodge Street tube/Euston Square tube/rail. **Rooms** 16 (2 en suite). **Rates** (incl English breakfast) *single* £33; *double* £46; *triple* £62; *quad* £84. **Credit** MC, £TC, V. **Map 6 K4**
Arosfa (which means 'place to stay' in Welsh) is run by the friendly Mr and Mrs Dorta, who offer basic but pleasantly decorated rooms in the former Georgian home of the artist John Everett Millais. There's a 2% surcharge on credit cards.
Hotel services *Garden. Lounge. Multilingual staff. Payphone.* **Room services** *TV. Washbasin.*

Ashlee House

261-265 Gray's Inn Road, WC1X 8QT (020 7833 9400/fax 020 7833 9677/info@ashleehouse.co.uk). King's Cross tube. **Rooms** 26 (175 beds). **Rates** (per person, incl breakfast) *4-6-bed room* £17; *8-10-bed room* £15; *16-bed room* £13; *twin* £22; *single* £34. **Map 6 M3**
This hostel-style accommodation caters mainly to young backpackers. The rooms (all with bunk beds) take between one and 16 people; the price per person decreases the more you share with. There's a large dining and self-catering area downstairs and staff are cheerful and accommodating.
Hotel services *Baggage store. Internet access. Laundry. Payphone. Safe. Self-catering facilities.* **Room services** *Washbasin.*
Website: www.ashleehouse.co.uk

Cartref House & James House

129 Ebury Street, SW1W 9QU & 108 Ebury Street, SW1W 9QD (020 7730 6176 & 020 7730 7338/ jandchouse@cs.com). Victoria tube/rail. **Rooms** (incl English breakfast) *Cartref* 11 (8 en suite); *James* 6 (3 en suite). **Rates** *single* £49-£60; *double* £65-£77; *triple* £82-£93; *quad* £110. **Credit** AmEx, MC, £TC, V. **Map 7 H10**
Under the same ownership, these B&Bs on a chic Georgian street provide bright, basic rooms and a cheery welcome.
Hotel services *Multilingual staff. No smoking throughout. Payphone.* **Room services** *Hairdryer. Tea/coffee. TV.*

Kensington's **Abbey House**. *See page 157.*

Garden Court Hotel

30-31 Kensington Gardens Square, W2 4BG (020 7229 2553/fax 020 7727 2749). Bayswater or Queensway tube. **Rooms** 32 (16 en suite). **Rates** (incl English breakfast) *single* £34-£48; *double* £52-£78; *triple* £72-£86; *quad* £78-£92. **Credit** MC, £TC, V. **Map 1 B6**

A popular family-run B&B overlooking a peaceful Victorian garden square. Rooms are comfortable, warm and clean. Additional features include an attractive paved garden and large lounge. One of the better quality hotels in this price range.

Hotel services *Garden. Lounge. Multilingual staff. Safe.* **Room services** *Hairdryer.*

The Generator

Compton Place (off 37 Tavistock Place), WC1H 9SD (020 7388 7666/fax 020 7388 7644/info@the-generator.co.uk). Russell Square tube. **Rooms** 217 (833 beds; none en suite). **Rates** (per person, incl breakfast) *single* £36-£38; *twin* £22-£26; *3-6-bed room* £18-£22; *7-8-bed room* £17-£21; *dorm-share* £15. **Credit** MC, V. **Map 6 K4**

Rooms and dorms at this former police barracks have taken on a prison cell theme right down to the bunk beds. Neon-lit, industrial-style communal areas include a huge games room, a self-service canteen, and an Internet access room. Guests can mingle in the lively downstairs bar (open until 2am). Ideal for backpackers, student groups and the more adventurous.

Hotel services *Baggage store. Bar. Internet access. No-smoking rooms. Safe.*
Room services *Washbasin.*
Website: www.the-generator.co.uk

Hampstead Village Guesthouse

2 Kemplay Road, NW3 1SY (020 7435 8679/fax 020 7794 0254/hvguesthouse@dial.pipex.com). Hampstead tube/Hampstead Heath rail. **Rooms** 6 (5 en suite).**Rates** *single* £40-£75; *double* £60-£100; *studio* £75-£135. **Credit** AmEx, DC, MC, £TC, V.

A real haven for eccentrics, this: located in a rambling Victorian Hampstead townhouse, each of its six rooms is filled with a fabulous array of books, antiques and family clutter, accumulated and lovingly arranged by its exuberant owner, Annemarie van der Meer. There is a separate outhouse with a tiny corner kitchenette, available for use as a private suite (sleeps one to five people). Guests should note that credit card payments are subject to a 5% charge.

Hotel services *Babysitting. Business services. Garden. Laundry. Multilingual staff. No smoking throughout.* **Room services** *Hairdryer. Iron. Refrigerator. Tea/coffee. Telephone. TV.*

Highfield Guesthouse

12 Dowanhill Road, SE6 1HJ (020 8698 8038/fax 020 8698 8039). Hither Green rail.
Rooms 3 (1 en suite) **Rates** (incl English breakfast) *single* £30-£45; *double/twin* £45-£65; *triple* £60-£65. **Credit** JCB, MC, £TC, V.

This immaculate little guesthouse boasts excellent facilities and comfortable rooms decked out in well-chosen IKEA-style furnishings. The owner, Frenchman Michel Tournier, goes to great lengths to accommodate his guests (he's happy to collect them from Hither Green station, which has frequent trains to central London). Rooms like these would be at least twice the price further north.

Hotel services *Garden. Multilingual staff. No-smoking rooms.* **Room services** *Hairdryer. Laundry. Radio. Refrigerator. Tea/coffee. Satellite TV.*

Jenkins Hotel

45 Cartwright Gardens, WC1H 9EH (020 7387 2067/fax 020 7383 3139/reservations@jenkinshotel.demon.co.uk). Russell Square tube/Euston tube/rail. **Rooms** 14 (7 en suite). **Rates** (incl English breakfast) *single* £45-£62; *double* £62-£72; *triple* £80. **Credit** MC, £TC, V. **Map 6 L3**

Three friendly black Labradors welcome guests into this recommended B&B located on a quiet, pretty Georgian crescent near the British Museum. Rooms are impeccably clean and airy.

Hotel services *Garden.* **Room services** *Hairdryer. Minibar. Refrigerator. Safe. Tea/coffee. Telephone. TV.*

London County Hall Travel Inn Capital

County Hall, Belvedere Road, SE1 7PB (020 7902 1600/fax 020 7902 1619). Waterloo tube/rail.
Rooms 313 (all en suite). **Rates** £62.95.
Credit AmEx, DC, MC, £$TC, V. **Map 8 M9**

One of two hotels in County Hall, the Travel Inn offers possibly the best-value rooms in central London. They all cost the same, regardless of whether they're for one, two, three or four people. OK, so they're not exactly brimming over with luxuries, but they are roomy and clean. The location is a bonus, right next to the British Airways London

Eye and just on the south side of Westminster Bridge. Potters restaurant serves breakfast and dinner, and snacks are available at the adjoining bar.
Hotel services *Bar. Currency exchange. Disabled rooms (16). Lift. Multilingual staff. No-smoking rooms. Restaurant. Safe.* **Room services** *Hairdryer (on request). Tea/coffee. Telephone. TV.*
Website: www.travelinn.co.uk

The Mad Hatter

3-7 Stamford Street, SE1 9NY (020 7401 9222/ fax 020 7401 7111/madhatter@fullers.demon.co.uk). Blackfriars tube/Waterloo tube/rail. **Rooms** 30 (all en suite). **Rates** *single/twin/double/family* £57.50-£78.50. **Credit** AmEx, DC, MC, £TC, V. **Map 11 N8**
A rash of Fuller's pubs with hotels attached has hit London, offering great value for money. Though the Mad Hatter is on a fairly busy road, the windows are double glazed so any noise from traffic is minimal. Rooms are large and pleasantly decorated in pastel hues. Three rooms are adapted for the disabled, and others have linked doors to the next rooms. Guests can get meals, including breakfast, in the pub.
Hotel services *Bar. Disabled rooms (3). Laundry. Lift. Multilingual staff. No-smoking rooms. Restaurant. Safe.* **Room services** *Satellite TV. Tea/coffee.*
Website: www.fullers.co.uk

Oxford House Hotel

92-94 Cambridge Street, SW1 (020 7834 6467/fax 020 7834 0225). Victoria tube/rail. **Rooms** 17 (none en suite). **Rates** (incl English breakfast) *single* £36; *double* £46-£48; *triple* £60-£63; *quad* £80-£84. **Credit** MC, £TC, V. **Map 7 H11**
This hotel is a real find: bright, comfortable accommodation just around the corner from Victoria Station. The shared facilities are clean and well kept.
Hotel services *Hairdryers (on request). Lounge. Multilingual staff. Payphone.*
Room services *Radio. Washbasin.*

Parkwood

4 Stanhope Place, W2 2HB (020 7402 2241/fax 020 7402 1574). Marble Arch tube. **Rooms** 17 (13 en suite). **Rates** (incl English breakfast) *single* £49.50-£69.50; *double* £64.50-£87.50; *triple* £77-£97. **Credit** MC, £TC, V. **Map 2 F6**
A quiet, centrally located B&B near Hyde Park and a just few minutes from Oxford Street. The spruce rooms are decorated in serene colours and floral prints. Rates may rise in 2000.
Hotel services *Lounge. Multilingual staff. No-smoking rooms. Terrace.* **Room services** *Radio. Satellite TV. Tea/coffee.*

St Margaret Hotel

26 Bedford Place, WC1B 5JL (020 7636 4277/ fax 020 7323 3066). Holborn or Russell Square tube. **Rooms** 64 (12 en suite). **Rates** (incl English breakfast) *single* £48.50; *double* £60-£78; *triple* £86.50. **Credit** MC, £$TC, V. **Map 6 L5**
A pleasant, characterful, family-run B&B with spacious rooms and obliging staff. Rooms at the back of the hotel have views of the Duke of Bedford's private gardens, to which all guests have access.
Hotel services *Garden. Hairdryer (on request). Lounge. Multilingual staff. Safe.*
Room services *Satellite TV. Telephone.*

Woodville House & Morgan House

107 Ebury Street, SW1W 9QU (020 7730 1048/fax 020 7730 2574) & 120 Ebury Street, SW1W 9QQ (020 7730 2384/fax 020 7730 8442). Victoria tube/rail. **Rooms** *Woodville* 12 (none en suite); *Morgan* 11 (3 en suite). **Rates** (incl English breakfast) *single* £42; *double* £60-£80; *triple* £80; *quad* £80-£100. **Credit** MC, £TC, V. **Map 7 H10**
Located close to Victoria Station, both these Georgian B&Bs are owned by exuberant couple Rachel Joplin and Ian Berry. Woodville House has traditional, flowery décor; Morgan is more contemporary. Families are very well catered for and one of the suites has an adjoining terrace that can double as a picnic area.
Hotel services *Babysitting. Hairdryer (on request). Iron. Kitchenette. Multilingual staff. Payphone. Terrace.* **Room services** *Tea/coffee (Morgan House only). TV.*
Website: www.woodvillehouse.co.uk

Women-only accommodation

Townsend House

126 Queen's Gate, SW7 5LQ (020 7589 9628/fax 020 7225 1458/platform@gfs.u-net.com). Gloucester Road tube. **Open** *phone enquiries* 9am-5pm Mon-Fri. **Rates** (B&B) *twin* £16; hostel: *single* £74 per week; *double/twin* £69 per week; *triple* £63 per week. **Credit** £TC. **Map 4 D10**
Run by the Girls' Friendly Society, Townsend House is a clean, conveniently located women-only B&B/ hostel. Most of the rooms in the house are given over to the long-stay hostel (one month minimum; for women aged 18-30 only); the B&B (14 days maximum) consists of a few rooms on the top floor, but all guests can use the house's amenities, which include a large kitchen, two large lounges, laundry facilities and a chapel. Look for the small 'GFS' sign on the front door.

Gay & lesbian accommodation

See page 267.

Youth hostels

Beds are either in twin rooms or in dormitories. If you are not a member of the International Youth Hostel Federation (IYHF), you'll have to pay an extra £1.70 a night to stay at hostels (after six nights you automatically become a member). Alternatively, join the IYHF for £12 (£6 for under-18s) at any youth hostel. Always phone hostels first to check the availability of beds. All the following hostels take MasterCard, Visa and travellers' cheques. You can become a member or book rooms through the IYHF's website (www.yha.org.uk).

City of London Youth Hostel *36-38 Carter Lane, EC4 (020 7236 4965/fax 020 7236 7681).*

St Paul's tube. **Beds** 199. **Reception open** 7am-11pm daily; 24-hour access. **Rates** (incl breakfast) £19-£26; £18-£21.50 under-18s. **Map 11 O6**

Earl's Court Youth Hostel *38 Bolton Gardens, SW5 (020 7373 7083/fax 020 7835 2034). Earl's Court tube*. **Beds** 155. **Reception open** 7am-11pm daily; 24-hour access. **Rates** (incl breakfast) £19.45; £17.15 under-18s. **Map 3 B11**

Hampstead Heath Youth Hostel *4 Wellgarth Road, NW11 (020 8458 9054/fax 020 8209 0546). Golders Green tube*. **Beds** 200. **Reception open** 6.45am-11pm daily; 24-hour access. **Rates** (incl breakfast) £19.70; £17.30 under-18s.

Holland House Youth Hostel *Holland House, Holland Walk, W8 (020 7937 0748/fax 020 7376 0667/hollandhouse@yha.org.uk). High Street Kensington tube*. **Beds** 201. **Reception open** 7am-11pm daily; 24-hour access. **Rates** (incl breakfast) £19.45; £17.15 under-18s. **Map 1 A8**

Oxford Street Youth Hostel *14 Noel Street, W1 (020 7734 1618/fax 020 7734 1657). Oxford Circus tube*. **Beds** 75. **Reception open** 7am-11pm daily; 24-hour access. **Rates** £19.45-£21.50; £15.90 under-18s. **Map 5 J6**

Rotherhithe Youth Hostel *Island Yard, Salter Road, SE16 (020 7232 2114/fax 020 7237 2919). Rotherhithe tube*. **Beds** 320. **Reception open** 7am-11pm; 24-hour access. **Rates** £22.15-£25.50; £18.65-£21.30 under-18s.

YMCAs

You may need to book months in advance to stay at a YMCA. Many specialise in long-term accommodation. A few of the larger hostels are listed below (all are unisex), but the National Council for YMCAs (020 8520 5599) can supply a full list. Prices are around £25-£30 per night for a single room and £40-£45 for a double.

Barbican YMCA *2 Fann Street, EC2 (020 7628 0697/fax 020 7638 2420). Barbican tube*. **Beds** 240. **Map 9 P5**

London City YMCA *8 Errol Street, EC1 (020 7628 8832/fax 020 7628 4080). Barbican tube*. **Beds** 111. **Map 9 F4**

Wimbledon YMCA *200 The Broadway, SW19 (020 8542 9055/fax 020 8542 1086). Wimbledon tube/rail*. **Beds** 110.

Staying with the locals

Staying in a Londoner's home is often more fun than being in an impersonal hotel. The following organisations can arrange accommodation (rates include breakfast).

At Home in London *70 Black Lion Lane, W6 9BE (020 8748 1943/fax 020 8748 2701/athomeinlondon@compuserve.com/ www.athomeinlondon.co.uk)*. **Open** *phone enquiries* 9.30am-5.30pm Mon-Fri. **Rates** £30-£56. **Credit** JCB, MC, £TC, V.

The Bulldog Club *14 Dewhurst Road, W14 OET (020 7371 3202/fax 020 7371 2015/jackson@ bulldogclub.u-net.com/www.bulldogclub.com)*. **Rates** from £85 per night. **Credit** AmEx, MC, V. Pay a £25 membership fee for three years and enjoy some of the most fabulous and exclusive B&Bs in the country.

Host and Guest Service *103 Dawes Road, SW6 7DU (020 7385 9922/fax 020 7386 7575/ www.host-guest.co.uk). Fulham Broadway tube*. **Open** 9am-5.30pm Mon-Fri. **Rates** from £16.50 per person; students from £85.90 per week. **Credit** MC, £TC, V. **Minimum stay** 2 nights.

London Bed & Breakfast Agency *71 Fellows Road, NW3 3JY (020 7586 2768/fax 020 7586 6567/stay@londonbb.com/www.londonbb.com)*. **Rates** £19-£41 per night. **Minimum stay** 2 nights.

London Homestead Services *Coombe Wood Road, Kingston-upon-Thames, Surrey KT2 7JY (020 8949 4455/fax 020 8549 5492)*. **Open** *phone enquiries* 9am-7pm daily. **Rates** *single* from £16; *double* from £32. **Credit** MC, £TC, V. **Minimum stay** 3 nights.

Self-catering/service apartments

It can be very expensive to rent accommodation in London, but if you're in a group, you may be able to save money by renting a flat. The following specialise in holiday lettings. See also the *Yellow Pages*.

Accommodation Outlet *2nd floor, 32 Old Compton Street, W1V 5PD (020 7287 4244/fax 020 7734 2249/holiday@outlet.co.uk/www.outlet.co.uk). Leicester Square or Tottenham Court Road tube*. **Open** 10am-6pm Mon-Fri; noon-5pm Sat. **Rates** *double studio* from £65 per night; *4-person apartment* from £103 per night. **Map 6 K6**

The Apartment Service *1st floor, 5-6 Francis Grove, SW19 4DT (020 8944 1444/fax 020 8944 6744). Wimbledon tube/rail*. **Open** 9am-6.30pm Mon-Fri. **Rates** *double studio* from £90 per night. **Credit** AmEx, MC, £TC, V.

Astons Apartments *31 Rosary Gardens, SW7 4NQ (020 7590 6000/fax 020 7590 6060/sales@ astons-apartments.com/www.astons-apartments.com). Gloucester Road tube*. **Open** 9am-6pm daily; *phone enquiries* 8am-9pm daily. **Rates** *single studio* £55 per night; *double studio* £78 per night. **Credit** AmEx, JCB, MC, £TC, V. **Map 3 C11**

Holiday Serviced Apartments *273 Old Brompton Road, SW5 9JA (020 7373 4477/fax 020 7373 4282/reservations@holidayapartments.co.uk/ www.holidayapartments.co.uk). Earl's Court tube*. **Open** 9.30am-6pm Mon-Fri. **Rates** *single/double studio* from £80 per night. **Credit** AmEx, MC, £TC, V. **Map 3 C11**

The Independent Traveller *Thorverton, Exeter, Devon EX5 5NT (01392 860807/fax 01392 860552/independenttrav@cs.com)*. **Rates** *apartments* £250-£2,000 per week. **Credit** MC, £TC, V. **Minimum stay** 3 nights. Properties in London and all over the UK.

London Holiday Accommodation Bureau *(tel/fax 020 8809 1899/07957 384924/ sales@londonholiday.co.uk).* **Rates** from £30 per night. **Credit** AmEx, MC, £TC, V.
Holiday apartments all over London, with airport/ tube pick-up, theatre tickets and a tour thrown in for good measure.

Palace Court Holiday Apartments *1 Palace Court, Bayswater Road, W2 4LP (020 7727 3467/fax 020 7221 7824). Notting Hill Gate or Queensway tube.* **Open** 8.30am-11pm daily. **Rates** *single studio* £56 per night; *double* £72 per night; *triple* £81 per night. **Credit** £TC.

Perfect Places *53 Margravine Gardens, W6 8RN (020 8748 6095/fax 020 8741 4213/permatch@ netcomuk.co.uk/www.perfectplaceslondon.co.uk). West Kensington tube.* **Rates** from £550 per week. **Credit** AmEx, MC, TC, V.
Kensington, Knightsbridge and Chelsea apartments.

University residences

During university vacations much of London's student accommodation is opened up to visitors, representing a basic but cheap place to stay.

Arcade Halls *The Arcade, 385-401 Holloway Road, N7 ORN (020 7607 5415/fax 020 7609 0052/ summerlets@unl.ac.uk). Holloway Road tube.* **Rooms** *self-contained flats (for 4-6).* **Rates** £14 per night; £77 per week. **Available** 3 July-4 Sept 2000.

Butlers Wharf LSE Residence *11 Gainsford Street, SE1 2NE (020 7407 7164/fax 020 7403 0847/butlers.wharf@lse.ac.uk). Tower Hill tube/London Bridge tube/rail.* **Rooms** *self-contained flats (sleeping up to 7)* 48. **Rates** from £20 per person (under-12s half-price). **Minimum stay** 4 nights. **Available** July-Sept. **Map 12 R9**

Cartwright University Halls *36 Cartwright Gardens, WC1H 9BZ (020 7388 3757/fax 020 7388 2552/carthalla@aol.com). Russell Square tube or Euston tube/rail.* **Rooms** *single* 153; *twin* 40. **Rates** *single* £30-£33; *twin* £42-£47. **Available** all year. **Map 6 L3**

Goldsmid House *36 North Row, W1R 1DH (020 7493 8911/fax 020 7491 0586). Marble Arch tube.* **Rooms** *single* 10; *twin* 120. **Rates** *single* £20; *twin* £28. **Available** June-Sept. **Map 5 G6**

High Holborn Residence *178 High Holborn, WC1V 7AA (020 7379 5589/fax 020 7379 5640/ high.holborn@lse.ac.uk). Holborn tube.* **Rooms** *single* 400; *twin* 48. **Rates** *single* £34; *twin* £57-£67. **Available** 8 July-27 Sept. **Map 6 M5**

International Students House *229 Great Portland Street, W1N 5HD (020 7631 8300/ 8310/fax 020 7631 8315/accom@ish.org.uk). Great Portland Street tube.* **Rooms** *single* 158; *twin* 107. **Rates** *single* £30; *twin* £22 per person; *dormitory* £9.99-£17.50. **Available** all year. **Map 5 H5**

King's Campus Vacation Bureau *King's College, Riddell House, St Thomas Campus, Lambeth Palace Road, SE1 7EH (020 7928 3777/fax 020 7928 5777/vac.bureau@kcl.ac.uk). Waterloo tube/rail.* **Rates** *single* £17-£33; *twin* £29-£47. **Available** 3 Apr-4 May, 19 June-15 Sept, 2000. King's has eight halls offering around 2,000 beds. **Map 11 N8**

Passfield Hall *1-7 Endsleigh Place, WC1H 0PW (020 7387 7743/3584/fax 020 7387 0419/ passfield@lse.ac.uk). Euston tube/rail.* **Rooms** *single* 100; *twin* 34; *triple* 7. **Rates** *single* £26.50; *twin* £45; *triple* £60. **Available** Easter, July-Sept. **Map 6 K4**

Walter Sickert Hall *29 Graham Street, N1 8LA (020 7477 8822/www.city.ac.uk/ems). Angel tube.* **Rooms** *single* 220; *executive single* 6; *executive twin* 3. **Rates** *single* £30; *executive single* £38; *executive twin* £55. **Available** 1 July-18 Sept 2000. **Map 9 P3**

Camping & caravanning

Crystal Palace Caravan Club Site *Crystal Palace Parade, SE19 1UF (020 8778 7155). Crystal Palace rail/3 bus.* **Open** *office Mar-Oct* 8.30am-8pm, *Nov-Feb* 9am-8pm, daily. **Rates** from £3.90; plus *caravan pitch* from £6; *car & tent pitch* from £3.50; *motorbike & tent pitch* £2.50; *bicycle/walker & tent pitch* £2; *electricity hook-up* £1.45-£2.20. **Credit** MC, £TC, V.
Room for 60 tent and 84 caravan pitches. There are good facilities plus fresh bread in the summer and restaurants nearby.

Lea Valley Campsite *Sewardstone Road, E4 7RA (020 8529 5689). Walthamstow Central tube/rail then 215 bus.* **Open** *Apr-Oct* 8am-10pm daily. **Rates** £5.40; £2.20 under-16s; *electricity hook-up* £2.25 per day. **Credit** MC, V.
Although this big site is 12 miles (19km) from central London it has good facilities and it's cheap. No single-sex groups.

Lea Valley Leisure Centre Camping & Caravan Park *Meridian Way, N9 0AS (020 8803 6900). Edmonton Green rail/W8 bus or Tottenham Hale tube/363 bus.* **Open** 8am-10pm daily. **Rates** £5.35; £2.25 5s-16s; *electricity hook-up* £2.30 per day. **Credit** MC, £TC, V.
Located behind a leisure centre, this is the ideal campsite for sport fiends. There are 160 touring caravan pitches and 100 tent pitches plus washing facilities, showers and a shop.

Tent City Acton *Old Oak Common Lane, W3 7DP (020 8743 5708/tentcity@ btinternet.com/www.tentcity.co.uk). East Acton tube.* **Open** *June-Sept* 24 hours daily. **Rates** £6; £3 under-12s; free under-5s; 10% discounts for groups. **Credit** £TC.
This venerable institution provides 320 beds in a tented hostel as well as 200 tent pitches. Free showers, toilets, washing and cooking facilities. All profits go to charity.

Tent City Hackney *Millfields Road, E5 0AR (020 8985 7656/tentcity@btinternet.com/ www.tentcity.co.uk). Liverpool Street tube/rail or Hackney Downs rail then 242 bus/38 bus.* **Open** *June-Sept* 24 hours daily. **Rates** £5 per person; £2.50 under-15s; free under-5s. **Credit** £TC.
This site is run by **Tent City Acton** *(see above)* and offers similar facilities including 90 beds in a tented

hostel and 200 tent pitches. At the time of going to press it was not certain whether the site would be open during 2000; phone or check the website.

Emergency accommodation

If you're left high and dry, the **Tonbridge Club** might be able to help.

Tonbridge Club *120 Cromer Street, WC1H 8BS (020 7837 4406). King's Cross tube/rail/Russell Square.* **Open** 9.30pm-midnight daily. **Rates** £5. **Map 6 L3**

By day it's a school club, by night it's the cheapest hostel in London. If you're stranded, the Tonbridge is a godsend. You'll have to sleep on a mattress on the gym floor, but there are hot showers, TV and a games room – all for just £5. Only foreign visitors and students are allowed to stay.

Longer stay

If you are planning on staying for months rather than weeks, it may work out cheaper to rent a place (although you'll normally have to pay a month's rent in advance and a further month's rent as a deposit). Even so, accommodation is still expensive and competition fierce. The best source for places to rent is *Loot*, published daily. Buy it as early as you can and get straight on the phone. Capital Radio publishes a flatshare list, available from the foyer (30 Leicester Square, WC2H 7LA; Leicester Square tube) every Thursday around 4pm. Also try *Time Out* magazine (available from Tuesdays in central London and Wednesday further out), and *Midweek*, free from tube stations on Thursdays.

As a rough guide, you're unlikely to get a studio (no separate bedroom or, often, kitchen) or a one-bedroom flat for less than £500 per month, and you'll have to settle for some of the less desirable suburbs. If you want to stay in a hip area like Notting Hill, expect to fork out £800-£1,200 per week; similar accommodation in Covent Garden costs £900-£1,300; if only Knightsbridge will do, prepare to stump up around £1,400 per month. If, however, you can stomach a room in a shared flat/house, you can find accommodation for less than £300 a month in the further reaches of the East End and south London, rising to around the £600-a-month level for Fulham or Hampstead.

Hotels by area

Note that this list does not include gay and lesbian hotels, youth hostels or YMCAs.

Bloomsbury

Academy Hotel, *p151*; **Arosfa**, *p157*; **Ashlee House**, *p157*; **Blooms**, *p149*; **Crescent Hotel**, *p154*; **The Generator**, *p158*; **Harlingford Hotel**, *p155*; **Jenkins Hotel**, *p158*; **Morgan Hotel**, *p155*; **myhotel bloomsbury**, *p150*; **St Margaret Hotel**, *p159*.

Chelsea & South Kensington

Blakes, *p146*; **Cranley Gardens Hotel**, *p153*; **Five Sumner Place**, *p153*; **The Gore**, *p149*; **Hotel 167**, *p155*; **Number Sixteen**, *p150*; **The Pelham**, *p150*; **Swiss House Hotel**, *p157*.

Covent Garden & Soho

Covent Garden Hotel, *p146*; **Hazlitt's**, *p150*; **One Aldwych**, *p147*; **St Martins Lane**, *p147*; **The Savoy**, *p149*.

Holborn & Clerkenwell

The Rookery, *p151*.

Knightsbridge & Belgravia

Abbey House, *p157*; **The Lanesborough**, *p147*; **Topham's Belgravia**, *p154*.

Marylebone

Dorset Square Hotel, *p149*; **Hart House Hotel**, *p155*.

Mayfair

The Metropolitan, *p147*; **No.5 Maddox Street**, *p150*.

South Bank

London County Hall Travel Inn Capital, *p158*; **The Mad Hatter**, *p159*.

Westminster & Victoria

Cartref House/James House, *p157*; **Oxford House Hotel**, *p159*; **Woodville House/ Morgan House**, *p159*.

North London

Hampstead Village Guesthouse, *p158*; **Sandringham**, *p154*.

South London

Highfield Guesthouse, *p158*; **The Plough**, *p155*; **Riverside Hotel**, *p155*.

West London

Abbey Court, *p151*; **Commodore Hotel**, *p151*; **Garden Court Hotel**, *p158*; **Gate Hotel**, *p154*; **The Halcyon**, *p146*; **The Hempel**, *p147*; **Kensington Gardens Hotel**, *p155*; **London Elizabeth Hotel**, *p153*; **Mornington Lancaster Hotel**, *p153*; **Parkwood**, *p159*; **Pembridge Court Hotel**, *p154*; **Portobello Hotel**, *p151*; **Rushmore**, *p157*; **30 King Henry's Road**, *p157*; **Vicarage Hotel**, *p157*.

Restaurants

Biriani, borscht, bacalao, bento – you name it, we got it.

The excellence of London's restaurants is unquestioned. Whether you fancy Michelin three-star haute cuisine or a bargain bowl of noodles, hanging out in the hippest new eaterie or noshing down with the cabbies in an unreconstructed caff, there is somewhere in the capital that will fulfill your gustatory needs. But be warned: there's still plenty of dross out there. If you want a taste of the good old, bad old days, you'll still have no trouble finding touristy rip-off joints serving up the sort of boiled-to-death slop you wouldn't feed your pets.

Eating out remains a favourite pastime for Londoners and, despite a glut of mega-seater restaurants opening in the last few years (and a not-always-enthusiastic uptake from punters), they still keep on coming (a 1,000-seater, **Sugar Reef**, opened in Great Windmill Street in Soho at the end of 1999). Yet diners are becoming more discerning about what and where they eat – on the one side this has led to a rash of health-oriented soup joints (*see page 177* **Souper snacks**) and noodle bars (spearheaded by the evergreen and ever-expanding **Wagamama** chain; *see page 183*), while on the other, chefs continue to experiment and develop. This can lead to wildcard brilliance such as that found at **Nobu** (*see page 177*) or more generalised improvements like the long-overdue development of India's myriad cuisines beyond the boring curry house fare.

PRACTICALITIES

Few places have strict dress codes these days; as a general rule, the pricier the joint, the smarter the clientele. It's only common sense that you don't turn up to Chez Nico wearing a Hawaiian shirt, yet even here you won't have to don a jacket and tie.

It's standard practice to pay ten per cent on top of the bill for service. Some restaurants will add this automatically (while insisting that it is 'optional'; so if service wasn't up to scratch don't hesitate to deduct the charge). In fact, it is becoming distressingly common to find 12.5 and even 15 per cent added. Be wary of places that include service in the bill but then leave the space for gratuity empty on your credit card slip.

The average prices below are for a three-course meal (or ethnic equivalent), excluding drinks and service, for one person. Note that the best-value restaurants below (£15 or less for a starter, main course and dessert) are marked **budget**. For further cheap options, *see page 184* **Dead-cheap dinners**. For restaurants geared towards children and families, *see page 236*. For a round-up of the city's best Internet cafés, *see page 346* **Cybercafés**. For more information, buy the annual *Time Out Eating & Drinking Guide* (£9).

Note that, for the following restaurants, if no credit cards are listed, none is taken.

Haute cuisine

Haute equals posh, generally. Expect formality in décor and service, high prices and classic, superlative food. Dress up and live it up. In addition to the places below, you can be assured of superb cooking at Pierre Koffmann's **La Tante Claire** (The Berkeley Hotel, Wilton Place, SW1; 020 7823 2003), **Pied à Terre** (23 Charlotte Street, W1; 020 7636 1178) and **L'Oranger** (5 St James's Street, SW1; 020 7839 3774).

Chez Nico at Ninety Park Lane

90 Park Lane, W1 (020 7409 1290). Hyde Park Corner or Marble Arch tube. **Lunch** noon-2pm Mon-Fri. **Dinner** 7-11pm Mon-Sat. **Set lunch** £25, £40, three courses. **Set dinner** £53 two courses, £64 three courses. **Credit** AmEx, MC, TC, V. **Map 7 G7**
Nico Ladenis' consummate mastery of flavours, colours and textures – whether classic French or with adroit touches of Asia and the Middle East – ensures exemplary standards of cooking in this sedate yet relaxed Mayfair drawing room.

Gordon Ramsay

68-69 Royal Hospital Road, SW3 (020 7352 4441/3334). Sloane Square tube. **Lunch** noon-2pm, **dinner** 6.45-11pm, Mon-Fri. **Average** £50.
Set lunch £28 three courses. **Set meal** £50 three courses, £65 seven courses. **Credit** AmEx, DC, JCB, MC, £TC, V. **Map 4 F12**
Since his dramatic parting (together with the entire kitchen and waiting staff) from Aubergine in 1998, ex-footballer and shy, retiring, Michelin two-star chef Ramsay has triumphantly set up on his own.

Oak Room

Meridien Hotel, 21 Piccadilly, W1 (020 7437 0202). Piccadilly Circus tube. **Lunch** noon-2.30pm Mon-Fri. **Dinner** 7-11.15pm Mon-Sat. **Average** £90.
Set lunch £37.50 three courses. **Set dinner** £55 three courses, £90 seven courses. **Credit** AmEx, JCB, MC, £TC, V. **Map 7 J7**
Be prepared to dig deep into your pockets to enjoy the stunning Michelin three-star cooking of Robert Reid at Marco Pierre White's flagship restaurant. Stick to the set lunch unless someone else is paying.

Stefano Cavallini Restaurant at the Halkin

Halkin Hotel, 5-6 Halkin Street, SW1 (020 7333 1234/1000). Hyde Park Corner tube. **Lunch** 12.30-2.30pm Mon-Fri. **Dinner** 7.30-10.30pm Mon-Sat; 7-10pm Sun. **Average** £50. **Set lunch** £23 three courses. **Set dinner** £55 six courses. **Credit** AmEx, DC, JCB, MC, £TC, V. **Map 7 G9**

One of London's very finest. Expect profound flavours, culinary skill and a refined light touch in understated, elegant surroundings. The set lunch is one of the best deals in town.

Modern European

The restaurants in this section represent the cutting edge of modern cuisine in London. Classical European cooking usually provides the base, but ingredients and inspiration are pillaged from around the world. In addition to those listed below, the **Red Room**, inside the huge Waterstone's bookstore at 203 Piccadilly (020 7851 2464) is also recommended.

Alastair Little

49 Frith Street, W1 (020 7734 5183). Tottenham Court Road tube. **Lunch** noon-3pm Mon-Fri. **Dinner** 6-11pm Mon-Sat. **Set lunch** £25 three courses. **Set dinner** £33 three courses. **Credit** AmEx, JCB, MC, £TC, V. **Map 6 K6**

Few people have had as big an impact on cooking in the capital as Alastair Little, and his small, informal Soho restaurant still knocks out beautifully rendered gutsy dishes like roast duck breast with butter beans and chorizo.

Branch: 136A Lancaster Road, W11 (020 7243 2220).

Andrew Edmunds

46 Lexington Street, W1 (020 7437 5708). Oxford Circus or Piccadilly Circus tube. **Lunch** 12.30-3pm Mon-Fri; 1-3pm Sat, Sun. **Dinner** 6-10.45pm Mon-Sat; 6-10.30pm Sun. **Average** £24. **Credit** AmEx, MC, £TC, V. **Map 5 J6**

This informal bistro is tiny, and its following of thirtysomething Soho workers loyal and large, but if you love simple, well-executed dishes, it's worth the squeeze.

Bank

1 Kingsway, WC2 (020 7379 9797). Covent Garden tube. **Breakfast** 7.30-10.30am Mon-Fri. **Brunch** 11.30am-3.30pm Sat, Sun. **Lunch** noon-3pm Mon-Fri. **Dinner** 5.30-11.30pm daily. **Average** £30. **Set meal** (5.30-7pm Mon-Sat) £13.90 two courses, £17.50 three courses. **Credit** AmEx, DC, MC, TC, V. **Map 6 M6**

It's huge, noisy and cost £5 million; but if you're in the mood, dining at Bank (on the likes of sea bream with black bean salsa and lime butter) is exhilarating. Service can be uncomfortably swift, however.

Bibendum

Michelin House, 81 Fulham Road, SW3 (020 7581 5817). South Kensington tube. **Lunch** noon-2.30pm Mon-Fri; 12.30-3pm Sat, Sun. **Dinner** 7-11.30pm Mon-Sat; 7-10.30pm Sun. **Average** £55. **Set lunch** (Mon-Fri) £23 two courses, £27.50 three courses; (Sat, Sun) £27.50 three courses. **Credit** AmEx, DC, MC, £TC, V. **Map 4 E10**

Sir Terence Conran's design and chef Simon Hopkinson's culinary skill made the name of this beautiful restaurant in the 1980s, and under Matthew Harris the kitchen continues to produce classic, unfussy cooking of the highest order.

Bluebird

350 King's Road, SW3 (020 7559 1000). Bus 19, 22, 49. **Brunch** 11am-4.30pm Sat, Sun. **Lunch** noon-3.30pm Mon-Fri. **Dinner** 6-11pm Mon-Sat; 6-10.30pm Sun. **Average** £33. **Set Sunday lunch** £17.50 three courses. **Set meal** (lunch, 6-7pm) £12.75 two courses, £15.75 three courses. **Credit** AmEx, DC, JCB, MC, TC, V. **Map 4 D12**

This former garage is now a gastro-complex consisting of a restaurant, bar, café, fruit and veg stall, food shop and cook shop. The buzzy first-floor restaurant is a relaxing spot for weekend brunch.

Circus

1 Upper James Street, W1 (020 7534 4000). Piccadilly Circus tube. **Open** *winter* noon-midnight Mon-Sat; noon-3pm Sun; *summer* noon-midnight Mon-Fri; 6pm-midnight Sat. **Average** £26. **Set meal** (noon-3pm, 5.45-7.30pm, 10.15pm-midnight) £14.75 two courses, £16.75 three courses. **Credit** AmEx, DC, MC, £TC, V. **Map 7 J6**

Circus may be trendily clinical in design but there's plenty of cockle-warming combos on the reliable menu – lamb with courgettes and tomatoes, and roast squab with shallots and Alsace bacon, for instance.

Clarke's

124 Kensington Church Street, W8 (020 7221 9225). Notting Hill Gate tube. **Lunch** noon-2pm, **dinner** 7-10pm, Mon-Fri. **Average** £29 lunch. **Set dinner** £42 four courses. **Credit** AmEx, MC, £TC, V. **Map 1 B7**

Sally Clarke brought Californian-style cooking to London, and her intimate, well-rounded restaurant remains a leading light after more than a decade. The menus change daily, but there's no choice for dinner, so phone first if you're a fussy eater. Great service.

Coast

26B Albemarle Street, W1 (020 7495 5999). Green Park tube. **Lunch** noon-2.45pm Mon-Fri; noon-3.30pm Sat. **Brunch** noon-4pm Sat, Sun. **Dinner** 6-11.45pm Mon-Sat. **Average** £35. **Set lunch** £19.50 two courses. **Credit** AmEx, DC, MC, £TC, V. **Map 7 H7**

Don your grooviest gear to visit this huge, stunningly designed goldfish bowl. Chef Stephen Terry combines ingredients in unusual yet inspired ways. Pricey, though.

The Fifth Floor

Harvey Nichols, Knightsbridge, SW1 (020 7235 5250). Knightsbridge tube. **Lunch** noon-3pm Mon-Fri; noon-3.30pm Sat, Sun. **Dinner** 6.30-11.30pm Mon-Sat. **Average** £30 dinner. **Set lunch** £23.50 three courses. **Credit** AmEx, DC, JCB, MC, £TC, V. **Map 4 F9**

Shop till you drop into this still-stylish, still-busy restaurant on the same floor as the bar, café and food shop. The spacious room isn't remarkable, but the menu, supplemented by daily specials, can be relied upon to come up with the goods.

French House Dining Room

1st floor, The French House, 49 Dean Street, W1 (020 7437 2477). Piccadilly Circus or Tottenham Court Road tube. **Lunch** noon-3pm, **dinner** 6-11.15pm, Mon-Sat. **Average** £23. **Credit** AmEx, DC, MC, £TC, V. **Map 6 K6**

An inimitable, unmissable slice of Soho, this tiny lacquered room is always packed with relaxed regulars who lap up Margot Clayton's tersely rendered dishes like ox tongue, carrots and green sauce.

The Glasshouse

14 Station Parade, Kew, Surrey (020 8940 6777). Kew Gardens tube/rail. **Lunch** noon-2.30pm daily. **Dinner** 7-10.30pm Mon-Sat. **Average** £17.50 lunch, £23.50 dinner. **Set lunch** £17.50 three courses. **Set dinner** £23.50 three courses. **Set Sunday lunch** £21.50 three courses. **Credit** AmEx, MC, £TC, V.

This place was a hit from the moment it opened in early 1999. The small, simple, modern dining room is a relaxed space in which to enjoy beautifully rendered gimmick-free dishes such as roast guinea fowl with boudin blanc.

Granita

127 Upper Street, N1 (020 7226 3222). Angel tube/ Highbury & Islington tube/rail. **Lunch** 12.30-2.30pm Wed-Sun. **Dinner** 6.30-10.30pm Tue-Sun. **Average** £20. **Set lunch** £11.95 two courses, £13.95 three courses. **Credit** MC, £TC, V. **Map 9 O3**

Lean, sleek Granita has matured into one of Islington's best restaurants. Dishes such as wok-fried squid with tamarind, lime and chilli sauce are as trendy as the uniforms worn by the charming, efficient staff.

The Ivy

1 West Street, WC2 (020 7836 4751). Covent Garden or Leicester Square tube. **Lunch** noon-3pm Mon-Sat; noon-3.30pm Sun. **Dinner** 5.30pm-midnight daily. **Average** £30. **Set lunch** (Sat, Sun) £15.50 three courses. **Credit** AmEx, DC, MC, £TC, V. **Map 6 K6**

Be prepared to book many months in advance to get a peak-time table at this beautifully restrained thespians' favourite. The menu is delightfully retro: nowhere will you get a classier Welsh rarebit, hamburger or fish and chips.

Mash

19-21 Great Portland Street, W1 (020 7637 5555). Oxford Circus tube. **Brunch** 11am-4pm Sat, Sun. **Lunch** noon-3pm Mon-Fri. **Dinner** 6-11.30pm Mon-Sat. **Average** £20. **Credit** AmEx, DC, MC, V. **Map 5 H5**

If you regard airport lounge décor of the 1970s as chic, Mash is for you. Offerings at Oliver Peyton's ever-on-the-pulse venue include bar snacks, cocktails, pizzas, pastas and options from the wood-burning oven. Beer is brewed on the premises.

Awfully good food at **Orrery**.

Odette's

130 Regent's Park Road, NW1 (020 7586 5486). Chalk Farm tube/31, 168 bus. Wine bar **Open** 12.30-2.30pm, 5.30-10.30pm, Mon-Sat; 12.30-2.30pm Sun. *Restaurant* **Lunch** 12.30-2.30pm Mon-Fri. **Dinner** 7-11pm Mon-Sat. **Average** £25. **Set lunch** (Mon-Fri) £10 three courses. **Credit** AmEx, DC, MC, £TC, V.

With its gorgeous display of gilded mirrors upstairs, and cosy pockets of space downstairs, Odette's could revive (or start) a relationship. And, happily, the quality of the food (not to mention a superb wine list) matches the setting.

Orrery

55 Marylebone High Street, W1 (020 7616 8000). Baker Street or Regent's Park tube. **Lunch** noon-3pm, **dinner** 7-11pm, daily. **Average** £40 dinner. **Set lunch** £23.50 three courses. **Set Sunday dinner** £28.50 three courses incl glass of champagne. **Credit** AmEx, DC, JCB, MC, £TC, V. **Map 5 G4**

The most understated – and underrated – of Sir Terence Conran's London restaurant portfolio. In the elongated first-floor restaurant there's an impressive emphasis on presentation from the *amuse-gueules* to the work-of-art desserts, and the execution is equally accomplished.

Oxo Tower Restaurant

Oxo Tower Wharf, Barge House Street, SE1 (020 7803 3888). Blackfriars, Southwark or Waterloo tube/rail. Brasserie **Lunch** noon-3.30pm daily. **Dinner** 5.30-11.30pm Mon-Sat; 6-10.30pm Sun. **Average** £30. **Set meal** (lunch, 5.30-7pm, Mon-Fri) £20 two courses. *Restaurant* **Lunch** noon-3pm Mon-Fri; noon-3.30pm Sun. **Dinner** 6-11pm Mon-Sat; 6.30-10.30pm Sun. **Average** £50. **Set lunch** £26.50 three courses. **Credit** AmEx, DC, JCB, MC, £TC, V. **Map 11 N7**

The Oxo Tower Restaurant is run by the people from Harvey Nichols' **Fifth Floor** (*see p165*). The fabulous views over the Thames from the eighth floor tend to overshadow the expensive, if usually reliable, food. The brasserie is cheaper (but still pricey). Both places are better suited for a business meal than a romantic dinner.

The People's Palace

Level 3, Royal Festival Hall, South Bank Centre, SE1 (020 7928 9999). Waterloo tube/rail. **Lunch** noon-3pm, **dinner** 5.30-11pm, daily. **Average** £23. **Set lunch** (Mon-Sat) £12.50 two courses, £17 three courses. **Set meal** (Sun, 5.30-7pm Mon-Sat) £15.50 two courses, £20 three courses. **Credit** AmEx, DC, MC, £TC, V. **Map 8 M8**

The dining option of choice if you're taking advantage of the entertainment at the South Bank Centre. There's a hint of airport lounge about the restaurant, but the mainly Mediterranean-influenced menu is reliable, the wine list is well chosen and the river views are fantastic.

Quaglino's

16 Bury Street, SW1 (020 7930 6767). Green Park tube. Bar **Open** 11.30am-1am Mon-Thur; 11.30am-2am Fri, Sat; noon-11pm Sun. **Average** £10. *Restaurant* **Lunch** noon-3pm daily. **Dinner** 5.30pm-midnight Mon-Thur; 5.30pm-1am Fri, Sat; 5.30-11pm Sun. **Average** £30. **Set meal** (noon-3pm, 5.30-6.30pm) £15.50 two courses, £19 three courses. **Credit** AmEx, DC, JCB, MC, £TC, V. **Map 7 J7**

Quag's sunken dining room, polished and gleaming, is as impressive as ever. The crustacea and upmarket comfort food (liver and bacon fishcakes, etc) usually hit the mark, but diners can feel they're just part of a highly efficient culinary machine.

Stephen Bull

5-7 Blandford Street, W1 (020 7486 9696). Bond Street tube. **Lunch** 12.15-2.30pm Mon-Fri. **Dinner** 6.30-10.30pm Mon-Sat. **Set lunch** £22 two courses, £26 three courses. **Set dinner** £27.50 three courses. **Credit** AmEx, DC, MC, V. **Map 5 G5**

One of the first exponents of 'Modern British' cooking, the self-taught Stephen Bull opened this, his original restaurant, in 1989. The menu changes frequently, and a decade or so on the cooking remains as skilful, controlled and satisfying as ever.

Branch: Stephen Bull Smithfield 71 St John Street, EC1 (020 7490 1750).

Sugar Club

21 Warwick Street, W1 (020 7437 7776). Oxford Circus or Piccadilly Circus tube. **Lunch** noon-3pm Mon-Sat; 12.30-3pm Sun. **Dinner** 6-10.30pm daily. **Average** £28. **Credit** AmEx, DC, JCB, MC, TC, V. **Map 7 J7**

Peter Gordon's virtuoso Pacific Rim cooking seems at home in these cool, contemporary surroundings. Dishes plunder the world's larder, but Gordon has the skill to pull together unlikely combinations.

Teatro

93-107 Shaftesbury Avenue, W1 (020 7494 3040). Piccadilly Circus tube. **Lunch** noon-3pm Mon-Fri. **Dinner** 6-11.45pm Mon-Sat. **Average** £35. **Set lunch** £15.50 two courses, £18 three courses. **Pre-theatre meal** (6-7.30pm) £15 two courses, £18 three courses. **Credit** AmEx, MC, £TC, V. **Map 6 K6**

Owned by ex-footballer Lee Chapman and actress Leslie Ash, Teatro is luvvie heaven. Yet food is up there with the best of them – standout dishes include fillet of salmon with vanilla soy dressing.

Afghan

Afghan Kitchen budget

35 Islington Green, N1 (020 7359 8019). Angel tube. **Meals** noon-midnight Tue-Sat. **Average** £8. **Map 9 O2**

Authentic, delicious, cheap Afghan food is served in this pint-sized diner overlooking Islington Green. You may have to share a table, and there's little choice on the short menu, but it's all good – and don't miss the Afghan chutney and pickles.

American

Arkansas Café budget

Unit 12, Old Spitalfields Market, E1 (020 7377 6999). Liverpool Street tube/rail. **Lunch** noon-3.30pm Mon-Fri; noon-4.30pm Sun. **Dinner** by arrangement. **Average** £9. **Credit** DC, MC, V. **Map 10 R5**

The best burgers and barbecued meats in town are doled out by genial, tall-hatted American Keir Helberg from his basic, informal café within Spitalfields Market.

Cactus Blue

86 Fulham Road, SW3 (020 7823 7858). South Kensington tube. **Brunch** noon-4pm Sat, Sun. **Dinner** 5.30-11.45pm Mon-Sat; 5.30-11pm Sun. **Average** £30. **Credit** AmEx, MC, £TC, V. **Map 4 D11**

This classy establishment is serious about its food and its design. Making full use of the palette of chillies, flavourings and regional ingredients that makes up Southwestern American cooking, Cactus Blue makes a welcome change from fajitas and tacos.

Dakota

127 Ledbury Road, W11 (020 7792 9191). Notting Hill Gate tube/52 bus. **Lunch** noon-3.30pm Mon-Fri. **Dinner** 7-11pm Mon-Sat; 7-10.30pm Sun. **Average** £23. **Credit** AmEx, JCB, MC, £TC, V.

It's hard not to be impressed by the Notting Hill outpost of this chain, from the room's off-white cool ambience to the stunning modern Southwestern American food. Sibling restaurants **Montana** (125-129 Dawes Road, SW6; 020 7385 9500), **Idaho** (13 North Hill, N6; 020 78341 6633), **Canyon** (Riverside, Richmond; 020 8948 2944), **Utah** (18 High Street, Wimbledon; 020 8944 1909) and newcomer **Congress** (North Court, 1 Great Peter Street, SW1; 020 7654 3000) continue the good work elsewhere.

Argentinian

La Pampa Grill

60 Battersea Rise, SW11 (020 7924 4774). Clapham Junction rail. **Meals** 6pm-midnight Mon-Sat; 6-11pm Sun. **Average** £20. **Credit** MC, £TC, V.

For a hearty chunk of Argentina, you'd be hard-pushed to do better than La Pampa Grill. The décor is unapologetically basic, the menu unabashedly meaty, the staff unrestrainedly solicitous and the atmosphere unreservedly fun.

Belgian

Belgo Centraal

50 Earlham Street, WC2 (020 7813 2233). Covent Garden tube. **Meals** noon-11.30pm Mon-Sat; noon-10.30pm Sun. **Average** £20. **Set lunch** £5. **Credit** AmEx, DC, JCB, MC, V. **Map 6 L6**

Celebrating the twin glories of Belgian culture – moules frites and beer – Belgo's extraordinary, noisy, *Blade Runner*-like basement restaurant is phenomenally and deservedly popular.

Branches: **Belgo Noord** 72 Chalk Farm Road, NW1 (020 7267 0718); **Belgo Zuid** 124 Ladbroke Grove, W10 (020 8982 8400).

Brazilian

Rodizio Rico

111 Westbourne Grove, W2 (020 7792 4035). Bayswater or Notting Hill Gate tube. **Lunch** 12.30-4.30pm Sat. **Dinner** 6.30-11.30pm Mon-Sat. **Meals** 12.30-11.30pm Sun. **Average** £18. **Set lunch** £9 two courses. **Set dinner** £10 (vegetarian), £16.50, two courses. **Credit** MC, £TC, V. **Map 1 B6**

For £16.50 you get hot starters, free range at the salad bar and then as much meat as you can eat, served up on sabres by men in outrageous trousers.

British

Boisdale

15 Eccleston Street, SW1 (020 7730 6922). Victoria tube/rail. **Lunch** noon-2.30pm Mon-Fri. **Dinner** 7-10.30pm Mon-Sat. **Average** £30. **Set meal** £12.90, £16.90, two courses. **Credit** AmEx, DC, MC, £TC, V. **Map 7 H10**

Excellent food with a Scottish theme (roast haggis with mash and neeps, and fish and chips in beer batter) is served at the intimate Boisdale. Snacks of a similar nature are served at the bar next door, which also boasts a fantastic selection of whiskies.

Greenhouse

27A Hay's Mews, W1 (020 7499 3331/3314). Green Park or Hyde Park Corner tube. **Lunch** noon-2.30pm Mon-Fri; 12.30-3pm Sun. **Dinner** 6.30-11pm Mon-Sat; 6.30-10pm Sun. **Average** £25 lunch, £35 dinner. **Set Sunday lunch** £19.50 three courses. **Credit** AmEx, DC, JCB, MC, £TC, V. **Map 7 H7**

The Mayfair mansion-block basement location and unremarkable décor aren't promising, but Gary Rhodes' one-time demesne is still a beacon of first-rate inventive Modern British cuisine.

Lindsay House

21 Romilly Street, W1 (020 7439 0450). Leicester Square or Piccadilly Circus tube. **Lunch** noon-2.30pm Mon-Fri. **Dinner** 6-11pm Mon-Sat. **Average** £30 lunch. **Set dinner** £42 three courses. **Credit** AmEx, DC, MC, £TC, V. **Map 6 K6**

Irish chef Richard Corrigan is a man with a vision and his constantly evolving Modern British cooking is never less than interesting, and often surprising. The townhouse setting is unusual and intimate.

Rules

35 Maiden Lane, WC2 (020 7836 5314). Covent Garden tube/Charing Cross tube/rail. **Meals** noon-11.30pm Mon-Sat; noon-10.30pm Sun. **Average** £35. **Set meal** (3-6pm Mon-Fri) £18.95 two courses. **Credit** AmEx, DC, MC, £TC, V. **Map 8 L7**

Founded in 1798, this ancient establishment exudes history and exclusivity, yet this is no Olde England theme restaurant. Imaginatively updated versions of British classics are expertly cooked and beautifully presented. A winner.

St John

26 St John Street, EC1 (020 7251 0848/4998). Farringdon tube/rail. Bar **Open** 11am-11pm Mon-Fri; 6-11pm Sat. **Average** £7. *Restaurant* **Lunch** noon-3pm Mon-Fri. **Dinner** 6-11pm Mon-Sat. **Average** £25. **Credit** AmEx, DC, JCB, MC, £TC, V. **Map 9 O5**

There's a rather stark, industrial feel to this converted smokehouse – but offal fans will be in innard heaven, enjoying dishes such as roast (veal) bone marrow and parsley salad, as well as less challenging fare. You can also eat at the bar.

Veronica's

3 Hereford Road, W2 (020 7229 5079). Bayswater or Queensway tube. **Lunch** noon-2.30pm Mon-Fri. **Dinner** 6-11.30pm Mon-Sat. **Average** £25. **Set meal** (lunch Mon-Fri, dinner Mon-Thur) £12.50 two courses, £16.50 three courses. **Credit** AmEx, DC, JCB, MC, £TC, V. **Map 1 B6**

Veronica Shaw's unique restaurant serves historic British dishes, using recipes from as far back as Roman times. The results are always interesting and the experience enjoyable and educational.

Burmese

Mandalay budget

444 Edgware Road, W2 (020 7258 3696). Edgware Road tube. **Lunch** noon-2.30pm, **dinner** 6-10.30pm, Mon-Sat. **Average** £11. **Set lunch** £3.50 one course, £5.90 three courses. **Credit** AmEx, DC, JCB, MC, £TC, V. **Map 2 E4**

The road to Mandalay may be the traffic-choked Edgware Road, but the warmth of Dwight and Gary Ally's welcome and the quality of their cooking ensure satisfied stomachs and smiles on faces.

Caribbean

Brixtonian Havana Club

11 Beehive Place, SW9 (020 7924 9262). Brixton tube/rail. **Lunch** noon-3pm daily. **Dinner** 7-10.30pm Mon-Thur, Sun; 7-11pm Fri, Sat. **Average** £21. **Credit** MC, £TC, V.

The current incarnation of ebullient Vincent Osborne's Brixtonian has proved a big hit. The high-ceilinged bar proffers a magnificent sweep of rums, and the small restaurant at one end offers spot-on Caribbean/'Black British' cooking.

The mussels and chips minimalism of **Belgo Zuid**. *See page 168.*

Mango Room budget

10 Kentish Town Road, NW1 (020 7482 5065). Camden Town tube. **Meals** noon-midnight daily. **Average** £15. **Credit** MC, V.

Lifting London-Caribbean food out of the region of solid home-cooking and into another realm, the Mango Room is also as cool a bar/restaurant as Camden can offer.

Chinese

See also page 179 **Singapore Garden II**.

Golden Harvest budget

17 Lisle Street, WC2 (020 7287 3822). Leicester Square or Piccadilly Circus tube. **Meals** noon-2.45am daily. **Average** £14. **Minimum** £5 from 5pm. **Set meal** £7-£15 per person (minimum two). **Credit** AmEx, DC, JCB, MC, £TC, V. **Map 8 K7**

This excellent restaurant expertly combines traditional flavours with novel ingredients. The proprietors also own Chinatown's fishmonger's, so seafood – pomfret, turbot, sea bass, carp – is a speciality. The seafood hot-pot (£20 a head) is worth every penny.

Hunan

51 Pimlico Road, SW1 (020 7730 5712). Sloane Square tube. **Lunch** noon-2.30pm, **dinner** 6-11pm, Mon-Sat. **Average** £27. **Set meal** £22-£100 per person (minimum two). **Credit** AmEx, MC, £TC, V. **Map 7 G11**

Possibly the only restaurant in London offering authentic western Chinese cooking. Be bold and ask the delightful maître d' Mr Peng to devise a feast for you, and insist on genuine full-blooded spicing.

Magic Wok

100 Queensway, W2 (020 7792 9767). Bayswater or Queensway tube. **Meals** noon-11pm daily. **Average** £16. **Set meal** £10.50-£22 per person (minimum two). **Credit** AmEx, DC, MC, £TC, V. **Map 1 C6**

Go for dishes from the specials list and you'll enjoy some of the best and most unusual Cantonese cooking in London, such as quail with special herbs and chilli and braised winter melon.

Mandarin Kitchen

14-16 Queensway, W2 (020 7727 9012). Bayswater or Queensway tube. **Meals** noon-11.30pm daily. **Average** £25. **Set meal** £10 per person (minimum two). **Credit** AmEx, DC, JCB, MC, £TC, V. **Map 1 C6**

Packed every night with smart Cantonese professionals, this longstanding restaurant has some of the best seafood in London; the lobster is superb.

Mr Kong

21 Lisle Street, WC2 (020 7437 7341/9679). Leicester Square or Piccadilly Circus tube. **Meals** noon-3am daily. **Average** £22. **Minimum** £7 after 5pm. **Set meal** £9.30 per person (minimum two)-£22 per person (minimum four). **Credit** AmEx, DC, JCB, MC, £TC, V. **Map 8 K7**

The setting may lack glamour and elbow room, but Mr Kong's menu is one of Chinatown's most enticing, with rarely found Cantonese specials such as sautéed pea-shoots with dried scallops.

New Diamond budget

23 Lisle Street, WC2 (020 7437 2517). Leicester Square or Piccadilly Circus tube. **Meals** noon-3am daily. **Average** £12. **Minimum** £7. **Set meals** £10-

Duck into the **New Four Seasons**.

£16 per person (minimum two). **Credit** AmEx, DC, JCB, MC, £TC, V. **Map 8 K7**
Mel Brooks' favourite Chinese restaurant doesn't look flash but knocks out some of the richest and most delicious sauces in the capital. Its long opening times are a bonus.

New Four Seasons

84 Queensway, W2 (020 7229 4320). Bayswater or Queensway tube. **Meals** noon-11.30pm Mon-Sat; noon-11pm Sun. **Average** £17. **Set meal** £11-£14 per person (minimum two). **Credit** AmEx, MC, £TC, V. **Map 1 C6**
Queensway now rivals Chinatown for the excellence of its Chinese food and, despite its somewhat dingy décor, the New Four Seasons offers a fabulous list of specials and possibly the best Cantonese roast duck in London.

Oriental

Dorchester Hotel, 55 Park Lane, W1 (020 7317 6328). Green Park, Hyde Park Corner or Marble Arch tube. **Lunch** noon-2.30pm Mon-Fri. **Dinner** 7-11pm daily. **Average** £35 lunch, £55 dinner. **Set lunch** £25 (dim sum) incl glass of wine. **Set dinner** £47-£90. **Credit** AmEx, DC, JCB, MC, £TC, V. **Map 7 G7**
It's pricey and blandly formal, but if only the highest standards of cooking will do, the Dorchester's Oriental is the one. Dishes such as stir-fried beef with lemongrass and black pepper are outstanding, and the restaurant's MSG-free policy is laudable.

Dim sum budget

London is one of the best places in the world to try one of the highlights of Cantonese cuisine, dim sum. These small, delicate dumplings and snacks are served from midday through the afternoon (never after 6pm) at low prices: expect to pay around £10 a head for a decent selection.

Golden Dragon

28-29 Gerrard Street, W1 (020 7734 2763). Leicester Square or Piccadilly Circus tube.
Meals noon-11.30pm Mon-Thur; noon-midnight Fri, Sat; 11am-11pm Sun. **Dim sum** noon-5pm Mon-Sat; 11am-5pm Sun. **Average** £8 dim sum, £20 full menu. **Minimum** £10. **Set meal** £10 per person (minimum two)-£20 per person (minimum five). **Credit** AmEx, DC, MC, £TC, V. **Map 8 K7**
A lively and ornate dim sum venue that offers classy versions of staples such as glutinous rice in lotus leaf and deep-fried squid, as well as some of the most stunning dumplings in town.
Branch: **Royal Dragon** 30 Gerrard Street, W1 (020 7734 0935).

Harbour City

46 Gerrard Street, W1 (020 7439 7859). Leicester Square or Piccadilly Circus tube. **Meals** noon-11.30pm Mon-Thur; noon-midnight Fri, Sat; 11am-11pm Sun. **Dim sum** noon-5pm Mon-Sat; 11am-5pm Sun. **Average** £8 dim sum, £17 full menu. **Set meal** £12.50-£20 per person (minimum two). **Credit** AmEx, DC, JCB, MC, £TC, V. **Map 8 K7**
This longstanding dim sum favourite offers an 'exotic' section including such rarely found treats as ducks' tongues in black bean and chilli sauce. Ask for a table on the lighter first floor.

Royal China

13 Queensway, W2 (020 7221 2535). Bayswater or Queensway tube. **Meals** noon-11pm Mon-Thur; noon-11.30pm Fri, Sat; 11am-10pm Sun. **Dim sum** noon-5pm Mon-Sat; 11am-5pm Sun. **Average** £10 dim sum, £29 full menu. **Set meal** £23, £29, per person (minimum two). **Credit** AmEx, DC, MC, £TC, V. **Map 1 C7**
Undoubtedly the finest dim sum in London – exquisite in flavour and presentation, and incredibly cheap. Come during the week for a quiet, leisurely meal; Sundays are more hectic, and queues are long.
Branch: 40 Baker Street, W1 (020 7487 4688).

Fish

fish!

Cathedral Street, SE1 (020 7836 3236). London Bridge tube/rail. **Lunch** 11.30am-3pm, **dinner** 5.30-11pm, Mon-Sat. **Average** £20. **Credit** AmEx, DC, JCB, MC, £TC, V. **Map 11 P8**
Sheltering beneath a remarkable glass construction within Borough Market, fish! offers a versatile, unpretentious menu majoring on the best market fish available, cooked in the manner of your choice and served with one of five simple sauces. Stock up on piscine goodies at the fish shop next door.

J Sheekey

28-32 St Martin's Court, WC2 (020 7240 2565). Leicester Square tube. **Lunch** noon-3pm Mon-Sat; noon-3.30pm Sun. **Dinner** 5.30pm-midnight daily. **Average** £30. **Set meals** (lunch Sat, Sun) £9.50 two courses, £13.50 three courses. **Credit** AmEx, DC, MC, V. **Map 8 K7**

Looking and feeling very much like The Ivy mark II (it has the same owners; *see p166*), J Sheekey offers the same classy dining experience (with a fish bias), marred by the same sittings policy.

Livebait

21 Wellington Street, WC2 (020 7836 7161). Covent Garden tube. **Lunch** noon-3pm, **dinner** 5.30-11.30pm, Mon-Sat. **Average** £32. **Set meal** (noon-3pm, 5.30-7pm, 10-11.30pm) £15.50 two courses. **Credit** AmEx, DC, JCB, MC, £TC, V. **Map 8 L7**

Livebait is one of the capital's most original and fun fish restaurants. The stunning tiled interior and seafood display of the Waterloo original have been replicated in this, the bigger Covent Garden branch. **Branch**: 41-43 The Cut, SE1 (020 7928 7211).

Fish & chips

Rock & Sole Plaice budget

47 Endell Street, WC2 (020 7836 3785). Covent Garden tube. **Meals** 11.30am-10pm Mon-Sat; 11.30am-9pm Sun. **Average** £10. **Credit** £TC. **Map 6 L6**

Open since 1871, Rock & Sole Plaice claims to be the oldest surviving fish and chip shop in London. Whatever the case, it's certainly the best place in the centre of town to sample the national dish.

Seashell budget

49-51 Lisson Grove, NW1 (020 7723 8703). Marylebone tube/rail. **Lunch** noon-2.30pm Mon-Fri, Sun. **Dinner** 5.15-10.30pm Mon-Fri. **Meals** noon-10.30pm Sat. **Average** £15. **Set meal** (until 7pm Mon-Sat, noon-3pm Sun) £10, £11 three courses. **Credit** AmEx, MC, £TC, V. **Map 2 E4**

Long a favourite of fish and chip connoisseurs (including many cab drivers, and Ken Hom), the two-floor, dark wood and chintz-decorated Seashell maintains a consistently loyal clientele.

Upper Street Fish Shop budget

324 Upper Street, N1 (020 7359 1401). Angel tube/ 4, 19, 30, 43 bus. **Lunch** noon-2.15pm Tue-Fri; noon-3pm Sat. **Dinner** 6-10.15pm Mon-Thur; 5.30-10.15pm Fri, Sat. **Average** £12. **Minimum** £7.50. **Credit** £TC. **Map 9 O1**

The imaginative, frequently changing menu here offers far more than the usual cod and chips. Not many chippies serve up deep-fried mussels and tempura. Puds, if you manage them, are equally fine.

French

Other French restaurants worthy of a visit include **Elena's L'Etoile** (30 Charlotte Street, W1; 020 7636 7189), **Amandier/Bistro Daniel** (26 Sussex Gardens, W2; 020 7262 6073) and **Saint M**, the pricey brasserie inside St Martins Lane hotel (*see page 147*).

Chez Bruce

2 Bellevue Road, SW17 (020 8672 0114). Wandsworth Common rail. **Lunch** noon-2pm Mon-Fri; 12.30-2.30pm Sat; 12.30-3pm Sun. **Dinner** 7-10.30pm Mon-Sat. **Set lunch** £21.50 three courses. **Set dinner** £25 three courses. **Credit** AmEx, DC, JCB, MC, V.

A Wandsworth restaurant where standards easily exceed many better-known West End places. The interior is plain, the atmosphere relaxed and Bruce Poole's cooking serious and seriously good.

Chez Lindsay budget

11 Hill Rise, Richmond, Surrey (020 8948 7473). Richmond tube/rail. **Meals** 11am-11pm Mon-Sat; noon-10pm Sun. **Average** £12.50. **Set lunch** (11am-3pm) £5.99 two courses. **Set meal** (11am-3pm, 6-11pm) £9.99 three courses. **Credit** MC, V.

Seafood and pancakes, the twin glories of Breton cooking, are presented with great verve in this relaxed restaurant. Try a scallop gallette, a cup of Breton cider and a sweet crêpe to follow.

Club Gascon

57 West Smithfield, EC1 (020 7253 5853). Barbican tube/Farringdon tube/rail. **Lunch** noon-2pm Mon-Fri. **Dinner** 7-10pm Mon-Fri; 7-10.30pm Sat. **Average** £30. **Set meal** £30 five courses. **Credit** MC, V. **Map 9 O5**

Specialising in the earthy goosefat-heavy cuisine of Gascony in south-west France, Club Gascon offers a blessed relief from self-conscious, over-elaborate experimentation. Simple, classic fare cooked with real flair and conviction. Book well in advance.

The Criterion

224 Piccadilly, W1 (020 7930 0488). Piccadilly Circus tube. **Lunch** noon-2.30pm Mon-Sat. **Dinner** 6-11.30pm Mon-Sat; 6-10.30pm Sun. **Average** £32. **Set meal** (noon-2.30pm, 6-6.30pm) £14.95 two courses, £17.95 three courses. **Credit** AmEx, DC, MC, £TC, V. **Map 8 K7**

As backdrops go, they don't come much more stunning than Marco Pierre White's Criterion. The glittering mosaics, giant drapes, hanging lanterns and mirrors match the textbook food.

L'Escargot

48 Greek Street, W1 (020 7437 2679). Tottenham Court Road tube. Ground-floor restaurant **Lunch** 12.15-2.15pm Mon-Fri. **Dinner** 6-11.30pm Mon-Sat. **Average** £26. **Set meal** (lunch, 6-7pm) £14.95 two courses, £17.95 three courses. *Picasso room* **Lunch** noon-2.15pm Tue-Fri. **Dinner** 7-11pm Tue-Sat. **Set lunch** £27 three courses. **Set dinner** £42 three courses. **Credit** AmEx, DC, JCB, MC, £TC, V. **Map 6 K6**

A Soho fixture for the last 70 years, this famed eating spot still has a special aura. The modern but ungimmicky food has moved with the times and can be enjoyed in the relaxed ground-floor restaurant or the pricier first-floor Picasso Room.

fish! *What more can you say? See page 171.*

Frith Street

63-64 Frith Street, W1 (020 7734 4545). Tottenham Court Road tube. **Lunch** noon-2.30pm Mon-Fri. **Dinner** 6-10.45pm Mon-Sat. **Average** £23.50. **Set meal** (lunch, 6-7pm) £15 two courses, £19.50 three courses. **Credit** AmEx, MC, V. **Map 6 K6**

Intimate and understated, yet spacious and cool, the design of Frith Street offers little distraction from Jason Atherton's superb cooking – confident, non-fussy and comforting.

Mirabelle

56 Curzon Street, W1 (020 7499 4636). Green Park tube. **Lunch** noon-2.30pm daily. **Dinner** 6-11.30pm Mon-Sat; 6-10.30pm Sun. **Average** £35. **Set lunch** £14.95 two courses, £17.95 three courses. **Credit** AmEx, DC, MC, V. **Map 7 H7**

Marco Pierre White has done a wonderful job of restoring the Mirabelle to a vision of 1930s splendour, and it's matched by the classic, fuss-free cooking. The set lunch is great value.

Rousillon

16 St Barnabas Street, SW1 (020 7730 5550). Sloane Square tube. **Lunch** noon-2.15pm Mon-Fri. **Dinner** 7-10.45pm Mon-Sat. **Set lunch** £16 three courses. **Set meals** £22 two courses, £25 three courses, £24 (vegetarian), £35 five courses. **Credit** AmEx, DC, JCB, MC, £TC, V. **Map 7 G11**

Almost without precedent for a French restaurant, Rousillon offers a menu for vegetarians, and a stunning one at that. Both meat and non-meat eaters can luxuriate in all that is sublime in French cooking.

Schnecke budget

58-59 Poland Street, W1 (020 7287 6666). Oxford Circus tube. **Meals** noon-11pm Mon-Thur; noon-11.30pm Sat; noon-10.30pm Sun. **Average** £14. **Credit** AmEx, DC, JCB, MC, V. **Map 5 J6**

It's wacky, it's kitsch, it's Alsatian – but thankfully, the menu of hearty fare stretches further than pickled cabbage, encompassing snails, tartes flambées (like rectangular pizzas) and great wines and beers.

Georgian

Little Georgia budget

2 Broadway Market, E8 (020 7275 0208). Bethnal Green tube/26, 48, 55, 106, 236 bus. **Lunch** 1-4pm Sun. **Dinner** 6.30-10.30pm Tue-Sat. **Average** £13.50. **Credit** MC, TC, V.

Occupying a pub conversion, Little Georgia's modern minimalism is tempered by a sprinkling of Georgian artefacts. Superb renderings of not-often-seen-in-London national dishes are served up by cheery staff in a relaxed atmosphere.

Global

Bali Sugar

33A All Saints Road, W11 (020 7221 4477). Westbourne Park tube. **Lunch** 12.30-2.30pm, **dinner** 6.30-11pm, daily. **Average** £27. **Credit** AmEx, DC, MC, V.

Plain walls and stripped wood floors offer little distraction from Bali Sugar's complex dishes, which, despite a multitude of flavours (many of them Asian), are executed with great skill and verve.

Helter Skelter

50 Atlantic Road, SW9 (020 7274 8600). Brixton tube/rail. **Dinner** 7-11pm Mon-Thur; 7-11.30pm Fri, Sat. **Average** £17. **Credit** AmEx, MC, £TC, V.

Sleek Helter Skelter may lie in backstreet Brixton, but the quality of the globe-trotting cooking and the friendly, professional service ensure a stream of returning youngish, hippish diners.

Jindivick

201 Liverpool Road, N1 (020 7607 7710). Angel tube. **Brunch** 10.30am-3.15pm Sat, Sun. **Lunch** noon-3pm Tue-Fri. **Dinner** 6-10.45pm Mon-Sat. **Average** £23. **Set meal** (noon-3pm Tue-Fri; 6-7.30pm Mon-Fri) £6.95 one course, £9.95 two courses, £11.95 three courses. **Credit** DC, MC, £TC, V. **Map 9 N1**

The award-winning brunch is one attraction at this clean, bright restaurant. The name is Australian Aboriginal, but the menu is becoming increasingly global in its influences.

The Lavender

171 Lavender Hill, SW11 (020 7978 5242). Clapham Junction rail. **Meals** noon-11.30pm Mon-Sat; noon-10.30pm Sun. **Average** £16. **Credit** AmEx, MC, V.

Bright, loud, full of confidence – and that's just the customers. The Lavender's a swinging, rainbow-painted bar-restaurant offering not just a sassy vibe and classy wine list, but fine modern global food.

Greek

Halepi

48-50 Belsize Lane, NW3 (020 7431 5855). Belsize Park or Swiss Cottage tube. **Lunch** noon-3pm Wed-Sat. **Dinner** 6-11pm Mon-Sat. **Meals** noon-11pm Sun. **Average** £20. **Set lunch** £10. **Credit** AmEx, DC, JCB, MC, TC, V.

It's official. There *is* such a thing as a modern Greek Cypriot restaurant. Contemporary minimal décor complements a wider than usual menu, which is particularly strong on fish.

The Real Greek

15 Hoxton Market, N1 (020 7739 8212). Old Street tube/rail/26, 48, 55, 149, 242 bus. **Lunch** noon-3pm, **dinner** 5.30-10.30pm, Mon-Sat. **Average** £25. **Credit** AmEx, MC, V. **Map 10 R3**

This is Greek food like you won't find anywhere else in town. In gastropub-like surroundings, Theodore Kyriakou's ambitious cooking shows just how moribund most of the capital's Hellenic eateries are.

Indian

Central London is not well equipped with Indian restaurants; the few good ones come at a price. For the most authentic subcontinental culinary and cultural experience, visit one of the unglamorous but vibrant centres of Indian London: Wembley, Southall or Tooting. Sunday lunchtime is the best time to see the locals promenading and snacking: take the tube to Tooting Broadway and cruise Upper Tooting Road and Tooting High Street, or the train to Southall and walk down The Broadway, or the tube to Alperton or Wembley Central and stroll down Ealing Road.

Café Spice Namaste

16 Prescot Street, E1 (020 7488 9242). Tower Hill tube/Tower Gateway DLR. **Lunch** noon-3pm Mon-Fri. **Dinner** 6.15-10.30pm Mon-Fri; 6.30-10pm Sat. **Average** £20. **Credit** AmEx, DC, JCB, MC, £TC, V. **Map 12 S7**

No pre-made standard curry pastes and stale popadums here – Cyrus Todiwala's bright, airy restaurant shows just how exquisite and extraordinarily diverse modern Indian cooking can be.

Branches: 247 Lavender Hill, SW11 (020 7738 1717).

Gifto's Lahore Karahi budget

162-164 The Broadway, Southall, Middlesex (020 8813 8669). Southall rail/207 bus. **Meals** noon-11.30pm Mon-Fri; noon-midnight Sat, Sun. **Average** £12. **Credit** AmEx, DC, JCB, MC, £TC, V.

Southall's premier Pakistani restaurant is a capacious, popular place where, in the open kitchen, a team of chefs slap nans in the tandoor, sear kebabs over charcoal and wield karahis over burners.

Karahi King budget

213 East Lane, North Wembley, Middlesex (020 8904 2760). North Wembley tube/245 bus. **Meals** noon-midnight daily. **Average** £12.

An out-of-the-way location means that gentrification is never likely to trouble Karahi King. Yet well-dressed Kenyan Asian families flock here, willing to overlook the cramped surroundings to enjoy some of the best karahi cooking in town.

Kastoori budget

188 Upper Tooting Road, SW17 (020 8767 7027). Tooting Bec or Tooting Broadway tube. **Lunch** 12.30-2.30pm Wed-Sun. **Dinner** 6-10.30pm daily. **Average** £15. **Credit** MC, V.

The best known of the several East African Gujarati restaurants along this busy road, the simply decorated, brightly lit Kastoori is notable for its attention to detail, especially in its distinct spicing.

Porte des Indes

32 Bryanston Street, W1 (020 7224 0055). Marble Arch tube. **Lunch** noon-2.30pm Mon-Fri; noon-3pm Sun. **Dinner** 7-11.30pm Mon-Sat; 7-10.30pm Sun. **Average** £40. **Set buffet lunch** £15. **Set meal** £31 three courses. **Credit** AmEx, DC, JCB, MC, £TC, V. **Map 2 F6**

A former Edwardian ballroom provides possibly the grandest setting for an Indian restaurant in London, and the imaginative menu comes close to matching the setting.

Rasa Samudra

5 Charlotte Street, W1 (020 7637 0222). Goodge Street tube. **Lunch** noon-2.45pm, **dinner** 6-10.45pm, Mon-Sat. **Average** £40. **Credit** AmEx, MC, £TC, V. **Map 5 J5**

By far the most expensive (and ambitious) of Siva Das Sreedharan's three-strong Rasa group, this is the place to come for exemplary Keralan seafood cooking. Unusual and exquisite.

Branches: **Rasa** 55 Stoke Newington Church Street, N16 (020 7249 0344); **Rasa W1** 16 Dering Street, W1 (020 7629 1346).

Tamarind

20 Queen Street, W1 (020 7629 3561). Green Park tube. **Lunch** noon-3pm Mon-Fri; noon-2.30pm Sun. **Dinner** 6-11.30pm Mon-Sat; 6-10.30pm Sun. **Average** £35. **Set lunch** £8.50-£16.50. **Set dinner** (6-7pm, 10.30-11.30pm, Mon-Sat) £16.50. **Credit** AmEx, DC, JCB, MC, £TC, V. **Map 7 H7**

One of London's finest Indian restaurants is housed in one of the city's most beautifully decorated basements. Chef Atul Kochhar's assured touch with the best and freshest ingredients ensures a (pricey) treat.

Vama

438 King's Road, SW10 (020 7351 4118). Sloane Square tube then 11, 22 bus. **Lunch** 12.30-3pm, **dinner** 6.30-11.30pm, daily. **Average** £25. **Set lunch** £6.95. **Credit** AmEx, DC, JCB, MC, £TC, V. **Map 4 D12**

This is an Indian-run enterprise but the look is more smart Italian restaurant than flock wallpapered curry house. The concise menu is also unusual, offering skilfully cooked dishes from the Pakistani borders with Afghanistan, and Baluchistan.

Zaika

257-259 Fulham Road, SW3 (020 7351 7823). South Kensington tube/14 bus. **Lunch** noon-2.30pm Mon-Fri. **Dinner** 6.30-10.30pm Mon-Sat. **Average** £28. **Set lunch** £9.95 two courses, £11.95 three courses. **Set meal** £20 five courses, £28 five courses incl wine. **Credit** AmEx, MC, JCB, £TC, V. **Map 4 D11**

Chef Vineet Bhatia is a big name and he lives up to his billing at this gorgeously attired Fulham Road restaurant packed with gorgeously attired Fulhamites. Expect tradition with a twist.

Italian

Great-value Italian eaterie chains with branches dotted throughout the centre of London include **Spaghetti House** and **Café Pasta**. See the *Yellow Pages* for branches.

Arancia

52 Southwark Park Road, SE16 (020 7394 1751). Elephant & Castle tube/rail then 1, 199 bus/South Bermondsey rail. **Lunch** 12.30am-3pm, **dinner** 7-11pm, Tue-Sat. **Average** £20. **Set meal** £7.50 three courses. **Credit** DC, JCB, MC, £TC, V.

Located in unfashionable Bermondsey, Arancia is a little more smart and polished than in its early days but it has lost none of its charm, and the shortish menu continues to feature excellent-value, confidently rendered earthy Italian classics.

Assaggi

The Chepstow, 39 Chepstow Place, W2 (020 7792 5501). Notting Hill Gate tube. **Lunch** 12.30-2.30pm, **dinner** 7.30-11pm, Mon-Sat. **Average** £33. **Credit** AmEx, DC, MC, JCB, £TC, V. **Map 1 B6**

So widely adored is this small restaurant that diners often have to book about a month in advance. The somewhat rudimentary décor doesn't seem quite in tune with the impeccable standards of the imaginative food and size of the bill.

Enoteca Turi

28 Putney High Street, SW15 (020 8785 4449). East Putney tube/Putney rail/14 bus. **Lunch** 12.30-2.30pm Mon-Fri. **Dinner** 7-11pm Mon-Sat. **Average** £22. **Credit** AmEx, DC, MC, V.

Enoteca, perched on a corner site, looks inviting in a spartan kind of way, and is particularly notable for its exceptional Italian wine list. The cooking is also handled with flair and care.

Ibla

89 Marylebone High Street, W1 (020 7224 3799). Baker Street, Bond Street or Regent's Park tube. **Lunch** noon-2.30pm, **dinner** 7-10.15pm, Mon-Sat. **Set meal** £15 two courses, £18 three courses. **Credit** AmEx, MC, V. **Map 5 G5**

An elongated S-shape provides the unusual setting for this thoroughly modern yet refreshingly untrendy Italian. The regularly changing set-price menu scores highly for quality and presentation.

Isola

145 Knightsbridge, SW1 (020 7838 1044). Knightsbridge tube. **Lunch** noon-3pm daily. **Dinner** 6pm-midnight Mon-Sat; 6-10.30pm Sun. **Average** £45. **Credit** AmEx, DC, MC, V. **Map 2 F9**

Oliver Peyton's newest restaurant (opened late 1999) is also his most mature to date. With Bruno Loubet in the kitchen, this is Italian cooking of the highest refinement and quality (and cost). The cheaper (but not *that* much cheaper) basement **Osteria** serves food all day.

Passione

10 Charlotte Street, W1 (020 7636 2833). Goodge Street tube. **Lunch** 12.30-2.30pm Mon-Fri. **Dinner** 7-10.30pm Mon-Sat. **Average** £22. **Credit** AmEx, JCB, MC, £TC, V. **Map 5 J5**

Passione, in defiance of its name, emits a cool, calm civility and serves up beautifully executed classic Italian dishes. The quality of ingredients is impeccable and their handling is assured.

Vasco & Piero's Pavilion

15 Poland Street, W1 (020 7437 8774). Oxford Circus or Tottenham Court Road tube. **Lunch** noon-3pm Mon-Fri. **Dinner** 6-11pm Mon-Fri; 7-11pm Sat. **Average** £25 (lunch). **Set dinner** £16.50 two courses, £19.50 three courses. **Credit** AmEx, DC, JCB, MC, £$TC, V. **Map 5 J6**

A reliable old Soho stager that delivers carefully executed dishes in a cosy, clubby atmosphere. Service is very friendly, particularly if you're one of the celeb regulars.

Zafferano

15 Lowndes Street, SW1 (020 7235 5800). Knightsbridge tube. **Lunch** noon-2.30pm, **dinner** 7-11pm, Mon-Sat. **Set lunch** £17.50 two courses, £20.50 three courses. **Set dinner** £26.50 two courses, £32.50 three courses, £36.50 four courses. **Credit** AmEx, DC, MC, £TC, V. **Map 4 F9**

One of London's best, smartest and most celebrity-packed restaurants. The food is well-nigh faultless, from imaginative pastas to more unusual dishes like sweetbreads in a Sicilian-style sweet and sour sauce.

Pizzerias budget

Of the chains, **Pizza Express** (with branches all over the city) remains the best, although the newer **ASK** chain is growing rapidly and gaining a reputation for reliable grub. Other good bets within central London include **Condotti** (4 Mill Street, W1; 020 7499 1308), **Pizza on the Park**

Souper snacks

Following piping hot on the cappuccino-foam-encrusted heels of the coffee bar explosion in London of the last few years comes another New York-inspired phenomenon: soup. It's cheap (who can resist a bargain?), it's healthy (who can miss a trend?), it's warming (who doesn't need that in this city?) and it can often taste pretty good too. All of the places below are reliably good, offering a daily changing selection of imaginative stomach-fillers. We list only the central London branches below.

Soup
1 Newburgh Street, W1 **Map 5 J6**;
37 Marylebone High Street, W1 **Map 5 G5**

Souperdouper
Euston Station, NW1 **Map 6 K3**; Baker Street Station, NW1 **Map 5 G4**; Main concourse, Victoria Station, SW1 **Map 7 H10**; Marylebone Station **Map 2 F4**

Soup Opera
17 Kingsway, WC2 **Map 6 M6**;
2 Hanover Street, W1 **Map 5 J6**

Soup Works
9 D'Arblay Street, W1 **Map 5 J6**;
58 Goodge Street, W1 **Map 5 J5**; 15 Moor Street, W1 **Map 6 K6**; 29 Monmouth Street, WC2 **Map 6 L6**

(11 Knightsbridge, SW1; 020 7235 5273), **Soho Pizzeria** (16-18 Beak Street, W1; 020 7434 2480), **Purple Sage** (90-92 Wigmore Street, W1; 020 7486 1912), **Medina's** (10 Clerkenwell Green, EC1; 020 7490 4041), **Spiga** (84-86 Wardour Street, W1; 020 7734 3444) and **La Spighetta** (43 Blandford Street, W1; 020 7486 7340). **Calzone** is a winning mini-chain, with branches in Notting Hill (2A Kensington Park Road; 020 7243 2003), Hampstead (66 Heath Street, NW3; 020 7794 6775), Chelsea (335 Fulham Road, SW10; 020 7352 9797), South Kensington (335 Fulham Road, SW10; 020 7352 9797) and Islington (35 Upper Street, N1; 020 7359 9191).

Japanese

Asakusa

265 Eversholt Street, NW1 (020 7388 8533). Camden Town or Mornington Crescent tube. **Dinner** 6-11.30pm Mon-Fri; 6-11pm Sat. **Average** £18. **Set dinner** £5.20-£18. **Credit** AmEx, DC, MC, £TC, V. **Map 5 J2**

Asakusa's winning combination of spot-on food, low prices and upbeat service draws in both Japanese and western diners. Booking advisable.

Kulu Kulu budget

76 Brewer Street, W1 (020 7734 7316). Piccadilly Circus tube. **Lunch** noon-2.30pm Mon-Fri; noon-3.45pm Sat. **Dinner** 5-10pm Mon-Sat. **Average** £12. **Credit** JCB, MC, £TC, V. **Map 7 J7**

A no-nonsense conveyor-belt sushi bar with thoroughly authentic, keenly priced, gimmick-free grub.

Matsuri

15 Bury Street, SW1 (020 7839 1101). Green Park or Piccadilly Circus tube. **Lunch** noon-2.30pm, **dinner** 6-10.30pm, Mon-Sat. **Average** £20 lunch, £40 dinner. **Set lunch** £6.50-£40. **Set dinner** £13-£55. **Credit** AmEx, DC, JCB, MC, £TC, V. **Map 7 J7**

Matsuri avoids the stuffiness of some top-notch Japanese places while matching all in the quality of food and service. Despite being in a basement, the dining area feels light and expansive.

Nobu

Metropolitan Hotel, 19 Old Park Lane, W1 (020 7447 4747). Hyde Park Corner tube. **Lunch** noon-2.15pm Mon-Fri. **Dinner** 6-10.30pm Mon-Sat. **Average** £30 lunch, £57 dinner. **Set lunch** £20-£40. **Set dinner** £60. **Credit** AmEx, DC, JCB, MC, £TC, V. **Map 7 H8**

If you thought you knew Japanese food, think again. South American influences are evident in dishes such as yellowtail sashimi with jalapeño garnish and citrus sauce. Superb and unique.

Ramen Seto budget

19 Kingly Street, W1 (020 7434 0309). Oxford Circus tube. **Lunch** noon-2.45pm, **dinner** 6-9.45pm, Mon-Fri. **Meals** noon-8.45pm Sat; noon-6.45pm Sun. **Average** £5. **Set meal** £4.50-£5.80. **Credit** V. **Map 5 J6**

The noodle line-up is augmented by a limited but decent selection of sushi, sashimi and tempura in this relaxed diner. Probably the best value in town.

Yo! Sushi

52 Poland Street, W1 (020 7287 0443). Oxford Circus tube. **Meals** noon-midnight daily. **Average** £16. **Credit** AmEx, DC, JCB, MC, £TC, V. **Map 5 J6**

Boasting the world's longest sushi conveyor belt (60m/176ft), sushi-making machines and robotic drinks trolleys, Yo! Sushi is not backward at coming forward. The food suffers somewhat in comparison, but for fun and novelty this place is hard to beat.

Yumi

110 George Street, W1 (020 7935 8320). Baker Street, Bond Street or Marble Arch tube. **Dinner** 5.30-10.30pm daily. **Average** £40. **Set dinner** £38-£85. **Credit** AmEx, DC, MC, £TC, V. **Map 5 G5**

Pronounced 'yoo-mee' but the food really is yummy (if pricey) – beautifully fresh and artfully presented. Staff are as refined as the cooking.

Tea time

The big attraction of afternoon tea is a chance to snoop inside hotels at which you'll never afford to stay. The hotels are in on this too, so you don't have to be a millionaire or a Hollywood star to gain entry. Dress codes of jacket and tie for men are the main rules at The Ritz, The Savoy and Claridges. Other hotels have this rule but don't appear to enforce it; check when phoning to book.

As for the food: quality scones, clotted cream, jam, cakes and sandwiches for nigh on £20 may sound expensive, but you are also paying for being treated like royalty in luxurious surroundings for up to two hours. During that time the world will seem an infinitely better place.

For the glitziest interior go to the **Waldorf Meridien**; for the cosiest setting, try **Brown's**; for top-notch tea and sandwiches, **The Lanesborough** impresses; the tastiest pastries and the best pianist can be found at **The Dorchester**; the best-value tea in town is at the low-key **Basil Street Hotel**; while the service at **Claridge's** can't be beaten. **The Ritz**, meanwhile, is the most popular: you'll need to book about three months in advance for a weekend.

Top tea at **The Lanesborough**.

Basil Street Hotel

Basil Street, SW3 (020 7581 3311). Knightsbridge tube. **Tea served** 3.30-5.45pm daily. **Set tea** £7.25, £11. **Credit** AmEx, DC, £TC, MC, V. **Map 4 F9**

Brown's

33-34 Albemarle Street, W1 (020 7518 4108). Green Park tube. **Tea served** two seatings: 3pm, 4.45pm, Mon-Fri; first come first served Sat, Sun. **Set tea** £18.95. **Credit** AmEx, DC, JCB, MC, £TC, V. **Map 7 J7**

Claridge's

Brook Street, W1 (020 7629 8860). Bond Street tube. **Tea served** 3-5.30pm daily. **Set tea** £22 Mon-Fri, £28.50 incl glass of champagne Sat, Sun. **Credit** AmEx, DC, MC, £TC, V. **Map 5 H6**

The Dorchester

54 Park Lane, W1 (020 7629 8888). Hyde Park Corner tube. **Tea served** 3-6pm, *high tea* 5-8pm, daily. **Set teas** £19.50, £25.50 incl glass of champagne; *high tea* £29.50. **Credit** AmEx, DC, JCB, MC, £TC, V. **Map 7 G7**

The Lanesborough

Hyde Park Corner, SW1 (020 7259 5599). Hyde Park Corner tube. **Tea served** 3.30-6pm daily. **Set teas** £19.50-£24.50. **Credit** AmEx, DC, JCB, MC, TC, V. **Map 7 G8**

The Ritz

Piccadilly, W1 (020 7493 8181). Green Park tube. **Tea served** 2-6pm daily; reserved sittings at 3.30pm, 5pm. **Set tea** £27. **Credit** AmEx, DC, JCB, MC, £TC, V. **Map 5 J7**

St James, Fortnum & Mason

181 Piccadilly, W1 (020 7734 8040). **Tea served** 3-5pm Mon-Sat. **Set teas** from £12.50, *high tea* £16.50, £18.95 incl glass of champagne. **Credit** AmEx, DC, JCB, MC, £TC, V. **Map 7 J7**

The Savoy

Strand, WC2 (020 7836 4343). Charing Cross tube/rail. **Tea served** 3-5.30pm daily. **Set tea** £19.50, £9.50 under-10s, Mon-Sat. **Tea dance** £23.50 Sun. **Credit** AmEx, DC, JCB, MC, £TC, V. **Map 8 L7**

Waldorf Meridien

Aldwych, WC2 (020 7836 2400). Covent Garden or Temple tube. **Tea served** 3-5.30pm Mon-Fri. **Tea dance** 2.30-5pm Sat; 4-6.30pm Sun. **Set teas** £21, £28 incl glass of champagne; £15, *tea dance* £25, £28 incl glass of champagne. **Credit** AmEx, DC, MC, £TC, V. **Map 8 M7**

Jewish

Solly's

148A Golders Green Road, NW11 (ground floor & takeaway 020 8455 2121/first floor 020 8455 0004). Golders Green tube. Ground floor **Lunch** 11.30am-3pm Fri. **Meals** 11am-11.30pm Mon-Thur, Sun; 11am-3pm Fri; one hour after sabbath-1am Sat. **Average** £17. **Set meal** £20 three courses. *First floor* **Dinner** 6.30-11.30pm Mon-Thur; *winter* one hour after sabbath-11.30pm Sat. **Meals** noon-11pm Sun. **Average** £20. **Set dinner** £20 four courses. **Credit** AmEx, DC, MC, £TC, V.

The upstairs dining room (said to be Europe's largest kosher restaurant) is decked out in Middle Eastern style, with murals, rugs and ornamental daggers. A well-executed menu and attentive service ensure a great evening out.

Korean

Greater London's main concentration of Korean residents – and restaurants – is in New Malden (20 minutes from Waterloo Station); try **Chisshine** (74 Burlington Road; 020 8942 0682) or, for lunch, **Erae Café** (169 High Street; 020 8949 0049).

Han Kang

16 Hanway Street, W1 (020 7637 1985). Tottenham Court Road tube. **Lunch** noon-3pm, 6-11pm, Mon-Sat. **Average** £20. **Set lunch** £5.90. **Credit** AmEx, DC, JCB, MC, £TC, V. **Map 6 K5**

A tatty backstreet linking Tottenham Court Road to Oxford Street is not a promising location but Han Kang survives by dint of its fine service and food, and *noraebang* (Korean karaoke) in the basement.

Kaya

42 Albemarle Street, W1 (020 7499 0622). Green Park or Piccadilly Circus tube. **Lunch** noon-3pm Mon-Sat. **Dinner** 6-11pm daily. **Average** £20 lunch, £30 dinner. **Set lunch** £13-£15. **Credit** AmEx, DC, JCB, MC, V. **Map 7 J7**

Kaya is London's prettiest Korean restaurant. Here, waitresses dressed in traditional costumes shuffle along to Korean folk music, and serve up authentic dishes such as *pibimbap*.

Malaysian & Indonesian

Melati budget

21 Great Windmill Street, W1 (020 7437 2745). Piccadilly Circus tube. **Meals** noon-11.30pm Mon-Thur, Sun; noon-12.30am Fri, Sat. **Average** £15. **Set meal** £17.50, £22.50, per person (minimum two). **Credit** AmEx, JCB, MC, £TC, V. **Map 8 K7**

This long-established, cramped but ever-popular Indonesian restaurant has a large Dutch following, so expect authentic cooking in big portions.

Selasih budget

114 Seymour Place, W1 (020 7724 4454). Edgware Road tube. **Lunch** noon-3pm Mon-Sat. **Dinner** 6-10.30pm daily. **Average** £12. **Set lunch** £4.95 one course. **Set meal** £20 (vegetarian), £25, per person (minimum two). **Credit** MC, V. **Map 2 F5**

An exotic interior, sarong-clad staff and exquisite food. Try the succulent *ikan pais* (grilled fish wrapped in banana leaf) or perfectly spiced *pajri nenas* (pineapple in a sweet and spicy curry).

Singapore Garden II

154-156 Gloucester Place, NW1 (020 7723 8233). Baker Street tube. **Lunch** noon-2.30pm daily. **Dinner** 6-10.30pm Mon-Thur, Sun; 6-11pm Fri, Sat. **Average** £20. **Set lunch** £6.95-£18.50 three courses. **Set dinner** £17.50-£30 per person (minimum two) four courses. **Credit** AmEx, DC, JCB, MC, V. **Map 2 F5**

This renowned venue has the sort of cross-cultural ambience you'd expect of a Singaporean restaurant. Both Chinese and Malaysian dishes are equally good.

Suan Neo

31 Broadgate Circle, EC2 (020 7256 5044). Liverpool Street tube/rail. **Meals** 11.30am-9.30pm Mon-Fri. **Average** £30. **Set meal** £25 three courses. **Credit** AmEx, DC, MC, V. **Map 10 Q5**

Suan Neo is furnished in a modern British style, with a cleverly lit low ceiling and lavishly set tables. The menu is inspiring, offering a wide choice of rarely found dishes.

Mediterranean

Bistro 190

190 Queen's Gate, SW7 (020 7581 5666). Gloucester Road or South Kensington tube. **Meals** 7am-midnight Mon-Fri; 7.30am-midnight Sat; 7.30am-11.30pm Sun. **Average** £20. **Credit** AmEx, DC, MC, £TC, V. **Map 4 D9**

This airy, high-ceilinged room, cluttered with pictures and prints, is a great spot to try simple but often inspired dishes such as poached salmon, rocket and lychee salad.

Snow's on the Green

166 Shepherd's Bush Road, W6 (020 7603 2142). Hammersmith tube. **Lunch** noon-3pm Mon-Fri. **Dinner** 6-11pm Mon-Sat. **Average** £20. **Set meal** £13.50 two courses, £15.50 three courses (6-8pm). **Credit** AmEx, DC, MC, V.

Sebastian Snow's sunny and serene restaurant offers a first-rate seasonally changing menu that can veer from the classics (squab pigeon with rösti) to the bizarre (banana and Nutella pizza).

Middle Eastern

Fairuz

3 Blandford Street, W1 (020 7486 8108). Baker Street tube. **Meals** noon-11.30pm daily. **Average** £18. **Set meal** £14.95 meze with arak, £24.95 two courses. **Credit** AmEx, DC, MC, £TC, V. **Map 5 G5**

A yellow-hued, intimate little place, Fairuz (named after the Lebanese diva) lacks the hauteur of many posh Lebanese restaurants yet is still very correct – and the food is reliably good.

Cafés, coffees & light lunches

London is now better supplied with quality cafés (from trad to trendy), coffee shops, soup bars (*see p177* **Souper snacks**) and lunch pit stops than it ever has been. If all you want is a shot of caffeine and a slice of cake, fast-growing chains **Aroma**, **Caffè Nero**, **Coffee Republic**, **Costa** and **Starbucks** have branches all over the centre of town. The capital's ground-breaking sandwich chain is **Pret a Manger**. The following represent a selection of central London's quirkier places to feed your face. For evening bargain meals, *see pages 184-5* **Dead-cheap dinners**.

Bloomsbury

Coffee Gallery *23 Museum Street, WC1 (020 7436 0455). Holborn or Tottenham Court Road tube.* **Open** 8am-5.30pm Mon-Fri; 10am-5.30pm Sat; noon-5.30pm Sun. **Afternoon tea served** 3-5.30pm. **Set tea** £3.40. **Credit** MC, £TC, V. **Map 6 L5**
Light lunches, coffee and superior cakes in this jolly, bright café near the British Museum.

October Gallery Café *24 Old Gloucester Street, WC1 (020 7242 7367). Holborn tube.* **Open** 12.30-2.30pm Tue-Sat. **Map 6 L5**
Global cooking and global art in a peaceful gallery.

Pâtisserie Deux Amis *63 Judd Street, WC1 (020 7383 7029). Russell Square tube/King's Cross tube/rail.* **Open** 9am-5.30pm Mon-Sat; 9am-1.30pm Sun. **Map 6 L3**
An oasis of sophistication in a drab area, offering filled baguettes, cakes, pastries and a Mediterranean ambience.

The City

See also **The Place Below** (*p188*) and **Arkansas Café** (*p167*).

Lococo *9A Cullum Street, EC3 (020 7220 7722). Monument or Bank tube.* **Open** 7am-5.30pm Mon-Fri. **Map 12 R7**
Atmospheric little coffee bar with good cakes.

Covent Garden

See also **Rock & Soul Plaice** (*p172*), **World Food Café** (*p188*) and **Food for Thought** (*p188*).

Hammock Café *186 Drury Lane, WC2 (020 7404 7808). Covent Garden or Holborn tube.* **Open** 9am-8pm Mon-Sat. **Map 6 L6**
Friendly little café with great, gutsy Brazilian food.

Juice *7 Earlham Street, WC2 (020 7836 7376). Covent Garden or Leicester Square tube.* **Open** 10am-10pm Mon-Sat; 10am-7pm Sun.
A café and juice bar on two floors. Great drinks, sandwiches, salads and cakes.

Neal's Yard Beach Café *13 Neal's Yard, WC2 (020 7240 1168). Covent Garden tube.* **Open** 11am-7pm daily. **Map 6 L6**
Colourful spot for brunchy snacks and great milkshakes. Slow service.

Photographers' Gallery Café *5 Great Newport Street (020 7831 1772). Leicester Square tube.* **Open** 11am-5.30pm Mon-Sat; noon-5.30pm Sun. **Map 8 K6**
Healthy lunchtime snacks amid photo exhibitions.

Holborn & Clerkenwell

Goodfellas *50 Lamb's Conduit Street, WC1 (020 7405 7088). Holborn tube/19, 38 bus.* **Open** 8am-7pm Mon-Fri; 10am-6pm Sat. **Map 6 M4**
Great sandwiches and an enormously popular lunchtime buffet (11.30am-2pm).

Lunch *60 Exmouth Market (020 7278 2420). Farringdon tube/rail.* **Open** 8.30am-4pm Mon-Fri; 10am-4pm Sat. **Credit** £TC. **Map 9 N4**
Tiny, modernist café/takeaway joint with good hot dishes, salads, filled bagels and wraps.

Saints' *1 Clerkenwell Road, EC1 (020 7490 4199). Barbican tube.* **Open** 8am-6pm Mon-Fri (no hot food after 4pm). **Map 9 O4**
Cheap and cheery lunch spot. Service can sometimes be slow.

Knightsbridge

Gloriette Pâtisserie *128 Brompton Road, SW3 (020 7589 4750).* **Open** 7am-7pm Mon-Sat; 9am-6pm Sun. **Credit** MC, V. **Map 4 E9**
A tiny, cosy place to tuck into Austrian sweets, pastries and exquisite cakes.

Marylebone

Delizioso *90B Cleveland Street, W1 (020 7383 0497). Great Portland Street tube.* **Open** 8am-5pm Mon-Fri; 9am-3pm Sat. **Map 5 J4**
A cut above the usual sandwich bar.

Mad Dog Café *35 James Street, W1 (020 7486 1511). Bond Street tube.* **Open** noon-11pm Mon-Sat; noon-6pm Sun. **Credit** AmEx, DC, JCB, MC, £TC, V. **Map 5 G6**
There's a masculine feel to this concrete-clad café, which offers global grub and hearty puds.

Pâtisserie Valerie at Sagne *105 Marylebone High Street, W1 (020 7935 6240). Baker Street or Bond Street tube.* **Open** 7.30am-7pm Mon-Sat; 9am-6pm Sun. **Credit** AmEx, DC, MC, £TC, V. **Map 5 G5**
Elegant café offering toothsome snacks and savouries, and fabulous cakes and tarts.

Mayfair & St James's

Richoux Coffee Co *171 Piccadilly, W1 (020 7629 4991). Green Park or Piccadilly Circus tube.* **Open** 7am-7pm Mon-Fri; 9am-7pm Sat, Sun. **Credit** AmEx, DC, MC, £TC, V. **Map 7 J7**
Spacious, chic coffee house with imaginative food.

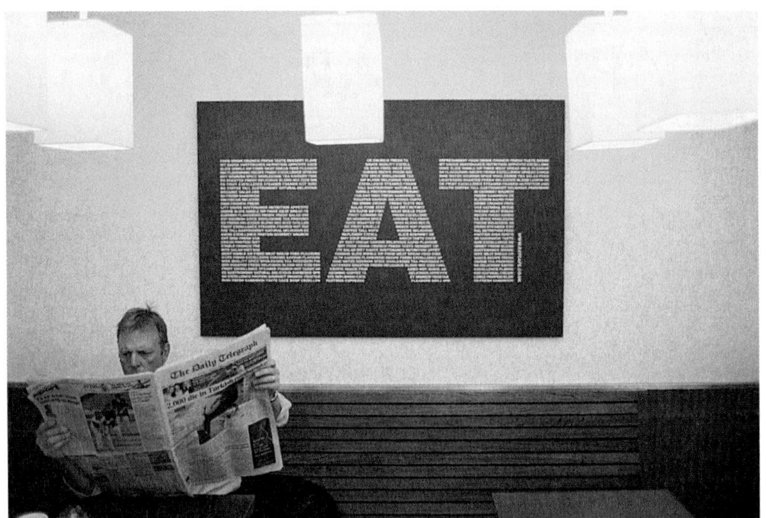

Victory Café *Basement, Gray's Antiques Market, South Molton Lane, W1 (020 7495 1587). Bond Street tube.* **Open** 10am-5.30pm Mon-Fri. **Map 5 H6**
An enjoyably quirky 1950s-style café in the depths of an antiques market. Food is more up to date.

Soho

For dim sum, *see p171. See also* **Mildred's** (*p188*), **Kulu Kulu** (*p177*) and **Ramen Seto** (*p177*).

Bar Italia *22 Frith Street, W1 (020 7437 4520). Leicester Square or Tottenham Court Road tube.* **Open** 24 hours Mon-Sat; 7am-4am Sun. **Map 6 K6**
Evergreen, ever-open Italian coffee bar.

Borders Café *Second floor, 203 Oxford Street, W1 (020 7292 1600). Oxford Circus tube.* **Open** 8am-10.30pm Mon-Sat; noon-5.30pm Sun. **Credit** AmEx, JCB, MC, £TC, V. **Map 5 J6**
US-oriented café-within-a-bookshop with views over Oxford Street and good drinks and snacks.

EAT *16A Soho Square, W1 (020 7287 7702). Tottenham Court Road tube.* **Open** 7am-6pm Mon-Fri; 10am-5pm Sat. **Map 6 K6**
Outstanding sarnies, muffins, cookies, coffees and other lunchables at this growing chain (*pictured*).

Maison Bertaux *28 Greek Street, W1 (020 7437 6007). Leicester Square, Piccadilly Circus or Tottenham Court Road tube.* **Open** 9am-8pm daily. **Credit** £TC. **Map 6 K6**
A wonderfully lost-in-time French café (it was founded in 1871). Exquisite pastries and a priceless atmosphere.

Pâtisserie Valerie *44 Old Compton Street, W1 (020 7437 3466). Leicester Square or Tottenham Court Road tube.* **Open** 8am-8pm Mon-Fri; 8am-7pm Sat; 9.30am-6pm Sun. **Credit** £TC. **Map 6 K6**
Wonderful savoury flans, cakes and pastries since 1926. The only problem is its huge popularity.
Branches: 215 Brompton Road, SW3; RIBA, 66 Portland Place, W1; 8 Russell Street, WC2.

Star Café *22 Great Chapel Street, W1 (020 7437 8778). Tottenham Court Road tube.* **Open** 7am-4pm Mon-Fri. **Map 6 K6**
Cosy oasis, just off Oxford Street, offering pastas, salads and five daily specials.

The South Bank

Konditor & Cook *Young Vic, 66 The Cut, SE1 (020 7620 2700). Southwark tube or Waterloo tube/rail.* **Open** 8.30am-11pm Mon-Fri; 10.30am-11pm Sat. **Credit** MC, V. **Map 11 N8**
Divine cakes from its own bakery and global grub are the attractions at this popular café.

RSJ Café *123 Stamford Street, SE1 (020 7928 5224). Southwark tube or Waterloo tube/rail.* **Open** 7am-6pm Mon-Fri. **Map 11 N8**
Superior sandwiches, some of them organic, and decent cakes and macaroons are offered here.

Westminster & Victoria

Café in the Crypt *Crypt of St Martin-in-the-Fields, Duncannon Street, WC2 (020 7839 4342). Charing Cross tube/rail.* **Open** *coffee bar* 10am-8pm Mon-Sat; noon-8pm Sun; *buffet* noon-3.15pm, 5-7.30pm, daily. **Map 8 K7**
Atmospheric spot, in the crypt of a church, dishing out good salads and sandwiches.

Jenny Lo's Tea House *14 Eccleston Street, SW1 (020 7259 0399). Victoria tube/rail.* **Open** 11.30am-3pm, 6-10pm Mon-Fri; noon-3pm, 6-10pm Sat. **Credit** £TC. **Map 7 H10**
Simply furnished noodle bar with a Chinese theme.

Maroush

21 Edgware Road, W1 (020 7723 0773). Marble Arch tube. **Meals** noon-2am daily. **Average** £27 (noon-10pm), £48 (10pm-2am). **Minimum** £48 after 10pm. **Credit** AmEx, DC, JCB, MC, £TC, V. **Map 2 F6**
This upmarket Lebanese restaurant has a wonderful sense of occasion and offers tremendous *meze* and thoroughly authentic versions of dishes such as *tawayeh*, a robust meat stew.

Patogh budget

8 Crawford Place, W1 (020 7262 4015). Edgware Road tube. **Open** noon-11.30pm daily. **Average** £8. **Credit** £TC. **Map 2 E5**
Not so much a restaurant as a cosy, chummy, New Age kebab shop, specialising in fresh Iranian grills. We defy anyone to finish the superb but unfeasibly large mixed grill.

North African

Momo

25 Heddon Street, W1 (020 7434 4040). Piccadilly Circus tube. **Brunch** 12.30-4.30pm Sat, Sun. **Lunch** 12.30-3pm Mon-Fri. **Dinner** 7-11pm Mon-Sat. **Average** £15 lunch, £30 dinner. **Set brunch** £15 four courses. **Set lunch** £12.50 two courses, £15.50 three courses. **Credit** AmEx, DC, MC, £TC, V. **Map 7 J7**
Momo has survived its original hype to emerge as one of London's best North African restaurants. The décor is as wonderful as the food, with a stone interior, candlelight and Arabic carved wooden screens.

Tajine budget

7A Dorset Street, W1 (020 7935 1545). Baker Street tube. **Lunch** noon-2.30pm Mon-Fri. **Dinner** 6-10.30pm Mon-Sat. **Average** £15. **Credit** MC, V. **Map 5 G5**
An unpretentious, warm-hearted restaurant that serves big portions of real Moroccan food such as aubergine *zaalouk* and a range of tagines.

Oriental

Birdcage

110 Whitfield Street, W1 (020 7323 9655). Goodge Street or Warren Street tube. **Lunch** noon-2.30pm Mon-Sat. **Dinner** 6-11.15pm Mon-Fri, Sun. **Set lunch** £26.50 three courses. **Set dinner** £38.50 three courses. **Credit** AmEx, DC, JCB, MC, V. **Map 5 J4**
Thai sculptures, birdcages and serving vessels of audacious weirdness are just part of this visually incredible restaurant. Michael von Hruschka's fusion cooking is equally unusual and often stunning.

Itsu

118 Draycott Avenue, SW3 (020 7584 5522). South Kensington tube/49 bus. **Meals** noon-11pm Mon-Sat; noon-10pm Sun. **Average** £20. **Credit** AmEx, JCB, MC, £TC, V. **Map 4 E10**
East meets west at this relaxed sushi-belted pit stop from Julian Metcalfe (the founder of the Pret a Manger sandwich bar chain). Help yourself to the likes of prawn sushi with Asian pesto.

Silks & Spice budget

23 Foley Street, W1 (020 7636 2718). Goodge Street tube. **Meals** noon-11pm Mon-Fri; 5.30-11pm Sat; noon-3pm, 5.30-10.30pm, Sun. **Average** £15. **Set lunch** £11 three courses per person (minimum two). **Set meal** £16.50-£22 three courses per person (minimum two). **Credit** AmEx, MC, £TC, V. **Map 5 J5**
Styling itself a Thai-Malaysian café-bar-restaurant, Silks & Spice is one of the most reliable oriental joints in town. The décor is warm-toned and the cooking imaginative and assured.
Branches: 42 Northampton Road, EC1 (020 7278 9983); 11 Queen Victoria Street, EC4 (020 7236 7222); 28 Chalk Farm Road, NW1 (020 7267 5751); 95 Chiswick High Road, W4 (020 8995 7991); 561 King's Road, SW6 (020 7833 5577).

Vong

Berkeley Hotel, Wilton Place, SW1 (020 7235 1010). Hyde Park Corner or Knightsbridge tube. **Brunch** 11.30am-2pm Sat, Sun. **Lunch** noon-2.30pm Mon-Sat. **Dinner** 6-11.30pm Mon-Sat; 6-10pm Sun. **Average** £38. **Set lunch** £16.50 two courses, £20 three courses. **Set dinner** (6-7.30pm, 10.30-11.30pm) £19.50 two courses. **Credit** AmEx, DC, JCB, MC, £TC, V. **Map 7 G8**
Oriental and western cuisines are fused magnificently in this minimally chic branch of Jean-Georges Vongerichten's celebrated New York restaurant. Save up and treat yourself – and don't pass on the stunning desserts.

Wagamama budget

101A Wigmore Street, W1 (020 7409 0111). Bond Street or Marble Arch tube. **Meals** noon-11pm Mon-Sat; 12.30-10.30pm Sun. **Average** £8. **Set meals** £8.25-£9.75. **Credit** AmEx, MC, £TC, V. **Map 5 G6**
Wagamama has become something of a London institution. Health- and money-conscious diners pack the long bench tables and slurp big bowls of ramen and plates of noodles. Queuing is often necessary, but it's worth the wait.
Branches: 4 Streatham Street, WC1 (020 7323 9223); 10A Lexington Street, W1 (020 7292 0990); 26-40 Kensington High Street, W8 (020 7376 1717); 11 Jamestown Road, NW1 (020 7428 0800).

Wok Wok budget

10 Frith Street, W1 (020 7437 7080). Piccadilly Circus or Tottenham Court Road tube. **Meals** noon-11pm Mon-Wed; noon-midnight Thur-Sat. **Dinner** 6-10.30pm Sun. **Average** £12. **Set lunch** £6.95 two courses. **Set meals** £14.50-£19.20 three courses per person (minimum six). **Credit** AmEx, DC, JCB, MC, £TC, V. **Map 6 K6**
Aiming to be a more upmarket (yet still very relaxed) noodle bar, Wok Wok provides a largely successful menu of stock South-east Asian dishes. Service is pleasantly breezy.
Branches: 7 Kensington High Street, W8 (020 7938 1221); 140 Fulham Road, SW10 (020 7370 5355); 67 Upper Street, N1 (020 7288 0333); 51-53 Northcote Road, SW11 (020 7978 7181); 67 Upper Street, N1 (020 7288 0333).

Dead-cheap dinners

In addition to our favourite places marked budget in this chapter, the majority of the central London venues below should be able to supply a good three-course meal (excluding drinks) for under £15 (and often less). For lighter snacks and lunch spots, *see page 180* **Cafés, coffees & light lunches**.

Bloomsbury

See also **Wagamama** (*p183*), **Navarro's Tapas Bar** (*p186*) and **Silks & Spice** (*p183*).

Diwana Bhel Poori House *121 Drummond Street, NW1 (020 7387 5556). Euston Square or Euston tube.* **Open** noon-11.30pm daily. **Credit** AmEx, DC, MC, £TC, V. **Map 5 J3**
Good south Indian veggie snacks. There are other bhel poori joints on the same street.

North Sea Fish Restaurant *7-8 Leigh Street, WC1 (020 7387 5892). Russell Square tube/ King's Cross tube/rail.* **Open** noon-2.30pm, 5.30-10.30pm, Mon-Sat. **Credit** AmEx, DC, MC, £TC, V. **Map 6 L3**
Retro Berni Inn décor but terrific fish and chips.

Chelsea

See also **Stockpot** (*below* **Knightsbridge**) and **Silks & Spice** (*p183*).

Chelsea Bun Diner *9A Limerston Street, SW10 (020 7352 3635). Bus 11, 19, 22, 31.* **Open** 7am-midnight Mon-Sat; 8am-midnight Sun. **Credit** MC, £TC, V. **Map 4 D12**
Fun, American-style diner with huge menu. Good breakfasts.

Chelsea Kitchen *98 King's Road, SW3 (020 7589 1330). Sloane Square tube.* **Open** 8am-11.30pm daily. **Map 4 F11**
Bargain-priced, no-nonsense stomach-fillers served in this clone of the **Stockpot** diners (*see below*).

The City

See also **Silks & Spice** (*p183*).

Noto Ramen House *Bow Bells House, 7 Bread Street, EC4 (020 7329 8056). Bank, Mansion House or St Paul's tube.* **Open** 11.30am-8.45pm Mon-Fri. **Credit** £TC. **Map 11 P6**
Authentically steamy Japanese noodle bar. Branch at 2-3 Bassishaw Highwalk, London Wall, EC2.

Covent Garden

See also **Rock & Soul Plaice** (*p172*) and **Food For Thought** (*p188*).

India Club *2nd floor, Strand Continental Hotel, 143 Strand, WC2 (020 7836 0650). Covent Garden or Temple tube.* **Open** noon-2.30pm, 6-11pm, Mon-Sat. **Credit** £TC. **Map 8 M7**
Unlicensed, quirky, utilitarian but priceless Indian diner of 50-years-plus vintage.

Knightsbridge

Stockpot *6 Basil Street, SW3 (020 7589 8627). Knightsbridge tube.* **Open** 9.30am-11pm Mon-Sat; noon-10.30pm Sun. **Map 4 F9**

Pie & mash budget

It may surprise some people to learn that London has its own indigenous cuisine. True, it lacks finesse, but the city's last bastions of pies, eels and mash (mostly in east London) offer delicious stomach-fillers at laughably low prices. Two of the finest are **G Kelly** (414 Bethnal Green Road, E2; 020 7739 3603) and **Manze's** (87 Tower Bridge Road, SE1; 020 7407 2985).

Polish

Patio budget

5 Goldhawk Road, W12 (020 8743 5194). Goldhawk Road or Shepherd's Bush tube.
Lunch noon-3pm Mon-Fri. **Dinner** 6pm-midnight daily. **Average** £10. **Set meal** £10.90 three courses incl glass of vodka. **Credit** AmEx, DC, JCB, MC, £TC, V.
A nondescript façade in an unpromising location masks a unique restaurant, where Ewa the enigmatic proprietress greets diners, and husband Michalik cooks up reassuring standards such as blinis and carp Polish-style. Short on frills, big on charm.

Wódka

12 St Alban's Grove, W8 (020 7937 6513). Gloucester Road or High Street Kensington tube.
Lunch 12.30-2.30pm Mon-Fri. **Dinner** 7-11.15pm daily. **Average** £20. **Set lunch** £10.90 two courses, £13.50 three courses. **Credit** AmEx, DC, MC, £TC, V. **Map 3 C9**
Jan Woroniecki is on a mission to modernise Polish food. The menu covers all the classics: hearty soups, stuffed cabbage and the rest, but innovatively combines them with the likes of olives and couscous.

Portuguese

Golborne Road, W10 (Ladbroke Grove tube) has the best of the Portuguese *pastelarias* (pâtisseries).

A Viga budget

127 Westbourne Park Road, W2 (020 7792 1399). Royal Oak or Westbourne Park tube. **Meals** noon-midnight daily. **Average** £12. **Credit** MC, £TC, V. **Map 1 A5**
No more than a hole in the wall, this street-level bar with bigger basement restaurant is the real McCoy. The stews are gutsy and warming and the tapas are first class. Service is low-key but solicitous.

Unfeasibly cheap, if uninspiringly basic, grub. Other Stockpots can be found at 18 Old Compton Street, W1; 40 Panton Street, SW1; 273 King's Road, SW3; 50 James Street, W1.

Marylebone

See also **Stockpot** (*above* **Knightsbridge**), **Wagamama** (*p183*), **Selasih** (*p179*) and **Patogh** (*p183*).

Giraffe *6-8 Blandford Street, W1 (020 7935 2333). Baker Street or Regent's Park tube.* **Open** 8am-midnight Mon-Fri; 9am-midnight Sat, Sun.
Second branch of the wonderfully inventive and versatile Hampstead café. Great for breakfast, lunch, a cuppa and a cake or dinner.

Soho

See also **Stockpot** (*above* **Knightsbridge**), **Wagamama** (*p183*), **Wok Wok** (*p183*) and **Melati** (*p179*).

Café Emm *17 Frith Street, W1 (020 7437 0723). Tottenham Court Road tube.* **Open** noon-3pm Mon-Fri; 5.30-10.30pm Mon-Thur; 5.30pm-12.30am Fri; 5pm-12.30am Sat; 5-10.30pm Sun. **Credit** MC, £TC, V. **Map 6 K6**
Relaxed vibe, huge portions, and a good vegetarian choice.

Ed's Easy Diner *12 Moor Street, W1 (020 7287 1951). Leicester Square or Tottenham Court Road tube.* **Open** 11.30am-midnight Mon-Thur, Sun; 11.30am-1am Fri, Sat. **Map 6 K6**
Ersatz '50s diner Americana and great burgers.

Hing Loon *25 Lisle Street, W1 (020 7437 3602). Leicester Square tube.* **Open** noon-11.30pm daily. **Credit** AmEx, MC, £TC, V. **Map 8 K7**
One of the best of Chinatown's many diners.

Pollo *20 Old Compton Street, W1 (020 7734 5917). Leicester Square or Tottenham Court Road tube.* **Open** noon-midnight daily. **Credit** £TC. **Map 6 K6**
Probably London's best known and most popular budget diner. Bags of atmosphere and reasonable pasta. Nearby, **Presto** (4 Old Compton Street) and **Centrale** (16 Moor Street) offer similar food in a less frenetic environment.

Tibetan Restaurant *17 Irving Street, W1 (020 7839 2090). Leicester Square tube.* **Open** noon-2.45pm Mon, Tue, Thur-Sat; 5-10.45pm Mon-Sat. **Credit** DC, MC, £TC, V. **Map 8 K7**
An other-worldly outpost of Tibet located just off Leicester Square.

The South Bank

See also **Konditor & Cook** (*p181*) and **Tas** (*p187*).

Gourmet Pizza Company *Gabriel's Wharf, 56 Upper Ground, SE1 (020 7928 3188). Southwark tube or Waterloo tube/rail.* **Open** noon-11pm Mon-Sat. **Credit** AmEx, DC, MC, £TC, V. **Map 11 N7**
Riverside pizzeria known for its adventurous toppings and often slow service.

Masters Super Fish *191 Waterloo Road, SE1 (020 7928 6924). Southwark tube or Waterloo tube/rail.* **Open** 5-10.30pm Mon; noon-11pm Tue-Thur; noon-11pm Fri, Sat. **Credit** MC, £TC, V. **Map 11 N8**
A well-worn old stager, Masters is a good bet for huge portions of fish and chips.

O Cantinho de Portugal

137 Stockwell Road, SW8 (020 7924 0218). Stockwell tube/Brixton tube/rail/2, 322, 345 bus. **Meals** 10am-midnight daily. **Average** £16. **Credit** £TC.
Choose between the light, modern restaurant and the shiny bar area, with green tiles, bright lights and droning TV, where undeniably authentic tapas for the brave might include pig's ear salad. An undilutedly Iberian experience.

Russian

Nikita's

65 Ifield Road, SW10 (020 7352 6326). Earl's Court or West Brompton tube/14, 31, 74 bus. **Dinner** 7.30-11.30pm Mon-Sat. **Average** £20. **Set meal** £18.50-£30.50 four courses. **Credit** AmEx, JCB, MC, £TC, V. **Map 3 C12**
Nikita's is delightfully over the top, from the theatrical décor to the story-book Russian classics, delineated in detail on the long menu. The owner, Mr Borsi, has overseen the fine spread of *zakuski* (hors d'oeuvres), chilled vodkas and caviar for more than 25 years.

South African

Springbok Café

42 Devonshire Road, W4 (020 8742 3149). Turnham Green tube. **Dinner** 6.30-11pm Mon-Sat. **Average** £17. **Credit** MC, £TC, V.
London's only exclusively South African restaurant offers such little-seen delights as peppered kudu, Plettenberg Bay linefish and zebra samosas. The quality of the cooking, however, has much more to offer than mere novelty, and the staff are usually delightful. One on its own.

Spanish

Cambio de Tercio

163 Old Brompton Road, SW5 (020 7244 8970). Gloucester Road tube. **Lunch** 12.30-2.30pm daily. **Dinner** 7-11.30pm Mon-Sat; 7-11pm Sun. **Average** £20, £14 tapas. **Credit** AmEx, MC, V. **Map 3 C11**
This stylish restaurant in a fashionable part of town is very popular, and it's easy to understand why when you sample Diego Ferrer's superb modern Spanish cooking.

Invasion of the gastropubs

Time was when the idea of eating in a pub appealed only to culinary masochists. A soggy, microwaved lard and gristle pie, a wilting spam sandwich or a reconstituted dried Vesta curry (with plenty of sultanas) used to be the most that anyone could hope to find on a pub menu. How times have changed. **The Eagle** in Farringdon blazed the trail, reopening in 1991 with a winning combination of bare-board bonhomie and seriously classy Mediterranean cooking. Within a few years everyone was jumping on the bandwagon, and today there's a stripped-down, wised-up gastropub on almost every street corner. Be warned that the prices in many of these places are the equivalent of those in good restaurants, and booking is often necessary. Most serve lunch and dinner every day (though usually only lunch on Sunday), but phone to check.

The Atlas *16 Seagrave Road, SW6 (020 7385 9129). West Brompton tube.* **Map 3 B12**

Belle Vue *1 Clapham Common Southside, SW4 (020 7498 9473). Clapham Common tube.* *See also p198.*

Builders Arms *13 Britten Street, SW3 (020 7349 9040). South Kensington tube.* **Map 4 E11**

Bull & Last *168 Highgate Road, NW5 (020 7267 3641). Kentish Town tube/rail then C2, 214 bus.*

The Chapel *48 Chapel Street, NW1 (020 7402 9220). Edgware Road tube.* **Map 2 E5** *See also p195.*

Duke of York *7 Roger Street, WC1 (020 7242 7230). Russell Sq tube.* **Map 6 M4** *See also p190.*

The Eagle *159 Farringdon Road, EC1 (020 7837 1353). Farringdon tube/rail/19, 38, 171A bus.* **Map 9 N4** *See also p195.*

The Engineer *65 Gloucester Avenue, NW1 (020 7722 0950). Chalk Farm tube/31, 168 bus.*

Lansdowne *90 Gloucester Avenue, NW1 (020 7483 0409). Chalk Farm tube/31, 168 bus.*

The Lord Stanley *51 Camden Park Road, NW1 (020 7428 9488). Camden Town tube or Camden Road rail then 29, 253 bus.*

Prince Bonaparte *80 Chepstow Road, W2 (020 7229 5912). Notting Hill or Westbourne Park tube/7, 20, 31 bus.* **Map 1 A5**

The Vine *86 Highgate Road, NW5 (020 7209 0038). Tufnell Park tube or Kentish Town tube/rail.*

The Westbourne *101 Westbourne Park Villas, W2 (020 7221 1332). Royal Oak or Westbourne Park tube.* **Map 1 B5** *See also p199.*

William IV *786 Harrow Road, NW10 (020 8969 5944). Kensal Green tube.*

Gaudí

63 Clerkenwell Road, EC1 (020 7608 3220). Farringdon tube/rail/55, 243 bus.
Lunch noon-2.30pm, **dinner** 7-10.30pm, Mon-Fri. **Average** £30. **Set lunch** £12.50 two courses, £15 three courses. **Credit** AmEx, DC, MC, £TC, V. **Map 9 N4**

The flamboyance of the Gaudí-esque décor of convoluted metalwork and multicoloured tiling is matched by the cooking of Nacho Martínez Jiménez – both are firmly based in a Spanish repertoire yet strikingly creative.

Moro

34-36 Exmouth Market, EC1 (020 7833 8336). Farringdon tube/rail. **Lunch** 12.30-2.30pm, **dinner** 7-10.30pm, Mon-Fri. **Average** £21. **Credit** AmEx, MC, £TC, V. **Map 9 N4**

Moro has deservedly attracted much attention since it opened in 1997. It is fashionably minimal and light, and offers an innovative, frequently changing menu incorporating influences mostly from Spain but also from North Africa.

Navarro's Tapas Bar budget

67 Charlotte Street, W1 (020 7637 7713). Goodge Street tube. **Lunch** noon-3pm Mon-Fri. **Dinner** 6-10.30pm Mon-Sat. **Average** £12. **Credit** AmEx, DC, JCB, MC, £TC, V. **Map 5 J5**

Navarro's tapas are among the most distinctive around. Especially suited to the pretty décor are the deliciously refreshing salads, while gutsier offerings like lentil and chorizo stew are equally good.

Sudanese

Mandola budget

139-141 Westbourne Grove, W11 (020 7229 6391). Notting Hill Gate tube/23 bus. **Meals** noon-11.30pm Mon-Sat; noon-10.30pm Sun. **Average** £12. **Unlicensed. Corkage** £1. **Credit** £TC. **Map 1 A6**

Booking is now essential at this simply decorated yet cosy Sudanese diner. The food is equally straightforward, but tasty, freshly prepared and with plenty of options for vegetarians. Bringing your own booze keeps the bill low.

Thai

Busabong Tree

112 Cheyne Walk, SW10 (020 7352 7534). Bus 11, 22, 31, 49, 319. **Lunch** noon-3pm daily. **Dinner** 6-11.15pm Mon-Sat. **Average** £22. **Set lunch** £9.95 three courses. **Set dinner** £22.25, £27.95, three courses. **Credit** AmEx, JCB, MC, £TC, V. **Map 4 D13**

A high class, soothing oriental design makes for a relaxing, elegant backdrop to the clear, precise flavours of the consistently first-rate cooking.

Sri Siam

16 Old Compton Street, W1 (020 7434 3544). Leicester Square or Tottenham Court Road tube. **Lunch** noon-3pm Mon-Sat. **Dinner** 6-11.15pm Mon-Sat; 6-10.30pm Sun. **Average** £25. **Set meal** £12.95-£19.95 per person (minimum two). **Credit** AmEx, DC, MC, £TC, V. **Map 6 K6**
A minimalist Thai restaurant may usually be a contradiction in terms in London, but Sri Siam's wood-strip floors and brightly painted walls are a refreshing setting for reliable food, including an impressively long vegetarian menu.

Tawana

3 Westbourne Grove, W2 (020 7229 3785). Bayswater, Queensway or Royal Oak tube. **Lunch** noon-3pm, **dinner** 6-11pm, daily. **Average** £16. **Set meal** £15.95. **Credit** AmEx, DC, MC, V. **Map 1 B6**
Kitted out like a Somerset Maugham vision of colonial Asia, Tawana's efficient, unobtrusive service, relaxing atmosphere and exemplary food make it one of the capital's top Thais.

Thai Bistro budget

99 Chiswick High Road, W4 (020 8995 5774). Turnham Green tube/27, 237, 267 bus. **Lunch** noon-3pm Mon, Wed, Fri-Sun. **Dinner** 6-11pm Mon-Sat; 6-10.30pm Sun. **Average** £15. **Credit** MC, V.
Vatcharin Bhumichitr's Thai Bistro has effortlessly established itself in Chiswick's competitive restaurantland. The minimal, canteen-like look is familiar, but the friendly staff and cheap, expertly cooked food are less common.

Thai Pot

1 Bedfordbury, WC2 (020 7379 4580). Covent Garden tube/Charing Cross tube/rail. **Lunch** noon-3pm Mon-Fri. **Dinner** 5.30-11.15pm Mon-Sat. **Average** £17. **Set lunch** £10 two courses. **Set meal** £15 three courses, £18 four courses. **Credit** AmEx, DC, MC, £TC, V. **Map 8 L7**
The unusually airy, neo-classical décor of Thai Pot makes a pleasant backdrop for a Thai menu that offers few surprises but competent, subtly spiced versions of Thai standards. The curries are particularly recommended.
Branch: **Thai Pot on the Strand** 148 Strand, WC2 (020 7497 0904).

Turkish

Many of London's best Turkish restaurants are the unprepossessing, unreconstructed kebab houses serving north London's Turkish community. A walk along Green Lanes or Stoke Newington Road in N16 can be a culinary revelation.

Efes I

80 Great Titchfield Street, W1 (020 7636 1953). Great Portland Street tube. **Meals** noon-11.30pm Mon-Sat. **Average** £20. **Set meal** £17 per person (minimum two). **Credit** AmEx, DC, JCB, MC, £TC, V. **Map 5 J5**
There's an air of Ottoman gentility to this spacious, elegantly furnished restaurant in Marylebone. The food is superb and tremendous value, particularly the meat dishes.

Istanbul Iskembecisi budget

9 Stoke Newington Road, N16 (020 7254 7291). Dalston Kingsland rail. **Meals** noon-5am daily. **Average** £12. **Credit** AmEx, DC, MC, V.
The signature dish here, *iskembe* (finely chopped tripe in soup), may not be to all tastes, but the wonderfully fresh ingredients in the meze and more mainstream main dishes, not to mention the solicitous service, will please most diners.

Iznik budget

19 Highbury Park, N5 (020 7354 5697). Highbury & Islington tube/rail/19 bus. **Meals** 10am-3.30pm Mon-Fri; 9am-3.30pm Sat, Sun. **Dinner** 6.30-11pm daily. **Average** £15. **Credit** MC, £TC, V.
The décor is as uncompromisingly oriental as Selim the Grim, whose portrait scowls down at customers as they enter. Iznik's food is equally reverent of Turkish culture and includes rarely seen, labour-intensive Ottoman lamb dishes.

Sofra Bistro

18 Shepherd Market, W1 (020 7493 5940). Green Park tube. **Meals** noon-midnight daily. **Average** £17. **Credit** AmEx, MC, £TC, V. **Map 7 H8**
Though the conditions are slightly cramped and the service rather temperamental, this Mayfair favourite dishes up a wide range of excellent Turkish dishes. Booking advisable.

Tas budget

33 The Cut, SE1 (020 7928 2111). Southwark tube or Waterloo tube/rail. **Meals** noon-11.30pm Mon-Sat; noon-10.30pm Sun. **Average** £15. **Set meal** £6.45-£17.95. **Credit** AmEx, MC, V. **Map 11 N8**
Proffering Turkish cuisine with a twist, rather than the standard classic dishes, Tas is a welcome change. Expect the likes of mussel soup with coriander and ginger, and inspired seafood casseroles.

Vegetarian

Other good restaurants for vegetarians include **Café Emm** (*page 185*), **Rousillon** (*page 173*), **Rasa W1** (*page 174*), **Mandola** (*page 186*) and **Sri Siam** (*page 187*).

Bah Humbug

The Crypt, St Matthew's Peace Garden, Brixton Hill, SW2 (020 7738 3184). Brixton tube/rail. **Brunch** 11am-5pm Sat, Sun. **Dinner** 5-11pm Mon-Thur; 5-11.30pm Fri, Sat. **Meals** 1-10.30pm Sun. **Average** £16. **Credit** MC, V.
Although it's in a crypt, Bah Humbug hums with life. Cool funk ricochets off the vaulted ceilings while Brixton trendies tuck into good veggie dishes such as crispy Cantonese mock duck (quorn). There's also a hip bar.

Blah Blah Blah

78 Goldhawk Road, W12 (020 8746 1337). Goldhawk Road tube/94 bus. **Lunch** noon-2.30pm, **dinner** 7-11pm, Mon-Sat. **Average** £16. **Unlicensed. Corkage** 95p per person.

Chef Andy Young turns out exquisite, light French-style dishes presented like works of art. The love of colour evident in the food extends to the décor.

Food For Thought budget

31 Neal Street, WC2 (020 7836 9072/0239). Covent Garden tube. **Breakfast** 9.30-11.30am Mon-Sat. **Lunch** noon-5pm daily. **Dinner** 5-8.30pm Mon-Sat. **Average** £8. **Minimum** £2.50 noon-3pm, 6-7.30pm. **Unlicensed. Corkage** no charge. **Credit** £TC. **Map 6 L6**

A long lunchtime queue, snaking out into Neal Street, testifies to Food For Thought's continuing popularity. On the ground floor is a takeaway; in the cramped downstairs diners sup from the daily changing menu offering quiches, salads and hot dishes.

The Gate

51 Queen Caroline Street, W6 (020 8748 6932). Hammersmith tube. **Lunch** noon-3pm Mon-Fri. **Dinner** 6-10.45pm Mon-Sat. **Average** £16. **Credit** AmEx, MC, £TC, V.

Tucked away in a quiet, leafy church courtyard, the Gate's sunflower-yellow walls and stripped-wood floor are a civilised setting in which to enjoy the elaborate, imaginative but not overambitious globally inspired menu. Probably London's best vegetarian restaurant.

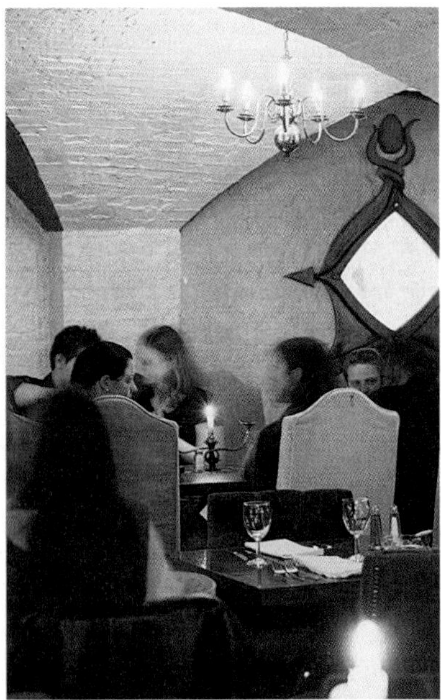

Bah Humbug's *veggie delights. See p187.*

Mildred's budget

58 Greek Street, W1 (020 7494 1634). Leicester Square or Tottenham Court Road tube. **Meals** noon-11pm Mon-Sat; noon-5pm Sun. **Average** £11. **Credit** £TC. **Map 6 K6**

This bustling, informal, friendly, long-established place bases its short menu around stir-fry, falafel and beanburger with salad, all of which are around a fiver. Expect to share a table.

The Place Below budget

St Mary-le-Bow, Cheapside, EC2 (020 7329 0789). St Paul's tube/Bank tube/DLR. **Open** 7.30am-2.30pm, **breakfast** 7.30-10.30am, **lunch** 10.30am-2.30pm, Mon-Fri. **Average** £12. **Credit** MC, £TC, V. **Map 11 P6**

Deep within the Norman crypt of the St Mary-le-Bow church (*see also p47*), this café offers a welcome escape from City life, as well as some decent vegetarian sustenance.

World Food Café budget

Neal's Yard Dining Room, 1st floor, 14 Neal's Yard, WC2 (020 7379 0298). Covent Garden or Leicester Square tube. **Meals** noon-5pm Mon-Sat. **Average** £10. **Credit** MC, V. **Map 6 L6**

One of the best choices for veggie food in the centre of town. Cooking is inventive and globally inspired, while the atmosphere is friendly and relaxed. Diners sit on high stools around the open kitchen.

Vietnamese

Huong-Viet budget

An Viet House, 12-14 Englefield Road, N1 (020 7249 0877). Bus 67, 149, 236, 242, 243, 243A. **Lunch** noon-3.30pm Mon-Fri, Sun; noon-4pm Sat. **Dinner** 5.30-11.30pm daily. **Average** £8. **Credit** JCB, MC, V.

This Vietnamese community centre and café offers an extensive menu of around 100 Vietnamese dishes, all freshly prepared with quality ingredients, served in big portions at low prices, in a basic but convivial dining room.

Saigon

45 Frith Street, W1 (020 7437 7109). Leicester Square tube. **Meals** noon-11.30pm Mon-Sat. **Average** £22. **Set meal** £15.75 per person two courses (minimum two), £19.35 per person three courses (minimum two). **Credit** AmEx, DC, MC, V. **Map 6 K6**

Long-established Saigon is as civilised an introduction to the food of Vietnam as you'll find in London. For an all-round taster, the set meals are good value.

Viet Hoa budget

70-72 Kingsland Road, E2 (020 7729 8293). Bus 26, 48, 55, 67, 149, 242. **Lunch** noon-3.30pm, **dinner** 5.45-11.30pm, daily. **Average** £8. **Set lunch** £3.95 two courses. **Credit** MC, V.

This huge, wonderfully unpretentious restaurant is deservedly popular. The décor may not be much to write home about, but do expect the admirably fresh, needle-sharp flavours of Vietnam in a relaxed, buzzy atmosphere. Service is efficient.

Restaurants by area

See also the eateries listed under **Tea time** (*page 178*), **Cafés, coffees & light lunches** (*page 180*), **Dirt-cheap dinners** (*page 184*) and **Invasion of the gastropubs** (*page 186*).

Bloomsbury

Birdcage, *p183*; **Navarro's Tapas Bar**, *p186*; **Passione**, *p175*; **Rasa Samudra**, *p174*; **Silks & Spice**, *p183*; **Wagamama**, *p183*.

Chelsea & South Kensington

Bibendum, *p165*; **Bistro 190**, *p179*; **Bluebird**, *p165*; **Busabong Tree**, *p186*; **Cactus Blue**, *p167*; **Calzone**, *p177*; **Cambio de Tercio**, *p185*; **Gordon Ramsay**, *p163*; **Itsu**, *p183*; **Vama**, *p175*; **Zaika**, *p175*.

City

Café Spice Namaste, *p174*; **The Place Below**, *p188*; **Silks & Spice**, *p183*; **Suan Neo**, *p179*.

Covent Garden

Bank, *p165*; **Belgo Centraal**, *p168*; **Food For Thought**, *p188*; **The Ivy**, *p166*; **Livebait**, *p172*; **Rock & Sole Plaice**, *p172*; **Rules**, *p168*; **J Sheekey**, *p172*; **Thai Pot**, *p187*; **World Food Café**, *p188*.

Holborn & Clerkenwell

Club Gascon, *p172*; **Gaudí**, *p186*; **Moro**, *p186*; **St John**, *p168*; **Stephen Bull Smithfield**, *p167*.

Knightsbridge

The Fifth Floor, *p165*; **Isola**, *p175*; **Pizza on the Park**, *p177*; **Vong**, *p183*; **Zafferano**, *p175*.

Marylebone

Efes I, *p187*; **Fairuz**, *p179*; **Ibla**, *p175*; **Mandalay**, *p168*; **Maroush**, *p183*; **Mash**, *p166*; **Orrery**, *p166*; **Patogh**, *p183*; **Porte des Indes**, *p174*; **Purple Sage**, *p177*; **Seashell**, *p172*; **Selasih**, *p179*; **Singapore Garden II**, *p179*; **La Spighetta**, *p177*; **Stephen Bull**, *p167*; **Tajine**, *p183*; **Wagamama**, *p183*; **Yumi**, *p177*.

Mayfair

Chez Nico at Ninety Park Lane, *p163*; **Coast**, *p165*; **Condotti**, *p177*; **The Criterion**, *p172*; **Greenhouse**, *p168*; **Kaya**, *p179*; **Matsuri**, *p177*; **Mirabelle**, *p173*; **Momo**, *p183*; **Nobu**, *p177*; **Oak Room**, *p163*; **Oriental**, *p171*; **Quaglino's**, *p167*; **Rasa W1**, *p174*; **Sofra Bistro**, *p187*; **Sugar Club**, *p167*; **Tamarind**, *p174*.

Soho & Chinatown

Alastair Little, *p165*; **Andrew Edmunds**, *p165*; **Circus**, *p165*; **French House Dining Room**, *p166*; **Frith Street**, *p172*; **Golden Dragon**, *p171*; **Golden Harvest**, *p169*; **Han Kang**, *p179*; **Harbour City**, *p171*; **Kulu Kulu**, *p177*; **Mildred's**, *p188*; **Mr Kong**, *p169*; **L'Escargot**, *p172*; **Lindsay House**, *p168*; **Melati**, *p179*; **New Diamond**, *p169*; **Ramen Seto**, *p177*; **Saigon**, *p188*; **Schnecke**, *p173*; **Soho Pizzeria**, *p177*; **Spiga**, *p177*; **Sri Siam**, *p187*; **Teatro**, *p167*; **Vasco & Piero's Pavilion**, *p175*; **Wagamama**, *p183*; **Wok Wok**, *p183*; **Yo! Sushi**, *p177*.

South Bank

fish!, *p171*; **Oxo Tower Restaurant**, *p166*; **The People's Palace**, *p167*; **Tas**, *p187*.

Westminster & Victoria

Boisdale, *p168*; **Hunan**, *p169*; **Rousillon**, *p173*; **Stefano Cavallini Restaurant**, *p165*.

North London

Afghan Kitchen, Islington, *p167*; **Asakusa**, Camden, *p177*; **Granita**, Islington, *p166*; **Halepi**, Belsize Park, *p174*; **Huong-Viet**, Dalston, *p188*; **Istanbul Iskembecisi**, Dalston, *p187*; **Iznik**, Highbury, *p187*; **Jindivick**, Islington, *p173*; **Karahi King**, Wembley, *p174*; **Mango Room**, Camden *p169*; **Odette's**, Primrose Hill, *p166*; **Solly's**, Golders Green, *p179*; **Upper Street Fish Shop**, Islington, *p172*; **Viet Hoa**, Hoxton, *p188*.

East London

Arkansas Café, Shoreditch, *p167*; **Little Georgia**, Bethnal Green, *p173*; **The Real Greek**, Hoxton, *p174*.

South London

Arancia, Bermondsey, *p175*; **Bah Humbug**, Brixton, *p187*; **Brixtonian Havana Club**, Brixton, *p168*; **Chez Bruce**, Wandsworth, *p172*; **Chez Lindsay**, Richmond, *p172*; **Enoteca Turi**, Putney, *p175*; **The Glasshouse**, Kew, *p166*; **Helter Skelter**, Brixton, *p173*; **Kastoori**, Tooting, *p174*; **La Pampa Grill**, Battersea, *p167*; **The Lavender**, Battersea, *p174*; **O Cantinho de Portugal**, Stockwell, *p185*.

West London

Assaggi, Notting Hill, *p175*; **Bali Sugar**, Notting Hill, *p173*; **Blah Blah Blah**, Shepherd's Bush, *p188*; **Clarke's**, Kensington, *p165*; **Dakota**, Notting Hill, *p167*; **The Gate**, Hammersmith, *p188*; **Gifto's Lahore Karahi**, Southall, *p174*; **Magic Wok**, Bayswater, *p169*; **Mandarin Kitchen**, Bayswater, *p169*; **Mandola**, Notting Hill, *p186*; **New Four Seasons**, Bayswater, *p171*; **Nikita's**, Earl's Court, *p185*; **Patio**, Shepherd's Bush, *p184*; **Rodizio Rico**, Bayswater, *p168*; **Royal China**, Bayswater, *p171*; **Snow's on the Green**, Hammersmith, *p179*; **Springbok Café**, Chiswick, *p185*; **Tawana**, Bayswater, *p187*; **Thai Bistro**, Chiswick, *p187*; **A Viga**, Notting Hill, *p184*; **Veronica's**, Bayswater, *p168*; **Wódka**, Kensington, *p184*.

Pubs & Bars

Victorian throwbacks, timeless taverns and futuristic style bars.

London has never had as great a variety of drinking dens as it has today. First it was the 1980s' wave of wine bars that challenged the hegemony of the smoky boozer; then in the 1990s followed the emergence of seriously stylish, thoroughly metropolitan bars and spruced-up pubs offering restaurant-quality food (for the best of the latter, *see page 186* **Invasion of the gastropubs**). Some of London's coolest new bars also double up as clubs late in the evening as DJs take the floor and dancing takes priority over drinking. For the pick of these places, *see page 244* **Club bars**. There's even talk of further liberalising Britain's still-archaic licensing laws. (At the moment, unless they have a late licence, pubs have to stop serving at 11pm from Monday to Saturday and 10.30pm on Sunday; for places where you can get a drink after these times, *see page 192* **Late-night liquor**).

But for some tastes the sweeping out of all that was once sacred in the British pub has gone too far. While the city's drinking scene was undoubtedly in need of a serious kick up the backside, there is also a worrying trend towards marketing-led homogeneity, with identikit pubs and bars spreading over the capital faster than fermenting yeast on a vat of ale. The ubiquity of barn-like **Pitcher & Piano** and **All Bar One** drinking halls, of **JD Wetherspoon** and **Firkin** pubs, and of **Balls Brothers**, **Corney & Barrow** and **Davy's** wine bars may offer a brand you recognise on almost every street corner (and often good-quality drinks), but they leave no room for individuality or idiosyncrasy. Lovers of the scruffy, friendly local pub are becoming an increasingly beleaguered tribe.

For bars that cater for a primarily gay or lesbian clientele, *see page 265*.

Central

Bloomsbury & Fitzrovia

Duke of York

7 Roger Street, WC1 (020 7242 7230). Russell Square tube/19, 38, 55 bus.
Open noon-11pm Mon-Fri; 7-11pm Sat.
Map 6 M4

Making a virtue of its original dinginess, this corner boozer still looks as if it should hold a few old geezers in flat caps nursing bitter. The fashionably eclectic food menu, however, betrays the Duke's ambition to move with the times.

Denim – *scary-looking but surprisingly inviting. It must be in the jeans. See page 192.*

The Lamb
Lamb's Conduit Street, WC1 (020 7405 0713). Russell Square tube. **Open** 11am-11pm Mon-Sat; noon-4pm, 7-10.30pm, Sun. **Map 6 M4**
Wonderfully old-fashioned pub that draws in a mixed crowd to enjoy the Young's beers and the splendid wooden bar with small, engraved, swivel-hinged glass panels dividing punter from publican.

Old Crown
33 New Oxford Street, WC1 (020 7836 9121). Holborn or Tottenham Court Road tube. **Open** 11am-11pm Mon-Sat. **Map 6 L5**
Decked out in distressed cream and green contemporary chic, the Old Crown offers a thoroughly modern, relaxed bar experience. It's a tiny place, although there are rooms upstairs. Good food.

Point 101
101 New Oxford Street, WC1 (020 7379 3112). Tottenham Court Road tube. **Open** 10am-2am Mon-Thur; 10am-2.30am Fri, Sat; noon-11.30pm Sun. **Map 6 K6**
This retro-feel bar beneath Centrepoint is prodigiously popular. Looking rather like a bus station from outside and a student union bar from within, the ground floor can seem a little desolate but livens up when the party crowd floods in for the nightly DJs.

Truckles of Pied Bull Yard
off Bury Place, WC1 (020 7404 5338). Holborn tube. **Open** 11am-10pm Mon-Fri; 11.30am-3pm Sat. **Map 6 L5**
One of the large chain of Davy's wine bars, this branch boasts a spacious two-floor interior and an attractive paved courtyard. All the classic bottles are sold, from claret to sherry to port. Good grub rounds things off.

Chelsea & South Kensington

Orange Brewery
37 Pimlico Road, SW1 (020 7730 5984). Sloane Square tube/11, 211 bus. **Open** 11am-11pm Mon-Sat; noon-10.30pm Sun. **Map 7 G11**
One of a growing number of microbreweries in London. Seasonal beers and special one-offs top up the range on tap. The place itself looks a bit too done-up in a tied-house make-over sort of way.

Phene Arms
9 Phene Street, SW3 (020 7352 3294). Sloane Square or South Kensington tube. **Open** 11am-11pm Mon-Sat; noon-10.30pm Sun. **Map 4 E12**
This excellent local, midway between King's Road and Chelsea Embankment, is full of (slightly eccentric) character, and has a fine summer terrace. Oh, and George Best has been spotted here.

The City

City Limits
16-18 Brushfield Street, E1 (020 7377 9877). Liverpool Street tube/rail. **Open** 11.30am-3pm, 5-10pm, Mon-Fri. **Map 10 R5**
Wine evangelist David Hughes' first-floor bar is a favourite of the slightly more sophisticated suits. Sample some unusual bottles in the small, airy and light bar room.

Jamaica Wine House
St Michael's Alley, off Cornhill, EC3 (020 7626 9496). Bank tube/DLR. **Open** 11am-11pm Mon-Fri. **Map 12 Q6**
This one-time haunt of London's rum merchants is a wonderfully theme-free drinking hole, despite its resemblance to a BBC Victorian costume drama set.

Old Dr Butler's Head
2 Mason's Avenue (between Coleman Street & Basinghall Street), EC2 (020 7606 3504). Bank tube/DLR/Moorgate tube/rail. **Open** 11am-11pm Mon-Fri. **Map 11 P6**
A classic, crusty old spit 'n' sawdust City pub. Constructed in 1610 by James I's physician William Butler, and rebuilt after the Great Fire, it's comfortingly dark and woody – and heaving at lunchtimes.

Water Poet
9 Stoney Lane, E1 (020 7626 4994). Liverpool Street tube/rail. **Open** 7.30am-11pm Mon-Fri. **Map 12 R6**
The drinking area of this popular ersatz New York bar is at one end of the long, low, white-painted room; the restaurant is at the other. Part of the Slug & Lettuce chain.

Ye Olde Mitre
1 Ely Court, off Ely Place, EC1 (020 7405 4751). Chancery Lane tube/Farringdon tube/rail. **Open** 11am-11pm Mon-Fri. **Map 9 N5**
A real step back in time. Down a forgotten alleyway stands this venerable sixteenth-century inn, complete with black beams and yellowing walls.

Covent Garden

The American Bar
Savoy Hotel, Strand, WC2 (020 7836 4343). Charing Cross tube/rail. **Open** 11am-11pm Mon-Sat; noon-3pm, 7-10.30pm, Sun. **Map 8 L7**
This art deco period piece is surprisingly relaxed for the cocktail bar of a five-star hotel. The drinks are first class, and come with endlessly replenished crisps and olives. Dress: jacket for men (no jeans).

Angel
61 St Giles High Street, WC2 (020 7240 2876). Tottenham Court Road tube. **Open** 11am-11pm Mon-Sat; noon-10.30pm Sun. **Map 6 K6**
The trendy bars are closing in, but this admirably scruffy trad pub (with tables outside in the garden) remains tremendously and deservedly popular. And the draught beer, for London, is astonishingly cheap.

Bar des Amis
11-14 Hanover Place, WC2 (020 7379 3444). Covent Garden tube. **Open** 11.30am-11pm Mon-Sat. **Map 6 L6**
A top-notch drinks list and a first-rate cheeseboard are two good reasons to patronise this agreeable basement wine bar.

Denim

4A Upper St Martin's Lane, WC2 (020 7497 0376). Leicester Square tube. **Open** noon-1am Mon-Sat; 3pm-midnight Sun. **Map 8 L6**

With its futuristic interior and womb-like red basement, Denim can't fail to make an impression. But, design aside, it also offers friendly service and decent bar snacks. Attracts a young crowd.

Freedom Brewing Company

41 Earlham Street, WC2 (020 7240 0606). Covent Garden tube. **Open** 11am-11pm Mon-Sat; noon-10.30pm Sun. **Map 6 L6**

Looking not unlike a pristine steamship engine room, this sizeable basement bar (formerly the Soho Brewing Company) is distinguished by its home-brewed beers and above-average food in the restaurant. There's a branch at 14-16 Ganton Street, W1.

Freud

198 Shaftesbury Avenue, WC2 (020 7240 9933). Covent Garden or Tottenham Court Road tube. **Open** 11am-11pm Mon-Sat; noon-10.30pm Sun. **Map 6 L6**

A basement bar, enhanced by huge candlesticks, distressed walls and slate tables. The cocktails aren't bad, there's a varied selection of international bottled beers and light dishes, and the clientele is agreeably disparate.

Fuel

21 The Market, Covent Garden, WC2 (020 7836 2137). Covent Garden tube. **Open** 10.30am-2am Mon-Sat; 10.30am-11.30pm Sun. **Admission** £5 after 10pm Fri, Sat. **Map 8 L6**

Red, brown and blue enliven the multi-arched stone cellar of this former fruit store. There are pizzas for the peckish, beers, cocktails and wines for the thirsty, and a mixed clientele.

Gordon's

47 Villiers Street, WC2 (020 7930 1408). Embankment tube or Charing Cross tube/rail. **Open** 11am-11pm Mon-Sat. **Map 8 L7**

Located in a dimly lit cellar, this classic wine bar scores highly for atmosphere. Prices are low, with fortified wines a strength. Fairly basic food sops up the booze admirably.

Lamb & Flag

33 Rose Street, WC2 (020 7497 9504). Covent Garden tube. **Open** 11am-11pm Mon-Thur; 11am-10.45pm Fri, Sat; noon-10.30pm Sun. **Map 8 L7**

A small, rickety pub tucked up a side alley. In the seventeenth century, Dryden was beaten up here – now it's a popular meeting place and one of the only decent pubs in Covent Garden. Upstairs is quieter – but not much.

Late-night liquor

Chucked out of the pub at 11pm? Here's a selection of central London places with late licences. The times listed are the official closing times, as opposed to when last orders are taken. Be aware that many of the venues below will have bouncers on the doors after hours, some of whom will have poor attitudes. If your face (and clothes) fit, you'll get in; if they don't, you won't, and there's no point arguing. For further late-opening places, *see pages 244* **Club bars**.

Bloomsbury & Fitzrovia

Point 101 *see p191.*

Sevilla Mía *22 Hanway Street, W1.* 1am Mon-Sat; midnight Sun. **Map 6 K5**

Covent Garden

Denim *see p192;* **Fuel** *see p192.*

Café Baroque *33 Southampton Street, WC2.* Midnight Mon-Sat. **Map 8 L7**

Covent Garden Wine Bar *1-2 The Piazza, WC2.* Midnight daily. **Map 8 L6**

La Perla *28 Maiden Lane, WC2.* Midnight Mon-Sat. **Map 8 L7**

Queen Mary *Victoria Embankment, WC2.* Midnight Fri, Sat; drinks in club until 2am. **Map 8 M7**

Roadhouse *Jubilee Hall, 35 The Piazza, WC2.* 3am Mon-Sat. **Map 8 L7**

Saint *8 Great Newport Street, WC2.* 1am Mon; 2am Tue-Thur; 3am Fri, Sat. **Map 8 K6**

Salsa! *96 Charing Cross Road, WC2.* 2am Mon-Sat. **Map 6 K6**

The Spot *29 Maiden Lane, WC2.* 1am daily. **Map 8 L6**

Holborn & Clerkenwell

Fluid *see p195;* **Match** *see p195.*

Mint *182-186 St John Street, EC1.* Midnight Mon-Sat. **Map 9 04**

Vic Naylor *38-40 St John Street, EC1.* Midnight Mon-Thur, Sat; 1am Fri. **Map 9 O5**

Marylebone

Mash *19-21 Great Portland Street, W1.* 1am Mon, Tue; 2am Wed-Sat. **Map 5 H5**

Mayfair

Trader Vic's *and* **Windows** *see p196.*

Dover Street *8-10 Dover Street, W1.* 3am Mon-Sat. **Map 7 J7**

Havana *17 Hanover Square, W1.* 2am Mon-Wed; 3am Thur-Sat; 1am Sun. **Map 5 H6**

Q Bar *12 New Burlington Street, W1.* 3am Mon-Sat. **Map 7 J7**

Holborn & Clerkenwell

Bleeding Heart

Bleeding Heart Yard, off Greville Street, EC1 (020 7242 8238). Chancery Lane tube or Farringdon tube/rail. **Open** noon-11pm Mon-Fri. **Map 9 N5**

Restored in recent years to its 1746 origins, this popular, jolly, informal and occasionally chaotic wine bar (with a smarter dining area) has a tremendous list, with plenty of choice under £15 a bottle.

Café Kick

43 Exmouth Market, EC1 (020 7837 8077). Farringdon tube/rail. **Open** 11am-11pm Mon-Sat. **Map 9 N4**

A shrine to table football, Café Kick is the scene of spirited contests on the (as the French would say) *babyfoot* tables. After joining battle, you can relax at the bar at the back with a bottle of beer or a cup of coffee.

Cicada

132-136 St John Street, EC1 (020 7608 1550). Farringdon tube/rail. Bar **Open** noon-11pm Mon-Fri; 6-11pm Sat. **Map 9 O5**

Cicada's pleasingly butch, modernist interior is a fine space, with rough-hewn surfaces and big windows. Pan-oriental food is available in the bar and restaurant. Trendy, but laid-back.

Atmospheric **Jerusalem Tavern**. *See p195.*

Soho

Cork & Bottle *see p196.*

Atlantic Bar & Grill *20 Glasshouse Street, W1.* 3am Mon-Sat. **Map 7 J7**

Bar Rumba *36 Shaftesbury Avenue, W1.* 3.30am Mon, Wed, Thur; 3am Tue; 4am Fri; 6am Sat; 2am Sun. **Map 8 K7**

Bar Soho *23-25 Old Compton Street, W1.* 1am Mon-Thur; 3am Fri, Sat. **Map 6 K6**

Circus *1 Upper James Street, W1.* 1.30am Mon-Thur; 3.30am Fri, Sat. **Map 7 J6**

De Hems *11 Macclesfield Street (between Shaftesbury Avenue & Gerrard Street), W1.* Midnight Mon-Sat. **Map 8 K6**

Detroit *35 Earlham Street, WC2.* Midnight Mon-Sat. **Map 6 L6**

Little Italy *21 Frith Street, W1.* 3am Mon-Sat. **Map 6 K6**

Lupo *50 Dean Street, W1.* Midnight Mon; 1am Tue; 2am Wed; 3am Thur-Sat. **Map 6 K6**

Mezzo *100 Wardour Street, W1.* 1am Mon-Thur, Sun; 3am Fri, Sat. **Map 6 K6**

Mondo *12-13 Greek Street, W1.* 3am Mon-Sat. **Map 6 K6**

O Bar *83 Wardour Street, W1.* 3am Mon-Sat. **Map 6 K6**

Sak *49 Greek Street, W1.* 2am Mon, Tue; 3am Wed-Sat. **Map 6 K6**

Signor Zilli *40-41 Dean Street, W1.* 1am Mon-Sat. **Map 6 K6**

Soho Spice *124-126 Wardour Street, W1.* 11.30pm Mon-Thur; 2.30am Fri, Sat. **Map 6 K6**

Tiger Tiger *29 Haymarket, SW1.* 3am Mon-Sat. **Map 8 K7**

South Bank

Auberge *see p197.*

Victoria

Boisdale *see p197.*

North London

Bar Gansa *see p197;* **Bierodrome** *see p197.*

East London

Cantaloupe *see p198;* **Great Eastern Dining Room** *see p198;* **Home** *see p198;* **Hoxton Square Bar & Kitchen** *see p198;* **Shoreditch Electricity Showrooms** *see p198.*

South London

Brixtonian Havana Club *see p198.*

West London

Wine Gallery *see p199.*

The Eagle

159 Farringdon Road, EC1 (020 7837 1353). Farringdon tube/rail. **Open** noon-11pm Mon-Sat; noon-5pm Sun. **Map 9 N4**

London's trail-blazing gastropub continues to be ridiculously popular: arrive early if you want any hope of a seat. Happily, the quality of the mainly Med dishes is high. Many wines are available by the glass.

Fluid

40 Charterhouse Street, EC1 (020 7253 3444). Farringdon tube/rail. **Open** noon-midnight Tue, Wed; noon-2am Thur, Fri; 6.30pm-2am Sat; 12.30pm-midnight Sun. **Map 9 O5**

A combination of cool design and Japanese food and drink, Fluid is yet another addition to the sky-rocketing number of trendy Clerkenwell bars. There are DJs Thursdays to Sundays. An admission charge may be required on certain nights, but this is never usually more than a couple of pounds.

Fox & Anchor

115 Charterhouse Street, EC1 (020 7253 4838). Farringdon tube/rail. **Open** 7am-11pm Mon-Fri. **Map 9 O5**

Note the opening hours of this unique pub: they are designed to meet the needs of workers at Smithfield's meat market (and, unintentionally, post-clubbers). The beer is good, and food is top-of-the-range butties with the emphasis on fried flesh.

Jerusalem Tavern

55 Britton Street, EC1 (020 7490 4281). Farringdon tube/rail. **Open** 9am-11pm Mon-Fri. **Map 9 O5**

All of Farringdon's media circus seem to squeeze into this tiny reconstructed Georgian parlour with its original fires, partitioned cubicles and distempered walls. A major reason is the outstanding beers from St Peter's Brewery in Suffolk.

L.e.d

171 Farringdon Road, EC1 (020 7278 4400). Farringdon tube/rail. **Open** noon-midnight Mon-Sat. **Map 9 N4**

Yet another minimalist Farringdon style bar. Warmth is provided by cheery staff and the crimson, womb-like basement lounge with its black '70s-style sofas, huge TV and Playstation consoles.

Match

45-47 Clerkenwell Road, EC1 (020 7250 4002). Farringdon tube/rail. **Open** 11am-midnight Mon-Fri; 6pm-midnight Sat. **Map 9 O4**

Match is that rare thing: a genuine, modern cocktail bar. Expect louche leather sofas, low lighting and a thoroughly '90s blend of funked-up and classic Martinis, short hits, (fresh) fruity confections and the frankly dangerous.

Knightsbridge

Grenadier

Old Barrack Yard, off Wilton Row, SW1 (020 7235 3074). Hyde Park Corner or Knightsbridge tube. **Open** noon-11pm Mon-Sat; noon-10.30pm Sun. **Map 7 G9**

Famed Bloody Marys, monster sausage baguettes, a 200-year-old pewter bar and the ghost of one of the Duke of Wellington's soldiers (flogged to death for cheating at cards) are among the draws here.

The Library

The Lanesborough Hotel, Hyde Park Corner, SW1 (020 7259 5599 ext 5681). Hyde Park Corner tube. **Open** 11am-11pm Mon-Sat; noon-10.30pm Sun. **Map 7 G8**

The Lanesborough's book-lined bar has an old-fashioned air at odds with the rest of the lavishly decorated hotel. Great cocktails, great service and complimentary nibbles of a high standard. Dress: no jeans or trainers.

Nag's Head

53 Kinnerton Street, SW1 (020 7235 1135). Hyde Park Corner or Knightsbridge tube. **Open** 11am-11pm Mon-Sat; noon-10.30pm Sun. **Map 7 G9**

A charming little chatterbox of a pub off Wilton Place, where staff are noticeably friendly and newcomers are made to feel welcome. In summer, the lack of space means that drinkers end up spilling out into the mews.

Marylebone

The Chapel

48 Chapel Street, NW1 (020 7402 9220). Edgware Road tube. **Open** noon-11pm Mon-Sat; noon-3pm, 7-10.30pm, Sun. **Map 2 E5**

This award-winning bar has a simple, bare-boarded interior, a pleasant shaded garden, plenty of wines by the glass, good cask-conditioned ales and excellent food.

Dover Castle

43 Weymouth Mews, W1 (020 7580 4412). Regent's Park tube. **Open** 11.30am-11pm Mon-Fri; noon-11pm Sat. **Map 5 H5**

A damn fine pub with good cheap Sam Smith's beer. Tucked away in a little mews, the Dover Castle has plenty of inviting nooks and bags of atmosphere.

Windsor Castle

29 Crawford Place, W1 (020 7723 4371). Edgware Road tube. **Open** 11am-11pm Mon-Sat; noon-10.30pm Sun. **Map 2 F5**

A classic boozer of the old school. OK, so Thai food is available, but everything else is firmly trad, from the friendly staff to the grizzled regulars to the huge collection of royal memorabilia on the walls and signed celebs' photos above the bar.

Mayfair

Claridge's Bar

Claridge's Hotel, Brook Street, W1 (020 7629 8860). Bond Street tube. **Open** 11am-11pm Mon-Sat; noon-10.30pm Sun. **Map 7 H6**

Ever-green aristo hotel Claridge's opened a stunning new art deco bar to celebrate its centenary in 1998. Make sure you dress up and enjoy (and don't look at the bill).

L.e.d... *another futuristic Farringdon bar. See page 195.*

Trader Vic's
Hilton Hotel, Park Lane, W1 (020 7493 8000 ext 420). Hyde Park Corner or Green Park tube. **Open** 5pm-1am Mon-Sat; 5-10.30pm Sun. **Map 7 G8**
Spectacularly tacky and very pricey, but if you're in the mood for cocktails and kitsch, this Hawaiian-themed basement bar can be tremendous fun. On the 28th floor, **Windows** bar offers one of London's most spectacular spots to gaze out over the city while you sup.

Ye Grapes
16 Shepherd Market, W1 (020 7499 1563). Green Park tube. **Open** 11am-11pm Mon-Sat; noon-10.30pm Sun. **Map 7 H8**
Unlike most Mayfair pubs, Ye Grapes draws in drinkers from all social strata. Décor is inoffensively olde worldy, and the atmosphere lively and chummy.

Soho

Alphabet
61-63 Beak Street, W1 (020 7439 2190). Oxford Circus tube. **Open** 11am-11pm Mon-Fri; 4.30-11pm Sat. **Map 7 J6**
Very hip at the time of its opening a few years ago, Alphabet has become something of a victim of its own success. The drinks are good, but claustrophobes steer clear.

Cork & Bottle
44-46 Cranbourn Street, WC2 (020 7734 7807). Leicester Square tube. **Open** 11am-midnight Mon-Sat; noon-10.30pm Sun. **Map 8 K7**
Don Hewitson's 30-year-old basement wine bar is one of London's finest. When busy (which is most of the time) it can feel cramped and airless, but brave the discomfort for the superb wine list and good food.

Dog & Duck
18 Bateman Street, W1 (020 7437 4447). Piccadilly Circus or Tottenham Court Road tube. **Open** noon-11pm Mon-Fri; 6-11pm Sat; 7-10.30pm Sun. **Map 6 K6**
A tiny, cosy, old-fashioned pub, with a lovely Edwardian interior, engraved mirrors and green-and-orange tilework. Seating is restricted to a few bar stools and benches.

The Dog House
187 Wardour Street, W1 (020 7434 2116/2118). Tottenham Court Road tube. **Open** 5-11pm Mon-Fri; 6-11pm Sat. **Map 6 K6**
An intimate basement space with alcove seating and a trendy but friendly crowd. There's a large selection of flavoured vodkas, from fruity versions to red-hot chilli pepper.

French House
49 Dean Street, W1 (020 7437 2799). Leicester Square tube. **Open** noon-11pm Mon-Sat; noon-10.30pm Sun. **Map 6 K6**
This tiny, heaving and enormously enjoyable establishment has long been a haunt of writers and artists. Don't ask for pints here – they only serve halves, plus wines and spirits.

South Bank

Anchor Bankside
34 Park Street, SE1 (020 7407 1577). London Bridge tube/rail. **Open** 11am-11pm Mon-Sat; noon-10.30pm Sun. **Map 11 P8**
A historic riverside tavern that is, perhaps, a little too much on the tourist trail, but nevertheless offers atmospheric, eccentrically shaped rooms, a Thames-side terrace and the knowledge that Dr Johnson wrote part of his dictionary on the premises.

Auberge

1 Sandell Street, off Cornwall Road, SE1 (020 7633 0610). Waterloo tube/rail. **Open** 11am-midnight Mon-Fri; noon-11pm Sat. **Map 11 N8**

A discreet side entrance admits you to this vaguely ecclesiastical-feeling café/bar specialising in Belgian beers. There's a resturant upstairs.

Fire Station

150 Waterloo Road, SE1 (020 7620 2226). Waterloo tube/rail. **Open** 11am-11pm Mon-Sat; noon-10.30pm Sun. **Map 11 N8**

This fiercesomely popular bar – with a good restaurant at the back – used to be, surprise, surprise, a fire station. The high ceilings partially make up for the packed floor space.

George Inn

77 Borough High Street, SE1 (020 7407 2056). Borough tube/London Bridge tube/rail. **Open** 11am-11pm Mon-Sat; noon-10.30pm Sun. **Map 11 P8**

One of London's most celebrated boozers, the George is the city's only surviving galleried coaching inn. Its labyrinthine layout, outdoor tables and genuine atmosphere pull in local workers and tourists in equal measures.

Studio Six

Gabriel's Wharf, 56 Upper Ground, SE1 (020 7928 6243). Waterloo tube/rail. **Open** noon-11pm Mon-Sat; noon-10.30pm Sun. **Map 11 N7**

Notable mainly for its wealth of outdoor, close-to-the-river seating, Studio Six also offers a good selection of drinks and decent food. The interior is very basic; go on a sunny day.

Victoria

Boisdale

15 Eccleston Street, SW1 (020 7730 6922). Victoria tube/rail. **Open** *Back Bar* noon-11pm Mon-Fri; *Macdonald Bar* noon-1am Mon-Sat; noon-10.30pm Sun. **Map 7 H10**

The bar at this great Franco-Scottish restaurant (*see p168*) has the largest collection of malt whiskies in London. And the range of champagnes and cigars is equally impressive. Suits predominate, but the atmosphere is friendly.

North

The Albion

10 Thornhill Road, N1 (020 7607 7450). Angel tube/Highbury & Islington tube/rail. **Open** 11am-11pm Mon-Sat; noon-10.30pm Sun. **Map 9 N1**

Ivy cascades down the broad front of this evergreen Barnsbury pub. There is a good-size garden at the back beneath another ivy canopy.

Bar Gansa

2 Inverness Street, NW1 (020 7267 8909). Camden Town tube. **Open** 10am-midnight Mon; 10am-1am Tue-Sat; 10am-11pm Sun.

A small, lively tapas bar. The narrow, brightly coloured space, filled with small tables decorated with flowers and candles, is very popular.

Bierodrome

173-174 Upper Street, N1 (020 7226 5835). Angel tube/Highbury & Islington tube/rail. **Open** noon-midnight Mon-Sat; noon-10.30pm Sun. **Map 9 O1**

The many-faceted joys of Belgian beer are celebrated in this tremendously fun bar, which extends back into a minimalist wood-panelled tunnel of a room.

The Clifton

96 Clifton Hill, NW8 (020 7624 5233). Maida Vale or St John's Wood tube. **Open** 11am-11pm Mon-Sat; noon-10.30pm Sun.

A smart, trad establishment in a fine St John's Wood house. The tables on the leafy front terrace make this an agreeable summer hangout, while the conservatory ensures it is a pub for all seasons.

Crown & Goose

100 Arlington Road, NW1 (020 7485 8008). **Open** 11am-11pm Mon-Sat; noon-10.30pm Sun.

One of the original stripped-down gastropubs, the Crown & Goose has a laid-back café-like atmosphere during the day which slowly transmutes into a more upbeat boozy vibe in the evenings.

The Flask

14 Flask Walk, NW3 (020 7435 4580). Hampstead tube. **Open** 11am-11pm Mon-Sat; noon-10.30pm Sun. **Map** *see p103.*

Delightfully unmessed-around-with, this Hampstead old-stager, with its no-frills public bar and relaxing lounge bar, offers both superior beer and food.

The Hollybush

22 Holly Mount, NW3 (020 7435 2892). Hampstead tube. **Open** noon-3pm, 5.30-11pm, Mon-Fri; noon-11pm Sat; noon-10.30pm Sun. **Map** *see p103.*

If you're looking for quiet conversation and an unspoilt bar full of nooks and crannies away from the ostentation of Hampstead village, this is the place to come.

O'Hanlons

8 Tysoe Street, EC1 (020 7837 4112). Angel tube or Farringdon tube/rail/19, 38, 171A bus. **Open** 11am-11pm Mon-Fri; noon-11pm Sat; noon-10.30pm Sun. **Map 9 N3**

Take one pint of O'Hanlons dry stout (an unpasteurised, unfiltered gem) and one leather armchair. Add a plate of oysters and home-made soda bread plus good conversation, and you have the ingredients of a classic evening.

Sauce

214 Camden High Street, NW1 (020 7482 0777). Camden Town tube. **Open** noon-11pm Mon-Fri; noon-11.30pm Sat; noon-4.30pm Sun.

A small, intimate organic bar. The stark design is enlivened by bright tablecloths and soft lighting, and the nutritious juices are balanced by a decent booze list. Good food too.

East

Cantaloupe

35-42 Charlotte Road, EC2 (020 7613 4411). Old Street tube/rail. **Open** 11am-midnight Mon-Fri; noon-midnight Sat; noon-10.30pm Sun. **Map 10 R4**

Cantaloupe caters for Hoxton's new inhabitants (designers, artists, photographers *et al*), but thankfully it's not too posey. The place is large, with benches in the bar and a small restaurant area with a weekly changing menu at the back.

The Grapes

76 Narrow Street, E14 (020 7987 4396). West Ferry DLR. **Open** noon-3pm, 5.30-11pm, Mon-Fri; 7-11pm Sat; noon-3pm, 7-10pm, Sun.

Established in 1583, rebuilt in 1720, the quiet, characterful Grapes is mercifully off the coach-party trail and is many people's pick of the East End riverside pubs.

Great Eastern Dining Room

54-56 Great Eastern Street, EC2 (020 7613 4545). Old Street tube. **Open** noon-midnight Mon-Fri; 6pm-midnight Sat. **Map 10 R4**

A fabulous, very NOW space in a former warehouse with a mix of retro and modern detailing, excellent food and good drinks.

Home

100-106 Leonard Street, EC2 (020 7684 8618). Old Street tube/rail. **Open** noon-midnight Mon-Fri; 6pm-midnight Sat; 3pm-midnight Sun. **Map 10 Q4**

Basically a large basement filled with knackered sofas, skip-worthy tables and a relaxed, unpretentious crowd who pack in for the mix of club and retro music, and the buzz. Not to be confused with the club of the same name.

Hoxton Square Bar & Kitchen

2-4 Hoxton Square, N1 (020 7613 0709). Old Street tube/rail. **Open** 11am-midnight Mon-Fri; noon-midnight Sat. **Map 10 R3**

A frighteningly cool, austerely decorated (walls of sand-textured concrete) hangout, softened somewhat by comfy chairs and comforting food.

Prospect of Whitby

57 Wapping Wall, E1 (020 7481 1095). Wapping tube. **Open** 11.30am-3pm, 5.30-11pm, Mon-Fri; 11.30am-11pm Sat; noon-10.30pm Sun.

With flagstone floors, cast-iron hearths, little round windows and a famous Elizabethan pewter bar, this is an archetypal olde worlde inn. Dating back to 1520, and having once served Samuel Pepys, the pub now plays host to gawping tourists.

Shoreditch Electricity Showrooms

39A Hoxton Square, N1 (020 7739 6934). Old Street tube/rail. **Open** 11am-11pm Mon-Wed; 11am-midnight Thur-Sat; noon-10.30pm Sun. **Map 10 R3**

There's no doubt as to the former function of this now ultra-hip bar. The décor mixes battered tables and chairs with clean-lined booths at the back and throws in a lurid alpine scene for good measure. And the beer and food are also cool.

South

Alma Tavern

499 Old York Road, SW18 (020 8870 2537). Wandsworth Town rail. **Open** 11am-11pm Mon-Sat; 10.30am-10.30pm Sun.

A beautifully renovated pub, with a big central bar and giant painted mirrors, and – to one side – a dining room with a huge pine table (serving international chow). The wine list is excellent.

Belle Vue

1 Clapham Common Southside, SW4 (020 7498 9473). Clapham Common tube. **Open** noon-11pm Mon-Sat; noon-10.30pm Sun.

A mix and match spread of tables and sofas, friendly staff and excellent food draw a young, amiable crowd to one of Clapham's most relaxed pubs. The choice of wine is better than the beer selection.

Bread & Roses

68 Clapham Manor Street, SW4 (020 7498 1779). Clapham Common or Clapham North tube. **Open** 11am-11pm Mon-Sat; noon-10.30pm Sun.

With bare boards, classy photos on the walls, and lots of light and space, this is a relaxed spot to drink and one of the best places in London to pass a Sunday, when music from a different African city is featured each week.

Brixtonian Havana Club

11 Beehive Place, SW9 (020 7924 9262). Brixton tube/rail. **Open** noon-1am Mon-Wed; noon-2am Thur-Sat; noon-midnight Sun.

More than 300 types of rum and killer cocktails are dispensed from behind the bar of this exuberant, high-ceilinged bar and restaurant (*see p168*).

Mayflower

117 Rotherhithe Street, SE16 (020 7237 4088). Rotherhithe tube/188, P11, P13 bus. **Open** noon-11pm Mon-Sat; noon-10.30pm Sun.

The Pilgrim Fathers' ship moored here at the start of its fateful journey, and, with its creaking wooden floors, small, wood-panelled rooms and narrow passages, you get the feeling that the pub has hardly changed at all since then.

North Pole

131 Greenwich High Road, SE10 (020 8853 3020). Greenwich rail. **Open** 5.30-11pm Mon; noon-11pm Tue-Sat; noon-10.30pm Sun. **Map** *see p121*.

At last, a cool bar in Greenwich. Sip a cocktail in the 'Leopard Lounge', gaze up at the goldfish swimming in the chandeliers or nibble on the excellent food in the first-floor restaurant.

The Ship

41 Jews Row, SW18 (020 8870 9667). Wandsworth Town rail/28, 295 bus. **Open** 11am-11pm Mon-Sat; noon-10.30pm Sun.

Inside, the perennially popular Ship is a beautiful big room with huge windows, bare boards, oak tables, a restaurant to one side and a smaller bar at the back. But it really comes into its own in summer when the barbecue is cranked up.

Sun & Doves

61-63 Coldharbour Lane, SE5 (020 7733 1525). Brixton tube/rail then 35, 45 bus or Oval tube then 36 bus. **Open** 11am-11pm Mon-Fri; noon-11pm Sat; noon-10.30pm Sun.

A bright, clean, reconstructed boozer offering unfancy food and a vibrant atmosphere. The patio is perfect for alfresco drinking of cocktails, beers, fruit juices and a balanced range of wines.

Trafalgar Tavern

Park Row, SE10 (020 8858 2437). Greenwich or Maze Hill rail. **Open** 11.30am-11pm Mon-Wed, Fri, Sat; 11.30am-11.30pm Thur; noon-10.30pm Sun. **Map** *see p121.*

Hardly unknown, but still one of the best pubs in Greenwich, the huge Trafalgar makes good use of its riverside location with great views out towards the Millennium Dome.

White Cross

Riverside, Richmond, Surrey (020 8940 6844). Richmond tube/rail. **Open** 11am-11pm Mon-Sat; noon-10.30pm Sun.

One of Richmond's best-known riverside pubs, the White Cross lives up to its billing. There's nothing reconstructed about the décor, the good Young's beers and the killer Sunday lunch.

West

Albertine

1 Wood Lane, W12 (020 8743 9593). Shepherd's Bush tube. **Open** 11am-11pm Mon-Fri; 6.30-11pm Sat.

A timeless, understated wine bar: battered wood tables, dripping candles stuck into old bottles, and huge platters of wholesome grub. The long and comprehensive wine list is a treasure trove of gems at notably low prices.

Anglesea Arms

35 Wingate Road, W6 (020 8749 1291). Goldhawk Road or Ravenscourt Park tube. **Open** 11am-11pm Mon-Sat; noon-10.30pm Sun.

Locals pack the small, smoke-filled pub, waiting patiently for one of the prized tables in the back room where Dan Evans and his team dish up back-to-basic platefuls of nosh.

Archery Tavern

4 Bathurst Street, W2 (020 7402 4916). Lancaster Gate tube. **Open** 11am-11pm Mon-Sat; noon-10.30pm Sun. **Map 2 D6**

A textbook example of a traditional London boozer. There's no muzak, just good ales, good conversation and a good mix of punters.

Churchill Arms

119 Kensington Church Street, W8 (020 7727 4242). High Street Kensington or Notting Hill Gate tube. **Open** 11am-11pm Mon-Sat; noon-10.30pm Sun. **Map 1 B8**

A deservedly popular, award-winning trad pub, packed with Churchill memorabilia and a lively, mixed crowd, and with a good Thai diner at the back.

The Cow

89 Westbourne Park Road, W2 (020 7221 0021). Westbourne Park tube. **Open** noon-11pm Mon-Sat; noon-10.30pm Sun. **Map 1 B5**

There's more of an Irish look than feel to Tom Conran's tiny local, though the voices heard here are Trustafarian rather than County Cork. Seafood gets top billing in the bar food line-up. There's a separately run restaurant upstairs.

The Dove

19 Upper Mall, W6 (020 8748 5405). Hammersmith tube. **Open** 11am-11pm Mon-Sat; noon-10.30pm Sun.

Three small, low-ceilinged rooms huddle round the tiny central bar of this unspoilt 300-year-old tavern that proudly eschews the paraphernalia of heritage theme pubs. A small terrace looks over the Thames.

The Elbow Room

103 Westbourne Grove, W2 (020 7221 5211). Bayswater, Notting Hill Gate or Westbourne Park tube/7, 23, 52 bus. **Open** noon-11pm Mon-Sat; noon-10.30pm Sun. **Map 1 B6**

A pool hall like no other, with an industrial look but a relaxed feel. The long bar area widens out to the rear, where there are pool tables. As many people come here to drink – and nibble snacks – as to play.

The Westbourne

101 Westbourne Park Villas, W2 (020 7221 1332). Royal Oak or Westbourne Park tube. **Open** 5-11pm Mon; noon-11pm Tue-Fri; 11am-11pm Sat; 11am-10.30pm Sun. **Map 1 B5**

Phenomenally popular gastrobar where the good food is matched by the beer selection. By day it's relaxed and civilised; by night the front terrace heaves with Notting Hill's trendiest.

White Horse

1 Parsons Green, SW6 (020 7736 2115). Parsons Green tube. **Open** 11am-11pm Mon-Sat; 11am-10.30pm Sun.

Known locally as the Sloaney Pony, this invariably heaving pub provides a spectacular range of beers (60 bottled varieties, including wheat beers, smoked beer from Bavaria and a few Trappist ales) and at least six real ales on tap.

Windsor Castle

114 Campden Hill Road, W8 (020 7243 9551). Kensington High Street or Notting Hill Gate tube. **Open** noon-11pm Mon-Sat; noon-10.30pm Sun. **Map 1 A8**

Three cosy interconnecting bars and a lovely walled garden are the draws at this famous old pub. Go on a summer's day, grab a plate of sausages and a pint and lap up the sun.

Wine Gallery

49 Hollywood Road, SW10 (020 7352 7572). Earl's Court tube. **Open** noon-4pm, 7pm-midnight, Mon-Sat; noon-4pm, 7-10.30pm, Sun. **Map 3 C12**

Almost unbelievably, this smart wine bar, with a sun-trap of a patio, sells its wines at retail prices (bottles start at £3.50 and champagne goes for around £17.50 upwards). You do, though, have to eat to enjoy this unique perk.

Shopping & Services

Though London is well known as a mecca for shopaholics, it's not always easy to sort the class from the dross. Here's a round-up of the city's best stores.

SHOPPING DISTRICTS

In addition to the longtime magnets for shoppers – **Oxford Street**, **Covent Garden**, **King's Road** – **Regent Street** is now increasingly joining the pack, with high-fashion newcomers such as **Zara** (*see page 207*) ousting the dull china shops and sweater shops that used to typify the street.

If it's big US-type malls you're after, nothing beats the humungous **Bluewater**, off junction 2 of the M25 at Greenhithe in Kent (08456 021021), which is set in 50 acres of parkland and includes more than 40 restaurants plus a 12-screen cinema. Alternatively, at junction 30/31 of the M25, just across the Thames from Bluewater at West Thurrock, Essex, is the smaller but perfectly adequate **Lakeside** (01708 869933).

YOUR RIGHTS

Statutory rights protect the consumer, and large or expensive items should come with a guarantee. You're entitled to a refund, replacement or credit note if goods are faulty (always keep the receipt). If you're returning goods for another reason, it's generally up to individual stores whether or not they refund your money. If you have a complaint about how your quibble was dealt with, report the offending trader to the **Trading Standards Department** of the relevant London borough. The **Office of Fair Trading** publishes free leaflets on all aspects of consumer purchase and runs a helpline (0345 224499; 9am-5pm Mon-Fri). The leaflets can also be obtained at **Citizens' Advice Bureaux** (*see page 325*). Staff at CABs should be able to advise you on your rights under the law.

LATE OPENING

Stores in central London are open late one night of the week (usually until 7pm or 8pm). As a rule of thumb, those in the West End (Oxford Street to Covent Garden) stay open late on Thursdays, while Wednesday is late opening in the chi-chi Chelsea/Knightsbridge/Kensington triangle.

Antiques

For **Bermondsey (New Caledonian) Market** and **Portobello Road Market**, *see page 223*. The following are arcades, featuring often hundreds of different stalls.

Admiral Vernon

141-149 Portobello Road, W11 (020 7727 5242). Notting Hill Gate tube. **Open** 5am-5pm Sat. **Credit** varies. **Map 1 A6**

One of London's smartest antiques arcades. Among the concessions you'll find textiles, lace, toys, oriental ceramics, art glass and fine drawings.

Alfie's Antique Market

13-25 Church Street, NW8 (020 7723 6066). Edgware Road tube/Marylebone tube/rail. **Open** 10am-6pm Tue-Sat. **Credit** varies. **Map 2 E4**

A sprawling multi-floor place (with almost 400 stalls), featuring, in the basement, paintings, art deco lighting, picture frames and pre-war kitchenalia. On the upper floors you'll find glass, prints, silver and much more. Cheaper than West End dealers.

Antiquarius

131-141 King's Road, SW3 (020 7351 5353). Sloane Square tube/19, 22, 319 bus. **Open** 10am-6pm Mon-Sat. **Credit** varies. **Map 4 F11**

Strengths at this antiques arcade, which boasts some 120 dealers, include art nouveau sculpture, photo frames, silver, jewellery and clocks.

Camden Passage

Camden Passage, off Upper Street, N1 (020 7359 0190). Angel tube. **Open** *indoor shops* 10am-5pm Tue, Thur, Fri; 8am-5pm Wed; 9am-5pm Sat; *outdoor stalls* 8am-2pm Wed; 8am-4pm Sat. **Credit** varies. **Map 9 O2**

In Islington, not Camden, this antiques-packed enclave has a number of specialist dealers, plus outdoor stalls on Wednesdays and Saturdays. At the northern end, the **Georgian Village** building contains some good art nouveau metalwork, blue and white ceramics and commemorative ceramics. **The Mall** is the most glamorous arcade with some fine porcelain, art pottery and watercolours.

Website: www.antiquescamdenpassage.co.uk

Grays Antiques Market & Grays in the Mews

58 Davies Street & 1-7 Davies Mews, W1 (020 7629 7034). Bond Street tube. **Open** 10am-6pm Mon-Fri; 11am-6pm Sat. **Credit** varies. **Map 5 H6**

Two locations: Grays Antiques Market specialises in antique jewellery (plus textiles, prints and some ceramics and glass), while Grays in the Mews is better suited to the bargain hunter. In the basement is a group of traders stocking pristine old toy cars and trains, plus a few dealers in antiquities. A new feature is **Biblion**, a purpose-built book room with 100 dealers selling antiquarian and second-hand books.
Website: www.graysantiques.com

London Silver Vaults

Chancery House, 53-64 Chancery Lane, WC2 (020 7242 3844). Chancery Lane tube. **Open** 9am-5.30pm Mon-Fri; 9am-1pm Sat. **Credit** AmEx, MC, V. **Map 6 M5**

These fascinating subterranean vaults, home to over 40 dealers, are packed with antique and modern silver. With prices from £20 to £20,000-plus, you should find something to suit you. Some traders also specialise in clocks and watches or jewellery.

Bookshops

It's also worth checking out the paperback-fest of the **Riverside Walk Market** (10am-5pm Sat, Sun and irregular weekdays) on the South Bank under Waterloo Bridge.

The big bookstore chains – **Waterstone's, Books etc** and **Borders** – have branches all over London; the largest are listed below.

General

Blackwell's

100 Charing Cross Road, WC2 (020 7292 5100). Tottenham Court Road tube. **Open** 9.30am-8.30pm Mon-Sat; noon-6pm Sun. **Credit** AmEx, MC, V. **Map 6 K6**

Although primarily known as an academic bookseller, Blackwell's has a huge selection of general titles, fiction and non-fiction.
Website: www.bookshop.blackwell.co.uk

Borders Books & Music

203 Oxford Street, W1 (020 7292 1600). Oxford Circus tube. **Open** 8am-11pm Mon-Sat; noon-6pm Sun. **Credit** AmEx, MC, V. **Map 5 J6**

An exhausting, exhaustive four-floor American-owned book store (plus a music department on the top floor, a café on the second and a **Paperchase** concession – *see p220* – on the ground). Unsurprisingly, it's particularly strong on American imports.

Foyles

113-119 Charing Cross Road, WC2 (020 7437 5660). Tottenham Court Road tube/14, 23, 24 bus. **Open** 9am-6pm Mon-Wed, Fri, Sat; 9am-7pm Thur. **Credit** AmEx, MC, £$TC, V. **Map 6 K6**

The sheer range of titles stocked makes Foyles well worth a visit; paperbacks are irritatingly arranged by publisher; staff could be a little less superior.

Where to find the old stuff...

Antiques shops in London are rarely solitary creatures, but tend to huddle together. If you fancy an afternoon's browsing, try the following enclaves.

Old Bond Street, New Bond Street, W1

Bond Street or Green Park tube.

Home to the top-notch shops and galleries. Gaze through their windows and dream.

Church Street, NW8

Edgware Road tube or Marylebone tube/rail.

Alfie's Antique Market (*see p200*) is at the eastern end, along with several shops full of nineteenth- and twentieth-century objects.

Kensington Church Street, W8

High Street Kensington tube.

Specialist dealers with some intimidatingly grand objects of desire.

King's Road/New King's Road, SW3, SW6

Fulham Broadway tube.

Everything from the sublime to the everyday is available on both these roads. Combine a trip with a visit to **Antiquarius** (*see p200*).

Lillie Road, SW6

Fulham Broadway or Hammersmith tube/ 11, 74 bus.

A cluster of shops offering a mixed bag of decorative antiques.

Portobello Road/Westbourne Grove, W11

Notting Hill Gate tube.

Push through the hordes who invade each Saturday; don't be afraid to haggle. *See p223.*

Tower Bridge Road, SE1

Borough or Tower Hill tube/London Bridge tube/ rail/Tower Gateway DLR.

Home to several furniture warehouses. There are a few bargains, but you'll have to be on your toes. A vast collection of antiques can be found at nearby **Bermondsey (New Caledonian) Market** (*see p223*).

Get your hands on **Micro Anvika**. See p205.

Waterstone's
203-206 Piccadilly, W1 (020 7851 2400). Piccadilly Circus. **Open** 8.30am-11pm Mon-Sat; noon-6pm Sun. **Credit** MC, V. **Map 7 J7**
Now back in the hands of founder Tim Waterstone as part of the HMV Media group, Waterstone's continues to be a feisty player in the bookselling game. This huge new flagship store is Europe's biggest bookstore, and boasts a café, juice bar, Internet area, lounge bar and the **Red Room**, serving great Modern European food.

Specialist

Books for Cooks
4 Blenheim Crescent, W11 (020 7221 1992). Ladbroke Grove tube. **Open** 9.30am-6pm Mon-Sat. **Credit** AmEx, DC, MC, £TC, V.
These pint-sized premises hold 8,000 books about food, and a tiny café. Also, cookery demonstrations.
Website: www.booksforcooks.com

Children's Book Centre
237 Kensington High Street, W8 (020 7937 7497). High Street Kensington tube. **Open** 9.30am-6.30pm Mon, Wed, Fri, Sat; 9.30am-6pm Tue; 9.30am-7pm Thur; noon-6pm Sun. **Credit** AmEx, MC, V. **Map 3 A9**
An attractive, well laid-out shop. The ground floor has reading material, tapes, CD-Roms and videos. In the basement are non-fiction books, games and toys.
Website: www.childrensbookcentre.co.uk

Cinema Bookshop
13-14 Great Russell Street, WC1 (020 7637 0206). Tottenham Court Road tube. **Open** 10.30am-5.30pm Mon-Sat. **Credit** MC, £TC, V. **Map 6 K5**
A huge collection of books (some rare), magazines and stills.

Daunt Books
83-84 Marylebone High Street, W1 (020 7224 2295). Baker Street or Bond Street tube. **Open** 9am-7.30pm Mon-Sat; 11am-6pm Sun. **Credit** MC, £TC, V. **Map 5 G5**
Three floors of (mainly) travel books in a beautiful wooden-floored shop. Friendly, helpful staff.
Branch: 193 Haverstock Hill, NW3 (020 7794 4006).

Edward Stanford
12-14 Long Acre, WC2 (020 7836 1321). Covent Garden or Leicester Square tube. **Open** 9am-7.30pm Mon, Wed, Thur, Fri; 9.30am-7.30pm Tue; 10am-7pm Sat. **Credit** JCB, MC, £TC, V. **Map 8 L6**
Venerable Stanford's is London's best source of maps and has an enviable selection of travel writing and guides, gazetteers and globes.

Forbidden Planet
71 New Oxford Street, WC1 (020 7836 4179). Tottenham Court Road tube. **Open** 10am-6pm Mon-Wed, Sat; 10am-7pm Thur, Fri. **Credit** AmEx, MC, £TC, V. **Map 6 L5**
Comics, mags and books (SF, fantasy, horror).

Gay's the Word
66 Marchmont Street, WC1 (020 7278 7654). Russell Square tube. **Open** 10am-6.30pm Mon-Sat; 2-6pm Sun. **Credit** AmEx, JCB, MC, £TC, V. **Map 6 L4**
London's only gay and lesbian bookshop offers a warm welcome and an impressive selection of fiction and biography.
Website: www.gaystheword.co.uk

Grant & Cutler
55-57 Great Marlborough Street, W1 (020 7734 2012). Oxford Circus tube. **Open** 9am-5.30pm Mon-Wed, Fri, Sat; 9am-7pm Thur. **Credit** MC, £TC, V. **Map 5 J6**
The leading foreign-language bookshop in town.
Website: www.grant-c.demon.co.uk

Serpentine Gallery Bookshop
Serpentine Gallery, Kensington Gardens, W2 (020 7298 1502). Lancaster Gate or South Kensington tube. **Open** 10am-6pm daily. **Credit** AmEx, JCB, MC, £TC, V. **Map 5 J4**
From Adorno to Zizek, the SG carries the most comprehensive stock of art and cultural theory books in central London.
Website: www.serpentinegallery.org

Silver Moon Women's Bookshop
64-68 Charing Cross Road, WC2 (020 7836 7906). Leicester Square tube. **Open** 10am-6.30pm Mon-Wed, Fri, Sat; 10am-8pm Thur; noon-6pm Sun. **Credit** AmEx, MC, £TC, V. **Map 8 K6**
'Europe's largest women's bookshop' stocks fiction by women writers, plus biographies and non-fiction. The lesbian section is in the basement.
Website: www.silvermoonbookshop.co.uk

Sportspages

Caxton Walk, 94-96 Charing Cross Road, WC2 (020 7240 9604). Leicester Square tube. **Open** 9.30am-7pm Mon-Sat; noon-6pm Sun. **Credit** AmEx, DC, MC, £TC, V. **Map 8 K6**

Books on sport, fanzines, magazines and videos.
Website: www.sportspages.co.uk

Talking Bookshop

11 Wigmore Street, W1 (020 7491 4117). Bond Street tube. **Open** 9.30am-5.30pm Mon-Fri; 10am-5pm Sat. **Credit** AmEx, JCB, MC, £TC, V. **Map 5 G6**

The largest selection of spoken-word CDs and tapes in the world.
Website: www.talkingbooks.co.uk

Zwemmer Media Arts

80 Charing Cross Road, WC2 (020 7240 4157). Leicester Square tube. **Open** 10am-6.30pm Mon-Fri; 10am-6pm Sat. **Credit** AmEx, DC, MC, £TC, V. **Map 8 K6**

Photography, cinema and design are the specialisations at this charming link in the Zwemmer chain of specialist shops.

Antiquarian/second-hand

See also page 201 **Gray's in the Mews: Biblion**.

Bertram Rota

1st floor, 31 Long Acre, WC2 (020 7836 0723). Covent Garden tube. **Open** 9.30am-5.30pm Mon-Fri (appointment recommended). **Credit** MC, £TC, V. **Map 6 L6**

Established in 1923, Bertram Rota offers a wide-ranging selection of first editions from the 1890s to the present day.

Maggs Brothers

50 Berkeley Square, W1 (020 7493 7160). Green Park tube. **Open** 9.30am-5pm Mon-Fri. **Credit** MC, V. **Map 7 H7**

London's most august antiquarian bookshop sells pre-twentieth-century books on travel, literature, natural history, early printing, bibliography and pre-1950 first editions. It's best to make an appointment.
Website: www.maggs.com

Skoob

15 Sicilian Avenue, WC1 (020 7404 3063). Holborn tube. **Open** 10.30am-6.30pm Mon-Sat; noon-5pm Sun. **Credit** AmEx, JCB, MC, V. **Map 6 L5**

Impeccably well-ordered stock of second-hand non-fiction books on the arts and sciences. Skoob is 'books' backwards, in case you didn't know.
Website: www.skoob.com

Ulysses

40 Museum Street, WC1 (020 7831 1600). Tottenham Court Road tube. **Open** 10.30am-6pm Mon-Sat; noon-6pm Sun. **Credit** AmEx, DC, JCB, MC, £TC, V. **Map 6 L5**

This smart shop has probably the biggest collection of modern first editions in town. Books are kept in glass cabinets, therefore it's not really a place for browsing.

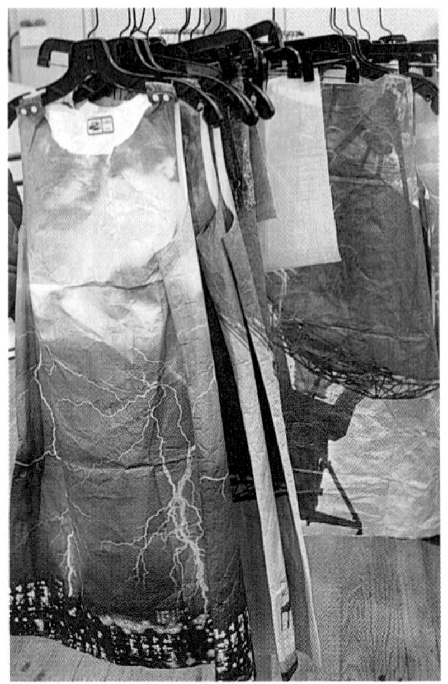

Groovy gear at **Urban Outfitters**. *See p210.*

Unsworths Bookseller

12 Bloomsbury Street, WC1 (020 7436 9836). Tottenham Court Road tube. **Open** 10am-8pm Mon-Sat; noon-8pm Sun. **Credit** AmEx, DC, JCB, MC, £TC, V. **Map 6 K5**

A roomy, modern interior holds remainders and out-of-print books as well as a decent antiquarian stock. The second-hand section is always worth a good browse.
Website: www.unsworths.com

Woburn Book Shop

10 Woburn Walk, WC1 (020 7388 7278). Russell Square tube/Euston tube/rail. **Open** 11am-6pm Mon-Fri; 11am-5pm Sat. **Credit** JCB, MC, £TC, V. **Map 6 K3**

One of the most fascinating bookshops in London run by affable owners with a special interest in anarchist and socialist subjects. The bow-fronted buildings along the street are a treat too.

Newsagents

A Moroni & Son

68 Old Compton Street, W1 (020 7437 2847). Piccadilly Circus tube. **Open** 7.30am-7pm Mon; 7.30am-9pm Tue-Sat; 8am-6pm Sun. **Map 6 K6**

This diminutive shop is packed from floor to ceiling with a vast array of up-to-date international newspapers and magazines.
Branch: 308 Regent Street, W1 (020 7580 3835).

Electronics

Tottenham Court Road, W1, is renowned for its electronics and computer shops. It's best to know what you are after and shop around for the best prices, and don't expect any social niceties from staff. It's worth asking for the cheapest price for a cash sale.

Computers & games

One of the best stockists of computer games is **Virgin Megastore** (*see page 228*).

Computer Exchange

32 Rathbone Place, W1 (020 7636 2666). Tottenham Court Road tube. **Open** 10am-6pm Mon-Sat. **Credit** MC, £TC, V. **Map 6 K5**

Tons of second-hand games, many of them reasonably current. The shop nearby, at 219 Tottenham Court Road, is a great source of used PCs and laptops. Prices are keen, and staff know what they're talking about.

Website: www2.cex.co.uk

Gultronics

52 Tottenham Court Road, W1 (020 7637 1619/ mail order 020 7436 3131). Tottenham Court Road tube. **Open** 9am-6pm Mon-Wed, Fri, Sat; 9am-7pm Thur. **Credit** AmEx, MC, £TC, V. **Map 6 K5**

From electric typewriters to fax machines and PCs, Gultronics stocks the lot, although laptops are undoubtedly what it does best. The special offers from week to week.

Branch: 45 New Oxford Street, W1 (020 7240 0070).

Micro Anvika

245 Tottenham Court Road, W1 (020 7636 2547). Goodge Street or Tottenham Court Road tube. **Open** 9.30am-6pm Mon-Wed, Fri, Sat; 9am-6.30pm Thur; 11am-5pm Sun. **Credit** AmEx, MC, £TC, V. **Map 6 K5**

A Mac specialist, although there's a decent range of PCs too. Good repair service. There are also shops at 16-17 and 53-54 Tottenham Court Road.

Hi-fi

The Cornflake Shop

37 Windmill Street, W1 (020 7631 0472). Goodge Street tube. **Open** 10am-6pm Tue, Wed, Fri, Sat; 10am-7pm Thur. **Credit** AmEx, MC, £TC, V. **Map 6 K5**

Mainly for buffs prepared to pay serious money for a system, but also stuff for separates fans on a budget.

Hi-Fi Experience

227 Tottenham Court Road, W1 (020 7580 3535). Tottenham Court Road tube. **Open** 10am-7pm Mon-Fri; 9am-6pm Sat. **Credit** AmEx, DC, MC, £TC, V. **Map 6 K5**

An excellent range of quality stock, eight demo rooms and expert staff. Home cinema a speciality.

Website: www.hifilondon.co.uk

Richer Sounds

2 London Bridge Walk, SE1 (020 7403 1201). London Bridge tube/rail. **Open** 10am-7pm Mon-Fri; 10am-5pm Sat. **Credit** MC, V. **Map 12 Q8**

Wide range of hi-fi separates at low prices, with a demo room. Branches all over London.

Website: www.richersounds.com

Antoni & Alison, *selling glad rags 'n' bags. See page 211.*

All the gorgeous shoes you could **Emma Hope** *for. See page 214.*

Photography

Jessops

63-69 New Oxford Street, WC1 (020 7240 6077). Tottenham Court Road tube. **Open** 9am-6pm Mon-Wed, Sat; 9am-8pm Thur; 9am-7pm Fri; 11am-5pm Sun. **Credit** AmEx, DC, MC, £TC, V. **Map 6 L5**

One of the biggest photographic shops in London, Jessops can cater for all your needs including film processing and repairs.

Website: www.jessops.com

Snappy Snaps

23 Garrick Street, WC2 (020 7836 3040). Leicester Square tube. **Open** 8.30am-6pm Mon-Fri; noon-5pm Sat. **Map 8 L7**

Probably the best of the high-street film processing chains.

Branches are too numerous to list here. Check the telephone directory for your nearest.

Fashion

Budget

Oxford Street is a good hunting ground for bargain seekers. Try **New Look** (nos.175 & 309; 020 7499 8497) for glitzy streetwear, **Tribe** (nos.67-71; 020 7494 1798) for natty lads' kit or **Jeffrey Rogers** (Unit G6, The Plaza, 120 Oxford Street; 020 7580 5545) for decent womenswear.

Amazon

1-22 Kensington Church Street, W8 (no phone). High Street Kensington tube. **Open** 10am Mon-Wed, Fri; 10am-7pm Thur; 9am-6pm Sat; noon-5pm Sun. **Credit** AmEx, DC, MC, V. **Map 1 B8**

A series of adjoining shops offering designerwear from the likes of Nicole Farhi, Jasper Conran and Calvin Klein with remarkable reductions.

H&M

261-271 Regent Street, W1 (020 7493 4004). Oxford Circus tube. **Open** 10am-7pm Mon-Wed, Sat; 10am-8pm Thur, Fri; noon-6pm Sun. **Credit** AmEx, MC, £TC, V. **Map 7 J7**

The Swedish chain's range of well-priced womenswear scores top marks for utility chic. The kids' clothes and ranges for bigger women are well worth a look too.

Branches are too numerous to list here. Check the telephone directory for your nearest.

Website: www.hm.com

Miss Selfridge

40 Duke Street, W1 (020 7318 3833). Bond Street tube. **Open** 10am-7pm Mon-Wed, Sat; 10am-8pm Thur, Fri; noon-6pm Sun. **Credit** AmEx, JCB, MC, £TC, V. **Map 5 G6**

Disposable fashion at disposable prices, primarily for teens, with a slant towards clubwear. Funky cosmetics are sold as well. Not surprisingly, there's a big concession of Miss Selfridge in Selfridges (*see p217*).

Design for life

London is packed with every big fashion name you can think of. If you've got the cash and the inclination to spend it in these places, you'll probably already know where they are. If you merely fancy a gawp at how the other 0.001 per cent live, then we list below where you'll find the major players.

If you want a wide range of labels under one roof, try **Harvey Nichols**, **Harrods** or **Liberty** (*see page 216*). Most shops are open 10am-6pm Monday to Saturday, with the Knightsbridge and South Kensington stores usually staying open until 7pm on Wednesday and the West End stores opening until 7pm on Thursday.

Chelsea, SW3
Sloane Square tube.
King's Road: Joseph (sale shop), World's End (Vivienne Westwood).

Covent Garden, WC2
Covent Garden tube.
Floral Street Agnès b, Jones (men), Paul Smith.
Long Acre Emporio, Nicole Farhi (men).

Knightsbridge, SW1, SW7
Knightsbridge tube.
Sloane Street Chanel, Christian Dior, Dolce & Gabbana, Giorgio Armani, Gucci, Hermès, Katharine Hamnett, MaxMara, Tomasz Starzewski, Tommy Hilfiger, Valentino.

Mayfair, W1
Bond Street tube.
Avery Row: Paul Smith (sale shop).
Brook Street: Comme des Garçons, Joseph, Pleats Please (Issey Miyake).
Conduit Street: Alexander McQueen, Moschino, Vivienne Westwood.
Davies Street: Vivienne Westwood.
New Bond Street: Calvin Klein, Donna Karan, Collezioni (Armani), Emporio, Fenwick, Louis Vuitton, MaxMara, Nicole Farhi (women), Polo Ralph Lauren, Thierry Mugler, Tommy Hilfiger, Yves Saint Laurent Rive Gauche.
Old Bond Street: DKNY, Gianni Versace, Prada.
South Molton Street: Browns, Pellicano.

South Kensington, SW1, SW3
South Kensington tube.
Brompton Road: Emporio, Issey Miyake, Betty Jackson, Paul Costelloe.
Draycott Avenue: Galerie Gaultier.
Sloane Avenue: John Rocha, Paul Smith.

Branches are too numerous to list here. Check the telephone directory for your nearest.

Pink Soda
22 Eastcastle Street, W1 (020 7636 9001). Oxford Circus tube. **Open** 10am-5pm Mon-Fri. **Map 5 J6**
This tiny shop is a mecca for fashion sophisticates and extroverts on a budget. Great, gleeful, finger-on-the-pulse gear for gals.

Top Shop/Top Man
214 Oxford Street, W1 (020 7636 7700). Oxford Circus tube. **Open** 9am-9pm Mon-Wed; 9am-9.30pm Thur-Sat; noon-6pm Sun. **Credit** AmEx, DC, MC, £TC, V. **Map 5 J6**
A revamp a couple of years ago left this as the world's largest fashion store. Rails of cheap, fashion-conscious clothes and shoes, some by top designers, plus a café and Essensuals hairdresser's.
Branches are too numerous to list here. Check the telephone directory for your nearest.

Zara
118 Regent Street, W1 (020 7534 9500). Oxford Circus or Piccadilly Circus tube. **Open** 10am-7pm Mon-Wed, Fri, Sat; 10am-8pm Thur; noon-6pm Sun. **Credit** AmEx, DC, MC, V. **Map 7 J7**
High-quality catwalk knock-offs at rock-bottom prices at this Spanish store. The impressive three-floor emporium adds to the glam feel.

Children

See also page 230 **Cheeky Monkey**.

Baby Gap/Gap Kids
146-148 Regent Street, W1 (020 7287 5095). Oxford Circus or Piccadilly Circus tube.
Open 9.30am-7.30pm Mon-Wed, Fri; 9.30am-8pm Thur; 9am-7pm Sat; noon-6pm Sun. **Credit** AmEx, MC, V. **Map 7 J7**
The clothes are spot-on, if a little pricey. Check the sale rail.
Branches are too numerous to list here. Check the telephone directory for your nearest.
Website: www.gap.com

Daisy & Tom
181 King's Road, SW3 (020 7352 5000). Sloane Square tube then 11, 19, 22 bus/49 bus.
Open 10am-6pm Mon, Tue, Thur, Fri; 10am-7pm Wed; 9am-6.30pm Sat; noon-6pm Sun. **Credit** AmEx, MC, £TC, V. **Map 4 E12**
There's an entire floor of hip clothes at this children's department store. Add in top toys, an in-store merry-go-round, a soda bar and a general hands-on play feel and you've got a winner.

Jigsaw Junior
97 Fulham Road, SW3 (020 7823 8915). South Kensington tube. **Open** 10am-6.30pm Mon-Sat; noon-6pm Sun. **4 D11**
Up-to-the-minute fashion for style-conscious kids with hefty moneyboxes. While parents shop, their offspring can play on the PlayStations, dive on a huge yellow rubber ball or play table football.

Branches: 126-7 New Bond Street, W1 (020 7491 4484); 190 Westbourne Grove, W11 (020 7229 8651); 83 Heath Street, NW3 (020 7431 0619); 41 George Street, Richmond, Surrey (020 8940 8386).

Trotters

34 King's Road, SW3 (020 7259 9620). Sloane Square tube. **Open** 9am-6.30pm Mon, Tue, Thur-Sat; 9am-7pm Wed; 10am-6pm Sun. **Credit** AmEx, MC, V. Great, trendy clothes for young fashion victims and admirably child-friendly service. There's also a hairdresser's and a children's library on site.
Branch: 127 Kensington High Street, W8 (020 7937 9373).

Fetish

Regulation

17A St Alban's Place, N1 (020 7226 0665). Angel tube. **Open** 10.30am-6.30pm Mon-Sat; noon-5pm Sun. **Credit** AmEx, MC, JCB, £TC, V. **Map 9 O2**
A massive warehouse packed with fetish gear and industrial clothing. There are 200 types of rubber and leather hoods alone.
Website: www.regulation-ltd.com

Mid-range

Egg

36 Kinnerton Street, SW1 (020 7235 9315). Hyde Park Corner or Knightsbridge tube.
Open 10am-6pm Tue-Sat. **Credit** AmEx, MC, £TC, V. **Map 7 G9**
Pricey, elegant clothing and beautiful accessories based largely on Chinese and Indian designs. A strange and seductive shop.

French Connection

99-103 Long Acre, WC2 (020 7379 6560). Covent Garden tube. **Open** 10am-7pm Mon-Wed, Fri, Sat; 11am-8pm Thur; noon-6pm Sun. **Credit** AmEx, DC, MC, £TC, V. **Map 8 L6**
A massive clothing store, with frequently stylish men's and women's ranges, toiletries and a café.
Branches are too numerous to list here. Check the telephone directory for your nearest.
Website: www.frenchconnection.com

Gap

30-31 Long Acre, WC2 (020 7379 0779). Covent Garden tube. **Open** 10am-8pm Mon-Wed, Sat; 10am-9pm Thur, Fri; noon-6pm Sun. **Credit** AmEx, JCB, MC, £TC, V. **Map 8 L6**
Nothing to thrill, perhaps, but a reliable first stop for nicely priced casuals.
Branches are too numerous to list here. Check the telephone directory for your nearest.
Website: www.gap.com

Hackett

137-138 Sloane Street, SW1 (020 7730 3331). Sloane Square tube. **Open** 9.30am-6pm Mon, Tue, Thur-Sat; 9.30am-7pm Wed. **Credit** AmEx, DC, JCB, MC, £TC, V. **Map 4 F10**
This huge emporium is the place to come for classic, but not po-faced English tailoring. In the Jermyn Street branch (no.87) Sloane meets Mod.
Branches are too numerous to list here. Check the telephone directory for your nearest.
Website: www.hackett.co.uk

Hobbs

Unit 17, Covent Garden Piazza, WC2 (020 7836 9168). Covent Garden tube. **Open** 10.30am-7pm Mon, Wed, Fri, Sat; 11am-7pm Tue; 10.30am-7.30pm Thur; noon-5pm Sun. **Credit** AmEx, DC, JCB, MC, £TC, V. **Map 8 L7**
Unadventurous but classically sleek and reliable staples and workwear are sold at this womenswear retailer. There's a range of shoes too.
Branches are too numerous to list here. Check the telephone directory for your nearest.

Jigsaw

126-127 New Bond Street, W1 (020 7491 4484). Bond Street tube. **Open** 10am-6.30pm Mon-Wed, Fri, Sat; 10am-7pm Thur. **Credit** AmEx, MC, £TC, V. **Map 5 H6**
Fashion meets art at Jigsaw's flagship store, designed by architect John Pawson. Artists exhibit their work amid the slick modern tailoring and quality fabrics. It's women-only at this branch; a large outlet at 9-10 Floral Street (020 7240 5651) in Covent Garden has a groovy range of menswear.
Branches are too numerous to list here. Check the telephone directory for your nearest.

Karen Millen

22-23 James Street, WC2 (020 7836 5355). Covent Garden tube. **Open** 10am-7.30pm Mon-Wed, Fri; 10am-8pm Thur; 10am-7pm Sat; 11am-6pm Sun. **Credit** AmEx, DC, JCB, MC, £TC, V. **Map 3 B9**
Smart suits and dresses with a twist, with much use made of interesting fabrics and wild colours. Sportswear and shoes are more recent additions.
Branches are too numerous to list here. Check the telephone directory for your nearest.

Monsoon

5-6 James Street, WC2 (020 7379 3623). Covent Garden tube. **Open** 10am-8pm Mon-Sat; 11am-6pm Sun. **Credit** AmEx, DC, JCB, MC, £TC, V. **Map 8 L6**
Lush, slightly ethnic clothes plus appealing dressier pieces adorned with colourful embroidery or beadwork.

Oasis

13 James Street, WC2 (020 7240 7445). Covent Garden tube. **Open** 10am-7pm Mon-Wed, Fri, Sat; 10am-8pm Thur; noon-7pm Sun. **Credit** AmEx, DC, JCB, MC, £$TC, V. **Map 8 L6**
Oasis will eventually interpret every important theme in the fashion world and bring it to the high street in a variety of fabrics.
Branches are too numerous to list here. Check the telephone directory for your nearest.

Ted Baker

1-4 Langley Court, WC2 (020 7497 8862). Covent Garden tube. **Open** 10am-7pm Mon-Wed, Fri; 10am-6.30pm Sat; 10am-7.30pm Thur; noon-5pm Sun. **Credit** AmEx, DC, MC, £TC, V. **Map 8 L6**

Shirts and ties are the standout items here, but all sorts of (men's and women's) clothes are stocked, including good clubby clobber in challenging fabrics.
Branch: 7 Foubert's Place, W1 (020 7437 5619).
Website: www.tedbaker.co.uk

Warehouse

96 King's Road, SW3 (020 7584 0069). Sloane Square tube. **Open** 10am-6.30pm Mon, Tue, Thur-Sat; 10am-7pm Wed; noon-6pm Sun. **Credit** AmEx, JCB, MC, £TC, V. **Map 4 F11**
A reliable high-street womenswear store that always responds quickly to new trends.
Branches are too numerous to list here. Check the telephone directory for your nearest.

Second-hand

Blackout II

51 Endell Street, WC2 (020 7240 5006). Covent Garden tube. **Open** 11am-7pm Mon-Fri; 11.30am-6.30pm Sat. **Credit** AmEx, DC, JCB, MC, £TC, V. **Map 6 L6**
Clothes from the 1950s to the 1980s – evening gowns hang alongside flares and ski pants. Tack, trash and glamour in equal measure.
Website: www.blackout2.com

Cornucopia

12 Upper Tachbrook Street, SW1 (020 7828 5752). Victoria tube/rail. **Open** 11am-6pm daily. **Credit** MC, V. **Map 7 J7**
A huge stock of twentieth-century womenswear in varying states of repair, plus a good range of ornamental jewellery. Something for every budget.

Oxfam Originals

26 Ganton Street, W1 (020 7437 7338). Oxford Circus tube. **Open** 11.30am-6.30pm Mon-Sat. **Map 5 J6**
The charity shop's range of oldies but goodies offers a well-chosen (and cleaned) selection of kit.
Branches: 123A King's Road, SW3 (020 7351 7979); 22 Earlham Street, WC2 (020 7836 9666).

Pandora

16-22 Cheval Place, SW7 (020 7589 5289). Knightsbridge tube. **Open** 9am-6pm Mon-Sat. **Credit** AmEx, JCB, MC, £TC, V. **Map 4 E9**
Probably London's largest and most famous dress agency, with sections devoted to the likes of Chanel, Armani and other big-name designers.

Steinberg & Tolkien

193 King's Road, SW3 (020 7376 3660). Sloane Square tube/11, 19, 22, 49 bus. **Open** 11.30am-7pm Mon-Sat. **Credit** AmEx, DC, JCB, MC, V. **Map 4 E12**
A massive and highly rated stock of second-hand gear and accessories, with a fine vintage designer clothing section.

Street

Boxfresh

2 Shorts Gardens, WC2 (020 7240 4742). Covent Garden tube. **Open** 10.30am-6.30pm Mon-Wed, Fri, Sat; 10.30am-7.30pm Thur; noon-5pm Sun. **Credit** AmEx, MC, V. **Map 6 L6**
Boxfresh currently favours a look on the casual side of sporty. As well as its own range, it can be relied upon to turn up interesting new labels. A womenswear range was launched relatively recently.
Website: www.boxfresh.co.uk

Burro

29 Floral Street, WC2 (020 7240 5120). Covent Garden tube. **Open** 10.30am-6.30pm Mon-Wed, Fri, Sat; 10.30am-7pm Thur; 1-5pm Sun. **Credit** AmEx, JCB, MC, £TC, V. **Map 8 L6**
Burro's Jarvis Cocker geek-chic is on the cusp between street and designer.

CM Stores

121 King's Road, SW3 (020 7351 9361). Sloane Square tube/11, 19, 22 bus. **Open** 10am-7pm Mon-Sat; noon-6pm Sun. **Credit** AmEx, MC, £TC, V. **Map 4 F11**
A vast open-plan space with enough hip streetwear labels to satisfy the fussiest workwear and clubwear devotee. It gets better and better.

Diesel

43 Earlham Street, WC2 (020 7497 5543). Covent Garden tube. **Open** 10.30am-7pm Mon-Wed, Fri, Sat; 10.30am-8pm Thur; 11.30am-7pm Sun. **Credit** AmEx, MC, £TC, V. **Map 6 L6**
Despite an ever-rising profile, Diesel isn't losing its cool. This Italian label keeps its finger on the pulse of new fabric technology and continues with the kitsch-retro look that made it famous.
Website: www.diesel.com

The Dispensary

25 Pembridge Road, W11 (020 7221 9290). Notting Hill Gate tube. **Open** 10.30am-6.30pm Mon-Sat. **Credit** AmEx, JCB, MC, £TC, V. **Map 1 A7**
A concise, fashion-forward collection of gear for men and women.
Branches: *womenswear* 9 Newburgh Street, W1 (020 7287 8145); *menswear* 15 Newburgh Street, W1 (020 7734 4095); 200 Kensington Park Road, W11 (020 7727 8797).

Duffer of St George

29 Shorts Gardens, WC2 (020 7379 4660). Covent Garden or Leicester Square tube. **Open** 10.30am-7pm Mon-Fri; 10.30am-6.30pm Sat; 1-5pm Sun. **Credit** AmEx, JCB, MC, £TC, V. **Map 6 L6**
For the achingly cool male, Duffer is a one-stop shop offering all the latest labels plus its own brand.

Shop

4 Brewer Street (basement), W1 (020 7437 1259). Leicester Square tube. **Open** 10.30am-6.30pm Mon-Sat. **Credit** AmEx, JCB, MC, £TC, V. **Map 7 J7**
Not your usual streetwear retailer, Shop has shelves and cabinets stuffed with sexy, fashion goods – Hysteric Glamour jeans, Stüssy T-shirts, Tocca slip dresses, etc.

Souled Out

Unit 25, Portobello Green Arcade, 281 Portobello Road, W10 (020 8964 1121). Ladbroke Grove or

Westbourne Park tube. **Open** 10am-6pm Mon; 11am-6pm Tue-Thur; 9am-6pm Fri, Sat. **Credit** AmEx, JCB, MC, £TC, V.
Ethnic floaty ensembles such as sari-bordered knee-length skirts, tunic dresses and tops.

Urban Outfitters

36-38 Kensington High Street, W8 (020 7761 1001). High Street Kensington tube. **Open** 10am-7pm Mon-Wed; 10am-8pm Thur; 10am-7pm Fri, Sat; noon-6pm Sun. **Credit** AmEx, JCB, MC, £TC, V. **Map 3 A9**
A great one-stop shop. Funky, affordable clobber, cosmetics, gadgets, magazines and homewares all under one roof.

Suit hire

Moss Bros

88 Regent Street, W1 (020 7494 0666). Oxford Circus or Piccadilly Circus tube. **Open** 9am-6pm Mon-Wed, Fri; 9am-7pm Thur, Sat; 11am-5pm Sun. **Credit** AmEx, DC, JCB, MC, £TC, V. **Map 7 J7**
This shop and the Covent Garden branch have the widest selection, but all Moss Bros stores have long been famed for their hire services.
Branches are too numerous to list here. Check the telephone directory for your nearest.
Website: www.mossbros.com

Underwear

Marks & Spencer (*see page 217*) also sells excellent-quality yet affordable undies, and has recently gone all raunchy with a range designed by Agent Provocateur.

Agent Provocateur

16 Pont Street, SW1 (020 7235 0229). Knightsbridge tube. **Open** 10am-6pm Mon-Sat. **Credit** AmEx, MC, £TC, V. **Map 4 F10**
Kitschy women's lingerie with 1950s pin-up appeal, most of it from France and the States. Staff are laid-back and the atmosphere is fun and informal.
Branch: 6 Broadwick Street, W1 (020 7439 0229).
Website: www.agentprovocateur.com

Rigby & Peller

22A Conduit Street, W1 (020 7491 2200). Oxford Circus tube. **Open** 9.30am-6pm Mon-Wed, Fri, Sat; 9.30am-7pm Thur. **Credit** AmEx, DC, JCB, MC, £TC, V. **Map 7 J6**
R&P might be corsetière to the Queen, but there's nothing snobby about the place – and the fitters are so skilled they can tell a woman's bra size by sight alone. In addition to its own-brand underwear, you'll find La Perla, Gottex and Prima Donna, plus swimwear and nightwear.
Branch: 2 Hans Road, SW3 (020 7589 9293).
Website: www.rigbyandpeller.com

Wolford

3 South Molton Street, W1 (020 7499 2549). Bond Street tube. **Open** 10am-6pm Mon-Wed, Fri, Sat; 10am-7pm Thur. **Credit** AmEx, DC, JCB, MC, £TC, V. **Map 5 H6**
Wolford has cornered the fashion-oriented hosiery market. Styles range from simple to sexy.
Branch: 28A Kensington Church Street, W8 (020 7937 2995).
Website: www.wolford.com

Unusual sizes

Base

55 Monmouth Street, WC2 (020 7240 8914). Leicester Square tube. **Open** 10am-6pm Mon-Sat. **Credit** AmEx, DC, MC, £TC, V. **Map 6 L6**
Sizes 16-28 are sold at Base, in both pricey and more affordable ranges.

High & Mighty

81-83 Knightsbridge, SW1 (020 7589 7454). Knightsbridge tube. **Open** 9am-6pm Mon, Tue, Thur-Sat; 9am-6.30pm Wed. **Credit** AmEx, DC, MC, £TC, V. **Map 4 F9**
Men over 6ft 2in (1m 88cm) and/or with waistlines measuring 44-60in (112cm-152cm) find salvation here. There are suits, shirts and casualwear.
Branches: 145-147 Edgware Road, W2 (020 7723 8754); The Plaza, 120 Oxford Street, W1 (020 7436 4861).
Website: www.highandmighty.co.uk

Sixteen 47

69 Gloucester Avenue, NW1 (020 7483 4174). Chalk Farm or Camden Town tube. **Open** 10am-6pm Tue-Sat. **Credit** MC, £TC, V.
Set up by comedian/actress Dawn French and designer Helen Teague, this shop aims to offer the 47% of British women who are size 16 or over something a bit different. Designs are unstructured, comfortable and fashionable.
Website: www.sixteen47.com

Fashion accessories & services

General

Accessorize

Unit 22, The Market, Covent Garden, WC2 (020 7240 2107). Covent Garden tube. **Open** 10am-8pm Mon-Sat; 11am-7pm Sun. **Credit** AmEx, DC, JCB, MC, £TC, V. **Map 8 L6/7**
The place that proves that seasonal trends can make it to the high street at a fraction of the price. Beaded, feathery, flowery jewellery, hats, bags, cosmetics and toiletries.
Branches are too numerous to list here. Check the telephone directory for your nearest.
Website: www.accessorize.co.uk

American Retro

35 Old Compton Street, W1 (020 7734 3477). Leicester Square tube. **Open** 10.30am-7.30pm Mon-Fri; 10.15am-7pm Sat. **Credit** AmEx, JCB, MC, £TC, V. **Map 6 K6**
This Soho stalwart (in business for more than a decade) sells a great range of wittily camp accessories, bags, hats and cool clothing.
Website: www.americanretro.com

Sumptuous smellies are the order of the day at the **Aveda Institute**. *See page 221.*

Antoni & Alison
43 Rosebery Avenue, EC1 (020 7833 2002). Farringdon tube/rail/19, 38, 341 bus.
Open 10.30am-6.30pm Mon-Fri; noon-4pm Sat. **Credit** MC, V. **Map 9 N4**
Cheeky accessories, original T-shirts plus full mens- and womenswear ranges are sold in this former Victorian electrical works.

Emma Bernhardt
301 Portobello Road, W10 (020 8960 2929). Ladbroke Grove tube. **Open** noon-5.30pm Tue; 10.30am-5.30pm Wed, Thur; 9.30am-5.30pm Fri; 10.30am-6pm Sat. **Credit** MC, V. **Map 1 A6**
Importer of all things Mexican, EB has created Latin kitsch in W10. Technicolor, cheap and cheery.

Octopus
King's Walk Mall, 122 King's Road, SW3 (020 7589 7715). Sloane Square tube. **Open** 9.30am-6.30pm Mon-Sat; noon-6pm Sun. **Credit** AmEx, MC, V. **Map 4 F11**
Everything from the wacky to the tacky can be found at this accessories emporium. Bouncy hand-made rubber lamps, mirrors, bow ties and braces are among the biggest sellers.
Branches: 54 Neal Street, WC2 (020 7836 2911); 28 Carnaby Street, W1 (020 7287 3916).

Dry cleaning, laundries & repairs

Buckingham Dry Cleaners
83 Duke Street, W1 (020 7499 1253). Bond Street tube. **Open** 8am-6pm Mon-Fri; 9.30am-12.30pm Sat. **Credit** MC, V. **Map 5 G6**
Exemplary service is Buckingham's trademark.

Danish Express
16 Hinde Street, W1 (020 7935 6306). Bond Street tube. **Open** 8.30am-5.30pm Mon-Fri; 9.30am-12.30pm Sat. **Credit** AmEx, DC, MC, V. **Map 5 G5**
Danish Express will collect and return laundry (£2 charge). The same-day service is at no extra charge if the item is brought in by 10am.

KS Tailoring Services
Lower ground floor, 13 Saville Row, W1 (020 7437 9345). Piccadilly Circus tube. **Open** 9am-6pm Mon-Fri; 9am-4pm Sat.
An experienced and reliable company that can mend and alter almost any garment.

Michael's Shoe Care
7 Southampton Row, WC1 (020 7405 7436). Holborn tube. **Open** 8am-6.30pm Mon-Fri. **Credit** AmEx, MC, £TC, V. **Map 6 M5**
A chain of cobblers offering most forms of shoecare, plus scarves, belts, umbrellas and briefcases.
Branches: 66 Ludgate Hill, EC4 (020 7248 4640); 9 Camomile Street, EC3 (020 7929 3887); 11A New London Street, EC3 (020 7265 1991).

Hats

See also page 226 **James Lock**.

Stephen Jones
36 Great Queen Street, WC2 (020 7242 0770). Covent Garden or Holborn tube. **Open** 11am-6pm Tue-Fri (or by appointment). **Credit** AmEx, DC, MC, £TC, V. **Map 7 J7**
Wit and wonder are Jones's specialities. Fabulously versatile unisex stuff. Prices £45-£250.

Eastern Colours of

Green St.

Brilliant Shopping

UPTON PARK UNDERGROUND

Jewellery

Angela Hale
5 The Royal Arcade, 28 Old Bond Street, W1 (020 7495 1920). Green Park tube. **Open** 10am-6pm Mon-Sat. **Credit** AmEx, JCB, MC, V. **Map 7 J7**
Original, special occasion, art deco and 1950s pieces are Angela Hale's forte.

Argenta
82 Fulham Road, SW3 (020 7584 4480). South Kensington tube. **Open** 9.30am-5.30pm Mon-Fri; 9.30am-5pm Sat. **Credit** AmEx, JCB, MC, V.
Map 4 D11
One of the biggest selections of jewellery (in silver and other special metals) in London with over 1,000 wedding and engagement rings, many by contemporary designers.
Website: www.argenta.co.uk

Butler & Wilson
189 Fulham Road, SW3 (020 7352 8255). South Kensington tube. **Open** 10am-6pm Mon, Tue, Thur-Sat; 10am-7pm Wed. **Credit** AmEx, JCB, MC, £TC, V. **Map 4 D11**
Costume jewellery at its glittering best.
Branch: 20 South Molton Street, W1 (020 7409 2955).
Website: www.butlerandwilson.co.uk

Electrum Gallery
21 South Molton Street, W1 (020 7629 6325). Bond Street tube. **Open** 10am-6pm Mon-Fri; 10am-5pm Sat. **Credit** AmEx, DC, JCB, MC, £TC, V.
Map 5 H6
One of the city's widest selections of modern craft jewellery, with work by over 100 international designers represented.

Frontiers
37 & 39 Pembridge Road, W11 (020 7727 6132). Notting Hill Gate tube. **Open** 11am-6.30pm Mon-Sat; noon-4pm Sun. **Credit** AmEx, DC, JCB, MC, £TC, V.
Map 1 A7
Antique and tribal jewellery from around the world (particularly Asia and North Africa) displayed in a spacious white-walled gallery.

The Great Frog
10 Ganton Street, W1 (020 7439 9357). Oxford Circus tube. **Open** 10.30am-6.30pm Mon-Sat. **Credit** AmEx, DC, JCB, MC, £TC, V. **Map 5 J6**
Silver and gold chunky rings, meaty bejewelled rings and other in-yer-face jewellery since 1971.

Into You
144 St John Street, EC1 (020 7253 5085). Angel tube/Farringdon tube/rail. **Open** noon-7pm Tue-Fri; noon-6pm Sat. **Credit** MC, £TC, V.
Map 9 O3
A welcoming tattoo and piercing parlour with a strong line in body jewellery, including classic designs and more ornamental pieces.
Website: www.into-you.co.uk

Janet Fitch
37A Neal Street, W1 (020 7240 6332). Covent Garden tube. **Open** 11am-7pm Mon-Sat; 1-6pm Sun. **Credit** AmEx, MC, £TC, V. **Map 6 L6**
A small chain stocking work by 300 or so contemporary designers.
Branches: 25A Old Compton Street, WC2 (020 7287 3789); 188A King's Road, SW3 (020 7352 4401); 1 The Market, Covent Garden, WC2 (020 7379 8666).

Lesley Craze Gallery/Craze 2/C2+
34-35 Clerkenwell Green, EC1 (Lesley Craze Gallery 020 7608 0393/Craze 2 020 7251 0381/C2+ 020 7251 9200). Farringdon tube/rail. **Open** 10am-5.30pm Mon-Sat. **Credit** AmEx, MC, £TC, V.
Map 9 N4
This showcase for British contemporary designers is packed with beautiful and unusual work. No.34 specialises in pieces made of precious metals; Craze 2 is dedicated to jewellery made from non-precious materials; C2+ features a range of textiles.

Tiffany & Co
25 Old Bond Street, W1 (020 7409 2790). Green Park tube. **Open** 10am-5.30pm Mon-Fri; 10am-6pm Sat. **Credit** AmEx, JCB, MC, £TC, V.
Map 7 J7
The most romantic of fine jewellers. Prices are serious, but the range is spirited, not stuffy.
Website: www.tiffany.com

Leather goods

Anya Hindmarch
91 Walton Street, SW3 (020 7584 7644). South Kensington tube. **Open** 10am-5.30pm Mon-Sat. **Credit** AmEx, MC, £TC, V. **Map 4 E10**
Elegant, fashionable bags at high prices.
Branch: 15-17 Pont Street, SW1 (020 7838 9177).

Bill Amberg
10 Chepstow Road, W2 (020 7727 3560). Notting Hill Gate or Westbourne Park tube. **Open** 10am-6pm Mon, Tue, Thur-Sat; 10am-7pm Wed. **Credit** AmEx, MC, V. **Map 1 A5**
Known for his beautiful, brightly coloured soft leatherwork, Bill's bags are popular with the fashion pack. His Notting Hill shop is filled with distinctive clutch and shoulder bags, as well as cosmetic cases, watch cases and travel slippers.

Mulberry
11-12 Gees Court, St Christopher's Place, W1 (020 7493 2546). Bond Street tube. **Open** 10am-6pm Mon-Wed, Fri, Sat; 10am-7pm Thur. **Credit** AmEx, DC, JCB, MC, £TC, V. **Map 5 H6**
This flagship store carries the complete Mulberry range: quintessentially British clothes, leather bags and accessories.
Branches: 41-42 New Bond Street, W1 (020 7491 3900); 185 Brompton Road, SW3 (020 7225 0313); 219 King's Road, SW3 (020 7352 1937).
Website: www.mulberry-england.co.uk

Osprey
11 St Christopher's Place, W1 (020 7935 2824). Bond Street tube. **Open** 11am-6pm Tue, Wed, Fri, Sat; 11am-7pm Thur. **Credit** AmEx, JCB, MC, £TC, V. **Map 5 H6**
Handmade, modern bags that look even more expensive than they are. There are beautiful belts too.

Petals for your petal at **The Wild Bunch**. *See page 215.*

Shoes

If you've got the cash, try two of the biggest names in fashion shoes: **Jimmy Choo** (20 Motcomb Street, SW1; 020 7235 0242) and **Manolo Blahnik** (49-51 Old Church Street, SW3; 020 7352 3863). For something rather more trad, *see page 226* **John Lobb**.

Camper

39 Floral Street, WC2 (020 7379 8678). Covent Garden tube. **Open** 10.30am-6.30pm Mon-Wed, Fri, Sat; 10.30am-7pm Thur; noon-5pm Sun. **Credit** AmEx, DC, JCB, MC, £TC, V. **Map 8 L6**
Stylish, comfy Majorcan-made shoes for both sexes.
Website: www.camper.es

Dr Marten Department Store

1-4 King Street, WC2 (020 7497 1460). Covent Garden tube. **Open** 10am-7pm Mon-Wed, Fri, Sat; 10.30am-8pm Thur; noon-6pm Sun. **Credit** AmEx, JCB, MC, £TC, V. **Map 8 L7**
Five floors of long-lasting footwear and clothing.

Emma Hope

53 Sloane Square, SW1 (020 7259 9566). Sloane Square tube. **Open** 10am-6pm Mon, Tue, Thur-Sat; 10am-7pm Wed. **Credit** AmEx, JCB, MC, V. **Map 4 F10**
Elegant shoes in a range of materials by one of Britain's best-known designers. There's a bridal collection too.
Branches: 33 Amwell Street, EC1 (020 7833 2367); 207 Westbourne Grove, W11 (020 7243 6233).

Natural Shoe Store

21 Neal Street, WC2 (020 7836 5254). Covent Garden tube. **Open** 10am-6pm Mon, Tue; 10am-7pm Wed-Fri; 10am-6.30pm Sat; noon-5.30pm Sun. **Credit** AmEx, DC, MC, £TC, V. **Map 6 L6**
Shoes here have been produced without cruelty or environmental damage, whenever possible.
Branch: 325 King's Road, SW3 (020 7351 3721).

Office

57 Neal Street, WC2 (020 7379 1896). Covent Garden tube. **Open** 10am-7pm Mon-Wed, Fri, Sat; 10am-8pm Thur; noon-6pm Sun. **Credit** AmEx, JCB, MC, £TC, V. **Map 6 L6**
Streety footwear from the relatively sober to the decidedly funky.
Branches are too numerous to list here. Check the telephone directory for your nearest.
Website: www.officelondon.co.uk

Patrick Cox

129 Sloane Street, SW1 (020 7730 8886). Sloane Square tube. **Open** 10am-6pm Mon, Tue, Thur-Sat; 10am-7pm Wed. **Credit** AmEx, MC, £TC, V. **Map 4 F10**
Inventive and unquenchably trendy, Cox's creations are so popular that people queue to buy his wares.

Shellys

266-270 Regent Street, W1 (020 7287 0939). Oxford Circus tube. **Open** 10am-7pm Mon-Wed, Fri; 10am-8pm Thur; 9.30am-7pm Sat; noon-6pm Sun. **Credit** AmEx, DC, JCB, MC, £TC, V. **Map 5 J6**
A huge range of streetsmart boots, shoes and trainers for men and women.
Branches are too numerous to list here. Check the telephone directory for your nearest.

Tailors

See also page 226 **Gieves & Hawkes**.

47/47A Carnaby Street

Carnaby Street, W1. Oxford Circus tube. **Map 5 J6**

Westminster Council has ensured that the traditional Soho trade of tailoring will not completely die out by making it impossible for anyone to use these buildings for any other purpose. Businesses here include **Keith Watson** (020 7437 2327), **Franco Santoro** (020 7437 8440) and **Brian Staples** (020 7734 5069).

Ozwald Boateng
9 Vigo Street, W1 (020 7734 6868). Piccadilly Circus tube. **Open** 10am-6pm Mon-Sat. **Credit** AmEx, JCB, MC, £TC, V. **Map 7 J7**
Needle-sharp tailoring for men with a marvellous line in arresting colours. Bespoke starts at £1,500; ready-to-wear from £895.

Richard James
31 Savile Row, W1 (020 7434 0605). Green Park or Piccadilly Circus tube. **Open** 10am-6pm Mon-Fri; 11am-6pm Sat. **Credit** AmEx, DC, MC, £TC, V. **Map 7 J7**
Unusually, a trendy, friendly tailor on Savile Row, offering sharp suits cut in anything from cashmere to denim. Clients have included Noel Gallagher of Oasis and Madonna.
Website: www.richardjames.co.uk

Timothy Everest
32 Elder Street, E1 (020 7377 5770). Liverpool Street tube/rail. **Open** 9am-5.30pm Mon-Fri; 9am-4pm Sat; also by appointment. **Credit** AmEx, MC, £TC, V. **Map 10 R5**
One of the best of the new breed of (trad with a modern slant) tailors, also selling accessories, shirts and shoes.

Umbrellas & walking sticks

James Smith & Sons
53 New Oxford Street, WC1 (020 7836 4731). Tottenham Court Road tube. **Open** 9.30am-5.25pm Mon-Fri; 10am-5.25pm Sat. **Credit** MC, £TC, V. **Map 6 K6**
There's a vast array of umbrellas and walking sticks at this beautiful old shop, which opened in 1857. Walking brollies can be cut to size while you wait.
Website: www.james-smith.co.uk

Watches

City Clocks
31 Amwell Street, EC1 (020 7278 1154). Angel tube. **Open** 8.30am-5.30pm Tue-Fri; 9.30am-2.30pm Sat. **Credit** AmEx, DC, MC, V. **Map 9 N3**
Any make of watch repaired, and antique pocket and wrist watches restored at this century-old business. Another good repairer is **CR Frost & Son** (60-62 Clerkenwell Road, EC1; 020 7253 0315).
Website: www.cityclocks.co.uk

Simon Carter
15 Quadrant Arcade, 80-82 Regent Street, W1 (020 7287 4363). Oxford Circus or Piccadilly Circus tube. **Open** 10.30am-6.30pm Mon-Thur; 10.30am-7.30pm Fri, Sat. **Credit** AmEx, JCB, MC, V. **Map 7 J7**
Carter makes and sells his own retro-style design watches, many influenced by the 1920s to 1960s. Prices start at around £100.

The Swatch Store
313 Oxford Street, W1 (020 7493 0237). Bond Street or Oxford Circus tube. **Open** 10am-7pm Mon-Wed, Fri, Sat; 10am-8pm Thur; noon-6pm Sun. **Credit** MC, V. **Map 5 H6**
Stockist of all the 160-plus Swatch watches. Prices start at £25.
Branch: 104-106 Long Acre, WC2 (020 7836 7868).
Website: www.swatch.com

Florists

See also page 223 **Columbia Road Flower Market**.

Wild at Heart
49A Ledbury Road, W11 (020 7727 3095). Notting Hill Gate or Westbourne Park tube. **Open** 10am-8pm Mon-Sat. **Credit** AmEx, MC, V. **Map 1 A6**
Fabulous, if pricey, flora, sold from a stylish shop. Don't miss the original branch within London's chicest public toilet nearby on Westbourne Grove.

The Wild Bunch
17 Earlham Street, WC2 (020 7497 1200). Covent Garden tube. **Open** 10am-7.30pm Mon-Sat. **Map 6 K6**
A winning florist operating from several stalls at Seven Dials. All manner of floral styles are sold, from florid tropical blooms to a bunch of daffs, with the same easygoing charm. Staff also wrap your flowers splendidly.

Woodhams at One Aldwych
1 Aldwych, WC1 (020 7300 0777). Covent Garden or Temple tube/Charing Cross tube/rail. **Open** 10am-7pm Mon-Fri; 10am-6pm Sat. **Credit** MC, V. **Map 8 M6**
You'd expect a flower shop within the effortlessly stylish One Aldwych hotel (*see p147*) to be impressive, and it certainly is. Bold colours, innovative, architectural arrangements.

Food & drink

For department-store food halls, *see pages 216-7.* For fish, *see page 171* **fish!**

Bakeries & pâtisseries

For other café-pâtisseries, *see also page 180.*

& Clarke's
122 Kensington Church Street, W8 (020 7229 2190). Notting Hill Gate tube. **Open** 8am-8pm Mon-Fri; 9am-4pm Sat. **Credit** AmEx, MC, £TC, V. **Map 1 B8**
This minute adjunct to Sally Clarke's restaurant is crammed with luxury goods (preserves, chocolate truffles, Neal's Yard cheeses). But the 35 or so breads, from fig and fennel to oatmeal and honey bread, are the draw.

Departments of commerce

At their worst, department stores are jacks of all trades but masters of none. Happily, London is supplied with plenty of examples of the other end of the scale, offering high-quality service and encouraging innovation. You'll find most stores in the Oxford Street/ Regent Street and Knightsbridge areas, but be aware that 'department store' can be misleading. With the exceptions of Harrods, John Lewis, Liberty and Selfridges, most stores are primarily clothes shops with other departments usually little more than an afterthought.

Dickins & Jones

224-244 Regent Street, W1 (020 7734 7070). Oxford Circus tube. **Open** 10am-6.30pm Mon, Tue; 10am-7pm Wed; 10am-8pm Thur; 10am-7pm Fri, Sat; noon-6pm Sun. **Credit** AmEx, DC, MC, £TC, V. **Map 5 J6**

After a refit, this House of Fraser fashion leader (devoted mainly to clothing and beauty) has transformed itself into one of the best-looking – if not exactly the most imaginative – stores in London. The menswear is rather dull, the womenswear variable, but the fashion accessories room is worth a look.

Branches: George Street, Richmond, Surrey (020 8940 7761); **Army & Navy Stores** 101 Victoria Street, SW1 (020 7834 1234); **DH Evans** 318 Oxford Street, W1 (020 7629 8800); **Barkers of Kensington** 63 Kensington High Street, W8 (020 7937 5432).

Fortnum & Mason

181 Piccadilly, W1 (020 7734 8040). Piccadilly Circus tube. **Open** 9.30am-6pm Mon-Sat. **Credit** AmEx, DC, JCB, MC, £$TC, V. **Map 7 J7**

F&M is the last word in 'la style anglaise', selling the rest of the world an idealised version of upper crust Britain at its most dapper and well behaved. The ground-floor food halls are the main draws at this beautiful, stately old store, which comes complete with fancy-dressed assistants. On the floors above are thoroughbred designer womenswear (YSL *et al*), sober, sensible blokes' gear, antiques and furniture. If you need to chill out after all that retail therapy, head to the **Fountain** for afternoon tea.

Harrods

87 Brompton Road, SW1 (020 7730 1234). Knightsbridge tube. **Open** 10am-6pm Mon, Tue, Sat; 10am-7pm Wed-Fri. **Credit** AmEx, DC, JCB, MC, £$TC, V. **Map 4 F9**

Harrods celebrated its 150th birthday in 1999. The fabulous food halls alone fill seven elaborately decorated rooms and cover 3,250sq m (35,000sq ft), although not all departments are as inspiring. There are 60 fashion departments, and the toys are always worth checking out. However, there's little here that isn't done better in Harvey Nichols or Peter Jones (although Harrods certainly covers a wider field), and many visitors find the security staff intimidating – you will probably be turned away if your clothing is deemed too skimpy (which includes shorts). Still, if you can face the heaving crowds, nothing beats the Harrods food halls at Christmas time.

Harvey Nichols

109-125 Knightsbridge, SW1 (020 7235 5000). Knightsbridge tube. **Open** 10am-7pm Mon, Tue, Sat; 10am-8pm Wed-Fri; noon-6pm Sun. **Credit** AmEx, DC, JCB, MC, £$TC, V. **Map 4 F9**

Heaven for serial spenders and style groupies. Fashion occupies most floor space; over 200 labels are featured, although there are few surprises. Foodies are well catered for by the basement Foundation brasserie and the fifth-floor complex (food hall, café, bar and restaurant; *see p165*). For a treat, head to the Aveda Urban Retreat on the fourth floor. Harvey Nicks' window displays are legendary.

John Lewis

278-306 Oxford Street, W1 (020 7629 7711). Oxford Circus tube. **Open** 9.30am-6pm Mon-Wed, Fri; 10am-8pm Thur; 9am-6pm Sat. **Credit** £TC. **Map 5 H6**

John Lewis majors on areas neglected by other stores, particularly homewares and haberdashery, and is famed for its 'never knowingly undersold' policy. Fashion tends to take a back seat, although it has been pepped up of late. Kitchenware too is a forte. **Peter Jones** on Sloane Square (020 7730 3434) is part of the same group but with added snob value.

Website: www.johnlewis.co.uk

Branches: Brent Cross Shopping Centre, NW4 (020 8202 6535); Wood Street, Kingston, Surrey (020 8547 3000).

Liberty

214-220 Regent Street, W1 (020 7734 1234). Oxford Circus tube. **Open** 10am-6.30pm Mon-Wed; 10am-8pm Thur; 10am-7pm Fri, Sat. **Credit** AmEx, DC, JCB, MC, TC, V. **Map 5 J6**

The Arts and Crafts heritage and faux-Tudor building give Liberty a certain quaint charm, but the store hasn't rested on its laurels. It is fast gaining a reputation for the funkiest women's fashion in London, and most departments (especially accessories, furniture, fabrics and jewellery) offer an above-average selection of goods. The small space of the cosmetics department, on the ground floor, is intelligently filled with a mix of cult and big names.

Marks & Spencer
458 Oxford Street, W1 (020 7935 7954). Bond Street or Marble Arch tube. **Open** 9am-8pm Mon-Fri; 9am-7pm Sat; noon-6pm Sun. **Map 5 G6**
Knickers and ready-made meals make up a hefty proportion of M&S's sales. Although it is pushing its homeware and furniture ranges, its strengths remain affordable, well-made clothes and upmarket food. Yet laurels have been sat on and M&S has lost its way in recent years, becoming staid and unexciting and losing the hitherto unshakeable loyalty of many core customers. Attempts have been made to halt this, not least among them the hiring of the people behind Agent Provocateur (*see p210*) to design some raunchy underwear. There is another big M&S on Oxford Street (no.173), near Oxford Circus. At long last, from spring 2000, M&S will start taking credit cards.
Website: www.marks-and-spencer.com
Branches are too numerous to list here. Check the telephone directory for your nearest.

Selfridges
400 Oxford Street, W1 (020 7629 1234). Bond Street or Marble Arch tube. **Open** 10am-7pm Mon-Wed; 10am-8pm Thur, Fri; 9.30am-7pm Sat; noon-6pm Sun. **Credit** AmEx, DC, JCB, MC, £$TC, V. **Map 5 G6**
Selfridges (*see picture*) contains one of the best of London's food halls – featuring a staggering range of international foodstuffs – as well as the biggest cosmetics hall in Europe. A major refit has spruced up the store for the twenty-first century and raised its fashion profile even further (unusually, both men and women are equally well catered for). Selfridges' range of cosmetics is unrivalled in London, offering lotions, potions and make-up from the big names plus harder-to-find Bobbi Brown, MAC and the like. A large section of the ground floor is taken up by **Spirit**, selling gear by, among others, Ted Baker, Diesel, Oasis, Warehouse, Red or Dead, Karen Millen and home-grown Miss Selfridge.

Konditor & Cook
22 Cornwall Road, SE1 (020 7261 0456). Waterloo tube/rail/27 bus. **Open** 7.30am-6.30pm Mon-Fri; 8.30am-2.30pm Sat. **Credit** MC, V. **Map 11 N8**.
A mouth-watering array of cakes and pastries is baked on the premises; breads are supplied by **& Clarke's** (*see p215*). Many can be sampled in the café of the same name in the **Young Vic** theatre on The Cut, SE1.
Branch: 10 Stoney Street, SE1 (020 7407 5100).

Pâtisserie Valerie
44 Old Compton Street, W1 (020 7437 3466). Tottenham Court Road tube. **Open** 7.30am-10pm Mon-Sat; 9.30am-7pm Sun. **Credit** AmEx, DC, MC, £TC, V. **Map 6 K6**
A Soho institution: this venerable pâtisserie has a fine range of pastries, cakes and tarts.
Branches: **Maison Sagne**, 105 Marylebone High Street, W1 (020 7935 6240); 215 Brompton Road, SW3 (020 7823 9971); RIBA, 66 Portland Place, W1 (020 7631 0467); **Café Valerie** 8 Russell Street, WC2 (020 7240 0064).

Beer

The Beer Shop
14 Pitfield Street, N1 (020 7739 3701). Old Street tube/rail. **Open** 11am-7pm Mon-Fri; 10am-4pm Sat. **Credit** MC, £TC, V. **Map 10 Q4**
A wide selection of draught and bottled beers, plus the kit you need to brew your own.

Cheese shops

See also page 226 **Paxton & Whitfield**.

Neal's Yard Dairy
17 Shorts Gardens, WC2 (020 7379 7646). Covent Garden tube. **Open** 9am-7pm Mon-Sat; 10am-5pm Sun. **Credit** JCB, MC, £TC, V. **Map 6 L6**
More than any other shop, NYD is responsible for the renaissance in British and Irish farmhouse cheeses. Most of them are matured in cellars under the shop and reach the counter in a state of rare perfection. Oils, chutneys and breads are also sold.
Branch: 6 Park Street, Borough Market, SE1 (020 7378 8195).

Coffee & tea

Algerian Coffee Stores
52 Old Compton Street, W1 (020 7437 2480). Leicester Square or Piccadilly Circus tube. **Open** 9am-7pm Mon-Sat. **Credit** AmEx, DC, JCB, MC, £TC, V. **Map 6 K6**
Dispensing coffee since 1887. Coffee beans, teas, chocolates and equipment are crammed into these Soho premises, which are steeped in charm.
Website: www.algcoffee.co.uk

The Tea House
15A Neal Street, WC2 (020 7240 7539). Covent Garden tube. **Open** 10am-7pm Mon-Wed, Sat; 10am-7.30pm Thur; 10.30am-7pm Fri; noon-6pm Sun. **Credit** AmEx, JCB, MC, £TC, V. **Map 6 L6**

A veritable temple to the goddess tea. Every imaginable type of infusion is here, plus a wide range of teapots.

R Twining & Co

216 Strand, WC2 (020 7353 3511). Temple tube/ Charing Cross tube/rail. **Open** 9.30am-4.30pm Mon-Fri. **Credit** AmEx, MC, V. **Map 6 M6**
Almost 300 years in the business, Twining & Co's long, thin shop stocks a great selection of classy tea blends. There's also a museum of the firm's history.

Whittard

65 Regent Street, W1 (020 7734 2170). Piccadilly Circus tube. **Open** 9.30am-6pm Mon-Wed; 9.30am-7pm Thur-Sat; 11am-5pm Sun. **Credit** AmEx, MC, £TC, V. **Map 7 J7**
Quirky teapots, cups and saucers, plus an impressive range of teas and coffees, from the traditional to the indulgent.
Branches are too numerous to list here. Check the telephone directory for your nearest.
Website: www.whittard.com

Confectioners

See also page 226 **Charbonnel & Walker**.

Godiva

247 Regent Street, W1 (020 7495 2845). Oxford Circus tube. **Open** 9.30am-7pm Mon-Sat; noon-6pm Sun. **Credit** AmEx, DC, MC, £TC, V. **Map 5 J6**
Don't come here if you're counting the calories: you won't be able to resist the luscious handmade, hand-filled and hand-finished chocs. Seasonal goodies are a speciality.
Branches: 150 Fenchurch Street, EC3 (020 7623 2287); Selfridges, 400 Oxford Street, W1 (020 7629 1234 ext 3798); Harrods, 87 Brompton Road, SW1 (020 7730 1234 ext 4199); Brent Cross Shopping Centre, NW4 (020 8203 8886).

Rococo

321 King's Road, SW3 (020 7352 5857). Sloane Square tube. **Open** 10am-6.30pm Mon-Sat; noon-5pm Sun. **Credit** AmEx, JCB, MC, £TC, V. **Map 4 D12**
Chantal Coady, of Chocolate Society fame, founded this chocaholic's paradise. Stock ranges from the serious (Valrhona rough-hewn slabs) to the frivolous (chocolate 'olives'). **The Chocolate Society** now has its own shop at 36 Elizabeth Street, SW1 (020 7259 9222).

Delicatessens

Bluebird

350 King's Road, SW3 (020 7559 1000). Sloane Square tube then 11, 19, 22, 49, 211, 319, 345 bus. **Open** 9am-8pm Mon-Wed; 9am-9pm Thur-Sat; noon-6pm Sun. **Credit** AmEx, DC, JCB, MC, £TC, V. **Map 4 D12**
Welcome to foodie heaven. Sir Terence Conran's gastrodome (for the restaurant, *see p165*) is built around the ground-floor food store, which contains a fabulous array of provisions including oils, fruit, vegetables and breads.

Carluccio's

28A Neal Street, WC2 (020 7240 1487). Covent Garden tube. **Open** 11am-7pm Mon-Fri; 11am-6pm Sat. **Credit** AmEx, MC, £TC, V. **Map 6 L6**
Beautifully packaged, pricey Italian groceries, plus exquisite fresh vegetables and prepared dishes.

Lina Stores

18 Brewer Street, W1 (020 7437 6482). Piccadilly Circus tube. **Open** 7am-5.45pm Mon-Fri; 7am-5pm Sat. **Credit** AmEx, JCB, MC, V. **Map 7 J7**
A small selection of almost every Italian deli item imaginable is sold at this Soho stalwart. Try the fresh tortelloni with fillings such as pumpkin or wild mushroom. Irreplaceable.

Villandry

170 Great Portland Street, W1 (020 7631 3131). Great Portland Street tube. **Open** 8.30am-10pm Mon-Sat; 11am-4pm Sun. **Credit** MC, V. **Map 5 H5**
Now that Villandry (the deli and the restaurant) has settled into its capacious new premises, there's room for an expanded selection of delectable cheeses, breads and choice foodstuffs from around the world.

Health & organic food

See also page 223 **Spitalfields Market**.

Freshlands

49 Parkway, NW1 (020 7428 7575). Camden Town tube. **Open** 8am-9.30pm daily. **Credit** MC, V.
This large shop is dedicated to the organic and unprocessed. There's a dizzying selection of vitamins, remedies, books, fresh food and naturally made produce.
Branches: 196 Old Street, EC1 (020 7250 1708); **Wild Oats** 210 Westbourne Grove, W11 (020 7229 1063).

Planet Organic

42 Westbourne Grove, W2 (020 7221 7171). Bayswater or Queensway tube. **Open** 9am-8pm Mon-Sat; 11am-5pm Sun. **Credit** JCB, MC, V. **Map 1 B6**
A gleaming, natural food supermarket. In addition to the ten or so aisles of groceries, there's a butcher's counter (with organic sausages), a fresh fish counter, an organic juice and coffee bar, and a mini-flower stall. Organic wines sold too.
Website: www.planetorganic.com

International

For the best Afro-Caribbean produce, *see page 222* **Brixton Market**. If you're after Chinese goodies, **Chinatown** remains the best place to go; try the immense **Loon Fung Supermarket** at 42-44 Gerrard Street. The best Turkish food in town is to be found along never-ending **Green Lanes** in N4 and N5 (Manor House or Turnpike Lane tube/29, 141, 171A bus), while north Indian specialities abound in **Southall** (Southall rail/83, 105, 207 bus). Pan-Asian delicacies are packed into the Japanese shopping mall **Oriental City** at 399 Edgware Road, NW9 (Colindale tube).

Simply Sausages' *beautiful bangers.*

Sausages

Simply Sausages

93 Berwick Street, W1 (020 7287 3482). Leicester Square or Tottenham Court Road tube. **Open** 8am-6pm Mon-Fri; 9am-6pm Sat. **Map 5 J6**
This shop makes marvellous bangers, some to centuries-old British recipes, others making use of ingredients from around the world.
Branch: 341 Central Markets, EC1 (020 7329 3227).

Wines & spirits

For everyday use, **Oddbins** (branches all over London – see the *Yellow Pages*) is hard to beat. *See also page 226* **Berry Bros & Rudd**.

Milroy's of Soho

3 Greek Street, W1 (020 7437 9311). Tottenham Court Road tube. **Open** 10am-7pm Mon-Fri; 10am-6pm Sat. **Credit** AmEx, DC, MC, £TC, V. **Map 6 K6**
Whisky galore: Milroy's stocks over 400 lines including a huge array of single malts, plenty of bourbons and a fine selection of Irish whiskies.

Furniture

The Conran Shop

Michelin House, 81 Fulham Road, SW3 (020 7589 7401). South Kensington tube. **Open** 10am-6pm Mon, Tue, Fri; 10am-7pm Wed, Thur; 10am-6.30pm Sat; noon-6pm Sun. **Credit** AmEx, MC, £TC, V. **Map 5 G5**
The ground floor of Sir Terence Conran's design mecca holds classic modern furniture (including the Conran Collection) and soft furnishings; accessories are confined to the basement.
Branch: 55 Marylebone High Street, W1 (020 7723 2223).
Website: www.conran.co.uk

Habitat

196 Tottenham Court Road, W1 (020 7631 3880). Goodge Street tube. **Open** 10am-6pm Mon-Wed; 10am-8pm Thur; 10am-6.30pm Fri; 9.30am-6.30pm Sat; noon-6pm Sun. **Credit** AmEx, MC, £TC, V. **Map 5 J4**
Sober but well-made furniture and home accessories are now the mainstay of what was the first high-street retailer to bring good, affordable, contemporary design to the masses.
Branches are too numerous to list here. Check the telephone directory for your nearest.
Website: www.habitat.net

Heal's

196 Tottenham Court Road, W1 (020 7636 1666). Goodge Street tube. **Open** 10am-6pm Mon-Wed; 10am-8pm Thur; 10am-6.30pm Fri; 9.30am-6.30pm Sat; noon-6pm Sun. **Credit** AmEx, DC, MC, £TC, V. **Map 6 K5**
One of London's oldest furniture stores, yet still one of the most fashionable. Several floors of stylish furniture, kitchenware and accessories, including pieces from the top design names.
Branch: 234 King's Road, SW3 (020 7349 8411).

Purves & Purves

80-81 & 83 Tottenham Court Road, W1 (020 7580 8223). Goodge Street or Warren Street tube. **Open** 9.30am-6pm Mon-Wed, Fri, Sat; 9.30am-7.30pm Thur. **Credit** AmEx, MC, £TC, V. **Map 5 J4**
Andrew and Pauline Purves mix the best of British design with a sprinkling of top European names. There's a refreshing lack of pretension in their two stores, one of which specialises in accessories.
Website: www.purves.co.uk

Tom Tom

42 New Compton Street, WC2 (020 7240 7909). Covent Garden, Leicester Square or Tottenham Court Road tube. **Open** noon-7pm Tue-Fri; 11am-6pm Sat. **Credit** AmEx, JCB, MC, £TC, V. **Map 6 K6**
A fun, eccentric shop stuffed to the gills with kitschy accessories and larger items such as post-war art (including works by Andy Warhol and Richard Hamilton), 1950s furniture and Charles and Ray Eames lounge chairs.

Gifts & stationery

In addition to the shops listed below, many of London's premier museums have excellent gift shops, in particular the **London Transport Museum** (*see page 85*), the **British Museum**

Don't rack your brains: go to **Purves & Purves** *for fab, funky furniture. See page 219.*

(*see page 64*) and the **Victoria & Albert Museum** (*see page 96*). *See also page 211* **Emma Bernhardt**.

BBC World Service Shop

Bush House, Strand, WC2 (020 7557 2576). Temple tube/Charing Cross tube/rail.
Open 9.30am-6pm Mon, Tue, Thur, Fri; 10am-6pm Wed; 10am-5.30pm Sat. **Credit** AmEx, MC, £TC, V. **Map 8 M6**
Wide range of BBC spin-offs plus books on a range of arts and media subjects.
Website: www.bbc.co.uk/worldservice

Graham & Green

4, 7, & 10 Elgin Crescent, W11 (020 7727 4594). Ladbroke Grove tube. **Open** 10am-6pm Mon-Sat; 11am-5pm Sun. **Credit** AmEx, DC, MC, £TC, V.
The stock here – funky jewellery, pens, china, fashion accessories, picture frames and the like – is all in the best possible taste.
Website: www.grahamandgreen.co.uk
Branch: 164 Regent's Park Road, NW1 (020 7586 2960).

Mysteries

11 Monmouth Street, WC2 (020 7240 3688). Tottenham Court Road tube. **Open** 10am-6pm Mon-Sat. **Credit** MC, £TC, V. **Map 6 L6**
New Age shop packed with books and pamphlets, spacey music, posters, jewellery, charms, candles and even a phrenology head.
Website: www.mysteries.co.uk

Neal Street East

5 Neal Street, WC2 (020 7240 0135). Covent Garden tube. **Open** 11am-7pm Mon-Wed; 10am-7.30pm Thur-Sat; noon-6pm Sun. **Credit** AmEx, JCB, MC, £TC, V. **Map 6 L6**
Huge range of oriental goods including Balinese animal carvings, embroidered Chinese dresses and Japanese cooking utensils.

Paperchase

213 Tottenham Court Road, W1 (020 7580 8496). Goodge Street tube. **Open** 9.30am-6.30pm Mon,Wed, Fri, Sat; 10am-6.30pm Tue; 9.30am-7.30pm Thur; 11am-5pm Sun. **Credit** AmEx, JCB, MC, £TC, V. **Map 6 K5**
A stationery chain with more verve than most. This revamped flagship store has a better-than-ever selection of cards, gift wrap, writing paper, pens, desk accessories and an art materials department.
Branches are too numerous to list here. Check the telephone directory for your nearest.

The Pen Shop

199 Regent Street, W1 (020 7734 4088). Oxford Circus tube. **Open** 9.30am-6pm Mon, Tue, Fri, Sat; 10am-6pm Wed; 9.30am-7pm Thur. **Credit** AmEx, DC, JCB, MC, V. **Map 7 J7**
A huge range of writing implements and accessories, ranging from the mundane (£2 ballpoint) to the monumental (£85,000 Mont Blanc).
Branch: 10 West Mall, Liverpool Street Station, EC2 (020 7628 4416).

The Tintin Shop

34 Floral Street, WC2 (020 7836 1131). Covent Garden tube. **Open** 10am-6pm Mon-Sat. **Credit** AmEx, DC, JCB, MC, £TC, V. **Map 8 L6**
Devoted to the world's most famous fictional Belgian (alongside Hercule Poirot, that is), the stock

at this tiny shop includes keyrings, T-shirts, towels and, of course, Hergé's comic books.
Branch: **The Big Kids Store** 394 King's Road, SW10 (020 7795 0801).

Health & beauty

Beauty services

The Green Room
21 Earl's Court Road, W8 (020 7937 6595). High Street Kensington tube. **Open** 9am-9pm Mon-Thur; 9am-6pm Fri, Sat; 10am-5pm Sun. **Credit** AmEx, JCB, MC, £TC, V. **Map 3 A9**
Body Shop products are used alongside the Green Room's own aromatherapy oils at these right-on salons. Facials, manicures, massage and natural tanning are all popular treatments.
Branches are too numerous to list here. Check the telephone directory for your nearest.

Porchester Spa
225 Queensway, W2 (020 7792 3980). Bayswater, Queensway or Royal Oak tube. **Open** *Women-only* 10am-10pm Tue, Thur, Fri; 10am-4pm Sun. *Men-only* 10am-10pm Mon, Wed, Sat. *Mixed* 4-10pm Sun. **Membership** £36.80 a year. **Admission** £13.50 members; £18.20 non-members. **Credit** MC, V. **Map 1 B5**
As well as being equipped with two steam rooms, a Jacuzzi, swimming pool, sauna and (purely for masochists) an ice-cold plunge pool, this spa has kept its splendid original 1920s features.

The Sanctuary
11-12 Floral Street, WC2 (020 7420 5151/gym 020 7240 0695). Covent Garden tube. **Open** *Health spa* 10am-6pm Mon, Tue, Sun; 9.30am-10pm Wed-Fri; 9.30am-8pm Sat. *Gym* 7am-9.30pm Mon-Fri; 10am-5pm Sat, Sun. **Membership** *Health spa* £1,392 per year. *Gym* full £600 per year (£60 per month) plus £175 joining fee; off-peak £445 per year (£44.50 per month) plus £150 joining fee. **Admission** £58 day visit; £35 evening visit (Wed-Fri). **Credit** AmEx, DC, MC, £$TC, V. **Map 8 L6**
This plant-filled, women-only haven is equipped with a gym, two pools, Jacuzzi, steam room, sauna, and offers more than 70 beauty treatments. You can become a member on the spot. A welcome touch of luxury in the city.
Website: www.thesanctuary.co.uk

Cosmetics & herbalists

For London's most venerable traditional perfumiers, *see page 226* **Penhaligon's** *and* **Floris**.

Aveda Institute
28-29 Marylebone High Street, W1 (020 7224 3157). Baker Street or Bond Street tube. **Open** 9.30am-7pm Mon-Fri; 9am-6pm Sat; noon-5pm Sun. **Credit** AmEx, JCB, MC, £TC, V. **Map 5 G5**
Aveda's covetable right-on lotions and potions may not be cheap, but you get what you pay for: 97% of ingredients are natural. Gorgeous flowers too.
Website: www.aveda.com

Crabtree & Evelyn
6 Kensington Church Street, W8 (020 7937 9335). High Street Kensington tube. **Open** 10am-6pm Mon-Wed, Fri, Sat; 10am-7pm Thur; 11am-5pm Sun. **Credit** AmEx, MC, £TC, V. **Map 1 B8**
Fanciful toiletries and gift foods, all beautifully packaged in a countrified nostalgic style. Ideal presents for the older woman in your life. The newer ranges of toiletries for gardeners and cooks have become very popular.
Branches are too numerous to list here. Check the telephone directory for your nearest.
Website: www.crabtree-evelyn.com

Jo Malone
150 Sloane Street, SW1 (020 7730 2100). Sloane Square tube. **Open** 10am-6pm Mon-Wed, Sat; 10am-7pm Thur, Fri. **Credit** MC, £TC. V. **Map 4 E10**
Gorgeous-smelling, sleekly packaged fragrances and matching body products. Sheer indulgence.
Website: www.jomalone.co.uk

Lush
Units 7 & 11, The Piazza, Covent Garden, WC2 (020 7240 4570). Covent Garden tube. **Open** 10am-7pm Mon-Sat; noon-6pm Sun. **Credit** AmEx, MC, £TC, V. **Map 8 L7**
Lush has made its name with its big tubs of freshly made enviro-friendly cosmetics, hunks of soap, wacky scents and fizzing bath bombes.
Branches: 123 King's Road, SW3 (020 7376 8348); 40 Carnaby Street, W1 (020 7287 5874).
Website: www.lush.co.uk

Neal's Yard Remedies
15 Neal's Yard, WC2 (020 7379 7222). Covent Garden tube. **Open** 10am-6pm Mon; 10am-7pm Tue-Fri; 10am-5.30pm Sat; 11am-5pm Sun. **Credit** AmEx, MC, £TC, V. **Map 6 L6**
Over 200 medicinal herbs, plus skincare products and toiletries. The range of aromatherapy oils is high quality. Staff know their stuff.
Branches: Chelsea Farmers' Market, Sydney Street, SW3 (020 7351 6380); 9 Elgin Crescent, W11 (020 7727 3998); 68 Chalk Farm Road, NW1 (020 7284 2039).

Nelsons Pharmacy
73 Duke Street, W1 (020 7629 3118). Bond Street tube. **Open** 9am-5.30pm Mon-Fri; 9am-4pm Sat. **Credit** MC, £TC, V. **Map 5 G6**
More than 2,000 remedies, including Bach Flower concoctions. There are aromatherapy oils, books and nutritional supplements. Homeopathic prescriptions are fulfilled by knowledgeable staff.

Space NK Apothecary
4 Thomas Neal Centre, 37 Earlham Street, WC2 (020 7379 7030). Covent Garden tube. **Open** 10am-7pm Mon-Wed, Fri, Sat; 10am-7.30pm Thur; noon-5pm Sun. **Credit** AmEx, DC, JCB, MC, V. **Map 6 L6**
Cutting-edge cosmetics, including Stila, Kiehl's and Laura Mercier, along with Diptyque candles, from Nicky Kinnaird's super-cool, super-successful and ever-expanding chain.

Market forces

There was a time when every London borough had its local street market – and was, to some degree, defined by it. Alas, many local markets are under threat from uncaring councils and supermarket competition. Listed here are some of the biggest and best of those that remain.

General

See also page 223 **Columbia Road Flower Market**.

Brick Lane Market

Brick Lane (north of railway bridge), Cygnet Street, Sclater Street, E1; Bacon Street, Cheshire Street, Chilton Street, E2. Aldgate East or Shoreditch tube or Liverpool Street tube/rail. **Open** 8am-1pm Sun. **Map 10 S5**

A sprawling East End institution, which kicks off at 6am with down-at-heel traders on Bethnal Green Road offering various old tat. At 7.30am things get under way on Sclater Street, given over to pet foods, provisions, electrical goods and tools. Off Cygnet Street, new bicycles, meat, fruit and vegetables are up for grabs. Brick Lane itself is where to find leather jackets, cheap jewellery, a fruit and veg stall and a jellied eel stand. Around Cheshire Street are cheap cassettes and household goods, lock-ups full of junk, and, further up, an indoor warehouse selling second-hand goods, collectibles and discount books. Great fun. Nearby **Dray Walk** has recently thrown up some interesting new shops, among them funky fashion stores and retro interiors shop Eat My Handbag Bitch.

Brixton Market

Electric Avenue, Pope's Road, Brixton Station Road, SW9. Brixton tube/rail. **Open** 8am-6pm Mon, Tue, Thur-Sat; 8am-3pm Wed.

Europe's largest collection of Afro-Caribbean foodstuffs is up for grabs at Brixton. Head for Electric Avenue or the slightly frayed charm of the Granville and Market Row arcades for the best of the provisions, including fab fish. But there's more than food here – reggae throbs out from the record stalls; incense and religious tracts are sold; and there's also second-hand clothes and bric-a-brac.

Camden Market

(020 7284 2084). Camden Town or Chalk Farm tube. **Camden Market** *Camden High Street, junction with Buck Street, NW1.* **Open** 9am-5.30pm Thur-Sun. **Camden Lock Market** *Camden Lock Place, off Chalk Farm Road, NW1.* **Open** 10am-6pm Sat, Sun (indoor stalls 10am-6pm Tue-Sun). **Stables Market** *off Chalk Farm Road, opposite junction with Hartland Road, NW1.* **Open** 8am-6pm Sat, Sun. **Camden Canal Market** *off Chalk Farm Road, south of junction with Castle Haven Road, NW1.* **Open** 10am-6pm Sat, Sun. **Electric Market** *Camden High Street, south of junction with Dewsbury Terrace, NW1.* **Open** 9am-5.30pm Sun.

Now London's fourth biggest tourist attraction, Camden Market has outposts in every bit of space on and off Chalk Farm Road between Camden Town tube and Hawley Street. First stop out of the tube, and south of the junction with Dewsbury Terrace, is the Electric Ballroom, with its laundered second-hand fashions. There are more clothes, new and second-hand, around Buck Street (this is 'Camden Market' proper). The Lock – a cobbled courtyard leading to the canal – attracts the most impenetrable crowds. Handmade crafts, hippyish clothes and vegetarian fast-food stalls are the highlights. Antiques, pine furniture, second-hand books, records and more clothes occupy the area off Chalk Farm Road. Come early if you want to avoid the crush, but there's such an enormous variety of stuff – and people – to look at, you can easily spend the whole day. Beware, though, that much of the market has become a victim of its own success, and you often have to look very hard for anything of quality or interest. Currently, there are big plans for Camden Market, so things may change.

Greenwich Market

Cutty Sark DLR or Greenwich DLR/rail. **Antiques Market** *Greenwich High Road, SE10.* **Open** 9am-5pm Sat, Sun. **Central Market** *off Stockwell Street, opposite Hotel Ibis, SE10.* **Open** *outdoor* 7am-6pm Sat; 7am-5pm Sun; *indoor (Village Market)* 10am-5pm Fri, Sat; 10am-6pm Sun. **Crafts Market** *College Approach, SE10.* **Open** *antiques* 7.30am-5pm Thur; *general* 9.30am-5.30pm Fri-Sun. **Food Market** *off Stockwell Street, opposite Hotel Ibis, SE10.* **Open** 10am-4pm Sat. **Map** *see p121*

A Sunday in Greenwich almost feels like a trip to the seaside, with fish and chip restaurants fighting for space with maritime souvenir shops. The covered section of the Crafts Market is filled with jumpers, porcelain dolls, model ships, and objects that straddle a line between skilled craftswork and tourist tat. The Camden-esque Central Market is more interesting, with goods ranging from high-quality second-hand clothing to bizarre junk shop ephemera. There's a couple of good bookshops in the indoor (Village Market) section, and a food court nearby. The antiques market has mainly twentieth-century bric-a-brac and collectibles.

Petticoat Lane Market

Middlesex Street and around, E1. Liverpool Street tube/rail. **Open** 9am-2pm Sun (Wentworth Street also open 10am-2.30pm Mon-Fri). **Map 12 R6**

Coachloads of tourists and bargain seekers cause pedestrian gridlock here every Sunday, making it hard to take full advantage of the huge range of budget clothes and shoes. The top end of the market, near Aldgate East tube, has a large area devoted to leather jackets. However, prices are rarely shown, so a bit of haggling may be in order.

Portobello Road Market

Portobello Road, W10, W11; Golborne Road, W10. Ladbroke Grove, Notting Hill Gate or Westbourne Park tube. **Antiques Market open** 4am-6pm Sat. **General Market open** 8am-6pm Mon-Wed; 9am-1pm Thur; 7am-7pm Fri, Sat. **Organic Market open** 11am-6pm Thur. **Clothes & Bric-a-brac Market open** 7am-4pm Fri; 8am-5pm Sat; 9am-4pm Sun. **Golborne Road Market open** 9am-5pm Mon-Sat. **Map 1 A6**

Despite Portobello's worldwide fame, and the gentrification of once-bohemian Notting Hill, a Saturday outing here is still rewarding, mainly because of the market's glorious diversity. This is really several markets rolled into one: the top end is of most interest to antiques buffs, with *objets*, jewellery, coins and medals, paintings, silverware and other collectibles. Further down the hill is a fruit and veg market (Mon-Sat), where prices are generally low. The next change comes under the Westway, where food gives way to clothes (second-hand and by young designers), jewellery, records and books. From here up to Golborne Road, the market becomes increasingly rundown, though it's still worth a look for bargains, and there are some great Portuguese cafés down here.

Walthamstow Market

Walthamstow High Street, E17. Walthamstow Central tube/rail. **Open** 8am-6pm Mon-Sat.

Walthamstow's answer to Petticoat Lane claims to be Europe's longest daily street market, with 450 stalls selling cheap clothing, fruit and veg, and household bits and bobs. As trad as they come.

Antiques

See also above **Camden**, **Greenwich** and **Portobello Road** markets.

Bermondsey (New Caledonian) Market

Bermondsey Square, SE1. Bermondsey tube. **Open** 5am-2pm Fri (starts closing around noon). **Map 12 Q10**

This market is a mecca for serious collectors and attracts dealers from all over the South-east, but most of the good stuff has gone by 9am.

Crafts

Apple Market

North Hall, Covent Garden Market, WC2 (020 7836 9136). Covent Garden tube. **Open** 9am-7pm Mon; 10.30am-7pm Tue-Sun. **Map 7 L8**

A decent range of handmade British arts and crafts are the mainstay of the Apple Market. On Mondays the stalls are given over to antiques and quality collectibles. The separately run Jubilee Market in Jubilee Hall on the south side of Covent Garden Piazza is only interesting on Mondays when the usual tourist tosh is replaced by jewellery, coins, medals, ornaments and the like.

Flowers

Columbia Road Flower Market

Columbia Road (between Gosset Street & the Royal Oak pub), E2. Old Street tube/rail/26, 48, 55 bus. **Open** 8am-1pm Sun. **Map 10 S3**

Without question the prettiest street market in town. Flowers, shrubs, bedding plants and other horticultural delights are spread in all directions. Shops lining the road stock garden accessories. The market has recently turned into a bit of a Sunday shopping mecca, also selling gifts, furniture, perfume, jewellery and the like.

Food

Berwick Street Market

Berwick Street & Rupert Street, W1. Leicester Square or Piccadilly Circus tube. **Open** 8am-6pm Mon-Sat. **Map 5 J6**

The best and cheapest selection of fruit and veg in central London in one of the last parts of Soho with a genuinely seedy feel. There are also good cheese, fish, bread, and herb and spice stalls.

Borough Market

Borough Market, between Borough High Street, Bedale Street, Winchester Walk & Stoney Street, SE10. London Bridge tube/rail. **Open** noon-6pm Fri; 9am-4pm Sat. **Map 11 P8**

This burgeoning food market (*see picture*) has gone from monthly to weekly. Stallholders include the **Fresh Olive Company**, **de Gustibus** and **Monmouth Coffee Company**. Nearby are **Konditor & Cook**, **Neal's Yard Dairy** (for both, *see p217*), and **fish!**, selling, well, fish, next to the diner of the same name (*see p171*).
Website: www.londonslarder.org.uk

Organic

Spitalfields Market

Commercial Street (between Lamb & Brushfield Streets), E1 (020 7377 1496). Liverpool Street tube/rail. **Organic Market open** 10am-5pm Fri, Sun. **General market open** 11am-3pm Mon-Fri; 10am-5pm Sun. **Map 10 R5**

Crafts and antiques stalls are set up through the week, but it's on Friday and (particularly) Sunday that the market comes alive with a dozen or so organic producers selling relishes, pickles, herbs and spices, breads and cakes, and fruit and vegetables. The food court offers cheap tasty food.

Branches: 7 Bishopsgate Arcade, 135 Bishopsgate, EC2 (020 7256 2303); 45-47 Brook Street, W1 (020 7355 1727); 307 King's Road, SW3 (020 7351 7209); 307 Brompton Road, SW3 (020 7589 8250); 73 St John's Wood High Street, NW8 (020 7586 0607).

Hairdressers

See also page 226 **GF Trumper**.

Fish

30 D'Arblay Street, W1 (020 7494 2398). Tottenham Court Road tube. **Open** 10am-7pm Mon-Wed, Fri; 10am-8pm Thur; 10am-5pm Sat. **Credit** MC, V. **Map 6 K6**

A style-conscious, youngish crowd are expertly coiffed in the friendly atmosphere of a former fishmonger's. Look out for the original tiles. Cuts start at £25.

Website: www.fishweb.co.uk

Essensuals

Basement of Top Shop, 214 Oxford Street, W1 (020 7631 3114). Oxford Circus tube. **Open** 9am-8pm Mon-Wed, Fri, Sat; 9am-9.30pm Thur; noon-6pm Sun. **Credit** AmEx, MC, V. **Map 5 J6**

Young, sleek and modern, this spin-off of Toni & Guy is cheaper than many of its nearest rivals (from £31 for a woman's cut and blow dry, £22 for men). Also offers makeovers and beauty treatments.

Vidal Sassoon

60 South Molton Street, W1 (020 7491 8848). Bond Street tube. **Open** 10.30am-6pm Mon, Tue, Wed, Fri; 10.30am-6.45pm Thur; 9am-5.15pm Sat. **Credit** AmEx, MC, £TC, V. **Map 5 H6**

The emphasis is on precision cutting at this world-famous, long-established chain. Call the VS School in 56 Davies Mews, W1 (020 7629 4635; appointments 10am-3pm Mon-Fri) for a bargain-priced cut from a (supervised) trainee. Otherwise, cuts start at £45.

Branches are too numerous to list here. Check the telephone directory for your nearest.

Opticians

Boots Opticians

127A Kensington High Street, W8 (020 7938 1620). High Street Kensington tube. **Open** 8.30am-6.30pm Mon-Sat; 11am-5pm Sun. **Credit** AmEx, JCB, MC, £TC, V. **Map 3 B9**

Not the greatest range of frames, but frequent sales, and Boots' ubiquitousness, make this a useful spec stop. One-hour service.

Branches are too numerous to list here. Check the telephone directory for your nearest.

Kirk Originals

36 Earlham Street, WC2 (020 7240 5055). Covent Garden tube. **Open** 10.30am-6.30pm Mon-Wed, Fri, Sat; 10.30am-7pm Thur. **Credit** AmEx, JCB, MC, V. **Map 6 L6**

Funky, trendy frames from Jason Kirk. His trend-setting chunky acetate specs now adorn the faces of countless celebs.

Website: www.kirkorig.co.uk

Vision Express

291 Oxford Street, W1 (020 7409 7880). Oxford Circus tube. **Open** 9.30am-7.30pm Mon-Wed, Fri; 9.30am-8pm Thur; 9am-7pm Sat; noon-6pm Sun. **Map 5 H6**

Offering 20-minute eye tests, Vision Express claims to be able to make an impressive 95% of its customers new glasses within the hour.

Branches are too numerous to list here. Check the telephone directory for your nearest.

Hobbies

The Bead Shop

21A Tower Street, WC2 (020 7240 0931). Leicester Square tube. **Open** 1-6pm Mon; 10.30am-6pm Tue-Fri; 11.30am-5pm Sat. **Credit** AmEx, JCB, MC, £TC, V. **Map 6 K6.**

A kaleidoscopic selection of beads, plus thread, thongs, findings and clasps.

Beatties

202 High Holborn, WC1 (020 7405 6285/8592). Holborn tube. **Open** 10am-6pm Mon; 9am-6pm Tue-Fri; 9am-5.30pm Sat. **Credit** AmEx, MC, £TC, V. **Map 6 L5**

Kits for all sorts of models, and everything a model railway enthusiast could require.

Branches are too numerous to list here. Check the telephone directory for your nearest.

London Dolls House Company

29 Covent Garden Market, WC2 (020 7240 8681). Covent Garden tube. **Open** 10.30am-7pm Mon-Sat; noon-5pm Sun. **Credit** AmEx, MC, £TC, V. **Map 8 L7**

Reproduction Victorian designs plus more modern dolls' houses and a large stock of accessories.

London Graphic Centre

16-18 Shelton Street, WC2 (020 7240 0095). Covent Garden tube. **Open** 9.30am-6pm Mon-Fri; 10.30am-6pm Sat. **Credit** AmEx, JCB, MC, £TC, V. **Map 6 L6**

Home to a great range of fine art, graphic and reprographic materials, and computer products.

Branches: 13 Tottenham Street, W1 (020 7637 2199); 254 Upper Richmond Road, SW15 (020 8785 9797).

Website: www.londongraphics.co.uk

Spink & Son

5 King Street, SW1 (020 7930 7888). Green Park tube. **Open** 9am-5.30pm Mon-Fri. **Credit** AmEx, MC, £TC, V. **Map 7 J8**

Britain's leading authority on coins and medals is also a fascinating and beautiful shop.

Stanley Gibbons International

399 Strand, WC2 (020 7836 8444). Covent Garden tube/Charing Cross tube/rail. **Open** 8.30am-6pm Mon-Fri; 9am-5.30pm Sat. **Credit** AmEx, DC, MC, V. **Map 8 L7**

Founded in 1856, the most famous – and biggest – name in philately has more than three million stamps for sale, a third of them £1 or less.

Victorian values

The gentleman's clubland of St James's, south of Piccadilly, and the southern part of Mayfair (*see also page 72*) contain a wonderfully anachronistic clutch of emporia where high prices are matched by superlative service and quality. Browsing in this time-warp wonderland, you can almost believe that Britain still has an empire.

Fashion

Gieves & Hawkes

1 Savile Row, W1 (020 7434 2001). Piccadilly Circus tube. **Open** 9am-7.30pm Mon, Tue, Thur; 10am-7.30pm; 9am-6pm Fri; 10am-6pm Sat. **Credit** AmEx, DC, JCB, MC, £TC, V. **Map 7 J7**
Venerable Savile Row tailors who are now focusing more on off-the-peg ranges. Expect to shell out at least £1,800 for a three-piece bespoke suit.
Branch: 18 Lime Street, EC3 (020 7283 4914).

James Lock

6 St James's Street, SW1 (020 7930 5849). Green Park tube. **Open** 9am-5.30pm Mon-Fri; 9.30am-5.30pm Sat. **Credit** AmEx, DC, JCB, MC £TC, V. **Map 7 J8**
This family business has been making hats to the highest standards since 1686. Past satisfied customers include Lord Byron and Harrison Ford.
Website: www.lockhatters.co.uk

John Lobb

9 St James's Street, SW1 (020 7930 3664). Green Park tube. **Open** 9am-5.30pm Mon-Fri; 9am-4.30pm Sat. **Credit** AmEx, JCB, MC, £TC, V. **Map 7 J8**
Expect to part with £1,500 and to wait eight months before you slip into a pair of John Lobb's fabulous men's shoes.

Turnbull & Asser

23 Bury Street, SW1 (020 7808 3000). Green Park or Piccadilly Circus tube. **Open** 9am-6pm Mon-Fri; 9.30am-6pm Sat. **Credit** AmEx, DC, JCB, MC, £$TC, V. **Map 7 J7**
T&A's bespoke and off-the-peg shirts have graced the backs of Winston Churchill and James Bond.
Branch: 71-72 Jermyn Street, SW1 (020 7808 3000).

Food & drink

Berry Bros & Rudd

3 St James's Street, SW1 (020 7396 9600/9666). Green Park tube. **Open** 9am-5.30pm Mon-Fri; 10am-4pm Sat. **Credit** AmEx, DC, JCB, MC, £TC, V. **Map 7 J8**
Venerable wine merchants Berry Bros is best known for its German and French wines, but has a comprehensive list that takes in good New World wineries.

Charbonnel & Walker

1 The Royal Arcade, 28 Old Bond Street, W1 (020 7491 0939). Green Park or Piccadilly Circus tube. **Open** 9am-6pm Mon-Fri; 10am-5pm Sat. **Credit** AmEx, DC, JCB, MC, £TC, V. **Map 7 J7**
Traditional hand-rolled chocolates. Don't miss the drool-worthy champagne truffles.

JJ Fox (St James's)

19 St James's Street, SW1 (020 7493 9009). Green Park tube. **Open** 9am-5.30pm Mon-Sat. **Credit** AmEx, DC, JCB, MC, £TC, V. **Map 7 J8**
This delightful, ancient, wood-panelled shop stocks a fabulous range of cigars – Churchill and Oscar Wilde have puffed away on Fox's prime merchandise in the past.
Website: www.jjfox.co.uk

Paxton & Whitfield

93 Jermyn Street, SW1 (020 7930 0259). Green Park or Piccadilly Circus tube. **Open** 9.30am-6pm Mon-Fri; 9am-5.30pm Sat. **Credit** AmEx, DC, MC, £TC, V. **Map 7 J7**
A pukka establishment with old-fashioned premises holding about 200 varieties of European cheeses, plus hams, pies, breads, teas, chutneys and pickles.
Website: www.cheesemonger.co.uk

Health & beauty

Floris

89 Jermyn Street, SW1 (020 7930 2885). Green Park or Piccadilly Circus tube. **Open** 9.30am-5.30pm Mon-Fri; 10am-5pm Sat. **Credit** AmEx, DC, JCB, MC, £TC, V. **Map 7 J7**
Traditional toiletries have been the business of this upmarket, elegant perfumier since 1730. Expect lots of floral scents for women and no-nonsense men's colognes.

GF Trumper

9 Curzon Street, W1 (020 7499 1850). Green Park tube. **Open** 9am-5.30pm Mon-Fri; 9am-1pm Sat. **Credit** AmEx, DC, JCB, MC, £TC, V. **Map 7 H7**
A Victorian ambience and obsequious staff perform treatments in the traditional manner at this high-class barbers. Also sells top-notch colognes.
Branch: 20 Jermyn Street, SW1 (020 7734 1370).

Penhaligon's

16-17 Burlington Arcade, W1 (020 7629 1416). Green Park or Piccadilly Circus tube. **Open** 9.30am-5.30pm Mon-Sat. **Credit** AmEx, DC, JCB, MC, £TC, V. **Map 7 J7**
Quintessentially English perfumes, toiletries and grooming products for men and women.
Branches: 20A Brook Street, W1 (020 7493 0002); 41 Wellington Street, WC2 (020 7836 2150); 8 Cornhill, EC3 (020 7283 0711); 18 Beauchamp Place, SW1 (020 7584 4008).
Website: www.penhaligons.co.uk

Home accessories

See also **The Conran Shop**, **Purves & Purves** and **Heal's** (*page 219*).

After Noah

121 Upper Street, N1 (020 7359 4281). Angel tube. **Open** 10am-6pm Mon-Sat; noon-5pm Sun. **Credit** AmEx, MC, £TC, V. **Map 9 O1**

A desirable mixture of second-hand and new household accessories and furniture with a neat sideline in jewellery.

Branch: 261 King's Road, SW3 (020 7351 2610).

Website: www.afternoah.com

Cath Kidston

8 Clarendon Cross, W11 (020 7221 4000). Holland Park tube. **Open** 10.30am-6pm Mon-Fri; 11am-6pm Sat. **Credit** JCB, MC, £TC, V.

New and second-hand items from or inspired by the 1950s: painted furniture, fabrics, utensils and crockery. Expect lots of floral prints and gingham.

Designers Guild

267-271 & 275-277 King's Road, SW3 (020 7351 5775). Sloane Square tube. **Open** 9.30am-5.30pm Mon, Tue; 10am-6pm Wed-Sat; noon-5pm Sun (nos.261-271 only). **Credit** AmEx, MC, £TC, V. **Map 4 E12**

Bright, energising colours are the hallmark of Tricia Guild's linen, crockery, glassware, soft furnishings and furniture.

David Wainwright

28 Rosslyn Hill, NW3 (020 7431 5900). Hampstead tube. **Open** 10am-7pm Mon-Sat; 11am-6.30pm Sun. **Credit** AmEx, DC, MC, V.

Desirable goods, including teak and bamboo coffee tables, from Rajasthan, Indonesia, Java and the Malaccan Straits.

Branches: 251 Portobello Road, W11 (020 7792 1988); 63 Portobello Road, W11 (020 7727 0707).

Divertimenti

45-47 Wigmore Street, W1 (020 7935 0689). Bond Street tube. **Open** 9.30am-6pm Mon-Wed, Fri; 9.30am-7pm Thur; 9.30am-6pm Sat. **Credit** AmEx, DC, MC, £TC, V. **Map 5 G6**

Seriously cool cookware.

Branch: 139-141 Fulham Road, SW3 (020 7581 8065).

Website: www.divertimenti.co.uk

Elephant

230 Tottenham Court Road, W1 (020 7637 7930). Goodge Street or Tottenham Court Road tube. **Open** 10am-6.30pm Mon-Fri; 10am-6pm Sat; 11am-5pm Sun. **Credit** MC, V. **Map 6 K5**

Good-value ethnic-inspired rugs, cushions, mirrors, vases and other home accessories are sold at this burgeoning chain.

Branches: 169-171 Queensway, W2 (020 7467 0630).

The Holding Company

241-245 King's Road, SW3 (020 7352 1600). Sloane Square tube then 11, 19, 22 bus. **Open** 10am-6pm Mon-Fri; 10am-7pm Sat; noon-6pm Sun. **Credit** AmEx, MC, £TC, V. **Map 4 D12**

A wonderful, inventive range of storage ideas.

Website: www.theholdingcompany.co.uk

Muji

187 Oxford Street, W1 (020 7437 7503). Oxford Circus tube. **Open** 10.30am-7pm Mon-Wed; 10.30am-8pm Thur; 10.30am-7.30pm Fri; 10am-7pm Sat; noon-6pm Sun. **Credit** AmEx, DC, JCB, MC, £TC, V. **Map 6 K6**

Pared-down designs in stationery, storage, kitchen and bathroom accessories, and clothing from this Japanese chain.

Branches are too numerous to list here. Check the telephone directory for your nearest.

Space

214 Westbourne Grove, W11 (020 7229 6533). Notting Hill Gate tube. **Open** 10am-6pm Mon-Sat. **Credit** MC, V.

This bright white shop sells all manner of funky home accessories from Jonathan Adler vases to the utterly gorgeous but ridiculously priced woolly beanbags (from £1,600).

Crafts

See also page 213 **Lesley Craze Gallery/ Craze 2/C2+**.

Contemporary Applied Arts

2 Percy Street, W1 (020 7436 2344). Tottenham Court Road tube. **Open** 10.30am-5.30pm Mon-Sat. **Credit** AmEx, MC, £TC, V. **Map 6 K5**

One of the largest, most varied and dynamic ranges of new craft/design work in London.

Website: www.caa.org.uk

Contemporary Ceramics

William Blake House, 7 Marshall Street, W1 (020 7437 7605). Oxford Circus tube. **Open** 10am-5.30pm Mon-Wed, Fri, Sat; 10am-7pm Thur. **Credit** AmEx, MC, £TC, V. **Map 5 J6**

The retail outlet of the Craft Potters' Association sells an inventive and affordable selection of its members' work. Regular exhibitions too.

Crafts Council Shop

44A Pentonville Road, N1 (020 7806 2559). Angel tube. **Open** 11am-6pm Tue-Sat; 2-6pm Sun. **Credit** AmEx, JCB, MC, £TC, V. **Map 9 N2**

The Crafts Council's headquarters house a small, attractive shop with a frequently changing stock of high-quality work in a variety of media.

Branch: Victoria & Albert Museum, Cromwell Road, SW7 (020 7589 5070).

Website: www.craftscouncil.org.uk

Gabriel's Wharf & Oxo Tower

Upper Ground, SE1 (recorded info 020 7401 2255). Waterloo tube/rail. **Open** 11am-6pm Tue-Sun. **Credit** varies. **Map 11 N7**

Gabriel's Wharf has two rows of design and craft shops/workshops including silversmiths, workers in papier mâché and ceramicists. A few hundred yards away, the **Oxo Tower** boasts a fine selection of outlets for individual artists' and designers' products, including ceramicist Caterina Fadda, Salt's 'modular' fabric window blinds, screens and wall hangings and Hive's rustic-minimalist furniture and *objets*.

Musical instruments

Denmark Street, off Charing Cross Road, WC2, has long been the mecca for musos.

Andy's Guitar Centre & Workshop

27 Denmark Street, WC2 (020 7916 5080). Tottenham Court Road tube. **Open** 10am-7pm Mon-Sat; 12.30-6.30pm Sun. **Credit** AmEx, DC, JCB, MC, £TC, V. **Map 6 K6**
Long-established retail and repair centre. Acoustic guitars upstairs; electric downstairs. Great vintage models: after all, this is where a number of guitar heroes come to buy and get their repairs done.
Website: andysguitarnet.com

Boosey & Hawkes

295 Regent Street, W1 (0800 731 4778/020 7580 2060). Oxford Circus tube. **Open** 9.30am-6pm Mon-Fri; 10am-5pm Sat. **Credit** AmEx, DC, MC, £TC, V. **Map 5 J6**
Specialists in classical sheet music.
Website: www.boosey.com/musicshop

Hobgoblin Music

24 Rathbone Place, W1 (020 7323 9040). Tottenham Court Road tube. **Open** 10am-6pm Mon-Sat. **Credit** AmEx, DC, JCB, MC, £TC, V. **Map 6 K5**
The spectrum of folk – from traditional Irish to Asian – by means of instruments, sheet music, CDs and so on.
Website: www.hobgoblin.com

Music & Video Exchange

56 Notting Hill Gate, W11 (020 7229 4805). Notting Hill Gate tube. **Open** 10am-8pm daily. **Credit** AmEx, DC, JCB, MC, £TC, V. **Map 1 A7**
There are plenty of bargains to be had at this well-stocked second-hand store, including pop and classical instruments.

Rayman

54 Chalk Farm Road, NW1 (020 7692 6261). Camden Town or Chalk Farm tube. **Open** 10.30am-6pm daily. **Credit** AmEx, MC, £TC, V.
Now relocated to Camden, Rayman still stocks a pan-world collection of instruments including pan pipes, *pinquillos* and rainsticks.

Turnkey & Soho Soundhouse

114-116 Charing Cross Road, WC2 (020 7379 5148). Tottenham Court Road tube. **Open** 10am-6pm Mon-Wed, Fri, Sat; 10am-7pm Thur. **Credit** AmEx, MC, £TC, V. **Map 6 K6**
Excellent prices on electronic equipment of all kinds, from PAs, lights and sampling equipment to guitars, amps and keyboards.
Website: www.turnkey.demon.co.uk

Music shops

Megastores

HMV

150 Oxford Street, W1 (020 7631 3423). Oxford Circus tube. **Open** 9am-8pm Mon-Sat; noon-6pm Sun. **Credit** AmEx, DC, MC, £TC, V. **Map 5 J6**
The ground floor holds rock, pop and soul sections; in the basement are jazz, soundtrack, classical, spoken word and world music sections. Less tiring than other megastores.
Branches: 363 Oxford Street, W1 (020 7629 1240); Trocadero, 18 Coventry Street, W1 (020 7439 0447).
Website: www.hmv.co.uk

Tower Records

1 Piccadilly Circus, W1 (020 7439 2500). Piccadilly Circus tube. **Open** 9am-midnight Mon-Sat; noon-6pm Sun. **Credit** AmEx, MC, £TC, V. **Map 7 J7**
In terms of sheer quantity, Tower is hard to beat. The choice of import CDs, particularly from Japan, is one of its most impressive features.
Branches: 62-64 Kensington High Street, W8 (020 7938 3511); Whiteley's, Queensway, W2 (020 7229 4550); 162 Camden High Street, NW1 (020 7424 2800).
Website: www.towerrecords.co.uk

Virgin Megastore

14-16 Oxford Street, W1 (020 7631 1234). Tottenham Court Road tube. **Open** 9am-9pm Mon-Sat; noon-6pm Sun. **Credit** AmEx, MC, £TC, V. **Map 6 K6**
Music still rules at this four-floor giant, but only just, as more and more space is taken over by computer games, plus videos and books (and even a travel agency). There's a decent classical selection on the top floor.
Branches: 225-229 Piccadilly, W1 (020 7930 4208); King's Walk Shopping Centre, King's Road, SW3 (020 7591 0957).

Specialist music shops

Cut a corner (Tottenham Court Road and Oxford Street – one of London's unloveliest corners) and dive into Hanway Street for second-hand sounds: at no.22 there's **On the Beat**, at no.36 **Division One**. Soho is also a music mecca – **Selectadisc** (no.34) and **Sister Ray** (no.94) are particularly strong on indie, **Reckless Records** (no.30) is good for quality mainstream, there's Jamaican music at **Daddy Kool** (no.12) and general cut-price CDs at **Mr CD** (no.80).

Black Market

25 D'Arblay Street, W1 (020 7437 0478). Oxford Circus tube. **Open** noon-7pm Mon; 11am-7pm Tue-Sat. **Credit** AmEx, MC, £TC, V. **Map 6 K6**
The music may be loud and the moodiness of the staff legendary, but the counter is always crammed three deep here. The biggest house tunes, 12in promo singles and drum 'n' bass are the main draws.
Website: www.blackmarket.co.uk

Ear, ear: it's **Virgin Megastore**. *See p228.*

Cheapo Cheapo Records
53 Rupert Street, W1 (020 7437 8272). Piccadilly Circus tube. **Open** 11am-10pm Mon-Sat. **Credit** £TC. **Map 8 K7**
The stuff of legends. They sell records! And they're cheap! 'Nuff said.

Harold Moores Records & Video
2 Great Marlborough Street, W1 (020 7437 1576). Oxford Circus tube. **Open** 10am-6.30pm Mon-Sat; noon-6.30pm Sun. **Credit** MC, £TC, V. **Map 5 J6**
A legendary vendor of rare classical records. There's a decent selection of CDs too.
Website: www.hmrecords.co.uk

Honest Jon's
276 & 278 Portobello Road, W10 (020 8969 9822). Ladbroke Grove tube. **Open** 10am-6pm Mon-Sat; 11am-5pm Sun. **Credit** AmEx, DC, JCB, MC, £TC, V. **Map 1 A6**
A favourite for black music, with jazz, soul, Latin, reggae and dance all well represented.

Intoxica!
231 Portobello Road, W11 (020 7229 8010). Ladbroke Grove tube. **Open** 10.30am-6.30pm Mon-Fri; 10am-6.30pm Sat; noon-5pm Sun. **Credit** AmEx, DC, MC, £TC, V. **Map 1 A6**
Intoxica! revels in the rare and esoteric, with nice lines in psychedelia, exotica and covetable jazz albums. Purchasing the kind of records that once went for pennies no longer comes cheap however, so expect to have to pay top dollar for some of the more desirable items.
Website: www.intoxica.co.uk

MDC Classic Music
437 Strand, WC2 (020 7240 2157). Charing Cross tube/rail. **Open** 9am-7pm Mon-Sat; noon-6pm Sun. **Credit** AmEx, MC, £TC, V. **Map 8 L7**
Unashamedly populist, MDC covers most branches of the classical world. Good for special offers.
Branches are too numerous to list here. Check the telephone directory for your nearest.
Website: www.mdcmusic.co.uk

Mole Jazz
311 Gray's Inn Road, WC1 (020 7278 0703). King's Cross tube/rail. **Open** 10am-6pm Mon-Thur, Sat; 10am-8pm Fri. **Credit** AmEx, DC, JCB, MC, £TC, V. **Map 6 M3**
Jazz from the early days to the hottest current artists: the ground floor has CDs and books; upstairs are second-hand LPs, with many collector's items.
Website: www.molejazz.co.uk

Rare Discs
18 Bloomsbury Street, WC1 (020 7580 3516). Holborn or Tottenham Court Road tube. **Open** 10am-6.30pm Mon-Sat. **Credit** AmEx, DC, MC, £TC, V. **Map 6 K5**
An unsurpassed collection of film soundtracks, plus shows and musicals, mainly on vinyl.

Rhythm Records
281 Camden High Street, NW1 (020 7267 0123). Camden Town tube. **Open** 10.30am-6.30pm Mon-Wed; 10.30am-7pm Thur, Fri; 10.30am-7.30pm Sat, Sun. **Credit** MC, V.
One of London's best selections of specialist independent music: hardcore punk, 1960s psychedelia, electronic, folk and country – on CD and vinyl.

Rough Trade
130 Talbot Road, W11 (020 7229 8541). Notting Hill Gate tube. **Open** 10am-6.30pm Mon-Sat; 1-5pm Sun. **Credit** AmEx, JCB, £TC, MC, V. **Map 1 A5**
A great selection of independent releases, from punk and hardcore to trip hop and world music. There's also a fabulous stock of fanzines.
Branch: 16 Neal's Yard, WC2 (020 7240 0105).
Website: www.roughtrade.com

Stern's African Record Centre
293 Euston Road, NW1 (020 7387 5550). Warren Street tube. **Open** 10.30am-6.30pm Mon-Sat. **Credit** AmEx, MC, £TC, V. **Map 5 J4**
African music from every country on the continent, on all formats. Sounds from other parts of the globe are increasingly represented.
Website: www.sternsmusic.com

Sport

The Kite Store
48 Neal Street, WC2 (020 7836 1666). Covent Garden tube. **Open** 10am-6pm Mon-Wed, Fri; 10am-7pm Thur; 10.30am-6pm Sat. **Credit** AmEx, MC, £TC, V. **Map 6 L6**

Over 100 different kites always in stock, from basic models to fantastic stunt designs. Staff are happy to advise novice flyers on the most suitable models.

Lillywhite's

24-36 Lower Regent Street, SW1 (020 7930 3181). Piccadilly Circus tube. **Open** 10am-8pm Mon-Wed, Fri; 10am-9pm Thur; 9am-7pm Sat; 11am-5pm Sun. **Credit** AmEx, JCB, MC, V. **Map 8 K7**

An all-rounder, with six floors containing everything from US brand-name leisurewear to specialist diving gear.

Skate Attack

95 Highgate Road, NW5 (020 7485 0007). Kentish Town tube. **Open** 9.30am-6pm Mon-Fri; 9am-6pm Sat; 10am-2pm Sun. **Credit** AmEx, MC, £TC, V.

Everything skate-like can be found at Skate Attack, the largest such shop of its kind in Europe. Also does repairs.

Website: www.skateattack.com

World of Football

119-121 Oxford Street, W1 (020 7287 5088). Oxford Circus or Tottenham Court Road tube. **Open** 10am-7pm Mon-Wed, Fri, Sat; 10am-8pm Thur; noon-6pm Sun. **Credit** AmEx, MC, £TC, V. **Map 5 J6**

Two-floor football megastore.

Website: www.hargreaves-sports.co.uk

YHA Adventure Shop

14 Southampton Street, WC2 (020 7836 8541). Covent Garden tube. **Open** 10am-6pm Mon, Tue; 10.30am-6pm Wed; 10am-7pm Thur, Fri; 9am-6.30pm Sat; 11am-5pm Sun. **Credit** AmEx, DC, JCB, MC, £TC, V. **Map 8 L7**

Good range of walking and camping gear.

Website: www.yhaadventure.co.uk

Toys, games & magic

It's also worth paying a visit to the toy and game departments of **Debenhams** (334-348 Oxford Street, W1; 020 7580 3000), **Harrods**, **Marks & Spencer**, **John Lewis** and **Selfridges** (for all, *see pages 216-7*). For computer games, *see page 205* **Electronics: Computers & games**. *See also page 207* **Daisy & Tom**.

Benjamin Pollock's Toy Shop

44 The Market, Covent Garden, WC2 (020 7379 7866). Covent Garden tube. **Open** 10.30am-6pm Mon-Sat; noon-5pm Sun. **Credit** AmEx, JCB, MC, £TC, V. **Map 8 L7**

Quaint and cluttered, this delightful shop specialises in old-style toys.

Website: www.pollocks-coventgarden.co.uk

Cheeky Monkey

202 Kensington Park Road, W11 (020 7792 9022). Notting Hill Gate tube. **Open** 9.30am-5.30pm Mon-Fri; 10am-5.30pm Sat. **Credit** AmEx, MC, £TC, V. **Map 1 A6**

A fine selection of new toys and nursery accessories, including handmade quilt and cot sets, nursery friezes and wooden toys. Good new and second-hand clothes too.

Branches: 24 Abbeville Road, SW4 (020 8673 5215); 1 Bennett Court, Bellevue Road, SW17 (020 8672 2025).

Davenport's Magic Shop

7 Charing Cross Underground Shopping Concourse, Strand, WC2 (020 7836 0408). Charing Cross tube/rail. **Open** 9.30am-5.30pm Mon-Fri; 10.15am-4pm Sat. **Map 8 L7**

This family business has been operating for over a century. The shop, in an unappetising subterranean arcade, provides for both professionals and newcomers, and staff are keen to encourage novices.

Disney Store

140-144 Regent Street, W1 (020 7287 6558). Oxford Circus tube. **Open** 10am-8pm Mon-Sat; noon-6pm Sun. **Credit** AmEx, JCB, MC, £TC, V. **Map 7 J7**

Get your Snow White dress, Hercules action figure or singalong videos here.

Branches are too numerous to list here. Check the telephone directory for your nearest.

Early Learning Centre

Unit 7, King's Mall, Hammersmith, W6 (020 8741 2469). Hammersmith tube. **Open** 9am-5.30pm Mon-Sat; 11am-5pm Sun. **Credit** AmEx, MC, £TC, V.

A chain of shops with large stocks of brightly coloured, chunky toys. As well as their own well-priced toys, stores carry the Duplo and Brio ranges.

Branches are too numerous to list here. Check the telephone directory for your nearest.

Website: www.elc.co.uk

Hamleys

188-196 Regent Street, W1 (020 7494 2000). Oxford Circus tube. **Open** 10am-8pm Mon-Fri; 9.30am-8pm Sat; noon-6pm Sun. **Credit** AmEx, DC, JCB, MC, £TC, V. **Map 7 J7**

As much tourist attraction as shop, Hamleys is five floors of noise, colour, beaming staff, crazed children and harassed parents. Plus points are London's biggest selection of board games, and a video arcade in the basement. Prices are high.

Branch: 3 The Plaza, Covent Garden, WC2 (020 7240 4646).

Website: www.hamleys.com

Tridias

25 Bute Street, SW7 (020 7584 2330). South Kensington tube. **Open** 9.30am-6pm Mon, Tue, Thur, Fri; 10am-6pm Wed, Sat. **Credit** MC, £TC, V. **Map 4 D10**

One of the UK's top traditional toy shops. Original, reasonably priced equipment: a good place to look for rainy-day activity toys, scientific toys and dressing-up gear.

Website: www.tridias.co.uk

Warner Brothers Studio Store

178-182 Regent Street, W1 (020 7434 3334). Oxford Circus tube. **Open** 10am-8pm daily. **Credit** AmEx, DC, JCB, MC, £TC, V. **Map 7 J7**

Bugs Bunny, Daffy Duck and chums are emblazoned on T-shirts, mugs and toothbrushes, or moulded into chunks of loud plastic.

Arts & Entertainment

Children

Capers with kids in the capital.

The British famously love their pets more than they do their children, so it may come as a surprise to find so much child-centred entertainment on offer in the capital. Romping in the park, zapping aliens in a mega video arcade, stroking an iguana, laughing at a puppet show – there's more than enough to keep your offspring entertained in town. For details of current events and activities, see London's monthly magazine for parents, *Kids Out*.

Grand days out

The past year has seen the closing of two of London's gems. Playtime ended at the London Toy and Model Museum in February 1999, and the Museum of the Moving Image on the South Bank closed in September 1999, but should be reopening, bigger and better, in 2003. These two museums aside, with plenty of child-friendly sights in all four corners of London, it's easy to plan whole days around one area. Most of the sights in bold have fuller entries elsewhere in the Guide; *see pages 349-55* **Index**.

SOUTH BANK

Start at the grand County Hall building, next to Westminster Bridge, which houses the **London Aquarium** (whose sharks are popular residents), the **FA Premier League Hall of Fame** (probably better suited to older footie fans) and the (expensive) video game palace of **Namco Station**. At its side, cantilevered out over the river, is the magnificent **British Airways London Eye** observation wheel. Outside Waterloo Station, in the middle of a huge roundabout, stands the state-of-the-art 480-seater **BFI London IMAX Cinema**, which opened in spring 1999. Nearby, on the South Bank, are the **Royal Festival Hall** (part of the South Bank Centre), where there are cafés, free foyer exhibitions and special events on summer weekends, the **National Film Theatre** and the **Royal National Theatre**. Stroll downstream to Gabriel's Wharf, with its shops, tearoom, restaurants, and open-air theatre and music events in the summer. The enigmatically named **Museum Of...**, meanwhile, has rotating exhibitions that are often of interest to older and younger visitors alike.

BANKSIDE

Continuing along the river... The magnificent new **Tate Modern** is likely to have child-oriented activities when it opens in May 2000 (details unavailable at time of going to press). Another building worth a gawp is the neighbouring **Shakespeare's Globe** (older children should enjoy the tours). Further along the river, close to London Bridge, is the wonderful reconstruction of Sir Francis Drake's **Golden Hinde**, where visitors can take part in Tudor or Stuart workshops with costumed guides. A little further downstream and 350 years on is **HMS Belfast**, back on the Thames after its trip down to Portsmouth in 1999 for a lick of paint. It's a great place for children, with seven huge decks to explore. While you're in the area, don't neglect to pop into lofty **Hay's Galleria** nearby to see David Kemp's wacky *The Navigators* sculpture. Dominating this part of the river is **Tower Bridge** and, on the north bank, the brooding bulk of the **Tower of London**. The **London Dungeon**, by London Bridge station, is not suitable for those of a sensitive disposition.

COVENT GARDEN

One of London's only pedestrianised areas. The old fruit and vegetable market is now full of shops, stalls and street entertainers, including several toy shops. The **Cabaret Mechanical Theatre**, on the lower level of the market, contains more than 60 visitor-operated quirky contraptions to keep even the most hyperactive child busy. Nearby are the **London Transport Museum** (surprisingly entertaining for kids), **Theatre Museum** and **St Paul's Church** garden (secluded and pretty, it's a good spot for a picnic, although it gets crowded when the sun's out).

PICCADILLY CIRCUS

The big attractions here include several examples of the thoroughly commercialised: **Rock Circus**, **Planet Hollywood** and the **Pepsi Trocadero**, which houses an **IMAX cinema**. There's enough to keep children happy all day, but the cost will leave parents reeling. Evenings are the best time to visit (all these places stay open late). Nearby is lively **Chinatown**, and the Leicester Square **cinemas** (*see page 259*).

TRAFALGAR SQUARE

A cheap option. Marvel at how long the kids enjoy feeding the pigeons, climbing on the lions (not real, of course), playing around the fountains and watching the world go by. Then cross the road to the **National Gallery**, which has excellent (free) trails for kids to follow, looking at paintings along the way. Nearby are the **National Portrait Gallery**, The Mall (leading to **Buckingham Palace**) and **St James's Park**, which, with its huge range of waterfowl, is a great place to birdspot. A two-in-one treat can be had at **St Martin-in-the-Fields**: go first to the Café in the Crypt, then burn off all that energy at the **Brass Rubbing Centre**.

THE CITY

Unsurprisingly, the financial district is not the most child-oriented area of London. A visit to **St Paul's Cathedral** is worthwhile, however. Climb to the dome for breathtaking City views (you need a head for heights and lots of stamina). There's also plenty of interest at the excellent **Museum of London** (which has regular workshops and film shows), and, between the two, **Postman's Park**, which is a sheltered spot for a picnic.

ROYAL LONDON

The first stop should be **Buckingham Palace** (the interior is open in summer only). The best place to see the **Changing of the Guard** is near the barracks in Birdcage Walk, while in the nearby **Royal Mews** you'll find groomed horses and lavish state coaches. If Queenie's not at home, she'll probably be at **Windsor Castle**, which makes for a lovely day out of London, as does **Hampton Court**. Whining children should be taken to the **Tower of London** and introduced to the story of the Princes in the Tower.

GREENWICH

Choose a fine day and take the riverboat to explore Greenwich and **Greenwich Park** (a 15-minute walk from the pier), which has recently been made more easily accessible by the extension of the DLR (Docklands Light Railway) down as far as Lewisham (Cutty Sark and Greenwich both serve the sights in this area). Located in the park itself are the excellent and recently extended **National Maritime Museum** (which has an interactive gallery for younger children), the **Queen's House** and the **Royal Observatory** (including a planetarium with shows every weekday), while within striking distance are the **Cutty Sark**, **Gipsy Moth IV** and **Greenwich Market**. Not far from here is the long-awaited **Dome**, which is filled with kid-friendly sights and activities; for more information including details on how to get there, *see page 124* **Dome sweet Dome?**

BOAT TRIPS

Cruise London's waterways. Trips run along the Regent's Canal in north London between Little Venice and **London Zoo** – phone the London Waterbus Company (020 7482 2550) or Jason's Trip (020 7286 3428) – and along the Thames between **Hampton Court** in the west and the **Thames Barrier** in the east, calling at all points and piers on the way (various companies run this route; phone 020 7345 5122 for details). *See also page 338-9.*

Cute kid at **Battersea Park Children's Zoo**. *See page 236. And the one on the right.*

MUSEUMS & COLLECTIONS

Of the Exhibition Road trio, the **Science Museum** is probably the most popular with kids. One of its major attractions is the Launch Pad, with hands-on experiments for tots to teenagers; it also organises Science Nights, when children can explore the museum after dark (ages 8-11; book ahead), and sleepovers. Not to be missed is the hands-on gallery, The Garden (for ages 3-6; phone first to check it's open). New for (summer) 2000 is the Wellcome Wing, housing new galleries and an IMAX cinema. The **Natural History Museum** is also a favourite with children, especially the Dinosaur section and the earthquake simulation in the Earth Galleries; Investigate, a hands-on gallery for children, which is due to open in spring 2000, will no doubt be another winner.

The mammoth scale of much of the ancient plunder in the **British Museum** impresses all ages; there's an excellent children's guide to the collections and the chance to take part in sleepovers with Egyptian or Native American themes. The Museum's monumental Great Court development (due to be completed towards the end of 2000) will incorporate a new Centre for Education, which itself includes a Centre for Young Visitors, with facilities for groups of schoolchildren and, at weekends and during school holidays, families.

The **Bethnal Green Museum of Childhood** is better suited to older children and adults who might want to peruse the back copies of the *Beano* and the grand Victorian dolls' houses. One of the city's quirkiest museums is the **Horniman Museum** in south London – exhibits include an impressive global collection of musical instruments and a stuffed walrus.

For something a bit different, take the kids to one of the superb talks on armour at the **Wallace Collection** (book well in advance), whose exhibition space is being expanded as part of an ambitious centenary project (due to finish in June 2000).

The phenomenal popularity of **Madame Tussaud's** shows no sign of diminishing, although its Chamber of Horrors is pretty tame if you've survived the **London Dungeon**.

Parks & playgrounds

London's parks are great fun for all ages. Below are a few not listed elsewhere in the Guide, but there are scores more. **Regent's Park** has two boating lakes (one for children), three playgrounds, an open-air theatre and **London Zoo**; **Kensington Gardens** boasts two playgrounds and the Round Pond for sailing model boats. Sprawling **Hampstead Heath** and **Parliament Hill** are great for views and kite-flying, while at **Richmond Park** the kids can indulge in a bit of deer-spotting. **Battersea Park** has an adventure playground and a small children's zoo (*see page 236*). **Alexandra Park** and **Clissold Park**, both in north London, and **Victoria Park**, the pride of east London, also have attractions specifically for children. Note that the various components of **Crystal Palace Park** (including a farmyard and boating lake) are under wraps for much of 2000; call 020 8778 9496 to find out what's open. All the parks mentioned below are free. For sporting activities available in the major parks, *see page 129*.

Coram's Fields

93 Guildford Street, WC1 (020 7837 6138). Russell Square tube. **Open** *Easter-Oct* 9am-8pm daily; *Nov-Mar* 9am-dusk daily. **Map 6 L4**

This seven-acre park has an under-fives play area, paddling pool, pets' corner with goats, sheep and a pig, and café. No dogs allowed, and no adults admitted without a child.

Highgate Wood

Muswell Hill Road, N6 (020 8444 6129). Highgate tube. **Open** 7.30am-one hour before dusk daily.

Nature trails, a great playground, a nature hut, loads of space to play and the veggie Oshobasho Café make this a top spot for kids with energy to burn.

Syon Park & London Butterfly House

Syon Park, Brentford, Middlesex (020 8560 0883/ Butterfly House 020 8560 0378/Snakes and Ladders 020 8847 0946/recorded info 020 8560 7272). Gunnersbury tube then 237, 267 bus. **Open** *May-Sept* 10am-5.30pm daily; *Oct-Apr* 10am-3.30pm daily. **Admission** *London Butterfly House* £3.30; £2 concs; £7.75 family; free under-3s; *Snakes and Ladders* from £2.85 under-5s; £3.95 over-5s weekdays & termtime. **Credit** MC, V.

Apart from a huge tropical greenhouse, there's a miniature steam train (Sun, spring-Oct), playground, the Aquatic Experience, featuring fish and reptiles, and the popular Snakes and Ladders adventure playground (10am-6pm daily). *See also p142.*

Supervised play areas

Kids Active

Kids Active has a handful of playgrounds across London where disabled and able-bodied children can play safely, supervised by fully trained staff. For a list, phone 020 7731 1435.

Indoor adventure playgrounds

Bramley's Big Adventure

136 Bramley Road, W10 (020 8960 1515). Ladbroke Grove or Latimer Road tube. **Open** 10am-6.30pm daily. **Admission** *weekends & school holidays* £4.25 over-5s; £3.25 under-5s; *weekdays & termtime* £3.50 over-5s; £2.75 under-5s. **Credit** MC, V.

This smart playground has a separate area for babies and under-fives and some excellent climbing equipment (with sound effects) for older children. There's coffee, food and magazines for accompanying adults. Children's parties from £1 per child.

The Playhouse

The Old Gymnasium, Highbury Grove School, corner of Highbury Grove & Highbury New Park, N5 (020 7704 9424). Highbury & Islington tube. **Open** 10am-6am Mon-Thur; 10am-7pm Fri-Sun. **Admission** £2.95; £2.20 third & subsequent children; £2.20 under-2s walking; £1.50 babies.

This medium-sized playroom has space for up to 70 children aged from six months to 12 years. Facilities include a three-level playframe, a 14-m (40-ft) slide, ball ponds, crawl tunnels and rope bridges. There's also a soft play area for under-fives.

Rascals Adventure Centre

Waterfront Leisure Centre, High Street Woolwich, SE18 (020 8317 5000). Woolwich Arsenal rail/177, 180 bus. **Open** 9.30am-6pm Mon-Fri; 9.30am-2pm Sat, Sun. **Admission** *members* £2.10 first child; £1.10 additional children (up to two only); *non-members* £3.10; £1.10 per session (up to two hours).

Up to 70 children can fling themselves around the play area, which is divided into a spacious soft play area for tinies and a large maze of runways, slides and other activities for five- to eight-year-olds. There's also a video corner to relax in. Note that a maximum of three children are admitted per adult. The Waterfront Leisure Centre also has excellent swimming facilities for kids.

Swimming

There are swimming pools and leisure centres all over London. Below we list some of the best for children as well as two venues specialising in classes. Note that by law a maximum of two children under the age of five per adult are allowed into a public pool. For more pools, *see page 288.*

Dolphin Swimming Club

ULU Pool, Malet Street, WC1 (020 8349 1844). Euston, Russell Square or Tottenham Court Road tube. **Open** 9.15am-2.45pm Sat, Sun. **Admission** *course of 11 30-min lessons* £203.50 individual; £101.75 two in a group; £64.90 five in a group. **Map 6 K4**

Swimming classes for children aged three and above with life-saving, diving, survival skills and synchronised swimming up to ASA gold standard.

Finchley Lido

Great North Leisure Park, High Road, N12 (020 8343 9830). Finchley Central or East Finchley tube. **Open** 6.45am-6.30pm Mon; 6.45am-9.30pm Tue, Thur, Fri; 6.45am-8pm Wed; 8am-4.30pm Sat, Sun. Last entry 30 mins before closing. **Closed** 8.30-9am Mon-Fri. **Admission** £2.60; £1.30-£1.90 concs; free under-5s.

As well as the 25-m main pool, there's a leisure pool with a wave machine, hot tubs, rapids, water jets, a shallow area for babies and slides for small children. On Tuesday from 4.30pm to 6pm kids can take part in a fun session with inflatables. The small outdoor pool is open from May to September. Children under eight must be accompanied by an adult.

Latchmere Leisure Centre

Burns Road, SW11 (020 7207 8004). Clapham Common tube then 345 bus/Clapham Junction rail then 49, 319, 344 bus. **Open** 7am-9.30pm Mon-Thur,

Branching out at **Highgate Wood**. *See page 234.*

Sun; 7am-6pm Fri; 7am-7.30pm Sat. **Admission** *9am-5pm* £2.20; *6-9pm* £2.55; £1.95 weekdays with under-5s; £1.65 concs; free under-5s, disabled.
A leisure pool with a beach, slides, wave machine and warm learners' pool, plus a gym and café.

Swimming Nature

Kensington Sports Centre, Walmer Road, W11 (020 7221 6520). Holland Park or Ladbroke Grove tube. **Open** *administration* 9.30am-5.30pm Mon-Fri. **Admission** *child lessons* £4-£30; *crash courses* £60-£145.
Dedicated, fun swimming classes for kids aged three to ten. Weekly term classes, which vary according to skill, and holiday courses are also offered, along with mother and baby sessions.
Branch: Queen Mother Sports Centre, Vauxhall Bridge Road, SW1 (020 7630 6871).

Waterfront Leisure Centre

High Street Woolwich, SE18 (020 8317 5000). Woolwich Arsenal rail/177, 180 bus. **Open** 7.15am-11pm Mon-Fri; 9am-10pm Sat; 9am-9.30pm Sun. **Admission** £1.20-£3.80; 95p-£2.80 children (additional charge for activities).
The Wild and Wet Adventure Park (open 3-8pm Mon-Fri; 9am-5pm Sat, Sun) has a 25-m fitness pool and four themed pools. Safari Oasis has interactive water toys for toddlers and a five-lane slide for all ages. Anaconda is a 65-m (103-ft) serpent-shaped slide; the ride is fast and in pitch black (children must be at least 1m/3ft 2in tall). The main leisure pool has a wave machine, rapids, jets, a 'volcano', a waterfall, a hot tub and entertainers in costumes who organise games. *See also p235* **Rascals Adventure Centre**.

Animal encounters

If your kids want to interact with animals, there are plenty of places in the city where they can see some cuddly (and not-so-cuddly) creatures. There are around 20 city farms in and around London. For a full list contact: The Federation of City Farms & Community Gardens, The Green House, Hereford Street, Bedminster, Bristol BS3 4NA (0117 923 1800/fax 0117 923 1900).

Battersea Park Children's Zoo

Battersea Park, SW11 (020 8871 7540). Sloane Square tube then 19, 137 bus/Battersea Park rail. **Open** *Apr-Sept* 10am-5pm daily (last entry 4.30pm); *Oct-Mar* 11am-3pm Sat, Sun. **Admission** £1.45; 70p-95p concs. **Map 4 F13**
A small zoo near the river. There are pony rides, a llama, a hillside infested with meerkats, monkey cages and lots of small animals, including pygmy goats, rabbits and a pot-bellied pig. The zoo also opens during half-term in February and October.

London Zoo

Regent's Park, NW1 (020 7722 3333). Camden Town tube then 274 bus. **Open** *Nov-Feb* 10am-4pm daily; *Mar-Oct* 10am-5.30pm daily.
Admission £8.50; £6-£7.50 concs; £26 family; free under-4s. **Credit** AmEx, MC, £$TC, V. **Map 5 G2**
One of the world's best-known zoos, London Zoo has a strong educational slant, even if most children are here to shriek at the gorillas, rhinos, elephants and wolves. This is especially true of the impressive new Web of Life glass pavilion, where the emphasis is on conservation. Bear Mountain, on Mappin Terraces, is a sure-fire hit. While you're here, you can adopt a little beast (animal, that is). Try to time your visit to coincide with one of the feeding times or animal shows (phone for details). *See also p69.*

New at the Zoo is **aka Rampage at London Zoo**, held from 10am to 1pm daily except Sunday, featuring art activities, zoo tours, games, fancy dress and playtimes for children aged five and over, all supervised and tutored by professionals. There are no sessions during January, but this is compensated for by extended hours during April and the summer months, when activities include volleyball and other sports in Regent's Park. Prices start at £15 per day (phone 020 7722 5909 for details).
Website: www.londonzoo.co.uk/londonzoo

Mudchute City Farm

Pier Street, Isle of Dogs, E14 (020 7515 5901/ horse-riding reservations 020 7515 0749). Crossharbour & London Arena DLR. **Open** 10am-4pm (pony rides 2-3pm) daily. **Admission** free (prices vary for pony rides).
Thirty-two acres of land packed with cows, goats, free-range chickens and horses.

Westway Stables

20 Stable Way, W10 (020 8964 2140). Latimer Road/Ladbroke Grove tube/rail.
Open 10am-6pm daily.
Riding lessons for all levels take place throughout the year, and during the holidays the centre runs an 'own a pony' week where children can look after and care for a pony all week and ride twice a day (£150 per week). There's also a day option for £35. Birthday parties are also catered for.

Theme parks

There are a number of major theme parks just outside London, including **Chessington World of Adventures**, **Thorpe Park** and **Legoland Windsor**. For these, and other family attractions outside the capital, *see pages 316.*

Eating with kids

London's restaurants are slowly picking up on the need for decent places for families to eat, with an increasing number now offering children's menus, entertainers and crèches. But it's still the themed venues that cater best for kids; our pick of the bunch are listed below.

Babe Ruth's

172-176 The Highway, E1 (020 7481 8181). Shadwell tube/DLR/D1, 100 bus. **Meals** noon-11pm Mon-Thur; noon-midnight Fri, Sat; noon-10.30pm Sun. **Credit** AmEx, £TC, MC, V.

This vast, family-friendly sports restaurant has games galore and a children's menu complete with puzzles on the back for £7.99. Kids can slam-dunk in the mini-basketball court or play on arcade games (£1 a go).
Branch: 02 Complex, Finchley Road, NW3 (020 7433 3388).

The Big Easy

332-334 King's Road, SW3 (020 7352 4071). Sloane Square tube then 11, 19, 22 bus.
Meals noon-midnight Mon-Thur; noon-12.30pm Fri, Sat; noon-11.30pm Sun. **Credit** AmEx, MC, £TC, V. **Map 4 D12**
This lively restaurant offers a hearty slice of American pie, plus facilities and offers for children that Uncle Sam would be proud of – crayons, high chairs and a kids' menu. An extra bonus is that one child under ten eats for free when accompanied by an adult (subsequent children each for £3.95). There's also a separate room for parties (Mon-Fri during the day).

Boiled Egg & Soldiers

63 Northcote Road, SW11 (020 7223 4894). Clapham Junction rail/45, 219, 319 bus.
Meals 9am-6pm Mon-Sat; 10am-5pm Sun.
Great kids' food in cosy surroundings. Parents will appreciate the all-day breakfasts (£4.50) too. There are toys and high chairs available, and a garden at the back for the summer.

Fatboy's Diner

Spitalfields Market, off Commercial Street, E1 (020 7375 2763). Liverpool Street tube/rail.
Meals 10am-4pm Mon, Tue; 10am-10pm Wed-Fri; 10am-5pm Sat; 9am-6pm Sun. **Map 10 R5**
A funky 1950s diner serving chunky chips and milk-shakes. The kids' menu offers meals for around £3. It's quieter on a Saturday, when staff are happy to arrange children's parties. Frazzled parents can get their own back by perusing the market (best on a Sunday; closed Saturday).

Maxwell's

8-9 James Street, WC2 (020 7836 0303). Covent Garden tube. **Meals** noon-midnight daily. **Credit** AmEx, DC, MC, £TC, V. **Map 8 L6**
Right near Covent Garden piazza, Maxwell's provides children's menus with themes at Christmas, Halloween and Thanksgiving. Staff usually don appropriate costumes, and there are colourings and quizzes to keep the littl'uns happy.
Branch: 76 Heath Street, NW3 (020 7836 0303).

Rainforest Café

20 Shaftesbury Avenue, W1 (020 7434 3111). Piccadilly Circus tube. **Meals** noon-10.30pm Mon-Thur; noon-11.30pm Fri; 11.30am-11.30pm Sat; 11.30am-10.30pm Sun. **Credit** AmEx, MC, V. **Map 8 K7**
Kids will love munching their American-style food to the sounds of wild animals, cascading waterfalls and even thunder and lightning. There's a set children's menu (£7.95), plus party bags, cakes, face painters and more for children's parties.

Smollensky's on the Strand

105 Strand, WC2 (020 7497 2101). Charing Cross tube/rail. **Meals** noon-midnight Mon-Wed; noon-12.30am Thur-Sat. **Credit** AmEx, DC, MC, £TC, V. **Map 8 L7**
This lively upmarket brasserie has loads of kids' entertainment, with clowns and magicians on weekend lunchtimes, a Punch and Judy show on Saturdays and a magic show on Sundays (both 2.30pm). There's also face painting (£4.50), a play area, Nintendo games, toys and crayons. Grown-ups, meanwhile, will appreciate the pianist (7pm-midnight Monday to Saturday), or the live jazz band on Sundays 8-10.30pm; £4.50 cover).

Sticky Fingers

1A Phillimore Gardens, W8 (020 7938 5338). High Street Kensington tube. **Meals** noon-11pm Mon-Thur, Sun; noon-11.30pm Fri, Sat. **Credit** AmEx, DC, MC, V. **Map 3 A9**
Bill Wyman's lively restaurant remains popular with kids for its burgers. There's a children's menu for around £5, plus a face-painter on Sundays. The food's nothing special but the service and ambience are fun. If the kids like this kind of thing, **Planet Hollywood** (Trocadero, 13 Coventry Street, W1; 020 7287 1000) and the **Hard Rock Café** (150 Old Park Lane, W1; 020 7629 0382) will also appeal.

TGI Friday's

6 Bedford Street, WC2 (020 7379 0585). Covent Garden tube/Charing Cross tube/rail. **Meals** noon-11.30pm Mon-Sat; noon-11pm Sun. **Credit** AmEx, MC, £TC, V. **Map 8 L7**
Having fun is compulsory in this loud venue, which has won awards for its family-friendliness. Staff are relentlessly cheerful and helpful. Kids have a choice of two menus (£6.25/£7.35) and can get their sticky paws on badges, crayons, balloons and toys. There's also face painting at weekends (1-5pm), plus a magician on Sundays. You *will* enjoy.
Branches are too numerous to list here: call 01908 669911 for your nearest branch.

Entertainment

Little Angel Theatre

14 Dagmar Passage, off Cross Street, N1 (020 7226 1787). Angel tube/Highbury & Islington tube/rail.
Performances *Sept-July* 11am, 3pm, Sat, Sun, half-terms & Christmas holidays. **Admission** £5-£7.50. **Credit** AmEx, MC, V. **Map 9 O1**
London's only permanent puppet theatre, founded in 1961, has seating for 110 people. It's a charming venue, with regular weekend shows by the resident company and visiting puppeteers. The minimum age is three, but some performances are suitable for older children only; phone to check.

London Symphony Orchestra Family Concerts

Barbican Centre, Silk Street, EC2 (020 7638 8891). Barbican tube. **Performances** once a term (usually Sun). **Admission** £6; £3 under-16s. **Credit** AmEx, MC, V. **Map 9 P5**

These concerts encourage children to learn about classical music in a fun and stimulating environment. During the interval, they can meet LSO players, who demonstrate their instruments in the foyer. Children are also invited to bring along an instrument and participate.

National Film Theatre

South Bank, SE1 (020 7928 3535). Embankment tube/Waterloo tube/rail. **Admission** £5.20; £3.70 concs; £1 under-16s accompanied by adults.
Credit AmEx, £TC, V. **Map 8 M7**
Matinées for children are held every Saturday and Sunday at 3-4pm.

Polka Theatre for Children

240 The Broadway, SW19 (020 8543 4888). Wimbledon South tube/Wimbledon tube/rail.
Admission £5-£10. **Credit** MC, V.
This beautiful purpose-built complex for under-13s has a 300-seat theatre, an Adventure Room for under-fives, a playground, café and two shops. The thriving company has put on several award-winning shows. There are regular workshops during term-time; phone for details. Closed in September.

Puppet Theatre Barge

Blomfield Road, W9 (020 7249 6876). Warwick Avenue tube. **Performances** *termtime* 3pm Sat, Sun; *school holidays & half-term* 3pm daily. **Admission** £6; £5.50 concs. **Credit** MC, V. **Map 2 D4**
Moored at Abingdon, Oxfordshire in June, Henley-on-Thames in July, Marlow in August, Richmond during the autumn and Little Venice in the winter, this unique floating marionette theatre stages regular family shows and performances for adults. Schools are accommodated and private performances are held by prior arrangement.

Unicorn Theatre for Children

Unicorn at the Pleasance Theatre, Carpenters Mews, North Road, N7 (020 7700 0702/7609 8753). Leicester Square tube. **Performances** *termtime* 10.15am, 1.30pm, Tue-Fri (phone to check); 11am, 2.30pm, Sat; 2.30pm Sun; *school holidays* phone to check. **Admission** £5-£10.
Credit AmEx, MC, £TC, V.
Founded in 1948, London's oldest professional children's theatre has left Great Newport Street and is at the Pleasance Theatre for the foreseeable future. It presents an adventurous programme of commissioned plays and other entertainment for children aged four to 12.

Annual events

There are few events in London geared specifically towards children, but youngsters normally enjoy such staples as the **Lord Mayor's Show**, which usually features a dazzling fireworks display (*see page 10*), **Trooping the Colour** (*see page 7*) and the **Changing of the Guard** (*see page 5*). Another sure-fire winner is the annual **Punch and Judy Festival** in Covent Garden (*see page 9*). For details of the puppet shows that take place in the summer in London's royal parks, phone 020 7298 2100. There are also several funfairs a year at **Alexandra Park** (*see page 108*), **Battersea Park** (*see page 132*), **Hampstead Heath** (*see page 105*) and **Clapham Common** (phone 020 8671 0994 for details).

Teddy Bears' Picnic

Battersea Park, SW11 (020 8871 8107). Battersea Park rail/49 bus. **Date** usually the first Fri afternoon in Aug. **Admission** free. **Map 4 F13**
An annual picnic, held for thousands of children and their furry friends. There are entertainers, and activities include face-painting and workshops.

Shopping for children

See pages 207 and *230.*

Taking a break

Childminders

6 Nottingham Street, W1 (020 7935 3000/2049).
Open 8.45am-5.45pm Mon-Wed; 8.45am-5.30pm Thur; 8.45am-5pm Fri; 9am-4.30pm Sat. **Map 5 G5**
A large agency with over 1,500 babysitters, mainly nurses, nannies and infant teachers (all with references), who live all over London and the suburbs.
Website: www.babysitter.co.uk

Pippa Pop-ins

430 Fulham Road, SW6 (020 7385 2458).
Open by appointment. **Fees** from £40 per day.
Credit AmEx, MC, £TC, V.
This friendly nursery school and kindergarten run by NNEB- and Montessori-trained nursery teachers and nannies also offers kids' parties, holiday activities, school runs and a crèche.

Universal Aunts

(daytime childminding 020 7738 8937/evening babysitting 020 7386 5900). **Open** 9.30am-5pm Mon-Thur; 9.30am-4pm Fri. **Rates** from £5.50 per hour (daytime).
This London agency, founded in 1921, can provide reliable people to babysit, meet children from trains, planes or boats, or take them sightseeing.

Information

For more information, see *Kids Out* magazine (available at all good newsagents or on subscription by calling 01454 620070). For local events, contact the relevant borough council.

Kidsline (020 7222 8070). **Open** *termtime* 4-6pm Mon-Fri; *school holidays* 9am-4pm Mon-Fri.
Information on films, shows, attractions and activities geared towards children.

Parentline (0808 800 2222). **Open** 9am-9pm Mon-Fri; 9.30am-5.30pm Sat; 10am-3pm Sun.
Free, confidential parent helpline.

The Register (020 7701 6111).
Fortnightly childcare listings magazine.

Clubs

Whether you're after a tiny underground sweatbox or a swanky new superclub, this city has the lot.

There are more places to dance in London than probably ever before. During 1999, three large-scale super-venues opened, while the continuing proliferation of late-opening club bars means an abundance of smaller DJ-led nightspots. Clubbing is now an essential part of mainstream British culture, but as well as the more commercial options there's always a new scene bubbling up from the underground, providing even the most established clubs with new ideas and fresh energy. British Asian musical culture, the breakbeat scene, new British house and the resurgence of hip hop have all kept alive the city's reputation for musical innovation, as has the evolving sound of UK garage (also known as 'speed garage'), itself a very local flavour. Go out in London and you might come across the latest hotbed of musical experimentation and find that it's only a few doors away from the most unapologetically glamorous superclub.

In the descriptions that follow we've focused on the actual venues, but be aware that in most places the precise music and style of a club will usually be different from night to night. We've highlighted particular nights worth looking out for, but for full details check out the extensive weekly club listings in *Time Out* magazine You'll also find events promoted on radio, on flyers and in the specialist club magazines. The more underground scenes are harder to infiltrate, though hanging around in record stores and tuning in to pirate radio are good places to start. As a rough guide, expect to pay around £3-£10 to get into a club, and if you're a student always ask about concessionary rates.

Up at the big house

All this diversity is fine, but it's still house music that packs the dancefloors at weekends. The most famous dance club in London is the **Ministry of Sound**. Situated south of the river near the Elephant & Castle (a rather grim part of town), it looks like a prison yard from the outside, yet draws all-night dancers like moths to a flame. Big-name guest DJs (from the USA and the UK) spinning garage and house are the principal attraction, but the sheer energy and enthusiasm of the place will take your breath away. On the downside, the queues can be long, the security crew at the door are rarely friendly and admission is £10-£15, but then you are paying to party on until 9am.

Thanks to the success of its 'brand' (it has its own magazine, record label and Internet radio broadcasts), the Ministry may well be high on visiting clubbers' itineraries. However, it is no longer unchallenged in the superclub stakes. With the opening of the **Scala**, **Home** and most recently **Fabric** (*see page 240* **Three of a kind**), with a combined capacity of 7-8,000, Londoners have a great deal more choice when it comes to venues large enough to boast impressive sound systems and big name visiting DJs.

The West End's **The End** is the most sophisticated dance venue in the heart of London; a cutting-edge homage to minimal styling and maximum sound quality. It's hosted by Mr C, of the techno-pop band The Shamen, who is often seen on the decks, and it boasts proper air-conditioning and spectacularly smart toilets, not to mention a monthly series of the best funky techno, drum 'n' bass

Catch **Scala** *fever. See page 240.*

Three of a kind

For the addresses of the following venues, see p246 **Clubs index**.

Typical – you wait ages for a superclub and then three come along at once. In fact, so dramatically did the **Scala**, **Home** and **Fabric** increase London's dancefloor capacity that sceptics were asking whether they could all survive. Well, so far there's been no question, as all three new venues have wowed the critics and packed in the punters.

The **Scala** (official capacity 800; cost to open £1.8m) was first out of the box, coming to life in spring 1999. A former fleapit cinema in King's Cross, famous for its all-night, six-film screenings, it was empty for several years until nightlife impresario Sean McCluskey turned it into the swank split-level club it is now. As well as club nights with a distinctly hip hop and breakbeat bias it hosts some dramatic one-off events plus regular live music, film screenings and even plays. Look out for Saturday's 'Sonic Mook Experiment', a fest of breaks and beats, and great hip hop monthly 'Scratch'.

The seven-storey nightpalace of **Home** (2,700; £8m) would probably be a very different club were it not smack in the middle of Leicester Square. Its glitzy LED video screen and tourist-friendly location are a natural deterrent to most Londoners, who prefer their nightlife on seedy backstreets in dodgy ex-warehouses. Home's guiding aim was to do everything that other clubs do, but better; hence even its restaurant has impressed food critics. So it's a shame that the elegant design and the excellent sound systems are left mostly to out-of-towners, at the weekends at least. At Home the music is centred around a residency by the world's most successful DJ (it's official), Paul Oakenfold, who is a business partner in the club and its 'musical director'. Oakey aims to create the kind of crowd loyalty he enjoyed at Liverpool's Cream and will be inviting a steady stream of outside guests including plenty of mega-jocks such as Danny Rampling and Pete Tong. As well as the banging weekends look out for 'Highrise' on a Thursday, one of the club's best nights, a seductive blend of deep house, funky breakbeats and more.

Thanks to the unique problems that came from its past life as a giant Victorian fridge, **Fabric** (2,500; £4.8m) wasn't quite fabricated in time for its much-advertised launch date (just one of the construction problems was that a couple of feet of cork insulation had to be removed from every inch of wall surface). However, it opened to great acclaim in October 1999 and has quickly become the city's most impressive venue for serious dancing. The beauty of this club is its sheer architectural brilliance: its grand, simple spaces are filled with world-class sound systems and not much else. No fuss, no fancy décor, just three vast rooms, a stream of great DJs, and a 24-hour music licence. Music policy is to avoid the overtly mainstream (although Sasha has a residency) and concentrate on more underground sounds, with an emphasis on bringing in DJs who appeal to the clubland cognoscenti such as Danny Tenaglia and François Kevorkian, as well as home-grown underground stars like Bill Brewster and Terry Francis. Finally, thanks to its unique 'Bodysonic' main dancefloor (the whole floor is a giant sub-bass loudspeaker), on a visit to Fabric you'll really feel the earth move.

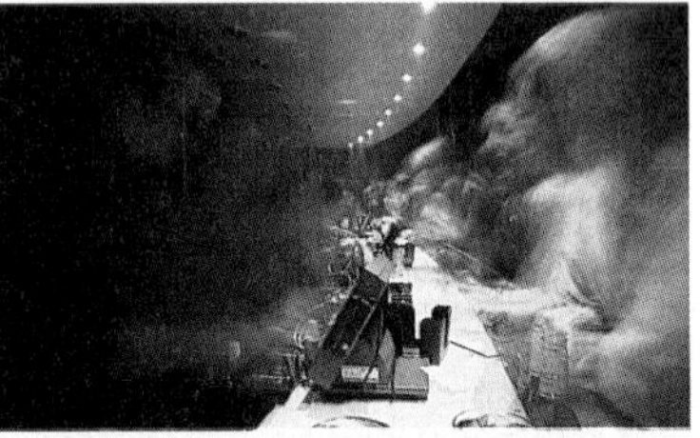

Top to bottom: **Home, Fabric, Scala.**

Doors of misperception

London clubs are notorious for the length of their queues and the whimsy of their door policies. Even the places that boast of giving their customers the finest service inside often treat you like cattle when you're waiting on the pavement. Unless you're a seasoned blagger or you really are on the DJ's guest list, the best approach is to grit your teeth and wait. And when it comes to contact with the door people the keywords are politeness and persistence. However, be aware that few clubs will tell you directly that you can't come in; if they deem you unsuitable they may simply let those behind you enter first. Only when you ask will they bring out the coded excuses such as 'it's a private party tonight' or 'it's not your kind of thing'. Unfair, unjustified, but in most cases completely legal.

Some places will go to extremes to ensure that you fit their idea of who should be in their club, hiring staff called 'door pickers' to sort out the good, the bad and the ugly. Certain gay clubs have been known to ask punters to snog a member of the same sex to prove their suitability; other clubs might ask you what DJ is playing tonight to see how clued-up you are. No one likes to be singled out, left cooling their heels outside, so to avoid such an experience, **phone the club in advance** to check that a specific night is on (club nights come and go with astonishing speed, so you could be queuing for the wrong thing entirely), and to find out the best time to arrive and whether there are any dress requirements. Note that most do not allow you in if you're wearing jeans and trainers; but be aware that even clubs with no dress code may exercise a subtle fashion fascism when it comes to allowing you through the door. However, if the door people think you look out of place, maybe they're right and you wouldn't enjoy what's inside. *Time Out* magazine is the best source to find out what's happening week to week. Good luck, and have a happy nightlife.

and deep house parties in London. The club also has a sister bar and restaurant, **AKA** (*see page 244* **Club bars**), right next door, which is a good pre-club joint or a place to go when you're too tired to dance any more.

Turnmills in Farringdon is famous for its 'underground' dance nights, but it has more nooks and crannies than your granny's cupboards and plenty of space to sit and chill out as well as sweat it out on the dancefloor. The full-on housey party, 'The Gallery' on Fridays, and the drunken revelry at the 'Headstart' on Saturdays are both ram-jammed popular. The latter closes at 3.30am, to be followed by 'Trade', a marathon, predominantly gay event that continues for the next ten hours until Sunday afternoon (*see page 265*). Most nights aren't quite so demanding on the stamina, usually finishing at a respectable 6am at weekends. Like The End, Turnmills has expanded over the past year, adding two floors, which dramatically improve the layout of the club.

Heaven, a maze of bars, dancefloors and corridors behind Charing Cross Station, had a major refit recently. It's London's most famous gay venue (*see page 264*); 'straight' clubbers are only likely to test its charms at the monthly parties – like 'Bedrock' on Thursdays, or at the popular mixed-gay 'There' on Fridays, where hard house meets new breakbeats on three dancefloors.

Other major dance venues worth checking out include **The Complex** (formerly the Blue Note; *see page 244*) and the **Fridge** (*see page 245*).

Dressed to kill

Let's assume that what you're really looking for is not the trendiest bar or the loudest sound system, but a nightclub where you can dress up and party in style. The West End's **Browns**, **Café de Paris** and **Stringfellows** spring to mind, while the **Roof Gardens** in Kensington is probably the most beautiful club location in the city. These are popular with people of all ages and positively encourage smart attire.

Browns is a sleek and chic two-floor club in Holborn that is best known as a haunt of celebrities and location for after-show parties. **Café de Paris**, a classic 1920s ballroom, has a lovely balcony, good for spying on the dancefloor below. There's a restaurant too, which is great if you want a hassle-free night out. The **Roof Gardens** is a members club (non-members are admitted on Thursday and Saturday; the £40 admission sounds steep but includes a three-course dinner) and has the atmosphere and appearance of a plush restaurant rather than a disco. It is six floors above ground and, as its name might suggest, boasts three stunning garden areas in addition to the restaurant and dancefloor. However, the place to go if you're all dressed up with, er, nowhere to go, is **The Emporium**, in the centre of town – it's known to be a hangout for celebs, and once had to refuse a request to hold a private party for Prince (or should that be The Artist…?) as it was too busy.

The samba scene

For the addresses of the following venues, see *p246* **Clubs index**.

London has a great selection of Latin clubs and one-nighters, and you don't have to be Jennifer Lopez or Ricky Martin to participate. Always welcoming to interested, enthusiastic strangers, these places tend to attract a broader age range and more cosmopolitan crowd than 'trendy' dance clubs and they're noticeably smarter too. Most of the dancers aren't Latinos, though regular dance classes and practice have transformed them into brilliant movers – don't be put off, as dance classes are often held before Latin clubs begin, so you can brush up your steps or learn a few beginner's moves to get you going…

Cuba, on Kensington High Street, is a good place to start. It's a relaxed club (and there's a restaurant and bar upstairs) with six nights of diverse Latin beats (Mon-Sat) often featuring live bands. If you're in the heart of the West End, then **Salsa!** on Charing Cross Road is a bar-cum-club that's well worth a visit, with a similarly broad range of nights aimed at dancers and Caipirinha-cocktail drinkers. If you're south of the river, the **Loughborough Hotel** in Brixton is a rambling corner pub that's been transformed into an excellent two-floor Latin venue (Thur, Fri). Close by in Vauxhall (just south of the river), **Club Soneros** is best known for putting on live Latin bands three nights a week (Thur-Sat); it has a 'no trainers or jeans' dress code.

Apart from the venues devoted to Latin rhythms, there are a couple of other long-running Latin one-nighters that are well worth checking. 'Rumba Pa'ti', **Bar Rumba** (Tue; *pictured above*), is ideal for beginners and has a young and dressed-down crowd. Meanwhile, 'Sunday School' at **Villa Stefano** (Sun) is pure 'hardcore salsa' for the real aficionados.

More famous and much less discreet is **Stringfellows**, another nightclub which can claim an à la carte (French) restaurant. It's a West End institution for suit-and-tie hedonists, and is hosted by the irrepressible self-styled 'king of clubs' – not to mention 'king of mullets' – Peter Stringfellow, and like its owner, it's neither new in town nor trendy. In fact, for most of the week (Monday to Thursday) it hosts table dancing; disco-house beats take over from the girls at weekends.

Mayfair play

Mayfair is quiet at night, so clubs here rely on reputation rather than passing trade, and are more stylish and comfortable than most other dance clubs. The **Hanover Grand** (just off Regent Street), with its balconied dancefloor upstairs and groovy bar below, is home to the best midweek R&B and hip hop ('Fresh 'n' Funky') on Wednesday, and seriously trendy dance nights on Thursday, Friday and Saturday, when only the most gorgeous club-people are likely to get past the style police on the door. **Legends**, near Piccadilly, is sleek and modern. Designed by Eva Jiricknа, the restaurant and bar upstairs have a huge window on to the street (if the area was busier it would be a perfect poseurs' parade) and a dressed-up, good-looking crowd bops to house dance beats at weekends.

Soho & Covent Garden

Dozens of bars, cafés, clubs and restaurants are situated in Soho and Covent Garden; the best way to explore is to cruise around on foot, although a few venues stand out. **Bar Rumba**, one of the best dance clubs in town, plays host to a series of excellent one-nighters: Monday has jazz, funk and drum 'n' bass; Tuesday, Latin; it's deep house on Wednesday; drum 'n' bass on Thursday; New Skool beats on Friday; and garage on Saturday. Each night is among the best of its type. Equally popular is **The Wag**, a stylish club on three floors that similarly plays host to a wide variety of music. Midweek sees indie-rock nights; Friday, an '80s retro session; while 'Blow Up' is one of the best parties around on Saturday, a night that takes its inspiration from '60s soul and pop, but that plays all kinds of 'lounge' tunes and big beat too.

The **Velvet Room**, on Charing Cross Road, is a luxuriously appointed 'club bar' that also hosts an excellent drum 'n' bass Wednesday-nighter ('Swerve') and a great techno and deep house night on Thursdays ('Ultimate BASE'). Stylish 'club' clothes should normally guarantee admission. Nearby, opposite the Centrepoint building, is **LA2**, home to 'Carwash' on Saturdays, the best disco night in town but one for which you must dress the part (ie like an extra from *Saturday Night Fever*).

Could this be **The End**? *See page 239.*

West is best

If you're staying in west or south-west London, then **Subterania** is an excellent night-time destination. Live music gigs entertain during the week and DJs spin funky sounds at the weekend to a trendy west London crowd – both Friday's 'Rotation' and Saturday's 'Soulsonic' are hard to get into unless you arrive early (and dress up for the latter). The **Leopard Lounge** on Fulham Broadway provides another good excuse not to hike up to the West End. It's a spacious and lavish club, predictably decked out with zebra- and leopard-skin décor (and full of flares-wearing '70s party people on Thursday nights).

North London nights

After being roundly hailed as the coolest place on earth a couple of years ago, the loft-loungers' paradise of Hoxton is now filled with trendy bars and restaurants, many of which encourage late drinking with DJs and a dancefloor. The Blue Note, one of the main reasons for Hoxton's trendiness, was forced to relocate by local authorities and now the only large club in the area is the **333**,

Club bars

The term 'club bar' has been coined to describe a growing number of bars that stay open later than 11pm, lay on DJs, have admission charges (after a certain time), and by doing all of this combine the conversation culture of pubs with the style, fashion and music of clubs. So if you're looking for somewhere that's musically credible and fills the gap between pre-club hangout and full-on all-nighter, here are some of our favourites. In addition to those below, *see also* **The Velvet Room** (*page 243* **Soho & Covent Garden**).

AKA

18 West Central Avenue, WC2 (020 7836 0110). Holborn or Tottenham Court Road tube.
Open 6pm-1am Tue; 6pm-3am Wed-Fri; 7pm-3am Sat. **Map 6 L6**
Highly rated bar and restaurant venture by former Shamen frontman Mr C, who also owns **The End** club (*see p239*) next door.

Blue Bar

257-259 Pentonville Road, N1 (020 7837 3218). King's Cross tube/rail. **Open** 5pm-1am Wed; 9pm-3am Thur-Sat; 7.30pm-1.30am Sun. **Map 6 M3**
A respite from the general sleaze of King's Cross, this funky hangout (formerly the Cross bar) offers decent grub and a chilled atmosphere before the music cranks up.

Bug Bar

The Crypt, St Matthew's Peace Garden, Brixton Hill, SW2 (020 7738 3184). Brixton tube/rail.
Open 7pm-1am Mon-Thur; 7pm-3am Sat; 7-11pm Sun. **Admission** £3 after 9pm; £5 after 11pm.
Laid-back yet resolutely alive, the perennially popular Bug Bar has regular entertainment such as bands, stand-ups and DJs.

Dogstar

389 Coldharbour Lane, SW9 (020 7733 7515). Brixton tube/rail. **Open** noon-1am Mon-Thur; noon-3am Fri, Sat; noon-11pm Sun. **Admission** £3 9-10pm, £4 10-11pm, £5 11pm-3am, Fri, Sat.
The burgeoning southside club crowd would be lost without this vibey and happening converted pub.

Dust

27 Clerkenwell Road, EC1 (020 7490 5120). Farringdon tube/rail. **Open** 11am-11pm Mon-Wed; 11am-midnight Thur, Fri; 6pm-midnight Sat; noon-6pm Sun. **Map 9 N4**
This classy DJ bar, within staggering distance of Turnmills (*see p241*), is a clever, simple space clad in wood and coppery paintwork. And the drinks and food are pretty good too.

Ego

23 Bateman Street, W1 (020 7437 1977). Tottenham Court Road tube. **Open** 5pm-1am Mon-Sat. **Map 6 K6**
This split-level bar in the heart of Soho is a tightly packed dance den filled with clubbers congregating for a night on the town.

a charmingly shabby venue that usually has a wonderful variety of entertainment ranged over its three floors, including poetry and jazz. On most nights of the week the sweaty cellar rocks to trancey house and techno.

The Blue Note washed up in Islington as **The Complex**, a four-floor venue that has most successfully caught the musical moods of the last couple of years; the diversity ranges from soulful funk to radical breakbeats, and often within the same night. The whole of the top level 'Love Lounge' is devoted to chilling out and socialising in a warm womb-red glow. Saturday night is one of the best places outside of an East End warehouse to see London's UK garage scene in full effect, in a freestyle feast of funk, swing and garage beats called 'Camouflage'.

Despite its location, in the wastelands behind King's Cross, **The Cross** has a reputation for great weekend dance parties, including 'Renaissance', the Midlands superclub that takes over each month, when the brick arches shake to the latest grooves. It's well worth a cab fare, but like so many of these clubs, it's already a hit with the locals, so arriving early is always a good idea. Across a small car park you'll find **Bagley's Studios**, a warren of connected rooms in an old film studio, which rocks to regular large-scale bashes, usually of a housey nature. Also near King's Cross, the **Scala** is proving itself extremely popular with a series of breakbeat and hip hop-related nights (*see page 240* **Three of a kind**).

The huge old music hall venue of the **Camden Palace** was transformed into a multi-level inferno of sound and light back in the early '80s. It's showing its age now but is still worth visiting for Tuesday's indie-rock club 'Feet First' and for some of the special events on Saturdays – otherwise leave it alone.

Southside stepping

There's a growing nightlife scene in and around Brixton. The biggest venue is **The Fridge**, a transformation of a former theatre that is hardly glamorous but can look spectacular with clever use of visuals and decor. Saturday is a major gay night but it goes 'straight' on Fridays for the trancey, techno all-nighter 'Escape From Samsara'. Right opposite The Fridge is **Mass**, a two-room nightclub high up a circular stairwell in a converted church. It's a great venue, boasting cutting

Embassy Bar

119 Essex Road, N1 (020 7226 9849). Angel tube/ 38, 56, 73, 171A bus. **Open** 5-11pm Mon-Thur; 5pm-1am Fri; 2pm-1am Sat; 2-10.30pm Sun. **Map 9 O1**

The Embassy Bar boasts suave, retro Hollywood-style glamour design and an up-to-the-minute music policy, with guest DJs putting in an appearance on Fridays and Saturdays.

Fridge Bar

1 Town Hall Parade, SW2 (020 7326 5100). Brixton tube/rail. **Open** 10am-2am Mon-Thur; 10am-4am Fri, Sat; 10am-12.30am Sun.

At weekends the Fridge Bar functions as an agreeable chill-down session for the club nights next door (*see p246* **Southside stepping**). A laid-back crowd add to the atmosphere.

Ion

165 Ladbroke Grove, W10 (020 8960 1702). Ladbroke Grove tube. **Open** noon-midnight daily.

This DJ bar is wonderfully light and airy, with a great terrace and decent restaurant on the mezzanine level.

Jerusalem

33-34 Rathbone Street, W1 (020 7255 1120). Tottenham Court Road tube. **Open** noon-2am Mon-Thur; noon-3am Fri, Sat. **Map 5 J5**

A capacious basement bar where massive chunks of wood serve as bench tables and trendy staff dish out trendy food and drinks to a trendy crowd. Pretty good DJs midweek.

Medicine Bar

181 Upper Street, N1 (020 7704 9536). Highbury & Islington tube/rail. **Open** 5pm-midnight Mon-Thur; noon-1am Fri, Sat; noon-11pm Sun. **Admission** (membership may be required) 7pm-1am Fri; 6pm-1am Sat.

A stylish and comfortable Islington hangout that fills up with pre-clubbers as the after-work drinkers begin to fade away.

Notting Hill Arts Club

21 Notting Hill Gate, W11 (020 7460 4459). Notting Hill Gate tube. **Open** 5pm-1am Mon-Sat; 4-11pm Sun. **Admission** £3-£5 8pm-1am Mon-Sat; 7-11pm Sun. **Map 1 A7**

A largish whitewashed basement that packs in local trustafarians and clubbed-out drinkers. Good DJs too.

The Social Bar

5 Little Portland Street, W1 (020 7636 4992). Oxford Circus tube. **Open** noon-midnight Mon-Sat; 5-10.30pm Sun. **Map 5 J5**

A smart, two-floor drinkery offering fine music nightly, The Social is the place you're most likely to spot a Manic Street Preacher or a Chemical Brother, plus more drunken record-biz press officers than you'll ever wish to see.

WKD

18 Kentish Town Road, NW1 (020 7267 1869). Camden Town tube/Camden Road rail. **Open** noon-2am Mon-Thur; noon-3am Fri, Sat; noon-1am Sun.

Varied live music and DJs from 9.30pm daily. The snack food is decent too.

edge line-ups, but often very little in the way of atmosphere thanks to rather undramatic sound and lighting. Smaller in scale but not in ambition are the 'club bars' (rather like a cross between pubs and clubs; *see also pages 244-5*). **The Dogstar** on Coldharbour Lane has set the trend; it's free to get in for most of the night and attracts some of London's most interesting DJs. **The Junction**, much further up Coldharbour Lane, and the **Bug Bar** (next to Mass) have a similarly adventurous line-up, while the **Fridge Bar** (adjacent to The Fridge, not surprisingly; *see page 245*) adopts a more global dance perspective.

Finally, hot on the heels of Scala, Fabric and Home (*see page 240* **Three of a kind**) comes **Grace**, a 2,000-capacity club, which opened in late 1999. Located off the Old Kent Road, the club makes a welcome change to an area not exactly renowned for its hip and happening nightlife. In addition to attracting big names in terms of DJs, the club also hopes to host barbecues when the weather's hot enough in summer.

Clubs index

Bagley's Studios *King's Cross freight depot, off York Way, N1 (020 7278 2777). King's Cross tube/rail.* **Map 6 L2**

Bar Rumba *36 Shaftesbury Avenue, W1 (020 7287 2715). Piccadilly Circus tube.* **Map 8 K7**

Browns *4 Great Queen Street, WC2 (020 7831 0802). Holborn tube.* **Map 6 L6**

Café de Paris *3 Coventry Street, W1 (020 7734 7700). Leicester Square or Piccadilly Circus tube.* **Map 8 K7**

Camden Palace *1A Camden High Street, NW1 (020 7387 0428). Camden Town or Mornington Crescent tube.*

Club Soneros *The Gallery, Bondway, SW8 (020 7820 0671). Vauxhall tube/rail.*

The Complex *1-5 Parkfield Street, N1 (020 7288 1986). Angel tube.* **Map 9 N2**

The Cross *Goods Way Depot, off York Way, N1 (020 7837 0828). King's Cross tube/rail.* **Map 6 L2**

Cuba *11-13 Kensington High Street, W8 (020 7938 4137). High Street Kensington tube.* **Map 3 A9**

The Emporium *62 Kingly Street, W1 (020 7734 3190). Oxford Circus tube.* **Map 5 J6**

The End *18A West Central Street, WC1 (020 7419 9199). Holborn or Tottenham Court Road tube.* **Map 6 L6**

Fabric *77A Charterhouse Street, EC1 (020 7490 0444). Farringdon tube/rail.* **Map 9 O5**

The Fridge *Town Hall Parade, Brixton Hill, SW2 (020 7326 5100). Brixton tube/rail.*

Grace *Olmar Street, off Old Kent Road, SE1 (020 7252 1199). Elephant & Castle tube/ London Bridge tube/rail then shuttle bus (phone for details).*

Hanover Grand *6 Hanover Street, W1 (020 7499 7977). Oxford Circus tube.* **Map 5 J6**

Heaven *under the arches, off Villiers Street, WC2 (020 7930 2020). Charing Cross tube/rail.* **Map 8 L7**

Home *1 Leicester Square, WC2 (020 8964 1999). Leicester Square tube.* **Map 8 K7**

The Junction *242 Coldharbour Lane, SW9 (020 7738 4000). Brixton tube/rail.*

LA2 *157 Charing Cross Road, WC2 (020 7434 0403). Tottenham Court Road tube.* **Map 6 K6**

Legends *29 Old Burlington Street, W1 (020 7437 9933). Oxford Circus tube.* **Map 6 K6**

Leopard Lounge *The Broadway, Fulham Road, SW6 (020 7385 0834). Fulham Broadway tube.* **Map 3 A13**

Loughborough Hotel *corner of Loughborough & Evandale Road, SW9 (no phone). Brixton tube/rail.*

Mass *at The Brix, St Matthew's Church, Brixton Hill, SW2 (020 7738 5255). Brixton tube/rail.*

Ministry of Sound *103 Gaunt Street, SE1 (020 7378 6528). Elephant & Castle tube/rail.* **Map 11 O10**

Roof Gardens *99 Kensington High Street (entrance in Derry Street), W8 (020 7937 7994). High Street Kensington tube.* **Map 3 B9**

Salsa! *96 Charing Cross Road, WC2 (020 7379 3277). Leicester Square tube.* **Map 6 K6**

Scala *278 Pentonville Road, N1 (020 7833 2022). King's Cross tube/rail.* **Map 6 L3**

Stringfellows *16-19 Upper St Martin's Lane, WC2 (020 7240 5534). Leicester Square tube.* **Map 8 L6**

Subterania *12 Acklam Road (under the Westway), W10 (020 8960 4590). Ladbroke Grove tube.*

333 *333 Old Street, EC1 (020 7739 5949). Old Street tube.* **Map 10 Q4**

Turnmills *63 Clerkenwell Road, EC1 (020 7250 3409). Farringdon tube/rail.* **Map 9 N4**

Velvet Room *143 Charing Cross Road, WC2 (020 7439 4655). Tottenham Court Road tube.* **Map 6 K6**

Villa Stefano *227 High Holborn, WC2 (020 7831 7318). Holborn tube.* **Map 6 L5**

The Wag *35 Wardour Street, W1 (020 7437 5534). Piccadilly Circus tube.* **Map 8 K7**

Comedy

Now here's a funny thing...

London? You've got to laugh. Well, when the capital offers more live comedy than any other city in the world, you really don't have a choice. In any one week (excepting, perhaps, August when many London-based comics head north for the Edinburgh Fringe Festival) dozens of clubs provide an exciting mixture of stand-up, improvisation and newcomer slots. Major clubs, such as the **Comedy Store** and **Jongleurs Battersea**, feature the biggest names in the business, while smaller venues combine established comics with specific newcomer competitions. Although the bulk of comedy is still based in pubs and only feature; on occasional nights of the week, over the last few years purpose-built venues have sprung up – an indication that stand-up is here to stay.

Check *Time Out* magazine for weekly listings of who's playing where. Below are some of the best comedy venues in town. At the end of this section we list the cream of the less-frequent comedy nights, as well as a brief introduction to the small but dedicated spoken word circuit.

Comedy

Backyard Comedy Club

231-237 Cambridge Heath Road, E2 (020 7739 3122). Bethnal Green tube. **Performances** 8.30pm Fri, Sat. **Admission** £10; £7 students, OAPs, ES40s. **Credit** MC, V.

Comedian Lee Hurst's purpose-built comedy club opened in a former dress factory in Bethnal Green in September 1998. His industry clout and avowed intention to treat comics with the respect they don't always command in other clubs means that consistently excellent bills are the norm. There's a disco after shows and a restaurant. New acts feature on the last Thursday of the month.

Banana Cabaret

The Bedford, 77 Bedford Hill, SW12 (020 8673 8904). Balham tube/rail. **Performances** 9pm Fri, Sat. **Admission** £10; £7 concs.

The Banana Cabaret is one of the most enterprising and enjoyable clubs on the London comedy scene, with two separate spaces running simultaneously in the same building on Saturday nights. It also serves as the current studio for the Mark Thomas Comedy Product. You need to arrive for the show by 8.45pm on Fridays and 8pm on Saturdays. Food orders are taken until 9pm. There's a disco and DJ until 2am after the show.

Website: www.bananacabaret.co.uk

Bearcat Club

Turk's Head, Winchester Road, Twickenham, Middlesex (020 8891 1852). St Margaret's rail. **Performances** 9.15pm Sat. **Admission** £8, £7 concs, members.

One of the longest established clubs around, with fine bills almost guaranteed.

Canal Café Theatre

The Bridge House, Delamere Terrace, W2 (020 7289 6054). Royal Oak or Warwick Avenue tube. **Performances** daily; phone for details. **Admission** varies; phone for details. **Annual membership** £1. **Credit** MC, V. **Map 1 C4**

Housed in an upstairs room in a pub next to the picturesque canal running through Little Venice, the Canal Café Theatre hosts a wide range of entertainment, from the long-running topical sketch show Newsrevue (Thur-Sun) to cabarets and serious drama. Food available till 10pm.

Chuckle Club

London School of Economics, Houghton Street, WC2 (020 7476 1672). Holborn tube. **Performances** 7.45pm Sat (during termtime). **Admission** £8; £6 students, OAPs, disabled, ES40s. **Map 6 M6**

The Chuckle Club has been operating from various venues for 15 years now, and is a reliable venue for top-quality performers. Its current location in the LSE bar means there's the added bonus of drinks at student prices.

Comedy Brewhouse

Camden Head, 2 Camden Walk, Camden Passage, N1 (020 7359 0851). Angel tube. **Performances** 9pm Fri, Sat. **Admission** £5; £4 students, OAPs, ES40s. **Map 9 O2**

Improv from the Laughing Cavaliers plus a selection of newish stand-ups.

Jongleurs – *what a larf. See page 248.*

Comedy Café

66 Rivington Street, EC2 (020 7739 5706). Old Street tube/rail. **Performances** 9pm Wed-Sat. **Admission** *Wed* free; *Thur* £3; *Fri* £10; *Sat* £12. **Credit** MC, V. **Map 10 R4**

One of the few clubs in London to have been customised for comedy. The free Wednesday shows are for new acts. There's an after-show club until 2am on Fridays and Saturdays. Food served up to 9pm.

Comedy Store

Haymarket House, 1A Oxendon Street, SW1 (020 7344 0234). Leicester Square or Piccadilly Circus tube. **Performances** 8pm Tue-Sun; also midnight Fri, Sat. **Admission** *Wed* £11, £8 concs; *Tue, Thur, Fri* £12, £8 concs; *Sat* £15; *Sun* £12, £8 concs. **Map 8 K7**

The most famous club in the country and the place where the new movement in comedy was launched in the late 1970s. All the best stand-ups appear here, particularly in the improvisation slots with the Comedy Store Players on Wednesdays and Sundays. Tuesday's innovative Cutting Edge show features a group of comics exploring different ways to interact on the same stage. Note that concessionary prices are only available to those who book in person.

Website: www.thecomedystore.co.uk

Cosmic Comedy Club

177 Fulham Palace Road, W6 (020 7381 2006). Hammersmith tube. **Performances** 9pm Tue, Thur; 8.30pm Fri, Sat. **Admission** *Tue* free; *Thur* £5; *Fri* £10; *Sat* £12. **Credit** MC, V.

A lovely, long-established, purpose-built club, offering a good mix of comedy styles. Tuesday nights are devoted to untried acts, with better-known faces appearing on other nights. Food is available and there's a disco until 2am on Fridays and Saturdays.

Website: www.cosmiccomedy.demon.co.uk

Downstairs at the King's Head

2 Crouch End Hill, corner of The Broadway, N8 (020 8340 1028/admin 01920 823265). Finsbury Park tube/rail then W7 bus. **Performances** 8.30pm Wed-Sun. **Admission** free-£7; free-£6 concs.

One of the oldest clubs in the capital and deservedly popular as the emphasis is on providing the best possible conditions for performers. Resident host is Huw Thomas, and there's a try-out night every other Thursday.

Upstairs at the EDT

East Dulwich Tavern, 1 Lordship Lane, SE22 (020 8299 4138). East Dulwich rail. **Performances** 9pm Mon, Thur, Sat. **Admission** *Mon, Thur* £3, £2 concs; *Sat* £6, £5 concs.

There's theatre, music and comedy at this well-run, long-established club. Reliable line-ups often feature some of the circuit's biggest names. Mondays are devoted to new material. All this and a relaxed, pleasant atmosphere – what more could you possibly want?

Jongleurs Battersea

The Cornet, 49 Lavender Gardens, SW11 (020 7564 2500). Clapham Junction rail. **Performances** 8.45pm Fri; 7.15pm, 11.15pm, Sat. **Admission** *Fri* £14, £11 OAPs, students, disabled, ES40s; *Sat* £12, £9 students, OAPs, disabled, ES40s. **Credit** MC, V.

One of the leading London comedy clubs, Jongleurs occupies an impressive first-floor hall, and presents varied line-ups – often of big names – that aren't confined to stand-up. Food is available, and there's an after-show disco on Fridays.

Website: www.jongleurs.com

Jongleurs Bow Wharf

221 Grove Road, E3 (020 7564 2500). Mile End tube. **Performances** 8.15pm Fri, Sat. **Admission** £12; £9 students, OAPs, disabled, ES40s. **Credit** MC, V.

The newest of the Jongleurs' venues, this purpose-built club features some of the bigger names on the comedy circuit. Late bar and disco until 1am. Food served.

Website: www.jongleurs.com

Jongleurs Camden Lock

Dingwalls, Middle Yard, Camden Lock, Camden High Street, NW1 (020 7564 2500). Camden Town or Chalk Farm tube. **Performances** 8.45pm Fri; 7.15pm, 11.15pm, Sat. **Admission** *Fri* £14, £11 students, OAPs, disabled, ES40s; *Sat* £12, £9 students, OAPs, disabled, ES40s. **Credit** MC, V.

A comfortable, purpose-built comedy venue based on the American model, with excellent bills, a late bar and food. Be sure to book in advance to guarantee a seat, and remember, those at the front should be prepared to join in. There's an occasional open slot, and a disco until 2am follows the show on Friday nights.

Website: www.jongleurs.com

Meccano Club

FW's, 2 Essex Road, N1 (020 7813 4478). Angel tube. **Performances** 9pm Fri, Sat. **Admission** £6; £5 students, ES40s. **Map 9 O2**

A splendid, unpretentious basement venue that the comics love to play, so you'll generally see them at their best here. An excellent – if at times chokingly smoky – evening is almost always guaranteed.

Up the Creek

302 Creek Road, SE10 (020 8858 4581). Greenwich DLR/rail. **Performances** 9pm Fri-Sun. **Admission** *Fri* £10, £6 concs, £2 local students; *Sat* £12, £8 concs; *Sun* £6, £4 concs, £2 local students. **Credit** AmEx, MC, V.

A fine, noisy, bearpit of a club that tests even the longest-established comics. Not for the faint-hearted. There's also food and a disco until 2am on Fridays and Saturdays.

Less-frequent clubs

One-off nights in venues that aren't dedicated to comedy tend to come and go with astonishing rapidity. Therefore, always phone first to check that the clubs listed below are still operating before setting out. Unless otherwise stated, the clubs listed take place weekly.

Aztec Comedy Club *The Borderland, 47-49 Westow Street, SE19 (020 8771 0885).* Fri.

BAC *Lavender Hill, SW11 (020 7223 2223).* Phone for details.

Bound & Gagged Palmers Green *The Fox, 413 Green Lanes, N13 (020 7483 3456).* Fri.

Bound & Gagged Tufnell Park *Tufnell Park Tavern, Tufnell Park Road, N7 (020 7483 3456).* Sat.

Buccaneers Comedy *The Hope, Tottenham Street, W1 (020 8761 5319).* Tue. **Map 5 J5**

Chiswick Comedy Club *Rowans Café Bar, Stile Hall Parade, Chiswick High Road, W4 (020 8742 1649).* Sat.

Comedy at Soho Ho *Crown & Two Chairmen, Dean Street, W1 (0956 996690).* Sat. **Map 6 K6**

Comedy Spot *The Spot, Maiden Lane, WC2 (020 7379 5900).* Mon. **Map 8 L7**

Downstairs at the Troubadour *The Troubadour, 265 Old Brompton Road, SW5 (020 7370 1434).* Tue. **Map 3 C11**

Fortnight Club *Moriarty's, 57 Liverpool Road, N1 (020 7837 5370).* Mon. **Map 9 N1**

Ha Bloody Ha *Ealing Studios (Whitehouse entrance) Ealing Green, St Mary's Road, W5 (020 8566 4067).* Fri.

Hampstead Comedy Club *The Washington, England's Lane, NW3 (020 7207 7256).* Sat.

Hecklers Comedy Club, *Upstairs at the Heathcote Arms, 344 Grove Green Road, E11 (020 8923 2127).* Sat.

Oranje Boom Boom *Upstairs at De Hems, Macclesfield Street, W1 (020 7437 2494).* Wed. **Map 8 K6**

Oval Comedy Club *The Grosvenor, Sidney Road, SW9 (020 7733 1799).* Wed.

Red Rose Comedy Club *129 Seven Sisters Road, N7 (020 7281 3051).* Sat.

Screaming Blue Murder *Dog & Fox, 24 High Street, Wimbledon Village, SW19 (020 8946 6565).* Fri.

Tut & Shive Cabaret *The Tut & Shive, 235 Upper Street, N1 (020 7359 7719).* Tue, Sun. **Map 9 O1**

Spoken word

One of the best sources for information on poetry readings and events is the **Poetry Society**, which hosts regular poetry-related bashes (and serves excellent food and wine) at its **Poetry Café** (22 Betterton Street, WC2; 020 7420 9880); check out the open mike evening (Tuesdays 7pm). The long-running **Apples & Snakes** group puts on fortnightly performances at the **BAC** in Battersea (*see above*). Presentations by **Express Excess** on Wednesdays at 8.30pm (The Enterprise, 2 Haverstock Hill, NW3; 020 7485 2659) are among the liveliest of the lot. **The Voicebox** (Level 5, Royal Festival Hall, SE1; 020 7960 4242) offers a range of talks and readings throughout the year, while **Vox'n'Roll** at Filthy McNasty's (68 Amwell Street, EC1; 020 7837 6067) intersperses celebrity readings of poetry and contemporary fiction with music and a packed pub atmosphere (8.30pm Tue-Thur). The **Blue Nose Poetry Club** (Quaker International Centre, 1-3 Byng Place, WC1; 020 8997 2127) has an open reading/workshop evening every other Tuesday. Finally, **Big Word**, formerly held on a Thursday at Finnegan's Wake, 2 Essex Road, N1, will be moving shortly: phone 020 7354 2016 for information.

Stewart Lee, *often seen doing the rounds.*

Contemporary Art

Catch some cutting-edge canvases around the capital.

London is amply supplied with world-class collections and major exhibition spaces (reviewed in various chapters of the Guide; for a list *see page 33*), but no art-lover should overlook the plethora of smaller galleries in which can be found everything from an Old Master to the latest installation.

The galleries of Mayfair are the commercial hub of the London art trade. More varied (in style and quality) work can be found elsewhere in the capital, particularly in east London. With Hackney holding the largest concentration of artists in Europe, this is, perhaps, not surprising, especially as many of the smaller galleries are artist-run or maintained on tiny budgets by members of the contemporary art world cognoscenti. Hackney's design and craft organisation **Hidden Art** can give you the lowdown on what's happening in the area (020 7729 3301; www.hiddenart.co.uk). Also included in this chapter are London's varied and scattered photography galleries.

Admission to all the galleries below is **free** unless otherwise stated. Some of the galleries close in August; phone to check.

Central: Mayfair

Annely Juda Fine Art

23 Dering Street, W1 (020 7629 7578/ ajfa@annelyjudafineart.co.uk). Bond Street tube. **Open** 10am-6pm Mon-Fri; 10am-1pm Sat. **Map 5 H6**

Annely Juda tends to favour abstract and expressionistic painting and sculpture. The gallery represents some of the biggest names in twentieth-century British art, such as Anthony Caro, Leon Kossoff and David Hockney, as well as more recent arrivals on the scene, such as the winner of the 1999 Jerwood Painting Prize, Prunella Clough.

Anthony d'Offay

9, 23 & 24 Dering Street, W1 (020 7499 4100). Bond Street or Oxford Circus tube. **Open** 10am-5.30pm Mon-Fri; 10am-1pm Sat. **Map 5 H6**

Since opening in 1980, d'Offay has become renowned for exhibitions of significant modern art. Work by big names can often be seen here, including Warhol, Lichtenstein and Richter along with more contemporary figures, such as Rachel Whiteread. D'Offay also owns a large space around the corner in Haunch of Venison Yard, to which the gallery will probably be moving towards the end of 2000. While you're in the area, also check out **Anthony Reynolds** just down the road (no.5), which focuses on British art.

Entwistle

6 Cork Street, W1 (020 7734 6440/ info@entwistle.net). Green Park or Piccadilly Circus tube. **Open** 10am-5.30pm Mon-Fri; 11am-4.30pm Sat. **Credit** AmEx, MC, V. **Map 7 J7**

Entwistle specialises in showing young British and American artists. Past exhibitions have ranged from Edward Lipski's sculptures and installations to realist photographic paintings by Jason Brooks. In early 2000, Entwistle will be showing work by **Dan Hays** (3 Mar-15 Apr) and **Jason Brooks** (21 Apr-3 June).

Victoria Miro

21 Cork Street, W1 (020 7734 5082/ vicmir@dircon.co.uk). Green Park or Piccadilly Circus tube. **Open** 10am-5.30pm Mon-Fri; 11am-1pm Sat. **Credit** AmEx, £TC. **Map 7 J7**

Victoria Miro's gallery – designed by Claudio Silvestrin – is well suited to the mixed clutch of contemporary artists she represents: Thomas Demand, Peter Doig, Andreas Gursky, Alex Hartley, Robin Lowe, Chris Ofili, Tracey Moffatt and Abigail Lane.

Waddington Galleries

11 & 12 Cork Street, W1 (020 7437 8611/ mail@waddington-galleries.com). Green Park or Piccadilly Circus tube. **Open** 10am-5.30pm Mon-Fri; 10am-1pm Sat. **Map 7 J7**

Leslie Waddington's galleries are one of the major forces to be reckoned with by modern and contemporary art dealers, and works of such masters as Picasso, Matisse and Dubuffet occasionally make an appearance. Peter Halley, Ben Nicholson and Patrick Heron had exhibitions here in 1999. In 2000 visitors will be treated to shows by **Ian Davenport** and **Michael Craig-Martin**.

Website: www.waddington-galleries.com

Central: other galleries

Eagle

159 Farringdon Road, EC1 (020 7833 2674). Farringdon tube/rail. **Open** 11am-6pm Wed-Fri; 11am-4pm Sat; also by appointment. **Credit** AmEx, £TC. **Map 9 N4**

A friendly and relaxed art space, upstairs from the trendy Eagle gastropub (*see p186*). Emma Hill established the gallery in 1991 with the aim of encouraging more of the non-gallery-going public to view (and hopefully buy) serious, frequently abstract, work. Exhibitors include Andrew Bick, Tom Hammick and Jeff Gibbons, and the gallery also has a small back catalogue of its own publications and limited edition artists' books by the likes of Bruce McLean, Terry Smith and Mel Gooding.

Frith Street

60 Frith Street, W1 (020 7494 1550/ frith-st@dircon.co.uk). Tottenham Court Road tube. **Open** 10am-6pm Wed-Fri; 11am-4pm Sat. **Map 6 K6**

Frith Street's four interlinked rooms provide an intimate space for exhibitions of contemporary artists from home and abroad. Juan Muñoz, master of precise drip painting Callum Innes, photographers Craigie Horsfield and John Riddy, and Turner-nominated Tacita Dean and Cornelia Parker are among recent exhibitors.

Jerwood Space

171 Union Street, SE1 (020 7654 0171). Borough or Southwark tube. **Open** 10am-6pm Mon-Sat; noon-6pm Sun. **Map 11 O8**

Opened in September 1998 in a former Victorian school building, the Jerwood Space (incorporating the Jerwood Gallery) concentrates on the work of Young British Artists. It has successfully attracted attention with a good line-up of shows, including the paintings of Glenn Brown and dumbpop – a group show of young British and European artists. Contenders for the annual **Jerwood Painting Prize** are given wall space throughout September and October (although the Prize show for 2000 was unconfirmed at the time of going to press).

Sadie Coles HQ

35 Heddon Street, W1 (020 7434 2227). Oxford Circus or Piccadilly Circus tube. **Open** 10am-6pm Tue-Sat. **Map 7 J7**

A cubby hole of a gallery in a cul-de-sac off Regent's Street, Sadie Coles HQ nevertheless seems to pack the place with fresh talent. Artists with wit, such as Sarah Lucas and Sue Williams, are favoured here.
Website: www.sadiecoles.com

White Cube

44 Duke Street, SW1 (020 7930 5373). Green Park tube. **Open** 10am-6pm Fri, Sat; Mon-Thur by appointment. **Map 7 J7**

With its floating ceiling and walls that don't quite reach the floor, the White Cube is something of an artwork in its own right. Designed by Claudio Silvestrin, Jay Jopling's one-room, box-like space has provided a focus for some of the most promising work of recent years. Jopling has a sure eye for artists of the future and his relentless self-promotion has put White Cube at the forefront of the contemporary art scene. If evidence is needed, witness his stable of artists, which includes Damien Hirst, Tracey Emin, Gary Hume, Turner-shortlisted Sam Taylor-Wood, Antony Gormley and Mona Hatoum.
Website: www.whitecube.com

North

Lisson

52-54 Bell Street, NW1 (020 7724 2739). Edgware Road tube. **Open** 10am-6pm Mon-Fri; 10am-5pm Sat. **Map 2 E5**

Though away from the flock, this open-fronted modernist gallery is well worth a visit. The Lisson offers space to the young and the established, and represents a number of sculptors of international repute including Sol Lewitt, Tony Cragg, Anish Kapoor, Richard Deacon, Robert Mangold, Dan Graham and Julian Opie, as well as promising newcomers Simon Patterson, Douglas Gordon, Jane and Louise Wilson, Christine Borland, Mat Collishaw and Jason Martin.

East

Anthony Wilkinson Gallery

242 Cambridge Heath Road (junction of Hackney Road), E2 (020 8980 2662/wilk@ndirect.co.uk). Bethnal Green tube. **Open** 11am-6pm Thur-Sat; noon-6pm Sun.

The three rooms of the Anthony Wilkinson Gallery are lit by a diffuse light that seems to benefit the discreet, minimalist work on show. In spirit, it is closest to the **Lisson** gallery (*see above*), albeit on a smaller scale and with a tighter budget.

The Approach

1st floor, Approach Tavern, 47 Approach Road, E2 (020 8983 3878). Bethnal Green tube.
Open noon-6pm Thur-Sun.

The room above the Approach Tavern is a haven for the young (well, youngish) pretenders of the art world, while the bar below caters mainly for those past pretending. It functions as more than just a place to hang paintings on the wall, however, and exhibitions are usually thoughtful and/or adventurous.

Chuck Close at **White Cube** *in late 1999.*

Chisenhale Gallery

64 Chisenhale Road, E3 (020 8981 4518/ mail@chisenhale.org.uk). Mile End or Bethnal Green tube/D6, 8, 277 bus. **Open** 1-6pm Wed-Sun.

A vast late-Victorian warehouse backing on to a canal provides a forum for innovative art forms. The **New Work UK** show – an annual open in July – consists of three one-week exhibitions of new British talent. Other recent shows have included Thomas Hirshorn, Tim Noble and Sue Webster, and a major group show of contemporary photography.

Website: www.chisenhale.org.uk

Flowers East

199-205 Richmond Road, E8 (020 8985 3333/ gallery@flowerseast.co.uk). Hackney Central rail or Bethnal Green tube then 106, 253 bus. **Open** 10am-6pm Tue-Sun. **Credit** AmEx, MC, V.

With four spaces – two at Flowers East and two at London Fields (282 Richmond Road, E8; 020 8533 5554) – Flowers has no shortage of room to show its varied, 30-strong stable. The art is mostly British and ranges from the abstract to the figurative; among those represented here are Nicola Hicks, Peter Howson and Patrick Hughes.

Website: www.flowerseast.co.uk

Gallery Westland Place

13 Westland Place, N1 (020 7251 6456/gallery@ westlandplace.co.uk). Old Street tube. **Open** 10am-6pm Mon-Sat. **Credit** AmEx, DC, JCB, MC, £TC, V.

Very new and barely tested, the remit for GWP seems wide – simply looking out for good contemporary art from across Europe. The first show brought together a group of artists from Scotland and England, while the second concentrated on a single German painter. There's tea and cakes too.

Interim Art

21 Herald Street, E2 (020 7254 9607). Bethnal Green tube. **Open** 11am-6pm Thur-Sun; and by appointment.

This important gallery in two rooms of a converted Victorian terraced house has made a broad shift in policy from innovative, international work towards Young British Artists. A risky strategy, perhaps, but Interim's reputation remains secure, with recent exhibitions by Gillian Wearing, Wolfgang Tillmans, Sarah Jones and Paul Noble.

Miltos Manetas' 'Lara Croft' at **Lux Gallery**.

Lux Gallery

1st floor, The Lux Centre, 2-4 Hoxton Square, N1 (020 7684 2785). Old Street tube.
Open noon-7pm Wed-Fri; noon-6pm Sat, Sun.
Map 10 R3

Less than two years old, the Lux Gallery is part of the Lux Centre, with its video and digital imaging studios, and repertory cinema. Not surprisingly, the gallery has a bias towards exhibiting video and film work, which it does with aplomb.

Matt's Gallery

42-44 Copperfield Road, E3 (020 8983 1771). Mile End tube. **Open** noon-6pm Wed-Sun.

The latest installations can be puzzled over at Matt's Gallery. Artists are given free rein to do what they will with the space, and the results range from the epistemic to the plain incomprehensible. In 2000 **Carl von Weiler** and **Elisabeth Ballet** will both be creating installations for the gallery.

Paton Gallery

282 Richmond Road, E8 (020 8986 3409). Bethnal Green tube then 106, 253 bus/London Fields rail/30, 38 bus. **Open** 11am-6pm Tue-Sat; noon-6pm Sun.

The dynamic Paton Gallery sells to New York's Metropolitan Museum, the Saatchi Gallery and major London corporate collections. Following considerable success in previous years, the Paton Gallery was represented by Rosie Snell, Kate Palmer, Ellie Howitt, Tim Ollivier and Alexander Guy at **ART2000** in Islington in January 2000, and will be exhibiting work by **Ellie Howitt**, **Alex Veness** and **Mary Mabutt** later in the year.

The Showroom

44 Bonner Road, E2 (020 8983 4115). Bethnal Green tube. **Open** 1-6pm Wed-Sun.

The peculiar, broken triangle space of The Showroom often dictates the kind of exhibit that functions best here; various artists have made work specifically for the space. The gallery provides a programme of four major exhibitions of newly commissioned work each year featuring established and emerging artists. For 2000 The Showroom is exhibiting **Claire Barclay**, **Alan Kane**, **Rachel Lowe** and **Eva Rothschild** among others.

South

Hales Gallery

70 Deptford High Street, SE8 (020 8694 1194/ halesgallery@btinternet.com). New Cross tube/ Deptford rail. **Open** 9am-5pm Mon-Sat.
Credit AmEx, MC, £TC, V.

Hales Gallery has been around since 1992, serving tea and sandwiches upstairs and spotlighting up-and-coming artists downstairs. Some of the artists represented by this commercial gallery have been garnering a fair degree of attention of late, including Tomoko Takahashi, Andrew Bick, Martin McGinn and Sarah Beddington. Hales is not entirely isolated; while you're in the area the **Museum of Installation (MOI)**, also on the High Street (no.175; 020 8692 8778), is worth a look.

The **South London Gallery** *shows off huge works by Julian Schnabel.*

Milch

2-10 Tinworth Street, SE11 (020 7735 7334/ milchgallery@yahoo.com). Vauxhall tube/rail.
Open phone for details.

Milch is a gallery headed by artists, curators and critics. The gallery's raison d'être is very much about commissioning new work from an impressively wide range of artists. In addition, Milch now co-hosts the **BT New Contemporaries**, a showcase for artists who have recently graduated (not confirmed for 2000 at time of going to press). Besides the large exhibition space, there are also seven studios.

South London Gallery

65 Peckham Road, SE5 (020 7703 9799/ mail@southlondonart.com). Oval tube then 36 bus or Elephant & Castle tube/rail then P3, 12, 171 bus.
Open 11am-6pm Tue, Wed, Fri; 11am-7pm Thur; 2-6pm Sat, Sun.

The large gallery room of the SLG has played host to an eclectic mix of shows in recent years, bringing in hot contemporary talent like Tracey Emin and Mark Quinn, and re-checking older heavyweights such as Julian Schnabel. Along with **Milch** in Vauxhall (*see above*), the South London Gallery co-hosts the excellent **BT New Contemporaries** show (Nov-Dec). Among the exhibitions to watch out for in 2000 are **On Stage** – a mix of videos and performances by artists and musicians (18 Apr-21 May), **Barbara Kruger**'s challenging **PowerPleasureDesireDisgust** (14 June-30 July) and work by **Leon Golub** (3 Nov-17 Dec). Admission to exhibitions is free but there are charges for some evening events.

Website: www.southlondonart.com

Other exhibition spaces

Architecture Association

36 Bedford Square, WC1 (020 7887 4000/arch-assoc@arch-assoc.org.uk). Tottenham Court Road tube. **Open** 10am-7pm Mon-Fri; 10am-3pm Sat. **Map 6 K5**

The Architecture Association often holds thought-provoking exhibitions that tend to look at architecture in its broadest context. In addition to shows, the association also hosts talks and discussions that tie in with exhibition themes.

Website: www.arch-assoc.org.uk

British Cartoon Centre

7 Brunswick Centre, Bernard Street, WC1 (020 7278 7172/fax 020 7278 4243/skp@escape.u-net.com). Russell Square tube. **Open** noon-6pm Mon-Fri. **Map 9 N5**

This centre is run by the charity Cartoon Art Trust, which organises and co-ordinates exhibitions and workshops for adults and children on cartoons, caricature, comics and animation. Lectures and demonstrations by professional cartoonists are held throughout the year; ring for details. Admission is free, but donations are gratefully received.

Crafts Council

44A Pentonville Road, N1 (020 7278 7700). Angel tube. **Open** 11am-6pm Tue-Sat; 2-6pm Sun. **Map 9 N2**

Housed in an elegantly converted Georgian house, the Council showcases the nation's craft output in a range of fields (textiles, wood, jewellery, furniture, ceramics). Exhibitions often take a theme and demonstrate work in that area. Spring 2000 sees the beginning of the **3 UP** programme, which will present the work of nine exhibitors in three shows (20 Jan-19 Mar, 6 Apr-4 June, 15 June-3 Sept), examining the relationship between craft traditions and contemporary practice. The finalists of the **Jerwood Applied Art Prize 2000: Jewellery** will be displayed from 14 September to 29 October. The Crafts Council is also responsible for the excellent **Chelsea Crafts Fair**, held in Chelsea Old Town Hall (17-22, 24-29 Oct).

RIBA

66 Portland Place, W1 (020 7580 5533). Oxford Circus or Regent's Park tube. **Open** 8am-6pm Mon, Wed-Fri; 8am-9pm Tue; 8am-5pm Sat. **Credit** MC, V. **Map 5 H5**
The Royal Institute of British Architects (RIBA) is housed in a monumental edifice built by Grey Wornham in 1934. The gallery celebrates the profession's great and good, in 1999 spotlighting the RIBA gold medal-winners Oscar Niemaeyer, as well as taking a long hard look at British housing in the twentieth century. The building contains a branch of the excellent Pâtisserie Valerie (*see p181*).
Website: www.riba.org

Photography

Association Gallery

Association of Photographers, 81 Leonard Street, EC2 (020 7739 6669/aop@dircon.co.uk). Old Street tube/rail. **Open** 9.30am-6pm Mon-Fri; noon-5pm Sat. **Credit** AmEx, MC, V. **Map 9 P4**
The two-floor Association Gallery showcases work (both commissioned and non-commissioned) for advertising and editorial purposes. It puts on a show every March of Association of Photographers award-winners and stages around 20 exhibitions of good contemporary photography each year.
Website: www.aophoto.co.uk

Camerawork

121 Roman Road, E2 (020 8980 6256/ info@camerawork.net). Bethnal Green tube.
Open 1-6pm Thur-Sat.
Camerawork's brief is a worthy one: to show adventurous, challenging, issue-based work; 1999's show by John Hansard exemplified this. In addition, it also offers extensive darkroom space and CD-Rom facilities to the public.

Hamilton's

13 Carlos Place, W1 (020 7499 9493/ photography@hamiltonsgallery.com). Bond Street or Green Park tube. **Open** 10am-6pm Tue-Sat.
Credit AmEx, MC, £$TC, V. **Map 7 H7**
Rubbing shoulders with Mayfair's fine art galleries, Hamilton's has always had an exclusive international clientele and exhibited high-profile photographers. This is photography as fine art – prices start at about £250. Choose from more than 3,000 prints by illustrious names such as Bailey, McCullin, Penn and Avedon. It's a great space, especially at the back, and has excellent exhibitions, concentrating on more fashionable contemporary names, from Peter Linbergh to the controversial Joel-Peter Witkin.
Website: www.hamiltonsgallery.com

Photofusion

17A Electric Lane, SW9 (020 7738 5774/ info@photofusion.org). Brixton tube/rail.
Open 10am-6pm Tue, Thur, Fri; 10am-8pm Wed; 11am-5pm Sat. **Credit** MC, V.
Aided by council and commercial grants, this co-operative has kept to its community roots and holds an impressive library of social documentary photos.
Website: www.photofusion.org

Photographers' Gallery

5-8 Great Newport Street, WC2 (020 7831 1772/ info@photonet.org.uk). Leicester Square tube.
Open 11am-6pm Mon-Sat; noon-6pm Sun.
Membership £25, £15 concs, per year.
Credit AmEx, DC, MC, V. **Map 8 K6**
In 1971, the Photographers' Gallery was the first of its kind to open in England. It has been promoting contemporary photography ever since, but is now moving away from social documentary and reportage. It has also been instrumental in encouraging national galleries to hold photographic shows in addition to mounting 24 of its own each year.
Website: www.photonet.org.uk

Special Photographers Company

21 Kensington Park Road, W11 (020 7221 3489/ info@specialphotographers.com). Ladbroke Grove or Notting Hill Gate tube. **Open** 10am-6pm Mon-Thur; 10am-5.30pm Fri; 11am-5pm Sat. **Credit** AmEx, MC, £TC, V. **Map 1 A6**
The Special Photographers Company gallery aims to represent serious snappers by exhibiting a wide range of work. Not limited by a specifically fine-art or documentary tradition, the gallery holds a large collection of prints from landscape to abstract (prices from £80). During 2000 the Company will exhibit reportage images of the East End, Charing Cross Road, and London during the Blitz by **Wolfgang Suschitzky** (6 Apr-27 May); contemporary installations combining poetry with 'diary' photos by **Jimmy Symonds** (1 June-22 July); and black and white music photographs from the mid-1960s by **John 'Hoppy' Hopkins**, including iconic images of the Rolling Stones and the Beatles (27 July-23 Sept).
Website: www.specialphotographers.com

Zelda Cheatle Gallery

99 Mount Street, W1 (020 7408 4448/ photo@zcgall.demon.co.uk). Bond Street or Green Park tube. **Open** 10am-6pm Tue-Fri; 11am-4pm Sat.
Credit AmEx, MC, V. **Map 7 G7**
Zelda Cheatle has a background in documentary work and a following of serious – particularly American – collectors. She shows some excellent international photography from the likes of Eve Arnold, Manuel Alvarez Bravo, Steve Pyke, Helen Sear and John Deakin.

Dance

Are you in the mood for dancing? Then the city has everything to keep you on your toes.

London's dance scene is becoming ever more exciting, with an enormous variety of shows, classes and workshops on offer and an increasing number of theatres and other performance spaces available. More and more companies from abroad, both established and new, are performing in the capital, giving the public a chance to experience a truly comprehensive and up-to-date panorama of what is going on in the dance world today.

The **Royal Opera House** reopened in December 1999 and now boasts, in addition to the refurbished main theatre, two brand-new performance spaces (*see page 256*). Other venues are being revamped: **The Place** is expected to shut down during much of the latter half of 2000 and the **South Bank Centre** is undergoing a long programme of renovation works, although this shouldn't interfere with the performance calendar.

As well as the performances and venues below, check the weekly listings in *Time Out*. The magazine's dance pages include detailed information on a gamut of fringe shows and more 'mainstream' productions, the latter often held at venues not used solely for dance events (such as *Lord of the Dance* at Wembley Arena, *Swan Lake* at the Royal Albert Hall, De La Guarda at Camden's Roundhouse, plus various dance-based shows and musicals such as *Chicago* and *The Lion King*; for more on these *see pages 295-7*).

The **London Dance Network Website** (www.london-dance.net) comprises some 50 artists, venues, producers and agencies whose brief is to promote up-to-the-minute awareness of the strength and diversity of dance in London. And make sure you drop by **Dance Books** at 15 Cecil Court, WC2 (off Charing Cross Road, close to the National Portrait Gallery; 020 7836 2314), the world's sole specialist shop for new and used dance books. CDs and videos about dance are also sold.

Finally, should Terpsichore inspire you to take a turn on the dancefloor yourself, London's range of dance classes is unrivalled (*see page 257*).

Major venues

Barbican Centre

Silk Street, EC2 (box office 020 7638 8891/enquiries 020 7638 4141). Barbican tube/Moorgate tube/rail. **Open** *box office* 9am-8pm daily. **Tickets** £6-£30. **Credit** AmEx, MC, £TC, V. **Map 9 P5**

This arts centre in the heart of the City has hosted some truly excellent shows since it entered the world of dance a couple of years back. The **Bite:00** season (May-Oct 2000) will include the award-winning **Compagnie Montalvo-Hervieu** with *Le Jardin de Io Io Ito Ito*, the **Ballet Atlantique Régine Chopinot** with *La Danse du Temps* in collaboration with the British artist Andy Goldsworthy, and the ineffable **Merce Cunningham** with the UK première of *Biped*, a Barbican co-commission set to music by Gavin Bryars.

Website: www.barbican.org.uk

ICA

The Mall, SW1 (020 7930 3647/membership enquiries 020 7873 0062/info@ica.org.uk/ tickets@ica.org.uk). Piccadilly Circus tube/Charing Cross tube/rail. **Open** *box office* noon-9.30pm daily. **Tickets** prices vary; average £8. **Credit** AmEx, DC, MC, V. **Map 8 K8**

The intimate space of the Institute of Contemporary Arts (ICA) is the setting for experimental, movement-based theatre and performance with an avant-garde flavour. A fine balance is struck between platforms for emerging talent and seasons for established British and international artists. The **London International Mime Festival** is also a regular visitor each January (*see also p10*). The price of a ticket includes day membership and access to the art gallery and hypertrendy café.

Website: www.ica.org.uk

London Coliseum

St Martin's Lane, WC2 (box office 020 7632 8300/ minicom 020 7836 7666). Leicester Square tube/ Charing Cross tube/rail. **Open** *box office* 24 hours daily. **Tickets** £2.50-£55; day tickets on sale to personal callers after 10am Mon-Fri; by telephone from 2.30pm Mon-Fri. **Credit** AmEx, DC, MC, £TC, V. **Map 8 L7**

The beautiful, spacious Coliseum is home to the **English National Opera** (ENO) for most of the year, and is usually visited by major dance companies over the summer and at Christmas. Summer 1999, for example, saw the Bolshoi performing a few immortal ballet classics, and, later in the year, the English National Ballet's *The Nutcracker*. In the June-July 2000 ENO season, watch out for **Mark Morris**, who will collaborate with the talented **Peter Sellars** on the staging of John Adams' *Nixon in China*, and will also stage his own dance group's interpretation of *Dido and Aeneas* by Purcell in a double bill with Virgil Thomson's *Four Saints in Three Acts*, as well as *L'Allegro, il Penseroso ed il Moderato* by Handel.

Website: www.eno.org

The Place

17 Duke's Road, WC1 (020 7387 0031/ placetheatre@easynet.co.uk). Euston tube/rail. **Open** *box office* 10.30am-6pm Mon-Fri; noon-6pm Sat. **Tickets** £7-£10. **Credit** MC, V. **Map 6 K3**

A venue entirely dedicated to contemporary dance, The Place will be under redevelopment for the second half of 2000. In the meantime, though, catch the **Spring Loaded** season (1 Mar-3 June), and, at the beginning of 2001, **Resolution!** (*see p258*). Facilities include a comprehensive dance video library, an information centre, top-notch dance training and evening classes for all levels of ability, and an excellent café serving vegetarian food.

Website: www.theplace.org.uk

Riverside Studios

Crisp Road, W6 (020 8237 1000/box office 020 8237 1111). Hammersmith tube. **Open** *box office* noon-7pm daily. **Tickets** £7-£15. **Credit** MC, V.

This leading arts and media centre occasionally hosts British contemporary dance and physical theatre, and visiting international companies, in three auditoria. There's a pleasant bar/café, restaurant and bookshop and wheelchair access to all ground-floor areas. The Riverside's major annual dance festival **Dance Umbrella** (*see p258*) takes place in October and November.

Royal Opera House

Bow Street, WC2 (box office/info 020 7304 4000/ enquiries 020 7240 1200/minicom 020 7212 9228/ webmaster@roh.org.uk). **Open** *box office* 10am-8pm Mon-Sat. **Tickets** £6-£150. **Credit** AmEx, DC, MC, V. **Map 8 L7**

This magnificent theatre has finally reopened, after a long and criticised programme of refurbishment and enlargement, dogged by management crises and strikes. In addition to the main theatre (home to the **Royal Ballet**), there is now the **Linbury Studio Theatre**, seating up to 420 people, staging lunchtime opera and music recitals, and the **Clore Studio Upstairs**, hosting dance workshops, events and small-scale performances for audiences of up to 200, programmed by Royal Ballet principal dancer Deborah Bull.

After so much negative publicity, the ROH is making a real effort to expunge its elitist image. The public now has access during the day to the restored **Vilar Floral Hall**, the new **Amphitheatre Bar** leading to a loggia with a view over Covent Garden Piazza, a shop and a coffee shop; there's also a programme of free lunchtime concerts and events, exhibitions, daily tours, conferences, study days and improved access for people with disabilities. In addition, ticket prices have been cut, though those for the best seats remain horrendously high. (Note that most of the cheapest tickets are for, not surprisingly, restricted view seats.)

The Royal Ballet's standards of performance may be rather variable and the programming not exactly adventurous, but you will have the chance to see stars of the calibre of Sylvie Guillem, Viviana Durante, Roberto Bolle and Carlos Acosta. In 2000 there will be an **Ashton** triple bill (Feb-Apr; including a new production of *Les Rendezvous*) and a not-to-be-missed **Diaghilev** triple bill (May) featuring works by Nijinska, Fokine and two by Nijinsky, created for Diaghilev's Ballet Russes. Look out also for a new ballet, *The Crucible*, by **William Tuckett** (Apr-May). In addition, the **Birmingham Royal Ballet** is set to return to the Royal Opera House in May/June and, as the Guide went to press, there were plans for summer seasons by the **Kirov Ballet Company** and the **Royal Ballet** (see its website: www.royalballet.org). *See also p270* **House party**.

Website: www.royaloperahouse.org

Sadler's Wells

Rosebery Avenue, EC1 (box office 020 7863 8000). Angel tube. **Open** *box office* 10am-8pm Mon-Sat. **Tickets** £7.50-£45. **Credit** AmEx, MC, V. **Map 9 N3**

Peacock Theatre, Portugal Street, off Kingsway, WC2 (box office 020 7863 8222). Holborn or Temple (closed Sun) tube. **Open** *box office* noon-8pm performance days, 10am-6pm when no performances, Mon-Sat. **Tickets** £7.50-£35. **Credit** AmEx, MC, V. **Map 6 M6**

An institution in the London dance world, Sadler's Wells now attracts world-class contemporary and classical dance companies to its totally rebuilt, ultra-modern theatre. Scheduled performances for 2000 include *Carmen*, by the **Northern Ballet Theatre** (21 Mar-1 Apr); the critically acclaimed Dutch company **Nederlands Dans Theater 2** (5-8 Apr); *The King*, a ballet about the life of Elvis Presley, performed by the **Peter Schaufuss Ballet** (27 Apr-6 May); and the first promenade performance at the Theatre by the **Rambert Dance Company** (31 May-10 June).

The considerably smaller, on-site **Lilian Baylis Theatre** has now reopened. The organisation is also retaining its second home, the more centrally located **Peacock Theatre** in Holborn, for younger companies and longer runs of more populist fare (tango, flamenco and urban street dance).

Website: www.sadlers-wells.com

South Bank Centre

South Bank, Belvedere Road, SE1 (box office 020 7960 4242/recorded info 020 7921 0682). Embankment tube/Waterloo tube/rail. **Open** *box office* 10am-9pm daily. **Tickets** £5-£60. **Credit** AmEx, DC, MC, V. **Map 8 M8**

This massive and rather austere arts complex with a wonderful view of the Thames is currently undergoing a series of improvements and restorations, although these won't, in theory, affect its excellent programming. British and international dance companies perform regularly at its three venues: the massive **Royal Festival Hall (RFH)**, the medium-sized **Queen Elizabeth Hall (QEH)** and the smaller **Purcell Room (PR)**. Highlights for 2000 include a collaboration between the SBC choreographer in residence, Jonathan Burrows, and the artist Anthony Gormley (Apr), a joint effort between William Forsythe's **Frankfurt Ballet** and Jan Lauwers' **Needcompany** (June), and a special

The Place *to go. See page 256.*

commission by the Royal Festival Hall and the Sydney Organising Committee for the 2000 Olympic Games for a show by the ground-breaking **DV8 Physical Theatre** to be performed in the host city and London. Every August the South Bank Centre hosts the free dance festival **Blitz**, and some of the higher-profile **Dance Umbrella** events can be seen here as well (*see p258*). *See also p271.*
Website: www.sbc.org.uk

Other venues

The Bhavan Centre

Old Church Building, Castletown Road, W14 (020 7381 3086). West Kensington tube. **Open** 9.30am-5.30pm daily. **Tickets** £5-£15. **Credit** MC, V.

This institute of Indian art and culture promotes, and sometimes hosts, traditional Indian dance performances, along with educational courses and classes in traditional Indian dance.

The Bull Theatre

68 High Street, Barnet, Herts (020 8449 0048). High Barnet tube. **Open** 10am-8.30pm Mon-Sat; 1-8.30pm Sun. **Tickets** £3-£10. **Credit** MC, V.

The Bull hosts a broad range of dance performances (approximately two a month), mostly by contemporary and world (especially Asian) dance companies.

Chisenhale Dance Space

64-84 Chisenhale Road, E3 (020 8981 6617/ mail@chisenhale.demon.co.uk). Bethnal Green or Mile End tube. **Open** *box office* 10am-6pm Mon-Fri. **Tickets** £4-£6; £3-£5 concs.

A seminal research centre for contemporary dance and movement-based performance of a more experimental, work-in-progress nature, Chisenhale also features a range of activities including workshops, often hosted by international artists, plus kids' classes.
Website: www.chisenhale.demon.co.uk

Cochrane Theatre

Southampton Row, WC1 (020 7242 7040). Holborn tube. **Open** *box office* 10am-6pm Mon-Fri; noon-6pm Sat. **Tickets** £4-£15. **Credit** MC, V. **Map 6 L5**

This small West End theatre programmes dance performances, from classical to contemporary.

Jacksons Lane Dancebase

269A Archway Road, N6 (020 8341 4421/ jacksonslane@pop3.poptel.org.uk). Highgate tube. **Open** 10am-10pm daily. **Tickets** £8; £6 concs. **Credit** MC, V.

This community centre presents an admirable number of dance performances and activities, with lots of contemporary and new dance from young British and international companies. During summer 2000, look out for **Zone 3**, a festival of cutting-edge contemporary dance, and **Mosaics** (the latter was unconfirmed at time of going to press; *see p258*).

Laban Centre

Laurie Grove, SE14 (020 8692 4070/ info@laban.co.uk). New Cross or New Cross Gate tube. **Open** 8.30am-5.30pm Mon-Fri; 9.15am-noon Sat. **Tickets** £5-£10; £3 concs.

The Laban Centre is an independent conservatory for dance training and research, which runs undergraduate and post-graduate courses, evening and weekend classes, specialist short courses and an international Easter and summer school. Other facilities include a dance library and a 'body-control studio' offering Pilates-based body conditioning. The centre is also home to the dynamic **Transitions** dance company. Shows featuring work by emerging contemporary dance choreographers are regularly presented in the **Bonnie Bird Theatre**. The centre publishes the excellent *Dance Theatre Journal* (available by mail order).
Website: www.laban.co.uk

Studio Theatre

North Westminster Community School, North Wharf Road, W2 (box office/enquiries 020 7641 8424/ studiot@globalnet.co.uk). Edgware Road tube. **Open** 10am-5pm Mon-Fri. **Tickets** £6; £4 concs. **Map 2 D5**

This theatre hosts about 20 dance shows a year, from traditional to contemporary. **Bullies Ballerinas** dance company is resident at the studio, while BiMa and Union Dance make regular appearances.

Dance classes

In addition to classes mentioned in the preceding section, the following places all offer dance classes to help you polish, and then strut, your stuff.

And that's just the tip of the iceberg in terms of what's available. For a list of accredited dance classes, call the **Council for Dance Education and Training** (020 8746 0076) or visit its website (www.cdet.org.uk). Look out too for **Feet First**, a programme of dance workshops, from Zulu to Cajun. It will be held from 10 June to 16 July at venues across town (call 020 7354 3030 for details).

Dance Attic

368 North End Road, SW6 (020 7610 2055). Fulham Broadway tube. **Membership** *daily* £1.50; *half year* £30; *annual* £50. **Classes** £3-£4. **Map 3 A12**
This centre in Fulham has a wide range of dance classes, including ballet, jazz, flamenco, lambada, salsa and hip hop, for all levels of expertise. There is also a gym if you're still feeling energetic. Membership is required.

Danceworks

16 Balderton Street, W1 (020 7629 6183). Bond Street tube. **Membership** *daily* 70p-£4; *monthly* £22; *annual* £50-£75. **Classes** £4-£6. **Map 5 G6**
Danceworks runs an incredible variety of dance classes (including Afro, contemporary, salsa, ballet and tango), as well as aerobics classes, yoga, Pilates, martial arts and various therapies. Some dance classes require membership.

Drill Hall

16 Chenies Street, WC1 (020 7637 8270). Goodge Street tube. **Courses** £25-£60. **Map 6 K5**
This central fringe venue provides classes in Egyptian, Latin American, tango, t'ai-chi, butoh, contemporary dance and more.

Greenwich Dance Agency

Borough Hall, Royal Hill, SE10 (020 8293 9741/ greenwich.dance@ukonline.co.uk). Greenwich rail/ DLR. **Classes** £3.40-£4; £3 concs.
Daily professional-level contemporary classes, workshops and occasional intensives run by established artists are offered here, as well as beginner/ intermediate adult classes in Egyptian, flamenco, jazz, salsa and other disciplines.
Website: web.ukonline.co.uk/greenwich.dance

Islington Arts Factory

2 Parkhurst Road, N7 (020 7607 0561). Caledonian Road or Holloway Road tube. **Membership** *term* £3; *annual* £8. **Classes** £3.50-£6.
Classes in ballet, Egyptian, jazz, contemporary, salsa and mime are held at this lively arts centre. Membership is required, but can be obtained on the day.
Website: www.cerbernet.co.uk/iaf

London School of Capoeira

Studio 8, The Place, 17 Duke's Road, WC1 (020 7281 2020). Euston tube/rail. **Classes** 8-10pm Tue, Wed, Fri. **Fees** *beginners' course* (four lessons) £75, £65 concs. **Map 6 K3**
Capoeira, which originated in Brazil, is becoming an increasingly popular fusion of dance, gymnastics and martial arts. Free demonstration sessions are held every Friday (8-10pm), and introductory workshops every month.

Morley College

61 Westminster Bridge Road, SE1 (020 7450 9232). Lambeth North tube. **Membership** *annual* £1.50. **Classes** £6-£14 one-day workshop; £7-£43 10 classes. **Map 8 M9**
A broad portfolio of dance classes and courses at all levels is held at this adult education centre. The setting is fairly spartan, but you can't complain about the prices, nor the efforts made to accommodate beginners. Membership is required.

Pineapple Dance Studio

7 Langley Street, WC2 (020 7836 4004). Covent Garden tube. **Membership** *daily* £1-£4; *annual* £45-£100. **Classes** £4-£6. **Map 6 L6**
Centrally located, this popular, trendy dance centre boasts a wide choice of classes, with an emphasis on ballet, jazz and commercial genres. There is also a gym for personal training, a studio for Pilates, treatments and therapists, a café and even a clairvoyant. Classes are for all levels. Membership is required.
Website: www.pineapple.uk.com

Festivals

The highly esteemed **Dance Umbrella** (020 8741 5881/www.danceumbrella.co.uk), which is now in its 22nd year, is one of the world's top contemporary dance festivals. Held for five weeks from early October, it features a stimulating mix of proven British and international companies (as well as a number of lesser-known discoveries), who perform at different venues across London. Merce Cunningham will be taking part in 2000 (*see page 255* **Barbican Centre**).

Since **The Place** (*see page 256*) will be closed for the second half of 2000, its habitual series of dance seasons will be reduced to two: **Spring Loaded** (1 Mar-3 June), an overview of British contemporary dance, featuring for the first time in 2000 a programme aimed specifically at children, and **Resolution!** in January and February 2001, a seven-week open platform for emerging British and European choreographers.

Each August the **South Bank Centre** (*see page 256*) hosts the month-long **Blitz**. Britain's biggest and most diverse community dance festival, it is a cornucopia of free dance performances, lectures and workshops. Also in August, **Sadler's Wells** (*see page 256*) and **Jacksons Lane Dancebase** (*see page 257*) co-present **Mosaics** (not confirmed at time of going to press). This ambitious season of small-scale events, with more than 30 young companies performing new dance and physical theatre, is a veritable dance-athon.

And, last but not least, a new arrival: thc **David and Goliath Festival**, a season created by the **Royal Opera House** (*see page 256*), which will present the work of independent artists in small-scale performances across a variety of artforms including dance. It will take place in the new **Clore Studio Upstairs**. *See also above* **Feet First**.

Film

The London movie scene is constantly developing. Our pick of the flicks highlights the best of the capital's cinemas and festivals.

Every conceivable cinematic taste is catered for in London. The centre of the industry and the best place to find a film is around Soho and the West End. The larger cinemas in Leicester Square generally show only blockbusters (*see page 260* **Size matters**) but they do it well – all have huge screens and state-of-the-art sound. If you're after more varied or international films, the smaller cinemas in the area have a fair selection, although you're probably better off choosing one of many repertory cinemas scattered around the city.

Films are classified under the following categories: **U** – suitable for all ages; **PG** – open to all, but parental guidance is advised; **12** – no one under the age of 12; **15** – no one under 15; **18** – no one under 18. Expect to pay £8-£10 for a first-run film in the West End; less in repertory cinemas. Some cinemas have concessionary rates for children, students and the unemployed, while many have reduced rates in the afternoons. It's a good idea to book by credit card for first-nighters, though you're generally charged a fee (around 50p) for this service. For cinema screening details, check the weekly listings in *Time Out* magazine.

Note that in late 1999 Virgin Cinemas were taken over by UGC and that, as this Guide went to press, they were in the process of being rebranded.

Best for...

- **glitzy premières**: Odeon Leicester Square; Empire
- **smoking**: Notting Hill Coronet
- **comfy surroundings**: Curzon Minema
- **international cinema**: Goethe Institut (subtitled German films); **Ciné Lumière** (subtitled French films)
- **cheap admission**: Prince Charles (cult films)
- **film buffs**: NFT (cinema classics)
- **taking children to**: Ritzy
- **bar for a pre-/post-film drink**: Curzon Soho; Ritzy

Cinemas

Mainstream & first-run

The central booking and information number for **Odeon** cinemas is **0870 505 0007**. You can also book tickets or check out what's on at your local Odeon cinema over the Internet, at www.odeon.co.uk. Other useful websites include those for **ABC** (www.abccinemas.co.uk), **Warner Village** (www.warnervillage.co.uk) and **Screen** cinemas (www.screencinemas.co.uk).

Bloomsbury & the City

ABC Tottenham Court Road *Tottenham Court Road, W1 (recorded info 020 7636 6148/credit card bookings 020 8795 6400). Tottenham Court Road tube.* **Map 6 K5**

Barbican Centre *Silk Street, EC2 (recorded info & bookings 020 7382 7000). Barbican or Moorgate tube.* **Map 9 P5**

Renoir *Brunswick Centre, Brunswick Square, WC1 (020 7837 8402). Russell Square tube.* **Map 8 L4**

Marylebone

Odeon Marble Arch *10 Edgware Road, W2. Marble Arch tube.* **Map 2 F6**

Screen on Baker Street *96 Baker Street, NW1 (020 7935 2772/recorded info 020 7486 0036). Baker Street tube.* **Map 5 G5**

Mayfair & St James's

ABC Panton Street *Panton Street, SW1 (recorded info 020 7930 0631/credit card bookings 020 8795 6401). Piccadilly Circus tube.* **Map 8 K7**

ABC Piccadilly *Piccadilly, W1 (recorded info 020 7287 4322). Piccadilly Circus tube.* **Map 7 J7**

Curzon Mayfair *38 Curzon Street, W1 (020 7369 1720). Green Park or Hyde Park Corner tube.* **Map 7 H8**

ICA Cinema *Nash House, The Mall, SW1 (recorded info 020 7930 6393/credit card bookings 020 7930 3647/www.ica.org.uk). Piccadilly Circus tube or Charing Cross tube/rail.* **Map 8 K8**

Odeon Haymarket *Haymarket, SW1. Piccadilly Circus tube.* **Map 8 K7**

Plaza *17-25 Regent Street, W1 (020 7930 0144/recorded info & credit card bookings 0870 603 4567/0990 888990). Piccadilly Circus tube.* **Map 8 K7**

Virgin Haymarket *Haymarket, W1 (recorded info & credit card bookings 0870 907 0712). Piccadilly Circus tube.* **Map 8 K7**

Soho to Leicester Square

Also in this area is the **Pepsi London IMAX Theatre** (*see page 261*).

ABC Shaftesbury Avenue *Shaftesbury Avenue, W1 (recorded info 020 7836 6279/ credit card bookings 020 8795 6403). Leicester Square or Tottenham Court Road tube.* **Map 6 K6**

ABC Swiss Centre *Swiss Centre, 10 Wardour Street, W1 (recorded info 020 7439 4470/ credit card bookings 020 8795 6402). Leicester Square or Piccadilly Circus tube.* **Map 8 K7**

Curzon Soho *93-107 Shaftesbury Avenue, W1 (credit card bookings 020 7734 2255/recorded info 020 7439 4805). Leicester Square or Piccadilly Circus tube.* **Map 8 K6**

Empire *Leicester Square, WC2 (recorded info & credit card bookings 0870 603 4567/0990 888990). Leicester Square or Piccadilly Circus tube.* **Map 8 K7**

Metro *Rupert Street, W1 (credit card bookings 020 7734 1506/recorded info 020 7437 0757). Leicester Square or Piccadilly Circus tube.* **Map 8 K7**

Odeon Leicester Square *Leicester Square, WC2. Leicester Square tube.* **Map 8 K7**

Odeon Mezzanine *adjacent to Odeon Leicester Square, WC2. Leicester Square tube.* **Map 8 K7**

Odeon West End *Leicester Square, WC2. Leicester Square tube.* **Map 8 K7**

Size matters

Screen size is generally proportional to the number of seats, so, if you want the full monty for *The Full Monty*, here's where you'll find the 15 biggest screens among the mainstream and first-run cinemas. London's two IMAX cinemas have the biggest screens of the lot (*see page 261*).

	Seats
Odeon Leicester Square	1,943
Empire 1	1,330
Odeon West End 2	838
Plaza 1	752
Chelsea Cinema	713
Odeon Swiss Cottage 1	686
ABC Shaftesbury Avenue 1	615
ABC Shaftesbury Avenue 2	581
Odeon Haymarket	566
Virgin Trocadero 1	548
Curzon Mayfair	542
Odeon Kensington 1	520
Odeon West End 1	503
Prince Charles	488
Virgin Haymarket	448

Prince Charles *Leicester Place, WC2 (recorded info 020 7437 8181). Leicester Square or Piccadilly Circus tube.* **Map 8 K7**

Virgin Trocadero *Trocadero, WC2 (recorded info & bookings 0870 907 0716). Leicester Square or Piccadilly Circus tube.* **Map 8 K7**

Warner Village West End *Leicester Square, WC2 (recorded info & bookings 020 7437 4347). Leicester Square tube.* **Map 8 K7**

Knightsbridge & Chelsea

Chelsea Cinema *206 King's Road, SW3 (020 7351 3742). Sloane Square tube.* **Map 4 E12**

Curzon Minema *45 Knightsbridge, SW1 (020 7369 1723/www.minema.com). Hyde Park Corner or Knightsbridge tube.* **Map 7 G9**

Virgin Chelsea *279 King's Road, SW3 (recorded info & credit card bookings 0870 907 0710). Sloane Square tube then 11, 19, 22 bus.* **Map 4 E12**

North London

ABC Hampstead *Pond Street, NW3 (info 020 7794 4000/credit card bookings 020 8795 6406). Hampstead Heath rail/24, C11 bus.*

Finchley Road Warner Village *Finchley Road, NW3 (box office & enquiries 020 7604 3066/ recorded info & advance bookings 020 7604 3110). Finchley Road tube.*

Odeon Camden Town *Parkway, NW1. Camden Town tube.*

Odeon Swiss Cottage *Finchley Road, NW6. Swiss Cottage tube.*

Screen on the Green *83 Upper Street (opposite Islington Green), N1 (020 7226 3520). Angel tube.* **Map 9 O2**

Screen on the Hill *203 Haverstock Hill, NW3 (020 7435 3366). Belsize Park tube.*

South London

Clapham Picture House *76 Venn Street, SW4 (recorded info 020 7498 2242/credit card bookings 020 7498 3323/www.picturehouse-cinemas.co.uk). Clapham Common tube.*

Greenwich Cinema *180 Greenwich High Road, SE10 (credit card bookings 020 8293 0101/recorded info 07626 919020). Greenwich rail.*

Ritzy *Brixton Oval, Coldharbour Lane, SW2 (recorded info 020 7737 2121/credit card bookings 020 7733 2229). Brixton tube/rail.*

Virgin Fulham Road *142 Fulham Road, SW10 (recorded info & credit card bookings 0870 907 0711). South Kensington tube.* **Map 4 D11**

West London

Gate Cinema *87 Notting Hill Gate, W11 (box office & enquiries 020 7727 4043). Notting Hill Gate tube.* **Map 1 A7**

Notting Hill Coronet *Notting Hill Gate, W11 (020 7727 6705). Notting Hill Gate tube.* **Map 1 A7**

Odeon Kensington *Kensington High Street, W8. High Street Kensington tube.* **Map 3 A9**

UCI Whiteleys *2nd floor, Whiteleys Shopping Centre, Queensway, W2 (recorded info & credit card bookings 0870 603 4567/0990 888990). Bayswater or Queensway tube.* **Map 1 C6**

The mighty **BFI London IMAX Cinema**.

Repertory

The following are distinguished by well-chosen, off-the-wall material. The **Phoenix** and **Watermans Arts Centre** also show new releases. Note that the **Everyman Cinema** in Hampstead was, as the Guide went to press, closed until further notice. *See also page 259* **ICA Cinema**, **Metro** and **Ritzy**.

Ciné Lumière *Institut Français, 17 Queensberry Place, SW7 (020 7838 2144/838 2146/ www.institut.ambafrance.org.uk). South Kensington tube.* **Map 4 D10**

Goethe Institut *50 Princes Gate, Exhibition Road, SW7 (020 7596 4000/www.goethe.de/london). South Kensington tube.* **Map 4 D9**

Lux Cinema *2-4 Hoxton Square, N1 (020 7684 0201/684 0200). Old Street tube/rail.* **Map 10 R3**

National Film Theatre (NFT) *South Bank, SE1 (020 7928 3232/www.bfi.org.uk). Embankment tube/ Waterloo tube/rail.* **Map 8 M7**

Phoenix *52 High Road, N2 (020 8444 6789/ recorded info 020 8883 2233). East Finchley tube.*

Rio Cinema *107 Kingsland High Street, E8 (020 7254 6677). Dalston Kingsland rail/30, 38, 56, 67, 76, 149, 242, 243 bus.*

Riverside Studios Cinema *Crisp Road, W6 (credit card bookings 020 8237 1111/ www.riversidestudios.co.uk). Hammersmith tube.*

Watermans Arts Centre *40 High Street, Brentford, Middlesex (020 8568 1176). Kew Bridge/ Brentford rail.*

IMAX

The capital has two IMAX cinemas – the **Pepsi London IMAX Theatre**, with 298 seats, and the visually more impressive 480-seater **BFI London IMAX Cinema**, which is ten storeys high. It also boasts the biggest film screen in Britain, with 80 million tiny holes allowing high-fidelity sound to filter through into the auditorium. The structure, which stands majestically on the roundabout just south of Waterloo Bridge, is built on springs to cut out the noise from surrounding traffic. Both cinemas show 2D as well as 3D features (don't be alarmed by the special headgear you have to wear for the latter: it's a vital part of the experience). The new Wellcome Wing at the **Science Museum**, due to open in June 2000, will also contain an IMAX cinema (*see page 97* **Three's company**).

BFI London IMAX Cinema

Waterloo Bullring, South Bank, SE1 (info 020 7902 1234/www.bfi.org.uk). Embankment tube/Waterloo tube/rail. GoSee Card member (see p32). **Map 8 M8**

Pepsi London IMAX Theatre

Pepsi Trocadero, Piccadilly Circus, W1 (info & bookings 020 7494 4153). Piccadilly Circus tube. **Map 8 K7**

Festivals

London's film industry has undergone a renaissance in recent years, with home-grown hits such as *Notting Hill* and *Lock, Stock and Two Smoking Barrels* making the capital once again a cinematic place-to-be.

The most high-profile festival in the capital (and one of the largest in the world) is the **London Film Festival** (2-16 Nov 2000; 020 7928 3232/ www.lff.org.uk or www.bfi.org.uk). During the festival over 150 feature films are screened across London's cinemas, centring around the NFT and the Odeon West End. The 1999 festival attracted Hollywood names including Spike Lee, Susan Sarandon and Tim Robbins.

The NFT also stages the **London Lesbian and Gay Film Festival** (30 Mar-13 Apr 2000; 020 7928 3232/www.llgff.org.uk or www.bfi.org.uk) with over 60 new and restored films from around the world each year, as well as many shorts and special events.

Raindance (13-26 Oct 2000; 020 7287 3833/ www.raindance.co.uk), held at the Metro cinema in Soho, showcases less established talent. It's Britain's largest festival devoted exclusively to independent film, with 85 per cent of the the content produced by first-time directors. The Metro is also home to the **Latin American Film Festival** (held in September; phone 020 7434 3357 for exact dates or check out the website at www.metrocinema.co.uk.)

Young directors often start off by directing 'shorts' and the capital now has several quality festivals that only cater for films less than ten minutes long. Among them are the **BBC British Short Film Festival** (in September; phone 020 8743 8000 ext 6222 for exact dates) and the **Rushes Short Film Festival** (29 July-4 Aug 2000; 020 7439 2397/www.rushes-soho-shorts-festival.co.uk).

Gay & Lesbian

Come this way.

The '90s saw an increase in the number of gay bars and cafés in London – particularly Old Compton Street and environs, in spite of the bombing of the Admiral Duncan pub – yet many bars in the centre and suburbs are throwing off their fortress exteriors in favour of open fronts and pavement tables. However, as we steam on into the new millennium there seems to be a jaded edge to many of the city centre watering holes. Freshness is to be found elsewhere. Homogeneous gay culture is being supplanted by a healthy heterodoxy, much of it away from Old Compton Street. Salsa, northern soul, rock, pop, bhangra, house, garage, funk, techno and Strauss waltzes – it's all out there for the gay and lesbian punter to savour, even if it means a night bus home from N19 or SE11. These days anything goes and 'queer' encompasses anything and everybody with leanings away from the straight and narrow.

Other positive signs are the increasingly visible lesbian and non-white gay scenes. We've already had the first lesbian beauty contest and Europe's first Black and Asian gay beauty contest, and we eagerly await more in the new millennium. In 1999 TV's Channel 4 gave us the no-punches-pulled drama *Queer as Folk*, *The Staying In Show*, a gay quiz show chaired by Amy Lamé and the sharp-tongued humour of avant-garde performer the Divine David – all of which are further indications of an increasingly confident and diverse culture.

Pride, one of London's biggest marches and festivals, has had a troubled recent history. The march and the post-march festival have effectively become two separate events. 1999's festival did eventually take place, in Finsbury Park. Entry was by advance ticket only and the same will undoubtedly apply in 2000. Check *Time Out* magazine nearer the time (July) for details. The burgeoning **Summer Rites** bash (020 7278 0995; *see also page 8*) is set to take place once again in Brockwell Park, near Brixton, on the first Saturday in August (with, possibly, a straight day on the Sunday). Expect plenty of events, live acts, market stalls, club-tents and a funfair.

London's lesbian and gay nightlife is well organised. Clubs advertise their events in the gay press and *Time Out* magazine, and in freebie publications (the 'gaypers') such as *Boyz*, *QX* and *Fluid*, whichare available in many of the bars and clubs listed below. Of the rest of the gay press, the *Pink Paper* is good for news and lifestyle features, while light relief can be had from (lipstick) lesbian mag *Diva* and fashion-led *Attitude*.

Admission prices vary from place to place and from night to night. The trendiest clubs often charge in excess of a tenner, depending on what time you get past the door. Keep an eye out for discount vouchers and flyers. At most pubs, though not all, admission is free.

Clubs

Soho is still the gay mecca, but recently clusters of gay nightlife have been appearing away from the West End, in places such as Brixton and Camden. Earl's Court, which was the centre of Gay London life in the 1970s, is also experiencing a renaissance. Clubs tend to come and go with bewildering speed, so be sure to phone ahead before you don your rubber gear. Note that venues that put on more than three nights a week are listed by venue; others are listed by the name of the club night.

Central London is served by an extensive network of night buses (bus numbers are prefixed with an N); only those for venues outside central London are listed below. 'Women only' means lesbians. Note that many bars also host excellent club nights; *see page 265*. Also worth looking out for is **Helmut Slang**, previously held at Gossips on a Wednesday; in spring 2000 it will move to a new venue in Soho and will take place on a Saturday (see *Time Out* or phone 020 7733 4506 for details).

100% Babe

147 Kentish Town Road, NW1 (07956 514574). Kentish Town tube. **Open** 7.30pm-midnight Sun.

Sunday-nighter for women and their gay male mates. DJ Blue spins the deep house and speed garage. *Website: www.wowbar.dircon.co.uk*

Addiction to DTPM

Fabric, 77A Charterhouse Street, EC1 (020 7251 8778). Barbican or Farringdon tube. **Open** 9pm-late Sun. **Map 9 O5**

A hip new home for the DTPM crew at this amazing venue (one of the new superclubs; *see p240* **Three of a kind**), pumping out funk, jazz, hard house, Latino and all.

The Artful Dodger

139 Southgate Road, N1 (020 7226 0841). Angel or Highbury & Islington tube. **Open** 6pm-midnight Mon-Wed; 6pm-1am Thur; 6pm-2am Fri, Sat; 1pm-midnight Sun. **Map 10 Q1**

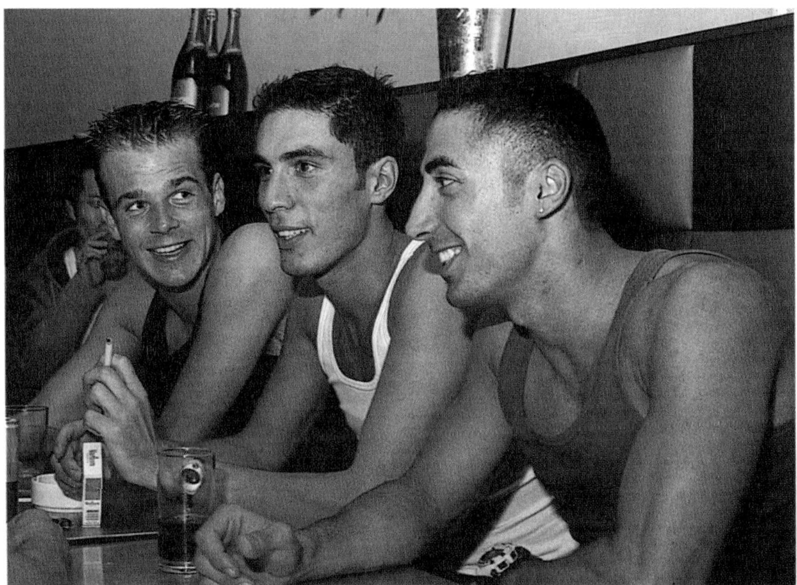

There's nothing like some **Coco Latté** *to keep you going in the evenings.*

Club Artful takes place on Fridays and Saturdays; there's an **Underwear Party** on Sunday from 3pm to midnight (£7, plus £5 membership for first timers – ouch!), which includes use of the minute sauna and gym downstairs. If, instead of your smalls, you'd rather a towel, try Wednesday's straightforwardly named **Towel Party**.

Club Travestie Extraordinaire

Stepney's, 373 Commercial Road (entrance in Aylward Street), E1 (020 8788 4154). Aldgate East tube. **Open** 9pm-2am every Sat.

Now on every Saturday, this TV/drag club has been running for 20 years and is as popular as ever, attracting not only TVs but gays, lesbians, straights – you name it. Fun disco tunes are expertly mixed by DJ Keith DeMaggio, and nights are often themed: check current listings for the latest. Regular cabaret.

Club V

The Garage, 20-22 Highbury Corner, N5 (020 7607 1818). Highbury & Islington tube/rail/N43 bus. **Open** 9pm-3am every other Sat.

An excellent alternative to **Popstarz** (*see p264*). DJs Mel, Neil, Phil and Sarit satisfy a mixed crowd with the Smashing Pumpkins and a host of other choice indie artists.

Coco Latté

59 Berkeley Square, W1 (07956 198267). Green Park tube. **Open** 10pm-3am Fri. **Map 7 H7**

Pricey, classy mixed gay night with funky house and chunky garage on the main floor and '70s classics and rare groove upstairs. Recommended.

Crash

Arch 66, Goding Street, SE11 (020 7278 0995). Vauxhall tube. **Open** 10.30pm-late Sat.

Busy, sexy south London cruise 'n' dance night. There are four bars, two dancefloors, two chill-out areas and a lot of muscle. Resident DJs include Tom Stephan, Antoine, Princess Julia and Alan X among others.

Exilio/Exilio Latino

229 Great Portland Street, W1 (0956 983320/ 07931 374391). Great Portland Street tube. **Open** 9pm-3am Fri, Sat. **Map 5 H4**

Wild Latin night on the last Friday of the month (Exilio Latino), and fortnightly on a Saturday (Exilio), with a mixed gay and lesbian crowd.

G.A.Y

The Astoria (LA1) & LA2, 157 Charing Cross Road, WC2 (020 7734 6963). Tottenham Court Road tube. **Open** 10.30pm-4am Mon, Thur; 11pm-4am Fri; 10.30pm-4.30am Sat. **Map 6 K6**

Jeremy Joseph hosts London's biggest gay trash bash, attracting mainly a young, unpretentious crowd. Monday's and Thursday's **G.A.Y Pink Pounder** at LA2 and Friday's **G.A.Y Camp Attack** ('70s/'80s music) at the Astoria have cheap drinks and entry (£1 or £2 with flyer) and are heavy on the cheese; for big commercial beats and bigger sound systems and PAs from the likes of, in the past, Boys Own and Steps, head for **G.A.Y** at the Astoria on Saturdays.

Website: www.g-a-y.co.uk

Waiting at the **Substation South** *on a Tuesday night. See page 265.*

Gay Tea Dance

The Limelight, Shaftesbury Avenue, W1 (020 7437 4303). Leicester Square tube. **Open** 6-11pm Sun. **Map 6 K6**

A Sunday institution, this feast of '70s, '80s and '90s pop is hosted by Dusty O, with a slightly harder sound downstairs.

Heaven

The Arches, Villiers Street, WC2 (020 7930 2020). Embankment tube/Charing Cross tube/rail. **Open** 10.30pm-3am Mon, Wed; 10.30pm-5am Fri; 10pm-5am Sat. **Map 8 L7**

The best-known and longest-established gay venue in town. A huge refurbishment a while back gave birth to a new sibling club, **Substation Soundshaft** (*see p265*), accessible from Heaven, and left the club itself with an extra bar, coffee bar and VIP lounge. Three floors, each with different music, keep a diverse crowd happy. Fabulous drag hostess Miss Kimberly manages the upstairs attitude-free lounge to the sound of oldies, disco and singalong tunes (and also **Powder Room** on a Wednesday), while the mid-floor offers the widest array of top-notch British DJs to entertain the New York house- and R&B-loving clientele. Downstairs, you'll find mainly tourists and out-of-towners, hoping to spot a star while listening to the latest techno/rave tunes. Monday's **Popcorn** offers a mix of bubblegum pop, disco trash and dance, and the Dakota cabaret bar (there's a friendly indie night, **Room Two**, in the Star Bar); **Fruit Machine** on Wednesdays finds soul in the Star Bar and some heavy funk downstairs. Friday night is **There**: hard house and techno beats. The ultimate night, though, is Saturday's **Heaven** itself: NY house and speed garage. Be warned, the club's popularity has moved it towards the mainstream, bringing in lots of non-gays and giving some of the staff an arrogance verging on the offensive.

Love Muscle

The Fridge, Town Hall Parade, Brixton Hill, SW2 (020 7326 5100). Brixton tube/rail/N2, N3, N35, N109 bus. **Open** 10pm-6am Sat.

The queues for this busy party night stretch into the distance. Once inside, expect dance and fluffy techno aimed at a mixed crowd of (mainly) muscle boys, disco dykes and club freaks. Superb light effects, steamy stage shows and a chill-out room are all part of the fun. If you last that long, then unwind with **Post Love Muscle** Sunday breakfast in the Fridge Bar (6am-11am).

Website: www.fridge.co.uk

Mis-shapes

Liquid Lounge, 256 Pentonville Road, N1 (020 7738 2336). King's Cross tube/rail. **Open** 5.30pm-3am Sat. **Map 6 M3**

A mixed gay club for 'mis-shapen types bullied at school' and alienated by the attitude of the gay scene – indie pop, funky rock, beaty swing.

Popstarz

Scala, 278 Pentonville Road, N1 (020 7833 2022). King's Cross tube/rail. **Open** 10pm-5am Fri. **Map 6 L3**

Simon Hobart's wonderful Popstarz has moved yet

again. Check out the indie and alternative in one room or the sounds of the '70s and '80s in the other. Or, if it all gets too much, retire to one of the two chill-out rooms.

Royal Vauxhall Tavern
Kennington Lane, SE11 (info 020 7737 4043). Vauxhall tube/rail/N2, N36, N44 bus. **Open** 9pm-2am Wed, Thur, Fri, Sat; 2pm-midnight Sun.
'Homosexualist rock 'n' roll' is played on the decks at mixed gay nights **Duckie** (Sat), presented by Amy Lamé; with the **Divine David** every fourth Friday of the month. Other nights are planned for later in 2000; check *Time Out* magazine for further details.

Substation Soundshaft
behind Heaven, Hungerford Lane, off Villiers Street, WC2 (no phone). Charing Cross tube/rail or Embankment tube. **Open** 10.30pm-3am Thur; 10.30pm-5am Fri. **Map 8 L7**
The latest in the Substation group, Soundshaft has two gay nights: Fat Tony and Slammer at **Twisted** on a Thursday, playing house, and **Spunk** on a Friday, where Tom Stephan and Antoine spin NY/garage/funk to the crowd.

Substation South
9 Brighton Terrace, SW9 (020 7737 2095). Brixton tube/rail/N2, N3, N37, N109 bus.
Open 10pm-3am Mon; 10.30pm-2am Tue; 10.30pm-3am Wed; 10.30pm-late Thur; 10.30pm-5am Fri; 10.30pm-6am Sat; 10pm-late Sun.
People who know what they want come here (as it were). It's strictly no-frills and down-to-business at Substation South. **Y-front** (Mon) is a men-only grope'n'grind fest – underwear only; **Massive** (Tue), 'for larger men and their admirers', and **Blackout** (Thur) are men-only cruise nights; **Boot Camp** (Wed) is for male fetish fans (uniforms, leather, jocks, boots), with proceeds to the Eddie Surman Trust. Weekends start up with gay/lesbian **Dirty Dishes** (Fri), followed by Saturday's the NY style house/garage of **Queer Nation** (mixed gay). On Sundays the indie kids flock in for fun-packed **Marvellous**, also mixed gay.

Sundays at Home
Home, 1 Leicester Square, W1 (020 8964 1999) Leicester Square tube. **Open** 4pm-midnight Sun.
Map 8 K6
Together with Fabric and Scala, Home was one of the new wave of superclubs to have opened in '99 (*see p240* **Three of a kind**). This huge club on seven floors offers a great, friendly atmosphere, courtesy of the mixed crowd of muscle boys and lipstick lesbians, normal drink prices and top-notch funky house. Recommended.

Trade
Turnmills, 63B Clerkenwell Road, EC1 (020 7250 3409). Farringdon tube/rail. **Open** 4am-noon Sun.
Map 9 N4
Muscle boys (pre)dominate at Trade on a Sunday morning, where DJs Alan Thompson, Malcolm Duffy *et al* spin the decks on the main floor, and, in the Lite Lounge, DJs Fat Tony and Sharp Boys, Chris McCoy and Guy Williams, are joined by live vocals. There's also a Members Area, and new lights and visuals.

Wig Out
The Tube, Falconberg Court, W1 (020 7287 3726). Tottenham Court Road tube. **Open** 10.30pm-5am Sat. **Map 6 K6**
This popular club, just off Sutton Row at the northern end of Charing Cross Road, is alive with '70s, '80s and '90s trash on a Saturday night, bringing in a happy clubby crowd.

Pubs & bars

Most of the places below are open to gay men and lesbians unless otherwise specified; we've tried to make clear which venues have less to offer female customers.

The Bar
Chariots House, Fairchild Street, EC2 (020 7247 5222). Old Street or Shoreditch tube/Liverpool Street tube/rail. **Open** 11am-11pm Mon-Sat; noon-10.30pm Sun. **Map 10 R4**
Large, airy café-bar adjoining Chariots Roman Spa. DJs and regular cabaret feature at The Bar. Friendly service and excellent food.

BarCode
3-4 Archer Street, W1 (020 7734 3342). Piccadilly Circus tube. **Open** 1pm-1am daily.
This popular bar was undergoing a radical refit at the time this Guide went to press. It promises to be more of a day and evening venue with an open glass front.

BJ's
White Swan, 556 Commercial Road, E14 (020 7780 9870). Limehouse DLR. **Open** 9pm-1am Mon; 9pm-2am Tue-Thur; 9pm-3am Fri, Sat; 5.30pm-midnight Sun. **Map 12 S6**
Busy local bar/club featuring discos and drag/cabaret on a Tuesday and Thursday, strip shows on a Monday and Wednesday, and a tea dance evening on Sundays.

The Box
32-34 Monmouth Street, WC2 (020 7240 5828). Leicester Square tube. **Open** *café* 11am-5.30pm Mon-Sat; noon-6.30pm Sun; *bar* 5.30-11pm Mon-Sat; 6.30-10.30pm Sun. **Map 6 L6**
Now six years old, this recently refurbished and expanded bar just off the Seven Dials in Covent Garden is light, bright and busy. Drinks, coffee, and food by cookery author Jane Pettigrew are served to a mixed crowd. A monthly changing series of paintings line the wall.

Brief Encounter
42 St Martin's Lane, WC1 (no phone). Charing Cross tube/rail. **Open** 11am-11pm Mon-Sat; noon-10.30pm Sun. **Map 8 K7**
Busy men's bar.

Let it all hang **First Out**.

Brompton's

corner of Old Brompton Road & Warwick Road, SW5 (020 7370 1344). Earl's Court tube. **Open** *bar* 6pm-2am Mon-Fri; 8pm-2am Sat; 5.30pm-midnight Sun; *club* 10.30pm-2am Mon-Thur; 10pm-2am Fri, Sat; 5.30pm-midnight Sun. **Map 3 B11**

A popular men's venue with two bars, and a cabaret stage. The bar, with a separate club (cabaret Mon, Thur), caters to gays and lesbians every night of the week except Tuesday when it's men only. Also check out **Privates on Parade**, with male strippers, on a Sunday.

Candy Bar

4 Carlisle Street, W1 (020 7494 4041). Tottenham Court Road tube. **Open** *bar* 5pm-midnight Mon-Thur; 5pm-2am Fri, Sat; 5-10.30pm Sun; *club* 8pm-midnight Mon-Thur; 8pm-2am Fri, Sat; 7-11pm Sun. **Map 6 K6**

The UK's first and only seven-nights-a-week lesbian bar hosts an exceptional series of club nights, including Wednesday's superbly named **Opportunity Knockers**; Thursday's old skool and rare groove **Tunes** and Friday's **Booby Trap**, with Camilla warming up the DJ spot for Princess Julia. **Dolly Mixtures** is Saturday's party night for girls, while **Precious Brown** on Sundays is soul, funk and rare groove with a dash of garage. Male guests are welcome every night. Note that the Candy Bar was planning to move in spring 2000, so phone before you set off.

Central Station

37 Wharfdale Road, N1 (020 7278 3294). King's Cross tube/rail. **Open** 5pm-2am Mon-Wed; 5pm-3am Thur; 5pm-4am Fri; noon-4am Sat; 11am-midnight Sun. **Map 6 L2**

This award-winning 'community pub' combines meeting place, cabaret and late-night cruising. **Bulk** (Wed) is a serious men-only night; **Handsome Devil** is a queer indie session (second Tue of month); while male latex-lovers can check out **Gummi** (second Sun of month), when the dress code is rubber gear only.

Website: www.centralstation.co.uk.

Duke of Clarence

140 Rotherfield Street, N1 (no phone). Angel tube then 38, 73, 56, 171A, 277 bus. **Open** 6pm-midnight Mon-Fri; 7pm-midnight Sat; 3-11.30pm Sun. **Map 9 P1**

Mixed gay pub with a separate women-only bar.

First Out

52 St Giles High Street, WC2 (020 7240 8042). Tottenham Court Road tube. **Open** 10am-11pm Mon-Sat; 11am-10.30pm Sun. **Map 6 K6**

The first lesbian and gay veggie eaterie in London. On Fridays, there's a pre-club night, **Girl Friday** (8-11pm; for women and male guests), described by the owners as 'house and garage with a funky twist'. Also has art exhibitions, which change monthly.

Freedom Café-Gallery-Bar

60-66 Wardour Street, W1 (020 7734 0071). Piccadilly Circus tube. **Open** 11am-3am Mon-Sat; 11am-midnight Sun. **Map 6 K6**

A busy joint that serves booze and food to a hip mixed crowd. There are various themed nights; see *Time Out* magazine for details.

Glass Bar

West Lodge, Euston Square Gardens, 190 Euston Road, NW1 (020 7387 6184). Euston tube/rail. **Open** 5pm-late Tue-Fri; 6pm-late Sat; 2-7pm Sun. **Map 5 J4**

London's largest women-only members bar (with a staggering 10,000 members), on two floors and with pub prices. No admission after 11.30pm.

The Hoist

Railway Arch, 47C South Lambeth Road, SW8 (020 7735 9972). Vauxhall tube/rail. **Open** 10pm-2am Wed; 10pm-3am Fri, Sat; 9pm-1am Sun.

Men's cruise bar. Dress: leather, rubber, uniform, etc.

King Edward VI

25 Bromfield Street, N1 (020 7704 0745). Angel tube. **Open** noon-midnight daily. **Map 9 N2**

Busy, mixed gay pub with café-bar upstairs, plus beer garden. Friendly, welcoming crowd.

King William IV

77 Hampstead High Street, NW3 (020 7435 5747). Hampstead tube. **Open** noon-11pm Mon-Sat; noon-10.30pm Sun.

Warm, friendly pub in the heart of Hampstead serving good food and with a nice beer garden.

Ku Bar

75 Charing Cross Road, WC2 (020 7437 4303). Leicester Square tube. **Open** noon-11pm Mon-Sat; 1-10.30pm Sun. **Map 8 K7**
A stylish edge-of-Soho bar, popular with a young, scene-friendly crowd.
Website: www.ku-bar.co.uk

Kudos

10 Adelaide Street, WC2 (020 7379 4573). Charing Cross tube/rail. **Open** 11am-11pm Mon-Sat; noon-10.30pm Sun. **Map 8 L7**
Smart, busy boys' bar. Large video screen downstairs, café upstairs.
Website: www.kudosgroup.com

Popstarz Liquid Lounge

275 Pentonville Road, N1 (no phone). King's Cross St Pancras tube. **Open** 5.30pm-2am Mon-Thur; 5.30pm-1am Fri; 5.30pm-3am Sat; 5.30pm-2am Sun.
Late night bar from the Popstarz crew, with live DJs, drinks at reasonable prices and nightly fixtures.

Retro Bar

2 George Court, off Strand, WC2 (020 7321 2811). Charing Cross tube/rail. **Open** noon-11pm Mon-Sat; noon-10.30pm Sun. **Map 8 L7**
Mixed gay indie/retro bar playing '70s, '80s, New Romantic, goth and alternative sounds. Look out also for theme nights, karaoke, tribute nights and DIY DJ nights (audition compulsory!).

Rupert Street

50 Rupert Street, W1 (020 7292 7141). Piccadilly Circus tube. **Open** noon-11pm Mon-Sat; noon-10.30pm Sun. **Map 8 K7**
Large, trendy, glass-fronted bar next to the Prowler emporium. Packed to the gills most evenings. Expect to pay upmarket drink prices. Also serves food.

West Central

29-30 Lisle Street, WC2 (020 7479 7981). Leicester Square tube. **Open** noon-11pm Mon-Sat; noon-10.30pm Sun; *basement bar* 10.30pm-2am Wed, Thur; 10.30pm-3am Fri, Sat. **Map 8 K7**
A newish and very happening three-floor bar. Every other Friday **Pop Machine I Love You** serves up the good, the bad and the fab of '70s and '80s music. Look out for Friday fortnightly, **Shinky Shonky**, slapstick fun with the Stuart Alexander Experience, and **Valley of the Dolly Birds** on the first Tuesday of the month (camp classic music for a mixed crowd).

Dining clubs

A relatively recent phenomenon, these increasingly popular organisations put together (for a price) civilised nights out in restaurants for those who are tired of the gay bar and club scene. The **Champagne Dining Club** (020 8696 0829/ champs@diningclub.freeserve.co.uk) organises lesbian-only evenings; the **Out and Out Dining Club** (020 8998 5674/www.outandout.co.uk) is strictly for the boys.

Sport

The Sauna Bar

29 Endell Street, WC2 (020 7836 2236). Covent Garden tube. **Open** noon-midnight daily. **Admission** £10 before 4pm Mon-Fri; £12 after 4pm Mon-Fri, all day Sat, Sun; £10 concs. **Credit** MC, £TC, V. **Map 6 L6**
Recently revamped and renamed, the former Covent Garden Health Spa is now primarily a sauna, with, it is claimed, the largest spa in Europe, plus a large relaxation area and all the other facilities we've come to expect of a gay men's sauna. Men only.

Soho Athletic Club

10-14 Macklin Street, WC2 (020 7242 1290). Holborn tube. **Open** 6.30am-10pm Mon-Fri; 10am-10pm Sat; noon-6pm Sun. **Membership** £325-£440 per year; £18-£22 per week; £6-£8 per day. **Map 6 L6**
A huge, friendly gym open to men and women, with excellent cardiovascular and resistance machines and plenty of free weights. It's become one of the first London gyms to embrace the new New York craze of spinning – low impact aerobics on exercise bikes. There's also normal aerobics, a therapy room and a beauty therapist on site. The real beauty is the hidden extras, which include the Revival Café and cable TV.

Accommodation

The **London Holiday Accommodation Bureau** (*see page 161*) can organise holiday apartments for gays and lesbians, and also throws in a free airport/tube pick-up, theatre tickets and a tour of Soho.

Accommodation Outlet

32 Old Compton Street, W1 (020 7287 4244/fax 020 7734 2249/homes@outlet.co.uk). Leicester Square tube. **Open** 10am-7pm Mon-Fri; noon-5pm Sat. **Map 6 K6**
A service for lesbian and gay flat-seekers, landlords and those looking for short-term holiday accommodation. It can find rooms in the West End from £45, as part of its holiday accommodation service.
Website: www.outlet.co.uk

Number Seven

7 Josephine Avenue, SW2 (020 8674 1880/ hotel@no7.com). Brixton tube/rail. **Rooms** 8 (all en suite). **Rates** *single* £59-£69; *double* £79-£99; *triple* £119; *quad* £129. **Credit** AmEx, MC, V.
A Victorian townhouse in a quiet tree-lined street in buzzing Brixton. Run by friendly John and Paul (and their dog Dougal), this small (though not cheap) B&B is clean and comfortable. Clubbers take note: it's handy for the **Fridge** (*see p241*) and **Substation South** (*see p265*).
Hotel services *Fax. Garden. Laundry. Parking. Safe.* **Room services** *Air-conditioning. Hairdryer. Radio. Refrigerator. Satellite TV. Tea/coffee. Telephone.*
Website: www.no7.com

Philbeach Hotel
30-31 Philbeach Gardens, SW5 (020 7373 1244/ 100756.3112@compuserve.com). Earl's Court tube.
Rooms 40 (14 en suite). **Rates** (incl Cont breakfast) *single* £35-£60; *double* £60-£85. **Credit** AmEx, DC, JCB, MC, £TC, V. **Map 3 A11**
A well-established gay hotel, particularly favoured by transvestites (there's a cross-dressing party every Monday). The interiors of some of the rooms are not quite up to scratch, but there is at least a late-opening bar and restaurant, Wilde about Oscar.
Hotel services *Bar. Fax. Garden. Laundry. Multilingual staff. Restaurant. Safe. TV Lounge.*
Room services *Room service (24 hours). Telephone. TV.*
Website: philbeach.freeserve.co.uk

Health & information

For further helplines, *see page 325.*

Audrey Lorde Clinic
Ambrose King Centre, Royal London Hospital, Whitechapel Road, E1 (020 7377 7312). Whitechapel tube. **Open** 9.30am-5pm Fri.
Weekly lesbian health clinic, offering smears, HIV testing, information and counselling.

Axis
Mortimer Market Centre, Mortimer Market, off Capper Street, W1 (020 7530 5050). Warren Street tube. **Open** 7-9pm Thur. **Map 5 J4**
Sexual health clinic for gay and bisexual men and women under 26. No appointment necessary. Also drugs information for gay men.

Bernhard Clinic
GU Medicine Department, Charing Cross Hospital, Fulham Palace Road, W6 (appointments 020 8846 1576/1577). Hammersmith or Baron's Court tube.
Open 2-7pm Wed.
Sexual health clinic for women.

Big Up Helpline
(020 7501 9315/info@bigup.co.uk).
Phone enquiries 6-8pm Tue, Thur.
An organisation run by and for gay African and Afro-Caribbean men, providing support and health information. Postal enquiries should be directed to: Unit 41, Eurolink Business Centre, 49 Effra Road, London SW2 1BZ.

Black Lesbian & Gay Helpline
(020 7620 3885/blgc@btinternet.com).
Phone enquiries 5.30-7.30pm Tue; 10am-1pm Thur; 11am-4pm Sat.
Also drop-in and advice.

The Jewish AIDS Trust
(020 8200 0369/jat@ort.org).
Information, counselling, financial, practical and social support and education.
Website: www.jat.ort.org

London Friend
(lesbian & gay 020 7837 3337/lesbian 020 7832 2782). **Phone enquiries** *lesbian & gay* 7.30-10.30pm daily; *lesbian* 7.30-10.30pm Mon-Thur, Sun.
Lesbian and gay helpline offering confidential information and support.

Weight to go: **Soho Athletic Club**. *See p267.*

London Lesbian Line
(020 7251 6911/minicom 020 7253 0924). **Phone enquiries** 2-10pm Mon, Fri; 7-10pm Tue-Thur.
Advice, info and support.

London Lesbian & Gay Switchboard
(020 7837 7324). **Phone enquiries** 24 hours daily.
Everything you want to know about queer life in the capital, but be prepared for a long wait before you get through.

Naz Project
(020 8741 1879). **Phone enquiries** 9.30am-5.30pm Mon-Fri.
The Naz Project serves the (gay and straight) Asian community, with counselling and information on HIV, AIDS and sexual health in South Asian, Middle Eastern, South American, Horn of African and North African languages.

Music: Classical & Opera

From huge swanky halls to ancient City churches, there are all manner of venues to hear your Handel.

The main auditorium at the **Barbican Centre**.

Not much changes when it comes to the city's classical music scene. The same old orchestras and ensembles still play in the same old concert halls to many of the same old punters. Sounds boring? It's exactly the opposite.

Classical music in London, despite the perennial financial worries of the big arts organisations, is as healthy as it's ever been. Quite aside from the four big orchestras – no other city can boast of such a surfeit of world-class large ensembles – there are plenty of smaller groups well worth the price of admission, and hundreds of young musicians plying their trade in and around the city.

The large ensembles are led by one of the finest orchestras in Europe, and easily the best in the capital – the **London Symphony Orchestra**, resident at the **Barbican Centre**. The **Philharmonia** is arguably second to the LSO of the London orchestra quartet, and based at the **Royal Festival Hall** (part of the **South Bank Centre**), which is also home to the improved **London Philharmonic Orchestra**. Meanwhile, the **Royal Philharmonic Orchestra** is unique in two respects: it doesn't benefit from state funding and isn't tied to any one venue. It's also rather less reliable than the others.

Quite aside from the bombast of these big four – not to mention the dozens of orchestras who visit the capital each year, both from within the UK and from abroad – there are dozens of smaller ensembles worth catching up with, such as the **London Sinfonietta**, the **Nash Ensemble** and the **Gabrieli Consort**. Add in a veritable cacophony of soloists (be sure to catch a recital at the wonderful **Wigmore Hall** while you're in town), two opera houses (including the newly reopened **Royal Opera House**), assorted choirs, concerts given by students of the three major London music colleges (the **Royal College of Music**, the **Guildhall School of Music & Drama** and **Trinity College of Music**) and some terrific festivals, and you'll be spoilt rotten.

LONDON STRING OF PEARLS MILLENNIUM FESTIVAL

Music plays a part in the huge programme of special events taking place across London in 2000. In addition to the special events listed in the entries below, there's the unique opportunity to experience Inigo Jones's magnificent **Banqueting House** on Whitehall (*see also page 87*), being used for something resembling its original purpose – with monthly Monday lunchtime concerts of seventeenth-century music. Tickets are £10; available in advance from 020 7839 8919 or on the door. For more details of the festival, call 020 7665 1540/020 7665 1558 or check out the website www.stringofpearls.org.uk. *See also page 8* **London's your oyster**.

Major venues

Barbican Centre

Silk Street, EC2 (box office 020 7638 8891/info 020 7638 4141). Barbican tube or Moorgate tube/rail.
Box office 9am-8pm daily. **Tickets** £6-£35.
Credit AmEx, MC, £TC, V. **Map 9 P5**

We say it every year, but we think you should be warned: take a map, compass and survival kit when you first venture into the Barbican Centre. A gargantuan concrete carbuncle with all the grace and elegance of a multi-storey car park, it's an absolute bugger to find your way around. Good thing, then, that the music is frequently outstanding. The Centre has finally rid itself of the aura of naffness that has long pervaded its music programme, with festivals such as 1998's Inventing America and the following

House party

Occasionally, the good things in life are worth waiting for. At the beginning of December 1999, the classical music world waited with the proverbial baited breath as the newly refurbished **Royal Opera House** (*see picture*) reopened. Hugely expensive renovations were finally completed (shock! horror! – on time and on budget) and the mismanagement and institutional snobbery that blighted the House for years seemed finally to be a thing of the past. Ticket prices were made far more affordable and, for the first time, the House became accessible to the public during the day for tours, exhibitions, free lunchtime concerts and access to the café, bar and shop.

So, how does the building shape up? Well, quite simply, she's a stunner. In addition to the grand **Vilar Floral Hall**, with a restaurant and champagne bar, opera-goers and the public alike can enjoy the sleek, inviting **Amphitheatre Bar and Restaurant**, and the **Terrace**, which overlooks Covent Garden market.

In terms of performances, the programme will be made up of the usual classics and the occasional modern work, with big-name singers promised. In 2000, look out for revivals of Strauss' **Der Rosenkavalier** (14 Mar-10 Apr), and Wagner's **Der fliegende Holländer** (24 Mar-11 Apr) and **Die Meistersinger von Nürnberg** (16-27 May), as well as the Royal Opera's first performances of Martinů's last major work, **The Greek Passion**, conducted by Charles Mackerras (25 Apr-8 May). As part of the **London String of Pearls Millennium Festival** (*see also page 8* **London's your oyster**), the House is staging **The Fleeting Opera**, a series of waterborne contemporary opera performances on barges on the Thames (first show 26 July 2000). They will be viewable for free from **Battersea Park** (*see page 132*). *See also pages 81 & 256.*

Royal Opera House

Covent Garden, WC2 (020 7304 4000). Covent Garden tube. **Box office** 10am-8pm Mon-Sat. **Tickets** £6-£150. **Credit** AmEx, DC, MC, £TC, V. **Map 6 L6**
Website: www.royaloperahouse.org

year's Only Connect series of collaborative concerts – slated to reappear in early 2001 – dragging the music programme into the twenty-first century. As resident orchestras go, the **London Symphony Orchestra** is one of the best, while the Centre also hosts regular concerts by guest orchestras. A programme of free music in the foyer, two cinemas, two theatres, assorted restaurants and one of the capital's best music libraries round things off nicely.
Website: www.barbican.org.uk

London Coliseum

St Martin's Lane, WC2 (box office 020 7632 8300/ fax credit card bookings 020 7379 1264/minicom 020 7836 7666). Leicester Square tube or Charing Cross tube/rail. **Box office** 24 hours daily. **Tickets** £2.50-£55; *day tickets* on sale to personal callers after 10am Mon-Sat and over the phone from 2.30pm Mon-Sat. **Credit** AmEx, DC, MC, £TC, V. **Map 8 L7**

The grandly named and grandly proportioned Coliseum is the home of the **English National Opera**, the matey cousin to the noticeably more stuffy Royal Opera. ENO, which hands over the Coliseum to ballet companies during the Christmas and summer seasons, likes to think of itself as an approachable, slightly populist company. To a large extent it's entitled to: in the past, ticket prices have tended to be considerably lower than the ROH's, while the productions could be considered more challenging than those at Covent Garden (although, now the new ROH has been unveiled, this distinction may be lost), and all the works are sung in English. In recent years, ENO has knocked out some fine productions in a return to the form that made it so popular in the 1980s. As part of the **London String of Pearls Millennium Festival** (*see also p8* **London's your oyster**), ENO is celebrating 400 years of opera with an ambitious run of ten consecutive new productions (Sept-Dec 2000), starting with Monteverdi's **The Coronation of Poppea** and concluding with Verdi's **Requiem**.
Website: www.eno.org

Royal Albert Hall

Kensington Gore, SW7 (box office 020 7589 8212/ info 020 7589 3203). South Kensington tube/9, 10, 52 bus. **Box office** 9am-9pm daily. **Tickets** £3-£150. **Credit** AmEx, MC, V. **Map 4 D9**

A much-loved London landmark, the Albert Hall stages events in just about any field you'd care to mention (there's even sport here from time to time). It merits mention in this chapter for hosting the Sir Henry Wood Promenade Concerts, better known as the **Proms**. Originally held at the Queens Hall, Langham Place, and only moved to Kensington after the Queens Hall was destroyed by bombing in 1941, the Wood of the title refers to the conductor who oversaw the first ever series of Proms in 1895. The annual series of concerts, held more or less nightly from July until September, encompasses everything you might expect (noted orchestras, classic works, the jingoistic Last Night) and many events you might not (jazz gigs, late-night early music recitals, world music). Tickets for the seatless 'Proms' area in front of the stage are dirt cheap.

St James's Church Piccadilly

197 Piccadilly, W1 (020 7734 4511). Piccadilly Circus tube. **Open** *enquiries* 10am-6pm Mon-Fri. **Admission** free-£17; tickets available at the door 1 hour before start of performance. **Credit** £TC. **Map 7 J7**

An odd yet delightful little Wren church, not far from the hubbub of Piccadilly Circus but, inside, as removed from the chaos outside as it's possible to be. The programme of events here is impressively varied, if hardly essential: aside from the fine lunchtime concerts (Mon, Wed, Fri) given by young musicians, there's also a series of talks and lectures each month. Look out too for the evening concerts: there's no set day/date plan, nor is there any real thread running through the programme, but the music is often delicious.

St John's Smith Square

Smith Square, SW1 (020 7222 1061). Westminster tube. **Box office** 10am-5pm Mon-Fri, or until start of performance on concert nights; from 6pm and at weekends for that evening's performance only. **Tickets** £5-£30. **Credit** MC, £TC, V. **Map 8 K10**

Situated in the heart of political London – the Houses of Parliament are a couple of minutes' walk away, while the HQ of the Conservative Party is in the square itself – St John's church has been a concert venue for almost 40 of its 270-plus years. It now hosts a regular programme of concerts of varying degrees of quality. Though the acoustics aren't great for larger ensembles and it's not an especially comfortable place – wrap up in winter – it's a winning venue boosted immeasurably by its crypt, which holds a lovely, secluded and even faintly romantic bar and restaurant.

Website: www.sjss.org.uk

St Martin-in-the-Fields

Trafalgar Square, WC2 (church 020 7930 0089/ concert info & box office 020 7839 8362). Charing Cross tube/rail. **Admission** *lunchtime concerts* donation requested; *evening concerts* £6-£16. **Credit** MC, £TC, V. **Map 8 L7**

One of those little curiosities that help to make London what it is, St Martin-in-the-Fields is not, as its name might suggest, set in an idyllic, pastoral location. Rather, it's right on Trafalgar Square overlooking one of the capital's most dangerous traffic hotspots. Once inside, though, it's easy to forget where you are, such is the tranquillity of the church. The series of lunchtime recitals (1.05pm Mon, Tue, Fri) largely features student musicians performing a wide range of music. This is supplemented by weekly concerts on Thursdays, Fridays, Saturdays and some Tuesdays at 7.30pm, invariably including baroque repertoire. The lovely **Café-in-the-Crypt** is a great place for lunch, though be sure to get there promptly as it fills up quickly during the week.

South Bank Centre

South Bank, Belvedere Road, SE1 (box office 020 7960 4242). Embankment tube or Waterloo tube/rail. **Box office** 10am-9pm daily. **Tickets** £5-£60. **Credit** AmEx, DC, MC, £TC, V. **Map 8 M8**

Were the programme of music not so good at this stalwart of London concert life, its location would still make it worth a visit. Its Thames-side situation affords lovely views along and across the river, especially at night. The umbrella name of the South Bank Centre encompasses three concert halls. The **Royal Festival Hall** is the largest, staging mainly symphony concerts and events at the more popular end of the spectrum, although the acoustics arguably don't suit amplified music. The **Queen Elizabeth Hall** is about a third of the size of the RFH, and takes care of chamber groups, semi-staged operas and the occasional idiosyncratic theatrical event. Finally, small chamber groups and recitals can be found in the comparatively cosy **Purcell Room**. In addition, there's a good-sized bookshop, free foyer music, an overpriced record store, a poetry library and performance room, several cafés, bars and restaurants, including the classy **People's Palace** (*see p167*).

Website: www.sbc.org.uk

Wigmore Hall

36 Wigmore Street, W1 (box office 020 7935 2141). Bond Street tube. **Box office** *personal callers Apr-Oct* 10am-8.30pm Mon-Sat; 10.30am-8pm Sun; *Nov-Mar* 10am-8.30pm Mon-Sat; 10.30am-5pm Sun; *telephone bookings Apr-Oct* 10am-7pm Mon-Sat; 1-6.30pm Sun; *Nov-Mar* 10am-7pm Mon-Sat; 1-4pm Sun. **Tickets** £5-£35. **Credit** AmEx, DC, MC, £TC, V. **Map 5 G6**

Built in 1901 for German piano manufacturer Friedrich Bechstein and seized as enemy property during World War I, the building at 36 Wigmore Street finally opened as the Wigmore Hall in 1917. The intimate auditorium is attractively decorated – the cupola over the stage, depicting the Soul of Music, is a wonder – and maintains a delightfully old-fashioned atmosphere. Long may it continue to do so, if it means the concerts and recitals – including the bargain-priced Monday lunchtime series that is recorded for transmission on BBC Radio 3 – continue to set such a superlative standard. The staff are friendly, the ticket prices are manageable and the acoustics are impeccable, while the occasional themed series adds a touch of spice. In short, it's a must-visit.

Festivals & open-air venues

London is blessed with a feast of music festivals good enough to gorge even the most voracious of music-lovers. From low-key lunchtime seasons at

City churches to large-scale outdoor events in London's parks, there's normally some sort of festival running at any given time. We've limited ourselves to listing the annual events, though the **Barbican** (*see page 269*), the **Royal Festival Hall** (*see page 271*) and, occasionally, the **Wigmore** (*see page 271*) all offer themed events and seasons throughout the year.

BOC Covent Garden Festival

Venues in and around Covent Garden, WC2 (info 020 7379 0870). **Tickets** free-£50. **Credit** AmEx, MC, £TC, V. **Date** 13 May-3 June 2000. **Map 6 L6**

An excellent festival packed with consistently interesting artists and inspired performer-venue juxtapositions. Many events are held in **St Paul's Church** (not to be confused with the cathedral) on the piazza, and nearby **Freemasons' Hall** and the **Peacock Theatre**. In 2000, the festival will include a number of special productions as part of the **London String of Pearls Millennium Festival** (*see also p8* **London's your oyster**), including Haydn's **Creation** in the courtyard of Somerset House, Gilbert and Sullivan's **Trial by Jury** at Bow Street Magistrates' Court and the Royal Courts of Justice, and **HMS Pinafore** from a boat on the River Thames; phone for details of dates and ticket prices.

Website: www.cgf.co.uk

Thank you for the music

When you're walking the streets of central London, spare a thought for the composers who trod the same thoroughfares centuries ago. Traditionally, foreigners have, on the whole, received a rough reception from the non-too-tolerant citizens of the capital. Yet, strangely, if that foreigner happened to have a musical talent they were welcomed with open arms. Londoners have long loved music.

Wolfgang Amadeus Mozart arrived in the city aged just six, when his father Leopold decided he needed 'to proclaim to the world a prodigy that God has vouchsafed to be born in Salzburg. And it becomes my obligation to convince the world of this miracle'. Of course, Leopold also figured that a 'Grand Tour', as the series of concerts became known, would also be an excellent way to make a quick buck. The Mozarts arrived in London in April 1764, finding lodgings in Cecil Court, a small street just off St Martin's Lane. After playing several recitals in front of assorted dignitaries, the family ended up at 180 Ebury Street in Belgravia, where they stayed for seven weeks and where Mozart junior wrote his first symphonies. In September 1765, they moved to 20 Thrift Street (now Frith Street) in Soho, remaining there for several months.

While in town, Mozart was taken under the wing of **Johann Christian Bach**, who shared a succession of Soho flats – at Meard Street, Carlisle Street and Golden Square – with viola da gamba wizard **Karl Friedrich Abel**, before marrying and moving to 80 Newman Street, just north of Oxford Street. JC was the son of JS and, though a less significant composer than his father, he was an extremely important figure on the London music scene of the time. It was he who started the first ever series of subscription concerts in London, and it was he who built the Hanover Square Rooms in Mayfair, the leading concert hall of its day (demolished in 1900).

Indeed, it was at the Hanover Square Rooms that **Franz Josef Haydn** gave his first ever London performances in 1791 at the invitation of **Johann Salomon**, who almost 30 years earlier had lured Mozart to London. During his 18-month stay, Haydn stayed with Salomon at 18 Great Pulteney Street in Soho, and enjoyed himself so much that he returned in 1794 and 1795, where he completed the wonderful set of 12 London symphonies that he'd begun during his first visit.

Moving north-west out of Soho through Marylebone, you'll find yourself near the home of much-loved British conductor **Thomas Beecham**, who lived at 21 Harley House, York Gate, just south of Regent's Park.

Felix Mendelssohn visited London regularly, staying at what is now 79 Great Portland Street (although his *Spring Song* was originally titled *Camberwell Green*, and was written after he had stayed briefly on nearby Denmark Hill, SE5).

And last but certainly not least, there's **George Frederick Handel**, who came to London for the first time in 1710 and moved here permanently in 1712. Handel first lodged at Burlington House (now the Royal Academy of Arts) on Piccadilly, before eventually moving to 25 Brook Street in Mayfair in 1720, where he remained until his death 39 years later (it's currently being converted into the Handel House Museum) and where he wrote the majority of his works, including the *Music for the Royal Fireworks*. Music, indeed, that is still performed regularly at outdoor summer concerts in London parks such as Kenwood and Marble Hill, with fireworks invariably accompanying proceedings. We think Georgie would approve.

City of London Festival

Venues in and around the City (festival box office 020 7638 8891/info 020 7377 0540).
Tickets free-£40. **Credit** AmEx, MC, £TC, V.
Date 20 June-13 July 2000.
Three weeks of wildly disparate events in and around London's financial district, at venues including the Barbican and St Paul's along with some City churches, livery halls and outdoor venues.
Website: www.city-of-london-festival.org.uk

Hampton Court Palace Festival

Hampton Court, East Molesey, Surrey (festival box office 020 7344 4444). Hampton Court rail/riverboat from Westminster or Richmond to Hampton Court Pier (Apr-Oct). **Tickets** £25-£85 (approx).
Credit AmEx, MC, V. **Date** 8-17 June 2000.
Less cutting-edge cultural event and more tourist attraction with bells on, the Hampton Court Palace Festival is a nice enough place to kill an evening with some so-so classical repertoire. *See also p135.*

Holland Park Theatre

Holland Park, Kensington High Street, W8 (box office 020 7602 7856). High Street Kensington or Holland Park tube. **Tickets** £10-£25. **Credit** AmEx, MC, £TC, V. **Date** June, Aug 2000. **Map 1 A8**
One of London's poshest parks – the electoral roll for the surrounding streets is practically a *Who's Who* of Britain's great and good – hosts music, opera, dance and theatre in its open-air theatre every year. When the weather holds, it's a treat. *See also p139.*

Kenwood Lakeside Concerts

Kenwood House, Hampstead Lane, NW3 (info 020 8233 5892/festival box office 020 7344 4444). Archway, Golders Green or Highgate tube/210 bus/ East Finchley tube then courtesy bus on concert nights. **Tickets** £5-£30 (approx); *day tickets box office* on site from 2pm on the day. **Credit** AmEx, MC, £TC, V. **Date** July, Aug 2000.
All the usual classical and baroque suspects are wheeled out every year at this series of outdoor musical events (concerts is not quite the right word). Bring a picnic, and try and go on a fireworks night.

Marble Hill Concerts

Marble Hill Park, Richmond Road, Twickenham, Middlesex (info 020 8233 5892/box office 020 7344 4444). St Margaret's rail or Richmond tube/rail then 33, 90, 290, H22, R70 bus. **Tickets** £10-£20.
Credit AmEx, MC, £TC, V. **Date** July, Aug 2000.
Almost identical to the **Kenwood** series (*see above*), the open-air Marble Hill festival, held on Saturdays in summer, offers undemanding repertoire in a pleasant location.

Spitalfields Festival

Christ Church, Commercial Street, E1 (box office 020 7377 1362). Aldgate or Aldgate East tube/Liverpool Street tube/rail. **Tickets** £3-£25. **Credit** MC, £TC, V. **Date** 5-23 June 2000, 18-22 Dec 2000. **Map 10 S5**
A maddening variety of twice-yearly musical treats take place in E1 – many concerts are held in Hawksmoor's **Christ Church Spitalfields** (*see p111*). One of London's best festivals.

City lunchtime concerts

Something of a hidden treat, the lunchtime concerts in the plethora of historic old churches scattered in and around the City are a wonderful way to while away a lunchtime. Many of the churches in the Square Mile have historic musical associations – the **Church of the Holy Sepulchre Without Newgate** on Giltspur Street even has a Musicians' Chapel – and maintain them, in a small way, with regular lunchtime concerts by local musicians, many of them students. The acoustics are often marvellous, the settings unique, and the musicians frequently excellent. What's more, concerts are normally either free or with an 'admission by donation' policy, though if you really like what you see, you can always pop across to the nearest pub afterwards and buy the performers a drink. The **City Information Centre** (020 7332 1456), just across the road from St Paul's Cathedral, can provide further details.

In addition to the venues below, regular lunchtime organ concerts are also held at several churches outside the City, including **Temple Church**, off Fleet Street, EC4 (020 7353 1736), **Grosvenor Chapel**, South Audley Street, W1 (01923 828522) and **St James's**, Clerkenwell Close, EC1 (020 7251 1190); phone for details.

St Anne & St Agnes

Gresham Street, EC2 (020 7606 4986).
St Paul's tube. **Performances** 1.10pm Mon, Fri.
Map 11 P6
Damaged in World War II and rebuilt during the 1960s, this red-brick church holds an erratic timetable of concerts.

St Bride's

Fleet Street, EC4 (020 7353 1301). Blackfriars tube/ rail. **Performances** 1.15pm Tue, Wed, Fri (except Aug, Advent, Lent). **Map 11 N6**
Performers at St Bride's are normally either professional musicians or senior students, with organists performing on Wednesdays. The spire of this Wren church is said to have been the inspiration for the design of the traditional layered wedding cake.

St Lawrence Jewry

Guildhall, EC2 (020 7600 9478). Bank or St Paul's tube. **Performances** 1pm Mon, Tue.
Map 11 P6
This Wren church, the local for the Corporation of London, has lunchtime piano recitals on Mondays and organ recitals on Tuesdays, plus a festival of lunchtime events in August.

St Margaret Lothbury

Lothbury, EC2 (020 7606 8330). Bank tube.
Performances 1.10pm Thur (except Aug).
Map 12 Q6
St Margaret's harmonious dark wood and cream interior focuses around the wonderful 1801 George England pipe organ. The church also holds the occasional evening concert; phone for details.

St Margaret Lothbury. *See page 274.*

St Martin within Ludgate

Ludgate Hill, EC4 (020 7248 6054). St Paul's tube or Blackfriars tube/rail. **Performances** 1.15pm Tue, Wed (occasional). **Map 11 O6**
Lunchtime recitals in this 1684 Wren church are somewhat irregular; phone for details.

St Mary-le-Bow

Cheapside, EC2 (020 7248 5139). Bank or St Paul's tube. **Performances** 1.05pm Thur. **Map 11 P6**
Escape the bustle of Cheapside by listening to the recitals at this beautiful white Wren church.

St Michael Cornhill

Cornhill, EC3 (020 7626 8841). Bank or Monument tube. **Performances** 1pm Mon. **Map 12 Q6**
It's believed that Handel once played the Renatus Harris organ at St Michael. Although you're unlikely to find anyone so notable there nowadays, the weekly organ recitals are still worth attending.

St Olave Hart Street

Hart Street, EC3 (020 7488 4318). Tower Hill tube/ Fenchurch Street rail. **Performances** 1.05pm Wed, Thur. **Map 12 R7**
Lovely St Olave's is where Samuel Pepys and his wife worshipped and are buried. Olave, incidently, was King Olaf of Norway, who fought with Ethelred the Unready against the Danes at the Battle of London Bridge in 1014 and was later canonised.

St Stephen Walbrook

39 Walbrook, EC4 (020 7283 4444). Bank tube or Cannon Street tube/rail. **Performances** 12.30pm Fri (except Good Friday and Friday nearest Christmas). **Map 11 P7**
Wren's glorious church is a suitable setting in which to hear the fabulous William Hill organ in action.

Other venues

Almeida Theatre

Almeida Street, off Upper Street, N1 (020 7359 4404). Angel tube or Highbury & Islington tube/rail. **Open** *personal callers* 9.30am-6.30pm Mon-Sat; *phone bookings* 24 hours daily. **Tickets** £6.50-£19.50. **Credit** AmEx, DC, MC, £TC, V. **Map 9 O1**
A teeny-weeny Islington theatre that mixes in small-scale opera and the occasional concert with its steady diet of theatre. *See also p297.*

Blackheath Halls

23 Lee Road, Blackheath, SE3 (box office 020 8463 0100). Blackheath rail/53, 54, 75, 108, 202 bus. **Box office** 10am-7pm Mon-Sat. **Tickets** £2.50-£50. **Credit** AmEx, MC, V.
Its leafy Blackheath location means that a trip down here is usually a pleasant experience. The music might be anything from pop and rap to regular classical or world music.
Website: www.blackheathhalls.com

Lauderdale House

Waterlow Park, Highgate Hill, N6 (020 8348 8716/ 020 8341 2032). Archway tube/143, 210, 271 bus. **Open** 11am-4pm Tue-Sun. **Tickets** £4-£7.
Halfway between stately home and country cottage, Lauderdale House – set in lovely **Waterlow Park** (*see p107*) – stages the occasional evening concert featuring London-based musicians.

Royal College of Music

Prince Consort Road, SW7 (020 7589 3643). South Kensington tube. **Map 4 D9**
London's leading music college stages chamber concerts every weekday during termtime (at around 1pm), with the occasional larger event in the evening. Most concerts are free and open to the public, and here, as at the other two big London music colleges, you get the chance to catch tomorrow's stars today.
Website: www.rcm.ac.uk

Resources

British Music Information Centre

10 Stratford Place, W1 (020 7499 8567). Bond Street tube. **Open** noon-5pm Mon-Fri. **Recitals** 7.30pm Tue, Thur (except Aug). **Tickets** £3-£5. **Map 5 H6**
If you want to find out anything about any British composer, this is where to head. The library holds books, scores, recordings (both audio and video), and there are occasional lectures. There are also twice-weekly recitals of modern British music.
Website: www.bmic.co.uk

National Sound Archive

British Library, 96 Euston Road, NW1 (020 7412 7440). Euston tube/rail. **Open** 10am-6pm Mon; 9.30am-8pm Tue, Wed; 9.30am-6pm Thur; 9.30am-5pm Fri, Sat. **Map 6 K3**
If you've ever made a record – or, perhaps, done a vox-pop for radio – then you'll be in here. Listening is free; it's advisable to call ahead with your request.
Website: www.bl.uk/collections/sound-archive

Music: Rock, Roots & Jazz

Whatever you want, whatever you like, it's all out there.

It's not an exaggeration to state that London's after-hours entertainment scene is driven by the live music on offer. Whether played by a living legend in front of 70,000 in Hyde Park, or before two dozen diners by a covers band restaurant, live music dominates night-time in the city, and not without good reason.

Of course, there's plenty of stuff in between these two extremes, which is where this chapter comes in. As *Time Out* magazine's weekly listings will prove, there are hundreds of potential Next Big Things in the city, all hoping to take the place of those acts who, on the very same night, are packing out the Brixton Academy or the Forum. Mix and match between these two extremes, then, and you'll get an excellent feel for the live music scene in London. You'll also, incidentally, have a terrific time.

Tickets

Prices for gigs vary greatly and can go as high as £50 for the stellar names. However, the average price ticket for a well-known band at most of the **Major venues** and **Club venues** listed below is between £10 and £15, while many lesser-known indie, jazz and folk groups can be seen for less than a fiver at the **Pubs & bars** we recommend. While tickets for the latter are usually available only on the door, it's advisable to buy tickets in advance for most other gigs: many sell out in double-quick time. Try to buy direct from the venue as it'll save on booking fees.

If the venue has sold out of tickets, you'll have to go via one of London's ticket agents, of which the biggest are **Ticketmaster** (020 7344 4444; www.ticketmaster.co.uk), **Ticketweb** (020 7771 2000; www.ticketweb.co.uk), **Stargreen** (020 7734 8932; www.stargreen.com), **ULU Ticketline** (020 7664 2030; ticketline@ulu.lon.ac.uk) and **First Call** (020 7420 1000; www.firstcalltickets.com). All these companies take all the major credit cards. Wherever possible, try to avoid buying from the fast-talking ticket touts who often hang around outside the bigger venues: you'll pay a fortune, and may not even end up with a legitimate ticket.

Major venues

In addition to the venues listed below, the **South Bank Centre** (*see page 271*), the **Royal Albert Hall** (*see page 270*) and, increasingly, the **Barbican Centre** (*see page 269*) all host rock and pop gigs, along with the occasional jazz bash.

Astoria (LA1)

157 Charing Cross Road, WC2 (box office 020 7434 0403). Tottenham Court Road tube. **Box office** 10.30am-5.30pm Mon-Sat; *by phone* 9am-7.30pm Mon-Sat. **Admission** £8-£15. **Credit** AmEx, MC, V. **Map 6 K6**

A thoroughly generic if pleasingly central rock venue, whose recent bills have been filled by everything from Melanie C and Steps (the latter at the popular G.A.Y night) to Ben Folds Five and – yikes! – The Mission. Lack of draught beer and a quite spectacularly ugly stairwell mural are two of the minuses; relatively decent views represent the main plus.

Brixton Academy

211 Stockwell Road, SW9 (020 771 2000). Brixton tube/rail. **Box office** 10am-8pm Mon-Fri; noon-6pm Sat; *by phone* 10am-6pm Mon-Fri; noon-6pm Sat. **Credit** MC,V.

Undoubtedly one of the best places to see bands in London, due largely to the fact that the steeply sloping floor does allow you to actually *see* them without having to stand on tippy-toes. It's surprisingly intimate for a venue its size (it holds over 4,000), though when the hall is at anywhere less than two-thirds full the cavernous interior means the sound quality is muddied by echo. Conveniently, there are bars at almost every corner of the hall.

Earl's Court Exhibition Centre

Warwick Road, SW5 (020 7373 8141). Earl's Court tube. **Box office** 9am-6pm Mon-Fri; 9am-2pm Sat. **Admission** £5-£50. **Credit** MC, V. **Map 3 A11**

The clue is in the name: it's an exhibition centre, and so was not really designed to host live music. To cynics, that's putting it mildly: horrendous acoustics, overpriced concessions and slightly less atmosphere than the moon make this one you might want to avoid.

Forum

9-17 Highgate Road, NW5 (info 020 7284 1001/ box office 020 7344 0044). Kentish Town tube/rail/

Brixton Academy. *See page 276.*

N2 bus. **Box office** 10am-6pm Mon-Sat; *by phone* 24 hours daily. **Admission** £5-£15. **Credit** AmEx, MC, V.
Perhaps the flagship venue in Vince Power's Mean Fiddler chain (of which much more later), the Forum is the capital's leading mid-sized venue. Decent sound and views help, of course, but the atmosphere's the thing: the Forum seems to draw out the best in its crowds, many of whom have been lubricating themselves before the show at the **Bull & Gate** (*see p281*) a few doors down.

Hackney Empire

291 Mare Street, E8 (020 8985 2424). Hackney Central rail/30, 38, 242, 277 bus. **Box office** 10am-6pm Mon-Sat. **Admission** £4-£25. **Credit** MC, V.
The gorgeous, historic Hackney Empire, beloved of legions of comics, actors and music-hall types, is on a perennial funding crusade: almost every month sees a benefit of some sort or other in a bid to stave off closure. Here's hoping it succeeds. Though it hosts more comedy and theatre than music, the rare gigs here are invariably a treat.
Website: www.hackneyempire.co.uk

London Arena

Limeharbour, Isle of Dogs, E14 (020 7538 1212). Crossharbour & London Arena DLR.
Box office 9am-7pm Mon-Fri; 10am-3pm Sat; *by phone* 9am-8pm Mon-Fri; 10am-3pm Sat.
Admission £5-£50. **Credit** MC, V.
Like **Earl's Court** (*see p276*) and **Wembley Arena** (*see below*), the London Arena is a mammoth (10,000-plus) aircraft hangar with almost no qualifications for hosting gigs: the acoustics are shocking, the concessions are even more overpriced than normal, and it's two blocks east of The Middle Of Nowhere. Christmas 1999 saw it host shows by the cutting-edge likes of Culture Club, Eurythmics and ABC. Which seems kind of appropriate, really.

Shepherd's Bush Empire

Shepherd's Bush Green, W12 (020 7771 2000). Shepherd's Bush tube. **Box office** 10am-6pm Mon-Fri; noon-6pm Sat; *by phone* 10am-8pm Mon-Fri; noon-6pm Sat. **Admission** £5-£20. **Credit** MC, V.
Something of a missed opportunity, yet still an above-average venue. The sound quality here is arguably the best in London, and the building itself (it used to be a BBC TV theatre) is a delight. However, only basketball players and those prescient enough to turn up on stilts will be able to see anything from the standing-only stalls area, while fire regulations mean the two balconies are both no-smoking areas (this is a rock venue, after all). Expect to see – or not, if you're downstairs – anyone from Iggy Pop to Nitin Sawnhey.

Wembley Arena, Stadium & Conference Centre

Empire Way, Wembley, Middlesex (020 8802 0802). Wembley Park tube/Wembley Central tube/rail.
Box office 24 hours daily. **Admission** £5-£100.
Credit AmEx, DC, MC, V.
The Stadium, which holds 70,000 for gigs by the likes of the Rolling Stones, will be closing soon (probably late summer 2000), which only leaves the 12,500-capacity Arena or – less often – the 7,500-capacity Conference Centre. For reasons of acoustics, transport, price and atmosphere, you might want to pass on both.

Club venues

100 Club

100 Oxford Street, W1 (020 7636 0933). Tottenham Court Road tube. **Open** 7.30pm-midnight Mon-Thur; noon-3pm, 8.30pm-2am, Fri; 7.30pm-1am Sat; 7.30-11.30pm Sun. **Admission** £5-£12.
Map 6 K6
Notorious for having hosted what many think was the first great punk gig, in 1976, as well as for '60s shows by the Stones and the Kinks, the impossibly central 100 Club now splits its evenings between trad jazz and cultish indie. Try not to get stuck behind a pillar.

Borderline

Orange Yard, Manette Street, off Charing Cross Road, W1 (020 7734 2095). Tottenham Court Road tube. **Box office** 4-7.30pm Mon-Fri. **Open** *gigs* 8-11pm Mon-Fri, some Sats; *club* 11.30pm-3am Mon-Sat. **Admission** *gigs* £5-£10; *club* £3-£8. **Credit** MC, V. **Map 6 K6**

Arguably one of the most underused venues in London, for although there are gigs here just about every night, most are by bands that both you and we have never heard of. Shame: it's a great little basement space in a great central location that, in the past, has played host to the likes of Counting Crows and, in a now-notorious secret gig, REM.

Dingwalls

Middle Yard, Camden Lock, Chalk Farm Road, NW1 (info 020 7267 1577/box office 020 7267 3142). Camden Town or Chalk Farm tube. **Open** *gigs* 7.30pm-midnight, nights vary. **Admission** £5-£12.

Still best known for its comedy gigs – Jongleurs sets up shop here every Friday and Saturday (*see p248*) – Dingwalls offers live music on an as-and-when basis. The multiple levels mean the venue is probably best suited to sit-down, table-top affairs, but the best bands do succeed in making the place feel like a music venue.

Embassy Rooms

161 Tottenham Court Road, W1 (020 7387 2414). Warren Street tube. **Box office** 11am-6pm Mon-Fri. **Open** *gigs* 8pm-midnight, nights vary. **Admission** £5-£20. **Credit** AmEx, MC, V. **Map 5 J4**

A delightful venue this, and one that finally seems to have settled on a purpose after previously attempting to do business as a Cockney-themed restaurant and a comedy club (when it was known as the Improv Theatre; there's still some stand-up to be found here). The mid-sized basement room is wider than it is long and the sound is great. Bands range from ABC to country-rockers Grand Drive.

The Garage

20-22 Highbury Corner, N5 (info 020 8963 0940/ box office 020 7344 0044). Highbury & Islington tube/rail. **Box office** 4-7pm Mon-Sat; *by phone* 24 hours daily. **Open** 8pm-midnight Mon-Thur; 8pm-3am Fri, Sat. **Admission** £4-£10. **Credit** AmEx, MC, V.

Another Mean Fiddler venue, and not one of the better ones. There's nothing wrong with the line-ups, mind: the Garage consistently puts on the bigger names in indie rock both from here and the US. However, the sound quality is usually terrible, the air-conditioning is worse and the door staff are surly. Smaller acts play at Upstairs At The Garage, a smaller room located… well, you work it out.

LA2

For listings, see p276 **Astoria (LA1)**.

The LA2 is only infrequently used as a live music venue, which is a bit of a shame. Though the views are not uniformly great, the sound usually is, and the place's multi-roomed, multi-floored layout makes it especially suited for clubs.

The **100 Club** *after one too many. See p277.*

Mean Fiddler

22-28A High Street, NW10 (info 020 8963 0940/ box office 020 7344 0044). Willesden Junction tube/rail. **Open** 8pm-2am Mon-Thur, Sun; 8pm-3am Fri, Sat. **Admission** £3-£15. **Credit** AmEx, MC, V.

The home of Vince Power's empire, this long-serving little venue has long drawn in locals with its mix of folksy, bluesy and just plain rocky fare. The Acoustic Room upstairs is the size of a broom cupboard and hosts the expected array of broken-hearted singer-songwriter types. Unless you live in north-west London, it's a bit of a hike.

Roadhouse

Jubilee Hall, 35 The Piazza, Covent Garden, WC2 (020 7240 6001). Covent Garden tube. **Open** 5.30pm-3am Mon-Sat; 5.30-10.30pm Sun; *gigs* 7-8pm daily; 10.30pm-midnight, days vary. **Admission** free-£15. **Credit** AmEx, DC, MC, V. **Map 8 L6**

Covers bands and ageing one- or two-hit wonders make up most bills at this rowdy, irredeemably naff Covent Garden spot, so if you ever wondered what happened to the likes of Limahl or The Real Thing, here's your chance to find out. Quite why you'd want to is another matter entirely.

Website: www.roadhouse.co.uk

Rock Garden

The Piazza, Covent Garden, WC2 (020 7240 3961). Covent Garden tube. **Open** 5pm-3am Mon-Thur; 5pm-4am Fri, Sat; 7pm-midnight Sun. **Admission** £4-£10. **Credit** AmEx, DC, MC, V. **Map 8 L6**

If its Covent Garden location hasn't already scared you off, the music here probably will: bands here are of the clueless up-and-coming variety, while the punters could be similarly pigeonholed. It's hard to believe that this was a prime venue in the late 1970s. *Website: www.rockgarden.co.uk*

The Social Bar

5 Little Portland Street, W1 (020 7636 4992). Oxford Circus tube. **Open** noon-midnight Mon-Sat; 5-10.30pm Sun; *gigs* 7.30pm Wed. **Admission** £3. **Map 5 J5**

A newish hangout, and an entirely welcome addition to the capital's music circuit. It's on the small side, mind, but don't let that put you off. Expect the likes of Ben & Jason to wow you over a pint or three. *See also p245.*

Sound Republic

Swiss Centre, Leicester Square (entrance at 10 Wardour Street), W1 (020 7287 1010). Leicester Square tube. **Open** noon-1am Mon-Thur, Sun; noon-3am Fri; noon-4am Sat; *gigs* 8pm, nights vary. **Admission** £8-£15. **Credit** AmEx, DC, MC, V. **Map 8 K7**

The Sound Republic hasn't really found its feet yet, at least not from a regular gigger's point of view: live music events here are still pretty scarce. However, given the millions of pounds invested in the place, expect the owners to turn things around some time soon.

Spitz

Old Spitalfields Market, 109 Commercial Street, E1 (020 7392 9032). Liverpool Street tube/rail. **Open** 5.30-11pm Mon; 11am-midnight Tue-Sun; *gigs* 7pm or 8pm Tue-Sun. **Admission** £4-£8. **Credit** MC, V. **Map 10 R5**

As close to an anything-goes venue as you'll find in London, the Spitz – named for its proximity to Spitalfields Market – is a bar, a restaurant, a café, an art gallery, a club and a live music venue. Expect, as they say, the unexpected, though mildly avant-garde jazz does tend to play a large part in proceedings. *Website: www.spitz.co.uk*

Subterania

12 Acklam Road, W10 (info 020 8963 0940/ box office 020 7344 0044). Ladbroke Grove tube. **Open** 8pm-2am, nights vary. **Admission** £5-£15. **Credit** AmEx, MC, V.

Another Mean Fiddler joint, Subterania concentrates mainly on club nights, with gigs few and far between. The '80s décor is looking a bit jaded now, but the atmosphere is usually good and the sound quality passable.

ULU (University of London Union)

Manning Hall, Malet Street, WC1 (020 7664 2030). Goodge Street tube. **Open** 8pm-midnight, nights vary. **Admission** £5-£10. **Credit** MC, V. **Map 6 K4**

The refurbishment of ULU may have smartened the place up a little, but the main hall itself has been left resembling nothing if not a gym at a modern comprehensive school. Still, the (invariably) indie bands who play here from time to time go down a treat with an audience buzzed up on the cheap beer (it's a university venue, after all).

A busy night at the bar at Camden's **Dingwalls**. *See page 278.*

Underworld

174 Camden High Street, NW1 (020 7482 1932). Camden Town tube. **Open** 7pm-3am, nights vary. **Admission** £3-£12.

A cut above the Camden pub venues on size alone: the labyrinthine corridors at Underworld eventually lead to a strange-shaped basement room spoilt mainly by the obtrusive pillars that prop up the World's End pub above it. Indie stuff dominates.

West One Four

3 North End Crescent, North End Road, W14 (020 7381 0444). West Kensington tube. **Open** 8.30pm-midnight Mon-Thur; 8.30pm-1.30am Fri, Sat; 7.30-11pm Sun. **Admission** £4-£8.

Formerly the Orange, this rather cumbersomely named club venue hosts a bunch of rather nondescript bands every week that are unlikely to get even the hardiest gig-goer excited: your best bet is probably the wheel-'em-on wheel-'em-off Original Songwriters event every Monday night. Do everything in your power to avoid the pub downstairs.

WKD

18 Kentish Town Road, NW1 (020 7267 1869). Camden Town tube/Camden Road rail. **Open** noon-2am Mon-Thur; noon-3am Fri, Sat; noon-1am Sun. **Admission** free-£7.

Café, bar, club, gallery… imagine a funkier, more Camden version of the **Spitz** (*see p279*) and you won't be far out. Reggae, soul and world music mix with more traditionally clubby stuff at this nice little spot. *See also p245.*

Pubs & bars

Bull & Gate

389 Kentish Town Road, NW5 (020 7485 5358). Kentish Town tube/rail. **Open** 11am-11pm Mon-Sat; noon-10.30pm Sun; *gigs* 8.30-11pm Mon-Sat; 8.30-10.30pm Sun. **Admission** £2-£5.

The quintessential Camden music venue, despite the fact it isn't even in Camden. The dingy but surprisingly spacious backroom regularly hosts three-bands-a-night extravaganzas featuring indie-ish ensembles you're unlikely to hear from ever again.

Camden Falcon

234 Royal College Street (entrance on Wilmot Place), NW1 (020 7485 3834). Camden Town tube. **Open** 2-11pm Mon-Sat; 4-10.30pm Sun; *gigs* 7.30-11pm Mon-Sat; 7-10.30pm Sun. **Admission** £3.50-£5.

A low-down-and-dirty alt-rock hovel that keeps NW1's indie kids happy on a nightly basis. If you're seeing a big-ish band here – and these things are, of course, relative – arrive early: admission to the venue is levied at the door of the pub, and on busy nights not everyone can fit in the tiny room where the bands actually play.

Dublin Castle

94 Parkway, NW1 (020 7485 1773). Camden Town tube. **Open** 11am-midnight daily; *gigs* 9pm-midnight Mon-Sat; 8.30-11pm Sun. **Admission** £3.50-£5.

Grimy, grotty and grubby: the perfect Camden indie venue, in other words. As expected, the back room – where the bands play – is tiny and, on busy nights, extremely uncomfortable. But hey! The bar's open until midnight.

Hope & Anchor

207 Upper Street, N1 (020 7354 1312). Highbury & Islington tube/rail. **Open** noon-1am daily; *gigs* 9-11pm daily. **Admission** £3.50-£5. **Map 9 O1**

Slightly smaller than a postage stamp, the Hope & Anchor started holding gigs again a couple of years back, having made its name in the 1970s with all manner of pub-rock affairs. Bands here tend to be at the early stage of their careers.

Station Tavern

41 Bramley Road, W10 (020 7221 9921). Latimer Road tube/295 bus. **Open** 11am-11pm Mon-Sat; noon-10.30pm Sun; *gigs* 9-11pm Mon-Sat; 2-5.30pm, 8.30-10.30pm, Sun. **Admission** free-£5.

A fairly nondescript pub that merits mention here for its nightly blues gigs. Don't expect Buddy Guy or BB King, though; do expect sweaty, noisy, down-and-dirty blues frolicking.

Water Rats

328 Gray's Inn Road, WC1 (020 7837 7269). King's Cross tube/rail. **Open** 8pm-midnight Mon-Sat; *gigs* 8.30-11pm Mon-Sat. **Admission** £4-£6. **Map 6 M3**

Back in its heyday, this slightly salubrious boozer hosted the Splash Club, a soon-to-be-legendary indie club that hosted bands almost nightly. Since the Splash folk left (to programme live music at the **Camden Falcon** – *see above* – incidentally) the live music here has dropped off. However, given its size – it's the largest of the pub venues – the bands that do play here tend to be at least a couple of rungs up the pop stardom ladder.

Roots venues

Acoustic Café

17 Manette Street, WC1 (020 7439 0831). Tottenham Court Road tube. **Open** 7pm-3am Mon-Sat; *gigs* 8.30pm-midnight. **Admission** £3-£4. **Map 8 L7**

A miniscule hole-in-the-wall type venue that's something of a poor man's **12 Bar Club** (*see p283*) but can throw up interesting newcomers, like hard-to-pigeonhole Hilary.

Africa Centre

38 King Street, WC2 (020 7836 1973). Covent Garden tube. **Open** *club* 9.30pm-3am Fri, Sat; *gigs* 9.30pm-3am Fri. **Admission** £6-£8. **Credit** MC, V. **Map 8 L7**

The Africa Centre plays host to top African bands most Friday nights as well as staging occasional gigs on other nights. During the day the ground-floor shop sells a range of African goods. There's also a specialist bookshop on the first floor and a basement restaurant/café.

Festival fun

While large-scale, big-name events such as **Glastonbury**, **Reading** and the **Notting Hill Carnival** (*see page 138*) dominate Britain's summer festival season, London offers plenty of smaller events. Most of the capital's fields and open spaces will, at some time during the year, stage some sort of bash: keep an eye on *Time Out* for details of festival line-ups. Phone the numbers below nearer the time to check dates and prices.

Charles Wells Cambridge Folk Festival

Cherry Hinton Hall Grounds, Cambridge (box office 01223 357851). **Date** 28 July-30 July 2000. **Tickets** £45 (approx). **Credit** AmEx, MC, V.
Easily the most relaxed and friendly of the summer wingdings, and in many ways the best. Of course, if folk, cajun, blues and gospel are not your bag, you may not enjoy yourself. But if your mind is even slightly open to hearing things outside your normal sphere of listening, and you like the idea of hanging around in the grounds of a lovely country house in one of England's prettiest cities with a bunch of like-minded individuals, then you should book your tickets now. Beards and woolly sweaters are not, despite initial impressions to the contrary, compulsory. Tickets go on sale in May.
Website: www.cam-folkfest.co.uk

Essential

Stanmer Park, Brighton, East Sussex (credit card bookings 01273 709709). **Date** 15-16 July 2000. **Tickets** £30. **Credit** AmEx, MC, V.
This relative newcomer evolved, somewhat surprisingly, from an annual campus barn dance (it takes place next to Sussex University campus). Although it's no longer a student event, the audience is generally youngish and laid-back. The weekend usually consists of a dance day and a roots day. Tickets are sold on a daily basis. No camping.

Fleadh

Finsbury Park, N4 (020 8961 5490/bookings 020 7344 0044). Finsbury Park tube.
Date July (phone to check). **Tickets** £30 (approx). **Credit** AmEx, MC, V.
Cynics frequently question the genuine Irishness of the Mean Fiddler-promoted Fleadh – pronounced 'flar'; it's Gaelic for 'party' – citing the fact that in recent years, this tremendously popular event has been headlined by the likes of James, Bob Dylan and The Pretenders. However, once you get past such quibbles, you'll probably have a blast, for the Fleadh is nothing if not a perfect excuse to get extremely drunk. Last year's line-up – the highlights of which were Elvis Costello, the Barenaked Ladies, John Prine and Ron Sexsmith – was quite possibly the best yet; with luck, 2000, the Fleadh's tenth anniversary, will offer similarly rich pickings.
Website: www.fleadhfestival.com

Glastonbury Festival

Worthy Farm, Pilton, Somerset (no phone at time this Guide went to press). **Date** usually late June.
The brainchild of farmer Michael Eavis, Glastonbury was first held in the 1960s, and has since spiralled out of control into the megalithic stoner-fest that generations of wasters have grown to love. The quality of Eavis' line-ups are legendary, though, to be honest, many people go more for the vibe than the music: a couple of years ago, Glastonbury sold out (that's almost 100,000 tickets) before it had even been announced who would be playing. However, expect about a zillion acts spread over about a million stages, from rock and folk to jazz and dance to world and cabaret. The box office opens in April (a phone number for bookings will be advertised in *Time Out* magazine from March).

Bread & Roses

68 Clapham Manor Street, SW4 (020 7498 1779). Clapham Common tube/37, 88, 133, 137, 345 bus. **Open** 11am-11pm Mon-Sat; noon-10.30pm Sun; *gigs* 1-5pm Sun. **Admission** free.
This fine pub hosts the Mwalimu Express, one of London's best world music events, taking in the live sounds and food of a different city each week. There are also family music workshops. *See also p198.*

Cecil Sharp House

2 Regent's Park Road, NW1 (020 7485 2206). Camden Town tube. **Open** *gigs* 7pm, nights vary. **Admission** £3-£6.
Folk music heaven, the more traditional the better. The folk club on Tuesdays is fun in a hey-nonny-nonny kind of way, but beware of frequent invitations to 'Join in on the refrain'.

Hammersmith & Fulham Irish Centre

Blacks Road, W6 (020 8563 8232). Hammersmith tube. **Open** *gigs* 8pm, nights vary. **Admission** £3-£6.
This small and friendly craic dealer plays hosts to all manner of Irish music events from free ceilidhs to biggish-name Irish acts like the Popes.

Swan

215 Clapham Road, SW9 (020 7978 9778). Stockwell tube. **Open** 5pm-midnight Mon-Wed; 5pm-2am Thur; 5pm-3am Fri; 7pm-3am Sat; 7pm-2am Sun; *gigs* 9.30pm daily. **Admission** £1.50-£6 (normally free Mon-Wed and before 9pm Thur, Sun).
An Irish – not, thankfully, Oirish – pub that specialises in semi-trad music most evenings, with big names and rock acts in the upstairs dancehall at weekends. Views are good even when the place is busy, and the atmosphere, like the music, is raucous.

Guildford Festival

Stoke Park, Guildford, Surrey (info 01483 536270). **Date** 28-30 July 2000. **Tickets** £25 per day (approx). **Credit** AmEx, MC, £TC, V.

Guildford stands apart from most of the other outdoor weekenders for a number of reasons. Firstly, and most importantly, it seems to operate slightly outside the music business throng inhabited by the Mean Fiddler fests and Glasto, and so the line-ups are less industry-led (and, some might say, less exciting). It's also considerably smaller than either Reading or Glasto, and offers a surprisingly intimate atmosphere. Expect a couple of big headline acts each day, a lot of filler, and an indubitably pleasant weekend.

Website: www.guildford-live.co.uk

Meltdown

Royal Festival Hall, on the South Bank, SE1 (020 7960 4242).
Date 16 June-2 July 2000. **Tickets** phone to check. **Credit** AmEx, DC, MC, V.

In many ways the Royal Festival Hall's flagship event, Meltdown consistently surprises, excites and infuriates in roughly equal measure. Each year, a guest artist curates two weeks' worth of programming in the Royal Festival Hall and the Queen Elizabeth Hall, which usually includes a few gigs by themselves and some one-off shows by fascinatingly obscure acts. Elvis Costello and Laurie Anderson are past curators, and, in 1999, Nick Cave (*see picture*) showcased such diverse talents as Antipodean violin-led dervishes Crucial Three together with the haunting minimalist classical music of reclusive composer Arvo Pärt. The 2000 festival offers the intriguing prospect of a festival programmed by legendary reclusive singer Scott Walker.

Website: www.sbc.org.uk

Reading Festival

Richfield Avenue, Reading, Berkshire (info 020 8963 0940/box office 020 7344 0044). **Date** 25-27 Aug 2000. **Tickets** £35 per day; £80 weekend. **Credit** AmEx, MC, V.

The end of the English summer is no longer marked by the leaves falling from the trees or the close of the cricket season. Rather, the Reading Festival, held over the August Bank Holiday weekend each year, has come to signal to every music-lover under 30 that autumn will soon be upon us. This three-day Mean Fiddler-organised fandango usually provides an excellent line-up spread over a plethora of stages, with the biggest of the big (Blur headlined in 1999) matching wits with the up-and-comers and flavours-of-the-month. The whole thing is utterly exhausting, but that's kind of the point.

V2000

Hylands Park, Chelmsford, Essex (info/credit card hotline 0870 165 5555/020 7344 4444).
Date usually Aug. **Tickets** phone for details. **Credit** AmEx, MC, V.

Equal parts music festival and mammoth weekend-long advertisement for Richard Branson's ubiquitous business empire (the 'V' of the title stands for 'Virgin'), The Festival Formerly Known As V99, V98, etc, has somehow found a place for itself in what was already an extremely busy summer festivals calendar. The line-ups over its five-year lifespan haven't really offered up too many surprises – think biggish indie bands ad nauseam – but the punters, younger than at most outdoor binges of this ilk, don't seem to mind too much. Keep an eye out for dates and further information about the festival in *Time Out* from early 2000 onwards.

12 Bar Club

22-23 Denmark Place, off Denmark Street, WC2 (info 020 7916 6989/box office 020 7209 2248). Tottenham Court Road tube.
Open 8pm-1.30am daily; *gigs* 9pm daily. **Admission** £5-£10. **Credit** MC, V. **Map 6 K6**

A gloriously postage-stamp-sized backroom just off Denmark Street's Tin Pan Alley, the popular 12 Bar is perhaps London's most intimate venue. It's split between two levels, neither holding more than 100 people at the absolute most. The music, incidentally, is often of a fine calibre: classy country and folk stuff is mixed in with the occasional full-scale band to excellent effect. It's well worth checking out the monthly Nashville Babylon alt-country gigs.

Website: www.12barclub.com

Union Chapel

Compton Terrace, N1 (020 7226 1686). Highbury & Islington tube/rail/N19, N65, N92 bus.
Open *gigs* 8pm, nights vary. **Tickets** £3-£13.

A church, basically, albeit one that stages semi-regular gigs. Expect everything from folk and electronica to indie and rock, though wrap up warm.

Jazz venues

606 Club

90 Lots Road, SW10 (020 7352 5953). Fulham Broadway tube/11, 22 bus. **Open** 7.30pm-1.30am Mon-Wed; 8.30pm-2am Thur-Sat; 8.30-11.30pm Sun; *gigs* 8pm-1am Mon-Wed; 9.30pm-1.30am Thur; 10pm-2am Fri, Sat; 9.30-11.30pm Sun. **Music charge** £5 Mon-Thur, Sun; £6 Fri, Sat. **Credit** MC, V. **Map 3 C13**

An unusual venue in that it (admirably) hosts mainly local and young jazz bands. There is no admission fee, just a music charge that funds the musicians and is added to your bill. On Fridays and Saturdays, visitors must have a meal; Monday to Thursday you can only consume alcohol if you eat (otherwise it's soft drinks). Food is good, if pricey.
Website: www.606club.co.uk

Bull's Head

373 Lonsdale Road, SW13 (020 8876 5241). Barnes Bridge rail. **Open** 11am-11pm Mon-Sat; noon-10.30pm Sun; *gigs* 8.30-11pm Mon-Sat; 2-4.30pm, 8-10.30pm, Sun. **Admission** £3-£10.
This delightful riverside boozer is something of a jazz landmark, and still offers up gigs by musos both from here and the US. There's nary a better place in the capital to while away a sunny summer's day.

Jazz Café

5 Parkway, NW1 (info 020 8963 0940/box office 020 7344 0044). Camden Town tube. **Open** 7pm-1am Mon-Thur; 7pm-2am Fri, Sat; 7pm-midnight Sun. **Admission** £6-£20. **Credit** AmEx, MC, V.
One of the best of the Mean Fiddler venues. The music is usually good, although the jazz tag is something of a misnomer – sounds will be anything from funk and soul to singer-songwriters. That it manages to create such a decent atmosphere despite the awful '80s décor and incessant nattering of the industry types on the balcony is only to its credit.
Website: www.jazzcafe.co.uk

Pizza Express Jazz Club

10 Dean Street, W1 (020 7439 8722/020 7437 9595). Tottenham Court Road tube. **Open** 7.45pm-midnight daily; *gigs* 9pm-midnight daily. **Admission** £8-£20. **Credit** AmEx, DC, MC, V. **Map 6 K6**
Excellent contemporary jazz can usually be found in the basement of this branch of Pizza Express, though most of their restaurants do offer live music in some shape or form. Mose Allison seems to play here almost every week.
Website: www.pizzaexpress.co.uk

Pizza on the Park

11 Knightsbridge, SW1 (020 7235 5273). Hyde Park Corner tube. **Open** 8.30am-midnight Mon-Fri; 9.30am-midnight Sat, Sun; *gigs* 9.15pm-midnight daily. **Admission** £10-£20.
Credit AmEx, DC, MC, V. **Map 7 G8**
A supremely tasteful and rather swanky pizza parlour in Knightsbridge that plays host to jazz artists at the decent end of mainstream. The finger-spot lighting is a treat, as are the pizzas.

Ronnie Scott's

47 Frith Street, W1 (020 7439 0747). Leicester Square or Tottenham Court Road tube.
Open 8.30pm-3am Mon-Sat; 7.30-10.30pm Sun; *gigs* 9.30pm daily. **Admission** £4-£20.
Credit AmEx, DC, MC, V. **Map 6 K6**
Mr Scott might have died a few years ago, but this Soho staple, started by Scott and Pete King some 40 years ago, is still going as strong as ever. The lights are low and the drinks are pricey, but the jazz is of the highest quality (acts play here for at least a week at a time). Be warned: the many expense-accounters who are drawn to the place for its fame do have a tendency to talk the whole way through.

Hammersmith & Fulham Irish Centre, *p282.*

Vortex

139-141 Stoke Newington Church Street, N16 (020 7254 6516). Stoke Newington rail/67, 73, 76, 106, 243 bus. **Open** 10am-11.30pm Mon-Thur; 10am-midnight Fri, Sat; 11am-11pm Sun; *gigs* 9-11.30pm daily. **Admission** free-£10. **Credit** MC, V.
A supremely relaxed venue that's a favourite of London's jazz community for the friendliness of the vibe, the cosiness of the room and the excellence of the mainly veggie food. Barking mad guitar hero Billy Jenkins plays here frequently, as does more mainstream vocalist Ian Shaw.

Best of the rest

Jazz is pretty much sewn up by the year's two big productions: the autumn **Soho Jazz Festival** (phone 020 7437 6437 for dates) and the **Oris London Jazz Festival** (phone 020 7405 5974 for dates). In addition, the **Coin Street Festival** (June-Sept; 020 7620 0544) offers a wide array of performances, and includes the **Latin American Gran Gran Fiesta** on 4 July (020 7620 0544). The festival usually ends with Thames-side fireworks.

Sport & Fitness

Let's get physical.

See the sport section of *Time Out* for the pick of the weekly action, as well as contacts and classes in all manner of activities, from archery to yoga. Alternatively, phone **Sportsline** (020 7222 8000) or contact your nearest leisure centre.

Participation sports

Baseball

British Baseball Federation

PO Box 45, Hessle, East Yorkshire HU13 0YQ (01482 643551).
The BBF runs the British Baseball League, which has northern and southern conferences, each with several divisions. There are teams all over London: write for details.

Bungee jumping

UK Bungee Club

Alexandra Palace, N22 (020 7731 5958). Alexandra Palace rail/Wood Green tube. **Open** every 2nd weekend, phone for times. **Cost** *jump* £50 (incl annual membership & insurance); *ride to viewing platform* £5.
The club has moved from Chelsea Bridge to Alexandra Palace on a temporary basis while it seeks a permanent venue for its 91-m (300-ft) tower. Jumps are currently from 52m (170ft).

Cycling

For bike hire, *see page 340.*

Herne Hill Velodrome

Burbage Road, SE24 (020 7737 4647). Herne Hill rail. **Open** *summer* 6-8.30pm Tue, Fri; *winter* 9am-1.30pm Sat. **Cost** £4.15; from £1.30 under-16s.
Founded over 100 years ago, Herne Hill Velodrome is the oldest cycle stadium in the country and the only velodrome in London. Riders of all standards can use the facilities, and bikes are available for hire. International events are occasionally staged here.

Lee Valley Cycle Circuit

Temple Mills Lane, E15 (020 8534 6085). Leyton tube. **Open** *summer* 8am-8pm daily, but check availability; *winter* 8am-3.30pm Mon-Fri. **Cost** *with bike hire* £4.15, £3 under-16s; *with own bike* £2.15, £1 under-16s.
BMX, road racing, time-trialing, cyclo-cross and mountain biking are catered for on various purpose-built tracks. There's also computerised cycle testing (£21 first test; £15 subsequently), while events from local to international calibre are held most weekends and on summer evenings.

Regent's Park Golf School. *See page 286.*

Golf

Ring the **English Golf Union** (01526 354500) for more information about courses in the capital. Those listed below are public courses where membership is not essential. All courses are 18-hole.

Courses

Airlinks *Southall Lane, Hounslow, Middlesex (020 8561 1418). Hayes & Harlington rail then 195 bus.* **Fees per round** £10 Mon-Fri; £16 Sat, Sun.

Brent Valley *Church Road, W7 (020 8567 1287). Hanwell rail.* **Fees per round** £7.50 Mon; £10 Tue-Fri; £14.50 before noon Sat, Sun; £12 after noon Sat, Sun.

Chingford Golf Course *Bury Road, E4 (020 8529 5708). Chingford rail.* **Fees per round** £10.40 Mon-Fri; £14.25 Sat, Sun; £5.20 under-18s, OAPs after 10am Mon-Fri.

Lee Valley Golf Course *Picketts Lock Lane, N9 (020 8803 3611). Ponders End rail.* **Fees per round** *members* £9 Mon-Fri; £11.80 Sat, Sun; *non-members* £11.30 Mon-Fri, £13.90 Sat, Sun.

Richmond Park *Roehampton Gate, Priory Lane, SW15 (020 8876 3205). Richmond rail.* **Fees per round** £5-£14 Mon-Fri; £5-£17.50 Sat, Sun (cost reduces the later in the day you play).

Stockley Park Golf Course *off Stockley Road (A408), Uxbridge, Middlesex (020 8813 5700). Heathrow Terminals 1, 2 & 3 tube then U5 bus.* **Fees per round** *Hillingdon residents* £21 Mon-Fri, £27 Sat, Sun; *non-residents* £23 Mon-Fri, £33 Sat, Sun.

Regent's Park Golf School

Outer Circle, Regent's Park, NW1 (020 7724 0643). Baker Street tube. **Open** 8am-9pm daily. **Membership** from £60, phone for details. **Map 5 G2**

Services include club adjustment, lessons with pros (£20 for 30 mins; £90 six lessons) and driving range sessions (*members* £2.50; *non-members* £5 for 50 balls). You can even have your golf swing computer-analysed, for £36.

Horse riding

See also page 236 **Mudchute City Farm**.

Hyde Park Stables

63 Bathurst Mews, W2 (020 7723 2813). Lancaster Gate tube. **Open** *summer* 10am-4.15pm Tue-Fri, 8.30am-4.15pm Sat, Sun; *winter* 10am-sunset Tue-Fri, 8.30am-sunset Sat, Sun. **Fees** *group lessons* £30 per hour, £25 children; *individual lessons* £50 per hour; *ride around Hyde Park* £30; £25 under-15s. Reservations essential. **Map 2 D6**

Smart but very pricey stables offering pleasant treks through Hyde Park.

Wimbledon Village Stables

24 High Street, SW19 (020 8946 8579). Wimbledon tube/rail. **Open** 8am-5pm Tue-Sun. **Fees** from £25 per hour Tue-Fri; £30 Sat, Sun.

These British Horse Society-approved stables have small classes and horses to suit both beginners and experienced riders of all ages from three upwards. Rides are on Wimbledon Common, Putney Heath and Richmond Park. Try to avoid weekends, when the stables are particularly busy.

Ice skating

Ice rinks need regular refreezing and sweeping. As a result, skating session times vary from day to day, and from season to season. Generally, sessions last two hours, and rinks are open from approximately 10am to 10pm; phone for more specific details.

Broadgate Ice Rink

Broadgate Circus, Eldon Street, EC2 (020 7505 4068). Liverpool Street tube. **Admission** £5; £3 under-16s, students, ES40s & OAPs. **Skate hire** £2; £1 under-16s, students, ES40s & OAPs. **Map 10 Q5**

Located in the heart of the City, London's only outdoor ice rink is compact, friendly and caters for skaters of all ages and abilities. Phone for details of private hire. Open late Oct-early April.

Lee Valley Ice Centre

Lea Bridge Road, E10 (020 8533 3154). Blackhorse Road tube then 158 bus/Walthamstow Central tube then 158 bus. **Admission** £4.40; £3.40 children. **Skate hire** £1.

Though awkward to get to by public transport, this is a large, well-maintained rink running popular disco nights.

Leisurebox

17 Queensway, W2 (020 7229 0172). Bayswater or Queensway tube. **Admission** £5. **Skate hire** £1. **Map 1 C6**

It's disco night on Fridays and Saturdays at this venerable Bayswater rink, while there are various after-school and family sessions at other times. There's tenpin bowling here too.

Streatham Ice Rink

386 Streatham High Road, SW16 (020 8769 7771). Streatham rail. **Admission** £4.50; £3.70 under-12s. **Skate hire** £1.50.

London's self-styled 'most famous ice rink' was refurbished at a cost of £2 million a few years ago, and offers spacious facilities for both novice and experienced skaters.

Karting

All the tracks below have bookable daytime and evening sessions; phone for details.

Daytona Raceway *Atlas Road, NW10 (020 8961 3616). North Acton tube.* **Rates** £20 15-min practice session; from £40 standard private entry fee for race.

Playscape Pro Racing *Battersea Kart Raceway, Hester Road, SW11 (020 7801 0110). Sloane Square tube then 19 bus.* **Rates** £37.50 per driver for two hours. **Map 4 E13**

Playscape Pro Racing *Streatham Kart Raceway, 390 Streatham High Road, SW2 (020 7801 0110). Streatham rail.* **Rates** £37.50 per driver for two hours.

Raceway *Central Warehouse, North London Freight Terminal, York Way, N1 (020 7833 1000). King's Cross tube/rail.* **Rates** £20 per driver for 15 mins; £30 per driver for 30 mins.

Trak 1 Racing *Unit 2A, Wyvern Way, Barnsfield Place, Uxbridge, Middlesex (01895 258410). Uxbridge tube.* **Rates** £35 per person per race meeting.

Softball

British Softball Federation

Bob Fromer, Birchwood Hall, Storridge, Malvern, Worcestershire WR13 5EZ (01886 884204).

There are 350 organised softball teams in London. National Development Officer Bob Fromer offers information both for beginners and seasoned players, ranging from contacts for local London teams, leagues and coaching sessions to advice on how to become an umpire.

Sport & leisure centres

Badminton, squash, swimming, exercise classes, gym and various indoor sports are on offer at public sports centres. There are usually discounts for members. You should phone well in advance if you're hoping to book a court or hall. For further centres, look in the *Yellow Pages* under 'Leisure Centres', or call **Sportsline** (020 7222 8000).

Admission prices for the following centres vary depending on the activity. Ask about membership rates if you're planning to use the facilities over a long period of time.

Chelsea Sports Centre

Chelsea Manor Street, SW3 (020 7352 6985). Sloane Square tube. **Open** 7am-10pm Mon-Fri; 8am-6.30pm Sat; 8am-10pm Sun. **Map 4 E12**

A 25-m swimming pool, a teaching pool, weights, badminton, yoga and exercise classes.

Jubilee Hall Leisure Centre

30 The Piazza, WC2 (020 7836 4835). Covent Garden tube. **Open** 7am-10pm Mon-Fri; 10am-5pm Sat, Sun. **Map 8 L7**

A large, well-equipped but busy gym with plenty of free weights is one of the main attractions here. Martial arts and exercise classes, and complementary therapy are also on offer.

Michael Sobell Leisure Centre

Hornsey Road, N7 (020 7609 2166). Finsbury Park or Holloway Road tube. **Open** 9am-11pm Mon-Fri; 9am-5pm Sat; 9am-9.30pm Sun.

The facilities at this north London centre are excellent, if showing signs of wear and tear, and include squash, trampolining, exercise classes, skating and a wide range of sports in the massive main arena.

Mornington Sports & Leisure Centre

142-150 Arlington Road, NW1 (020 7267 3600). Camden Town tube. **Open** 7am-9pm Mon-Fri; 10am-5pm Sat, Sun. **Map 5 J2**

The usual range of team sports (volleyball, basketball and football) are offered at this small centre, as well as a gym and plenty of exercise classes.

Porchester Centre

Queensway, W2 (general enquiries 020 7792 2919/ spa 020 7792 3980). Bayswater or Queensway tube. **Open** 7am-10pm Mon-Fri; 8am-8pm Sat, Sun.

Swimming, gym, exercise classes and squash are on the programme. The Porchester Spa includes art-deco-style relaxation areas, Turkish hot rooms, Russian steam rooms, sauna, plunge pool and a range of complementary therapies.

Seymour Leisure Centre

Seymour Place, W1 (020 7723 8019). Edgware Road or Marble Arch tube. **Open** 7am-10pm Mon-Fri; 7am-8pm Sat; 8am-8pm Sun. **Map 2 F5**

This 1930s-style centre has a swimming pool, sports hall, fitness room, steam and sauna suite, plus a Courtney's gym operating to a separate tariff. The popular 'Move It' programme of exercise classes is justly renowned.

Swiss Cottage Sports Centre

Winchester Road, NW3 (020 7413 6490). Swiss Cottage tube. **Open** 7am-9.30pm Mon-Fri; 8am-7.30pm Sat, Sun.

As well as a gym and two indoor swimming pools, there are facilities for squash, badminton and five-a-side football.

Queen Mother Sports Centre

223 Vauxhall Bridge Road, SW1 (enquiries 020 7630 5522/bookings 020 7630 5511). Victoria tube/rail. **Open** 6.30am-10pm Mon-Fri; 8am-8pm Sat, Sun. **Map 7 J10**

This popular centre boasts a well-equipped gym, two exercise studios, badminton, swimming and diving, martial arts and beauty treatments.

Park life

London's parks offer a wealth of sporty activities. Note that some facilities must be booked in advance; phone for details. Here's a list of what's on offer at six of the main parks:

Battersea Park

See p132 (020 8871 7530). **Map 4 F13**

Athletics track. Boating lake. Cycle/rollerblading tracks. Football, rugby & softball pitches. Tennis courts.

Hampstead Heath

See p105 (020 7485 3873). **Map** *see p103.*

Athletics track. Bowls. Cycle paths. Football, cricket & hockey pitches. Horse riding. Kite flying. Model boat sailing pond. Putting. Swimming ponds (women's, men's & unisex). Tennis courts.

Hyde Park

See p95 (020 7298 2100). **Map 2 E7**

Boating. Boules & bowls. Cycle tracks. Fishing. Horse-riding paths. Putting. Tennis courts.

Regent's Park

See p70 (020 7486 7905). **Map 5 G2**

Athletics track. Boating lakes. Football, hockey & rugby pitches (winter). Golf school. Softball, cricket & rounders pitches (summer). Tennis courts & school.

Richmond Park

See p134 (020 8948 3209).

Cycle & pedestrian paths (shared). Fishing. Horse riding. Model aeroplane field. Model boat sailing pond. Swimming pool (outdoor).

Victoria Park

See p116 (020 8533 2057).

Athletics track. Bowls. Cycle & pedestrian paths. Cricket & softball pitches. Fishing. Football, mini-football & rugby pitches. Model boating lake. Tennis courts.

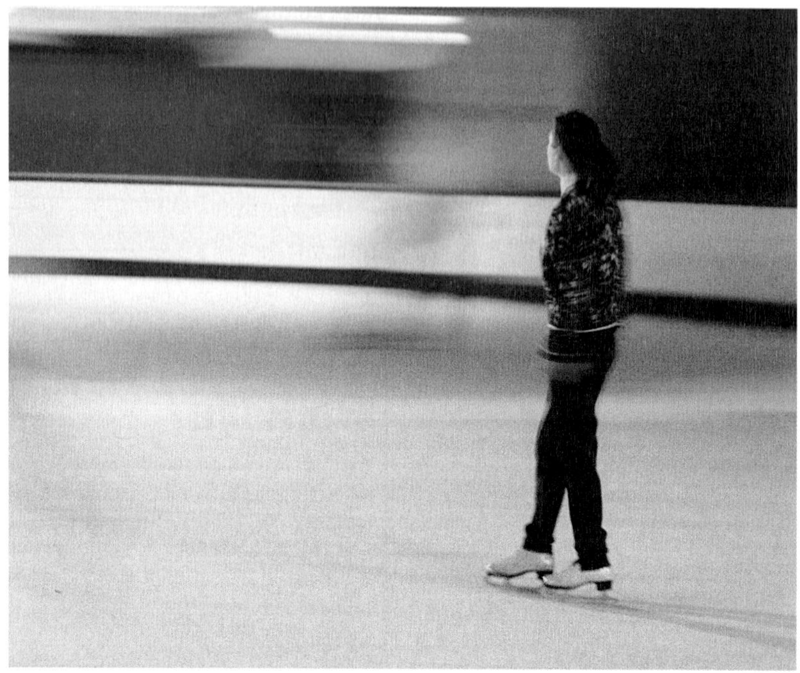

Solo dancing out on the ice at **Leisurebox***'s disco night. See page 286.*

Swimming (indoor)

To find your nearest swimming pool, try the *Yellow Pages* or **Sportsline** (020 7222 8000). A few of the better-known ones follow (*see also page 287* **Sport & leisure centres**). For pools that are particularly suitable for children, *see page 235*.

Highbury Pool *Highbury Crescent, N5 (020 7704 2312). Highbury & Islington tube/rail.* **Open** 6.30am-9pm Mon-Fri; 7.30am-7pm Sat; 7.30am-9pm Sun. *Women only* 7-9pm Tue. **Admission** £2.70; £1.20 under-16s; free under-4s.

Ironmonger Row Baths *Ironmonger Row, EC1 (020 7253 4011). Old Street tube.* **Open** 7.30am-8pm Mon-Fri; 10am-6.30pm Sat, Sun. **Admission** £2.70; £1.20 under-16s; free under-3s. **Map 9 P4**

Oasis Sports Centre *32 Endell Street, WC2 (020 7831 1804). Covent Garden or Holborn tube.* **Open** *indoor pool* 6.30am-6.45pm Mon-Fri; 9.30am-5pm Sat, Sun; *outdoor pool* 7.30am-9pm Mon-Fri; 9.30am-5.30pm Sat, Sun. **Admission** £2.80; £1.10 under-16s; free under-5s. **Map 6 L6**

Swimming (outdoor)

See also above **Oasis Sports Centre** and *page 235* **Finchley Lido**.

Brockwell Lido *Dulwich Road, SE24 (020 7274 3088). Herne Hill rail.* **Open** *May-Sept* 6.45-10am, noon-7pm, Mon-Fri; 11am-7pm Sat, Sun. **Admission** *morning* £1.50, £1 children; *afternoon* £3, £2 children.

Hampstead Heath Ponds *Hampstead Heath, NW3 (020 7485 4491). Hampstead tube/Gospel Oak or Hampstead Heath rail/C2, C11, 214 bus.* **Open** 7am-dusk daily. **Admission** free.

Parliament Hill Lido *Hampstead Heath, Gordon House Road, NW5 (020 7485 3873). Gospel Oak rail/C11 bus.* **Open** *Apr-Sept* 7-9.30am, 10am-7pm, daily. **Admission** £1-£3; free 7-9.30am.

Richmond Pools on the Park *Old Deer Park, Twickenham Road, Richmond, Surrey (020 8940 0561). Richmond tube/rail.* **Open** *May, Sept* 6.30am-8pm Mon-Fri; 8am-6pm Sat; 7am-6pm Sun; *June-Aug* 6.30am-10pm Mon, Wed, Fri; 6.30am-9pm Tue, Thur; 7am-7pm Sat, Sun. **Admission** £2.30-£3.20.

Serpentine Lido *Hyde Park (020 7298 2100). Hyde Park Corner, Knightsbridge, Lancaster Gate or Marble Arch tube.* **Open** usually for two months over summer; phone for times and admission prices.

Tooting Bec Lido *Tooting Bec Road, Tooting Bec Common, SW16 (020 8871 7198). Tooting Bec tube/Streatham rail.* **Open** *May-Oct* 10am-8pm daily. **Admission** £2.40, £1.90 children Mon-Fri; £2.95, £2.10 children Sat, Sun.

Tennis

Many London parks have tennis courts, which usually cost little or nothing to play on (*see page 287* **Park life**). Private facilities and coaching are more pricey, but **Sportsline** (020 7222 8000) may be able to help you find a bargain. If you want to test out your ground shots on grass, then you can phone or write (enclosing a stamped self-addressed envelope) to the Information Department at the **Lawn Tennis Association**, Queen's Club, London W14 9EG (020 7381 7000) for its leaflets on where to play. These are published on a county-by-county basis: Middlesex includes central London, while Essex, Surrey and Hertfordshire cover outlying areas.

Islington Tennis Centre

Market Road, N7 (020 7700 2100). Caledonian Road tube. **Open** 7am-10pm Mon-Fri; 8am-10pm Sat, Sun. **Fees** *outdoor courts* £5-£6 per hour; *indoor courts* £13.50-£15 per hour.

The centre provides two floodlit outdoor courts and six indoor courts for general use. Coaching courses are held at the centre itself, and during the summer at Highbury Fields, for beginners and players of all standards, priced £20-£38.

Tenpin bowling

Tenpin bowling is becoming increasingly popular, both as a competitive sport and for a fun night out. Here are a few of the capital's best bowling centres; for other choices look in the *Yellow Pages*. All have food and drink facilities, of fast-food style and quality. Prices vary from place to place and depending on the time of day, but average about £5 per game – which includes the hire of soft-soled bowling shoes. *See also page 286* **Leisurebox**.

Airport Bowl *Bath Road, Harlington, Middlesex (020 8759 1396). Hatton Cross tube.* **Open** 10am-late Mon-Fri; 8am-late Sat, Sun. **Lanes** 36.

GX Superbowl *15-17 Alpine Way, E6 (020 7511 4440). East Ham tube then 101 bus/Beckton DLR.* **Open** 10am-midnight daily. **Lanes** 22.

Rowans Bowl *10 Stroud Green Road, N4 (020 8800 1950). Finsbury Park tube/rail.* **Open** 10.30am-1am Mon-Thur; 10.30am-3.30am Fri, Sat; 10.30am-1.30am Sun. **Lanes** 24.

Streatham Mega Bowl *142 Streatham Hill, SW2 (020 8671 5021). Streatham Hill rail.* **Open** 10am-midnight daily. **Lanes** 36.

Watersports

Times and prices vary; phone for details.

Capital Rowing Centre

Polytechnic Boathouse, Ibis Lane, W4 (0973 314199). Chiswick rail. **Open** daily.

Capital offers friendly and accessible tuition for virgin oarspeople.

Docklands Sailing & Watersports Centre

Millwall Dock, Westferry Road, E14 (020 7537 2626). Crossharbour & London Arena DLR. **Open** 9.30am-11pm Mon-Fri; 9.30am-5pm Sat, Sun.

Dragon-boat racing, sailing, rowing and canoeing.

Docklands Watersports Club

Gate 14, King George V Dock, Woolwich Manor Way, E16 (020 7511 7000). Gallions Reach DLR/ North Woolwich rail. **Open** 10am-dusk Wed-Sun.

Popular with jet-skiers of all standards.

Lee Valley Watersports Centre

Banbury Reservoir, Harbet Road, E4 (020 8531 1129). Angel Road rail. **Open** 10am-dusk daily.

Windsurfing, sailing, water-skiing and canoeing.

Yoga

The following places are open daily; it's always best to phone to check what's on offer in the way of classes and treatments. *See also page 287* **Chelsea Sports Centre**.

Iyengar Institute

223A Randolph Avenue, W9 (020 7624 3080). Maida Vale tube.

Iyengar is a particularly focused and precise style of yoga, with classes for all standards plus remedial sessions and 'yoga days'.

Yogahome

Bliss Studios, 11 Allen Road, N16 (020 7249 2425). Canonbury rail.

Yogahome is typical of London's new crop of cool yoga spaces, with classes in almost every style at prices from around £5.

Yoga Therapy Centre

Homeopathic Hospital, 60 Great Ormond Street, WC1 (020 7419 7195). Russell Square tube.
Map 6 L4

Founded by the Yoga Biomedical Trust (a registered charity), the Yoga Therapy Centre provides treatment for asthma, hypertension, arthritis, diabetes, ME, menstrual problems and stress-related illness. Remedial classes are available for asthma and back pain, tailored sessions for pregnancy, while general classes run at weekday lunchtimes and evenings.

Spectator sports

Basketball

This fast-expanding sport has a number of teams in the capital. The **London Towers** play in the elite Dairylea Dunkers Championship. For details, phone the **English Basketball Association** (0113 236 1166).

London Towers

Crystal Palace National Sports Centre, Ledrington Road, SE19 (020 8776 7755). Crystal Palace rail. **Admission** £7; £5 children.

Boxing

Details of big fights are fly-posted throughout the city. Seats can cost anything from £20 to £200, or even more for a big world-title bout. Most London promotions take place in the East End at **York Hall**, Old Ford Road, E2 (020 8980 2243), while major championship fights are often staged at bigger venues like the **Royal Albert Hall**, **Earl's Court**, **Wembley Arena** or **London Arena** (*see page 277*). For information on where and when to see boxing in London, phone the **British Boxing Board of Control** (020 7403 5879).

Cricket

County Championship matches are staged over four days, so if you haven't got much spare time it's advisable to catch one of the limited-overs matches in the Benson & Hedges Cup, NatWest Trophy or CGU National League. The season runs from April to September.

Lord's

St John's Wood Road, NW8 (MCC info 020 7289 1611/tickets 020 7432 1066). St John's Wood tube.
Lord's is the spiritual and administrative home of the game. It's the headquarters of the Marylebone Cricket Club (MCC) – governing body of the sport – and Middlesex County Cricket Club, and hosts Test matches and all the major cup finals. You don't need to buy tickets in advance for regular county games, and admission costs less than £10. A stunning new addition to the ground is the futuristic NatWest Multimedia Centre, built to give commentators a better view of the pitch. For the **MCC Museum**, *see p102*.

Foster's Oval

Kennington Oval, SE11 (020 7582 7764). Oval tube.
The Oval is the more populist of the two major venues in London, easily recognisable by the gasometer dominating one side of the ground. The final game in each summer's Test series is traditionally played here. The ground is also home to Surrey County Cricket Club, for whose games admission costs less than £10. Surrey have experimented with Australian-style day-night matches, and more will be held this summer.

Football

Tickets for Premier League matches are becoming increasingly scarce for casual spectators. Every match at Arsenal is a sell-out; similarly, it would be unwise to turn up at Chelsea, Tottenham or West Ham on the off chance of gaining admission. However, London clubs also feature in all three divisions of the Nationwide League, where tickets are cheaper and more readily available. At this lower level, all clubs offer concessions for kids and OAPs. The prices quoted below are for adult non-members buying on a match-by-match basis.

Clubs

Arsenal *Arsenal Stadium, Avenell Road, N5 (020 7413 3366). Arsenal tube.* **Tickets** £15-£37. FA Carling Premiership.

Barnet *Underhill Stadium, Barnet Lane, Barnet, Hertfordshire (020 8449 6325). High Barnet tube.* **Tickets** *standing* £8; *seats* £14. Nationwide League Division 3.

Brentford *Griffin Park, Braemar Road, Brentford, Middlesex (020 8847 2511). Brentford rail.* **Tickets** *standing* £10; *seats* £14. Nationwide League Division 2.

Charlton Athletic *The Valley, Floyd Road, SE7 (020 8333 4010). Charlton rail.* **Tickets** £15. Nationwide League Division 1.

Chelsea *Stamford Bridge, Fulham Road, SW6 (020 7386 7799). Fulham Broadway tube.* **Tickets** £24-£26. FA Carling Premiership. **Map 3 B13**

Crystal Palace *Selhurst Park, Park Road, SE25 (020 8771 8841). Selhurst rail.* **Tickets** £16-£25. Nationwide League Division 1.

Fulham *Craven Cottage, Stevenage Road, SW6 (020 7893 8383). Putney Bridge tube.* **Tickets** *standing* £12; *seats* £16. Nationwide League Division 1.

Leyton Orient *Matchroom Stadium, Brisbane Road, E10 (020 8926 1111). Leyton tube.* **Tickets** *standing* £11; *seats* £13-£15. Nationwide League Division 3.

Millwall *The Den, Zampa Road, SE16 (020 7231 9999). South Bermondsey rail.* **Tickets** £13-£17. Nationwide League Division 2.

Queens Park Rangers *Rangers Stadium, South Africa Road, W12 (020 8740 2575). White City tube.* **Tickets** £17-£19. Nationwide League Division 1.

Tottenham Hotspur *White Hart Lane, High Road, N17 (0870 012 0200). White Hart Lane rail.* **Tickets** £20-£46. FA Carling Premiership.

Watford *Vicarage Road, Watford, Hertfordshire (01923 496010). Watford High Street rail.* **Tickets** £22-£30. FA Carling Premiership.

West Ham United *Boleyn Ground, Green Street, E13 (020 8548 2700). Upton Park tube.* **Tickets** £26-£42. FA Carling Premiership.

Wimbledon *Selhurst Park, Park Road, SE25 (020 7413 3388). Selhurst rail.* **Tickets** £20-£22. FA Carling Premiership.

Golf

Two of the UK's most famous courses lie within easy reach of London. Wentworth is the venue for the World Matchplay tournament every October. Phone for details.

Sunningdale *Ridgemount Road, Sunningdale, nr Ascot, Berkshire (01344 621681). Sunningdale rail.*

Wentworth *Wentworth Drive, Virginia Water, Surrey (01344 842201). Virginia Water rail.*

Greyhound racing

Greyhounds chase a dummy hare around the track, and punters place bets on likely-looking dogs between beers. It's great fun for an evening out, and very user-friendly for the uninitiated. All tracks have several bars and restaurants.

Catford Stadium *Adenmore Road, SE6 (020 8690 8000). Catford or Catford Bridge rail.* **Races** 7.30pm Thur, Sat. **Admission** £4.

Romford Stadium *London Road, Romford, Essex (01708 762345). Romford rail.* **Races** 7.35pm Mon, Wed, Fri; 11am Sat. **Admission** £2-£4.

Walthamstow Stadium *Chingford Road, E4 (020 8531 4255). Walthamstow Central tube.* **Races** 7.30pm Tue, Thur, Sat. **Admission** £2-£4.50.

Wimbledon Stadium *Plough Lane, SW19 (020 8946 8000). Wimbledon Park tube.* **Races** 7.30pm Tue, Fri, Sat. **Admission** £3-£4.50.

Horse racing

The horse-racing season is roughly divided into flat racing (Apr-Sept) and National Hunt (jumps) racing (Oct-Apr). Evening meetings are held during the summer months. All courses cater for everyone from dedicated punters to day-tripping families, with plenty of places to eat and drink. There's no compulsion to bet, although it adds to the fun if you risk a small wager or two.

Ascot

High Street, Ascot, Berkshire (01344 622211). Ascot rail. **Admission** *silver ring* £5; *grandstand* £8-£13; *members* £12-£20.
Big hats invade Britain's premier flat racing course in June for one of the highlights of the society calendar, the **Royal Meeting**, when the Queen drops in for a flutter and admission prices rocket. In 2000, the Royal Meeting will be held from 20 to 23 June (Ladies' Day is on the 22nd). Early booking is essential. *See also p7.*

Epsom

Epsom Downs, Epsom, Surrey (01372 726311). Tattenham Corner or Epsom Downs rail. **Admission** £5-£16.
The **Oaks** and the **Derby** are both run at Epsom (9 and 10 June 2000 respectively) – one of the world's oldest and most idiosyncratic flat racing courses. In contrast to the exclusive Royal Meeting at Ascot, 'Derby Day' is the traditional Londoners' day out, with pearly kings, jellied eels, palm readers and a funfair all adding to the bustling atmosphere. *See also p7.*

Kempton Park

Staines Road East, Sunbury-on-Thames, Surrey (01932 782292). Kempton Park rail. **Admission** £5-£14.
This popular course holds meetings throughout the year. An annual highlight is the **King George VI Stakes**, run on Boxing Day (26 Dec).

Sandown Park

Esher Station Road, Esher, Surrey (01372 463072). Esher rail. **Admission** £5-£17.
Generally considered the best equipped of the south-east tracks and a regular award-winner to prove it, Sandown's major occasions include the **Whitbread Gold Cup** (29 Apr 2000) and the **Coral Eclipse Stakes** (8 July 2000).

Windsor

Maidenhead Road, Windsor, Berkshire (01753 865234). Windsor & Eton Riverside rail. **Admission** £4-£15.
Overlooked by the brooding bulk of Windsor Castle, this course takes advantage of its picturesque Thames-side setting with a shuttle boat service operating to and from the town before and after meetings. The figure-of-eight course, with a head-on view of the last five furlongs, can make it difficult to work out which horse is winning, though in the balmy ambience of the popular evening meetings you may not care.

Ice hockey

London Knights

London Arena, Limeharbour, E14 (020 7538 1212). Crossharbour DLR. **Admission** £10-£15; £6-£15 children.
The London Knights were created in 1998 as part of British ice hockey's ambitious expansion programme, and play in the Sekonda Superleague. The season runs from September to March, with games most weekends.

Slough Jets

Ice Arena, Montem Lane, Slough, Berkshire (01753 821555). Slough rail. **Admission** £7; £4 children.
Slough play in the lower-grade British National League, but with just as many imports from North America as the bigger teams.

Motor sport

Wimbledon Stadium

Plough Lane, SW17 (020 8946 8000). Wimbledon Park tube. **Admission** £8; £4 under-14s, OAPs.
Bangers, hot rods and stock cars provide family-oriented motorised mayhem on Sunday evenings. The season takes a break in June and July.

Rugby league

London Broncos

Stoop Memorial Ground, Langhorn Drive, Twickenham, Middlesex (020 8410 5005). Twickenham rail.
Owned by Richard Branson's Virgin, the Broncos are the only professional rugby league team outside the game's traditional northern heartland and work hard to dispel local indifference to the 13-a-side code. The Super League season runs from March to September.

Rugby union

The oval-ball revolution has brought professional status and a steady increase in playing standards, but clubs are finding it hard to sustain large squads on gates of around 3-5,000. Many leading internationals play their club rugby here, notably with Harlequins, London Irish, London Wasps and Saracens. The Allied Dunbar Premiership and lower-grade Jewson National League seasons run from August to May, and most games are played on Saturday and Sunday afternoons.

Clubs

Blackheath *Rectory Field, Charlton Road, SE3 (020 8858 1578). Blackheath rail.* **Admission** *standing* £10, *seats* £12. Jewson National League Division 1.

Harlequins *Stoop Memorial Ground, Langhorn Drive, Twickenham, Middlesex (020 8410 6000). Twickenham rail.* **Admission** £12-£20. Allied Dunbar Premiership Division 1.

London Irish *Stoop Memorial Ground, Langhorn Drive, Twickenham, Middlesex (0870 887 0232).* **Admission** £12-£16. Allied Dunbar Premiership Division 1.

London Wasps *Rangers Stadium, South Africa Road, W12 (020 8743 0262). White City tube.* **Admission** £11-£16. Allied Dunbar Premiership Division 1.

London Welsh *Old Deer Park, Kew Road, Richmond, Surrey (020 8940 2368). Richmond tube/rail.* **Admission** *standing* £8; *seats* £11. Allied Dunbar Premiership Division 2.

Rosslyn Park *Upper Richmond Road, Priory Lane, Roehampton, SW15 (020 8876 1879). Barnes rail.* **Admission** £5. Jewson National League Division 1.

Saracens *Vicarage Road Stadium, Watford, Hertfordshire (01923 496200). Watford High Street rail.* **Admission** £12-£25. Allied Dunbar Premiership Division 1.

Twickenham

Whitton Road, Twickenham, Middlesex (020 8892 2000/box office 020 8831 6666). Twickenham rail.
Twickenham is the home of English rugby, hosting internationals and major cup finals. The stadium has been magnificently rebuilt in recent years, raising capacity to 60,000 and making it the country's most impressive modern venue. Tickets for matches in the Six Nations Championship (Jan-Mar) are distributed via affiliated clubs and are almost impossible for casual spectators to obtain. Those for cup finals and other matches are easier to come by (phone the box office for details). For the **Museum of Rugby**, *see p135*.

Tennis

All England Lawn Tennis Club (Wimbledon)

PO Box 98, Church Road, SW19 (020 8944 1066/ recorded info 020 8946 2244). Southfields tube.
Gaining admission to the one-they-all-want-to-win is among life's more troublesome tasks. Seats on Centre and Number One courts are allocated by ballot: write (enclosing an SAE) for an application form between 1 September and 31 December. For most people, the outside courts are a cheaper but still enjoyable proposition. You'll need hours to spare for the inevitable queuing, but once you're in, the freedom to wander from court to court means you're never far from the action. Later in the day, you can buy returned show-court tickets for a fraction of their face value, with proceeds going to charity. Wimbledon is from 26 June to 9 July 2000.

Queen's Club

Palliser Road, W14 (020 7385 3421). Barons Court tube.
These attractive west London grass courts host the Stella Artois tournament, featuring most of the stars from the men's circuit as they limber up for the Big One down the road at Wimbledon. Book ahead, as it's very popular both with spectators and corporate hospitality companies. It will be held from 12 to 18 June 2000.

Major stadiums

Crystal Palace National Sports Centre

Ledrington Road, SE19 (020 8778 0131). Crystal Palace rail.
London's only major athletics stadium is in need of a complete overhaul, but it still stages a Grand Prix track-and-field meeting every summer. The sports centre itself hosts a huge variety of events and tournaments including basketball, netball, martial arts, hockey and weightlifting. Following repeated threats of closure, Crystal Palace was reprieved in late 1997 and has since been made a Grade II listed building.

London Arena

Limeharbour, E14 (box office 020 7538 1212). Crossharbour & London Arena DLR/D8, D9 bus.
In the shadow of Canary Wharf, the Arena provides an impressively modern and comfortable setting for major indoor sports. Londoners know it best as the home of ice hockey's Knights (*see p291*). Big boxing promotions are often staged here.

Wembley Stadium/Wembley Arena

Empire Way, Wembley, Middlesex (020 8900 1234). Wembley Park tube/Wembley Stadium rail.
Open *box office* 9am-9pm Mon-Sat; 9am-7pm Sun.
The transformation of legendary but down-at-heel Wembley Stadium (capacity 80,000) into a multipurpose, state-of-the-art venue capable of hosting major world championships (including, perhaps, the World Cup in 2006) was dealt a blow in late 1999, when it was decided that the new stadium would host only football matches, not athletics, as was originally planned. The famous ground with the twin towers has staged the FA Cup Final (*see p6*) since 1923, and is also the venue for international matches, rugby league's Challenge Cup Final and pop concerts. The indoor Wembley Arena accommodates a wide range of sports, including show jumping, boxing and basketball.

Theatre

The good, the bad and the Lloyd Webber musical.

London theatre consists of far more than the glitzy, long-running commercial shows and the handful of big-name dramas that pack out West End theatres nightly – there's also a huge amount of talent out there away from the neon of Shaftesbury Avenue. Many theatre-going Londoners' most memorable nights have been in grotty pub theatres in unglamorous parts of town; although, in truth, many of their worse theatrical moments are likely to have been in similar surroundings. Here, we attempt to provide a guide to the best and most interesting board-stomping in town.

In this chapter productions and theatres are split into three categories: 'West End', 'Off-West End' and 'The Fringe'. '**West End**' refers to the part of central London lying to the west of the City, where most of the big musicals and major dramas can be found, but it also refers to the cultural status of its leading theatres (the **Royal National Theatre**, for example, is classified as 'West End' even though it is located south of the river). The most reliable of West End venues with repertory rather than fixed, long-running programmes are the building-based companies such as the **Royal National Theatre** (three stages in the South Bank Centre), the **Royal Shakespeare Company** (during the winter months, two theatres in the **Barbican** and one at the **Young Vic**) and **Shakespeare's Globe**, which has settled down as more than just a heritage gimmick. The **Royal Court**, meanwhile, is the country's most dynamic new writing theatre, now re-installed in its Sloane Square home. Note that the long-term future of the **Old Vic** (The Cut, SE1; 020 7928 2651), known for its exciting and challenging work, still depends upon the raising of funds. Productions are likely to take place during 2000, however; keep an eye out in *Time Out* for information.

'**Off-West End**' refers to the next rung down in terms of financial means and it is this section that generally provides the best mix of quality and originality. These theatres are usually heavily subsidised, paying minimum wages or, in some cases, no wages at all. Top writers, directors and actors are lured instead by the prospect of artistic liberty. But even these places have their own pecking order, with wealthier theatres like the **Young Vic** and the **Almeida** leading the pack. Theatres such as **The Gate** and the **King's Head**, by contrast, are often dependent on fresh-out-of-drama-college hopefuls prepared to work for nothing to make their names.

'**The Fringe**', meanwhile, is scattered all over London – it is a theatrical underclass where standards are much more variable. There is, of course, a lot of good work to be found, and many of the biggest names in British theatre cut (and, in some cases, broke) their teeth here. But finding such shows is, in practice, like winning the lottery. Among the best are theatres such as **The Finborough**, **The New End** and **The Grace**, struggling in adverse financial circumstances to develop bold artistic policies.

Finally, it is the nature of theatre that it is a constantly changing landscape. To keep abreast of what's best to see and where, *Time Out* magazine, with full, up-to-date listings and reviews, is an indispensable guide.

INFORMATION & TICKETS

Tickets for West End musicals can be the most difficult to obtain and are easily the most expensive, at £10-£35. In association with many theatre box offices, **Ticketmaster** (020 7344 4444) and **First Call** (020 7420 0000) provide advance tickets, but watch out for those big bad booking fees, which can bump up the price by ten per cent or more. The cheapest option is to buy your tickets in person with cash direct from the theatre. You can also book tickets for many shows over the Internet: www.ticketmaster.co.uk, www.tickets-direct.co.uk and www.stoll-moss.com are three useful websites.

Note that in the listings below, the hours given in brackets after the phone number are the times that bookings are taken over the phone. If no hours are specified here, then the phone line for booking is open the same hours as the box office.

The West End

Building-based repertory companies

Royal Court Theatre (English Stage Company)

Sloane Square, SW1 (020 7565 5000). Sloane Square tube. **Box office** 10am-6pm Mon-Sat. **Tickets** 10p-£25; all tickets £5 Mon. **Credit** AmEx, MC, £TC, V. **Map 7 G11**

The Royal Court is the undisputed epicentre of new writing in Britain. Having been in exile in the West End, it now returns to its long-time Sloane Square home after a £25-million refurbishment. It boasts two spanking new performing spaces – the

Going cheap

● The **Half-Price Ticket Booth** in the Clocktower Building by the south entrance to the gardens in Leicester Square, WC2, has discounted tickets for most West End shows. Tickets for some are as little as half-price, plus a £2 service charge (£1.25 on tickets under £12.50). These are sold on a first-come, first-served basis (cash only), restricted to four per person. Beware of touts and be sure you go to the right booth, not one of the similar-looking, more expensive outlets in Leicester Square.

● Matinée performances are much cheaper than evenings, although, in some instances, understudies replace stars. Seats for Monday to Thursday evening performances in the West End tend to be cheaper than Friday or Saturday nights.

● Pay for a restricted-view seat in the stalls (not all theatres have them), then quietly slip into a better seat when the lights go down. Of course, this won't work if the auditorium is full or the ticket-holder of the seat to which you've moved turns up late (and is bigger than you).

● The cheapest seats are usually in the 'gods' at the top of the theatre, but visibility can become faint – especially if vertigo sets in.

● Buy tickets direct (in person or by phone) from the theatre's box office to save on insidious 'booking fees' of 10% and more.

● Go to previews of West End and Off-West End shows. Tickets are considerably cheaper and, despite the melodramatic assertions of highly strung luvvies, there's usually no difference between a preview and the 'real' thing: a turkey's a turkey no matter how long it's cooked.

● The **Royal National Theatre** sells a number of the cheapest tickets (£10-£12) for shows on the day from 10am at the box office (limited to two per person; queues start as early as 8am for the popular shows), plus remainder tickets for evening shows on the night (from two hours before the performance starts).

● Some theatres have reduced-price nights. For example, the **BAC** has a 'pay what you can' night on Tuesdays, the **Royal Court** has some standing tickets for as little as 10p, while all tickets on a Monday are £5, and the **Theatre Royal Stratford East** has traditionally the lowest concessionary rates around for the unwaged, students and pensioners. Also, it's often worth scanning the Society of London Theatres' well-presented and informative website for details of periodic deals (www.officiallondontheatre.co.uk).

● Look out for occasional special offers in *Time Out*'s weekly magazine.

imaginatively entitled 'Upstairs' (small studio theatre) and 'Downstairs' (proscenium arch main stage) – as well as a snazzy new restaurant and bar.
Website: www.royalcourttheatre.com

Royal National Theatre

South Bank, SE1 (box office 020 7452 3000/info 020 7452 3400). Waterloo tube/rail. **Box office** 10am-8pm Mon-Sat. **Tickets** *Olivier & Lyttelton* £10-£29; *Cottesloe* £12, £18, £20. **Credit** AmEx, DC, MC, V. **Map 8 M7**

Under the captaincy of populist ex-RSC and West End musical maestro Trevor Nunn, Britain's leading theatre has established a core repertory company to perform its catch-all diet of musicals, classics and contemporary drama. Set in the concrete mausoleum of the South Bank Centre, the RNT contains three theatres: the **Olivier**'s large, open platform for the big shows, the **Lyttelton**'s traditional proscenium arch for medium-sized productions, and the newly refitted **Cottesloe**'s flexible studio space accommodating smaller, more cutting-edge productions. The Theatre is currently being redeveloped, with new investment in sound, scenery, staging and lighting systems, and a totally new exterior performance space, **Theatre Square**.
Website: www.nt-online.org

Royal Shakespeare Company

Barbican Centre, Silk Street, EC2 (box office 020 7638 8891). Barbican tube/Moorgate tube/rail.
Box office 9am-8pm daily. **Tickets** £9-£33.
Credit AmEx, MC, £TC, V. **Map 9 P5**

The RSC is the principal custodian of Shakespeare's legacy in Britain, but it also stages works by new and classical writers of relevance to the Bard, as well as doing a sideline in money-spinning musicals like *Les Misérables*. Aside from national tours, it divides its time between its main home in Stratford-upon-Avon at the **Royal Shakespeare Theatre**, the **Swan** and **The Other Place** (*see p116*), and, between October and May, the Barbican Centre (the huge **Barbican Theatre** and the more intimate space of **The Pit**) and now also the **Young Vic** in Waterloo (*see p300*). In 2000 productions of **Timon of Athens**, **Antony and Cleopatra** and **Othello** are running until the first week of April; while Chekhov's **The Seagull** and a new play by David Greig, **Victoria**, are on from 18 April to 13 May.
Website: www.rsc.org.uk

Shakespeare's Globe

New Globe Walk, SE1 (020 7401 9919). Blackfriars or Southwark tube. **Box office** 10am-5pm Mon-Fri.
Tickets £5-£25. **Credit** AmEx, MC, £TC, V.
Map 11 O7

Under the guidance of actor Mark Rylance, this fascinating venue has established itself as a serious theatre, staging plays from May to September in the open-air theatre replicating Shakespeare's original Globe theatre. With all the background noise of modern life and the transient interest of coach parties, the theatre is no great friend of artistic nuance. However, the venue provides interesting insights into how Shakespeare dealt with mob dynamics, and

Mamma Mia! *Must be a top West-End production. See page 297.*

the productions are nothing if not fun. The Inigo Jones Theatre, a replica Jacobean indoor playhouse, will be used to stage plays in winter when it is completed in 2000. *See also p41.*
Website: www.shakespeares-globe.org

Long-runners & musicals

Most theatres have evening shows Monday to Saturday (starting 7.30-8pm) and matinées on one weekday (usually Wednesday), Saturday and sometimes Sunday. Phone the theatres for details.

An Inspector Calls

Garrick Theatre, 2 Charing Cross Road, WC2 (020 7494 5085; 24 hours daily). Leicester Square tube. **Box office** 10am-8pm Mon-Sat. **Tickets** £10-£27.50. **Credit** AmEx, MC, V. **Map 8 K7**
Stephen Daldry's production of JB Priestley's previously stale old repertory warhorse rediscovered as an expressionist psychological and social parable.

Art

Wyndhams Theatre, Charing Cross Road, WC2 (020 7369 1736; 9am-9pm daily). Leicester Square tube. **Box office** 10am-8pm Tue-Sat. **Tickets** £9.50-£29.50. **Credit** AmEx, DC, MC, V. **Map 8 K7**
Yasmina Reza's lightweight satire of three men whose friendship is blown apart when one buys an overpriced painting.

Blood Brothers

Phoenix Theatre, Charing Cross Road, WC2 (020 7369 1733; 9am-9pm daily). Tottenham Court Road tube. **Box office** 10am-7.45pm Mon-Sat. **Tickets** £11.50-£32.50. **Credit** AmEx, DC, MC, V. **Map 6 K6**
Willy Russell's grand, ambitious melodrama, filled with Scouse sentiment and toe-tapping songs, has notched up an impressive 11 years in the West End.

Buddy

Strand Theatre, Aldwych, WC2 (020 7930 8800; 10am-8pm Mon-Sat, 12.30-4pm Sun). Charing Cross tube/rail. **Box office** 10am-6pm Mon; 10am-8pm Tue-Sat; 12.30-4pm Sun. **Tickets** £10-£30 (half-price Fri matinée). **Credit** MC, V. **Map 6 M6**
A jolly, nostalgic review of the songs that made Buddy Holly world-famous before his early death in a plane crash.

Cats

New London Theatre, Drury Lane, WC2 (020 7405 0072; 24 hours daily). Covent Garden or Holborn tube. **Box office** 10am-7.45pm Mon-Sat. **Tickets** £10.50-£35. **Credit** AmEx, DC, MC, V. **Map 6 L6**
Based on TS Eliot's *Old Possum's Book of Practical Cats*, Andrew Lloyd Webber's patchwork show is London's longest-running musical (19 years).

Chicago

Adelphi Theatre, Strand, WC2 (Ticketmaster 020 7344 0055; 24 hours daily). Charing Cross tube/rail. **Box office** 10am-8pm Mon-Sat. **Tickets** £16-£36. **Credit** AmEx, MC, V. **Map 8 L7**
Kander and Ebb's well-praised cabaret and dance satire of Al Capone's city.

Complete Works of William Shakespeare/Complete History of America (both abridged)

Criterion Theatre, Jermyn Street, W1 (020 7369 1737; 9am-9pm Mon-Sat, 10am-6pm Sun). Piccadilly Circus tube. **Box office** 10am-8pm Tue-Sat; 10am-4pm Sun. **Tickets** £10-£25. **Credit** AmEx, DC, MC, V. **Map 7 J7**
The RSC (Reduced Shakespeare Company), American iconoclasts of the Bard's oeuvre and their own national history, started as a fringe act but have now been in the West End for five years.

Les Misérables

Palace Theatre, Shaftesbury Avenue, W1 (020 7434 0909; 24 hours daily). Leicester Square tube. **Box office** 10am-8pm Mon-Sat. **Tickets** £7-£35. **Credit** AmEx, DC, MC, V. **Map 6 K6**

Boubil and Schonberg's 15-year-old money-spinner idealises the struggle between paupers and villains in Victor Hugo's revolutionary Paris.

The Lion King

Lyceum Theatre, Wellington Street, WC2 (0870 243 9000; 8.30am-10pm Mon-Fri, 8.30am-9.30pm Sat, 10am-8pm Sun). Charing Cross or Holborn tube. **Box office** 10am-8pm Mon-Sat. **Tickets** £15-£35. **Credit** AmEx, MC, V. **Map 8 L7**

Wildly acclaimed Disney extravaganza about the lion cub struggling to grow up. The 'animals' are the real show-stopper; the rest is seen-it-all-before Hollywood hype.

Mamma Mia!

Prince Edward Theatre, Old Compton Street, W1 (020 7447 5400; 24 hours daily). Leicester Square tube. **Box office** 10am-7pm Mon-Sat. **Tickets** £15-£35. **Credit** AmEx, MC, V. **Map 6 K6**

Hugely popular nostalgic '70s romance set on a Greek island, designed to link Abba's greatest hits into a continuous story. Note that, at the time of going to press, tickets were sold out until at least June 2000.

The Mousetrap

St Martin's Theatre, West Street, WC2 (020 7836 1443). Leicester Square tube. **Box office** 10am-8.15pm Mon-Sat. **Tickets** £11-£26. **Credit** AmEx, MC, V. **Map 6 K6**

Absurdly long-running murder mystery from the mistress of suspense, Agatha Christie.

Phantom of the Opera

Her Majesty's Theatre, Haymarket, SW1 (020 7494 5000/5400; 24 hours daily). Piccadilly Circus tube. **Box office** 10am-6pm Mon-Sat. **Tickets** £10-£35. **Credit** AmEx, MC, V. **Map 8 K7**

Lloyd Webber's renowned and long-running non-autobiographical musical about the hideously deformed theatre-goer who becomes obsessed with a beautiful opera singer.

Spend, Spend, Spend

Piccadilly Theatre, Denman Street, W1 (020 7369 1734; 9am-9pm Mon-Sat, 10am-6pm Sun). Piccadilly Circus tube. **Box office** 10am-8pm Mon-Sat. **Tickets** £15-£35. **Credit** AmEx, DC, MC, V. **Map 7 J7**

The rags-to-riches-to-rags story of Viv Nicholson who won the equivalent of £3m on the pools in 1961 is brought to vivacious life in Steve Brown and Justin Greene's witty, gutsy production.

Starlight Express

Apollo Victoria Theatre, Wilton Road, SW1 (020 7416 6070; 8.30am-10pm Mon-Fri, 8.30am-9pm Sat, 10am-8pm Sun). Victoria tube/rail. **Box office** 10am-8pm Mon-Sat. **Tickets** £8-£30. **Credit** AmEx, MC, V. **Map 7 H10**

Revamped Lloyd Webber musical depending less on the music than the spectacle of the cast flying round on rollerblades impersonating trains.

Whistle Down the Wind

Aldwych Theatre, Aldwych, WC2 (020 7416 6003; 8.30am-10pm Mon-Fri, 8.30am-9pm Sat, 10am-8pm Sun). Covent Garden tube. **Box office** 10am-8pm Mon-Sat. **Tickets** £10-£35. **Credit** AmEx, DC, MC, V. **Map 8 M6**

Lloyd Webber's '50s-set musical about an adolescent girl and a runaway killer has been critically deplored – but it's booking way ahead just the same.

The Witches of Eastwick

Drury Lane Theatre, Catherine Street, WC2 (020 7494 5000; 24 hours daily). Covent Garden tube. **Box office** 10am-8pm Mon-Sat. **Tickets** £12.50-£37.50. **Credit** AmEx, MC, £TC, V. **Map 6 L6**

Cameron Mackintosh's new musical comedy, which fills the space that *Miss Saigon* left in late 1999, is derived from the Jack Nicholson film derived from the John Updike book. Opens 13 June 2000.

The Woman in Black

Fortune Theatre, Russell Street, WC2 (020 7836 2238). Covent Garden tube. **Box office** 10am-8pm Mon-Sat. **Tickets** £9.50-£25. **Credit** AmEx, MC, V. **Map 6 L6**

Susan Hill's ghost story performed by just two actors has become a persistently popular West End spine-chilling potboiler.

Off-West End

Almeida

Almeida Street, N1 (020 7359 4404; 24 hours daily). Angel tube/Highbury & Islington tube/rail. **Box office** 9.30am-6pm Mon-Sat. **Tickets** £7-£21.50. **Credit** AmEx, DC, MC,V. **Map 9 O1**

For more than ten years now actor-directors Ian McDiarmid and Jonathan Kent have maintained a steady flow of lively, highbrow drama involving actors as big as Kevin Spacey and Cate Blanchett.

Website: www.almeida.co.uk

BAC

Lavender Hill, SW11 (020 7223 2223; 10.30am-7pm Mon-Sat, 4-7pm Sun). Clapham Junction rail/77, 77A, 345 bus. **Box office** 10.30am-6pm Mon; 10.30am-9pm Tue-Sat; 4-7pm Sun. **Tickets** £4-£12.50; 'pay what you can' Tue. **Credit** MC, V.

Situated in a crusty Victorian town hall and under the tenacious directorship of Tom Morris, BAC (Battersea Arts Centre) lives up to its self-appointed status as the 'National Theatre of the Fringe'. It contains three theatres (main house and two studios), carrying much of the capital's best fringe work while also promoting a lot of physical, experimental and visual theatre.

Website: www.bac.org.uk

The Bush

Shepherd's Bush Green, W12 (020 8743 3388; 10am-8pm Mon-Sat). Goldhawk Road or Shepherd's Bush tube. **Box office** 6.30-8pm Mon-Fri; 7-8pm Sat. **Tickets** £7-£11. **Credit** MC, V.

This is the second most important venue for new writing in London – and perhaps even England – after the Royal Court Theatre. Dedicated to new

Phantom of the Opera. *See page 297.*

plays, often by first-time writers, The Bush is the springboard for many young writers into the bigger theatres (such as Conor McPherson, author of *The Weir*). Seating is on a large squidgy bank, so the best seats are at the back where you won't get anyone's knees in your neck.

Donmar Warehouse

41 Earlham Street, WC2 (020 7369 1732; 9am-9pm Mon-Sat, 10am-6pm Sun). Covent Garden tube.
Box office 10am-8pm Mon-Sat. **Tickets** £14-£24. **Credit** AmEx, DC, MC, V. **Map 6 L6**
Under the artistic direction of Sam Mendes, the Donmar Warehouse has continued to put out a combination of old and new plays, visiting and in-house shows produced to a very high standard, at West End prices. Nicole Kidman and William H Macy are among the major names to have appeared here in recent years.

Drill Hall

16 Chenies Street, WC1 (020 7637 8270; 11am-7pm Mon-Sat, 11am-6pm Sun). Goodge Street tube.
Box office 10am-7.30pm Mon-Fri; 11am-7.30pm Sat. **Tickets** £6-£12. **Credit** AmEx, DC, MC, V. **Map 6 K5**
London's biggest, loudest and liveliest gay and lesbian theatre stages its own work and shows from all over the world. Monday evenings are women-only from 6pm and Thursday is no-smoking day, but this is not a hostile or separatist venue. There's a popular vegetarian café in the basement.

The Gate

The Prince Albert, 11 Pembridge Road, W11 (020 7229 0706). Notting Hill Gate tube.
Box office 10am-6pm Mon-Fri. **Tickets** £6-£12. **Credit** MC, V. **Map 1A7**
Located above a pub, The Gate has an estimable reputation for producing high-quality, low-budget world drama (past and present) on a shoestring. One of its other hallmarks is radical set designs. Young actors and directors sell loved ones down the river to work here for nothing.

Hampstead Theatre

Avenue Road, NW3 (020 7722 9301). Swiss Cottage tube. **Box office** 10am-7.30pm Mon-Sat. **Tickets** £9-£17. **Credit** MC, V.
More Swiss Cottage roundabout than Hampstead, but, despite being housed in what looks like a glorified caravan, do not be deceived: the Hampstead Theatre under the artistic direction of Jenny Topper is widely respected for its contemporary drama.
Website: www.hampstead-theatre.co.uk

King's Head

115 Upper Street, N1 (020 7226 1916). Angel tube/Highbury & Islington tube/rail.
Box office 10am-8pm Mon-Sat; 10am-4pm Sun. **Tickets** £4-£14. **Credit** MC, V. **Map 9 O1**
London's oldest pub theatre stages a variable diet of small-scale musicals and revues in the evening (preceded by optional, cheap and cheery dinners) as well as lunchtime plays (short shows taken with burger and chips). The unspoilt pub's late licence (midnight) and impromptu musical evenings make it a busy all-round winner, although it is currently under threat, thanks to the local council withdrawing funding.

Lyric

King Street, W6 (020 8741 2311; 10am-7pm Mon-Sat). Hammersmith tube. **Box office** 10am-8pm Mon-Sat. **Tickets** £5-£18. **Credit** AmEx, DC, MC, V.
The Lyric, although not strictly a producing house, has established a serious reputation for more alternative mainstream work. Other productions on the large proscenium main stage (often classified as West End) tend to feature major touring companies, while the studio space is usually taken by smaller-scale touring productions.
Website: www.lyric.co.uk

Open Air Theatre

Regent's Park, NW1 (020 7486 2431/1933). Baker Street tube. **Repertory season** May-Sept, phone for details. **Tickets** £8-£22. **Credit** AmEx, DC, MC, V. **Map 5 G3**
A well-equipped theatre with a buffet bar and barbecue in a leafy Regent's Park bower, this is a delightful venue for watching plays in summer months. Usually very popular (and not just with tourists), the company has a robust reputation – although its productions are at the mercy of the English weather, it is remarkable how few of the mixed repertory shows are cancelled. You can always count on a couple of alfresco Shakespeares, one musical and a family show as well as Sunday concerts.
Website: www.open-air-theatre.org.uk

Orange Tree

1 Clarence Street, Richmond, Surrey (020 8940 3633). Richmond tube/rail. **Box office** 10am-7pm Mon-Sat. **Tickets** £5-£14.50. **Credit** MC, V.
This small, smart bear pit of a venue has been flourishing under the directorship of Sam Walters and his prescribed diet of wholesome, closely directed (often) costume drama in the round with little or no set.

Riverside Studios

Crisp Road, W6 (020 8237 1111/1000; 24 hours daily). Hammersmith tube. **Box office** noon-9pm daily. **Tickets** £6-£22.50. **Credit** MC, V.
With one hangar-like space and one studio, the Riverside boasts a repertory cinema and its own gallery while hosting a commendable range of international travelling theatre, art, dance and larger-scale domestic works, usually with an avant-garde tilt. Recent revamping has been made possible by money from Chris Evans' resident TV show *TFI Friday*.
Website: www.riversidestudios.co.uk

Theatre Royal Stratford East

Gerry Raffles Square, E15 (020 8534 0310). Stratford tube/rail. **Box office** 10am-8pm Mon-Sat. **Tickets** £5-£15. **Credit** AmEx, MC, V.
Going back to Joan Littlewood in the 1950s with shows like *Oliver!* and *Oh! What A Lovely War*, the

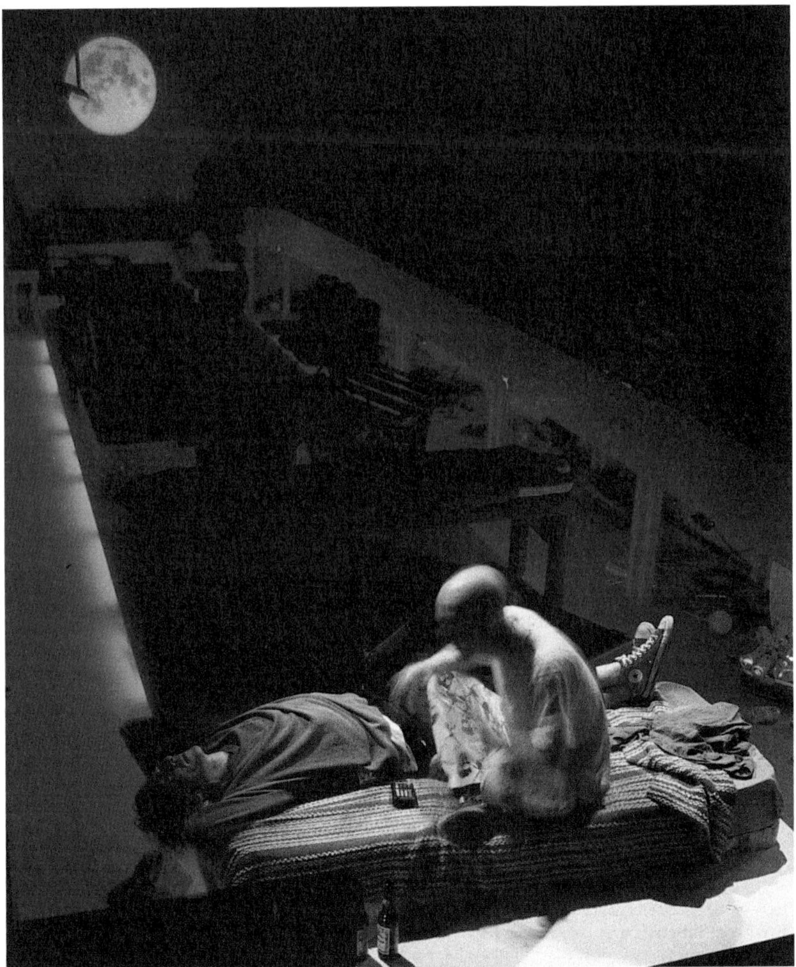

Performers at **The Gate** *like to take things lying down. See page 298.*

Theatre Royal Stratford East has been a consistent powerhouse of popular community-oriented drama, musicals and revue. Now driven by the passionate Philip Hedley it continues to produce vigorous, popular work for its racially mixed audiences, while simultaneously launching West End hits like *East is East*. The theatre has been under redevelopment for some time and is due to reopen in autumn 2000 next to a big all-mod-cons Arts Centre with gallery, cinema and performance spaces. A musical is planned to coincide with the reopening.

Tricycle

269 Kilburn High Road, NW6 (020 7328 1000). Kilburn tube. **Box office** 10am-8pm Mon-Sat. **Tickets** £8.50-£15. **Credit** MC, V.

A smaller-scale West London rival to the Theatre Royal Stratford East, the Tricycle specialises in high-quality Black and Irish drama, musical and revue aimed at its local population. Under the directorship of Nicholas Kent, the theatre maintains a strong identity as well as one of Kilburn's more agreeable bars with its own art gallery and super-comfy cinema. In 1999 *Trainspotting*'s Jonny Lee Miller (Sick Boy) trod the boards here in a production of *Four Nights in Knaresborough*.

Young Vic

66 The Cut, SE1 (020 7928 6363). Southwark tube. **Box office** 10am-7pm Mon-Sat. **Tickets** £7-£21. **Credit** MC, V. **Map 11 N8**

Artistic director Tim Supple has turned around the fortunes of this theatre standing in the shadow of the venerable Old Vic, making it an altogether more thrusting venue with a well-proportioned studio space and a large main house playing host to touring companies as big as the Royal Shakespeare Company and names as big as Jude Law. In 2000 look out for a production of *Tales from Ovid* by Ted Hughes (22 June-22 July).

Website: www.youngvic.org

The Fringe

Keep an eye on the selection of venues below for some of the better examples of London's ever-simmering fringe.

The Bridewell *Bride Lane, off Fleet Street, EC4 (020 7936 3456). Blackfriars tube/rail.* **Box office** noon-7pm Tue-Sat. **Map 11 N6**

A good-sized theatre with a decent mixture of musicals and new works, often produced by national theatre companies.

Chelsea Centre *King's Road, SW10 (020 7352 1967; 10am-9pm Mon-Sat). Sloane Square tube then 11, 22, 211 bus/Earl's Court tube then 328 bus.* **Box office** 7-9pm Mon-Sat. **Map 3 C13**

This large, versatile but rather under-exploited space looks set for fuller artistic usage and architectural development thanks to Lottery funding.

Etcetera Theatre *Oxford Arms, 265 Camden High Street, NW1 (020 7482 4857). Camden Town tube.* **Box office** 10am-8pm Tue-Sun.

Classic tiny pub theatre with a perennially lively programme of works by ambitious young theatre folk. Two different shows a night (phone for details).

The Finborough *Finborough Arms, Finborough Road, SW10 (020 7373 3842). Earl's Court tube.* **Box office** 11am-8.30pm daily. **Map 3 B12**

Pub venue nurturing new writing, some of which has gone on to the West End and Broadway.

Grace Theatre *Latchmere Pub, 503 Battersea Park Road, SW11 (020 7223 3549). Clapham Junction rail.* **Box office** 9am-11pm daily.

Burgeoning, ambitious venue whose thrusting programme is raising its profile.

Jermyn Street Theatre *16B Jermyn Street, SW1 (020 7287 2875). Piccadilly Circus tube.* **Box office** 11am-7pm Mon-Fri; 1-7pm Sat. **Map 7 J7**

Small studio theatre in the heart of the West End that mixes its own ambitious cocktails of musicals, revues and classics.

New End Theatre *27 New End, NW3 (020 7794 0022). Hampstead tube.* **Box office** 10am-8pm Mon-Fri; 1-8pm Sat, Sun.

Small, very Hampstead theatre staging increasingly adventurous work to increasingly high standards.

Oval House *52-54 Kennington Oval, SE11 (020 7582 7680/www.ovalhouse.dircon.co.uk). Oval tube.* **Box office** 10am-9pm Tue-Fri; 3-9pm Sat.

London's second gay and lesbian venue after the Drill Hall (*see p298*) has two theatres hosting work often by respected, subsidised companies.

Pleasance Theatre *Carpenters Mews, North Road (off Caledonian Road), N7 (020 7609 1800). Caledonian Road tube.* **Box office** 10am-6pm daily.

This offshoot of one of the Edinburgh Fringe Festival's most successful venues is a large, commercially ambitious fringe theatre with generally sound productions.

Southwark Playhouse *62 Southwark Bridge Road, SE1 (020 7620 3494/www.southwark-playhouse.co.uk). Borough tube/35, 40, 133, 344 bus.* **Box office** 11am-7.30pm Mon-Sat. **Map 11 P8**

This small theatre in Bankside aims high with its ambitious programme of writing and music. The results are often mixed.

Tristan Bates Theatre *The Actors Centre, 1A Tower Street, WC2 (020 7240 6283). Leicester Square tube.* **Box office** 10am-8pm daily. **Map 6 K6**

Thanks to its situation in the busy Actors Centre, this theatre's otherwise poorly appointed stage hosts commendable work. Book at least 48 hours before.

Warehouse Theatre *Dingwall Road, Croydon (020 8680 4060/www.uk-live.co.uk/warehouse_theatre). East Croydon rail.* **Box office** 10am-5pm Mon; 10am-8.30pm Tue; 10am-10pm Wed-Sat; 3-7pm Sun.

Alternative, suburban theatre (a little more suburban than alternative) funded for its mix of conventional and unconventional new plays.

White Bear *138 Kennington Park Road, SE11 (020 7793 9193). Kennington tube.* **Box office** 10am-6pm Mon-Sat; noon-6pm Sun.

Occupying the back room of a seedy bar, this can be fringe theatre at its most depressing, but it can also rise to adventurous and original heights.

Trips Out of Town

Trips Out of Town

London: been there, done that. Now it's time to get out.

Myriad though the thrills of the big city are, there comes a time when we all need to escape the traffic, the noise, the pollution and the crush. Many visitors (and most Londoners) are unaware of the attractions lurking outside the M25 – and how easily accessible they are. For a more in-depth look at getaways within easy reach of London, get a copy of the *Time Out Book of Weekend Breaks* (Penguin, £12.99).

PLANNING A TRIP

The best place to start is at the new **British Travel Centre** (*see below*). Here you can get guidebooks, free leaflets and advice on any destination in the UK and Ireland you can book rail, bus, air or car travel, reserve tours, theatre tickets and accommodation; there's even a bureau de change, a branch of Thomas Cook, a ticket agency and a bookshop. Visitors are strongly advised to visit the tourist information centre in the town they visit as soon as they arrive, which will provide leaflets, further information about accommodation and where to eat, and details of local attractions.

British Visitor Centre

1 Regent Street (south of Piccadilly Circus), SW1 (no phone). Piccadilly Circus tube. **Open** *June-Sept* 9.30am-6.30pm Mon-Fri; 9am-5pm Sat; 10am-4pm Sun; *Oct-May* 9.30am-6.30pm Mon-Fri; 10am-4pm Sat, Sun. **Credit** AmEx, MC, V. **Map 8 K7**
Personal callers only.

Getting there

Most of the places of interest we list in this chapter are within an hour and a half's rail journey of London (although some will then require a further bus or taxi ride). In the listings for each destination, we include the approximate train (and, where appropriate, coach) journey time.

By train

To find out train times and ticket prices, call National Rail Enquiries on **0845 748 4950**. (If you want to reserve your tickets in advance by credit card, ask the operators on the above line for the appropriate number.) Always make sure you ask about the cheapest ticket for the journey you are planning. The **rail travel centres** in all of London's mainline stations (as well as in Heathrow and Gatwick airports and the British Travel Centre, for which *see above*) will also be able to help with timetable information and ticket booking. The train journey times we give in the listings below are the fastest available.

If you want timetable information over the web, go to www.virgintrains.co.uk. Rail tickets for any train operator in the UK can be bought on the Net at www.thetrainline.com.

London mainline rail stations

Charing Cross *Strand, WC2.* **Map 8 L7**
For trains to and from south-east England (including Dover, Folkestone and Ramsgate).

Euston *Euston Road, NW1.* **Map 6 K3**
For trains to and from the north and north-west of England, and a suburban line to Watford.

King's Cross *Euston Road, N1.* **Map 6 L2**
For trains to and from the north and north-east of England and Scotland, and suburban lines to north London and Hertfordshire.

Liverpool Street *Liverpool Street, EC2.* **Map 10 R5**
For trains to and from the east coast (including Harwich) and Stansted Airport; also trains to East Anglia and suburban services to east and north-east London.

Paddington *Praed Street, W2.* **Map 2 D5**
For trains to and from the south-west, west, and south Wales and the Midlands.

Victoria *Terminus Place, SW1.* **Map 7 H10**
For fast trains to and from the Channel ports (Folkestone, Dover, Newhaven); also trains to and from Gatwick Airport, plus suburban services to south and south-east London.

Waterloo *York Road, SE1.* **Map 8 M8**
For fast trains to and from the south and south-west of England (Portsmouth, Southampton, Dorset, Devon), plus suburban services to south-west London.

By coach

Coach and bus travel is almost always cheaper than rail travel, but almost always slower. **National Express** (0870 580 8080) runs routes to most parts of the country; its coaches depart from Victoria Coach Station on Buckingham Palace Road, five minutes' walk from Victoria rail and tube stations. **Green Line** buses (020 8668 7261) operate within an approximate 40-mile (64-km) radius of London. Their main departure point is Eccleston Bridge, SW1 (Colonnades Coach Station, behind Victoria Station).

Victoria Coach Station

164 Buckingham Palace Road, SW1 (0171 730 3466). Victoria tube/rail. **Map 7 H11**

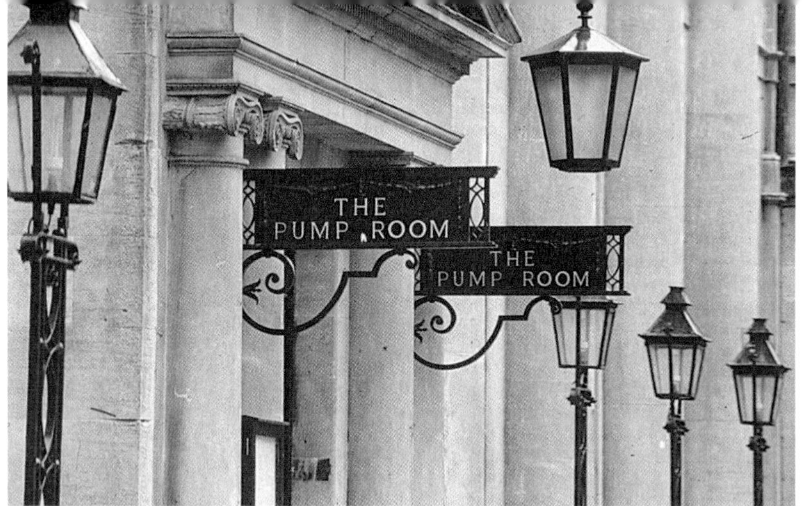

A cup of char goes down nicely in the Pump Room, **Bath**.

Britain's most comprehensive coach company **National Express** – which runs services to destinations all over England, Scotland and Wales – and **Eurolines** (01582 404511) – which travels to the Continent – are based at Victoria Coach Station. There are many other companies operating to and from London (some departing from Marble Arch). *See also p337.*

By car

If you are in a group of three or four people, it may be cheaper (and more flexible) to hire a car (*see page 340*). And if you plan to take in several sights within an area, then this is probably the only realistic way of getting around. The road directions given in the listings below should be used in conjunction with a map. (Note that, for example, 'J13 off M11' means 'come off the M11 motorway at junction 13'.)

How this chapter is arranged

This chapter has been split into nine broad categories: **Town & city breaks**, **Castles**, **Country houses**, **Family attractions**, **Gardens**, **Homes of the famous**, **Life on the ocean wave**, **Out in the country** and **Seaside**.

Opening times & admission prices

For main entries below we include full details of opening times, admission and transport details, but be aware that these can change without notice. If you are planning a trip around one particular sight, **always phone first to check that it is open**. Many attractions close down during the winter (typically between November and March inclusive), although major sights are open year round. We supply phone numbers for sights listed within entries; again, phone first to find out opening times. In the 'Where to stay' sections, the accommodation prices listed are the range for a double room. **Note that credit cards are only accepted where specified**.

Town & city breaks

Bath

Bath is a stunner; a sleek, immaculately groomed supermodel of a city. With its slender Georgian streets, tanned stone, beautifully proportioned curves and voluptuously hilly situation it puts most of frumpy, flyblown Britain to shame. It's no surprise that this is the only city in the UK with the distinction of being a World Heritage Site.

The Romans, realising the curative powers of the local hot springs, called the city Aquae Sulis. For hundreds of years, the Roman baths were buried under medieval buildings but were rediscovered in the eighteenth and nineteenth centuries. The **Roman Baths Museum** (01225 477785) offers an excellent acoustiguide tour of what are the most impressive non-military Roman remains in Britain – made all the more evocative by the fact that the waters still bubble up from the earth here (250,000 gallons a day at 46.5°C), just as they did 2,000 years ago. You can taste the waters in the adjoining **Pump Room** (which was immortalised by Jane Austen), but a pot of Earl Grey might go down better.

Overlooking the baths is **Bath Abbey**, a fifteenth-century rebuilding of an earlier Norman structure, itself built on the site of a Saxon church where Edgar, the first king of a united England, was crowned in 973. It's a beautifully light, harmonious building, boasting some fine fan vaulting and stained glass.

Bath has close on 20 museums, most of them excellent. These include **The Building of Bath Museum** on Lansdown Road (01225 333895), the highlight of which is a spectacular model of the city, and, in Bennett Street, the **Museum of East Asian Art** (01225 464640), which contains a fine collection of Chinese jade carvings. Opposite, in the grand **Assembly Rooms** (once the social focus of Georgian high society in Bath), there's the renowned **Museum of Costume** (01225 477789), illustrating posh togs that have been made since the late sixteenth century. The **American Museum** (01225 460503) at Claverton Manor, which offers a fascinating series of reconstructed seventeenth- to nineteenth-century American domestic interiors, is well worth the short trip out of town (bus 18).

But Bath's greatest attraction is simply its streets, the grandest of which is the much-photographed **Royal Crescent**, a breathtaking sweep of 30 houses designed by John Wood the Younger (1767-75). No.1 Royal Crescent (01225 428126) is furnished in authentic period style with a fully restored Georgian garden and is open to the public. Nearby is the magnificent **Circus**, which was designed by the elder John Wood and completed by his like-named son, composed of three crescents forming a circle. In terms of its exquisite proportions (its diameter is exactly that of Stonehenge) and architectural detail, it's an even finer creation than Royal Crescent. Stand in the middle and try out the powerful echo.

Mighty **Canterbury Cathedral**. *See p307.*

Not all of Bath's streets are so imposing – there are also plenty of narrow alleyways, particularly in the area to the north of **Abbey Churchyard**, an open space popular with street entertainers. There is plenty of good shopping too, centred largely around Milsom, Union and Stall streets and Southgate.

The **River Avon** adds greatly to the appeal of the city and is spanned by **Pulteney Bridge**, an Italianate masterpiece by Robert Adam, which recalls the bridges of Florence and Venice. There are walks beside the river and the adjacent Kennet and Avon Canal. Boats may be hired in summer from the Boating Station on Forester Road.

Further information

Getting there *by train* from Paddington (1 hour 15mins); *by coach* National Express (3 hours 20mins); *by car* J18 off M4 then A46, use park 'n' rides to get into the centre.

Where to stay: Haydon House (9 Bloomfield Park; 01225 444919; £70-£90) offers superior B&B and splendid breakfasts; five minutes' drive from the centre. **Holly Lodge** (8 Upper Oldfield Park; 01225 424042; £79-£89) is another classy B&B. Regency elegance in the centre of town is provided at the **Queensberry Hotel** (Russell Street; 01225 447928; £120-£185). A more affordable central option is **Harington's Hotel** (8-10 Queen Street; 01225 444804; £78-£98).

Where to eat & drink: Sally Lunn's Refreshment House & Museum (01225 461634) in North Parade Passage is the oldest house in Bath; here you can sample the famous buns made fashionable by Sally Lunn in the 1680s. The best of Bath's many restaurants are top-rank curry house **Jamuna** at 9-10 High Street (01225 464631), Michelin two-star **Lettonie** at 35 Kelston Road (01225 446676), the **Moon & Sixpence** wine bar/bistro at 6A Broad Street (01225 460962), the fine French fare of **Clos du Roy**, next to the Theatre Royal (01225 444450), the classy, cosy **Moody Goose** (01225 466688) on Kingsmead Square and the excellent bargain-priced **Hullaballoos** at 36 Broad Street (01225 443323). Popular pubs include the **Coeur de Lion** in Northumberland Place, the **Boater** on Argyle Street (by the river) and the **Saracen's Head** on Broad Street.

Tourist Information Centre Abbey Chambers, Abbey Churchyard (01225 477101). **Open** *Oct-Apr* 9.30am-5pm daily; *May-Sept* 9.30am-6pm Mon-Sat; 10am-4pm Sun.

Brighton

'Brighton looks like a town that is constantly helping the police with their enquiries,' said Keith Waterhouse, and it is as a roguish, flamboyant, even tarty city that Brighton has come to be known. It is appropriate that its best-known sight is the outrageous **Royal Pavilion** (01273 290900). Its bizarre blend of architectural styles – Indian,

Sun, sea, shingle... and two boys waving, on **Brighton Beach**.

Chinese, Gothic – was conceived by John Nash in 1823 for the Prince Regent (later George IV), and it stands in gardens that have been restored to their original Georgian condition. The adjacent **Brighton Museum & Art Gallery** (01273 290900) is home to a good crop of twentieth-century and ethnic art and artefacts.

Brighton has much else to offer the visitor. The English Channel for a start: it may be freezing cold most of the year and the beach steep and pebbly rather than sandy, but it's still the sea. The gaudy **Palace Pier** is packed with archetypal seaside attractions – slot machines, funfair, fish and chips. On a clear day you can gaze west from the top of the helter skelter to the Isle of Wight, or along the shore to the derelict West Pier (currently undergoing restoration) and genteel Hove.

Between the piers, beachfront arches house cafés, bars and clubs – notably the **Zap** (01273 821588) and **Honey** (01273 202807) clubs. Contrast these with the neighbouring **Brighton Fishing Museum** (01273 723064) and crafts shops or the **Sea Life Centre** (01273 604234).

When the sea loses its fascination, lose yourself in **The Lanes**, a warren of antique and specialist shops punctuated by pubs and cafés, between West Street and the Old Steine. If these prove too expensive, cross North Street and explore the vibrant **North Laine** area for vintage clothing, street fashion, records, kitsch and cafés of every kind, or visit the **Duke of York's** (01273 626261) at Preston Circus, quite possibly the cosiest independent cinema in the UK.

However, there's more to Brighton than sea, sights and shops. More and more people come (and return) here for the atmosphere – an eclectic cocktail of traditional seaside resort and liberal lifestyles. Brighton will embrace anyone – as the town's large gay community, anarchists, artists, eccentrics and celebs will testify.

Further information

Getting there *by train* from Victoria (from 50mins), or from King's Cross (1 hour 10mins); *by coach* National Express (1 hour 50mins); *by car* M23 then A23.

Where to stay: The Adelaide (51 Regency Square; 01273 205286; £65-£82) is old, four-star and mid-priced; the **Twenty One** (21 Charlotte Street; 01273 686450; £60-£65) offers a friendly welcome and a tasty breakfast; the poshest place in town remains **The Grand** (King's Road; 01273 321188; £195-£220); the other end of the scale is **Brighton Backpackers** (75-76 Middle Street; 01273 777717; from £10 per person).

Where to eat & drink: For food, try the enticing Anglo-Asian dishes at the unpromisingly sited **Black Chapati** (12 Circus Parade, New England Road; 01273 699011), north of the rail station, the inspired vegetarian café **Terre à Terre** at 71 East Street (01273 729051) or the first-rate French food at **La Fourchette** at 101 Western Road (01273 7322556). Drink in **The Cricketers**, 15 Black Lion Street, the **Pump House** at 45 Market Street or the **Regency Tavern**, Russell Square, modelled loosely on the Royal Pavilion. The Lanes are lined with pubs.

Events Second in the UK only to Edinburgh, the **Brighton Festival** (01273 292951) fills the first three

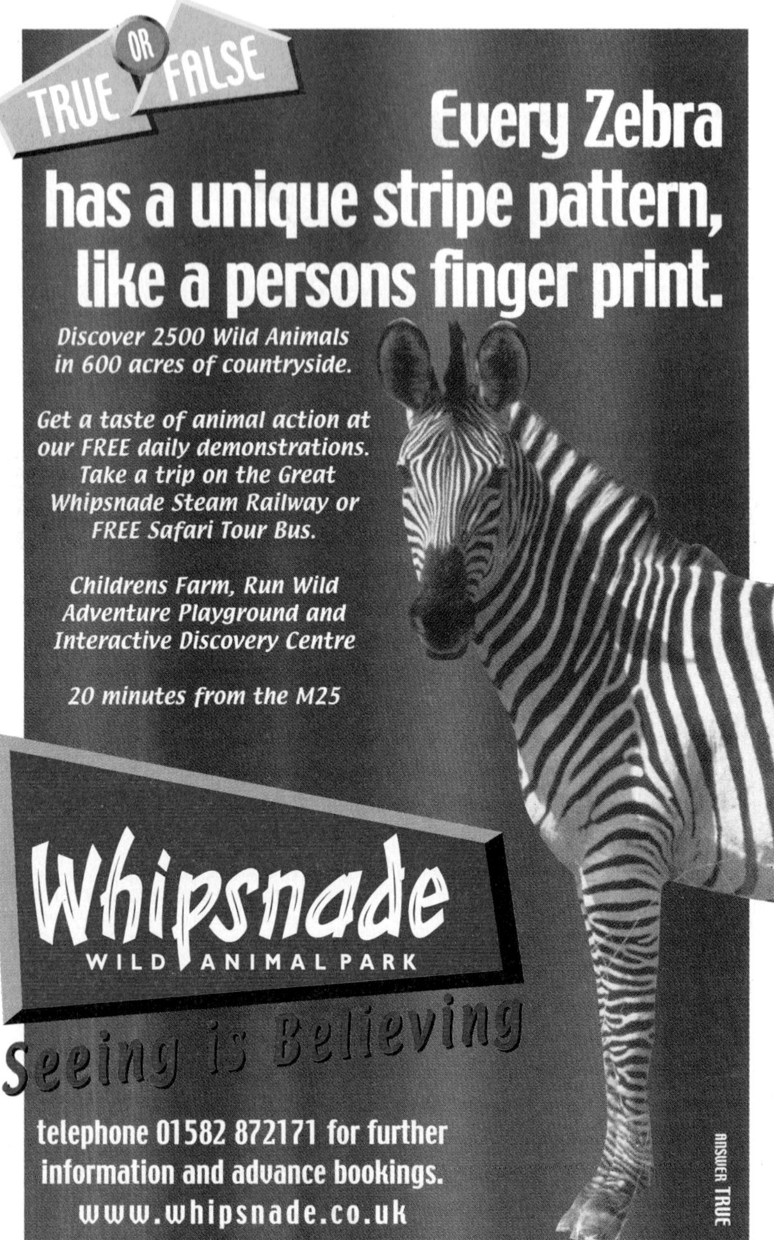
TRUE OR FALSE
Every Zebra
has a unique stripe pattern,
like a persons finger print.
Discover 2500 Wild Animals
in 600 acres of countryside.
Get a taste of animal action at
our FREE daily demonstrations.
Take a trip on the Great
Whipsnade Steam Railway or
FREE Safari Tour Bus.
Childrens Farm, Run Wild
Adventure Playground and
Interactive Discovery Centre
20 minutes from the M25
Whipsnade
WILD ANIMAL PARK
Seeing is Believing
telephone 01582 872171 for further
information and advance bookings.
www.whipsnade.co.uk
ANSWER TRUE

weeks of May with theatre, comedy, art, music and literature. On Sundays throughout the year Madeira Drive on the seafront hosts diverse events – notably the **London to Brighton Bike Ride** in June and the **London to Brighton Veteran Car Run** in November. Monthly listings guides *Impact* and *The List* are available from newsagents, or find out what's going down by tuning in to Surf 107FM (6.30-7pm Mon-Fri). For gay listings, see the monthly *G Scene* or visit Scene 22 (129 St James Street; 01273 626682).

Tourist Information Centres
10 Bartholomew Square (01273 292599/ www.brighton.co.uk). **Open** *July, Aug* 9am-6.15pm Mon-Fri; 10am-6pm Sat; 10am-4pm Sun; *Sept-June* 9am-5pm Mon-Fri; 10am-5pm Sat; 10am-4pm Sun.
Hove Town Hall, Church Road, Hove (01273 292589). **Open** 9am-5pm Mon-Fri.

Cambridge

There is a casual air to Cambridge that lingers in the stonework of the old town centre, that drifts in the breeze above the waters of the River Cam and permeates the grassy glades that edge the town to the south and west and encroach upon parts of the centre that should, by rights, be built up with houses and roads and multi-storey car parks.

The **university** has dominated life in Cambridge since the fourteenth century. The oldest of the colleges is **Peterhouse** on Trumpington Street, endowed in 1284. The original hall still survives, though most of the present buildings are nineteenth century. Just up the road is **Corpus Christi**, founded in 1352. Its Old Court dates from that time and is linked by a gallery to the eleventh-century **St Bene't's Church**, the oldest building in town. Just across the road is fifteenth-century **Queens'**. Most of the original buildings survive and the inner courts are wonderfully picturesque.

Next to Queens' is, logically enough, **King's**, founded by Henry VI in 1441, and renowned for its **chapel** (1446-1515; 01223 331155). Considered one of the greatest Gothic buildings in Europe, the chapel's interior, containing its original stained glass, is breathtaking. Famous King's alumni include EM Forster, Rupert Brooke and John Maynard Keynes. To the north is **Trinity**, founded in 1336 by Edward III and refounded by Henry VIII in 1546. The apple tree outside the gate is a direct descendant of the one that dropped its fruit on Sir Isaac Newton's head to such inspirational effect. A fine collection of Tudor buildings surrounds the Great Court where, legend has it, Lord Byron used to bathe naked in the fountain with his pet bear. Wittgenstein studied and taught at Trinity; the library where he occasionally worked, designed by Wren, is open to visitors for two hours after lunch each day. Further on, at the corner of Bridge Street and St John's Street, is the **Round Church** (the oldest of the four remaining round churches in England) and now also home to the **Cambridge Brass Rubbing Centre**.

Behind the main group of colleges is **The Backs**, a series of beautiful meadows, some still grazed by cows, bordering the willow-shaded **River Cam**, which is spanned by several fine footbridges. It's a perfect spot for summer strolling, or you can hire a punt and drift lazily along the river.

The city also has its non-collegiate attractions: visit the **Fitzwilliam Museum** on Trumpington Street (01223 332900) for its outstanding collections of antiquities and Old Masters; climb the tower of **Great St Mary's Church** on King's Parade for far-reaching views; take a short walk to the **Scott Polar Research Institute** (01223 336540) in Lensfield Road; admire the **Botanic Gardens** (01223 336265) in Bateman Street; or simply wander along the charming streets. Unsurprisingly, Cambridge is an excellent place to buy books – new, second-hand and antiquarian.

Further information

Getting there *by train* from King's Cross (50mins); *by coach* National Express (1 hour 50mins); *by car* J11 or J12 off M11.

Where to stay: Cambridge is short on characterful accommodation. Two decent options are **Arundel House** (01223 367701; £65-£92.50) at 53 Chesterton Road, a fine early Victorian terrace overlooking the Cam, and **De Freville House** (01223 354993; £50-£55) at 166 Chesterton Road.

Where to eat & drink: For posh nosh, try the quality French cooking at **Midsummer House** (01223 369299) on Midsummer Common, the global cuisine at **22 Chesterton Road** (01223 351880) or the bargain-priced oriental goodies at **Dojo** in Miller's Yard, Mill Lane (01223 363471). Sup a jar in the comfy, well-worn **Eagle** on St Bene't Street or the rowing-mad (no-smoking) **Free Press** on Prospect Row, which also offers decent lunchtime food.

Events The city hosts the **Cambridge Shakespeare Festival** during July and August. Performances are held mainly outside, and remain as true to the text as possible.

Tourist Information Centre
The Old Library, Wheeler Street (01223 322640/ www.cambridge.gov.uk/leisure/index.htm).
Open *Apr-Oct* 10am-6.30pm Mon-Fri; 10am-5pm Sat; *Nov-Mar* 10am-5.30pm Mon-Fri; 10am-5pm Sat.

Canterbury

When St Augustine converted King Ethelbert to Christianity in 597, Canterbury became the cradle of English Christianity: long stretches of its medieval walls still stand and the magnificent **cathedral** (01227 762862), with its superb stained glass, stone vaulting and vast Norman crypt, is now the Mother Church of Anglicans worldwide. A plaque near the altar marks the spot where Archbishop Thomas à Becket was murdered in 1170 by four overzealous knights who had overheard King Henry II moaning, 'Will no one rid me of this turbulent priest?' Becket's tomb has been a site of pilgrimage ever since. **Trinity Chapel**

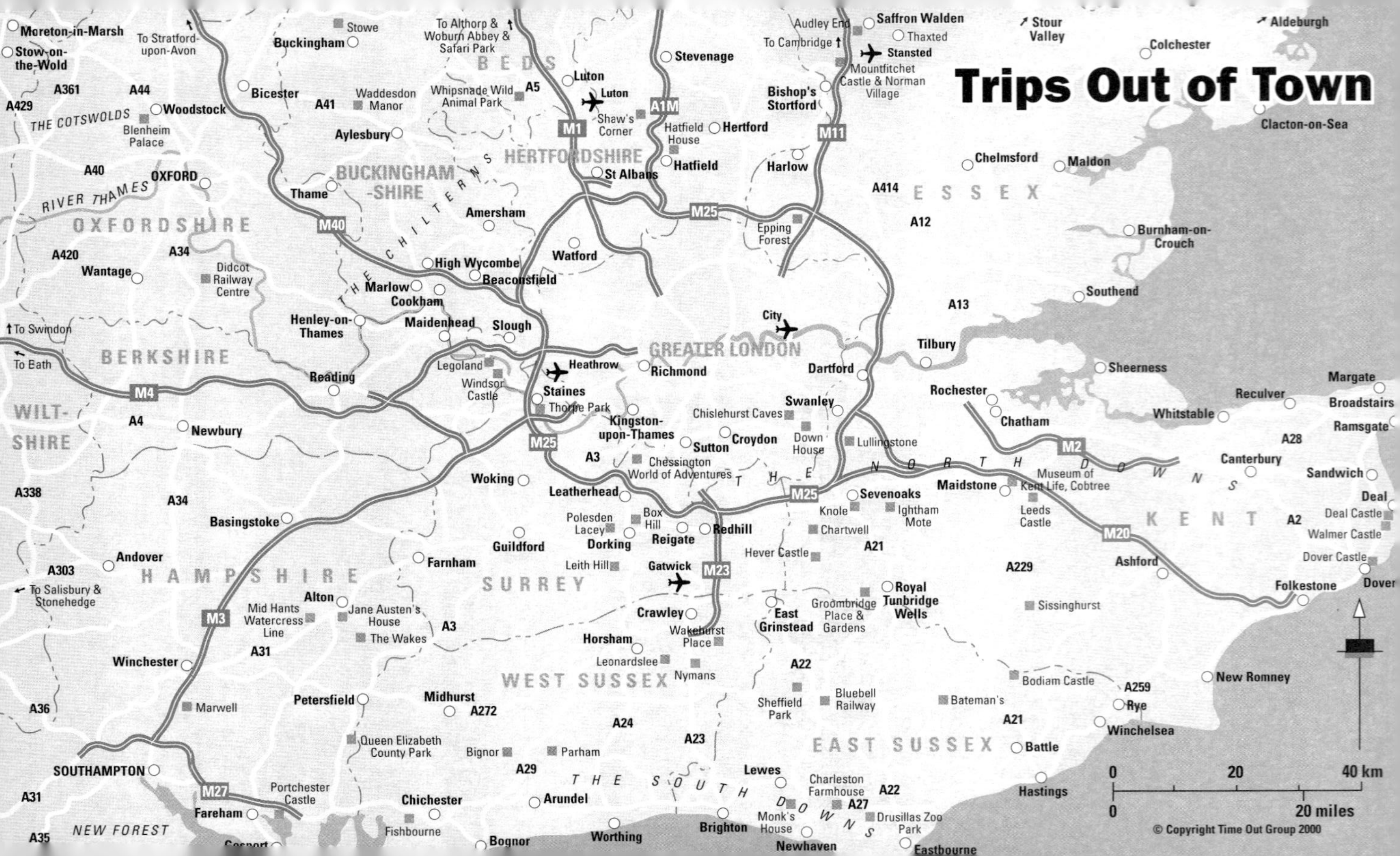
Trips Out of Town
Moreton-in-Marsh
Stow-on-the-Wold
To Stratford-upon-Avon
A361
A44
A429
THE COTSWOLDS
Woodstock
Blenheim Palace
Stowe
Buckingham
Bicester
A41
Waddesdon Manor
Aylesbury
To Althorp & Woburn Abbey & Safari Park
BEDS
Whipsnade Wild Animal Park
A5
Luton
M1
Shaw's Corner
A1M
Stevenage
Hatfield House
Hertford
Hatfield
HERTFORDSHIRE
St Albans
Audley End
Saffron Walden
To Cambridge
Thaxted
Stansted
Mountfitchet Castle & Norman Village
Bishop's Stortford
M11
Harlow
Stour Valley
Aldeburgh
Colchester
Clacton-on-Sea
A40
OXFORD
RIVER THAMES
OXFORDSHIRE
BUCKINGHAM-SHIRE
Thame
M40
THE CHILTERNS
Amersham
M25
Epping Forest
Chelmsford
Maldon
A414
ESSEX
A12
Burnham-on-Crouch
A420
A34
Didcot Railway Centre
Wantage
Watford
High Wycombe
Beaconsfield
Marlow
Cookham
Maidenhead
Slough
Henley-on-Thames
Southend
A13
To Swindon
To Bath
BERKSHIRE
M4
Reading
Legoland
Windsor Castle
Heathrow
Staines
Thorpe Park
GREATER LONDON
City
Richmond
Dartford
Tilbury
Sheerness
Margate
Broadstairs
Ramsgate
Reculver
Whitstable
Rochester
Chatham
Swanley
Chislehurst Caves
Down House
Kingston-upon-Thames
Croydon
Sutton
Lullingstone
M2
A28
Canterbury
Sandwich
WILT-SHIRE
A4
Newbury
A3
Chessington World of Adventures
NORTH DOWNS
Maidstone
Museum of Kent Life, Cobtree
Deal
A338
A34
Woking
Leatherhead
Sevenoaks
Knole
Ightham Mote
Leeds Castle
KENT
A2
Deal Castle
Walmer Castle
Basingstoke
Polesden Lacey
Box Hill
Redhill
Reigate
Dorking
Guildford
Chartwell
A21
M20
Dover Castle
Andover
Farnham
Leith Hill
Gatwick
M23
Hever Castle
A229
Ashford
Dover
Folkestone
A303
HAMPSHIRE
SURREY
To Salisbury & Stonehenge
Alton
Mid Hants Watercress Line
Jane Austen's House
The Wakes
A3
Crawley
East Grinstead
Groombridge Place & Gardens
Royal Tunbridge Wells
Sissinghurst
M3
A31
Horsham
Wakehurst Place
Winchester
Leonardslee
Nymans
A22
WEST SUSSEX
Bodiam Castle
New Romney
A259
Rye
Marwell
Petersfield
Midhurst
A272
Sheffield Park
Bluebell Railway
Bateman's
A21
A36
A24
A23
Winchelsea
Queen Elizabeth County Park
Bignor
Parham
EAST SUSSEX
Battle
SOUTHAMPTON
A29
THE SOUTH DOWNS
Lewes
Charleston Farmhouse
A22
Hastings
M27
Portchester Castle
Chichester
Arundel
A27
A31
Fareham
Fishbourne
Monk's House
Drusillas Zoo Park
NEW FOREST
A35
Gosport
Bognor
Worthing
Brighton
Newhaven
Eastbourne
0
20
40 km
0
20 miles
© Copyright Time Out Group 2000

contains the site of the original shrine plus the tombs of Henry IV and the Black Prince.

The small city centre can become overcrowded in summer but still retains its charm. **Eastbridge (St Thomas's) Hospital** (01227 471688), on the High Street, dates from the twelfth century and contains a medieval mural, sundry antique treasures and a crypt; there are the remains of a Roman townhouse and mosaic floor at the **Roman Museum** on Butchery Lane (01227 785575); and the **Royal Museum & Art Gallery** (01227 452747) on the High Street covers the history of the area. **King's School** is where Elizabethan playwright Christopher Marlowe, author of *Dr Faustus*, was educated.

Further information

Getting there *by train* from Victoria to Canterbury East (1 hour 20mins), or from Charing Cross to Canterbury West (1 hour 30mins); *by coach* National Express (1 hour 50mins); *by car* A2 then M2 and A2.

Where to stay: Try the 600-year-old **Falstaff** (01227 462138; £95-£105) at 8-10 St Dunstan's Street or the flower-strewn B&B **Magnolia House** (01227 765121; £72-£95) at 36 St Dunstan's Terrace.

Where to eat & drink: If you fancy Italian, go to **Tue e Mio** at 16 The Borough (01227 761471), or oriental, try **Bistro Vietnam** at 72 Castle Street (01227 760022), or Mexican, sample **Café des Amis du Mexique** at 95 St Dunstan's Street (01227 464390), or classy French cooking, head for **La Bonne Cuisine** (01227 351880) in the Canterbury Hotel at 71 New Dover Road. Drink in the young and lively **Three Tuns** in Castle Street, the **Bell & Crown** in Palace Street or the **Bishop's Finger** on St Dunstan's Street. Canterbury is stuffed with tearooms and coffee shops.

Tourist Information Centre 34 St Margaret's Street (01227 766567/www.canterbury.co.uk). **Open** *July, Aug* 9.30am-5.30pm daily; *Sept-June* 9.30am-5pm Mon-Sat.

Oxford

Founded by the Saxons, Oxford began its development in the early eighth century around a priory established by St Frideswide on the site where Christ Church now stands. Its slow but steady growth in importance and influence received the royal seal of approval when Henry I built his Palace of Beaumont there in the early twelfth century, at much the same time as the first students were beginning to gather. Their numbers were boosted in 1167 when Paris University was closed to the English, and by the end of the century Oxford was firmly established as England's first university town. Today, the university comprises a federation of 41 independent colleges and halls, many occupying architecturally spectacular buildings.

Most are usually open to the public, and a shortlist of the finest includes **Christ Church**, with its famous Tom Tower, and a chapel so grand that it serves as Oxford's cathedral. Nearby **Merton**, founded in 1264, boasts a marvellous medieval library and garden, but **University College** was Oxford's first college, endowed in 1249. **Magdalen** (pronounced, for no apparent reason, 'mórd-lin') is often said to be the loveliest college. Its extensive grounds include a deer park and a meadow where the rare snakeshead fritillary still blooms every April.

Other centres of academia in Oxford include the **Ashmolean Museum** (01865 278000) in Beaumont Street, and the **Bodleian Library** (01865 277000) off Broad Street, begun in 1598. The elegant **Radcliffe Camera** is England's earliest example of a round reading room (1737). You can see, hear and smell the history of academe at **The Oxford Story** (01865 790055) on Broad Street, a popular animatronic 'dark-ride' giving a one-hour introduction to the university's history.

But Oxford is as much town as gown, and there's more to see than centres of learning. The **Museum of Modern Art** (01865 722733) in Pembroke Street has established an international reputation for its pioneering exhibitions of contemporary and twentieth-century work. At the other extreme, the **Pitt Rivers Museum of Archaeology & Anthropology** (01865 270927) on Parks Road is a remarkable Victorian pile crammed with one of the strangest collections of ancient ethnic artefacts in the world.

Little Clarendon Street and the recent development at Gloucester Green offer some interesting specialist shops. Best of all is the classy **Covered Market**, linking High Street and Market Street. Opened in 1774, it's a foodie's delight. If shopping for antiques, you should investigate Park End Street between the bus and railway stations.

The countryside pushes green fingers into the heart of the town, with the **Oxford Canal**, the **River Thames** (sometimes called the Isis, from the Latin 'Thamesis') and the **Cherwell** (pronounced 'Chár-well') providing opportunities for strolling and punting. For the classic view of Matthew Arnold's 'dreaming spires' you must climb Boar's Hill three miles to the south-west.

Further information

Getting there *by train* from Paddington (1 hour), then use your rail ticket for a free ride into the centre on one of Oxford's pioneering electric buses (every 10mins); *by coach* frequent, cheap, fast services from several London departure points; details from National Express (1 hour 40mins), Stage Coach (01865 727000) and Oxford Bus Company (01865 785400); *by car* J8 off M40 then A40; use the park 'n' rides.

Where to stay: The **Norham Guesthouse** (01865 515352; £55), at 16 Norham Road, offers reliable B&B within 15 minutes' walk of the centre. The ever-popular seventeenth-century **Old Parsonage** (01865 310210; £145-£195) at 1 Banbury Road, one-time home to the undergraduate Oscar Wilde, is a more upmarket alternative, with a good bar and food.

Get your rocks off at hippy hangout **Stonehenge**.

The city's classiest new accommodation is the sleekly luxurious **Old Bank Hotel** (01865 799599; £155-£195) at 92-94 High Street.

Where to eat & drink: There's upmarket fare in somewhat basic surroundings at the riverside **Cherwell Boat House** (01865 552746) off Bardwell Road; classy Italian cooking at **Il Cortile** at the Bath Place Hotel (01865 791812) off Holywell Street and Raymond Blanc's swish, metropolitan brasserie **Le Petit Blanc** (01865 510999) at 71-72 Walton Street. Oxford is well supplied with taverns – the busy sixteenth-century **King's Arms** at 40 Holywell Street can be overwhelmed by students but has good beer and decent pub grub; there's good food at the **White House** behind the station; or try the **Eagle & Child**, favoured watering hole of CS Lewis and JRR Tolkien.

Tourist Information Centre The Old School, Gloucester Green (01865 726871/www.oxford.gov.uk). **Open** *Easter-Oct* 9.30am-5pm Mon-Sat; 10am-3.30pm Sun; *Nov-Easter* 9.30am-5pm daily.

Salisbury & Stonehenge

In its first incarnation Salisbury was an Iron Age hill fort, subsequently taken over by the Romans, the Saxons and finally the Normans. The latter called it Sarum and built a castle and cathedral, but the site at **Old Sarum**, still worth a visit for its impressive ruins (01722 335398), wasn't big enough for both to co-exist happily and in 1220 the bishop embarked on the building of a new cathedral two miles to the south. The settlement that grew up around it became New Sarum, now Salisbury.

The **cathedral** (01722 555120) took only 38 years to complete, so it's unusually consistent in style, except for the spire, the tallest in Britain, which was added in 1334. The cathedral library contains one of only four original copies of the Magna Carta (1215) and, in the north aisle, you can see the country's oldest working clock (1386). Cathedral Close is a haven of peace lined with beautiful houses and lawns to soothe the eye. Many of the houses are thirteenth century but with Georgian façades. Two of the finest are **Malmesbury House** (01722 327027) and **Mompesson House** (01722 335659), both of which are open to the public, while the **Salisbury & South Wiltshire Museum** (01722 332151), in the King's House, is one of the country's most enjoyable local museums.

The town centre is a jumble of jettied, gabled, timber-framed buildings overhanging narrow streets. Names such as Butcher Row, Fish Row and Poultry Cross hint at Salisbury's true character as a regional trading centre; it really comes alive on market days (Tuesdays and Saturdays), as it has for the past 400 years.

For all its considerable charms, it seems that most visitors to Salisbury are just stopping off on their way to **Stonehenge** (01980 624715), a World Heritage Site about ten miles (16km) to the north, near Amesbury. Why it was built we don't know, and never will. How it was built is staggering enough. Construction began around 3000BC and continued intermittently over a period of 1,500 years. The stones were transported over land and water (from Pembrokeshire and the Marlborough Downs) using sledges and rafts. It has been estimated that each of the largest stones would have required 500 men to pull the sledge, and 100 more to lay rollers in front of it. What remains today is only a small part of the original complex. Stonehenge is only one of more than 500 known prehistoric sites in an area of just ten square miles (26sq km).

Further information

Getting there *by train* from Waterloo to Salisbury (1 hour 20mins); *by coach* National Express (2 hours 45mins); *by car* J8 off M3 then A303 and A338; *local buses* Wilts & Dorset (01722 336855) is the main operator and runs daily services to Stonehenge from Salisbury bus and rail stations.

Where to stay: The **Old Mill at Harnham** (01722 327517; £80) offers comfy rooms in a great location outside Salisbury. In the city, you could stay at the fourteenth-century **Old Bell Hotel** on St Ann's Street (01722 327958; £50-£75) or the even older **Red Lion** on Milford Street (01722 323334; £101-£115).

Where to eat & drink: Excellent Indian food can be had at **Asia** at 90 Fisherton Street (01722 327628) or sophisticated modern European fare at **LXIX** (01722 340000) at 67-69 New Street. The fourteenth-century **Haunch of Venison**, on Minster Street, is the oldest tavern in town, and serves decent food; the **King's Arms** on St John Street isn't much younger; while the **New Inn** is also anything but new and puts on a good spread.

Tourist Information Centre Fish Row, Salisbury (01722 334956). **Open** *May* 9.30am-5pm Mon-Sat; 10.30am-4.30pm Sun; *June, Sept* 9.30am-6pm Mon-Sat; 10.30am-4.30pm Sun; *July, Aug* 9.30am-7pm Mon-Sat; 10.30am-5pm Sun; *Oct-Apr* 9.30am-5pm Mon-Sat.

Stratford-upon-Avon

Where there's a Will... there's a thriving tourist industry. In many people's minds Stratford *is* Shakespeare. Born here in 1564, the playwright returned later in life and died in the town in 1616. Top of the list for visitors are the Shakespeare properties, five picturesque Tudor houses that function as museums and are worth visiting in their own right. There are three in the town centre: **Shakespeare's Birthplace** (01789 204016) on Henley Street; **Hall's Croft** (01789 204016), home of his daughter Susanna, on Old Town; and **Nash's House** (01789 204016), on Chapel Street, which belonged to the first husband of his granddaughter. Its garden contains the foundations of **New Place**, Shakespeare's last home, which was demolished in 1759.

A mile and a half away at Shottery, and accessible from Stratford by public footpath, is **Anne Hathaway's Cottage** (01789 204016), where Shakespeare's wife lived before she married the Bard. The girlhood home of his mother, **Mary Arden's House** (01789 204016), is at Wilmcote, a pleasant 3½-mile (5½-km) stroll along the towpath of the Stratford Canal. Both may also be reached by bus, and there are trains to Wilmcote.

Shakespeare was educated at **Stratford Grammar School**, which you can see on Church Street, and he was buried in **Holy Trinity Church**, which has a fine riverside setting and supposedly the playwright's tomb (although the whereabouts of his body are disputed). The dramatist's most meaningful memorials are his plays, and the **Royal Shakespeare Theatre** is the place to see them (tickets sell out fast though). The adjoining **Swan Theatre** stages a variety of classics, while **The Other Place** is for modern and experimental work. For bookings call 01789 403403. If you can't get a ticket, make do with a backstage tour or a visit to the **RSC Collection**, a museum of props and costumes (tours 01789 403405).

Relief from all things Shakespearian is easily achieved. Stratford has been a market town since 1169 and, in a way, that's still what it does best. See it on a Friday, when the awnings go up over the stalls at the top of Wood Street, and locals flock in from the outlying villages. And wander round the town centre, which still maintains its medieval grid pattern. Many fine old buildings survive, among them **Harvard House** on the High Street, dating from 1596. It was the home of Katharine Rogers who married Robert Harvard of London. It was their son John who founded Harvard University.

The town's charms are enhanced by the presence of the **River Avon** and the **Stratford Canal**. The canal basin is usually crammed with narrowboats and there are walks beside both waterways.

Further information

Getting there *by train* from Paddington (2 hours 10mins); *by coach* National Express (2 hours 45mins) or Guide Friday (01789 294466) from Euston; *by car* J15 off M40 then A46.

Where to stay: The pick of the many B&Bs is **Caterham House** (01789 267309; £76-£80) at 58 Rother Street, close to the Royal Shakespeare Theatre. Another good choice is **Victoria Spa Lodge** (01789 267985; £60) on Bishopton Lane.

Where to eat & drink: Among the many eating options is the excellent bistro fare at **The Opposition** (01789 269980) on Sheep Street, the imaginative, highly rated **Russon's** (01789 268822) at 8 Church Street and the popular modern cooking at **Desport's** at 13-14 Meer Street (01789 269304). Drink with the thespians at the **Dirty Duck** (aka the **Black Swan**) on Waterside, or the heavily beamed **Garrick** on the High Street.

Tourist Information Centre Bridgefoot (01789 293127/www.shakespeare-country.co.uk). **Open** *Easter-Oct* 9am-6pm Mon-Sat; 11am-5pm Sun; *Nov-Easter* 9am-5pm Mon-Sat.

Castles

See also page 322 **Walmer, Deal & Dover**.

Arundel

West Sussex (01903 882173). **Getting there** *by train* from Victoria (1 hour 30mins); *by car* A24 then A280 and A27. **Open** *Apr-last Fri in Oct* noon-5pm Mon-Fri, Sun (last entry 4pm). **Admission** £6.70; £4.20 5s-15s; £5.70 OAPs; £18 family.

Arundel's picturesque hilltop setting inevitably draws in summer crowds, but the medieval settlement remains one of the region's most charming and least spoiled towns. The major sight is the castle, home of the Dukes of Norfolk since the sixteenth century. The original structure was Norman, but it has been rebuilt many times, most recently in the nineteenth century. There's plenty to see inside, including the imposing Barons Hall and some good paintings by Van Dyck and Holbein. Don't miss the unusual Fitzalan Chapel in the grounds. It contains the tombs of past dukes (the leading Catholic family in post-Reformation England) and is separated from the altar of the main (Anglican) church of St Nicholas by a glass screen and an iron grille – it paid to be discreet about your Catholicism in those days.

Arundel also has its own neo-Gothic nineteenth-century **cathedral**, more impressive outside than in, plus some agreeable shopping streets and a handful of decent alehouses – try the busy Eagle on Tarrant Street.

Five miles (8km) north-east of Arundel is **Parham**, a near-perfect Elizabethan house in a near-perfect English country setting, beneath the South Downs (01903 742021). A couple of miles west of Parham are the evocative remains of **Bignor Roman Villa** (01798 869259), site of the longest surviving extent of mosaic pavement in the country. Further west towards Chichester is the brilliant outdoor **Sculpture at Goodwood** (01243 538449). The £10 admission fee may be offputting, but no one interested in modern art should pass up the opportunity to stroll around the 40 or so exhibits of this stunning collection of contemporary sculpture, set in 20 acres of woodland.

Bodiam

nr Robertsbridge, East Sussex (01580 830436).
Getting there *by train* Charing Cross to Robertsbridge (1 hour 15mins), then 10-min taxi journey; *by car* J5 off M25 then A21. **Open** *mid-Feb-Oct* 10am-6pm/dusk daily (last entry 5pm); *Nov-mid-Feb* 10am-4pm daily (last entry 3pm). **Admission** £3.60; £1.80 5s-15s; £9 family. **Credit** AmEx, MC, V.

All that remains of fourteenth-century Bodiam Castle is its shell, yet this is one of southern England's most evocative castles. It's great fun exploring the ruins, with their turreted tower, thick walls, moat and drawbridge. At the beginning of the twentieth century the castle was a favourite excursion for society in search of the picturesque and it retains a romantic appeal. The surrounding countryside is also a treat. Great for kids.

Hever

Hever, nr Edenbridge, Kent (01732 865224).
Getting there *by train* Victoria to Edenbridge (1 hour), then 5-min taxi journey, or Victoria to Hever (1 hour), then 1-mile walk; *by car* J5 off M25 then B2042 and B269 or J6 off M25 then A22, A25 and B269. **Open** *castle Mar-Nov* noon-6pm (last entry 5pm) daily; *Dec-Feb* noon-4pm (last entry 3pm) daily; *gardens* 11am-6pm daily. **Admission** £7.30; £4 5s-16s; £6.20 OAPs; £18.60 family; *garden only* £5.80; £3.80 5s-16s; £4.90 OAPs; £15.40 family. **Credit** MC, V.

Eight miles (13km) north-west of Tunbridge Wells, in the magnificent gardens of this enchanting, double-moated, thirteenth-century castle, Henry VIII is said to have courted Anne Boleyn. The ill-fated queen certainly spent much of her childhood here. More recently, the American millionaire William Waldorf Astor bought the estate (in 1903) and spent a huge amount of time, money and effort in restoring the place. The grounds now boast splendid Italianate gardens with loggia, classical sculpture and a colonnaded piazza, as well as a large lake and rose garden. One of Hever's most popular attractions, a water maze (open Apr-Oct), invites bravehearts to reach a folly in the middle of a large pond, by means of stepping stone paths, while avoiding water obstacles made by jets of water.

Leeds

Broomfield, nr Maidstone, Kent (01622 765400).
Getting there *by train* Victoria to Bearsted (1 hour), then 10-min bus transfer; *by car* J8 off M20. **Open** *Mar-Oct* 10am-6pm daily (last entry 5pm); *Nov-Feb* 10am-4pm daily (last entry 3pm). **Admission** *castle* £9.30; £6 under-15s; £7.30 OAPs; £25 family; *park only* £7.30; £4.50 under-15s; £5.80 OAPs; £20 family. **Credit** MC, V.

Leeds Castle, five miles (8km) east of Maidstone, is stunningly sited on two small islands in the midst of a lake. Built by the Normans nearly 900 years ago, it was converted into a royal palace by Henry VIII and now contains a mishmash of medieval furnishings, paintings, tapestries and, bizarrely, the world's finest collection of antique dog collars. The castle's greatest attractions, however, are external. Apart from the flower-filled gardens, there's the Culpeper Garden (an outsize cottage garden), an aviary containing over 100 rare bird species and, best of the lot, the maze, which centres on a spectacular underground grotto adorned with stone mythical beasts and shell mosaics. Facilities for disabled visitors are good (a leaflet is available in advance). Special events are held throughout the year (phone for details). The combined train journey, transfer and entrance ticket (book at Victoria Station) is the best deal going; £18.50 for an adult, £9.25 child.

Six miles (10km) from Leeds Castle (and a mile north of Maidstone) is the excellent **Museum of Kent Life** (01622 763936) at Sandling, an award-winning open-air re-creation of ye olde Kent complete with an oast house, hop gardens, an eighteenth-century farmhouse, hop-pickers' huts, working craftspeople and an adventure playground. The **North Downs Way** (*see p321*) is also within easy reach of Leeds Castle.

Lewes

169 High Street, Lewes, East Sussex (01273 486290). **Getting there by train** Victoria to Lewes (1 hour); *by car* M23 then A23 and A27. **Open** 10am-5.30pm/dusk Mon-Sat; 11am-5.30pm/dusk Sun. **Admission** £3.50; £1.80 5s-15s; £3 OAPs; £10 family. **Credit** MC, V.

Lewes is blessed with a handsome town centre and a fine setting amid the South Downs. There are splendid views of the countryside from the towers of the ruined eleventh-century castle. The admission price includes entry to the **Barbican House Museum** (same hours), a distinctly superior town museum, opposite the castle entrance. Also worth a look while you're in town is Tudor **Anne of Cleves House** (01273 474610). Henry VIII's queen was given the house as part of her divorce settlement, although she never actually lived here. The oak-beamed bedroom is stunning. Lewes' **Bonfire Night** celebrations (5 November) are famed, not only because of their scale and extravagance, but also because they commemorate the 17 Protestants burned here in 1556 as part of Mary I's crackdown on the new religion, rather than Guy Fawkes' 1605 plot to blow up James I and Parliament (*see p15*).

View over superb countryside from **Bignor Roman Villa**. *See page 312.*

Rochester

The Keep, Rochester, Kent (01634 402276).
Getting there *by train* from Victoria (45mins); *by car* A2. **Open** *Apr-Sept* 10am-6pm daily; *Oct-Mar* 10am-4pm daily. **Admission** £3.50; £2.50 5s-15s, OAPs, students; £9.50 family. **Credit** MC, V.

Rochester, Chatham and Gillingham form an almost continuous urban sprawl known as the Medway Towns. The hilly setting is lovely; the towns themselves are, in the main, distressingly ugly. Yet this is an area rich in history. **Rochester**'s biggest draw is its **castle**. Commanding a wide bend on the River Medway, the vast keep of Rochester, built in the late eleventh century by the architect of the White Tower in London, is one of the finest Norman castles in the country. Its early history was particularly lively, including occupation by Wat Tyler and his ragged-trousered forces in the Peasants' Revolt of 1381.

The castle dominates the town, and overlooks the small but beautiful **cathedral**. Also Norman in origin, it has been much altered over the centuries, but retains some splendid early paintings. Charles Dickens spent his youth in Rochester and, although he was not overly impressed with the place, it appeared in a number of his works (variously disguised as 'Mudfog' and 'Dullborough'); his last, unfinished novel The *Mystery of Edwin Drood* was set here. The entertaining **Charles Dickens Centre** in Eastgate House on the High Street is well worth a look (01634 844176). The **Guildhall Museum** (01634 848717), making the most of the area's rich history, is also worth visiting. **Gad's Hill Place** at Higham (3 miles/5km from Rochester; 01474 822366) is where Dickens lived from 1857 until his death in 1870 and has been evocatively preserved.

Windsor

High Street, Windsor (01753 831118).
Getting there *by train* Paddington to Slough, then change for Windsor Central (45mins); Waterloo to Windsor Riverside (1 hour); *by car* J6 off M4.
Open *Mar-Oct* 9.45am-5.15pm daily; *Nov-Feb* 10am-4.15pm daily. **Admission** Mon-Sat £10; £5 5s-15s; £7.50 OAPs; £22.50. Sun £8.50; £4 5s-15s; £6.50 OAPs; £18.50 family.
Credit AmEx, MC, £TC, V.

The largest castle in England squats bulkily above the Thames near Slough. There has been a royal home here since William the Conqueror built the first fortifications in 1070 to protect the western approaches to London, although the modern edifice is a hotchpotch thrown up by various monarchs' fancies down the ages. George V liked the place so much that he changed his family name in 1918 to Windsor (Saxe-Coburg-Gotha being none too popular during a war against Germany). Not to be missed is **Queen Mary's Dolls' House**, designed by Edward Lutyens and built over three years by 1,500 craftsmen, to such detail that even the toilets flush. The **State Apartments** have reopened following the 1992 fire. The Perpendicular Gothic **St George's Chapel** is where Henry VIII is buried. There are other royal tombs inside – as well as the most beautiful roof you may ever see.

Country houses

For information about **Althorp**, the Spencer family home and the burial place of Diana, Princess of Wales, phone 01604 592020 or visit the website at www.althorp.com. Note that the house is open only during July and August.

Audley End

Saffron Walden, Essex (01799 522399).
Getting there *by train* Liverpool Street to Audley End (1 hour) then 1-mile walk or 2-min taxi ride; *by car* J8 off M11 then B1383. **Open** *Apr-Sept* 11am-5pm Wed-Sun; *Oct guided tours only* 10am-3pm Wed-Sun.

Admission £6; £3 5s-16s; £4.50 OAPs, students; £15 family. **Credit** MC, V.

The magnificent Jacobean mansion of **Audley End** was the largest house in the country when it was built for Thomas Howard, 1st Earl of Suffolk, in 1614. It was later owned by Charles II, but given back to the Howards in the eighteenth century, who demolished two-thirds of it to make the place more manageable. More than 30 rooms are open to the public today, many of which have been restored to Robert Adam's 1760s designs. 'Capability' Brown landscaped the grounds. Phone to book a guided tour.

Saffron Walden (1 mile/1.5km from Audley End) is an appealing market town containing many timber-framed houses with decorative plastering (known as 'pargeting'). Eight miles (13km) southwest of here is the village of **Thaxted**, where Gustav Holst wrote much of *The Planets* and site of a superb three-tiered, half-timbered Guildhall, dating from the fifteenth century (01371 831339). There are many other fine villages and much great walking in the area.

Blenheim Palace

Woodstock, Oxfordshire (01993 811325).
Getting there *by train* Paddington to Oxford (1 hour) then 30-40-min bus ride; *by car* J8 off M40 then A40 and A44. **Open** *palace & gardens mid-Mar-Oct* 10.30am-5.30pm (last entry 4.45pm) daily, *park* 9am-5pm daily. **Admission** £8.50; £4.50 5s-15s; £6.50 OAPs; £22 family; *park only* £6 per car (including occupants), £2 adult, £1 concs.
Credit AmEx, DC, MC, V.

As a prize for beating the French at the Battle of Blenheim, John Churchill, Duke of Marlborough, was promised the money to build this immense, extravagant baroque fantasy. Its construction was acrimonious, as Parliament refused to stump up all the necessary cash and Churchill's wife quarrelled with the architect, Sir John Vanbrugh (she had wanted Wren for the job). Baroque masterpiece it may be, but the scale of the building means that it overwhelms rather than charms, and the speedy tours of the plush, antique-packed interior don't leave much time for reflection. The gardens, landscaped by the ubiquitous 'Capability' Brown, are splendid (and contain a butterfly house, adventure play area, maze, putting greens and mini-train). Winston Churchill was born at Blenheim in 1874 (five rooms are dedicated to the wartime PM) and is buried with his wife and parents in the nearby church at **Bladon**.

The handsome, well-scrubbed Oxfordshire town of **Woodstock** has a long history of royal connections but now chiefly services visitors to Blenheim and the Cotswolds. It's an agreeable refreshment stop. If you want to avoid the worst of the crowds, try the Black Prince pub on Oxford Street, just north of the centre.

Hatfield House

Hatfield, Hertfordshire (01707 262823).
Getting there *by train* from King's Cross to Hatfield (25mins); *by car* J4 off A1(M). **Open** *house late Mar-Sept* noon-4pm Tue-Thur; 1-4pm Sat, Sun; *gardens late Mar-Sept* 10.30am-6pm Tue-Sun.
Admission £6; £3 5s-15s; *gardens only* £5.

Hatfield House is one of the largest and most impressive Jacobean mansions in the country. Built in 1607-11 for Sir Robert Cecil (and remaining in the hands of his family today), it stands on the site of Tudor Hatfield Palace, where Elizabeth I spent much of her childhood. Cecil demolished most of the sixteenth-century building, although one wing survives. The grand interior contains some fine furniture and wonderful Tudor and Jacobean portraits. Outside, the seventeenth-century formal gardens were laid out by John Tradescant. The entrance to the house is opposite the rail station.

Knole

Sevenoaks, Kent (01732 450608). **Getting there** *by train* Charing Cross to Sevenoaks (31mins); *by car* J5 off M25. **Open** *Apr-Oct* noon-4pm Wed-Sat (last entry 3.30pm); 11am-5pm Sat (last entry 4.30pm); *garden Mar-Sept* noon-4pm 1st Wed of month.
Admission £5; £2.50 5s-17s; £12.50 family; £2.50 parking; garden only £1. **Credit** MC, V.

With fast connections to London, Sevenoaks is well placed to allow easy access to a number of sights in north-west Kent. As a town, it has little to entice visitors beyond the massive noble pile of Knole. The house was largely created by Archbishop of Canterbury Thomas Bourchier in 1456 and carefully planned to be in harmony with the calendar (seven courtyards, 52 staircases, 365 rooms – only 13 of which are open to the public). Knole was again remodelled by the Sackville family in 1605 and it has remained in the family ever since. Deer roam the vast grounds.

Polesden Lacey

Dorking Road, Surrey (01372 458203).
Getting there *by train* Waterloo to Westhumble or Dorking (40mins) then 10-min taxi ride; *by car* A3 then A243 and A24. **Open** *house Mar-Oct* 1.30-5.30pm Wed-Sun; *grounds* 11am-6pm/dusk daily.
Admission £6; £3 5s-16s; £15 family; *grounds only* £3; £7.50 family.

Three miles (5km) west of **Box Hill** (*see p321*) is the Regency villa of Polesden Lacey. This was the honeymooning ground for the Queen Mother and the late George VI more than 70 years ago. Tucked into the folds of the North Downs, the house and gardens give way to splendid views over woodland and commons. Within the grounds, tree-lined walks, walled rose gardens and a charming thatched bridge over a typical Surrey sunken lane all make for a right royal day out.

Waddesdon Manor

Waddesdon, nr Aylesbury, Buckinghamshire (01296 651211). **Getting there** *by train* Marylebone to Aylesbury (53mins) then bus; *by car* J9 off M40 then A41. **Open** *house Apr-June, Sept, Oct* 11am-4pm Thur-Sun; *July, Aug* 11am-4pm Wed-Sun.
Admission £9; £7.50 5s-16s; *grounds only* £3; £1.50 5s-16s. **Credit** MC, V.

Five miles (8km) north-west of Aylesbury, château-like Waddesdon Manor looks fantastically out of place in the English countryside. Built by the obscenely wealthy Rothschild family between 1874 and 1889, the house contains a magnificent collection of seventeenth- and eighteenth-century decorative arts. Panelling from nineteenth-century Parisian houses lines the walls, Savonnerie and Aubusson carpets cover the floors, and fine gold boxes, rare books and majolica are among the exhibits. The star attraction is one of the world's finest selections of Sèvres porcelain. The splendid rococo aviary in the grounds is also worth a look, as are the Rothschild wine-packed cellars (where tastings are on offer).

Woburn Abbey

Woburn, Bedfordshire (01525 290666). **Getting there** *by train* Euston to Bletchley (30mins) then 25-min taxi ride; *by car* J13 off M1 then A4012. **Open** *26 Mar-1 Oct* 11am-4pm Mon-Sat; 11am-5pm Sun; *2 Oct-29 Oct* 11am-4pm Sat; 11am-5pm Sun; 2 Jan-25 Mar 11am-4pm Sat, Sun. **Admission** £7.50; £3-£6.50 concs. **Credit** MC, V.

Home of the Dukes of Bedford for more than 350 years, eighteenth-century Woburn Abbey is hugely popular with daytrippers, due in large part to its **Safari Park** (half-price admission with a ticket for the abbey; *see p317*). The abbey itself – so called because it was built on the foundations of a twelfth-century Cistercian monastery – is a grand old house, containing some superb Tudor portraits.

Glorious **Sculpture at Goodwood**. *See p312.*

Family attractions

Many of the other destinations in this chapter are great for families – particularly the castles and seaside towns.

Chessington World of Adventures

Leatherhead Road (A243), Chessington, Surrey (01372 729560/recorded info 01372 727227). **Getting there** *by train* Waterloo to Chessington South (30mins); *by coach* Flightline 777 bus from Victoria Coach Station (1 hour); *by car* J9 off M25 or A3. **Open** *5 Apr-1 Aug, Sept-29 Oct* 10am-5.15pm daily (last entry 3pm); *Aug* 10am-9pm daily (last entry 7pm). **Admission** £19.50; £15.50 4s-13s; £9.50-£10.50 concs; free under-4s; £59 family. **Credit** AmEx, MC, V.

This frenetic 26-hectare (65-acre) theme park and zoo is certainly fun (if a little tacky), but boy do you pay through the nose for the pleasure. If you take the train to get here, hang on to your tickets as there's usually reduced-price admission for rail passengers. Attractions include Rameses Revenge, the Vampire (a suspended rollercoaster), the Safari Skyway Monorail, and the Rattlesnake, a rollercoaster ride 'that bites back'! Make sure you arrive early to preempt the worst of the queues.

Website: www.chessington.co.uk

Chislehurst Caves

Chislehurst, Kent (020 8467 3264). **Getting there** *by train* Charing Cross to Chislehurst (23mins); *by car* A222. **Open** 45-min tour every hour 10am-4pm Wed-Sun (daily during school hols); 90-min tour 2.30pm Sun. **Admission** 45-min tour £3; £1.50 concs; 90-min tour £5; £2.50 concs.

On the outskirts of south-east London, and close to Chislehurst rail station, are the highly recommended Chislehurst Caves. Take a lamplight tour (45 or 90mins) through this maze of ancient manmade chalk tunnels and caves. Previous occupants include Druids, Romans and wartime Londoners sheltering from air raids.

Drusillas Zoo Park

Alfriston, East Sussex (01323 870656). **Getting there** *by car* A22 then A27 or M23 then A23 and A27. **Open** *Apr-Oct* 10am-5pm daily; *Nov-Mar* 10am-4pm daily. **Admission** £6.95; £5.75 3s-12s; £5.25 OAPs. **Credit** MC, V.

This deceptively large wildlife park is imaginatively designed. Children and agile adults can scramble through tunnels to re-emerge in mini-domes amid meerkats or rats. It's an impressively clean and well-organised place – almost to the point of military precision; you have to wind your way along a pre-ordained path to earn that cuppa in the café at the end, where there is also a huge playground with (free) activities including gargantuan slides and train rides.

Legoland Windsor

Winkfield Road, Berkshire (0870 504 0404). **Getting there** *by train* Paddington to Windsor Central, change at Slough (30mins) or to Windsor & Eton Riverside (49mins) then shuttle service (small charge); *by car* J6 off M4, J3 off M3 or J13 off M25, then follow signs; *by coach* Green Line runs a daily service from Victoria (020 8668 7261). **Open** *mid-Mar-Oct* 10am-6pm daily. **Admission** £17; £14 3s-12s; £11 OAPs; free under-3s. **Credit** AmEx, MC, V.

Modelled on the Danish original, Legoland is a slick affair and a sure-fire hit with most two- to 12-year-olds. The huge site is split into different activity zones. In Miniland, there are miniature versions of famous European buildings. Duplo Gardens has a water-play area and cascades of chunky plastic, while the Castleland adventure area has the Dragon Knight's rollercoaster ride. Kids can get their Legoland licence in the Driving School, before heading on to Wild Woods to pan for gold and ride the Pirate Falls. Phone for details of special events and for an advisory sheet on facilities and access for guests with disabilities.
Website: www.legoland.co.uk

Mountfitchet Castle & Norman Village

Stansted Mountfitchet, Essex (01279 813237). **Getting there** *by train* Liverpool Street to Stansted Mountfitchet (45mins); *by car* J8 off M11 then A120 and B1383. **Open** *castle mid-Mar-mid-Nov* 10am-5pm daily; *toy museum mid-Jan-mid-Dec* 10am-4pm daily. **Admission** *castle* £4.50; £3.50 2s-14s; £3.80 OAPs; *toy museum* £3.50; £2.50 2s-14s, £3.20 OAPs. **Credit** MC, V.
Stansted Mountfitchet, eight miles (13km) south of Saffron Walden, is the site of this superb award-winning reconstruction of an eleventh-century Norman castle, which vividly brings history to life. There is also a good toy museum (with over 50,000 exhibits) in the village. A great place for kids.

Thorpe Park

Staines Road, Chertsey, Surrey (0870 5880880/ 01932 569393). **Getting there** *by train* Victoria to Staines, change at Clapham Junction (45 mins), or Hatton Cross tube, then link bus; *by car* J11 or J13 off M25. **Open** phone to check. **Admission** phone to check. **Credit** AmEx, DC, MC, V.
A Disneyesque theme park in Surrey, attracting around one million visitors a year. The pleasantly landscaped site covers 202 hectares (500 acres) and rounds up the usual suspects: rides, stunt shows, a working farm, 'fungle jungle' adventures, ghost rides, oversized and overfriendly cartoon characters and, if you can face it, No Way Out, a backwards ride in the dark.

Whipsnade Wild Animal Park

nr Dunstable, Bedfordshire (0870 520 0123). **Getting there** *by train* King's Cross to Luton (33mins) or Euston to Hemel Hempstead (25mins), then bus or 20-min taxi ride; *by car* J9 off M1 then A5 and B4540. **Open** *Apr-Oct* 10am-6pm Mon-Sat; 10am-7pm Sun; *Nov-Mar* 10am-4pm Mon-Sat. **Admission** £9.50; £7 3s-15s; £7 OAPs. **Credit** AmEx, MC, V.
Set in 243 hectares (600 acres) of beautiful parkland, Whipsnade is one of Europe's largest conservation centres. It is home to over 2,500 animals (many of them endangered species), including wallabies, Chinese water deer, elephants, lemurs and a hippo pool. Kids especially love the Runwild Play Area, Children's Farm and Great Whipsnade Railway, but there are many attractions that adults can enjoy too, including the Birds of the World demonstration, Squirrel Monkey Island and Tiger Falls.

Woburn Safari Park

Woburn Park, Bedfordshire (01525 290407). **Getting there** *by car* J13 off M1. **Open** *11 Mar-29 Oct* 10am-5pm daily; *Nov-10 Mar* 11am-3pm Sat, Sun. **Admission** *summer* £12; £8.50-£9 concs; free under-3s; *winter* £6.50; £5-£5.50 concs; free under-3s. **Credit** MC, V.
The Duke of Bedford's vast grounds have been turned over to a grand safari park, home to lions and tigers and bears… and monkeys and rhinos. There are five adventure playgrounds to explore (and two designed for under-fives). Children should enjoy the full programme of animal demonstrations and feeding times, including training sessions with the park's three Asian elephants. Other attractions include Rainbow Landing (where visitors can be swooped at by rainbow lorikeets) and the new walk-through squirrel monkey exhibit. While you're here, you might also want to look at **Woburn Abbey** (half-price admission with a ticket for the Safari Park; *see p316*).
Website: www.woburnsafari.co.uk

Gardens

Groombridge Place Gardens

Groombridge, Kent (01892 863999). **Getting there** *by rail* Charing Cross to Tunbridge Wells (53mins) then 10-min taxi ride; *by car* J5 off M25 then A21, A264 and B2110. **Open** *Easter-Oct* 9am-6pm daily. **Admission** £6.50; £5.50 3s-12s, OAPs; £20 family. **Credit** AmEx, MC, V.
It comes as little surprise that this medieval site has inspired artists and writers over the centuries (including filmmaker Peter Greenaway and Sir Arthur Conan Doyle for *The Valley of Fear*). Though the current house, which dates from the seventeenth century, is closed to the public, visitors can explore the surrounding parkland. With a listed walled garden set against a seventeenth-century moated mansion, walks through the award-winning 'Enchanted Forest', spring-fed pools and waterfalls giving way to dramatic views over the Weald, the possibilities for waxing lyrical are endless. A great place for kids.

Leonardslee

Lower Beeding, West Sussex (01403 891212). **Getting there** *by train* Victoria to Horsham (1 hour 8mins) then 15-min taxi ride; *by car* M23 then A23 and B2110. **Open** *Apr-Oct* 9.30am-6pm daily. **Admission** phone to check.
Perhaps the most charming of Sussex gardens, Leonardslee, set in a wooded valley three miles (5km) south-west of Nymans (*see below*), is particularly impressive for its floral displays. Six lakes, originally built in the sixteenth century to provide water power for iron foundries, are linked by paths; deer and wallabies roam free.

Nymans

Handcross, West Sussex (01444 400321). **Getting there** *by train* Victoria to Three Bridges (35mins) then 10-min taxi ride; *by car* M23 then A23

and B2114. **Open** *Mar-Oct* 11am-6pm/dusk Wed-Sun; *Nov-Mar* 11am-4pm Sat, Sun. **Admission** £2.50-£5; £1.25-£2.50 5s-18s. **Credit** MC, V.
Four miles (6km) south of Crawley is one of the finest of all English gardens. Set high on the edge of the Sussex Weald, Nymans is a showpiece of rare shrubs and trees. Highlights include the walled garden, the hidden sunken garden and some wonderful woodland walks. Parts of the house are now open to the public.

Sheffield Park

nr Uckfield, East Sussex (01825 790231).
Getting there *by train* Victoria to Hayward's Heath (45mins) then 15-min taxi ride; *by car* J10 off M23 then A264, A22 and A275. **Open** *Jan, Feb* 10.30am-4pm Sat, Sun; *Mar-Oct* 10.30am-6pm Tue-Sun; *Nov, Dec* 10.30am-4pm Tue-Sun. **Admission** £4.20; £2.10 5s-17s; £10.50 family.
The major draw of the sleepy heart of Sussex is its array of splendid gardens. The most majestic of these is Sheffield Park, located ten miles (16km) north of Lewes. Yet another eighteenth-century 'Capability' Brown creation, the gardens were modified in the early twentieth century but retain a grand landscape feel. There are five lakes connected with cascades and waterfalls in the early spring, fine specimens of azalea and rhododendron in early summer, and autumn hues from rare trees. Close by is the southern terminus of the nine-mile (14-km) **Bluebell Railway** (01825 722370) and the lovely village of **Fletching**. The Griffin Inn here is a great spot for lunch.

Sissinghurst

Sissinghurst, Cranbrook, Kent (01580 712850).
Getting there *by train* Charing Cross to Staplehurst (53mins) then 10-min taxi ride; *by car* J5 off M25 then A21 and A262. **Open** *Apr-mid-Oct* 1-6.30pm Tue-Fri; 10am-5.30pm Sat, Sun. **Admission** £6; £3 5s-15s. **Credit** AmEx, MC, V.
Sissinghurst is the greatest of the Kent gardens. Here Vita Sackville-West and her husband Harold Nicolson transformed a ruined sixteenth-century mansion (closed to the public) and grounds into a paradise of colour and fragrance. Alas, the edenic lure of Sissinghurst is so powerful that coachloads of trippers frequently swamp the place and timed tickets are the norm.

Stowe

Buckinghamshire (gardens 01280 822850/house 01280 818280). **Getting there** *by train* Euston to Milton Keynes (40mins) then bus to Buckingham (30mins) then 10-min taxi ride; *by car* J10 off M40 then A43 and A422 or J14 off M1 then A5 and A422. **Open** *gardens 29 Mar-4 July* 10am-5pm Wed-Sun (last entry 4pm); *5 July-10 Sept* 10am-5pm Tue-Sun; *10 Sept-29 Oct* 10am-5pm/dusk Wed-Sun (last entry 4pm); *2 Dec-23 Dec* 10am-4pm daily (last entry 3pm); *house 29 Mar-21 Apr, 3 July-8 Sept* 2-5pm Mon-Fri; noon-5pm Sat, Sun. **Admission** *gardens* £4.60; £2.50 concs; £11.50 family; *house* £2; £1 child.
Three miles (5km) north-west of Buckingham, Stowe is possibly the most important and spectacular eighteenth-century landscaped garden in the country. Its 132 hectares (325 acres) were first laid out in 1680 but transformed over the following 100 years by tree-plantings, (six) lake-makings and (32) temple-buildings. To 'Capability' Brown's naturalistic landscape-shaping were added monuments by almost every big-name architect of the time, including James Gibbs, John Vanbrugh and William Kent. Little of the interior of the house can be seen because it is occupied by Stowe School. Buckingham itself is a relatively lively town, with some jumping, studenty pubs.

Homes of the famous

For **Gad's Hill Place** (Dickens), *see page 313*; for **Flatford Mill** (Constable), *see page 321*.

Bateman's

Burwash, Etchingham, East Sussex (01435 882302).
Getting there *by car* J5 off M25 then A21 and A265. **Open** *Apr-1 Nov* 11am-5pm Mon-Wed, Sat, Sun (last entry 4.30pm). **Admission** £5; £2.50 5s-14s; £12.50 family. **Credit** MC, V.
Rudyard Kipling lived at Bateman's from 1902 until his death in 1936. The seventeenth-century house has been preserved as the author left it, and the attractive grounds contain a watermill that Kipling converted to generate electricity.

Charleston Farmhouse & around

nr Firle, East Sussex (01323 811265).
Getting there *by train* Victoria to Lewes (1 hour 5mins) then 10-min taxi ride; *by car* M23 then A23 and A27. **Open** *Apr-June, Sept, Oct* 2-6pm Wed-Sun; *July, Aug* 11.30am-6pm Wed-Sat, 2-6pm Sun. Last entry 1hr before closing. **Admission** £5.50; £3.50 5s-16s, OAPs, students; garden only £2; £1 5s-16s, OAPs, students. **Credit** MC, V.
Six miles (10km) east of Lewes stands this shrine for Bloomsbury Groupies. Virginia Woolf's sister **Vanessa Bell** moved here with her husband **Clive** and lover **Duncan Grant** during World War I so that the two men, as conscientious objectors, could become farm labourers and, thus, be exempt from military service. Admission includes a guided tour of the house, which is hung with superb paintings by the likes of Picasso and Renoir, as well as more minor daubings.

Four miles (6km) west of here is another Bloomsbury site – **Monk's House** in Rodmell, home of **Leonard** and **Virginia Woolf** from 1919 (01892 890651; Apr-Oct 2-5.30pm Wed, Sat; £2.50, £1.25 5s-16s). Close by is the spot on the River Ouse where Virginia drowned herself in 1941, walking into the water, her pockets full of stones. She and Leonard (who lived here until his death in 1969) are both interred in the garden.

Chartwell

Westerham, Kent (recorded info 01732 866368/ 01732 868381). **Getting there** *by train* Charing Cross to Sevenoaks (33mins) then Chartwell Explorer bus; *by car* J5 off M25 then A25 and B2026 or J6 off M25 then A22, A25 and B2026. **Open** *Apr-June*

11am-5pm Wed-Sun; *July, Aug* 11am-5pm Tue-Sun; *Sept-29 Oct* 11am-5pm Wed-Sun. Last entry 4.15pm. **Admission** £5.50; £2.75 5s-16s; £13.75 family. **Credit** V.

Six miles (9km) west of Sevenoaks lies one of the South-east's most-visited sights: Chartwell, home of **Winston Churchill**. The wartime PM lived in the much-restored Tudor building from 1924 until his death in 1965 and it contains a large hoard of Churchillabilia. Guided tours are available on Wednesday mornings; phone for details.

Down House

Luxted Road, Downe, Kent (info 01689 859119). **Getting there** *by train* Charing Cross to Orpington (23mins) then 20-min taxi ride; *by car* A223 or A21. **Open** *1 Apr-30 Sept* 10am-6pm Wed-Sun; *Oct* 10am-5pm Wed-Sun; *Nov, Dec, Feb, Mar* 10am-4pm Wed-Sun. **Admission** £5.50; £4.10 concs; £2.80 child. **Credit** MC, V.

A couple of miles outside Orpington is the recently restored home of probably the most significant figure of the nineteenth century: **Charles Darwin**. The naturalist's world-shaking theory of evolution was partly written in this large house, where he lived for 40 years. On the ground floor are the original drawing room and study; the first floor houses temporary topical exhibitions.

Jane Austen's House

Chawton, Hampshire (01420 832262). **Getting there** *by train* Waterloo to Alton (1 hour); *by car* J5 off M3 then B3349. **Open** *Mar-Dec* 11am-4.30pm daily; *Jan, Feb* 11am-4.30pm Sat, Sun. **Admission** £2.50; 50p 8s-18s; £2 OAPs, students. **Credit** MC, V.

A mile south-west of Alton is the village of Chawton, where **Jane Austen** lived between 1809 and 1817. She wrote or revised all of her six books in this modest red-brick house, which now contains a collection of Austen first editions and other memorabilia.

Alton is one terminus of the **Mid Hants Watercress Line**, which runs steam trains between here and Alresford (01962 733810). Four miles (6km) to the south of Chawton is **Little Selborne**, where eighteenth-century naturalist **Gilbert White**'s house **The Wakes** (01420 511275) has been preserved as a memorial to his pioneering work.

Shaw's Corner

Ayot St Lawrence, Hertfordshire (01438 820307/ 01494 755567). **Getting there** *by train* from King's Cross to Welwyn North (55mins) then 10-min taxi ride; *by car* J6 off A1(M). **Open** *Apr-Oct* 1-5pm Wed-Sun. **Admission** £3.30; £1.65 5s-16s; £8.25 family.

George Bernard Shaw lived for more than 40 years (until his death in 1950) in the village of Ayot St Lawrence amid some of Hertfordshire's prettiest scenery. The playwright's house has been preserved much as he left it, and his famous revolving writing shed, which turned to follow the path of the sun, was restored to full working order in 1998. Works undertaken by Shaw here include *St Joan* and *Pygmalion*.

Life on the ocean wave

Portsmouth Historic Dockyard

HM Naval Base, College Road, Hampshire (023 9286 1512). **Getting there** *by train* Waterloo to Portsmouth Harbour (1 hour 30mins); *by car* A3 or M3 then M27. **Open** *Mar-Oct* 10am-5.30pm daily (last entry 4.30pm), *Nov-Feb* 10am-5pm daily (last entry 4pm). **Admission** *all-ships ticket* £11.90; £8.90 5s-14s; £10.40 OAPs; £28.25 family (phone for details of charges to individual attractions).

Portsmouth is rich in naval associations but poor in looks (the two are connected: its importance as a port meant it was bombed to bits during World War II). The city's greatest draw is undoubtedly the **Historic Ships**. This encompasses a number of museums and three ships: Britain's first armoured battleship, HMS *Warrior*, dating from 1860; Nelson's flagship at Trafalgar, HMS *Victory*; and Henry VIII's *Mary Rose*, which sank in front of the King while engaging the French just off the coast in 1545.

It is also worth making the short ferry journey to Gosport to look around the claustrophobic vessels in the **Royal Navy Submarine Museum** (023 9252 9217). Military enthusiasts can press on to the **D-Day Museum** on Clarence Esplanade (023 9282 7261), centred around the 83-m (272-ft) embroidery commemorating Operation Overlord, in which Portsmouth played a major role. Next to the museum is **Southsea Castle** (023 9282 7261), from which Henry VIII may have watched his beloved *Mary Rose* sink beneath the waves. A mile further along the front is the **Royal Marines Museum** (023 9281 9385), complete with junior assault course.

Portsmouth's one non-military attraction is **Dickens' Birthplace** at 393 Commercial Road, north of the town centre (023 9282 7261). There's not a lot to see, though, beyond a couple of recreated rooms.

World Naval Base

The Historic Dockyard, Chatham, Kent (01634 823800). **Getting there** *by train* Victoria to Chatham then 1-mile walk, 2-min taxi ride or bus; *by car* J2 off M25 then A2. **Open** *Apr-Oct* 10am-5pm daily (last entry 4pm); *Feb, Mar, Nov* 10am-4pm Wed, Sat, Sun (last entry 3pm). **Admission** £8.50; £5.50 5s-15s; £6.30 OAPs; £22.50 family. **Credit** MC, V.

Close neighbour to **Rochester** (*see p313*), **Chatham**, founded by Henry VIII, had become England's biggest naval base within 100 years. Not surprisingly, the town's major attraction is the excellent **World Naval Base**, a restored Georgian river dockyard with a 'Sail and Colour Loft', where you can learn how flags and sails are made. Vessels to explore include restored sloops, gunships and paddle steamers. Other attractions are the dockyard's shire-horses and a collection of naval guns. Nearby **Fort Amherst** (01634 847747) was built to defend the dockyard in the mid-eighteenth century and extended during the Napoleonic Wars. There are tunnels, nature trails, barracks and batteries to be explored and occasional military re-enactments to enjoy on Sundays. Chatham town itself is decidedly lacking in the charm department.

Out in the country

Despite appearances, London's sprawl does not go on forever. There's wonderful walking country within easy reach of the city, particularly in the North Downs, south of London; the Chilterns to the north-west; and the Cotswolds to the west. For further details, see below.

Shameless self-promotion it may be, but we recommend the pocket-sized *Time Out Book of Country Walks* (Penguin, £9.99) for walking enthusiasts. The book details 52 walks in the countryside around London.

Country Lanes *9 Shaftesbury Street, Fordingbridge, Hampshire SP6 1JF (01425 655022).* Take the train from London and be met at your destination by representatives from Country Lanes who will then lead you on cycling or walking tours of the New Forest, the Cotswolds, Dorset and other areas. There are day trips, short breaks and six-day tours. Write or phone for a brochure.

The Chilterns

Getting there *by train* from Paddington to Henley (55mins); Paddington to Maidenhead then change for Marlow (55mins); *by car Henley/Marlow* J8 off M4 then A404(M) and A4130 or J4 off M40 then A404 and A4155; *Wendover* J20 off M25 then A41 and A4011 or A40 and A413.

Stretching in a broad arc around the north-west of London, the Chilterns rarely receive more than a glance out of the window from tourists powering through to Oxford and Stratford. Yet this gently hilly region has some great walking and excellent pubs (if also some charmless towns) and is easily and quickly accessible from the capital.

At the place where Oxfordshire, Berkshire and Buckinghamshire meet is cocky little **Henley** (tourist office: 01491 578034). This wealthy commuter burg becomes the centre of braying-toff life for five days at the end of June when the Henley **Royal Regatta** hits town (*see p7*), but is otherwise most useful as a base from which to explore the wonderful villages and countryside to the north. Some of the best walking in the Chilterns can be found around **Frieth** and **Nettlebed**, and the Prince Albert pub in the former and Carpenters Arms in Crocker End near the latter are good spots to hole up with a pint after a hike. There's also fine walking further north around **Wendover**.

Another good (if very popular) place from which to explore the southern Chilterns and the Thames Valley, **Marlow** is a relaxed little town with some good Georgian architecture and a fine pub – the Two Brewers on St Peter's Street – where Jerome K Jerome wrote part of *Three Men in a Boat*. Other notable literary residents have included Percy and Mary Shelley and TS Eliot.

The cutesy village of **Cookham**, four miles (7km) east of Marlow, is famed as the home of one of Britain's greatest and most idiosyncratic twentieth-century painters, **Stanley Spencer**. Several of his deceptively naïve, sex-and-God-obsessed works are displayed in the **Stanley Spencer Gallery** (01628 520890) on the High Street.

Stowaway to **Stowe**. *See page 318.*

The Cotswolds

Getting there *by train* Paddington to Moreton-in-Marsh (1 hour 20mins); *by car* M40 then A40 and A44.

Nowhere in England is there such a harmonious relationship between buildings and landscape as in the Cotswolds. The enchanting stone villages and incomparable 'wool churches' that characterise the area were built by the medieval merchants who grew rich from the profits of the local wool trade. Routinely described as 'honey-coloured', the stone is actually extremely variable, yet its ubiquitous use helps to unify a region that sprawls generously over six counties.

Parts of the Cotswolds suffer horrible congestion on summer weekends, but it's always localised. While crowds buzz around **Bourton** and **Bibury**, equally charming villages such as **Stanton** and **Stanway** slumber gently on, almost undisturbed. The small Cotswold towns are often even more memorable than the villages. Places such as **Stow-on-the-Wold**, whose elegant seventeenth-century houses look down on The Square (the tourist information centre is found here; 01451 831082); **Winchcombe**, with its gargoyle-encrusted church and its wonderful setting; **Broadway**, where cottage gardens of wisteria, clematis and old roses spill out on to the High Street; and, best of all, **Chipping Campden**, with its 600-year-old houses and glorious wool church.

Chipping Campden is also the starting point of the long-distance footpath, the **Cotswold Way**. Fortunately, Cotswold footpaths are as suitable for Sunday strollers as hardened hikers. Well-maintained and waymarked, they converge on every town and village. The ancient Eight Bells Inn in Chipping Campden (01386 840371), the Old White Lion in Winchcombe (01242 603300) and the pricier Grapevine Hotel in Stow-on-the-Wold (01451 830344) are all recommended bases. For **Stratford-upon-Avon**, *see p311*.

Epping Forest

Information Centre, High Beech, Loughton, Essex (020 8508 0028). **Getting there** *by train* Loughton tube then 2-mile walk or 5-min taxi ride; *by car* J26 off M25. **Open** *Apr-Oct* 10am-5pm Mon-Sat; 11am-5pm Sun; *Nov-Mar* 11am-3pm Mon-Fri; 10am-dusk Sat; 11am-dusk Sun.

The 2,430 hectares (6,000 acres) left of this once massive ancient forest are still mighty impressive, and perfect for walking, cycling, horse riding, picnicking, blackberrying and mushrooming. Wander down wheelchair- (and buggy-) friendly paths, among ancient oaks adjacent to the visitors' centre and around Connaught Water. The friendly staff can offer suggestions for walks around the acres, or supply leaflets and a detailed map to help with explorations. Be warned that the visitors' centre is a two-mile uphill walk from Loughton tube station. You're best off buying a map of the forest beforehand (try **Edward Stanford**; *see p203*), having a coffee in Loughton town when you get off the tube, and then walking to the information centre through the forest rather than along the main roads. Alternatively, continue on the tube for a couple of stops to Theydon Bois, a pretty, largely unspoiled village with a green and duck pond, and wander into the forest from there.

Website: www.eppingforest.org

The North Downs

Getting there *by train* Waterloo to Westhumble or Dorking (40mins) then 10-min taxi ride; *by car* A3 then A243 and A24.

The bones of the landscape of England south of London are the Downs – North and South – long chalk ridges facing each other across the Weald. The South Downs are more spectacular, but the North Downs are much closer to the capital; so close that you can enjoy some of the South-east's best views little more than 20 miles (32km) from the heart of London.

A long-distance footpath, the **North Downs Way**, runs for 140 miles (224km) from Farnham in Surrey to the White Cliffs of Dover. Opportunities for shorter walks are plentiful, and the ancient market town of **Dorking** is a good centre. There's easy access from here to **Box Hill**, which has been a popular picnic spot since the days of Charles II – avoid weekends if you can. The William IV pub in nearby Mickleham is a popular place for liquid and solid refreshment. Not far away is **Polesden Lacey** (*see p315*) and **Ranmore Common**, which offers good walks on the south slopes of the Downs. Another good spot for walking, six miles (9km) south-west of Dorking, is **Leith Hill**, the highest point in south-east England.

The Stour Valley

Essex & Suffolk. **Getting there** *by train* Liverpool Street to Sudbury (1 hour 7mins); *by car* J28 off M25, then A12 and A134.

Despite its dour reputation, parts of Essex are very pretty, particularly where the county meets Suffolk at the Stour (pronounced 'stoo-er') Valley. This tranquil, gently undulating region is known for its good walking, handsome towns and villages (impressively built on the wealth of the area's medieval wool and weaving trade) and, most of all, as **John Constable** country. The birthplace of Britain's best-loved painter at **East Bergholt** is long gone, so the Constable heritage industry is now based around **Flatford Mill**, the house his father owned, and the setting for *The Hay Wain.*

Good-looking **Sudbury**, the biggest town in the Stour Valley, makes a decent base for touring a region where the chief pleasures are the soothing landscape and the fine architecture. Among the area's most beguiling villages are **Long Melford**, **Castle Hedingham**, **Kersey** and medieval picture-postcard-perfect **Lavenham** (the Great House French restaurant with rooms is a good place to eat and sleep; 01787 2047431; from £140 including dinner, bed and breakfast). If you're in the area, treat yourself to a meal at the wonderful White Hart in Great Yeldham near Halstead (01787 237250).

Thames Path

The Thames Path follows a 180-mile (288-km) stretch of river from its source near Kemble in Gloucestershire via the Cotswolds, Oxford, the Chilterns, Windsor and through London to the Thames Barrier at Woolwich. Set up by the Countryside Commission, the Path is claimed to be the only long-distance route that follows a river for most of its length. You can join it at any point and enjoy the riverside scenery for a short walk or a longer hike.

Leaflets are available from tourist information centres, although it's worthwhile buying a copy of the *National Trail Guide: The Thames Path* by David Sharp (Aurum Press, £12.99), which includes Ordnance Survey maps and details of public transport and refreshment stops.

Seaside

See also page 304 **Brighton**.

Aldeburgh

Suffolk. **Getting there** *by car* J28 off M25 then A12 and A1094.

There can be something otherworldly about the Suffolk coast, and the little town of Aldeburgh is a perfect spot to experience its uniqueness and escape the capital's crowds – that is unless you come when the place is overwhelmed by visitors to the world-famous **Aldeburgh Festival** of classical music (9-25 June 2000), **Proms** (1-31 Aug 2000) and **Aldeburgh Poetry Festival** (3-5 Nov 2000; phone 01728 453435 for details of all). Local boy **Benjamin Britten** founded the music festival in 1948 and is buried in the churchyard by the side of his long-term partner, the tenor Peter Pears; the two of them lived in Crag House on Crabbe Street from 1947 to 1957. The tourist office on the High Street (01728 453637) can help with places to stay, or try B&B at Ocean House (01728 452094; £55-£65). There are a number of good restaurants in town, including the Lighthouse (01728 453377), which isn't and never was a lighthouse. Other beguiling spots on the Suffolk coast include Orford and Southwold.

Hastings & Battle

Getting there *by train* from Charing Cross or Victoria (1 hour 30mins-2 hours); *by car* M25 then A21.

Apart from having the most famous battle on British soil named after it, there is little of distinction about **Hastings**. Its fading-resort air sits oddly with an arty quarter popular with painters and the still-active fishing port. Of the sprinkling of museums, the commandingly situated ruins of the **Norman castle** hold **The 1066 Story** (01424 781112), an explanation of William the Conqueror's invasion. More exciting is the **Smugglers' Adventure** (01424 422964) in St Clement's Caves. Until the early nineteenth century, smuggling was one of Hastings' major industries, and the caves, once used for stashing contraband, now contain some excellent dioramas detailing the nefarious activities of the locals. The tourist office is in Queens Square (01424 781111).

The literally named town of **Battle**, five miles (8km) inland, gives a big clue as to the actual spot where William and King Harold slugged it out for the English crown more than 900 years ago. To thank God for his victory William built **Battle Abbey** (01424 773792) on the spot where Harold was killed. The abbey is in ruins now, but wonderfully evocative ruins they are, and an audio-visual display gives a low-down of the battle and the demise of the English King (who was clubbed to death, not shot in the eye with an arrow as a misinterpretation of the Bayeux Tapestry popularly led us to believe). The town itself is rather touristy, but the fourteenth-century **Almonry** (01424 772727) on the High Street is worth a look for the Battle of Hastings model and the 300-year-old Guy Fawkes effigy, which is paraded through the streets on the Saturday nearest to 5 November.

Rye

East Sussex. **Getting there** *by train* Charing Cross to Ashford then change for Rye (1 hour 40mins); *by car* J10 off M20 then A2070 and A259 or J5 off M25 then A21 and A268.

When is a seaside town not a seaside town? When the river it sits on silts up, the sea retreats and it finds itself two miles inland. Such is the case with the wonderful town of Rye, one of the original Cinque Ports. The skew-whiff little houses tumbling down steep streets are tremendously snappable (as is cobbled Mermaid Street) – a fact that draws the summer hordes to Rye and has resulted in rather too much commercialisation. Still, this is a great place to visit, and is rich with literary connections. Radclyffe Hall and EF Benson lived here, as did **Henry James**, whose former residence **Lamb House** (01797 224982) is open to the public. Also worth a peek are **Rye Castle** (01797 226728) and **Rye Art Gallery** (01797 222433). Two of the best B&Bs in town are Jeake's House on Mermaid Street (01797 222828) and Little Orchard House on West Street (01797 223831). Eating options in Rye include the Landgate Bistro (01797 222829) and the Mermaid inn (01797 223065).

If you want to avoid the Rye crowds, you need only travel a couple of miles south-west to **Winchelsea**, another little town abandoned by the sea. It was planned on a grid pattern by Edward I in the thirteenth century and contains a wonderfully evocative ruined church. There's a shingly beach a mile or so south of here.

Walmer, Deal & Dover

Getting there *by train* from Charing Cross to Walmer, Deal or Dover Priory (1 hour 40mins-2 hours); *by car Walmer and Deal* J13 off M20 then A258; *Dover* J13 off M20.

Part of the chain of coastal forts built by Henry VIII to protect Britain from the fury aroused in the remaining Catholic countries of Europe by the Reformation, Walmer and Deal, only a mile apart, make a satisfying comparison. **Walmer Castle** (01304 364288), next to the beach where Julius Caesar landed in 55BC, has been converted into a stately home for the Warden of the Cinque Ports (HM the Queen Mother) with splendid gardens. **Deal Castle** (01304 372762) remains almost unchanged: a sturdy, menacing structure (shaped like a Tudor rose) with long gloomy passages.

Eight miles (13km) to the south, **Dover Castle** (01304 211067) was once the most strategically important castle in Britain, dominating the narrowest point of the English Channel, and has been in constant use for the last 800 years. Within the cliffs on which it perches are a warren of tunnels to explore. Walking along the castle's walls you are closer to that distressingly Eurosceptic island spirit of complacent security than almost anywhere else in the land. Other attractions in not-very-attractive Dover include the **White Cliffs Experience** (01304 214566), which recreates the town in Roman times and during World War II, and the informative **Dover Museum** (01304 201066), which boasts a newly opened Bronze Age Gallery, displaying an impressive 3,550-year-old boat and other Bronze Age artefacts.

Whitstable

Kent. **Getting there** *by train* from Victoria (1 hour 15mins); *by car* J7 off M2 then A99.

Much of the north Kent coast is not particularly appealing, but the civilised little town of Whitstable is an exception. The seafront, looking out on to a neat shingle beach, is unobtrusive and well mannered, but most people come to Whitstable to eat. The town has long been famous for its oysters (previously considered a poor man's food), and fine seafood now fills the menus of a number of excellent restaurants, the pick of which is probably the **Whitstable Oyster Fishery Company** (01227 276856), which also offers quirky, characterful rooms for the night at the **Hotel Continental** (01227 280280) just a few hundred metres away. You can brush up on your bivalve knowledge in the **Whitstable Oyster & Fishery Exhibition** (01227 276856) or of the town itself in the **Whitstable Museum & Gallery** (01227 276998). Margate and, round the headland, Broadstairs and Ramsgate, are within easy reach of Whitstable.

Directory

Resources A-Z

Customs

When entering the UK, non-EU citizens and anyone buying duty-free goods should be aware of the following import limits:

- 200 cigarettes **or** 100 cigarillos **or** 50 cigars **or** 250 grams (8.82 ounces) tobacco;
- 2 litres still table wine **plus either** 1 litre spirits or strong liqueurs (over 22 per cent alcohol by volume) **or** 2 litres fortified wine (under 22 per cent abv), sparkling wine or other liqueurs;
- 60cc/ml perfume;
- 250cc/ml toilet water;
- other goods to the value of £145 for non-commercial use;
- the import of meat, meat products, fruit, plants, flowers and protected animals is restricted or forbidden;
- no restrictions on import and export of currency.

Since the Single European Market agreement came into force at the beginning of 1993, people over the age of 17 arriving from an EU country have been able to import limitless goods for their own personal use, if bought tax-paid (not duty-free). But Customs officials may need convincing that you do not intend to sell any of the goods.

Embassies

For other embassies, consulates and high commissions check the telephone directory and *Yellow Pages* under 'Embassies'.

American Embassy *24 Grosvenor Square, W1 (020 7499 9000). Bond Street or Marble Arch tube.* **Open** 8.30am-5.30pm Mon-Fri. **Map 7 G7**

Emergencies

In the event of a serious accident, fire or incident, call **999** and specify whether you require ambulance, fire service or police. *See also below* **Health**.

Australian High Commission *Australia House, Strand, WC2 (020 7379 4334/www.australia.org.uk). Holborn or Temple tube.* **Open** 9.30am-3.30pm Mon-Fri. **Map 8 M6**

Canadian High Commission *38 Grosvenor Street, W1 (020 7258 6600). Bond Street tube.* **Open** 8-11am Mon-Fri. **Map 7 H7**

New Zealand High Commission *80 Haymarket, SW1 (020 7930 8422). Piccadilly Circus tube.* **Open** 9am-5pm Mon-Fri. **Map 8 K7**

South African High Commission *South Africa House, Trafalgar Square, WC2 (020 7451 7299/www.southafricahouse.com). Charing Cross tube/rail.* **Open** 8.45am-12.45pm. **Map 8 K7**

Health

Free emergency medical treatment under the National Health Service (NHS) is available to:

- European Union nationals, plus those of Iceland, Norway and Liechtenstein. People from these countries are also entitled to specific treatment for a non-emergency condition on production of form E112.
- Nationals (on production of a passport) of Bulgaria, Czech and Slovak Republics, Gibraltar, Hungary, Malta, New Zealand, Russia, former Soviet Union states (except Latvia, Lithuania and Estonia) and the former Yugoslavia.
- Residents, irrespective of nationality, of Anguilla, Australia, Barbados, British Virgin Islands, Channel Islands, Falkland Islands, Iceland, Isle of Man, Montserrat, Poland, Romania, St Helena, Sweden, Turks & Caicos Islands.
- Anyone who at the time of receiving treatment has been in the UK for the previous 12 months.
- Anyone who has come to the UK to take up permanent residence.
- Students and trainees whose course requires them to spend more than 12 weeks in employment during their first year. Students and others living in the UK for a settled purpose for more than six months may be accepted as ordinarily resident and not liable to charges.
- Refugees and others who have sought refuge in the UK.
- Anyone formally detained by the Immigration Authorities.
- People with HIV/AIDS at a special clinic for the treatment of sexually transmitted diseases. The treatment covered is limited to a diagnostic test and counselling associated with that test.

There are no NHS charges for the following:

- Treatment in Accident & Emergency departments.
- Certain district nursing, midwifery or health visiting.
- Emergency ambulance transport.
- Diagnosis and treatment of certain communicable diseases including STDs.

Directory

- Family planning services.
- Compulsory psychiatric treatment.

Any further advice should be obtained from the Patient Services Manager at the hospital where treatment is to be sought.

Accident & emergency

Below are listed most of the hospitals with 24-hour accident & emergency departments. Those within central London are marked on the maps at the back of this Guide by a white cross on a red square.

Charing Cross Hospital
Fulham Palace Road, W6 (020 8846 1234). Barons Court or Hammersmith tube.

Chelsea & Westminster Hospital
369 Fulham Road, SW10 (020 8746 8000). Bus 14, 73, 211. **Map 3 C12**

Guy's Hospital
St Thomas Street (entrance Snowsfields, off Weston Street), SE1 (020 7955 5000). London Bridge tube/rail. **Map 11 P8**

Hackney & Homerton Hospital
Homerton Row, E9 (020 8510 5555). Homerton rail/22B bus.

Royal Free Hospital
Pond Street, NW3 (020 7794 0500). Belsize Park tube/Hampstead Heath rail.

Royal London Hospital
Whitechapel Road, E1 (020 7377 7000). Whitechapel tube.

St George's Hospital
Blackshaw Road, SW17 (020 8672 1255). Tooting Broadway tube.

St Mary's Hospital
Praed Street, W2 (020 7886 6666). Paddington tube/rail. **Map 2 D5**

St Thomas's Hospital
Lambeth Palace Road, SE1 (020 7928 9292). Waterloo tube/rail or Westminster tube. **Map 8 M9**

University College Hospital
Grafton Way, WC1 (020 7387 9300). Euston Square or Warren Street tube. **Map 5 J4**

Whittington Hospital
St Mary's Wing, Highgate Hill, N19 (020 7272 3070). Archway tube.

Contraception/ abortion

Family planning advice, contraceptive supplies and abortions are free to British citizens on the National Health Service. This also applies to EU residents and foreign nationals living, working and studying in Britain. If you decide to go private, contact one of the organisations listed below. You can also phone 020 7837 4044 for your nearest branch of the **Family Planning Association**.

British Pregnancy Advisory Service

7 Belgrave Road, SW1 (020 7828 2484). Victoria tube/rail.
Open phone first for an appointment; phone lines 8am-8pm Mon-Fri; 8.30am-6pm Sat; 9.30am-1pm Sun. **Map 7 H10**
Contraception advice, contraceptives and the morning-after pill are available. The service carries out pregnancy tests and makes referrals to BPAS nursing homes for private abortions.
Website: www.bpas.demon.co.uk

Brook Advisory Centre

233 Tottenham Court Road, W1 (enquiries 020 7323 1522/ helpline 0800 018 5023). Tottenham Court Road tube. **Open** enquiries 9.30am-7.30pm Mon-Thur; 9.30am-3pm Fri; noon-2pm Sat. **Map 6 K5**
There are 13 Brook Advisory family planning clinics in central London. Call the above number to find your nearest. Advice is given on contraception, sexual health and abortion with referral to an NHS hospital or private clinic. This branch offers a walk-in clinic noon-6pm Mon-Thur; noon-2pm Fri, Sat. Brook is primarily aimed at young people (it's free for under-21s).

Marie Stopes House

Family Planning Clinic/ Well Woman Centre
108 Whitfield Street, W1 (family planning 020 7388 0662/ termination 0845 300 8090). Warren Street tube. **Open** 9am-5pm Mon, Thur-Sat; 9am-8pm Tue, Wed. **Map 5 J5**
Contraceptives, treatment and advice for gynaecological complaints, counselling for sexual problems and referral for abortion. Fees vary. There's a walk in clinic 10am-12.30pm Sat.
Website: www.mariestopes.org.uk

Dental services

Dental care is free under the NHS to the following British residents:

- Under-18s.
- Under-19s in full-time education.
- Pregnant women and those with a baby under the age of one when treatment begins.
- People receiving Income Support, Jobseeker's Allowance, Family Credit or Disability Working Allowance.

All other patients, NHS or private, must pay. NHS charges start from around £4 for a check-up or a filling. To find an NHS dentist, get in touch with the local Health Authority or a Citizens' Advice Bureau (*see page 325*). Private dentists can charge whatever they like. We list emergency services below.

Dental Emergency Care Service

(020 7955 2186). **Open** 8.45am-3.30pm Mon-Fri.
The Dental Emergency Care Service refers callers to a surgery open for treatment (private or NHS).

Guy's Hospital Dental School

Guy's Tower, St Thomas Street, SE1 (020 7955 4317). London Bridge tube/rail. **Open** 9am-3pm Mon-Fri. **Map 12 Q8**
Walk-in dental emergency service. Free, except weekends (phone first).

Doctors & medication

If you are a British citizen or working in the UK, you can go to any general practitioner (GP). If you are not visiting your usual GP, you will be asked for details of the doctor with whom you are registered. People who are ordinarily resident in the UK, including overseas students, can also register with an NHS doctor.

Many drugs cannot be bought over the counter. A pharmacist will dispense medicines on receipt of a prescription from a GP. An NHS prescription costs £5.90 at present (some people, such as children under the age of 16 and people over 60, are exempt from paying, and contraception is free). If you are not eligible to see an NHS doctor, you will be charged cost price for medicines prescribed by a private doctor.

Great Chapel Street Medical Centre

13 Great Chapel Street, W1 (020 7437 9360/gcs.medical@virgin.net). Tottenham Court Road tube.

Open 11am-12.30pm Mon, Tue, Thur; 2-4pm Mon-Fri (phone for available times). **Map 6 K6**
Walk-in NHS surgery for anyone without a doctor.

Medicine: complementary

British Homeopathic Association

27A Devonshire Street, W1N 1RJ (020 7935 2163). **Open** *phone enquiries* 1.30-5pm Mon-Fri.
The BHA will give you the address of your nearest homeopathic chemist and doctor (send a 60p stamped self-addressed envelope for a list).

Physiotherapy

Chartered Society of Physiotherapy

14 Bedford Row, WC1R 4ED (020 7242 1941/csp@csphysio.org.uk). **Open** *phone enquiries* 9am-5pm Mon-Fri.
The professional body of physiotherapists. The CSP can check whether any practitioner is a qualified member.
Website: www.csp.org.uk

STDs/HIV/AIDS

NHS Genito-Urinary Clinics (such as the **Centre for Sexual Health**; *see below*) are affiliated to major hospitals. They provide free, confidential treatment of sexually transmitted diseases (STDs) and other problems such as thrush and cystitis. They offer information and counselling about HIV and other STDs and can conduct a confidential blood test to determine HIV status. *See also below* **Helplines & information**, and *page 324* **Contraception/abortion**.

AIDS Helpline

(0800 567123/minicom 0800 521261). **Open** 24 hours daily.
A free and confidential information service. The helpline (0800 917 227) caters for various languages at 6-10pm on the days indicated: Gujarati (Mon), Urdu (Tue), Arabic (Wed), Hindi (Fri), Punjabi (Sat) and Cantonese (Sun).

Body Positive

14 Greek Street, W1 (020 7287 8010/helpline 0800 616212). Tottenham Court Road or Leicester Square tube. **Open** 9am-9pm Mon; 9am-7pm Tue-Thur; 9am-6pm Fri; noon-5pm Sat; *helpline* 7-10pm Mon-Fri; 4-10pm Sat, Sun. **Map 6 K6**
Run by and for people who are HIV-positive and their families, Body Positive offers complementary therapies and counselling by appointment. Courses are available for those who have been recently diagnosed and a newsletter is published monthly.
Website: www.bodypositive.org.uk

Centre for Sexual Health

Genito-Urinary Clinic, Jefferiss Wing, St Mary's Hospital, Praed Street, W2 (020 7886 1697). Paddington tube/ rail. **Open** 8.45am-5pm Mon; 8.45am-6pm Tue, Fri; 10.45am-6pm Wed; 8am-1pm Thur; 10am-noon Sat; new patients must arrive at least 30mins before closing. **Map 2 D5**
Walk-in clinic; free and confidential.

Terrence Higgins Trust

52-54 Gray's Inn Road, WC1 (admin 020 7831 0330/helpline 020 7242 1010/legal line 020 7405 2381). **Open** *helpline* noon-10pm daily; *legal line* 7-9pm Mon, Wed.
The Trust advises and counsels those with HIV/AIDS, their relatives, lovers and friends. Free leaflets about AIDS are available. The Trust also gives advice about safer sex.
Website: www.tht.org.uk

Helplines & information

See also above **STDs/HIV/AIDS**. For gay and lesbian helplines *see page 268*.

Alcoholics Anonymous

(020 7833 0022). **Open** *helpline* 10am-10pm daily.
A helpline for the London area. Operators put you in touch with a member in your area who can act as an escort to your first meeting.
Website: www.alcoholics-anonymous.org.uk

Capital Radio Helpline

(020 7484 4000). **Open** *helpline* 10am-10pm Mon-Fri; 10am-4pm Sat, Sun.
This helpline tackles queries about anything. If the staff can't answer your query themselves, they'll put you in touch with someone who can. It's always busy, so keep trying.

Childline

Freepost 1111, London N1 OBR (0800 1111/020 7239 1000). **Open** *phone lines* 24 hours daily.
Free and confidential national helpline for children and young people in trouble or danger.
Website: www.childline.org.uk

Just Ask

50 Crispin Street, E1 (020 7247 0180). Liverpool Street tube/rail. **Open** *counselling* 10am-9pm Mon-Thur; 10am-5pm Fri; *helpline* 10am-6pm Mon-Thur (after-hours answerphone). **Map 12 R6**
Counselling is targeted at people aged 35 and under who are homeless, unemployed or on a low income, but advice will be given to anyone with a personal problem. Closed in August.

London Rape Crisis Centre

(020 7837 1600).
Free, confidential rape counselling. Due to cuts in funding, there are no set opening times for this phone line.

Medical Advisory Service

(020 8994 9874). **Open** 6-9pm Mon-Fri.
Helpline for most medical problems.

MIND

Granta House, 15-19 Broadway, E15 (020 8519 2122/info line 020 8522 1728/0345 660163/info@mind.org.uk). **Open** *info line* 9.15am-4.45pm Mon-Fri.
Callers to the mental health charity MIND will be referred to one of 34 London groups. MIND's legal service advises on maltreatment, wrongful detention and sectioning.
Website: www.mind.org.uk

Narcotics Anonymous

(020 7730 0009). **Open** 10am-10pm daily.
Run by members of the fellowship, this helpline offers advice and informs callers of their nearest meeting.
Website: www.ukna.org

National Association of Citizens' Advice Bureaux

Greater London Office, 136-144 City Road, EC1 (020 7549 0800). **Open** *phone enquiries* 9am-5pm Mon-Fri.
CABs are run by local councils, and offer free advice on legal, financial and personal matters. The above office does not give advice itself but will direct callers to their nearest CAB.

Rape and Sexual Abuse Centre

(020 8239 1122). **Open** noon-2.30pm, 7-9.30pm, Mon-Fri; 2.30-5pm Sat, Sun.
Offers support and information to those who have experienced rape or sexual abuse.

Refuge Helpline

(0990 995443). **Open** 24 hours daily.
Refuge referral for women suffering domestic violence. An after-hours answerphone gives alternative numbers for immediate help.

Rights of Women

(020 7251 6577). **Open** 2-4pm, 7-9pm, Tue-Thur; noon-2pm Fri.
This service provides legal advice for women.

Samaritans

(020 7734 2800). **Open** 24 hours daily.
The Samaritans will listen to anyone with emotional problems. It's a popular service so do persevere when phoning.

Victim Support

National Office, Cranmer House, 39 Brixton Road, SW9 (0845 303 0900/ fax 020 7582 5712). Oval tube. **Open** *support line* 9am-9pm Mon-Fri; 9am-7pm Sat, Sun.
Victims of crime are put in touch with a volunteer who provides emotional and practical support, including information on legal procedures and advice on compensation. Interpreters can be arranged.

Insurance

Insuring personal belongings is highly advisable, and difficult to arrange once you have arrived in London, so organise it before you leave home.

Medical insurance is often included in travel insurance packages, and it's important to have it unless your country has a reciprocal medical treatment arrangement with Britain (*see page 323*). EU citizens (and those from Iceland, Norway and Liechtenstein) are entitled to free emergency healthcare in hospitals under the NHS. Those wanting specific treatment under the NHS will need form E112, while citizens of these countries studying in the UK for less than six months are entitled to full NHS treatment if they have form E128.

Left luggage

Airports

Gatwick Airport
(South Terminal 01293 502014/ North Terminal 01293 502013).

Heathrow Airport
(Terminal 1 020 8745 5301/ Terminal 2/3 020 8759 3344/ Terminal 4 020 8745 7460).

London City Airport
(020 7646 0000).

Luton Airport
(01582 423289).

Stansted Airport
(01279 663213).

Railway stations

In order to find out which train stations have the facilities to store luggage call 020 7928 5151.

Lost property

Always inform the police if you lose anything (to validate insurance claims). See the *Yellow Pages* for your nearest police station. Only dial the emergency number (999) if violence has occurred. A lost passport should be reported to the police and to your embassy (*see pages 328 & 323*).

Airports

The following lost property offices deal only with items lost in the airports concerned. For property lost on the plane contact the airline or handling agents dealing with the flight.

Gatwick Airport
(01293 503162).

Heathrow Airport
(020 8745 7727).

London City Airport
(020 7646 0640/020 7646 0782).

Luton Airport
(01582 423289).

Stansted Airport
(01279 680500).

Buses & tubes

London Transport *Lost Property Office, 200 Baker Street, NW1 (recorded info 020 7486 2496). Baker Street tube.* **Open** 9.30am-2pm Mon-Fri. **Map 5 G4**
Allow three days from the time of loss. If you lose something on a bus, call 020 7222 1234 and ask for the phone numbers of the depots at either end of the route. Pick up a lost property form from any tube station.

Railway stations

If you have lost property in an overground station or on a train, call 020 7928 5151; an operator will connect you to the appropriate station.

Taxis

Taxi Lost Property *15 Penton Street, N1 (020 7833 0996). Angel tube.* **Map 9 N2**
This office deals only with property that has been found in registered black cabs. For items lost in a minicab you will have to contact the office from which you hired the cab.

Money

For the time being at least the nation's currency remains the pound sterling (£). One pound equals 100 pence (p). 1p and 2p coins are copper; 5p, 10p, 20p and the seven-sided 50p coins are silver; the £1 coin is yellowy-gold; the £2 coin is silver in the centre with a circle of yellowy-gold around the edge. Paper notes are as follows: blue £5, orange £10, purple £20 and red £50. Note, though, that you will probably find an increasing number of places pre-empting the Government and accepting euros – but don't rely on this.

You can exchange foreign currency at banks and bureaux de change (*see page 328*). If you're here for a long stay, you may need to open a bank or building society account. To do this, you'll probably need to present a reference from your bank at home, and certainly a passport as identification.

Banks

Minimum opening hours are 9.30am-3.30pm Monday to Friday, but most branches close at 4.30pm. Cash can be obtained at any time from ATMs outside most banks, which you'll also find in some major tube and train stations.

Exchange and commission rates vary considerably; it pays to shop around. Commission is sometimes charged for cashing travellers' cheques in foreign currencies, but not for sterling travellers' cheques, provided you cash the cheques at a bank affiliated to the issuing bank (get a list when you buy your cheques). Commission is charged if you change cash into another currency. You always need identification, such as a passport, when exchanging travellers' cheques.

Bureaux de change

You will be charged for cashing travellers' cheques or buying and selling foreign currency at a bureau de change. Commission rates, which should be clearly displayed, vary. **Chequepoint** (13 London branches), **Lenlyn** (25 London branches) and **Thomas Cook** (149 London branches; many within Midland Bank) are reputable bureaux. Major rail and tube stations in central London have bureaux de change, and there are many in tourist areas. Most are open 8am-10pm, but those listed below are open 24 hours daily.

Chequepoint

548 Oxford Street, W1 (020 7723 1005). Marble Arch tube. **Map 5 G6**

222 Earl's Court Road, SW5 (020 7370 3238). Earl's Court tube. **Map 3 B10**

2 Queensway, W2 (020 7229 0093). Queensway tube. **Map 1 C6**

Lost/stolen credit cards

Report lost or stolen credit cards immediately to both the police and the 24-hour services listed below. Inform your bank by phone and in writing.

American Express *(01273 696933).*

Diners Club/Diners Club International *(general enquiries & emergencies 01252 513500/ 0800 460800).*

Eurocard *(00 49 697 933 1910). This German number will accept reversed charges in an emergency.*

JCB *(020 7499 3000).*

MasterCard *(0800 964767).*

Switch *(0113 277 8899).*

Visa/Connect *(0800 895082).*

Money transfers

Western Union

(0800 833833).

The old standby for bailing cash-challenged travellers out of trouble – but it's certainly pricey. Expect to pay a whopping 10%-plus commission.

Police & security

The police are a good source of information about the locality and are used to helping visitors find their way. If you have been robbed, assaulted or involved in an infringement of the law, look under 'Police' in the phone directory for the nearest police station, or call directory enquiries (free from public payphones) on 192.

If you have a complaint to make about the police, there are several things you can do. Make sure that you take the offending police officer's identifying number, which should be prominently displayed on his or her epaulette. You can then register a complaint with the **Police Complaints Authority**, 10 Great George Street, SW1P 3AE (020 7273 6450). Alternatively, contact any police station or visit a solicitor or a Law Centre.

Violent crime is relatively rare in London, but, as in any major city, it is unwise to take any risks. Thieves and pickpockets specifically target unwary tourists. Use common sense and follow these basic rules:

- **Keep** your wallet and purse out of sight. Don't wear a wrist wallet (they are easily snatched). Keep your handbag securely closed.
- **Don't** leave a handbag, briefcase, bag or coat unattended, especially in pubs, cinemas, department stores or fast-food shops, on public transport, at railway stations and airports, or in crowds.
- **Don't** leave your bag or coat beside, under or on the back of your chair.
- **Don't** put your bag on the floor near the door of a public toilet.
- **Don't** wear expensive jewellery or watches that can be easily snatched.
- **Don't** keep your passport, money, credit cards, etc, together. If you lose one, you'll lose all.
- **Don't** put your purse down on the table in a restaurant or on a shop counter while you scrutinise the bill.
- **Don't** carry a wallet in your back pocket.
- **Don't** flash your money or credit cards around.
- **Avoid** parks after dark. Late at night, travel in groups of three or more.

Postal services

Post office opening hours are usually 9am-5.30pm Monday to Friday; 9am-noon Saturday, with the exception of **Trafalgar Square Post Office** (24-28 William IV Street, WC2; 020 74849304; Charing Cross tube/rail), which is open 8am-8pm Monday to Thursday; 8.30am-8pm Friday; 9am-8pm Saturday. The busiest time of day is usually 1-2pm. Listed below are the other main central London post offices.

There's a central number for all post office enquiries (**0345 223344**) or check the website www.postoffice.co.uk.

43-44 Albemarle Street, W1 (020 7493 5620). Green Park tube. **Map 7 J7**

111 Baker Street, W1 (020 7935 3701). Baker Street tube. **Map 5 G5**

202 Great Portland Street, W1 (020 7636 9935). Great Portland Street tube. **Map 5 H4**

32A Grosvenor Street, W1 (020 7629 2480). Bond Street tube. **Map 7 H7**

3-9 Heddon Street, W1 (020 7734 5556). Piccadilly Circus tube. **Map 7 J7**

19 Newman Street, W1 (020 7636 9995). Tottenham Court Road tube. **Map 5 J5**

43 Seymour Street, W1 (020 7723 0867). Marble Arch tube. **Map 2 F6**

Poste restante

If you intend to travel around Britain, friends from home can write to you care of a post office, where mail will be kept at the enquiry desk for up to one month. Your name and 'Poste Restante' must be clearly marked on the letter above the following address: Post Office,

24-28 William IV Street, London WC2N 4DL. Bring ID when you come to collect mail.

Stamp prices

You can buy stamps at all post offices and also at many newsagents. Current prices are 19p for second-class and 27p for first-class letters and letters to EU countries. Postcards cost 36p to send within Europe and 45p to countries outside Europe. Rates for other letters and parcels vary according to weight and destination.

Public holidays

On public holidays (known as bank holidays) many shops remain open, but public transport services are less frequent. The exception is Christmas Day, when almost everything closes down.

New Year's Eve Sun 31 Dec 2000.
New Year's Day Mon 1 Jan 2001.
Good Friday Fri 21 Apr 2000; Fri 13 Apr 2001.
Easter Monday Mon 24 Apr 2000; Mon 16 Apr 2001.
May Day Holiday Mon 1 May 2000; Mon 7 May 2001.
Spring Bank Holiday Mon 29 May 2000; Mon 28 May 2001.
Summer Bank Holiday Mon 28 Aug 2000; Mon 27 Aug 2001.
Christmas Day Mon 25 Dec 2000; Tue 25 Dec 2001.
Boxing Day Tue 26 Dec 2000; Wed 26 Dec 2001.

Religion

Anglican

St Paul's Cathedral
For listings details see p54.
Services 7.30am, 8am, 12.30pm, 5pm, Mon-Fri; 8am, 8.30am, 12.30pm, 5pm, Sat; 8am, 10.15am, 11.30am, 3.15pm, 6pm, Sun. **Map 11 O6**
Times vary due to special events, phone to check.

Westminster Abbey
For listings details see p90.
Services 7.30am, 8am (Holy Communion), 12.30pm, 5pm (choral evensong, except Wed), Mon-Fri; 8am, 9.20am, 3pm (evensong), Sat; 8am, 10am (sung matins), 11.15am (abbey eucharist), 3pm (evensong), 5.45pm organ recital, 6.30pm (evening service), Sun.
Map 8 K9

Baptist

Bloomsbury Central Baptist Church
235 Shaftesbury Avenue, WC2 (020 7240 0544). Tottenham Court Road tube. **Open** 10am-4pm daily; *Friendship Centre* (closed Aug) 11.30am-2.30pm Tue; 10.30am-8.30pm Sun (closed during services). **Services** 11am, 6.30pm, Sun.
Map 6 L6
Website: www.bloomsbury.org.uk

Buddhist

Buddhapadipa Temple
14 Calonne Road, SW19 (020 8946 1357). Wimbledon tube then 93 bus. **Open** *temple* 1-6pm Sat; 10am-6pm, Sun; *meditation retreat* 7-9pm Tue, Thur; 4-6pm Sat, Sun.
Website: www.buddhapadipa.org

Catholic

Brompton Oratory
For listings details see p93.
Services 7am, 7.30am, 8am (Latin mass), 10am, 12.30am, 6pm, Mon-Fri; 7am, 7.30am, 8am, 10am, 6pm, Sat; 7am, 8am, 9am, 10am (tridentine), 11am (sung Latin), 12.30pm, 4.30pm, 7pm, Sun. **Map 4 E10**

Westminster Cathedral
For listings details see p91.
Services eight daily masses Mon-Fri; seven daily masses Sat; 7am, 8am, 9am, 10.30am, noon, 5.30pm, 7pm, Sun. **Map 7 J10**

Hindu

Swaminarayan Hindu Mission
105-119 Brentfield Road, NW10 (enquiries to Amrish Patel on 020 8961 5031). Neasden tube or Harlesden tube/rail. **Open** 9am-6.30pm daily. **Services** 11.45am, 7pm, daily.
In addition to a large prayer hall, this huge complex provides north-west London's Hindu community with a social and cultural centre, comprising a conference hall, a marriage suite, sports facilities, a library and a health clinic. *See also p142.*

Islamic

London Central Mosque
146 Park Road, NW8 (020 7724 3363). Baker Street tube/74 bus. **Open** dawn-dusk daily. **Services** phone to check.

East London Mosque
82-92 Whitechapel Road, E1 (020 7247 1357). Aldgate East or Whitechapel tube. **Open** phone to check. **Services** *Friday prayer* 1.30pm (1pm in winter). **Map 12 S6**
Website: www.eastlondon-mosque.org.uk

Jewish

Liberal Jewish Synagogue
28 St John's Wood Road, NW8 (020 7286 5181). St John's Wood tube. **Open** *enquiries* 9am-5pm Mon-Thur; 9am-1pm Fri. **Services** 6.45pm Fri; 11am Sat.

West Central Liberal Synagogue
109 Whitfield Street, SW1 (020 7636 7627). Warren Street tube. **Services** 3pm Sat. **Map 5 J4**

Methodist

Methodist Central Hall
Westminster Central Hall, Storey's Gate, SW1 (020 7222 8010). St James's Park tube. **Open** *Chapel* 9am-5pm Mon-Fri. **Services** 12.45pm Wed; 10am, 11am, 6.30pm, Sun. **Map 8 K9**
Website: www.wch.co.uk

Quaker

Religious Society of Friends (Quakers)
Friends House, 173-177 Euston Road, NW1 (020 7387 3601). Euston tube/rail. **Open** 8.30am-9pm Mon-Fri. **Meetings** 11am Sun.
Map 6 K3
Website: www.quaker.org.uk

Telephones

The codes for London are changing in 2000. The old 0171 and 0181 codes will be replaced by a new code **020** with a **7** or **8** added to the original seven-digit number to create a new eight-digit number. For example, 0171 813 3000 becomes 020 7813 3000. The old and new systems will actually run in parallel until 14 October 2000, after which only the new numbers will work.

If you want to call a London number from within London, you omit the 020 code and dial the last eight digits (eg 7813 3000; although prior to 22 April 2000 you will need to include the 020 code). If you are calling from outside the UK, you omit the first 0 of the 020 code and dial 00 44 (the UK code), then 20 for London, then the eight digit number (eg 00 44 20 7813 3000). To dial a mobile number you need the full code.

In this Guide we list only the new numbers. For help and information call 0800 224 2000.

International dialling codes

Australia (*00 61*); **Austria** (*00 43*); **Belgium** (*00 32*); **Brazil** (*00 55*);

Canada *(00 1)*; **Czech Republic** *(00 42)*; **Denmark** *(00 45)*; **France** *(00 33)*; **Germany** *(00 49)*; **Greece** *(00 30)*; **Hong Kong** *(00 852)*; **India** *(00 91)*; **Iceland** *(00 354)*; **Ireland** *(00 353)*; **Israel** *(00 972)*; **Italy** *(00 39)*; **Japan** *(00 81)*; **Netherlands** *(00 31)*; **New Zealand** *(00 64)*; **Norway** *(00 47)*; **Portugal** *(00 351)*; **South Africa** *(00 27)*; **Spain** *(00 34)*; **Sweden** *(00 46)*; **Switzerland** *(00 41)*; **USA** *(00 1)*.

Operator services

Operator

Call **100** for the operator in the following circumstances: when you have difficulty in dialling; for an early-morning alarm call; to make a credit card call; for information about the cost of a call; and for help with international person-to-person calls.

Dial **155** if you need to reverse the charges (call collect) or if you can't dial direct, but be warned that this service is very expensive.

Directory enquiries

Dial **192** for any number in Britain, or **153** for international numbers. Phoning directory enquiries from a private phone is expensive, and only two enquiries are allowed per call. However, if you phone from a public call box, calls are free.

International telemessages/telegrams

Call **0800 190190** to phone in your message and it will be delivered by post the next day (£8.99 for up to 50 words, an additional £1 for a greeting card). There is no longer a domestic telegram service, but you can still send telegrams abroad. Call the same number if you urgently need to contact someone abroad.

Talking Pages

This 24-hour free service lists the numbers of thousands of businesses in the UK. Dial **0800 600900** and say what type of business you require, and in what area of London.

Public phones

Public payphones take coins, credit cards or prepaid phonecards (sometimes all three). The minimum cost is 10p, but some payphones (such as counter-top ones found in many pubs) require a minimum of 20p.

British Telecom phonecards

Available from post offices and many newsagents. **Cost** 10p per unit; cards in denominations of £2, £5, £10 and £20.

Call boxes with the green Phonecard symbol take prepaid cards. A notice in the call box tells you where to find the nearest stockist. A digital display shows how many units you have remaining on your card.

Telephone directories

There are three phone directories for London: two for private numbers and one for companies. These are available at post offices and libraries. Hotels have them too and they are issued free to all residents, as is the *Yellow Pages* directory, which lists businesses and services.

Time & the seasons

Every year in spring (26 Mar 2000; 25 Mar 2001) the UK puts its clocks forward by one hour to give British Summer Time (BST). In autumn (29 Oct 2000; 28 Oct 2001) the clocks go back by one hour to rejoin Greenwich Mean Time (GMT).

Prepare yourself for the unpredictability of the British climate. For some guidance try **Weathercall** on 0891 500401 (50p per minute at all times). The figures in the chart opposite have been provided by the Met Office and give a rough indication of what to expect.

Spring extends approximately from March to May, though winter often seems to stretch well beyond February. March winds and April showers may turn up either a month early or a month late. May is generally very pleasant.

Summer – June, July and August – can be unpredictable. Searing heat one day followed by sultry greyness and thunderstorms the next. The combination of high temperatures, humidity and the city's pollution can create problems for anyone with hayfever or breathing difficulties – so head for the open spaces.

Autumn starts in September, although the weather can still have a mild, summery feel. Real autumn comes with October when the leaves start to fall. Then the cold sets in and November hits with a reminder that London is situated on a fairly northerly latitude.

Winter may contain the odd mild day, but don't bank on it. December, January and February are generally pretty chilly in London, although snow is rare. A crisp, sunny winter's day in the capital is hard to beat.

Tipping

In Britain it's accepted that you tip in taxis, minicabs, restaurants (some waiting staff are forced to rely heavily on gratuities), hairdressers, hotels and some bars (not pubs) – ten per cent is normal, with some restaurants adding up to 15 per cent. Be careful to check whether service has been added automatically to your bill. Too many restaurants include service in the bill and then leave the space for a gratuity on your credit card slip blank.

Tourist information

The **London Tourist Board** (LTB; 020 7932 2000) runs the information centres listed below; these centres can supply a free map of central London. You can also ring **London Line 2000** (09068 663344; calls cost 60p per minute), a recorded information service with several different lines providing information on events and entertainment for adults and children. See also its website www.londontown. com. The opening times below are for winter; hours are usually extended for the rest of the year.

Heathrow Terminals 1, 2, 3 *Tube station concourse, Heathrow Airport.* **Open** 8am-6pm daily.

Liverpool Street Station *Tube station concourse, EC2.* **Open** 8am-6pm daily. **Map 10 R5**

Victoria Station *Victoria Station forecourt, SW1.* **Open** 8am-7pm Mon-Sat; 8am-6pm Sun. **Map 7 H10**

Waterloo International Terminal *Arrivals Hall, SE1.* **Open** 8.30am-10.30pm daily. **Map 8 M8**

For information on travel in the rest of Britain, *see page 302*. There are also tourist information offices in Greenwich (*see page 122*), next to St Paul's (*see page 50;* **Map 11 06**) and on the south side of London Bridge (**Map 12 Q8**).

Weather report

Average daytime temperatures, rainfall and daily hours of sunshine in London

	Jan	Feb	Mar	Apr	May	June
Temperature °C/°F	6/43	6/43	8/46	10/50	13/55	16/61
Rainfall mm/in	45/1.8	30/1.2	43/1.7	37/1.5	47/1.9	44/1.8
Hours of sunshine	1.9	2.5	3.3	5.3	6.3	6.2
	July	**Aug**	**Sept**	**Oct**	**Nov**	**Dec**
Temperature °C/°F	19/66	19/66	16/61	13/55	9/48	7/45
Rainfall mm/in	46/1.8	42/1.7	39/1.6	56/2.2	46/1.8	49/2.0
Hours of sunshine	6.7	6.6	5.0	3.5	2.3	1.5

Visas

Citizens of EU countries do not require a visa to visit the UK; citizens of other countries, including the USA, Canada and New Zealand, require a valid passport for a visit of up to six months.

To apply for a visa, and to check your visa status **before you travel**, contact the British Embassy, High Commission or Consulate in your own country. The visa allows you entry for a maximum of six months. For information about work permits, which must be arranged before entering the UK, *see page 332*.

To obtain visas to other countries, contact the embassies concerned (*see page 323*), or have the paperwork handled for you – for a fee – by **Rapid Visa** or **Ferguson Snell**. However, certain countries, including Italy, Canada, Guyana and Japan, require personal applications.

Ferguson Snell & Associates

10/11 Heathfield Terrace, W4 4JE (020 8747 3004/ fs@fergusonsnell.co.uk). Chiswick Park tube. **Open** 9am-5.30pm Mon-Fri.

Ferguson Snell will sort out work permits and extensions to your UK visa for up to six months. It charges from £350 for the service and also arranges visas for other countries.
Website: www.fergusonsnell.co.uk

Home Office

Immigration & Nationality Directorate, Block C, Whitgift Centre, Wellesley Road, Croydon CR0 1AT (0870 606 7766). **Open** *phone enquiries* 8.45am-4.45pm Mon-Thur; 8.45am-4.30pm Fri.

The immigration department of the Home Office deals with queries about immigration matters, visas and work permits for citizens from Commonwealth and a few other countries. If all you require is an application form, then call 0870 241 0645.
Website: www.homeoffice.gov.uk/ind/hpg.htm

Rapid Visa

Adventure Travel Centre, 135 Earl's Court Road, SW5 (020 7373 3026). Earl's Court tube. **Open** 9am-5.30pm Mon-Fri; 9.30am-12.30pm Sat. **Credit** £TC. **Map 3 B11**

Can arrange visas for most countries.

Working in London

Finding temporary employment in London can be a full-time job in itself. But providing you can speak English well, are an EU citizen or have a work permit, you should be able to find something in catering, labouring, bar/pub or shop work. Graduates with an English or foreign-language degree could try teaching. If your English isn't great, there's always the mind-numbing distributing of free magazines. You can also try for seasonal work in tourist spots; local councils sometimes take on summer staff such as play-group leaders or swimming pool attendants. Ideas can be found in *Summer Jobs in Britain*, published by Vacation Work, 9 Park End Street, Oxford OX1 1HJ (£9.99 plus £1.50 p&p). The **Central Bureau for Educational Visits & Exchanges** (*see page 332*) has other publications.

To find work, look in the *Evening Standard*, local and national papers and news-agents' windows. Employers advertise vacancies on Jobcentre noticeboards; there is often temporary and unskilled work available. Most districts of London have a Jobcentre; look in *Yellow Pages* under 'Employment Agencies'.

For office work, sign on with temp agencies. If you have good shorthand, typing (40 words per minute upwards) or wordprocessing skills, and dress the part, such agencies might find you well-paid assignments. If you're desperate, try one of the fast-food chains.

Work for foreign visitors

With few exceptions, citizens of non-European Economic Area (EEA) countries (*see below*) need a work permit before they are legally able to work in the UK. One of the advantages of working in the UK is the opportunity to meet people, but for any employment it's essential that you speak reasonable English. For office work you need a high standard of English and relevant skills.

Work permits

EEA citizens, residents of Gibraltar and certain categories of other overseas nationals do not require a work permit. However, others who wish to come to the UK to work must obtain a permit before setting out.

The prospective employer who has a vacancy that they are unable to fill with a resident or EEA national must apply for a permit to the Department for Education & Employment (*see below*). Permits are issued only for jobs that carry a high level of skill and experience. The employer must be able to demonstrate to the DfEE that there is no resident/EEA labour available.

There is a Training & Work Experience Scheme that enables non-EEA nationals to come to the UK for training towards a professional or specialist qualification, or to undertake a short period of managerial-level work experience. Again, this should be applied for before coming to the UK. Listed below are other possibilities.

Au pairs

The option of au pairing is only open to citizens of certain countries (*see below*) who are aged between 17 and 27. Try contacting an agency in your own country or look in *Yellow Pages* under 'Employment Agencies'. Such work usually provides free accommodation, but wages tend to be low. The following countries are included in the **Au Pair Scheme**: Andorra, Bosnia-Herzegovina, Croatia, Cyprus, Czech Republic, Faroe Islands, Greenland, Hungary, Macedonia, Malta, Monaco, San Marino, Slovak Republic, Slovenia, Switzerland and Turkey.

Sandwich students

Students at a recognised UK university or college can undertake work placements that are essential to obtain their qualifications. Approval for such placements must be obtained by the college from the DfEE's **Overseas Labour Service** (*see below* **Department for Education & Employment**).

Students

Visiting students from the US, Canada, Australia or Jamaica can get a blue BUNAC card enabling them to work in the UK for up to six months. BUNAC cards are not difficult to obtain, but they must be acquired before entering the country. Contact the Work in Britain Department of the **Council on International Educational Exchange** or call **BUNAC** (*see below*), a non-profit-making organisation that arranges work exchange programmes for students from these countries. BUNAC students should obtain an application form OSS1 (BUNAC) from BUNAC before starting work in the UK. This should be submitted to the nearest Jobcentre to obtain permission to work.

Non-EEA nationals in the UK as students who wish to take casual part-time or vacation employment unconnected to their course of study must obtain the permission of their local Employment Service Jobcentre. The Jobcentre will provide an application form (OSS1) for completion by the student, their college and the prospective employer.

Voluntary workers

Voluntary work in youth hostels (*see p159*) can provide board, lodging and some pocket money. For advice on voluntary work with charities contact the **Home Office** (*see below*).

Working holidaymakers

Citizens of Commonwealth countries, aged 17-27, may apply to come to the UK as a working holidaymaker. This allows them to take part-time work without a DfEE permit. They must contact their nearest British Diplomatic Post to obtain the necessary entry clearance before travelling to the UK.

Useful addresses

BUNAC

16 Bowling Green Lane, EC1 (020 7251 3472/www.bunac.org). Farringdon tube/rail.

Central Bureau for Educational Visits & Exchanges

British Council, 10 Spring Gardens, SW1 (020 7930 8466). Charing Cross tube/rail. **Open** 9am-5pm Mon-Fri. **Map 8 K8**
This office deals with the organisation of visits outside the UK, but otherwise you can obtain copies of its useful publications.
Website: www.britishcouncil.org

Council on International Educational Exchange

Work in Britain Department, 205 East 42nd Street, New York, NY 10017, USA (00 1 212 822 2600).

Department for Education & Employment

Overseas Labour Service, Level 5, Moorfoot, Sheffield S1 4PQ (0114 259 4074/sec.ols@dfee.gov.uk). **Open** *phone enquiries* 9am-5pm Mon-Fri.
Not open to personal visits, but you can call the above enquiry line. Employers seeking work permit application forms should phone 0990 210224 or visit the website.
Website: www.dfee.gov.uk/ols

Home Office

Immigration & Nationality Directorate, Block C, Whitgift Centre, Wellesley Road, Croydon CR0 1AT (0870 606 7766). **Open** *phone enquiries* 8.45am-4.45pm Mon-Thur; 8.45am-4.30pm Fri.
Will give advice on whether a work permit is required.
Website: www.homeoffice.gov.uk/ind/hpg.htm

Overseas Visitors Records Office

180 Borough High Street, SE1 (020 7230 1208). Borough or Elephant & Castle tube/London Bridge tube/rail. **Open** 9am-4.30pm Mon-Fri. **Map 11 P9**
Formerly the Aliens Registration Office run by the Metropolitan Police, the Overseas Visitors Records Office charges £34 to register a person if they have a work permit.

Getting to London

By air

Gatwick Airport

(01293 535353). About 30 miles (50km) south of central London, off the M23.

Three rail services link Gatwick to London. The **Gatwick Express** to Victoria Station takes about 30-35 minutes and runs 24 hours daily, every 15 minutes, then every hour between 12.30am and 5am. Tickets cost £10.20 single, £20.40 return (valid for one month), £11.70 day return (after 9.30am); half-price for under-15s; free for under-5s.

Connex South Central also runs a service between Gatwick and Victoria, with trains running approximately every 15 minutes during the day and every hour between 1am and 4am. It takes between three and eight minutes longer than the Gatwick Express but, on the plus side, tickets are cheaper, costing £8.20 single, £16.40 return (valid for one month), £8.30 day return (after 9.30am); half-price for under-15s; free for under-5s.

There is also a **Thameslink** service that might be more convenient if you are staying in the Bloomsbury area or want to connect with trains at King's Cross or Euston. It runs via Blackfriars, City Thameslink, Farringdon and King's Cross, and frequency and journey times vary depending on the time of day. Tickets (to King's Cross) cost £9.50 single, £19 return.

The **Jetlink 777** bus (020 8668 7261/01737 242411) to Victoria Coach Station (*see p302*) is the cheapest option, but the journey time is about 90 minutes. Buses run 5am-8pm daily, every one or two hours (phone to check). Tickets cost £8 single, £12 return (valid for three months); half-price under-15s; free under-5s.

If you really want your hand held from airport to hotel, you could try **Berkeleys Hotel Connections** (book by phone 01442 251400, fax 01442 255656 or on the website www.berkeleys.co.uk). For £18 per person each way (£16 if booked on the Internet) you go to the welcome desk on the Gatwick Express concourse where you'll be guided to the Gatwick Express train, met at the other end at Victoria Station and taken on to your hotel by minibus.

Forget **taxis** unless you are seriously wealthy – you could end up paying £90 and the journey to central London takes at least an hour.

Heathrow Airport

(0870 000 0123). About 15 miles (24km) west of central London, off the M4.

The **Heathrow Express** service (0845 6001515; 15-20 minutes to Paddington Station) is the quickest and most efficient way of travelling between Heathrow and central London (you can get a taxi at Paddington for your onward journey). The train can be boarded at one of the airport's two underground stations (Terminals 1, 2 & 3 or Terminal 4). Tickets cost £12 each way (£22 return); half-price for under-15s (free if ticket purchased before boarding); free for under-5s. Many airlines, including British Airways, American Airlines and United Airlines, now have check-in desks at Paddington, for both hand-luggage and luggage for the hold.

A longer but far cheaper journey is by tube on the **Piccadilly Line** (50-60mins to Piccadilly Circus). Tickets to central London cost £3.40 one way (£1.40 under-16s). Trains run from about 5.30am to 11.30pm Mon-Sat, 6am-11pm Sun. There's a tube station at Terminal 4 and one for Terminals 1, 2 & 3.

The **Airbus Heathrow Shuttle** (020 7222 1234/020 8400 6655) runs two buses an hour (5am-10.30pm) from all four terminals at Heathrow to 17 points within central London (journey time is about 1hr 45mins to King's Cross). These special double-deckers have ample room for luggage and are all accessible to wheelchair users. Tickets cost £7 single, £12 return (£3 single, £5 return, concs; under-16s free).

There's also the friendly, efficient **Berkeleys Hotel Connections** service (book by phone 01442 251400, fax 01442 255656 or on the website www.berkeleys.co.uk). Terminal 1 and 2 passengers will be met from their flights (Terminal 3 and 4 passengers should go to the welcome desks in the arrivals area). All will be taken to a minibus that will drive them to their hotels. The service costs £12 per person each way (£11 if booked on the Internet).

Taxi fares to central London are high (around £45) and the journey time is about 45-60 minutes (often far longer during the rush hour).

London City Airport

(020 7646 0000). 9 miles (14km) east of central London, Docklands.

Silvertown & City Airport rail station, on the Silverlink Line (*see p339*), is a couple of minutes' walk from the terminal. Its services are approximately every 20 minutes and run via Stratford (interchange with the Central Line tube). Most people travel to London on the blue-and-white **Airbus** service (020 7222 1234), which goes to Liverpool Street Station (30mins journey time) via Canary Wharf. The shuttle bus leaves every 10 minutes 6.50am-9.10pm Mon-Fri, 6.50am-10pm Sat, 11am-10pm Sun; tickets cost £5 to Liverpool Street Station (£2 to Canary Wharf). The journey by **taxi** to the City takes about 30-40 minutes and costs around £21.

Luton Airport

(01582 405100). About 30 miles (50km) north of central London, off the M1 at junction 10.

The building of Luton Airport Parkway rail station enables people to travel direct from the airport to central London. The service, run by Thameslink (national rail enquiries 08457 484950), calls at a number of central London stations including King's Cross. Trains leave every 5-10 minutes, take 30-40 minutes and cost £9 single. Cheap day returns (after 9.30am Mon-Fri) cost £10.10.

For a cheaper but longer journey, the **Green Line** coach service (020 8668 7261) runs from Luton to Victoria Station at 40 minutes past each hour. The journey takes 90 minutes, and costs £7.20 single, £11.80 return (valid for 3 months); half-price under-15s; free for under-5s.

A **taxi** from the airport into central London takes at least an hour and will set you back around £65.

Stansted Airport

(01279 680500). About 35 miles (60km) north-east of central London, off the M11.

The quickest way to get to London is on the **Stansted Express** train (08457 484950) to Liverpool Street Station; the journey time is 40-45 minutes. Trains leave between every 15 and 30 minutes depending on the time of day. Tickets cost £11 single, £12.80 day return (after 9.30am Mon-Fri), £16.10 return within five days (after 9.30am), £22 open return; half-price under-15s.

Jetlink 777 buses run to Victoria Coach Station; the journey takes about 1 hour 40 minutes, with stopoffs at Hendon Central and Finchley Road tube stations and Marble Arch. Prices are £9 single, £13 return (valid for three months), half-price under-16s. By car, the journey to central London takes about an hour.

A **taxi** to central London will cost around £80.

By train

Eurostar

Waterloo International Terminal, SE1 (0990 186186). Waterloo tube/rail. **Map 8 M8**

Probably the most fun way to reach (and escape from) London is via the Channel Tunnel and Eurostar. The company now operates five routes – Paris, Disneyland Paris, Brussels, Lille and the ski train, which goes to Bourg St Maurice and Moutiers (Saturdays only).

Standard class fares to Brussels and Paris range from £65 for a weekend day return (£105 for first class) to £270. If you book at least 14 days in advance and stay two nights or over a Saturday, then the Leisure Apex 14 fare is a bargain £69 return. Look out also for special offers.

Journey time to Paris is three hours, Brussels two hours 40 minutes, the tunnel section taking a measly 22 minutes. Services are frequent: there are currently between 16 and 19 trains a day to Paris from Monday to Saturday, and either ten or 11 to Brussels. On Sundays, there's still a range of services: between ten and 12 trains run to Paris and seven or eight to Brussels.

Getting around London

LT Travel Information Centres

All the information below can be accessed on London Transport's website www.londontransport.co.uk or by phoning **020 7222 1234**. London Transport (LT) centres provide maps and information about the tube, buses and Docklands Light Railway (DLR). You can find them in the following stations:

Euston 7.15am-6pm Mon-Sat; 8.30am-5pm Sun. **Map 6 K3**

Hammersmith Bus Station 7.15am-6pm Mon-Fri; 8.15am-6pm Sat.

Heathrow Airport *Terminals 1, 2 & 3 tube station* 6.30am-7pm Mon-Sat; 7.15am-7pm Sun. *Terminal 1* 7.15am-10pm Mon-Sat; 8.15am-10pm Sun. *Terminal 2* 7.15am-5pm Mon-Sat; 8.15am-5pm Sun. *Terminal 4* 6am-3pm Mon-Sat; 7.15am-3pm Sun.

King's Cross 8am-6pm Mon-Sat; 8.30am-5pm Sun. **Map 6 L2**

Liverpool Street 8am-6pm Mon-Fri; 8.45am-5.30pm Sat, Sun. **Map 10 R5**

Oxford Circus 8.45am-6pm Mon-Sat. **Map 5 J6**

Piccadilly Circus 8.45am-6pm daily. **Map 8 K7**

St James's Park 8.15am-5.30pm Mon-Fri. **Map 8 K9**

Victoria 7.45am-7pm Mon-Sat; 8.45am-7pm Sun. **Map 7 H10**

Fares & Travelcards

Bus and tube fares are based on a zone system. There are six zones stretching 12 miles (20km) out from the centre of

Directory

Trips & tours

Balloon tours

Adventure Balloons *London Road, Winchfield Park, Hartley Wintney, Hampshire, RG27 8HY (01252 844222).* **Flights** *Apr-Oct* morning & evenings daily, weather permitting. **Fares** £125-£175 per person. **Credit** MC, V.
Drift over the capital from the launch site a couple of miles from Tower Bridge.
Website: www.adventureballoons.co.uk

Bicycle tours

See p340.

Bus tours

Big Bus Company *(020 8944 7810/0800 169 1365).* **Open-top bus tours** three different routes, 40mins-1hr; all with live commentary.
Departures every 15mins from Green Park, Victoria and Marble Arch *summer* 8.30am-7pm daily; *winter* 8.30am-4.30pm daily. **Pick-up** Green Park (near The Ritz Hotel); Marble Arch (Speaker's Corner); Victoria (outside Royal Westminster Hotel, Buckingham Palace Road, SW1). **Fares** £15; £6 children; tickets are valid for 24 hours, and are interchangeable between routes, allowing you to hop on and off the bus at over 50 different locations.
Website: www.bigbus.co.uk

London Pride *(01708 631122).* **Departures** *Apr-Sept* phone to check; *Oct-Mar* 8.30am-6pm daily; *grand tour* 1hr 30mins. **Fares** *from* 50p; £12 (for all tours), £6 5s-15s, valid 24 hours. Also routes from Buckingham Palace, Russell Square to the South Kensington museums, Bayswater to Euston Station and Bloomsbury to Tate Gallery.
Website: www.londonpride.co.uk

Original London Sightseeing Tour *(020 8877 1722).* **Departures** *summer* 9am-7pm daily; *winter* 9.30am-5pm daily. **Pick-up** Victoria Street; Grosvenor Gardens; Marble Arch (Speaker's Corner); Baker Street tube (forecourt); Haymarket (at bus stop L); Charing Cross Station (Strand); Charing Cross. **Fares** £12.50; £7.50 concs.
Website: www.theoriginaltour.com

Helicopter tours

Cabair Helicopters *Elstree Aerodrome, Hertfordshire (020 8953 4411). Elstree rail.* **Flights** *from* 11.30am Sun. **Fares** £125 per person for 30mins. **Credit** MC, £TC, V.
Website: www.cabair.com

Personal tours

Tour Guides *(020 7495 5504).* Tailor-made tours with Blue Badge guides for individuals, small or large groups, on foot, by car, coach or boat.

River tours

See p338-9 **Riverboat services**.

Specialist tours

Architectural Dialogue *(020 7267 7697).* **Departures** 10.15am Sat; 10.45am Sun. **Meeting point** outside gates of Royal Academy of

London. Beware of on-the-spot £10 fines for anyone caught travelling without a valid ticket.

Note that for most visitors to London, the **Travelcard** (*see below*) is by far the cheapest way of getting around (although it is not valid before 9.30am Mondays to Fridays).

Adult fares

The single **underground** fare for adults within Zone 1 is £1.50; for Zones 1 and 2, £1.80; rising to £3.50 for an all-zone single fare. Single **bus** fares are 70p for a journey outside Zone 1 and £1 for a journey within Zone 1 or which crosses the Zone 1 boundary. Buying individual tickets is the most expensive way to travel. If you are likely to make three or more journeys in one day, or if you are staying in London for more than a day, it's always better value to buy a Travelcard (*see below*).

Child fares

On all buses, tubes and local trains, children are classified as under 16. Under-5s travel free. Under-16s pay a child's fare until 10pm; after 10pm (buses only) they pay an adult fare. Fourteen- and 15-year-olds must carry Child Rate Photocards, available from any post office: take a passport-size photo and proof of age (passport or birth certificate) with you. The single **underground** fare for children in Zone 1 is 60p; for Zones 1 and 2, 80p; rising to £1.50 for an all-zone ticket. Single child **bus** fares are 40p anywhere in London.

One-Day LT Cards

One-Day LT Cards will only be of interest **if you intend to travel during peak times** (ie before 9.30am on weekdays) and make several journeys during the day. They are valid on buses (but not N-prefixed night buses), underground services (although not those running to and from Bakerloo Line stations north of Queen's Park; this section of track is not run by London Transport) and Docklands Light Railway (DLR) services, but **not** on overland rail services or airbuses. The cards cost £5 for Zones 1 & 2; £6 for Zones 1-4 and £7.50 for zones 1-6 (child £2.50 Zones 1 & 2; £3 Zones 1-4; £3.30 Zones 1-6).

Travelcards

The most economical way to get around London is with a **Travelcard** (although note that they are not valid before 9.30am on weekdays). These can be used on the tube sytem, buses (except N-prefixed night buses), rail services, Docklands Light Railway and some Green Line bus services. Travelcards can be bought at all tube and rail stations and also at appointed newsagents. The most convenient cards for short-term visitors are the One-Day or One-Week Travelcards; monthly tickets are also available.

One-Day Travelcards can be used after 9.30am Mon-Fri and all day at weekends. You can make unlimited journeys within the zones you select. They cost £3.90 for Zones 1 & 2; £4.10 for Zones 1-4; £4.70 Zones 1-6 (£2 for a child all-zone ticket). Note that these tickets are not valid on N-prefixed night buses. If you'll be travelling on consecutive weekend days, it's probably worth getting a **Weekend Travelcard** (*see below*).

One-Week Travelcards offer unlimited journeys throughout the selected zones for seven days, including use of N-prefixed night buses. Weekly Travelcards cost £15.30 for

Directory

Arts, Piccadilly, W1 (Piccadilly Circus tube). **Duration** 3hrs (and occasional one-day tours; phone for details). **Tickets** £18.50; £13 students. *Advance booking advisable.*

Beatles Walks *(020 7624 3978).*
Beatles Magical Mystery Tour **Departures** 2pm Wed; 11am Thur, Sun. **Pick-up** Dominion Theatre, Tottenham Court Road, W1 (Tottenham Court Road tube). *Beatles In My Life Tour* **Departures** 11am Tue, Sat. **Meeting point** Baker Street tube (Baker Street exit). **Duration** (both) 2 hrs 30mins. **Tickets** (both) £4.50; £3.50 concs.

Garden Day Tours
(01935 815924/from USA 1 800 873 7145/ www.gentlejourneys.co.uk). **Departures** *May-Sept* 8.45am Tue-Sun (return 6.30pm). **Meeting point** Victoria Coach Station. **Tickets** £54 per day (lunch not incl).

Jack the Ripper Mystery Walk
(020 8558 9446/mobile 07957 388280).
Departures 8pm Wed, Sun. **Duration** 2hrs. **Meeting point** Aldgate tube. **Tickets** £5; £3.50 concs.

London Show Boat
Departures *May-Oct* 7pm Thur-Sun; *Nov-Apr* 7pm Fri, Sat (return 10.30pm). **Meeting point** Westminster Pier. **Tickets** £42 per head including one drink, four-course meal, half-bottle of wine, live show and dancing.

Royal & Celebrity Tour *(01932 854721).*
Departures Wed, Fri, Sat (phone for times). **Pick-up** Victoria Station (Tourist Information Centre). **Duration** phone for details. **Tickets** £18.

Taxi tours

Black Taxi Tours of London *(020 7289 4371).*
Cost £65.
A tailored two-hour tour for up to five people.

Walking tours

Ever-increasing numbers of companies and individuals are running (often themed) walks around London. One of the best and longest established is **The Original London Walks** (020 7624 3978/www.walks.com), which encompasses walks on everything from Sherlock Holmes to riverside pubs to ghosts. Also recommended is **ZigZag Audio Tours** (020 7435 3736/ www.zigzagtours.com), which offers two anecdote-filled self-guided walks in various languages, one in the City and one around the royal sights of London. For £7.95, it will deliver a Walkman with a tour on cassette to your home or hotel. Other walk companies include: **Citisights** (020 8806 4325); **Historical Tours** (020 8668 4019), **Capital Walks** (020 8650 7640), **Cityguide Walks** (01895 675389) and **Stepping Out** (020 8881 2933). There are even art guided tours in Hebrew (020 7586 1455).

If you want to do it yourself, the excellent **Green Chain** walks connect many of the green spaces of south-east London (020 8312 5884).

The *Time Out Book of London Walks* (£9.99) details 30 walks by writers around the capital.

Tube, bus & train enquiries

The tube and buses in Greater London are run by London Transport (LT), which has a 24-hour telephone enquiry service: call London Travel Information on **020 7222 1234** (often engaged, so keep trying, or settle for the 24-hour recorded information line on 020 7222 1200).

For information on overland rail services, both in London and the UK, call national rail enquiries on **08457 484950**.

Zone 1; £18.20 for Zones 1 & 2; £21.70 for Zones 1-3; £26.80 for Zones 1-4; £32.40 for Zones 1-5; £35.40 for all zones (child £6.50 Zone 1; £7.50 Zones 1 & 2; £10 Zones 1-3; £12.50 Zones 1-4; £13.70 Zones 1-5; £15 Zones 1-6).

Weekend Travelcards allow travel on consecutive weekend days or public holidays (not valid on N-prefixed night buses). The cost is £5.80 for Zones 1 & 2; £6.10 Zones 1-4; £7 Zones 1-6 (child £3 Zones 1-6).

Family Travelcards are available for families and groups of one or two adults travelling with between one and four children. They are valid after 9.30am Mon-Fri, and all day weekends and public holidays (but not on N-prefixed night buses) and cost £2.60 for Zones 1 & 2; £2.70 Zones 1-4; £3.10 Zones 1-6 (child 80p Zones 1-6).

Carnet

If you're planning on making a lot of short-hop journeys within Zone 1 over a period of several days, it makes sense to buy a carnet of ten tickets for £11 (£5 for children). This brings down the cost of each journey to £1.10 rather than the standard £1.50. Note that if you exit a station outside of Zone 1 and are caught with only a carnet ticket, you are liable to a £10 penalty fine.

Photocards

Photocards are required for all bus passes and Travelcards except one-day versions. Child-rate photocards are required for five-15-year-olds using child-rate Travelcards and bus passes. Fourteen and 15-year-olds need a child-rate photocard if buying any ticket at child-rate.

Buses

Certain routes still use the venerable 30-year-old red Routemaster buses (the ones you can hop on and off), but modern buses are taking over: they are cheaper to run as they are operated by a single driver/conductor, although this can make them slower. Travelling by bus is one of the most pleasurable ways of getting about (and getting to know) London, although progress can be very slow during the morning and evening rush hour.

Night buses

Night buses are the only form of public transport that runs through the night. They operate from around 11pm to 6am, about once an hour, on most routes. All pass through central London, and the majority stop at Trafalgar Square, so head there if you're unsure which bus to get. Night buses have the letter 'N' before their number (note that One-Day Travelcards, Weekend Travelcards, Family Travelcards and One-Day LT cards – *see page 335* – are not valid on night buses). Pick up a free map and timetable from one of the LT Travel Information Centres (*see page 330*).

Night bus fares from central London start at £1.50. Note that there are no child fares on night buses.

Green Line buses

Green Line buses (020 8668 7261/www.greenline.co.uk) serve the suburbs and towns within a 40-mile (64-km) radius of London. Their main departure point is Eccleston Bridge, SW1 (Colonnades Coach Station, behind Victoria).

Stationlink bus

The red-and-yellow Stationlink buses (020 7222 1234) are convenient for the disabled, the elderly, people laden with luggage or those with small children. The service connects all the main London rail termini (except Charing Cross) on a round trip. Buses run every hour from about 9am to 7pm (phone for details). The fare is £1 for adults, 50p for 5s-15s.

The underground

Travelling on the tube is the quickest way to get around London (although short distances may be faster on foot). However, lines frequently suffer from delays, escalators are sometimes out of action and, occasionally, there are station and line closures (typically at the weekend because of engineering work). Smoking is illegal anywhere on the underground system. Crime is not a major problem on the tube, although you would be wise to avoid getting into an empty carriage on your own, and beware of pickpockets.

Using the system

Tickets can be purchased from a station ticket office or self-service machines. (Unfortunately, staff in ticket offices rarely speak foreign languages and can be remarkably gruff and unhelpful.) You can buy most tickets, including carnets and One-Day LT Cards (*see p338*), from self-service machines, but for anything covering a longer period you need to show a valid photocard to a ticket officer. Note that, because of staff shortages,

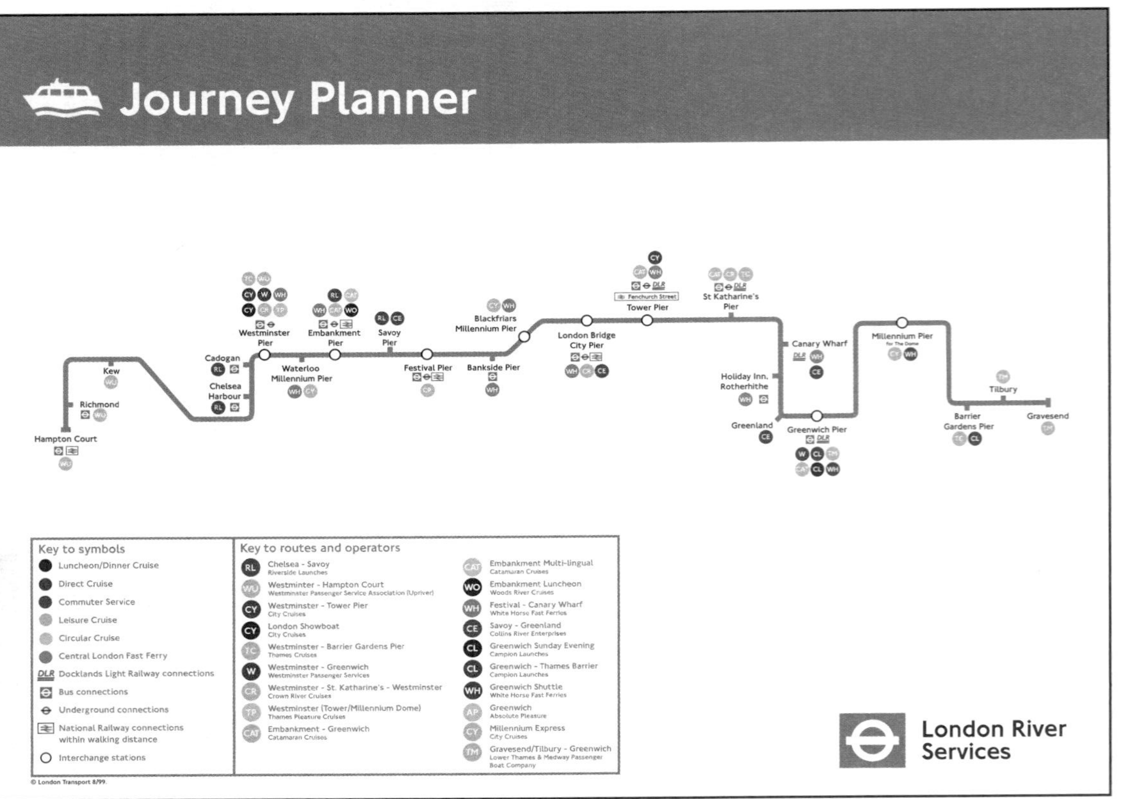
Journey Planner
Hampton Court
Richmond
Kew
Cadogan
Chelsea Harbour
Westminster Pier
Waterloo Millennium Pier
Embankment Pier
Savoy Pier
Festival Pier
Blackfriars Millennium Pier
Bankside Pier
London Bridge City Pier
Tower Pier
Fenchurch Street
St Katharine's Pier
Holiday Inn, Rotherhithe
Canary Wharf
Greenland
Greenwich Pier
Millennium Pier
Barrier Gardens Pier
Tilbury
Gravesend
Key to symbols
Luncheon/Dinner Cruise
Direct Cruise
Commuter Service
Leisure Cruise
Circular Cruise
Central London Fast Ferry
DLR Docklands Light Railway connections
Bus connections
Underground connections
National Railway connections within walking distance
Interchange stations
Key to routes and operators
RL Chelsea - Savoy
Riverside Launches
WU Westminter - Hampton Court
Westminster Passenger Service Association (Upriver)
CY Westminster - Tower Pier
City Cruises
CY London Showboat
City Cruises
TC Westminster - Barrier Gardens Pier
Thames Cruises
W Westminster - Greenwich
Westminster Passenger Services
CR Westminster - St. Katharine's - Westminster
Crown River Cruises
TP Westminster (Tower/Millennium Dome)
Thames Pleasure Cruises
CAT Embankment - Greenwich
Catamaran Cruises
CAT Embankment Multi-lingual
Catamaran Cruises
WO Embankment Luncheon
Woods River Cruises
WH Festival - Canary Wharf
White Horse Fast Ferries
CE Savoy - Greenland
Collins River Enterprises
CL Greenwich Sunday Evening
Campion Launches
CL Greenwich - Thames Barrier
Campion Launches
WH Greenwich Shuttle
White Horse Fast Ferries
AP Greenwich
Absolute Pleasure
CY Millennium Express
City Cruises
TM Gravesend/Tilbury - Greenwich
Lower Thames & Medway Passenger Boat Company
© London Transport 8/99.
London River Services

Riverboat services

At long last, the Thames is finally fulfilling its potential as a viable method of transport. Often overlooked, the river offers a speedy way of getting about, and is less congested than other modes of transport. The map opposite shows the main riverboat services that operate on the Thames. The times of services vary greatly, but, as a general rule, most operate every 20 minutes to one hour between about 10.30am and 5pm. Services tend to be more frequent and run later during the summer. Call the individual operators listed below for precise details of schedules and fares. The names in bold below are the names of piers; the central ones are marked on the maps at the back of this Guide.

Westminster–Greenwich (50mins)
Westminster Passenger Services 020 7930 4097.

Westminster–Tower (30mins)
City Cruises 020 7930 9033.

Westminster–Festival (5mins)–**London Bridge City** (20mins)–**St Katharine's** (5mins)
Crown River Cruises 020 7936 2033.

Westminster–(Thames) Barrier Gardens (1hr 10mins)
Thames Cruises 020 7930 3373.

Westminster–Kew (1hr 30mins)–**Richmond** (30mins)–**Hampton Court** (1hr 30mins)
Westminster Passenger Service Association 020 7930 2062.

Embankment–Tower (30mins)–**St Katharine's** (5mins)–**Greenwich** (25mins)
Catamaran Cruises 020 7987 1185.

Rotherhithe Holiday Inn–Canary Wharf (5mins)–**London Bridge City** (15mins)–**Blackfriars** (5mins)
White Horse Fast Ferries 01474 566220.

Savoy–London Bridge City (6mins)–**Canary Wharf** (10mins)–**Greenland** (4mins)
Collins River Enterprises 020 7488 4306.

Savoy–Cadogan (18mins)–**Chelsea** (2mins)
Riverside Launches 01342 317402.

Greenwich–(Thames) Barrier Gardens (25mins)
Campion Launches 020 8305 0300.

Lunch & dinner cruises
Lunch cruises daily from Embankment (1hr-1hr 15mins)
Woods River Cruises 020 7480 7770/ Bateaux London 020 7925 2215.
Dinner cruises (2 days a week to daily) from Westminster, Embankment and Savoy (2hrs 30mins-4hrs)
City Cruises 020 7237 5134/Bateaux London 020 7925 2215/Silver Sturgeon (Woods River Cruises 020 7480 7770).

ticket offices in some of the less busy stations often close early (around 7.30pm).

Put your ticket through the automatic checking gates (and pull it out of the top to open the gates). If you have a single journey ticket, it will be retained by the gate at the exit station. There are 12 underground lines, colour-coded on the tube map.

The much-delayed £1.9-billion Jubilee Line extension finally opened in late 1999 and now links Green Park in the West End to Stratford in east London via Waterloo, Bermondsey, North Greenwich (for the Dome) and Canary Wharf.

Underground timetable

Tube trains run daily, starting at around 5.30am Mon-Sat, 7.30am Sun. The only exception is Christmas Day, when there is no service. Generally you won't have to wait more than ten minutes for a train; during peak times the service should run every couple of minutes. Times of last trains vary; usually 11.30pm-1am Mon-Sat, and 11.30pm Sun. The only all-night public transport is by **night bus** (*see above*). If you want to avoid the worst of the rush-hour crush, don't travel between about 8am and 9.30am and 4.30pm and 6.30pm.

Docklands Light Railway (DLR)

(020 7363 9700).
The DLR is administered as part of the tube system. Its driverless trains run on a raised track from Bank (Central Line/Waterloo & City Line) or Tower Gateway, close to Tower Hill tube (Circle and District Lines), to Stratford, Beckton and down the Isle of Dogs to Island Gardens. During 1999 this latter branch was extended south across (or, rather, under) the Thames to Greenwich and on to Lewisham. Trains run from 5.30am to around 12.30am Mon-Fri; 6am-12.30am Sat; 7.30am-11.30pm Sun.

The DLR is keen to promote itself as much as a tourist attraction as a transport system. To this end it offers 'Sail and Rail' tickets that combine unlimited travel on the DLR with a riverboat trip between Greenwich and Westminster Piers (boats departing from 10.30am to 6.30pm; *see above*) plus discounts on selected museums and sights. Starting at Tower Gateway, special trains leave on the hour (from 10am) with a DLR tour guide giving passengers the low-down on the area as the train glides along. Tickets cost approximately £8.50 for adults, £4.50 for children.
Website: www.dlr.co.uk

Rail services

Independently owned commuter services run out of all of London's mainline rail stations (*see page 302*). Travelcards are valid on these services within the relevant zones. The **Silverlink Line** (01923 207258 or national rail enquiries 08457 484950/ www.silverlinktrains.com) is a useful and relatively underused overground service that carves a huge arc through the north of the city, running from Richmond (in the south-west) to North Woolwich (in the east).

Directory

On yer bike!

Two wheels good, four wheels bad? An increasing number of Londoners think so. The issue has received high-profile attention in recent years through street-party-cum-road-blocks – or 'organised coincidences' – arranged by direct-action groups and coalitions such as **Critical Mass** (fax 020 7326 0353/ www.critmass.org.uk) and **Reclaim the Streets** (020 7281 4621; rts@gn.apc.org/ www.gn.apc.org/rts) in protest at soaring pollution levels and appalling road congestion.

However, despite the efforts of some local councils, London remains, on the whole, an unfriendly place for bike-riding commuters who, mostly without cycle lanes, have to contend with pitted roads and pit-bull motorists. A safety helmet, filter-mask and determined attitude are advisable. However, cyclists shouldn't forget that they have as much responsibility as motorists for driving safely. So no jumping those red lights.

London Cycling Campaign

228 Great Guildford Business Square, 30 Great Guildford Street, SE1 0HS (020 7928 7220). **Open** *phone enquiries* 2-5pm Mon-Fri.

Get the definitive guide to pedalling around London, *On Your Bike*, and the *Cyclists' Route Map* (£4.95 for both), from the London Cycling Campaign. It includes tips on maintenance, security and the law. Members of the LCC enjoy a host of other benefits (membership from £5.50).

Website: www.lcc.org.uk/lcc

Cycle hire & storage

Bikepark

11 Macklin Street, WC2 (020 7430 0083/bikepark@easynet.co.uk). Covent Garden or Holborn tube. **Open** 8.30am-7pm Mon-Fri; 10am-6pm Sat. **Hire** £10 first day; £5 second day; £3 per day thereafter. **Deposit** £200. **Credit** MC, £TC, V. **Map 6 L6**

Leave your bike in secure parking (50p per hour; £2 for 24 hours; £20 a month), and make use of the changing facilities at this branch (there are showers at the Chelsea branch). There's also a repair service and you can hire a hybrid or mountain bike and accessories for commuting or touring. Season tickets also available.

Branch: **Bikepark Chelsea** The Courtyard, 250 King's Road, SW3 (020 7565 0777).

Website: www.bikepark.co.uk

London Bicycle Tour Company

1A Gabriel's Wharf, 56 Upper Ground, SE1 (020 7928 6838/ enquiries@londonbicycle.com). Blackfriars tube/rail or Southwark tube. **Open** *Easter-Oct* 10am-6pm daily; *Nov-Easter* by appointment. **Hire** £2.50 per hour; £10 first day; £5 per day thereafter. **Deposit** £100 (unless paying by credit card). **Credit** AmEx, DC, MC, £TC, V. **Map 11 N7**

In addition to bike hire, this company, as the name implies, conducts daily bicycle tours (approx three hours). Its West End tour on Sundays costs £11.95, and it also offers weekend breaks in the countryside around London.

Website: www.londonbicycle.com

The line connects with the tube network at several stations. Trains run about every 20 minutes Mon-Sat, every 30 minutes Sun. It offers a refreshing alternative to the tube with great views of London's back gardens.

Driving

If you've heard that driving in central London is tough, just wait till you try to find somewhere to park. If you park illegally, you'll probably get a £60-£80 parking ticket (which will be reduced by 50 per cent if you pay within 14 days) or find your car has been immobilised by a yellow triangular wheel clamp, or it may be towed away and impounded. The retrieval procedure, to put it mildly, is no easy ride (*see page 342*).

Car hire

To hire a car you must have at least one year's driving experience with a full current driving licence. If you are an overseas visitor, your current driving licence is valid in Britain for a year. Prices for car hire vary considerably; always ring several competitors for a quote (see *Yellow Pages*). Below are two of the most reputable companies.

Avis *(Central reservations 0990 900500).* **Open** 24 hours daily. **Credit** AmEx, DC, MC, £TC, V.

You must be over 23. Chauffeur-driven cars are also available. Rental prices vary within different areas of London.

Website: www.avis.com

Europcar BCR *30 Woburn Place, WC1 (020 7255 2339). Russell Square tube.* **Open** 8am-6pm Mon-Fri; 8am-1pm Sat. **Credit** AmEx, DC, MC, £TC, V. **Map 6 L4**

You must be over 23 to hire a car at BCR. Cheapest rental is £36 per day inclusive. There is a £150 deposit on all rentals.

Website: www.eurocar.com

Motorbike hire

Scootabout *1-3 Leeke Street, WC1 (020 7833 4607). King's Cross tube/rail.* **Open** 9am-6pm Mon-Fri. **Credit** MC, £TC, V. **Map 6 M3**

Any British driving licence or foreign motorbike licence qualifies you to drive a 50cc moped. The hire charge for these starts at £15.50 per day; £91.50 per week. Hiring an ST1100 Pan European costs £71.50 per day; £365 per week. All rental prices include 250 miles per day, with excess mileage at 10p a mile, AA cover, insurance and VAT. Helmet hire costs £2 per day, and £12 per week. Note

Access all areas

Compared to some European cities, such as Madrid and Rome, London is relatively friendly to the mobility-impaired. But this is only relative. While many of the capital's sights make provision for wheelchair users, the great headache for those who have problems getting around is transport.

London Transport publishes a booklet called *Access to the Underground*, which gives information on lifts and ramps at individual underground stations. It's available free from LT ticket offices or from LT's Unit for Disabled Passengers (172 Buckingham Palace Road, SW1 9TN; 020 7918 3312/fax 020 7918 3876/ lt.udp@ltbuses.co.uk) and at LT Travel Information Centres (*see page 334*). The unit also provides details on buses and Braille maps. All DLR stations have wheelchair access.

We thoroughly recommend *Access in London* by Gordon Couch, William Forrester and Justin Irwin (Quiller Press, 1996). Admirably comprehensive, it includes detailed maps of step-free routes and accessible tube stations. There are tips on travelling around, a guide to adapted loos, sections on accommodation, shopping and entertainment. The guide is available at some bookshops, for £7.95, or free of charge (although a donation is appreciated) from Access Project, 39 Bradley Gardens, W13 8HE or by calling 020 7250 3222.

The organisations below offer help to disabled visitors to London. For information about services for disabled students, *see page 345* **National Bureau for Students with Disablities**.

Artsline

54 Chalton Street, NW1 (tel/ minicom 020 7388 2227/fax 020 7383 2653). Euston tube/rail. **Open** 9.30am-5.30pm Mon-Fri. **Map 6 K3**

Information on disabled access to arts and entertainment events in London and on adapted facilities in cinemas, art galleries, theatres, etc.
Website: www.dircon.co.uk/artsline

Can Be Done

7-11 Kensington High Street, W8 5NP (020 8907 2400). **Open** 9am-5.30pm Mon-Fri; noon-1pm Sat. **Map 3 A9**

This small tour operator can tailor holidays and tours in London to the needs of disabled people.
Website: www.canbedone.co.uk

DAIL (Disability Arts in London)

Diorama Arts Centre, 34 Osnaburgh Street, NW1 (020 7916 6351/minicom 020 7691 4201/fax 020 7916 5396/dail@dail.dircon. co.uk/www.dail.dircon.co.uk). **Open** 10.30am-6.30pm Mon-Fri.

Produces a monthly magazine containing listings, reviews and articles on the arts and the disabled (voluntary subscription of £10 per year). DAIL is part of LDAF (London Disability Arts Forum; 020 7916 5484), which organises events for disabled people in London.

DIAL (National Association of Disablement Information & Advice Lines)

(01302 310123). **Open** 9am-5pm Mon-Thur; 9am-4pm Fri.

Has details of local groups in the UK that can offer free information and advice on all aspects of disability.

William Forrester

1 Belvedere Close, Guildford, Surrey, GU2 6NP (01483 575401).

William Forrester is a London Registered Guide and, as a wheelchair user himself, has extensive experience in leading tours in the capital for disabled individuals and groups. Book early.

Greater London Action on Disability (GLAD)

336 Brixton Road, SW9 (020 7346 5800/infoline 020 7346 5819/ minicom 020 7346 5811). Brixton tube/rail. **Open** *general phone enquiries* 9am-5pm Mon-Fri; *infoline* 1.30-4.30pm Mon, Wed, Fri.

GLAD is a voluntary organisation providing, via local associations, valuable information for disabled visitors and residents. Its publications include the fortnightly *Update*, containing extracts from articles in the national newspapers and magazines that relate to the disabled, and the monthly *London Disability News*.

Holiday Care Service

For listings details, see p145.

An advisory service specialising in holiday accommodation for disabled visitors.

Royal Association for Disability & Rehabilitation (RADAR)

12 City Forum, 250 City Road, EC1 (020 7250 3222). Old Street tube/rail. **Open** 8am-5pm Mon-Fri. **Map 9 P3**

The central organisation for disabled voluntary groups. Through RADAR you can get advice on almost any aspect of life. The Association publishes *Bulletin*, a monthly newsletter, which has articles on news-oriented subjects such as housing and education.
Website: www.radar.org.uk

Tripscope

Brentford Community Resource Centre, Alexandra House, 241 High Street, Brentford, Middlesex, TW8 0NE (tel/minicom 08457 585641/020 8994 9294/ tripscope@cableinet.co.uk). **Open** *phone enquiries* 9am-4.45pm Mon-Fri.

Jim Bennett and Adrian Drew's information/advice service for the elderly and disabled can help with all aspects of getting around London, the UK and overseas. It's chiefly an enquiry line, but you can write in or e-mail them if you have difficulty with the phone.
www.justmobility.co.uk/tripscope

Wheelchair Travel & Access Mini Buses

1 Johnston Green, Guildford, Surrey GU2 6XS (01483 233640/ info@wheelchair-travel.co.uk).

An excellent source of converted vehicles for hire, including adapted minibuses (with or without driver), plus cars with hand controls and 'Chairman' cars.
Website: www.wheelchair-travel.co.uk

that bikes can only be hired if a credit card is handed over for security.
Website: www.hgbmotorcycles.co.uk

Clamping

The immobilising of vehicles by attaching a clamp to one wheel is becoming an increasingly common way of combating illegal parking in London. If you've been clamped, call the Clamping and Vehicle Section 24-hour hotline (020 7747 4747). There will be a label attached to the car telling you which payment centre to phone or visit. Some boroughs let you pay over the phone with a credit card, others insist you go in person. Either way, you'll have to stump up a £38 clamp fee and pay a parking fine of £30-£40.

Staff at the payment centre promise to de-clamp your car within the next four hours but can't tell you exactly when. You are also warned that if you don't remove your car within one hour of its being de-clamped, they will clamp it again. This means you may have to spend quite some time waiting by your car.

Any appeals against clamping, removal and ticketing can be made by calling 020 7747 4700.

Vehicle removal

If your car has mysteriously disappeared, chances are that, if it was legally parked, it's been nicked; if not, it's probably been hoisted on to the back of a truck and taken to a car pound, and you're facing a stiff penalty: a fee of £125 is levied for removal, plus £15 per day if you don't collect it within 24 hours. To add insult to injury, you'll probably get a parking ticket of £30-£40 when you collect the car. To find out where your car has been taken and how to retrieve it call 020 7747 4747.

24-hour car parks

NCP (020 7404 3777/ www.ncp.co.uk) has a number of (phenomenally expensive) 24-hour car parks in and around central London, including:

Arlington House, Arlington Street, SW1 *(020 7499 3312).* **Rates** £12 for 3 hours; £23.50 for 6 hours; £34 for 9 hours; £39 for 12 hours; £48 for 24 hours. **Map 7 J8**

21 Bryanston Street, W1 *(020 7499 0313).* **Rates** £6.20 for 2 hours; £11.50 for 4 hours; £17 for 6 hours; £23.50 for 9 hours; £34 for 24 hours. **Map 2 F6**

2 Lexington Street, W1 *(020 7734 0371).* **Rates** £7.50 for 2 hours; £14.80 for 4 hours; £20.50 for 6 hours; £30 for 9 hours; £37 for 24 hours. **Map 7 J7**

Car breakdown

If you are a member of a motoring organisation in another country, check to see if it has a reciprocal agreement with a British organisation.

AA (Automobile Association)

119-121 Cannon Street, EC4 (info 0990 500600/breakdown 0800 887766/new members 0800 444999). **Open** 24 hours daily. **Credit** MC, V.
You can call the AA if you break down. Become a member on the spot, and it will cost you £78 to join. The first year's roadside service membership starts at £43.
Website: www.theaa.co.uk

Environmental Transport Association

Freepost KT4021, Weybridge, Surrey KT13 8RS (01932 828882). **Open** *office* 8am-6pm Mon-Fri; 9am-4pm Sat; *breakdown service* 24 hours daily. **Credit** MC, V.
The green alternative, if you don't want part of your membership fees used for lobbying the government into building more roads, as happens with the AA and RAC. Basic membership is £20 a year for individuals and £25 for families.
Website: www.eta.co.uk

RAC

RAC House, 1 Forest Road, Feltham TW13 TRR (emergency breakdown 0800 828282/office & membership 0990 722722). **Open** *office* 8am-9pm Mon-Fri; 9am-5pm Sat; 10am-4pm Sun; *breakdown service* 24 hours daily. **Credit** AmEx, DC, MC, V.
Ring the general enquiries number and ask for the Rescue Service. Membership costs from £39 for basic cover to £140 for the most comprehensive, plus £75 for European cover.
Website: www.rac.co.uk

Taxis

Black cabs

Licensed London taxis are called black cabs (even though some of them are not black). They all have a yellow 'For Hire' sign and a white licence plate on the back of the vehicle. Drivers of black cabs must pass 'The Knowledge' to prove they know the name of every street in central London, where it is and the shortest route to it. Any complaints or enquiries should be made to the Public Carriage Office (020 7230 1631/lost property 020 7833 0996; 9am-4pm Mon-Fri). Remember to note the number of the offending cab. When a taxi's 'For Hire' sign is switched on, it can be hailed in the street (though, annoyingly, some cabbies switch off the sign even when free, picking up fares as they please). **Radio Taxis** (020 7272 0272) and **Dial a Cab** (020 7253 5000) both run 24-hour services for black cabs.

Minicabs

Minicabs (saloon cars) are generally cheaper than black cabs, especially at night and weekends. However, the drivers are usually unlicensed, untrained, sometimes uninsured, not always reliable and very occasionally dangerous. There are, though, plenty of trustworthy firms – always ask for a recommendation. Ask the price when you book and confirm it with the driver when the car arrives. Minicabs can't legally be hailed in the street: avoid drivers touting for business (common at night) as it's illegal and can be very risky. **Addison Lee** (020 7387 8888) is one of the bigger, more reliable companies, and it also claims to do pick-ups from all areas. Women travelling alone may prefer to use **Lady Cabs** (020 7254 3501/020 7923 7599), which employs only women drivers.

Business services

The proudly pink *Financial Times* (daily) is the most authoritative newspaper for facts and figures in the City and all over the world. If you are after in-depth analysis, and some considered domestic and international news, try *The Economist* magazine (weekly).

Communications

British Monomarks

Monomarks House, 27 Old Gloucester Street, WC1 (020 7419 5000/020 7404 5011/fax 020 7831 9489/bm@monomark.co.uk). Holborn tube. **Open** 9.30am-5.30pm Mon-Fri. **Credit** AmEx, MC, £$TC, V. **Map 6 L5**

British Monomarks services include mail forwarding, e-mail, fax and 24-hour telephone answering.

Conferences

London Tourist Board

Glen House, Stag Place, SW1 (020 7932 2010/fax 020 7932 2013). Victoria tube/rail. **Open** 9am-5.30pm Mon-Fri. **Map 4 J9**

The LTB runs a venue enquiry service for conventions or exhibitions. Request (by letter or fax) its free guide, *Convention & Exhibition London*, which lists hotels and centres that host events, together with their facilities.

Website: www.londontown.com

Queen Elizabeth II Conference Centre

Broad Sanctuary, SW1 (020 7222 5000/enquiries 020 7798 4000/ fax 020 7798 4200). St James's Park tube. **Open** 8am-6pm Mon-Fri; 24-hour conference facilities. **Map 8 K9**

This unattractive, purpose-built centre close to the Houses of Parliament has some of the best conference facilities in the capital. There are rooms with capacities from 30 to 1,100, and communications equipment is available including a TV studio equipped to broadcast specifications.

Website: www.qeiicc.co.uk

Equipment hire

ABC Business Machines

59 Chiltern Street, W1 (020 7486 5634). Baker Street tube. **Open** 9am-5.30pm Mon-Fri; 9.30am-12.30pm Sat. **Credit** JCB, MC, £TC, V. **Map 5 G5**

Fax machines, answerphones, computers, photocopiers and audio equipment are among the items on hire at ABC.

Secretarial

Reed Employment, Staff Agency

143 Victoria Street, SW1 (020 7834 1801/fax 020 7821 5593). Victoria tube/rail. **Open** 8am-6pm Mon-Fri. **Map 7 J10**

Reed supplies secretarial, computing, accountancy and technical services to registered companies. This branch specialises in secretarial and administration services.

Website: www.reed.co.uk

Typing Overload

67 Chancery Lane, WC2 (020 7404 5464/fax 020 7831 0878). Chancery Lane tube. **Open** 9.30am-5.30pm Mon-Fri. **Credit** AmEx, DC, MC, £$TC, V. **Map 6 M5**

Come here for a speedy and professional typing service for any job that can be done on a wordprocessor. **Branch**: 35 Brompton Road, SW3 (020 7823 9955).

Translation

Central Translations

2-3 Woodstock Street, W1 (020 7493 5511). Bond Street tube. **Open** 9am-5pm Mon-Fri. **Map 5 H6**

Be it typesetting, proofreading, translation or the use of an interpreter, Central can work with almost every language under the sun.

www.centraltranslations.co.uk

1st Translation Company

24 Holborn Viaduct, EC1 (020 7329 0032/fax 020 7329 0035). Chancery Lane tube. **Open** 10am-6pm Mon-Fri. **Map 11 N5**

More than 50 languages can be translated. Interpreters cost £220-£500 per day.

Website: www.1st-translation-co.com

Media

Newspapers

National newspapers fall broadly into three categories. At the lofty, serious news end of the scale are the broadsheets – the rightish-wing *Daily Telegraph* and *The Times* are balanced by the (increasingly unindependent) *Independent* and the *Guardian*. All have bulging Sunday equivalents (except the *Guardian*, but it does have a sister Sunday paper, the *Observer*). The right-wing middle-market leader has long been the *Daily Mail* (and *Mail on Sunday*), although its rival, the *Daily Express*, has made huge efforts to claw back its market share and currently sells around a million copies a day, about half that of the *Daily Mail*. At the bottom of the pile are the most popular papers of them all: the tabloids. Still undisputed leader of the rat pack is the *Sun* (and the Sunday *News of the World*), selling around three and a half million copies daily (more than half the daily total of all newspapers sold). The *Daily Star* and the *Mirror* are the other main lowbrow contenders. The *People* and the *Sunday Mirror* provide sleaze on Sunday. London's only daily paper, which comes out in several editions through the day, is the right-wing *Evening Standard*, a sort of *Mail* for London. In 1999, a free morning paper for London, *Metro*, was launched. Distributed at tube stations, it contains just enough news and features to occupy the average commuter journey.

Magazines

There are more than 6,500 titles available. The women's market is the most profitable (and saturated), with *Marie Claire* and *Cosmopolitan*, both selling close to half a million copies a month, leading the way. The men's market continues to expand, with *Loaded* doing particularly well at the moment. Style magazines, such as *i-D* and *Dazed and Confused*, have established themselves in a profitable niche. Weekly TV listings magazines are also big winners: *Time Out* also includes London-related features and interviews, while glossy *Heat* is heavy on film and TV features. If you're looking for something more serious and hard-hitting, there's not much to choose from. *The Spectator*, the *New Statesman* and *Prospect* are the closest you will get. *Private Eye* offers a fortnightly satirical look at politics and news. *The Big Issue*, sold on the street by homeless people, is also worth a look. *The Economist* covers international political and business issues, and you'll find the international editions of *Time* and *Newsweek* at most newsagents.

Radio

BBC Radio 1 *98.8 FM.* Youth-oriented music station – pop, rock, dance and more unusual genres.

BBC Radio 2 *89.1 FM.* Fairly bland, middle-of-the-road – both the music and the DJs.

BBC Radio 3 *91.3 FM.* The BBC's classical music station.

BBC Radio 4 *93.5 FM, 720 MW, 198 LW.* Speech-only station, particularly loved for its six-mornings-a-week *Today* news programme.

BBC Radio 5 Live *693, 909 MW.* News and sport, 24 hours a day. Live coverage of major sporting events.

BBC GLR (Greater London Radio) *94.9 FM.* By far the best and most intelligent London station. Despite the good music and entertaining chat, GLR's future currently hangs in the balance.

BBC World Service *648 MW.* Transmitted worldwide but available in the UK for a distillation of the best of all the other BBC stations.

Capital FM *95.8 FM.* London's liveliest commercial station offers music, quizzes and ads.

Capital Gold *1548 MW.* Plays '60s to '80s pop.

Choice FM *96.9 FM.* South London soul station.

Classic FM *100.9 FM.* Classical easy listening.

Country *1035 MW.* Nuff said.

Heart *106.2 FM.* More MOR music, less talk.

Jazz FM *102.2 FM.* There's still *some* jazz left on this station, which had to go mainstream in order to survive.

Kiss *100.0 FM.* Dance music for the seriously funked up.

Liberty *963 MW.* Liberty took over from the women's station, Viva!

London Newstalk (LBC) *1152 MW.* Phone-ins and chat.

News Direct *97.3 FM.* 24-hour news, weather, motoring and business information.

Spectrum *558 MW.* Researched, produced and presented by various ethnic communities.

Talk Radio *1053, 1089 MW.* As the name implies…

Virgin *105.8 FM.* Adult rock.

XFM *104.9 FM.* Indie music station.

Television

The next generation of television in the UK will be digital. Sky Digital, ONdigital and various digital cable TV companies currently offer services that reproduce and expand on the established analogue offerings listed below. Sky Digital currently has 170 channels and ONdigital about 30, with additional online shopping, banking and information services in the pipeline.

BBC1

BBC1 represents all that is 'Auntie BBC' – the Corporation's mass-market station. There are no commercials. There's a smattering of soaps and game shows, also the odd quality programme. Daytime programming, however, stinks.

BBC2

In general, BBC2 is also free of crass programmes. That doesn't mean the output is riveting, just not insulting. It offers a cultural cross-section and plenty of documentaries; recently it has also been competing with Channel 4 in the Friday-night comedy stakes.

ITV – Carlton

Mass-appeal programmes punctuated by frequent commercial breaks. It's not quite the lowest common denominator, more the highest possible audience. Any successful formula is repeated *ad infinitum*. The odd sparkler of a drama.

ITV – London Weekend Television

LWT takes over from Carlton at the weekend to offer much of the same – if not more downmarket – stuff.

Channel 4

C4's output includes some pretty mainstream fare, especially its extremely successful US imports, but it still comes up with some gems of programmes, particularly its films.

Channel 5

Britain's newest terrestrial channel. So far, output has failed to match the hype, except for viewers for whom made-for-TV films and re-runs pass as entertainment.

Satellite & cable

Bravo B-movies and cult TV.

CNN News and current affairs reporting, the American way.

Discovery Channel Science and nature documentaries.

Eurosport One of three sport-only channels; marginal-interest events.

FilmFour This admirable Channel 4 venture shows 12 hours of films every day, including independent flicks and director's cuts.

Granada Plus News, views, current affairs – like Radio 5 Live but on TV.

History Channel Self-explanatory.

Movie Channel More films.

MTV Rock/pop channel that borrows from its US counterpart.

Paramount US & British sitcoms.

Performance Dance, theatre and opera, plus interviews.

QVC Home shopping channel.

Sky Movies Blockbusters and interview snippets.

Sky Movies Gold Classic movies.

Sky News 24-hour news and features.

Sky One Channel with general appeal.

Sky Sports Major sporting events. There are also Sky Sports 2 and Sky Sports 3.

TNT Cartoons and classic repeats.

UK Arena Classical concerts and all things arts-related.

UK Gold Buys wholesale from BBC and ITV, repeating yesterday's successes.

UK Horizon Science documentaries.

UK Living For those who spend all day at home.

UK Style Shopping, fashion, cooking.

VH-1 Rock station featuring extensive album coverage.

Students

Being a student in London can be an exciting, if initially daunting, not to mention, disconcertingly expensive, affair. Whether you are here to study or just visiting, *Time Out*'s annual *Student Guide* magazine, available in many bookshops and newsagents, provides a comprehensive low-down on what London has to offer students and how to survive in the big city.

Throughout this Guide, entry prices for students at museums, art galleries, sights, sports venues and other places are usually designated 'concs' ('concessions'). You'll have to show ID – an NUS or ISIC card – to get these rates. Students (whether EU citizens or not) wanting, or needing, to find work in the UK as a way of boosting their funds, *see page 331* **Working in London**.

National Bureau for Students with Disabilities

Chapter House, 18-20 Crucifix Lane, SE1 (0800 328 5050). **Open** *phone enquiries* 1.30-4.30pm Mon-Fri.
Information and advice.

Universities

Brunel University *Clevedon Road, Uxbridge, Middlesex (01895 274000/Students Union 01895 462200). Uxbridge tube.*

City University *Northampton Square, EC1 (020 7477 8000/ Students Union 020 7505 5600). Angel or Barbican tube.* **Map 9 O3**

Guildhall University *2 Goulston Street, E1 (020 7320 1000/Students Union 020 7320 2233). Aldgate East tube.* **Map 12 S6**

South Bank University *Borough Road, SE1 (020 7928 8989/Students Union 020 7815 6060). Elephant & Castle tube.* **Map 11 O9**

University of East London (Stratford Campus) *Romford Road, E15 (020 8590 7722/Students Union ext 4210). Stratford tube/rail.*

University of Greenwich *Wellington Street, SE18 (020 8331 8000/Students Union 020 8331 8268). Woolwich Arsenal rail.*

University of Kingston *Penrhyn Road, Kingston, Surrey (020 8547 2000/Students Union 020 8255 2222). Kingston rail.*

University of London (*see below*).

University of Middlesex *Trent Park, Bramley Road, N14 (020 8362 5000/Students Union 020 8362 6450). Cockfosters or Oakwood tube.*

University of North London *166-220 Holloway Road, N7 (020 7607 2789/Students Union 020 7753 3367). Holloway Road tube.*

University of Westminster *309 Regent Street, W1 (020 7911 5000). Oxford Circus tube.* **Map 5 H4**

University of London

Many students in London attend one of the 34 colleges, spread across the city, that make up the huge University of London; only the six largest are listed below. All London universities (except Imperial College) are affiliated to the **National Union of Students (NUS)**.

NUS London Regional Office *(020 7272 8900/www.nus.org.uk).* **Open** 9.30am-5pm Mon-Fri.

Goldsmiths' College *Lewisham Way, SE14 (020 7919 7171/ Students Union 020 8692 1406). New Cross/New Cross Gate tube/rail.*

Imperial College *Exhibition Road, SW7 (020 7589 5111/Students Union 020 7594 8060). South Kensington tube.* **Map 4 D9**

King's College *Strand, WC2 (020 7836 5454/Students Union 020 7836 7132). Temple tube.* **Map 8 M7**

London School of Economics (LSE) *Houghton Street, WC2 (020 7405 7686/Students Union 020 7955 7158). Holborn tube.* **Map 6 M6**

Queen Mary & Westfield College (QMW) *Mile End Road, E1 (020 7975 5555/Students Union 020 7975 5390). Mile End or Stepney Green tube.*

University College London (UCL) *Gower Street, WC1 (020 7387 7050/Students Union 020 7387 3611). Goodge Street or Warren Street tube/Euston tube/rail.* **Map 6 K4**

Student bars

Many student unions will only let in students with the relevant ID, so be sure to carry your NUS or ISIC card with you at all times to ensure entry. Below are the six best student bars in the capital, which offer a good night out at friendly prices.

Imperial College

Beit Quad, Prince Consort Road, SW7 (020 7589 5111). South Kensington tube. **Open** noon-2pm, 5-11pm, Mon, Tue, Thur; noon-2pm, 5pm-midnight, Wed; noon-2pm, 5pm-1am, Fri; 12.30-11pm Sat; 12.30-10.30pm Sun (times vary out of termtime). **Map 4 D9**
No-frills union hospitality at its most basic and best. Imperial has a large union, a fact reflected in its excellent entertainments programme. The main bar, Da Vinci's, is lively and friendly, with cheap beer and constant MTV. Imperial is the only college in the UK not to be affiliated to the NUS, so check if you'll be able to get in before you go.

International Students House

229 Great Portland Street, W1 (020 7631 8300 ext 744). Great Portland Street tube.
Open noon-2pm, 5-11pm, Mon-Thur; noon-2pm, 5pm-2am, Fri; 5.30-11pm Sat; 7-10.30pm Sun. **Map 5 H4**
Part refuge, part social mecca, ISH attempts to be all things to all students – and it largely succeeds. Aside from keeping rooms to rent for visiting students on a long- or short-term basis (*see p161*), there are also sports facilities, eateries and a bar, which holds events throughout the year, including a decent club night on Fridays. Look out too for the heavily subsidised Travel Club. Some colleges automatically enroll their students here: check first before forking out.

King's College

Macadam Building, Surrey Street, WC2 (020 7836 7132). Temple tube. **Open** *Waterfront* noon-11pm Mon-Fri; 8-11pm Sat. *Tutu's* 9pm-2am Fri; 10pm-2am Sat. **Map 8 M7**
King's is the best student venue in London: no question. This is all the more surprising when you consider that it was once an utter dump. Now, though, there's the refurbished and always lively and entertaining Waterfront Bar, which also serves pretty decent food, and Tutu's, a 600-capacity live venue that puts on some great bands every couple of weeks.

School of Oriental & African Studies (SOAS)

Thornhaugh Street, WC1 (020 7637 2388). Goodge Street or Russell Square tube. **Open** noon-2pm, 5-9pm, Mon-Fri. **Map 6 K4**
A capacious, scruffy bar with a great atmosphere most nights of the week.

Cybercafés

For a congenial atmosphere, good food and friendly service, **Global Café** is the pick of the city's Internet cafés. If cheap Net access is a greater priority to you than first-rate cappuccinos and toothsome cakes, then head to one of the branches of **easyEverything**, the mega Net store that took the capital by storm during 1999 thanks to its astonishingly low prices (both branches listed below are open 24 hours daily, more are springing up all the time). They're not licensed to serve alcohol (neither is **Shoot'n'Surf**); all the other places listed below will let you surf beer in hand. For the cheapest Net access (free, in fact), in addition to music and decent food, head for **The Vibe Bar**; for the cosiest surfing space go to the **Buzz Bar**; and in order to see where the phenomenon started check out the pioneering **Cyberia Cyber Café**.

Buzz Bar

95 Portobello Road, W11 (020 7460 4906/mike@portobellogold.com). Notting Hill Gate or Ladbroke Grove tube. **Open** 10am-9pm Mon-Fri; 10am-7pm Sat; noon-7pm Sun. **Net access** £5 per hour. **Terminals** 7. **Credit** DC, MC, £TC, V. **Map 1 A6**
Website: www.buzzbar.co.uk

Café Internet

22-24 Buckingham Palace Road, SW1 (020 7233 5786/cafe@cafeinternet.co.uk/www.cafeinternet.co.uk). Victoria tube/rail. **Open** 7am-9pm Mon-Fri; 10am-8pm Sat, Sun. **Net access** £2 per hour; *Internet training* from £15 per half hour. **Terminals** 30. **Credit** AmEx, MC, £TC, V. **Map 7 H10**

Cyberia Cyber Café

39 Whitfield Street, W1 (020 7681 4200/cyberia@easynet.co.uk/www.cyberiacafe.net). Goodge Street tube. **Open** 9am-9pm Mon-Fri; 11am-7pm Sat; 11am-6pm Sun. **Net access** £3 per half hour; £6 per hour. **Terminals** 19. **Credit** MC, £TC, V. **Map 6 K5**

The beer's cheap – which goes some way towards compensating for the decidedly dodgy décor – there are three pool tables, and they even serve pies. What more could you want?

University of London Union (ULU)

Malet Street, WC1 (020 7664 2000). Goodge Street or Russell Square tube. **Open** noon-11pm Mon-Fri; noon-1am Fri, Sat; noon-10.30pm Sun. **Map 6 K4**
The big London student venue. Of the two decent bars, Room 101 is a cod-wine bar; the Duck & Dive is a more pubby bar where you can also get food – and where there's often a band or two playing on a Friday or Saturday.

University of North London

166-220 Holloway Road, N7 (020 7607 2789 ext 2532). Holloway Road tube. **Open** 11am-11pm Mon, Tue, Thur; 11am-2am Wed; 11am-late Fri; 11am-6am Sat.
In keeping with the university's reputation for design, the Rocket Bar is in a postmodern style. The free Big Fish club is held in the huge function hall upstairs every Wednesday night.

Money-saving tips

London can be an expensive place. But don't despair – student status can turn out to be a money-saver. First, you need a student card: either a **National Union of Students (NUS) Card** (available to only those studying at a UK university), or, if you don't have an NUS card (but have some other form of student ID), then get an **International Student Identity Card (ISIC)**, available from most students' unions or student travel agencies.

Both cards work as a passport to savings on all sorts of goods and services in town, from clothing to cheap haircuts and driving lessons. Check the NUS website (www.nus.org.uk) for details of the latest savings available. Be aware that while some organisations advertise their student discounts heavily, others are rather more coy: a flash of your student card, wherever you are, might just net you a considerable discount.

Entertainment

Many cultural events in London – from indie gigs to art exhibitions – offer some form of student reduction. For details of current discounted events, see *Time Out*'s weekly student section, or the free fortnightly newspaper *London Student*.

London cinemas are queuing up to give students concessions. Most **ABC** and **Virgin** cinemas in central London offer cheap tickets for students all day every day (though there are some exceptions). Many other West End movie houses have discounts for everyone, not just students, while most rep houses, including the estimable **National Film Theatre** (020 7928 3232), have reduced-price tickets for students.

Many big classical music venues operate a student standby scheme. Most concerts at the **Royal Festival Hall** (020 7960 4242) have discounted student tickets – in advance or standby. Major cultural centres, including the **English National Opera** (020 7632 8300) and the **Barbican Centre** (020 7638 8891), plus lesser-known venues such as **Wigmore Hall** (020 7935 2141), run their own student standby schemes for some, if not all, performances.

Student theatre buffs needn't despair: some of the big houses run some sort of discount scheme (*see page 294*).
Another useful innovation is the **Stage Pass** (020 7379 6722/www.stagepass.yandm.org.uk),

easyEverything
9-13 Wilton Road, SW1 (opposite Victoria Station) (020 7233 8456). Victoria tube/rail. **Open** 24 hours daily. **Net access** £1 30mins-2hrs (rate varies depending on number of other users). **Terminals** over 400. **Map 7 H10**
Branch: 9-16 Tottenham Court Road, W1 (020 7436 1206).

Global Café
15 Golden Square, W1 (020 7287 2242/ dbcox@hotmail.com/www.globalcafe.net). Oxford Circus or Piccadilly Circus tube. **Open** 8am-midnight Mon-Fri; 10am-midnight Sat; noon-11pm Sun. **Net access** no charge (must buy a drink); access for 1hr or longer if not busy. **Terminals** 10. **Map 7 J7**

Intercafé
25 Great Portland Street, W1 (020 7631 0063/ managers@intercafe.co.uk/www.intercafe.co.uk). Oxford Circus tube. **Open** 7.30am-7pm Mon-Fri; 9.30am-5pm Sat. **Net access** £3 per half hour; £5 per hour. **Terminals** 9. **Credit** MC, £TC, V. **Map 5 J5**

Shoot'n'Surf
13 New Oxford Street, WC1 (020 7419 1183/ info@shootnsurf.co.uk/www.shootnsurf.co.uk). Holborn or Tottenham Court Road tube. **Open** 11am-7pm daily. **Net access** £1.50 per 15 mins; £3 per half hour. **Terminals** 12. **Credit** AmEx, MC, V. **Map 6 L5**

The Vibe Bar
The Truman Brewery, 91 Brick Lane, E1 (020 7247 1685/claudine@vibe-bar.co.uk/www.vibe-bar.co.uk). Aldgate East tube. **Open** 11am-11pm Mon-Sat; noon-11pm Sun. **Net access** no charge. **Terminals** 4. **Credit** AmEx, MC, V. **Map 10 S5**

Webshack
15 Dean Street, W1 (020 7439 8000/ webmaster@webshack-cafe.com/ www.webshack-cafe.com). Tottenham Court Road tube. **Open** 9am-11pm Mon-Fri; 10am-11pm Sat; 1-8pm Sun. **Net access** £3 per half hour; £5 per hour. **Terminals** 20. **Credit** DC, MC, V. **Map 6 K6**

World Café
394 St John Street, EC1 (020 7713 8883/ theworldcafe@earthling.net/www.worldcafe.smallplanet.co.uk). Angel tube. **Open** 11am-8pm Mon-Fri; noon-6pm Sat. **Net access** £3 per half hour; £5 per hour. **Terminals** 6. **Credit** AmEx, MC, V. **Map 9 O3**

available to anyone aged 16-29 for £15 a year. This gives discounts on a variety of shows and, unlike the standby schemes in Theatreland, lets you buy discounted seats in advance.

Travel

Increased competition is resulting in cheaper than ever travel to many destinations around the globe (less so, alas, within Britain), and for students (and under-26s in general) savings can be huge. Surprisingly, the cheapest way of travelling is often by air. As well as the places below (which specialise in cheap air, rail and coach fares for students and young people), the **International Students House Travel Club** (020 7631 8300) runs a heavily subsidised travel programme.

STA Travel
6 Wrights Lane, W8 (Europe 020 7361 6161/worldwide 020 7361 6262/guides & brochures 020 7361 6166/www.statravel.co.uk). High Street Kensington tube.
Open 9am-6pm Mon-Fri; 10am-4pm Sat. **Map 3 B9**
Branches: 86 Old Brompton Road, SW7 (020 7581 4132); 117 Euston Road, NW1 (020 7465 0484); 38 Store Street, WC1 (020 7580 7733); 11 Goodge Street, W1 (020 7436 7779).

Trailfinders
194 & 215 Kensington High Street, W8 (Europe & transatlantic 020 7937 5400/long haul 020 7938 3939/3366/ www.trailfinders.com). High Street Kensington tube. **Open** 9am-6pm Mon-Wed, Fri, Sat; 9am-7pm Thur; 10am-6pm Sun. **Map 3 A9**
Branch: 42-50 Earl's Court Road, W8 (020 7938 3366).

Usit Campus
52 Grosvenor Gardens, SW1 (0870 240 1010/www.usitcampus.co.uk). Victoria tube/rail. **Open** 9am-6pm Mon-Fri; 10am-5pm Sat; 10am-4pm Sun. **Map 7 H10**
Branches: 32 Store Street, WC1 (020 7580 5522); 14 Southampton Street, WC2 (020 7836 3343); 174 Kensington High Street, W8 (020 7938 2188).

English language classes

Aspect Covent Garden Language Centre
3-4 Southampton Place, WC1 (020 7404 3080/fax 020 7404 3443/ 114007.3020@compuserve.com). Holborn tube. **Map 6 L5**
As well as offering English language courses, this educational centre puts students in touch with host families.

Central School of English
1 Tottenham Court Road, W1 (020 7580 2863/fax 020 7255 1806/ efl@cselond.demon.co.uk). Tottenham Court Road tube.
Map 6 K5
Students can benefit from one-to-one tuition in this long-established school.
Website: www.edunet.com/cselond

Frances King School of English
77 Gloucester Road, SW7 (070 0011 2233/fax 070 0011 3344/ info@francesking.co.uk). Gloucester Road tube. **Map 2 F9**
A study year in London and teacher training courses are just two of the special programmes available here.
Website: www.francesking.co.uk

London Study Centre
Munster House, 676 Fulham Road, SW6 (020 7731 3549/fax 020 7731 6060/lsc.uk@btinternet.com). Parsons Green tube.
This long-established centre has such useful courses as English for Tourism.

Sels College
64-65 Long Acre, WC2 (020 7240 2581/fax 020 7379 5793/ english@sels.co.uk). Covent Garden tube. **Map 6 L6**
Founded in 1975, Sels places an emphasis on tuition in small groups.
Website: www.sels.co.uk

Shane English School
59 South Molton Street, W1 (020 7499 8533/fax 020 7499 9374/ info@shane-english.co.uk). Bond Street tube. **Map 5 H6**
Intensive daytime and evening English courses are offered by this school just off Oxford Street.
Website: www.saxoncourt.com

Further Reading

Fiction

Peter Ackroyd *Hawksmoor/The House of Doctor Dee/Dan Leno & the Limehouse Golem/ Great Fire of London*
Intricate studies of arcane London.

Jonathan Coe *The Dwarves of Death*
Mystery, music, mirth, malevolence.

Norman Collins *London Belongs to Me*
Witty saga of goings-on in Kennington in the 1930s.

Wilkie Collins *The Woman in White*
A midnight encounter has dire consequences.

Joseph Conrad *The Secret Agent*
Anarchism in seedy Soho.

Charles Dickens *Oliver Twist/David Copperfield/ Bleak House/Our Mutual Friend*
Four of the master's most London-centric novels.

Sir Arthur Conan Doyle *Complete Sherlock Holmes*
Reassuring sleuthing shenanigans.

Christopher Fowler *Soho Black*
Walking dead in Soho.

Graham Greene *The End of the Affair*
Adultery, Catholicism and Clapham Common.

Patrick Hamilton *20,000 Streets Under the Sky/ Hangover Square*
Yearning romantic trilogy set among Soho sleaze/ Love and death in darkest Earl's Court.

Alan Hollinghurst *The Swimming Pool Library*
Evocation of gay life around Russell Square.

Stewart Home *Come Before Christ and Murder Love*
Paranoia, food sex and tour-guide psycho-rap.

Maria Lexton (ed) *Time Out Book of London Short Stories*
London-based writers pay homage to their city.

Colin MacInnes *City of Spades/Absolute Beginners*
Coffee and jazz, Soho and Notting Hill.

Michael Moorcock *Mother London*
Love-letter to London.

Iris Murdoch *Under the Net*
Adventures of a talented but wastrel writer.

Courttia Newland *The Scholar*
Life is full of choices for a kid on a West London estate.

Kim Newman *The Quorum*
Intrigue surrounds Docklands-based media magnate.

George Orwell *Keep the Aspidistra Flying*
Saga of struggling writer and reluctant bookshop assistant.

Derek Raymond *I Was Dora Suarez*
Blackest London noir.

Geoff Ryman *253*
The lives of passengers on a Bakerloo Line train.

William Sansom *Selected Short Stories*
Lyrical tales of Londoners at large.

Will Self *Grey Area*
Short stories.

Iain Sinclair *Downriver/Radon Daughters/ White Chappell, Scarlet Tracings*
The Thames's own Heart of Darkness by London's laureate/William Hope Hodgson via the London Hospital/Ripper murders and bookdealers.

Muriel Spark *The Ballad of Peckham Rye*
The devil incarnate spreads mayhem in Peckham.

Evelyn Waugh *Vile Bodies*
Satire on the too-shamemaking antics in 1920s Mayfair.

Angus Wilson *The Old Men at the Zoo*
London faces down oblivion.

Virginia Woolf *Mrs Dalloway*
Joyce's *Ulysses* transplanted to London, this time with a female lead.

Non-fiction

Felix Barker & Ralph Hyde *London as it Might Have Been*
Schemes that never made it past the drawing board.

Daniel Farson *Soho in the Fifties*
Affectionate portrait of the many pubs and characters of Soho.

The Handbook Guide to Rock & Pop London
The pop sites, from the Beatles to Oasis.

Derek Hammond *London, England – A Day-tripper's Travelogue from the Coolest City in the World*
Witty, enthusiastic celebration of the capital.

Samantha Hardingham *London: A Guide to Recent Architecture*
Excellent pocket-sized guide.

Stephen Inwood *A History of London*
Recent, readable, encyclopaedic London biog.

Jack London *The People of the Abyss*
Extreme poverty in the East End.

Nick Merriman (ed) *The Peopling of London*
Fascinating account of 2,000 years of settlement.

George Orwell *Down and Out in Paris and London*
Autobiographical account of waitering and starving.

Samuel Pepys *Diaries*
Fires, plagues, bordellos and more.

Roy Porter *London – A Social History*
All-encompassing history of London.

Iain Sinclair *Lights Out For the Territory*
Time-warp visionary walks across London.

Richard Trench *London Under London*
Investigation of the subterranean city.

Ben Weinreb/Christopher Hibbert (eds) *Encyclopaedia of London*
Fascinating, thorough, indispensable.

Index

Note: *Page numbers in* **bold** *indicate the section giving key information on the topic; italics indicate photographs.*

b

t

Advertisers' Index

Please refer to the relevant sections for addresses/telephone numbers

Maps

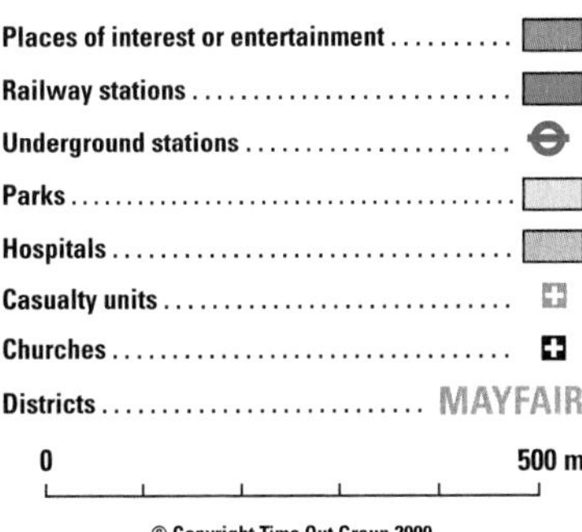
Places of interest or entertainment
Railway stations
Underground stations
Parks
Hospitals
Casualty units
Churches
Districts
MAYFAIR
0
500 m

London Overview

A10
EDMONTON
A112
A104
M11
London (Stansted)
NORTH CIRCULAR ROAD
Great Cambridge Road
WOODFORD
CHIGWELL
A406
Southend
Road
TOTTENHAM
William Morris Gallery
Forest Road
Epping Forest
HARRINGAY
High Road
Green Lanes
WALTHAMSTOW
A12
Eastern Ave
Cambridge Park
FINSBURY PARK
Seven Sisters Road
STAMFORD HILL
A104
LEYTONSTONE
Wanstead Park
A118
WANSTEAD
A107
CLAPTON
LEYTON
A12
Leytonstone
STOKE NEWINGTON
Stoke Newington Road
DALSTON
A11
FOREST GATE
ILFORD
Road
HACKNEY
Sutton House
River Lea
STRATFORD
High Rd
HIGHBURY
Map 9
Map 10
New North Rd
Kingsland Road
A102(M)
West Ham Park
BARKING
ISLINGTON
HOXTON
Victoria Park
Stratford High St
WEST HAM
Map 6
Museum of Childhood
BOW
EAST HAM
A13
City Road
SHOREDITCH
MILE END
Bow Rd
PLAISTOW
BETHNAL GREEN
Mile End Rd
Ragged School Museum
A12
NEWHAM
Liverpool Street
Whitechapel Rd
STEPNEY
Newham Way
A406
CITY
WHITECHAPEL
East India Dock Road
CANNING TOWN
BECKTON
St Paul's Cathedral
LIMEHOUSE
Blackwall Tunnel
London City Airport
Tower of London
Tower Bridge Rd
WAPPING
Canary Wharf
North Woolwich Rd
Albert Rd
Waterloo
River Thames
Dome
THAMESMEAD
ROTHERHITHE
ISLE OF DOGS
Thames Barrier
Woolwich Ferry
Map 11
Map 12
BERMONDSEY
New Kent Rd
A102(M)
Woolwich Road
Maryon Park
Map 8
A206
WOOLWICH
Royal Naval College
Old Kent Road
Romney Road
Academy Road
CHARLTON
KENNINGTON
DEPTFORD
Cutty Sark
National Maritime Museum
Museum of Artillery
A205
PLUMSTEAD
CAMBERWELL
GREENWICH
Greenwich Park
Camberwell New Rd
Peckham Rd
Queens Road
Royal Observatory
Shooters Hill Road
A207
Brixton Rd
NEW CROSS
Lewisham Way
Oxleas Park
PECKHAM
NUNHEAD
BLACKHEATH
Well Hall Rd
BRIXTON
Lordship Lane
LEWISHAM
Lee High Rd
East Rochester Way
A2
Dulwich Picture Gallery
Peckham Rye
Lewisham High St
Eltham Road
ELTHAM
Brockwell Park
DULWICH
Westhorne Ave
N
SOUTH CIRCULAR ROAD
Horniman Museum
Brownhill Road
Christchurch Rd
Dulwich Common
London Road
Stanstead Rd
Sidcup Road
A205
FOREST HILL
CATFORD
A20
0
1
2
3 miles
0
1
2
3
4
5 km
Crystal Palace Park
CRYSTAL PALACE
© Copyright Time Out Group 2000
A21
BROMLEY

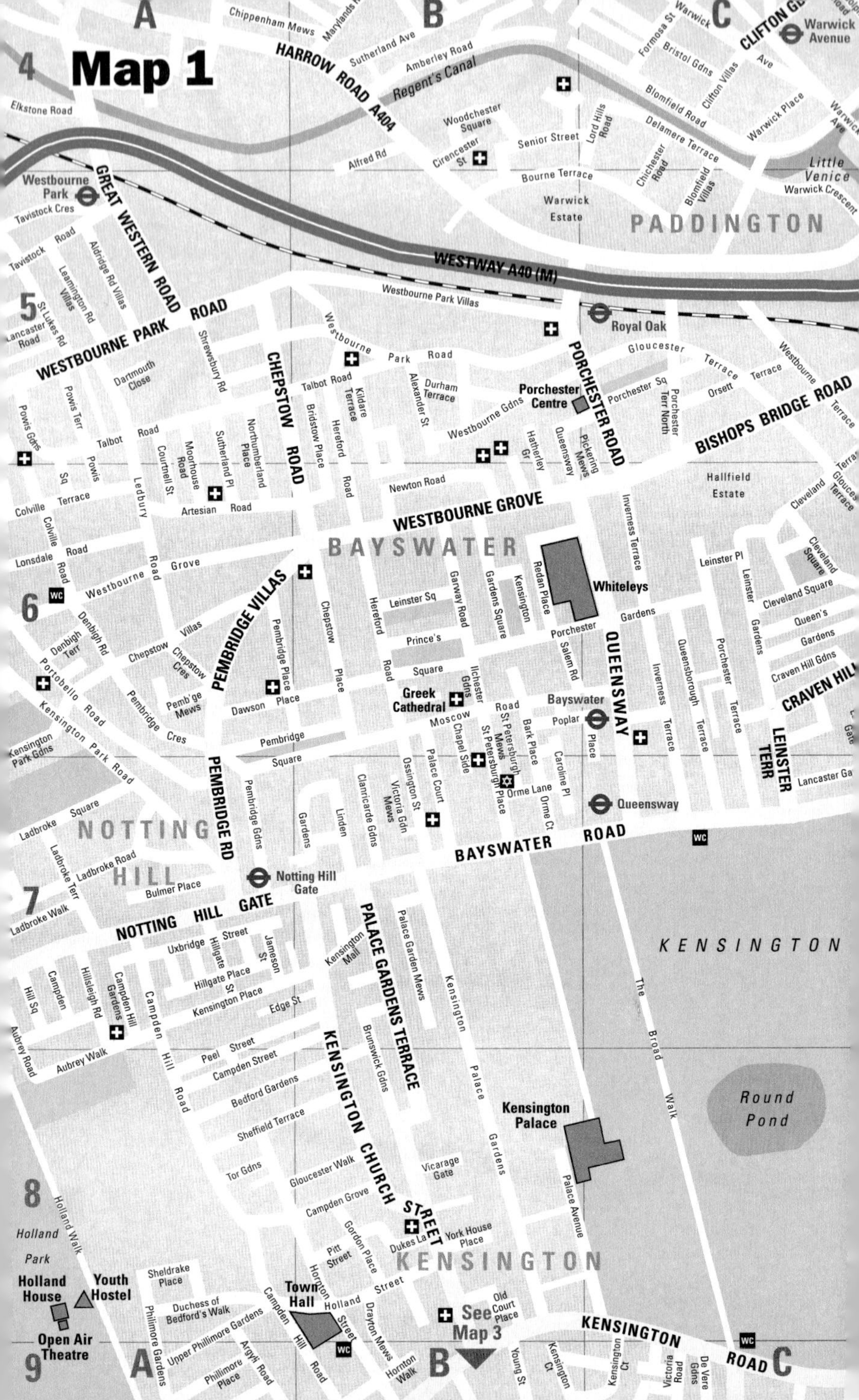

Map 1
A
B
C
4
5
6
7
8
9
Chippenham Mews
Marylands Rd
Harrow Road A404
Sutherland Ave
Amberley Road
Regent's Canal
Warwick
Formosa St
Bristol Gdns
Clifton Gdns
Clifton Villas
Warwick Avenue
Warwick Ave
Blomfield Road
Delamere Terrace
Warwick Place
Little Venice
Warwick Crescent
Elkstone Road
Woodchester Square
Cirencester St
Alfred Rd
Senior Street
Lord Hills Road
Bourne Terrace
Chichester Road
Blomfield Villas
Warwick Estate
PADDINGTON
Westbourne Park
Great Western Road
Tavistock Cres
Tavistock Road
Aldridge Rd Villas
Leamington Rd Villas
St Lukes Rd
Lancaster Road
Westway A40 (M)
Westbourne Park Villas
Royal Oak
Westbourne Park Road
Shrewsbury Rd
Dartmouth Close
Chepstow Road
Talbot Road
Kildare Terrace
Alexander St
Durham Terrace
Porchester Road
Porchester Centre
Gloucester Terrace
Porchester Sq
Porchester Terr North
Orsett Terrace
Westbourne Terrace
Bishops Bridge Road
Powis Gdns
Powis Terr
Powis Sq
Talbot Road
Ledbury Road
Courtnell St
Moorhouse Road
Sutherland Pl
Northumberland Place
Bridstow Place
Hereford Road
Westbourne Gdns
Hatherley Gr
Queensway
Pickering Mews
Hallfield Estate
Cleveland Terr
Gloucester Terrace
Colville Terrace
Artesian Road
Newton Road
Westbourne Grove
BAYSWATER
Inverness Terrace
Colville Road
Lonsdale Road
Westbourne Grove
Pembridge Villas
Leinster Sq
Garway Road
Gardens Square
Kensington
Redan Place
Whiteleys
Leinster Pl
Leinster Gardens
Cleveland Square
Cleveland Square
Queen's Gardens
Craven Hill Gdns
Craven Hill
Denbigh Terr
Denbigh Rd
Chepstow Villas
Chepstow Cres
Chepstow Place
Pembridge Place
Hereford Road
Prince's Square
Porchester Gardens
Salem Rd
Queensway
Queensborough Terrace
Porchester Terrace
Portobello Road
Kensington Park Road
Pembridge Cres
Pemb'ge Mews
Dawson Place
Greek Cathedral
Ilchester Gdns
Moscow Road
Bayswater
Poplar Place
Leinster Terr
Kensington Park Gdns
Pembridge Square
Chapel Side
St Petersburgh Mews
St Petersburgh Place
Bark Place
Caroline Pl
Orme Lane
Orme Ct
Lancaster Ga
Ladbroke Square
NOTTING HILL
Pembridge Rd
Pembridge Gdns
Gardens
Linden
Clanricarde Gdns
Victoria Gdn Mews
Ossington St
Palace Court
Queensway
Bayswater Road
Ladbroke Road
Ladbroke Terr
Bulmer Place
Notting Hill Gate
Ladbroke Walk
Palace Gardens Terrace
Palace Garden Mews
KENSINGTON
Uxbridge Street
Hillgate Street
Jameson St
Kensington Mall
Hillgate Place
Kensington Place
Edge St
Campden Hill Gardens
Hillsleigh Rd
Campden Hill Sq
Campden Hill Road
Kensington Palace Gardens
The Broad Walk
Aubrey Road
Aubrey Walk
Peel Street
Campden Street
Kensington Church Street
Brunswick Gdns
Bedford Gardens
Sheffield Terrace
Kensington Palace
Round Pond
Tor Gdns
Gloucester Walk
Vicarage Gate
Palace Avenue
Holland Walk
Campden Grove
Gordon Place
York House Place
Holland Park
Pitt Street
Dukes La
Holland House
Youth Hostel
Sheldrake Place
Hornton Street
Town Hall
Holland Street
Old Court Place
See Map 3
Duchess of Bedford's Walk
Campden Hill Road
Drayton Mews
Kensington Road
Open Air Theatre
Phillimore Gardens
Upper Phillimore Gardens
Phillimore Place
Argyll Road
Hornton Walk
Young St
Kensington Ct
Victoria Road
De Vere Gdns
WC

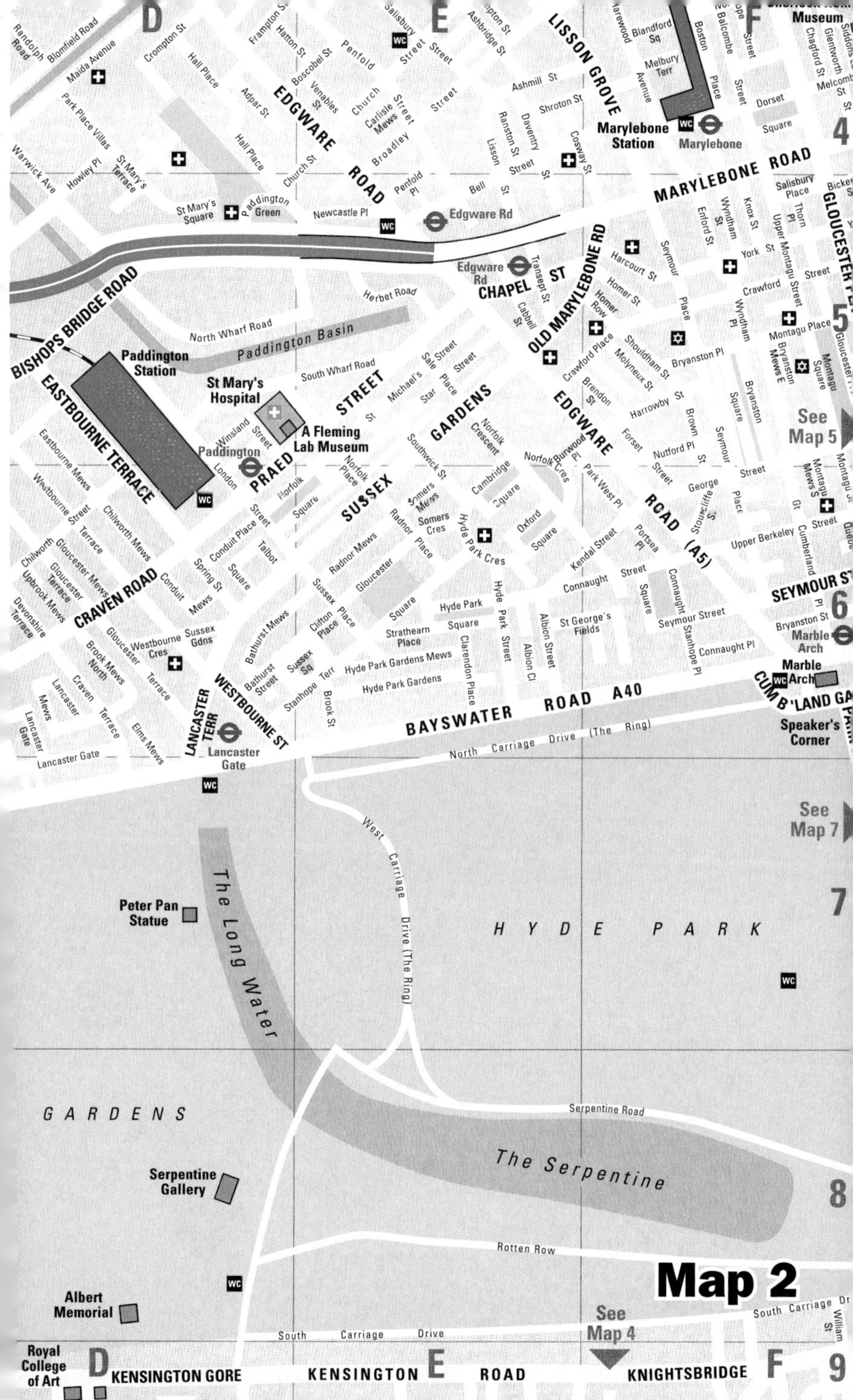

D
E
F
Museum
LISSON GROVE
EDGWARE ROAD
Randolph Road
Blomfield Road
Maida Avenue
Crompton St
Hall Place
Frampton St
Hatton St
Boscobel St
Venables St
Penfold Street
Salisbury Street
Ashbridge St
Church Street
Carlisle Mews
Broadley Street
Blandford Sq
Melbury Terr
Boston Place
Balcombe Street
Chagford St
Glentworth St
Melcombe St
Dorset Square
Ashmill St
Shroton St
Ranston St
Daventry Street
Lisson Street
Cosway St
Bell St
Marylebone Station
Marylebone
MARYLEBONE ROAD
Salisbury Place
Thorn Pl
GLOUCESTER PL
Park Place Villas
Adpar St
Warwick Ave
Howley Pl
St Mary's Terrace
St Mary's Square
Paddington Green
Church St
Newcastle Pl
Penfold Pl
Edgware Rd
Enford St
Wyndham St
Knox St
Upper Montagu Street
York St
Harcourt St
Seymour Place
Transept St
CHAPEL ST
OLD MARYLEBONE RD
Homer St
Homer Row
Crawford Street
Wyndham Pl
Montagu Place
Bryanston Mews E
Montagu Square
Gloucester Pl
BISHOPS BRIDGE ROAD
Herbet Road
Cabbell St
North Wharf Road
Paddington Basin
Paddington Station
South Wharf Road
St Mary's Hospital
Sale Street
Star Place
St Michael's Street
Crawford Place
Shouldham St
Molyneux St
Bryanston Pl
Bryanston Square
Bryanston
Brendon St
Harrowby St
Brown St
Seymour
See Map 5
EASTBOURNE TERRACE
Eastbourne Mews
Westbourne Street
Chilworth Mews
Winsland Street
A Fleming Lab Museum
Paddington
London
PRAED STREET
Norfolk Place
Norfolk Square
Southwick St
SUSSEX GARDENS
Norfolk Crescent
Norfolk Cres
Burwood Pl
Park West Pl
Forset St
Nutford Pl
George Street
Montagu Mews S
Cambridge Square
Somers Mews
Somers Cres
Radnor Place
Hyde Park Cres
Oxford Square
ROAD (A5)
Stourcliffe St
Upper Berkeley Street
Cumberland Gt
Chilworth St
Gloucester Mews
Gloucester Terrace
Upbrook Mews
Devonshire Terrace
CRAVEN ROAD
Conduit Place
Conduit Mews
Talbot Square
Spring St
Radnor Mews
Gloucester Square
Sussex Place
Kendal Street
Portsea Pl
Connaught Street
Connaught Square
Connaught Pl
SEYMOUR ST
Bryanston St
Marble Arch
Westbourne Cres
Sussex Gdns
Bathurst Mews
Clifton Place
Hyde Park Square
Strathearn Place
Hyde Park Street
Albion Street
Albion Cl
St George's Fields
Seymour Street
Stanhope Pl
Brook Mews North
Craven Terrace
Lancaster Mews
Lancaster Gate
Sussex Sq
Bathurst Street
Stanhope Terr
Brook St
Hyde Park Gardens Mews
Hyde Park Gardens
Clarendon Place
WESTBOURNE ST
LANCASTER TERR
Lancaster Gate
Elms Mews
BAYSWATER ROAD A40
CUMB'LAND GA
Speaker's Corner
North Carriage Drive (The Ring)
WC
See Map 7
West Carriage Drive (The Ring)
The Long Water
Peter Pan Statue
HYDE PARK
GARDENS
Serpentine Road
The Serpentine
Serpentine Gallery
Rotten Row
Map 2
Albert Memorial
See Map 4
South Carriage Drive
William St
Royal College of Art
KENSINGTON GORE
KENSINGTON ROAD
KNIGHTSBRIDGE
4
5
6
7
8
9

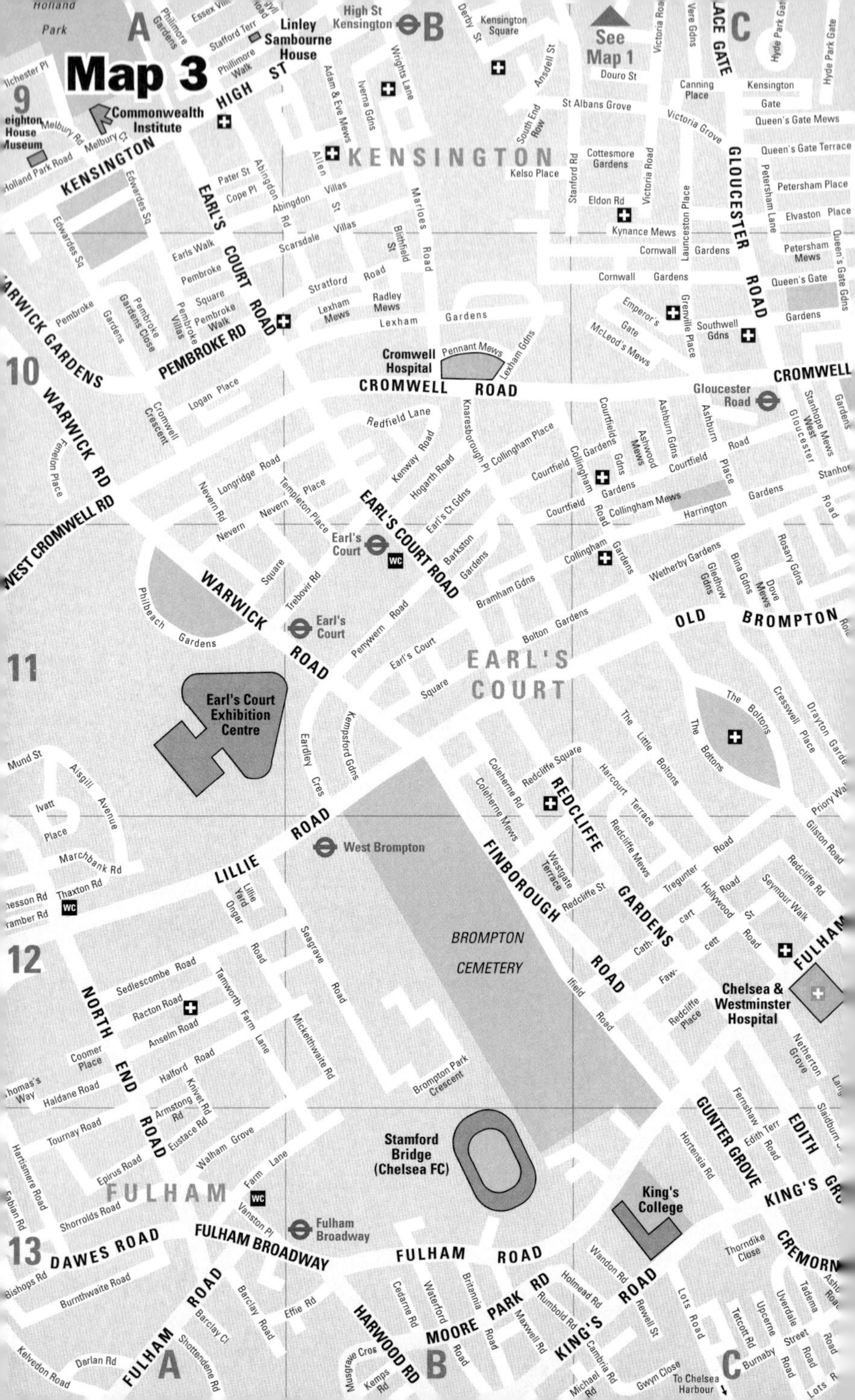

Map 3
See Map 1
KENSINGTON
EARL'S COURT
FULHAM
BROMPTON CEMETERY
Commonwealth Institute
Linley Sambourne House
Cromwell Hospital
Earl's Court Exhibition Centre
Stamford Bridge (Chelsea FC)
King's College
Chelsea & Westminster Hospital
High St Kensington
Gloucester Road
Earl's Court
West Brompton
Fulham Broadway
HIGH ST
KENSINGTON
CROMWELL ROAD
WARWICK GARDENS
WARWICK RD
WEST CROMWELL RD
WARWICK ROAD
EARL'S COURT ROAD
PEMBROKE RD
GLOUCESTER ROAD
OLD BROMPTON
LILLIE ROAD
REDCLIFFE GARDENS
FINBOROUGH ROAD
NORTH END ROAD
FULHAM BROADWAY
FULHAM ROAD
DAWES ROAD
HARWOOD RD
MOORE PARK RD
KING'S ROAD
GUNTER GROVE
EDITH
CREMORNE
To Chelsea Harbour
A
B
C
9
10
11
12
13

Royal Albert Hall
Royal College of Art
Royal College of Music
Imperial College of Science and Technology
Goethe Institute
Science Museum
Victoria & Albert Museum
Brompton Oratory
Natural History Museum
Harrods
KNIGHTSBRIDGE
See Map 2
See Map 7
South Kensington
Michelin House
Royal Marsden Hospital
Royal Brompton Hospital
CHELSEA
Chelsea College of Art & Design
Chelsea Old Town Hall
Chelsea Royal Hospital
National Army Museum
Chelsea Antiques Market
Bluebird
Carlyle's House
Chelsea Old Church
Crosby Hall
Chelsea Physic Garden
River Thames
Peace Pagoda
Zoo
BATTERSEA PARK
Chelsea Wharf
Lots Road Power Station
Map 4

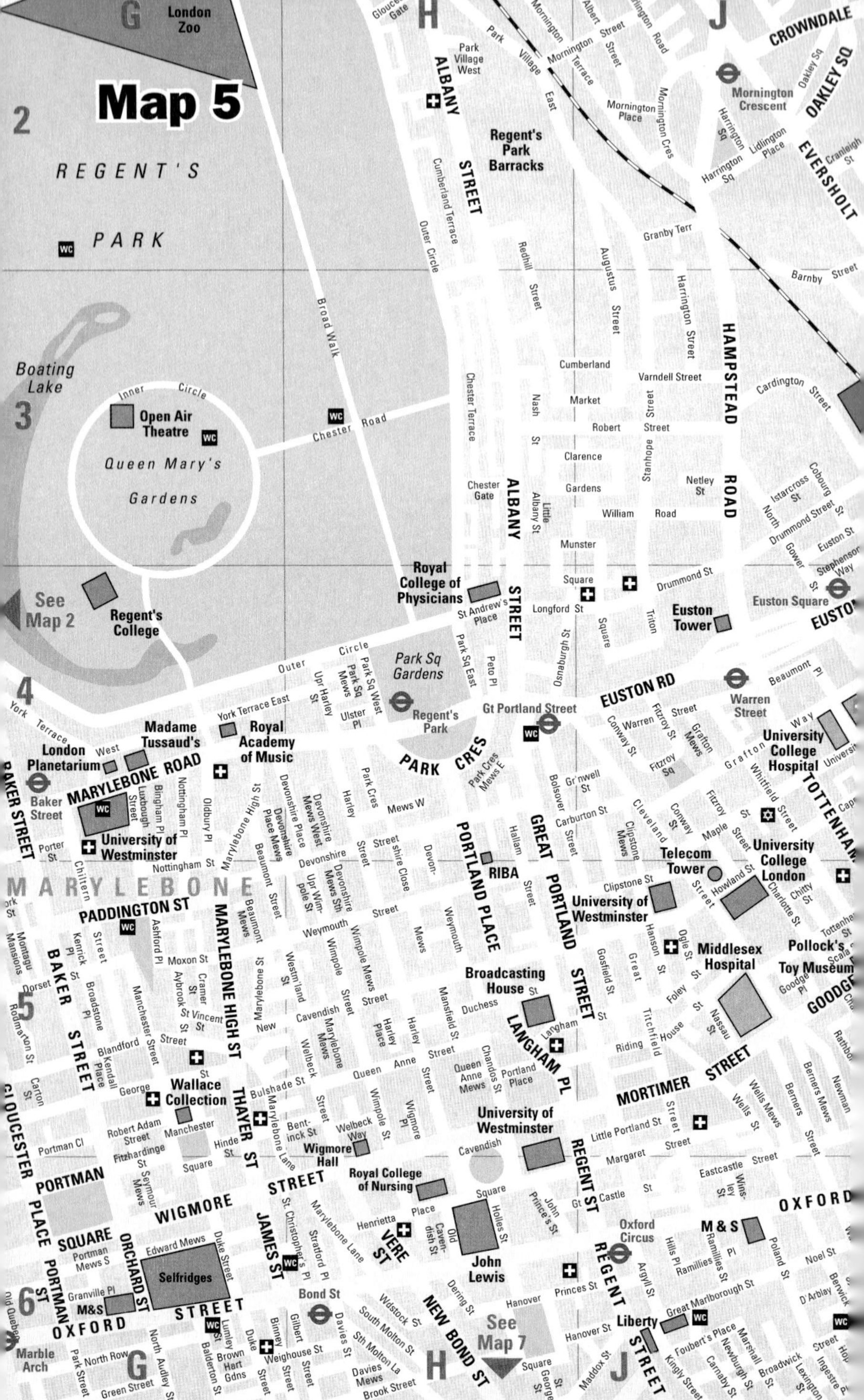

Map 5
London Zoo
REGENT'S PARK
Boating Lake
Open Air Theatre
Queen Mary's Gardens
Inner Circle
Chester Road
Broad Walk
Outer Circle
See Map 2
Regent's College
Royal College of Physicians
Regent's Park Barracks
Park Village West
ALBANY STREET
Mornington Crescent
CROWNDALE
OAKLEY SQ
EVERSHOLT
HAMPSTEAD ROAD
Euston Tower
Euston Square
EUSTON RD
Warren Street
Gt Portland Street
Regent's Park
Park Sq Gardens
PARK CRES
Madame Tussaud's
London Planetarium
Royal Academy of Music
MARYLEBONE ROAD
Baker Street
University of Westminster
University College Hospital
TOTTENHAM
MARYLEBONE
PADDINGTON ST
MARYLEBONE HIGH ST
PORTLAND PLACE
RIBA
GREAT PORTLAND STREET
Telecom Tower
University College London
Middlesex Hospital
Pollock's Toy Museum
Broadcasting House
LANGHAM PL
MORTIMER STREET
Wallace Collection
THAYER ST
Wigmore Hall
WIGMORE STREET
Royal College of Nursing
University of Westminster
REGENT ST
Oxford Circus
OXFORD
M & S
John Lewis
Selfridges
PORTMAN SQUARE
ORCHARD ST
OXFORD STREET
Bond St
NEW BOND ST
See Map 7
Liberty
Marble Arch
BAKER STREET
GLOUCESTER PLACE

Map 6
K
L
M
2
3
4
5
6
See Map 9
See Map 8
St Pancras Gardens
Camley St Natural Park
Regent's Canal
Battle Bridge Basin
Canal Museum
Goldington Cres
Medburn St
Goldington St
Charrington
Platt St
St Pancras Road
Goods Way
York Way
Crinan St
New Wharf Road
All Saints St
Killick St
Caledonian Road
Carnegie St
Muriel St
Wynford Road
Wharfedale Road
Cranleigh St
Chalton
Bridgeway St
Werrington
Aldenham St
Purchese Street
Coopers Lane
Battle Bridge Rd
Cheney Rd
Balfe St
Railway St
King's Cross Station
Northdown St
Calshot Street
Priory Green
Rodney
Collier Street
Cumming St
Polygon Road
Brill Place
St Pancras Station
Midland Road
Caledonia St
Keystone Cres
Pentonville Road
Street
British Library
Ossulston Street
Phoenix Road
Drummond Cres
Chalton Street
Euston Station
Doric Way
Churchway
King's Cross St Pancras
Cressfield St
Birkenhead Street
Thameslink Station
St Chad's Place
Leeke St
King's Cross Rd
Lorenzo St
Weston Rise
Penton Rise
Vernon Rise
Percy Circus
Britannia Street
Wicklow St
Euston Road
Belgrave St
Argyle St
St Chad's St
Argyle Sq
Argyle Street
Swinton St
Great Percy
Euston
Grafton Pl
Bidborough St
Judd Street
Tonbridge St
Whidborne St
Gray's Inn Road
Acton St
Wharton Street
Melton St
Duke's Rd
Flaxman Terr
Hastings St
Thanet St
Sandwich St
Cartwright Gardens
Cromer Street
Harrison Street
Regent Square
Frederick St
Ampton St
Cubitt Street
Granville Square
Upr Woburn Pl
Woburn Walk
Burton Street
Leigh St
Wakefield St
Seaford St
Sidmouth St
Endsleigh Gardens
Endsleigh St
Road
Wellcome Foundation
Gower Place
Gordon St
Taviton St
Tavistock Place
Hunter St
St George's Gardens
Heathcote St
Eastman Dental Hospital
Pakenham St
Kenton St
Tavistock Square
Mecklenburgh
Wren St
Calthorpe St
Mount Pleasant Sorting Office
University College London
Gordon Square
Woburn Place
Marchmont Street
Handel St
Brunswick Centre
Grenville St
Brunswick Square
Coram's Fields
Square
Doughty Street
Gough Street
Herbrand Street
Coram St
Lansdowne Terr
Percival David Foundation
Gower Street
Petrie Museum of Egyptian Archaeology
Woburn Square
Bedford Way
Bernard Street
Colonnade
Guilford Street
Great Ormond St Hospital
Doughty Mews
Brownlow Mews
Dickens' House
Coley St
Chenies M
Huntley St
Torrington Place
Malet Street
Torrington Square
University of London
Russell Square
Lamb's Conduit Street
Millman St
Roger St
North Mews
John St
John's Mews
Elm St
Gray's Inn Road
Ridgmount Gdns
Bloomsbury
Queen Square
Great Ormond
Orde Hall St
Rugby St
Northington St
King's Mews
Goodge Street
North Crescent
Chenies St
Ridgmount St
Senate House
Russell Square
Dombey St
Emerald St
Gt James St
Keppel St
Montague Pl
Bedford Place
Old Gloucester St
Boswell St
New North St
Harpur St
Theobald's Road
Alfred Pl
Court Road
Store Street
Gower Mews
South Crescent
Bedford Square
Montague St
British Museum
Southampton Row
Bloomsbury Square
Red Lion Square
Red Lion St
Princeton St
Bedford Row
Jockey's Field
Raymond Buildings
Gray's Inn Gardens
Whitfield Street
Windmill St
Bayley St
Morwell St
Bloomsbury St
Great Russell Street
Drake St
Sandland St
Brownlow St
Percy Street
Gilbert Pl
Bury Pl
Bloomsbury Way
Sicilian Ave
Fisher St
Procter St
Eagle St
Rathbone Place
Gresse St
Stephen St
Bedford Ave
Great Russell St
Coptic St
Little Russell St
Museum St
Barter St
Soton Pl
Catton St
High Holborn
Holborn
Chancery Lane
Stone Buildings
Hanway Pl
Hanway St
Bainbridge St
Dyott St
Streatham St
New Oxford Street
Sir John Soane's Museum
Whetstone Park
Tottenham Court Road
New Oxford Street
West Central St
Newton St
Lincoln's Inn Fields
Street
Soho St
Charing Cross Road
Andrew Borde St
Earnshaw St
Bucknall St
Grape St
High Holborn
Stukeley St
Remnant St
Lincoln's Inn Fields
Lincoln's Inn
Soho
Sutton Row
St Giles High St
Shaftesbury Avenue
Drury Lane
Macklin St
Parker St
Great Queen Street
Kingsway
Dean St
Chapel St
Denmark St
Goslett Yd
Manette St
Flitcroft St
New Compton St
Covent Garden
Freemasons' Hall
Wild Ct
Lincoln's Inn Fields
Serle Street
New Square
Carlisle St
Soho Square
Greek Street
Frith Street
Stacey St
Phoenix St
Endell St
Betterton St
Museums of the Royal College of Surgeons
Portugal St
St Anne's Ct
Bateman St
Moor St
Shorts Gdns
Neal St
Arne St
Gt Queen
Wild Street
Keeley St
Kemble St
Kean St
Carey St
Royal Courts of Justice
Grange Ct
Clement's Inn
Seven Dials
Earlham St
Monmouth St
Tower St
Mercer St
Shelton St
Langley St
Long Acre
Bow St
Royal Opera House
Floral St
Russell St
Drury Lane
LSE
Aldwych
St Clement Danes
Meard St
Bourchier St
Old Compton Street
Romilly St
Cambridge Circus
West St
Peter Street

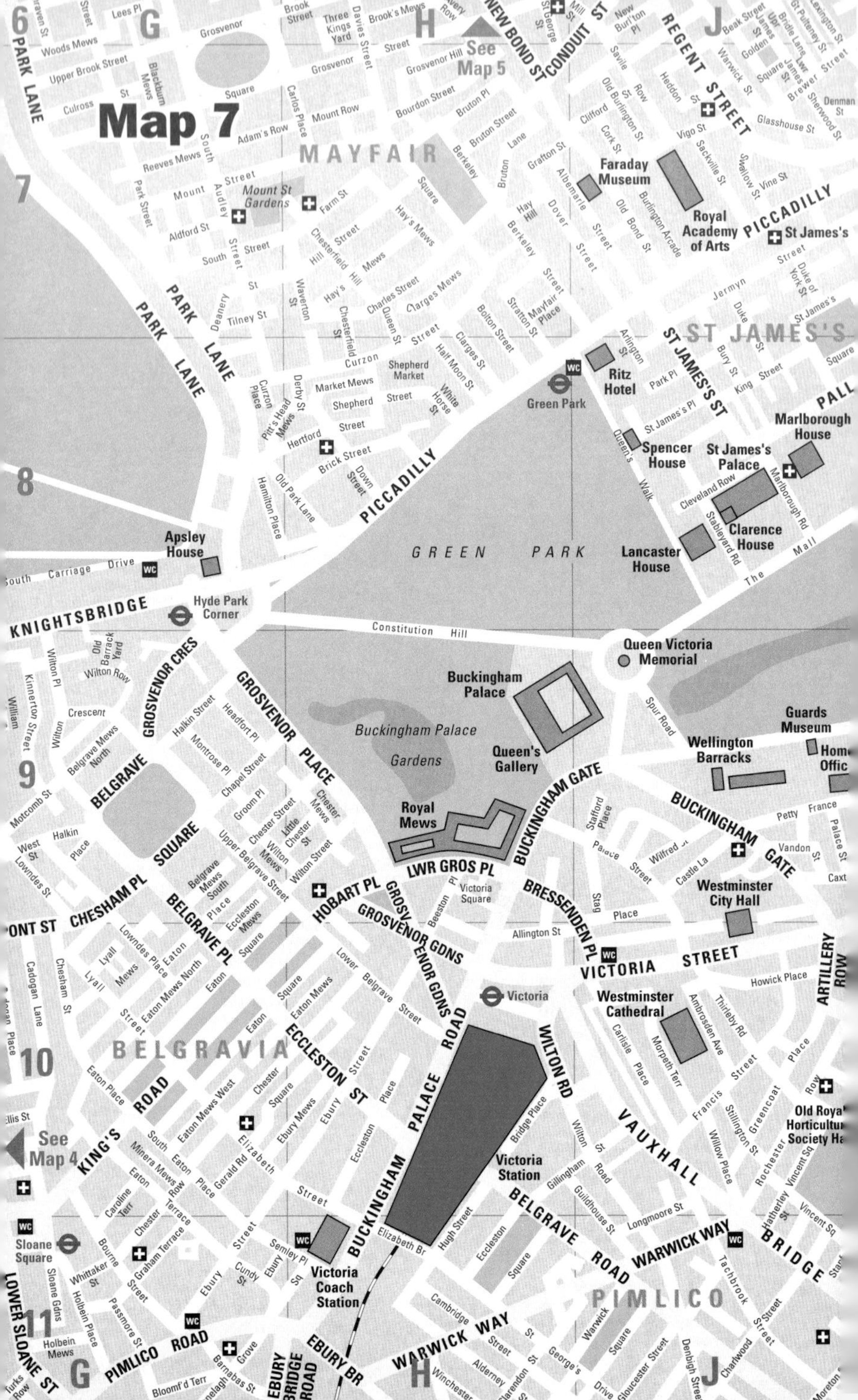

Map 7
MAYFAIR
ST JAMES'S
BELGRAVIA
PIMLICO
GREEN PARK
Buckingham Palace Gardens
See Map 5
See Map 4
Faraday Museum
Royal Academy of Arts
Ritz Hotel
Green Park
Spencer House
St James's Palace
Marlborough House
Clarence House
Lancaster House
Apsley House
Hyde Park Corner
Queen Victoria Memorial
Buckingham Palace
Queen's Gallery
Royal Mews
Guards Museum
Wellington Barracks
Westminster City Hall
Victoria
Westminster Cathedral
Victoria Station
Victoria Coach Station
Sloane Square
Old Royal Horticultural Society Hall
PICCADILLY
PARK LANE
KNIGHTSBRIDGE
GROSVENOR PLACE
BUCKINGHAM GATE
VICTORIA STREET
BUCKINGHAM PALACE ROAD
VAUXHALL BRIDGE
KING'S ROAD
PIMLICO ROAD

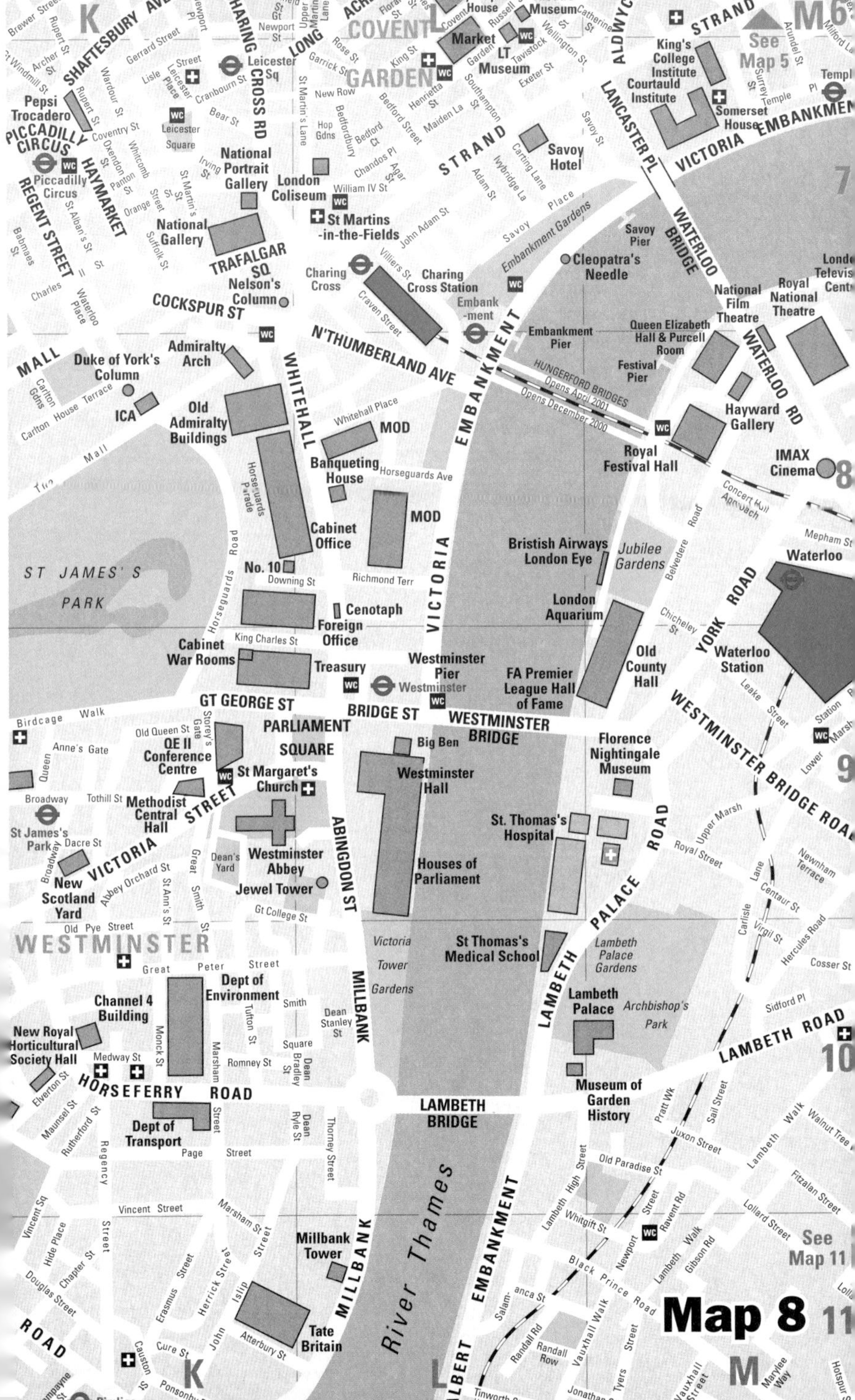

K
L
M
COVENT GARDEN
See Map 5
Map 8
See Map 11
SHAFTESBURY AVE
CHARING CROSS RD
LONG ACRE
STRAND
ALDWYCH
LANCASTER PL
VICTORIA EMBANKMENT
Royal Opera House
Theatre Museum
Market
LT Museum
King's College Institute
Courtauld Institute
Somerset House
Leicester Sq
Leicester Square
Pepsi Trocadero
PICCADILLY CIRCUS
Piccadilly Circus
HAYMARKET
REGENT STREET
National Portrait Gallery
London Coliseum
National Gallery
St Martins -in-the-Fields
TRAFALGAR SQ
Nelson's Column
Charing Cross
Charing Cross Station
Savoy Hotel
Savoy Pier
Embankment Gardens
Cleopatra's Needle
WATERLOO BRIDGE
COCKSPUR ST
Embankment
N'THUMBERLAND AVE
EMBANKMENT
Embankment Pier
HUNGERFORD BRIDGES
Opens April 2001
Opens December 2000
Festival Pier
Queen Elizabeth Hall & Purcell Room
National Film Theatre
Royal National Theatre
WATERLOO RD
Hayward Gallery
Royal Festival Hall
IMAX Cinema
MALL
Duke of York's Column
Admiralty Arch
WHITEHALL
ICA
Old Admiralty Buildings
MOD
Banqueting House
Horseguards Ave
Horseguards Parade
Cabinet Office
No. 10
Downing St
Richmond Terr
VICTORIA
Bristish Airways London Eye
Jubilee Gardens
London Aquarium
ST JAMES'S PARK
Cenotaph
Foreign Office
King Charles St
Cabinet War Rooms
Treasury
Westminster Pier
Westminster
FA Premier League Hall of Fame
Old County Hall
YORK ROAD
Waterloo
Waterloo Station
GT GEORGE ST
PARLIAMENT SQUARE
BRIDGE ST
WESTMINSTER BRIDGE
WESTMINSTER BRIDGE ROAD
Birdcage Walk
QE II Conference Centre
Big Ben
Westminster Hall
Florence Nightingale Museum
St Margaret's Church
Methodist Central Hall
VICTORIA STREET
St James's Park
New Scotland Yard
Westminster Abbey
Jewel Tower
ABINGDON ST
Houses of Parliament
St. Thomas's Hospital
LAMBETH PALACE ROAD
WESTMINSTER
Victoria Tower Gardens
St Thomas's Medical School
Lambeth Palace Gardens
Dept of Environment
Channel 4 Building
MILLBANK
Lambeth Palace
Archbishop's Park
New Royal Horticultural Society Hall
LAMBETH ROAD
HORSEFERRY ROAD
LAMBETH BRIDGE
Museum of Garden History
Dept of Transport
River Thames
Millbank Tower
EMBANKMENT
Tate Britain
ALBERT
Pimlico

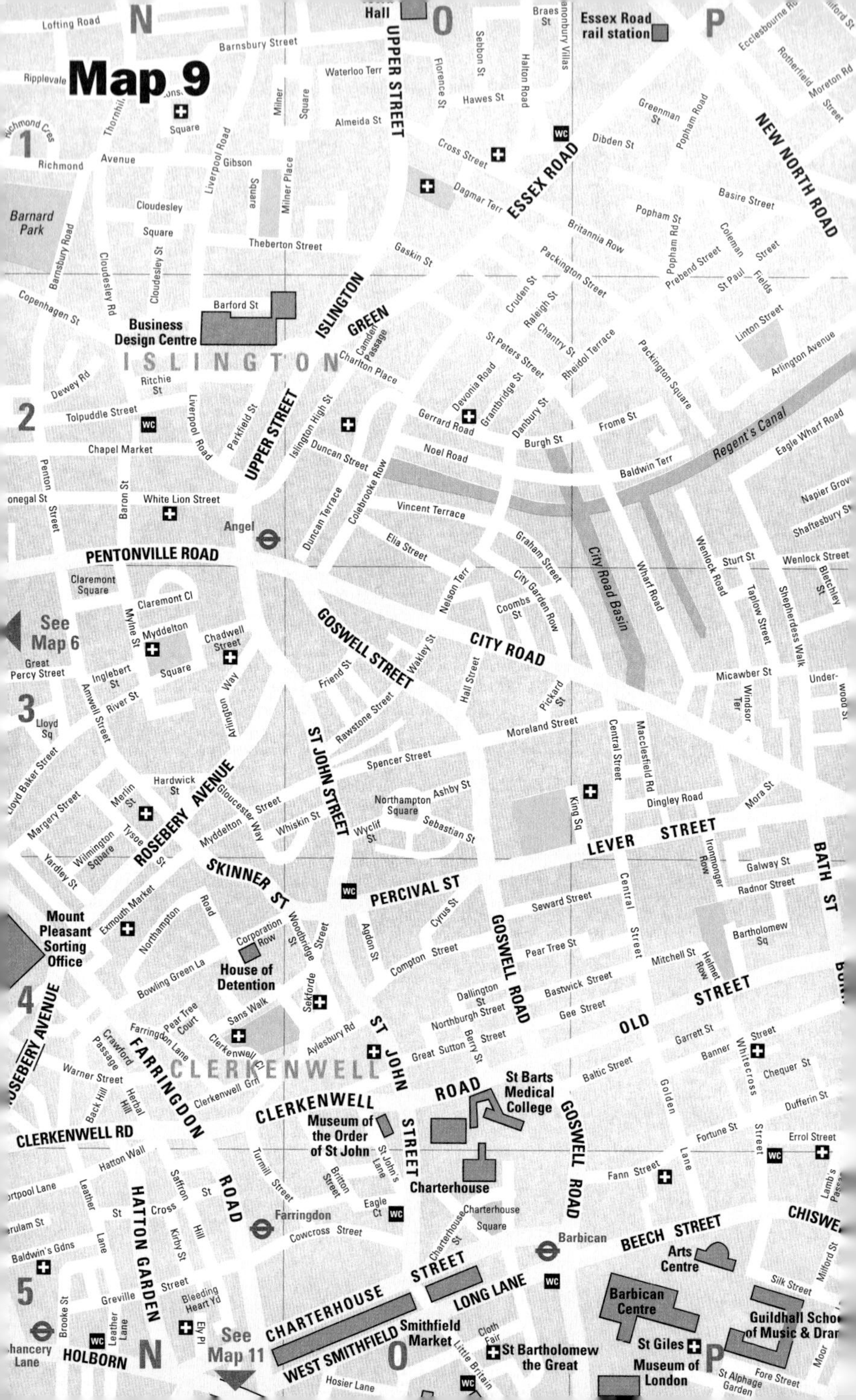

Map 9
N
O
P
1
2
3
4
5
Lofting Road
Barnsbury Street
Hall
UPPER STREET
Braes St
Canonbury Villas
Essex Road rail station
Ecclesbourne Rd
Rotherfield Street
Moreton Rd
Ripplevale
Waterloo Terr
Milner Square
Florence St
Sebbon St
Halton Road
Hawes St
Greenman St
Popham Road
NEW NORTH ROAD
Richmond Cres
Thornhill
Square
Almeida St
Cross Street
WC
Dibden St
Richmond Avenue
Liverpool Road
Gibson Square
Milner Place
Dagmar Terr
ESSEX ROAD
Basire Street
Barnard Park
Cloudesley Square
Popham St
Britannia Row
Coleman Street
Barnsbury Road
Cloudesley Rd
Cloudesley St
Theberton Street
Gaskin St
Packington Street
Popham Rd
Prebend Street
St Paul Fields
Copenhagen St
Barford St
ISLINGTON GREEN
Cruden St
Raleigh St
Linton Street
Business Design Centre
Camden Passage
Chantry St
St Peters Street
Rheidol Terrace
Packington Square
Arlington Avenue
ISLINGTON
Charlton Place
Dewey Rd
Ritchie St
Devonia Road
Grantbridge St
Tolpuddle Street
Liverpool Road
Parkfield St
UPPER STREET
Islington High St
Gerrard Road
Danbury St
Frome St
Regent's Canal
Eagle Wharf Road
Chapel Market
Duncan Street
Noel Road
Burgh St
Baldwin Terr
Penton Street
Colebrooke Row
Napier Grove
Donegal St
Baron St
White Lion Street
Vincent Terrace
Shaftesbury St
Angel
Duncan Terrace
Elia Street
Graham Street
City Road Basin
Wharf Road
Wenlock Road
Sturt St
Wenlock Street
PENTONVILLE ROAD
Claremont Square
Claremont Cl
Nelson Terr
City Garden Row
Taplow Street
Bletchley St
Mylne St
Myddelton Square
Chadwell Street
GOSWELL STREET
Coombs St
Shepherdess Walk
See Map 6
Great Percy Street
Inglebert St
Wakley St
CITY ROAD
Amwell Street
River St
Arlington Way
Friend St
Hall Street
Pickard St
Micawber St
Under-wood St
Lloyd Sq
Windsor Ter
Rawstone Street
ST JOHN STREET
Moreland Street
Central Street
Macclesfield Rd
Lloyd Baker Street
Spencer Street
Hardwick St
ROSEBERY AVENUE
Gloucester Way
Northampton Square
Ashby St
King Sq
Dingley Road
Mora St
Margery Street
Merlin St
Street
Whiskin St
Sebastian St
Tysoe St
Myddelton Street
Wyclif St
LEVER STREET
Ironmonger Row
BATH ST
Wilmington Square
Galway St
Yardley St
SKINNER ST
PERCIVAL ST
Radnor Street
Seward Street
Exmouth Market
Mount Pleasant Sorting Office
Northampton Road
Corporation Row
Woodbridge St
Street
Cyrus St
Agdon St
GOSWELL ROAD
Pear Tree St
Bartholomew Sq
House of Detention
Bowling Green La
Compton Street
Mitchell St
Helmet Row
Sekforde Street
Dallington St
Bastwick Street
OLD STREET
ROSEBERY AVENUE
Sans Walk
Northburgh Street
Gee Street
Pear Tree Court
Farringdon Lane
Aylesbury Rd
Garrett St
Crawford Passage
FARRINGDON
Clerkenwell Cl
ST JOHN
Great Sutton Street
Berry St
Banner Street
Whitecross Street
Chequer St
CLERKENWELL
Warner Street
Clerkenwell Grn
Baltic Street
Back Hill
Herbal Hill
CLERKENWELL ROAD
St Barts Medical College
Dufferin St
CLERKENWELL RD
Museum of the Order of St John
STREET
GOSWELL ROAD
Golden Lane
Fortune St
Hatton Wall
Turnmill Street
St John's Lane
Britton Street
Errol Street
Portpool Lane
Leather Lane
Saffron Hill
HATTON GARDEN
ROAD
Charterhouse
Fann Street
Lamb's Passage
Cross St
Eagle Ct
Charterhouse Square
CHISWELL
Kirby St
Farringdon
Charterhouse St
Barbican
BEECH STREET
Baldwin's Gdns
Cowcross Street
Arts Centre
Milford St
STREET
LONG LANE
Silk Street
Greville Street
Bleeding Heart Yd
CHARTERHOUSE
Barbican Centre
Guildhall School of Music & Drama
Brooke St
Leather Lane
Ely Pl
See Map 11
WEST SMITHFIELD
Smithfield Market
Cloth Fair
St Bartholomew the Great
St Giles
Museum of London
Moor
Chancery Lane
HOLBORN
Little Britain
Hosier Lane
St Alphage Garden
Fore Street

Map 10
Q
R
S
1
2
3
4
5
DALSTON
HAGGERSTON
HOXTON
SHOREDITCH
Mapledene Rd
Lavender Gr
Holly St
Road
Moreton Rd
Halliford Street
Almorah Rd
Cleveland Road
Northchurch Road
Ufton Road
Lawford Road
De Beauvoir Road
De Beauvoir Square
Mortimer Rd
Southgate Gr
Downham Road
Southgate Road
Sherbourne St
Balmes Road
Hertford Road
KINGSLAND ROAD
Haggerston Road
Albion Square
Albion Drive
Queensbridge Road
Shrubland Road
Livermore Rd
Lee Street
Scriven St
Brownlow Rd
Acton Mews
Stean St
Clarissa St
De Beauvoir Crescent
Whitmore Road
Wilton Square
Baring Street
Dunston Rd
Pownall Row
Regent's Canal
Orsman Road
Halcomb St
Penn St
Bridport Place
Hyde Rd
Poole St
Mill Row
Phillipp Street
Laburnun Road
Whiston Road
NEW NORTH ROAD
Shoreditch Park
Hemsworth St
Hoxton Street
Nuttall St
Hows Street
Thurtle Rd
Kent St
Haggerston Park
Wimbourne St
Cropley Street
Mintern Street
Pitfield Street
Ivy St
Geffrye Street
Ormsby Street
Pearson Street
Appleby Street
Weymouth Ter
Queensbridge Road
Purcell St
Stanway Street
Buckland St
Regan Way
Wenlock Street
Cherbury St
Geffrye Museum
Dunloe Street
Murray Grove
Crondall Street
Shenfield St
Falkirk Street
Cremer Street
HACKNEY ROAD
New North Rd
Cadell Cl
Horchio St
Ravenscroft Street
Shipton Street
Provost Street
Fanshaw St
Nazral St
Union Wk
KINGSLAND ROAD
Bevenden St
EAST ROAD
Nile Street
Vestry St
Haberdasher St
Long St
Columbia Road
Quilter St
Buttesland St
Waterson St
Chart St
Moorfields Eye Hospital
Baches St
Pitfield Street
Chart St
Hoxton
Hoxton Street
Drysdale St
COLUMBIA ROAD
Wellington Row
GOSSET ST
Corsham St
Charles Square
Hoxton Square
Brunswick Place
Boot St
Peerless Street
Austin St
Virginia Rd
Chambord St
OLD STREET
Cranwood St
Old Street
Calvert Ave
Arnold Circus
Swanfield Street
Brick Lane
Padbury Ct
Satchwell St
OLD STREET
Rivington Street
Charlotte Road
CURTAIN RD
Boundary Street
Bateman's Row
Mallow St
Cowper St
Willow St
GREAT EASTERN STREET
Leonard Street
Club Row
Old Nichol Street
Granby St
Featherstone St
Chilton St
John Wesley's House
Bunhill Fields Burial Grounds
Tabernacle Street
Paul Street
Luke Street
Phipp St
New Inn Yard
Redchurch Street
BETHNAL GREEN ROAD
Bacon Street
CITY ROAD
Epworth St
Scrutton St
Holywell Lane
SHOREDITCH HIGH STREET
SCLATER ST
CHESHIRE ST
Shoreditch
ROW
Bonhill St
Holywell Row
Curtain Road
Hearn St
Plough Yard
Wheeler St
Pedley St
Bunhill Fields
Worship Street
Worship Street
Fleur de Lis St
Quaker Street
Code St
Buxton Street
Finsbury Square
Dysart St
Christopher St
Snowden St
Blossom St
Elder St
Calvin St
Grey Eagle St
BRICK LANE
Spital St
Hunton St
Deal St
ST
Clifton Street
Earl St
Pindar St
Appold Street
Primrose St
Folgate Street
Woodseer St
Sun Street
Sun Street
Spital Sq
Lamb St
COMMERCIAL ST
Hanbury Street
Ropemaker Street
Finsbury Pavement
Lackington St
Wilson Street
Broadgate Centre
Liverpool Street Station
Steward St
Spitalfields Market
Wilkes St
Princelet Street
See Map 12
South Place
Fournier St
Moorfields
MOORGATE
Moorgate
Eldon St
Brushfield Street
Gun St
Christ Church
Heneage St
Finsbury
Artillery Lane

Map 11
5
N
O
P
6
7
8
9
10
Furnival St
Fetter Lane
New Fetter La
HOLBORN VIADUCT
Cock Lane
Giltspur St
Little Britain
ALDERSGATE ST
LONDON WALL
See Map 9
Cursitor St
New St
SHOE LANE
FARRINGDON ST
St Bartholomew's Hospital
National Postal Museum
Noble St
Alder Square
Basinghall Ave
Aldermanbury
CHANCERY LANE
Bream's Bldgs
Stone St
Old Bailey
Haberdashers' Hall
Love Lane
Wood Street
Fetter Lane
Gough Sq
ST BRIDE ST
Fleet Lane
NEWGATE ST
ANGEL ST
Goldsmiths' Hall
Guildhall
Basinghall St
Coleman Street
Limeburner La
Old Bailey
Cutters Hall
Foster Lane
Gresham
Street
Dr Johnson's House
Stationers' Hall
Warwick Lane
Paternoster Square
Gutter La
Wood Street
Milk St
St Dunstan
FLEET STREET
LUDGATE HILL
Paternoster Row
St Paul's
Trump St
King St
Ironmonger Lane
Grocers' Hall
Prince Henry's Room
St Bride's
Bride Lane
NEW BRIDGE ST
St Paul's Cathedral
NEW CHANGE
CHEAPSIDE
St Mary -le-Bow
Old Jewry
Bank
Middle Temple Lane
Inner Temple La
Old Mitre Ct
Whitefriars St
Dorset Rise
Pilgrim St
Ludgate Lane
ST PAUL'S CHYD
Watling St
Bread St
Temple Church
Bouverie St
Bridewell Place
City Thames-link station
Blackfriars
Carter Lane
City Information Centre
Bow Lane
Crown Office Row
Tudor Street
Apothecaries' Hall
St Andrews Hill
College of Arms
CANNON ST
STREET
Godliman St
Temple of Mithras
Walbrook
Middle Temple
Inner Temple
Temple Ave
Carmelite St
John Carpenter St
St Andrews by the Wardrobe
QUEEN
VICTORIA
Mansion House
London Stone
CANNON STREET
Blackfriars
Castle Baynard Street
Garlickhythe
Queen
College Hill
Cannon Street
VICTORIA EMBANKMENT
UPPER
Hill
Painters' Hall
Skinners La
Blackfriars Millennium Pier
White Lion
THAMES
St James
College St
STREET
High Timber St
Skinners' Hall
River Thames
BLACKFRIARS BRIDGE
Millennium Bridge (Opens May 2000)
Vintners' Hall
See Map 8
Oxo Tower Wharf
Cannon Street Station
SOUTHWARK BRIDGE
Gabriel's Wharf
Bankside Gallery
Tate Modern
Shakespeare's Globe
Bankside Pier
Ground
Upper
Upper Ground
Rennie St
Bankside
Rose Theatre
Broadwall
Hopton St
Holland St
New Globe Wk
Bear Gdns
Clink Exhibition
Golden Hinde
London Television Centre
Duchy
STREET
BANKSIDE
Park
Street
Clink St
Coin
Paris Gardens
Emerson St
Vinopolis, City of Wine
STAMFORD
Street
Hatfields
Sumner
Street
SOUTHWARK BRIDGE ROAD
Porter St
Southwark Cathedral
St
Aquinas St
Colombo St
SOUTHWARK STREET
Zoar St
Great Guildford St
Park St
Maiden Lane
Stoney Street
Theed
Street
Burrell St
Chancel St
Bear Lane
Thrale St
Cornwall
Whittlesey St
Waterloo East Station
Meymott
St
Gt Suffolk St
Lavington St
BOROUGH
Roupell Street
Brad Street
Joan Street
Scores St
Gambia St
ROAD
Ewer St
Keppel Row
SOUTHWARK ST
Borough Market
Exton St
Greet St
Hatfields
Southwark
UNION STREET
Road
Wootton St
UNION ST
Way
WATERLOO
Sandell St
Young Vic Theatre
THE CUT
Risbor St
Pepper St
BOROUGH HIGH STREET
Copperfield Street
London Fire Brigade Museum
Ayres St
Redcross
Old Vic Theatre
Street
Loman St
Pocock St
Great Suffolk Street
Sawyer St
Newcomen Street
Waterloo Station
Mitre Rd
Ufford
Surrey Row
Little Dorrit Court
Mermaid Ct
Lwr Marsh
Webber
Chaplin Cl
Pocock Street
MARSHALSEA RD
Tennis St
ROAD
Street
Valentine Pl
Rushworth St
Glass Hill Street
Sturge St
ROAD
St George the Martyr
Gray St
Barons Pl
BLACKFRIARS
Lant Street
Borough
BAYLIS ROAD
Coral St
Webber Row
Webber Street
Gt Suffolk St
TABARD ST
LONG LANE
Street
Street
Silex St
BRIDGE
Lambeth North
Pearman
Street
Lancaster Street
King James St
BOROUGH HIGH ST
NEBRASKA ST
Burdett St
Morley
Gerridge St
Dodson St
Library St
Stones End St
Street
Cole Street
Pilgrimage St
St. George's Circus
BOROUGH
SOUTHWARK
ROAD
Swan
Trinity
Trinity Street
GREAT
Tabard Street
WESTMINSTER BRIDGE ROAD
Rotary St
Keyworth Street
Church Sq
DOVER
Oakey Lane
King Edward Walk
LONDON ROAD
Doyle St
NEWINGTON CAUSEWAY
Avon St
Merrick Square
LAMBETH ROAD
Gladstone Street
HARPER ROAD
South Bank University
ST GEORGE'S ROAD
GARDEN ROW
Imperial War Museum
Geraldine Mary Harmsworth Park
Tiverton St
Bath Terrace
Falmouth Road
Spurgeon St
Burbage Close
KENNINGTON
Street
Rockingham
London College of Printing
Elephant & Castle
Deverell St
Brook Drive
West Square
Falmouth Rd

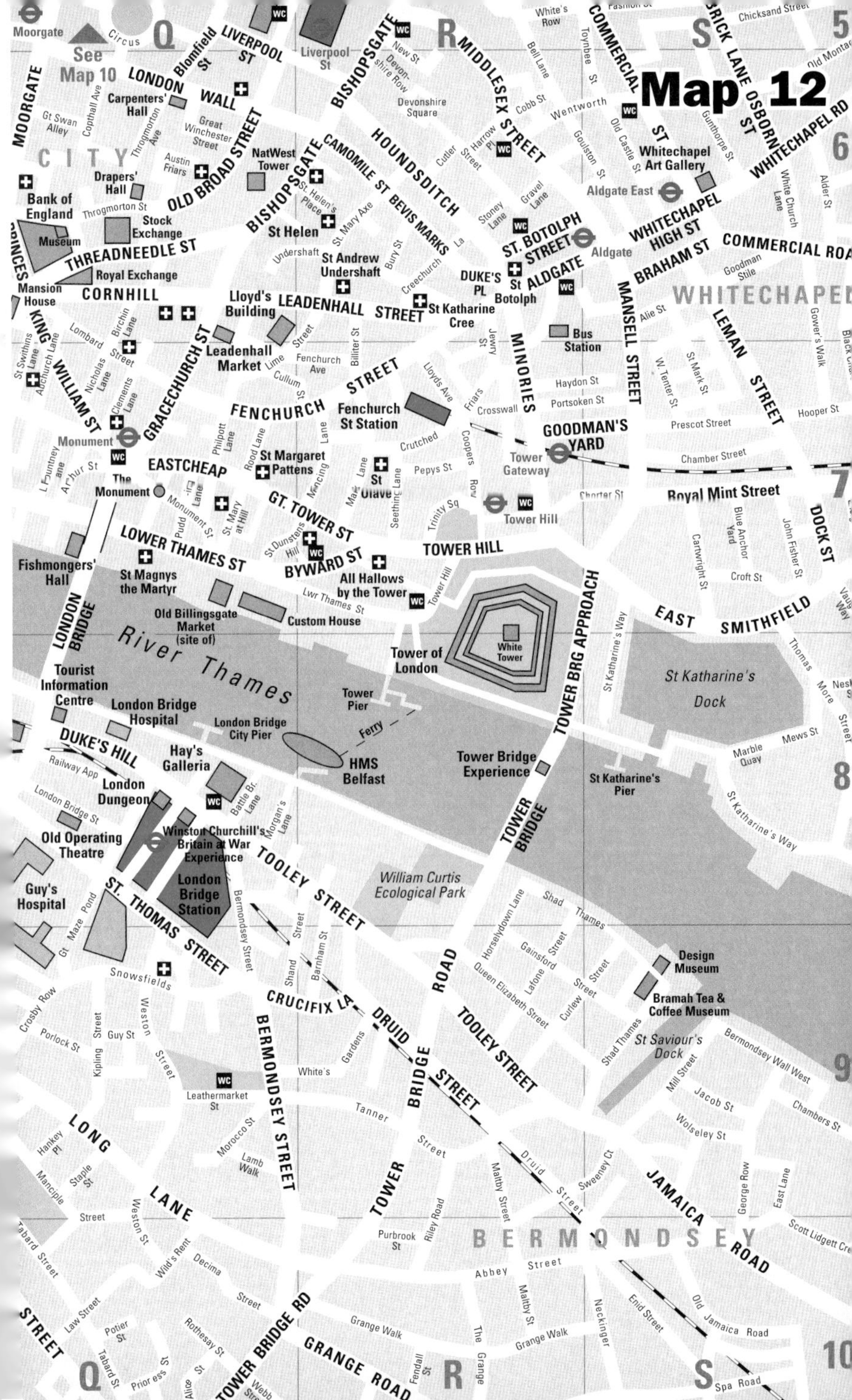
Map 12
See Map 10
Q
R
S
Q
R
S
5
6
7
8
9
10
Moorgate
Circus
Blomfield St
LIVERPOOL ST
Liverpool St
BISHOPSGATE
New St
Devonshire Row
Devonshire Square
MIDDLESEX STREET
White's Row
Bell Lane
COMMERCIAL ST
Toynbee St
BRICK LANE
OSBORN ST
Chicksand Street
Old Montague
MOORGATE
LONDON WALL
Carpenters' Hall
Copthall Ave
Gt Swan Alley
Throgmorton Ave
Great Winchester Street
OLD BROAD STREET
Austin Friars
NatWest Tower
CITY
Drapers' Hall
Throgmorton St
Stock Exchange
Bank of England
Museum
PRINCES
THREADNEEDLE ST
Royal Exchange
Mansion House
CORNHILL
KING WILLIAM ST
St Swithins Lane
Abchurch Lane
Lombard Street
Nicholas Lane
Birchin Lane
Clements Lane
GRACECHURCH ST
Leadenhall Market
Lloyd's Building
LEADENHALL STREET
Lime Street
Cullum St
Fenchurch Ave
Billiter St
BISHOPSGATE
St Helen's Place
St Helen
Undershaft
St Andrew Undershaft
St Mary Axe
CAMOMILE ST
BEVIS MARKS
HOUNDSDITCH
Bury St
Creechurch La
St Katharine Cree
Cutler Street
Harrow Pl
Cobb St
Wentworth
Old Castle St
Goulston St
Gunthorpe St
Whitechapel Art Gallery
WHITECHAPEL RD
Aldgate East
White Church Lane
Alder St
Stoney Lane
Gravel Lane
ST. BOTOLPH STREET
Aldgate
WHITECHAPEL HIGH ST
COMMERCIAL ROAD
DUKE'S PL
St Botolph
ALDGATE
BRAHAM ST
Goodman Stile
WHITECHAPEL
MANSELL STREET
Alie St
LEMAN STREET
Gower's Walk
Black Church
Jewry St
MINORIES
Bus Station
Haydon St
Portsoken St
W. Tenter St
St Mark St
Hooper St
Prescot Street
Chamber Street
FENCHURCH STREET
Fenchurch St Station
Lloyds Ave
Friars
Crosswall
GOODMAN'S YARD
Tower Gateway
Monument
The Monument
EASTCHEAP
Philpott Lane
Rood Lane
Lane
St Margaret Pattens
Mincing Lane
Mark Lane
St Olave
Seething Lane
Crutched
Pepys St
Coopers Row
Trinity Sq
Tower Hill
Chorter St
Royal Mint Street
Blue Anchor Yard
John Fisher St
DOCK ST
L Pountney Lane
Arthur St
Monument St
Pudding Lane
St. Mary at Hill
GT. TOWER ST
St Dunstens Hill
LOWER THAMES ST
BYWARD ST
TOWER HILL
Cartwright St
Croft St
Fishmongers' Hall
St Magnys the Martyr
All Hallows by the Tower
Lwr Thames St
Custom House
Old Billingsgate Market (site of)
TOWER BRG APPROACH
St Katharine's Way
EAST SMITHFIELD
Vaughan Way
LONDON BRIDGE
River Thames
Tower of London
White Tower
Thomas More Street
St Katharine's Dock
Nesham St
Tourist Information Centre
London Bridge Hospital
London Bridge City Pier
Tower Pier
Ferry
HMS Belfast
Tower Bridge Experience
St Katharine's Pier
Marble Quay
Mews St
DUKE'S HILL
Railway App
London Bridge St
London Dungeon
Hay's Galleria
Battle Br. Lane
Morgan's Lane
TOWER BRIDGE
St Katharine's Way
Winston Churchill's Britain at War Experience
Old Operating Theatre
Guy's Hospital
London Bridge Station
TOOLEY STREET
William Curtis Ecological Park
Horselydown Lane
Shad Thames
Gainsford Street
Lafone Street
Queen Elizabeth Street
Curlew Street
Design Museum
Bramah Tea & Coffee Museum
ST. THOMAS STREET
Maze Pond
Gt Maze Pond
Bermondsey Street
Shand Street
Barnham St
ROAD
TOOLEY STREET
Snowsfields
Crosby Row
Porlock St
Kipling Street
Guy St
Weston Street
CRUCIFIX LA
DRUID STREET
Gardens
BERMONDSEY STREET
BRIDGE
St Saviour's Dock
Shad Thames
Mill Street
Bermondsey Wall West
Jacob St
Chambers St
Wolseley St
Leathermarket St
White's
Tanner Street
LONG LANE
Hankey Pl
Staple St
Manciple Street
Morocco St
Lamb Walk
TOWER
Maltby Street
Druid Street
Sweeney Ct
JAMAICA ROAD
George Row
East Lane
Scott Lidgett Cres
Weston St
Wild's Rent
Decima Street
Purbrook St
Riley Road
BERMONDSEY
Abbey Street
Tabard Street
STREET
Law Street
Potier St
Rothesay St
TOWER BRIDGE RD
Grange Walk
Maltby St
Neckinger
Enid Street
Old Jamaica Road
GRANGE ROAD
The Grange
Fendall St
Grange Walk
Tabard St
Prioress St
Alice St
Webb Street
Spa Road

Street Index

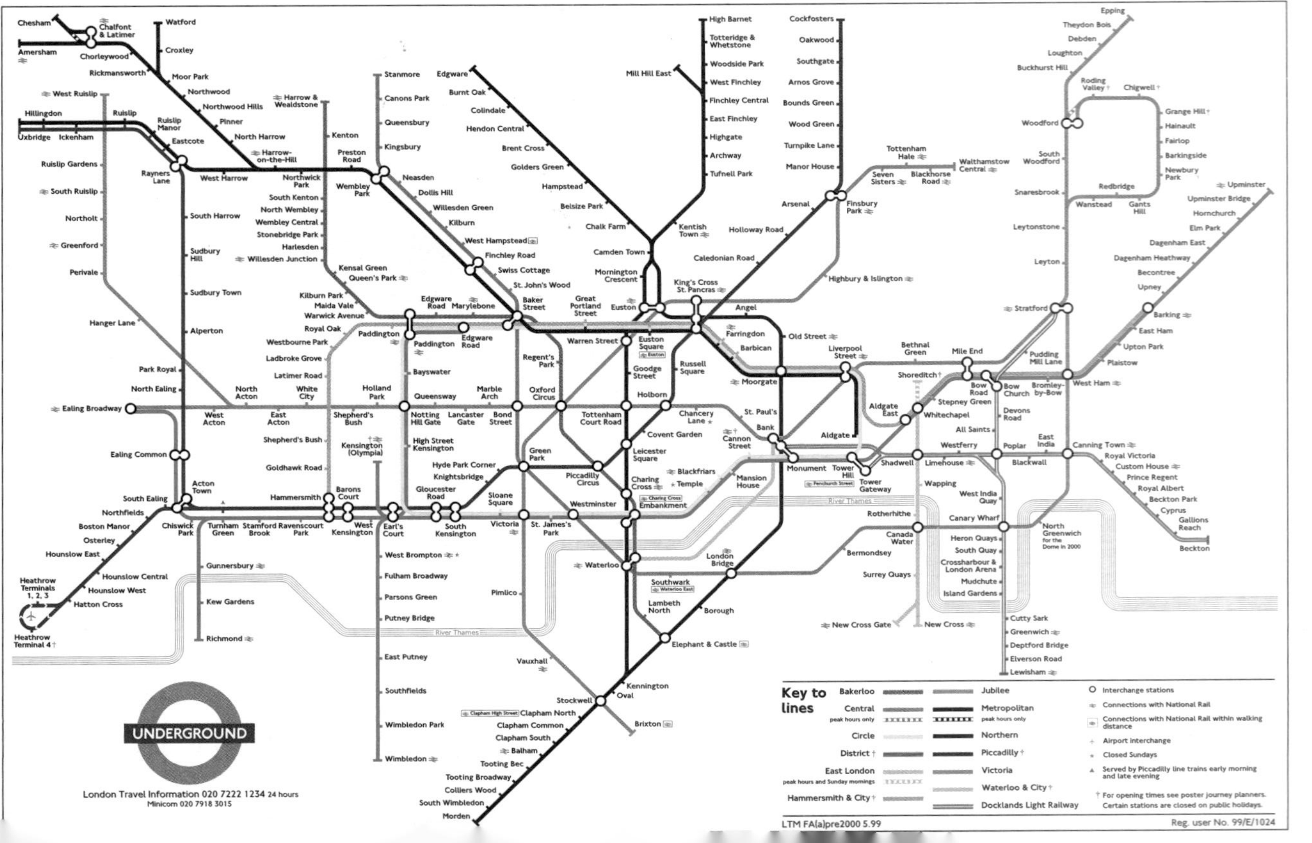

Chesham
Chalfont & Latimer
Amersham
Chorleywood
Watford
Croxley
Rickmansworth
Moor Park
Northwood
Northwood Hills
Pinner
North Harrow
Harrow-on-the-Hill
Harrow & Wealdstone
West Ruislip
Hillingdon
Ruislip
Ruislip Manor
Uxbridge
Ickenham
Eastcote
Ruislip Gardens
Rayners Lane
West Harrow
South Ruislip
Northolt
Greenford
Perivale
Hanger Lane
South Harrow
Sudbury Hill
Sudbury Town
Alperton
Park Royal
North Ealing
Ealing Broadway
Ealing Common
South Ealing
Northfields
Boston Manor
Osterley
Hounslow East
Hounslow Central
Hounslow West
Hatton Cross
Heathrow Terminals 1, 2, 3
Heathrow Terminal 4
Stanmore
Canons Park
Queensbury
Kingsbury
Kenton
Preston Road
Northwick Park
South Kenton
North Wembley
Wembley Central
Stonebridge Park
Harlesden
Willesden Junction
Wembley Park
Neasden
Dollis Hill
Willesden Green
Kilburn
West Hampstead
Finchley Road
Swiss Cottage
St. John's Wood
Edgware
Burnt Oak
Colindale
Hendon Central
Brent Cross
Golders Green
Hampstead
Belsize Park
Chalk Farm
Camden Town
Mornington Crescent
Mill Hill East
High Barnet
Totteridge & Whetstone
Woodside Park
West Finchley
Finchley Central
East Finchley
Highgate
Archway
Tufnell Park
Kentish Town
Cockfosters
Oakwood
Southgate
Arnos Grove
Bounds Green
Wood Green
Turnpike Lane
Manor House
Arsenal
Finsbury Park
Holloway Road
Caledonian Road
Highbury & Islington
Tottenham Hale
Seven Sisters
Blackhorse Road
Walthamstow Central
Kensal Green
Queen's Park
Kilburn Park
Maida Vale
Warwick Avenue
Royal Oak
Westbourne Park
Ladbroke Grove
Latimer Road
Paddington
Edgware Road
Marylebone
Baker Street
Great Portland Street
Euston
King's Cross St. Pancras
Angel
Farringdon
Barbican
Old Street
Bayswater
Queensway
Holland Park
North Acton
White City
West Acton
East Acton
Shepherd's Bush
Goldhawk Road
Kensington (Olympia)
Notting Hill Gate
Lancaster Gate
Marble Arch
Bond Street
Regent's Park
Oxford Circus
Warren Street
Euston Square
Goodge Street
Russell Square
Holborn
Tottenham Court Road
Moorgate
Liverpool Street
Chancery Lane
St. Paul's
Bank
Covent Garden
Leicester Square
Cannon Street
High Street Kensington
Hyde Park Corner
Knightsbridge
Green Park
Piccadilly Circus
Charing Cross
Blackfriars
Temple
Mansion House
Monument
Tower Hill
Tower Gateway
Aldgate
Aldgate East
Acton Town
Hammersmith
Barons Court
Gloucester Road
Sloane Square
Chiswick Park
Turnham Green
Stamford Brook
Ravenscourt Park
West Kensington
Earl's Court
South Kensington
Victoria
St. James's Park
Westminster
Embankment
Gunnersbury
Kew Gardens
Richmond
West Brompton
Fulham Broadway
Parsons Green
Putney Bridge
East Putney
Southfields
Wimbledon Park
Wimbledon
Pimlico
Vauxhall
Waterloo
Southwark
Lambeth North
London Bridge
Borough
Elephant & Castle
Kennington
Oval
Stockwell
Brixton
Clapham North
Clapham Common
Clapham South
Balham
Tooting Bec
Tooting Broadway
Colliers Wood
South Wimbledon
Morden
River Thames
Bethnal Green
Mile End
Shoreditch
Stepney Green
Whitechapel
Bow Road
Bow Church
Bromley-by-Bow
Pudding Mill Lane
Stratford
West Ham
Shadwell
Limehouse
Westferry
All Saints
Devons Road
Poplar
East India
Blackwall
Canning Town
Wapping
Rotherhithe
Canada Water
Bermondsey
Surrey Quays
New Cross Gate
New Cross
West India Quay
Canary Wharf
Heron Quays
South Quay
Crossharbour & London Arena
Mudchute
Island Gardens
Cutty Sark
Greenwich
Deptford Bridge
Elverson Road
Lewisham
North Greenwich
for the Dome in 2000
Royal Victoria
Custom House
Prince Regent
Royal Albert
Beckton Park
Cyprus
Gallions Reach
Beckton
Epping
Theydon Bois
Debden
Loughton
Buckhurst Hill
Roding Valley
Chigwell
Woodford
Grange Hill
Hainault
Fairlop
Barkingside
Newbury Park
South Woodford
Snaresbrook
Redbridge
Wanstead
Gants Hill
Leytonstone
Leyton
Upminster
Upminster Bridge
Hornchurch
Elm Park
Dagenham East
Dagenham Heathway
Becontree
Upney
Barking
East Ham
Upton Park
Plaistow
UNDERGROUND
London Travel Information 020 7222 1234 24 hours
Minicom 020 7918 3015
Key to lines
Bakerloo
Central
peak hours only
Circle
District
East London
peak hours and Sunday mornings
Hammersmith & City
Jubilee
Metropolitan
peak hours only
Northern
Piccadilly
Victoria
Waterloo & City
Docklands Light Railway
Interchange stations
Connections with National Rail
Connections with National Rail within walking distance
Airport interchange
Closed Sundays
Served by Piccadilly line trains early morning and late evening
For opening times see poster journey planners. Certain stations are closed on public holidays.
LTM FA(a)pre2000 5.99
Reg. user No. 99/E/1024